ATLAS OF THE THIRD WORLD

Second Edition

Edited by
George Kurian

Facts On File
New York • Oxford

Atlas of the Third World

second edition

Copyright © 1992 by George Kurian

Facts On File, Inc.   Facts On File Limited
460 Park Avenue South   Collins Street
New York NY 10016   Oxford OX4 1XJ
USA   United Kingdom

Library of Congress Cataloging-in-Publication Data

Kurian, George Thomas.
  Atlas of the Third World.

  1. Natural resources—Developing countries—Maps.
2. Developing countries—Economic conditions—Maps.
3. Developing countries—Social conditions—Maps.
I. Title.
G1046.G1K8 1989   912'.19724   88-675259
ISBN 0-8160-1930-4

A British CIP catalogue record for this book is available from the British Library.

Australian CIP data available on request from Facts On File.

Facts On File books are available at special discounts when purchased in bulk quantities for businesses, associations, institutions or sales promotions. Please call our Special Sales Department in New York at 212/683-2244 (dial 800/322-8755 except in NY, AK or HI) or in Oxford at 865/728399.

Electronic Publishing Services provided by Christos Moschovitis & Associates, Inc.
AMIS/EDP, Computer Graphics, Multimedia, and *Electronic Pubishing* firm in Brooklyn, New York
Manufactured by Arcata Graphics Company/Kingsport
Printed in the United States of America

10 9 8 7 6 5 4 3 2 1

This book is printed on acid-free paper.

CONTENTS

INTRODUCTION TO THE SECOND EDITION v
INTRODUCTION vii

PART I: THEMATIC PROFILES
PROLOGUE 1
POLITICAL DIVISIONS 5
POPULATION 11
ECONOMIC CONDITIONS 23
BURDEN OF DEBT 31
FOOD AND AGRICULTURE 39
INDUSTRY 54
ENERGY 57
LABOR 62
ENVIRONMENT 66
TRADE 71
DEFENSE 77
EDUCATION 83
HEALTH 87
MEDIA AND COMMUNICATIONS 98

PART II: COUNTRY PROFILES
AFGHANISTAN 104
ALGERIA 108
ANGOLA 112
ARGENTINA 114
BANGLADESH 118
BENIN 122
BOLIVIA 126
BRAZIL 128
BURKINA 132
CAMBODIA 134
CAMEROON 136
CHAD 140
CHILE 144
COLOMBIA 148
CONGO 152
COSTA RICA 154
CUBA 156
DOMINICAN REPUBLIC 160
ECUADOR 162
EGYPT 166
EL SALVADOR 170
ETHIOPIA 174
GABON 178
GHANA 182
GUATEMALA 186
GUINEA 190
GUYANA 192
HAITI 196
HONDURAS 198
INDIA 202

INDONESIA 206
IRAN 210
IRAQ 214
IVORY COAST 218
JAMAICA 222
JORDAN 226
KENYA 230
KOREA, NORTH 234
KOREA, SOUTH 236
LAOS 240
LEBANON 242
LIBERIA 244
LIBYA 248
MADAGASCAR 252
MALAWI 256
MALASIA 260
MAURITANIA 264
MAURITIUS 266
MEXICO 268
MOROCCO 272
MOZAMBIQUE 276
MYANMAR 278
NEPAL 282
NICARAGUA 286
NIGER 290
NIGERIA 292
PAKISTAN 296
PANAMA 300
PERU 304
PHILIPPINES 306
SAUDI ARABIA 311
SENEGAL 314
SIERRA LEONE 318
SINGAPORE 322
SOMALIA 324
SRI LANKA 328
SUDAN 332
SYRIA 336
TANZANIA 340
THAILAND 344
TUNISIA 348
TURKEY 352
UGANDA 356
URUGUAY 360
VENEZUELA 362
VIETNAM 366
YEMEN ARAB REPUBLIC 368
YEMEN, PEOPLE'S DEMOCRATIC REPUBLIC OF 370
ZAIRE 372
ZAMBIA 376
ZIMBABWE 378
INDEX 381

INTRODUCTION TO
THE SECOND EDITION

The second edition of the ATLAS OF THE THIRD WORLD is designed, just as the first, to provide a state of the Third World report in graphic form. The data on which its charts and maps are based relate to the critical lustrum from 1983 to 1990. Together they present a picture of the Third World on the eve of the last decade of the 20th century.

In 1984, when the first edition of ATLAS was published, the world was just coming out of a deep recession, the last in a series that had battered the fragile economies of the developing nations since the beginning of the 1970s. This recession signaled the end of the free-spending third quarter of the century. The ripple effects of the recession, spreading rapidly through the less developed economies, have left permanent scars, whereas the more developed economies have been able to readjust their economic policies and regain a degree of stability. The seventies had established the interdependence of the regional economies but the middle eighties have effectively decoupled the weaker economies from the stronger ones and created new fault lines that may have strong implications for the 21st century. At the end of the eighties, Third World nations not only remained as milch cows for developed nations but their national resources were indentured to those of the superpowers by unbearable levels of debt.

The 1984–90 lustrum was characterized by contradictory trends: on the one hand there were significant improvements in political stability, population growth, food, health and education as a direct result of developments and policies initiated in the 1960s and 1970s. On the other, there was a process of disdevelopment by which the Third World nations were being subject to increasing economic instability, deteriorating terms of trade, unmanageable levels of inflation and unemployment (the discomfort index) and a virtual drying up of external capital flows. The poorest nations of the world—numbering according to the UN some 40—had become much poorer by the end of the decade and their problems had defied conventional economic solutions. The eighties also witnessed a phenomenon unprecedented in history, as dropout nations, as Lebanon and Cambodia, ceased to function altogether and the combined effects of civil strife and economic chaos left them in shambles. A number of other countries are also candidates for this basketcase category, although their national economies are still functioning and are not totally extinct. They include Bangladesh, Chad, Ethiopia and Afghanistan. These nations represent a category that may well be called the Disabled World.

In the 1970s and early 1980s Third World observers held that the backwardness of the developing world was due principally to certain structural weaknesses that they identified as political authoritarianism, uncontrolled population growth, and inadequate food, health and education. Yet, it is precisely in these areas that major advances were made in the middle eighties. Political repression is no longer a major issue in the Third World. Authoritarianism has virtually disappeared from the Latin American scene. In Asia, Pakistan and the Philippines have been reclaimed for democracy. In Africa, dictatorship is everywhere in the retreat, although the level of freedom is still not any higher than it was in the 1970s.

Along with an improvement in the political climate there has been a winding down of the many wars that have plagued the Third World. (Since World War II virtually all wars have been fought on Third World soil). The year 1988 could be regarded as an *annus mirabilis* because more wars were concluded (or came close to a negotiated settlement) in that year than in any other in modern history. These included the withdrawal of the Soviet troops from Afghanistan, the proposed withdrawal of Vietnamese from Cambodia, the UN–imposed truce in the Gulf War, agreement on a plebiscite in Western Sahara, the possibility of a negotiated peace in the civil war in Angola, de-escalation of the civil war in Nicaragua, and the ending of the civil war in Chad with the expulsion of Libyan invaders.

Similarly, although population growth rates have not dropped significantly in low-income and lower middle-income countries, fertility rates have dropped between 1980 and 1986 from 6.6 to 6.1 in the former and from 6.3 to 3.9 in the latter and this bodes well for future growth rates. Crude birth rates also have dropped per 1,000 from 46 to 43 in low-income countries and from 44 to 35 in lower middle-income countries during the same period.

In health the indicators are as encouraging. Between 1965 and 1981 the number of persons per physician has dropped from 26,620 to 17,670 in the least developed countries and from 17,340 to 7,880 in the lower middle-income countries. The daily calorie supply per capita has increased between 1965 and 1985 from 1,998 to 2,100 in the least developed countries and from 2,117 to 2,511 in the lower middle-income countries. Between 1965 and 1985 the primary, secondary and tertiary enrollment ratios have climbed from 44 to 67, from 9 to 22 and from 1 to 5 in the least developed countries and from 75 to 104, 16 to 42, and 4 to 13 in the lower middle-income countries. With 1979–81=100, the average index of food production per capita in 1984–86 was 101 in the least developed countries and 105 in the lower middle-income countries, comparable to the figure of 103 for developed countries. Fertilizer consumption has increased between 1970 and 1985 from 80 to 234 grams per hectare of arable land in the least developed countries and from 150 to 422 grams per hectare of arable land in the lower middle-income countries.

Yet, despite measurable progress in these areas, the overall performance of the least developed countries has been dismal. Per capita GNP has remained virtually stationary in the 1980s at $200 for the least developed countries and $750 for the middle-income countries as against $12,960 for developed countries. Between 1965–80 and 1980–86 GDP growth rate has actually declined from 3.1% to 2.9% for the least developed countries and from 6.5% to 1.8% for the lower middle-income countries. The average annual growth rate of GNP per capita during 1965–86 was only 0.5% for the least developed countries, which means that it will take them over 1,200 years to catch up with the 1986 figure for developed countries. The inflation rates have been even more alarming. Between 1980 and 1986 the average annual rate was 19.1% for the least developed countries, 22.9% for the lower middle-income countries and 56.8% for the upper middle-income countries as against 2.3% for the developed countries. Particularly affected are low-income African countries that were caught in a punishing bind between rising interest rates, falling export earnings and closed bank doors. Paradoxically, declining oil prices also confronted high-income oil producers with severe problems of adjustment and introduced them for the first time in two decades to the whiplash of fiscal austerity. A few countries have been able to readjust their economic policies and thus maintain reasonable growth levels during this decade. Among them is India, which is in a class by itself. Although one of the poorest countries of the world in per capita GNP, India exhibits at the same time some of the characteristics of an advanced economy with a high level of political stability, a highly educated segment of the labor force, a large domestic market and, since the 1970s, self-sufficiency in food.

Debt may be the single most critical problem in the Third World in the 1990s. In nominal terms, total debt for all Third World countries reached $1.245 trillion, or 48% of the combined GNP of these countries. Between 1980 and 1987 fifty developing countries have renegotiated their foreign debts through multilateral negotiations. In all, $390 billion of maturities have been renegotiated since 1980, $321 billion with commercial banks and $68 billion with official creditors. Particularly in Africa, slow growth, compounded by poor economic policies and depressed commodity prices, have played a major role in exacerbating the debt problem. Twenty-two countries in Africa are now identified by the World Bank as "debt-distressed," a new addition to the development glossary. They suffered a 17% decline in per capita GDP between 1980 and 1986 with exports declining by 50% during the same period. External debt was 108% of GDP in the debt-distressed countries in 1986, compared with 47% in other sub-Saharan African countries and 61% in Latin America.

At the root of the poor performance of developing countries has been their failure to adjust to external developments coupled with the magnitude of the economic shocks. Some countries have adopted or continued to pursue policies that produce unnecessary conflicts between short-term stabilization and longer-term growth. One of the main problems is fiscal. Public spending in the developed countries has remained high because it is tied to what is perceived as socially desirable goals, as, for example, food subsidies and indexing of wages. Spending cuts were often made in the area of investment, which, in turn, slowed medium-term growth. Many heavily indebted countries are finding it difficult to reduce current expenditures because of large interest payments on outstanding debts. The burden on the national budget is particularly heavy for those countries that failed to direct previously borrowed funds into efficient and productive activities. As few developing countries have full-fledged bond markets, most of them have financed their budget deficits by borrowing from the banking system or printing more money. Large increases in the money supply generated by fiscal deficits have been the main cause in the rapid increase in inflation in most Latin American and some Asian and African countries. Governments and central banks have sometimes tried to suppress the symptoms of inflation by overvaluing domestic currencies and controlling the prices of politically sensitive goods and services. This has added to the public sector deficit and thus has exacerbated, rather than reduced, inflation. Nearly all developing countries control interest rates and ration credit according to various planning priorities. Inefficient interest rates have led to an absolute shortage of savings, thus jeopardizing future growth. Most of the credit is channeled to relatively inefficient public enterprises and programs, and the private sector is left to compete for the remaining smaller share of nonallocated or nonsubsidized credit. Adjustment of interest rates is also necessary to stem capital flight, which is a major problem in a number of heavily indebted countries.

In the 1960s and 1970s, public authorities in the Third World undertook expensive prestige projects that have yielded low returns. In an effort to trim public expenditures in the 1980s, they have swung to the other extreme and suspended programs essential to keeping existing capital stock in working order. In much of sub-Saharan Africa, the basic infrastructure—highways, waterworks, railroads and power—is in a state of disrepair and in many cases in worse condition than 20 years ago. Thus the Third World is entering the 1990s with its substantial achievements of the 1960s and 1970s threatened by a very inhospitable economic environment.

Appropriately, a new section has been included in the ATLAS on debt. The section on environment has been expanded in recognition of its growing importance. The section on law enforcement in the first edition has been deleted for lack of space. Innovations in the edition include the provision of referential statistical data along with bar and pie charts, and full source citations with many maps and charts and graphs. In the second part, Vietnam, about which more information is available today than five years ago, is added to bring the total number of countries to 81.

The project was shepherded by Dr. Eleanora von Dehsen, director of special projects at Facts On File. Work on the ATLAS was smooth and easy, in a manner typical of her relaxed and legato personality. Tribute is also due to Robert Wolf, who handled the detailed technical aspects of the work with meticulous attention. Above all, my gratitude is due to Edward W. Knappman, without whose encouragement and support, this work would not have been possible.

George Thomas Kurian

INTRODUCTION

THE ATLAS OF THE THIRD WORLD presents a comprehensive selection of maps and statistical information in graphic form organized under topical headings to depict important aspects of the current economic and social conditions in the Third World and their underlying historical dynamics. It is designed to be self-sufficient in scope but in many ways it supplements the ENCYCLO-PEDIA OF THE THIRD WORLD (three volumes, Facts On File, 1992).

The ATLAS is divided into two parts: The 14 chapters of the First Part examine certain broad topics that have been identified as the critical issues affecting Third World development. Many indicators in this section are presented as a series of observations covering the past decade (in some cases, the past two decades) and allow the reader to gauge the direction of possible trends. In certain instances, by extrapolating available data, the statistician can function as a minor prophet and determine what conditions would develop if present trends were allowed to continue undisturbed. The Second Part presents charts and maps on 81 countries of the world with narrative introductions. Because of the complex interactions of factors affecting national life, it is interesting to read and compare country maps and charts, especially those relating to either neighboring countries, such as India and Pakistan, Ethiopia and Somalia, Bolivia and Peru, or to countries with different political systems, such as Mozambique and Zambia or North and South Korea.

Three broad types of indicators may be distinguished among those presented in the Second Part. The first describes the country's natural resources, including land area; the second the country's population—the key that determines all other indicators; and the third the country's social and economic performance as well as what is generally described as the quality of life. The first is the given in the equation of economic development, the second the fulcrum of growth and the third the engine of progress. If we think of development as a pyramid, the first indicator would form the base, the second the middle building block and the third the apex. No country in the developed or developing world possesses all three in their ideal shape or form, and developmental strategy consists in managing available resources to produce the most desirable quality of life. It should, however, be borne in mind that there are other elements in the equation which cannot be presented graphically because they are essentially nonquantifiable, such as the will to achieve growth or the ruling political ideology. Nevertheless, the charts and maps presented in each country chapter provide as complete a picture of the state of the country's economy as is possible using existing data.

The purpose of the ATLAS is to present a graphic report on the state of the Third World. To do so, we shall examine the picture under 11 headings.

1. DEVELOPMENT

The underlying theme in this ATLAS—the common thread that binds the more than 1,000 maps and charts—may be described as Development. (The word "development" has been chosen instead of "growth" because not all development is growth.) In the 1960s economists envisioned development as a linear process divided into stages, from "take-off" to "high mass consumption," with intermediate stages requiring such acrobatic feats as "breaking the vicious circle" and "catching up." All countries were seen as starting from the same point and facing the same obstacles as they proceeded over the same course. Some would simply move faster than others, the slower ones following at a distance and catching up later. The poorer countries could learn from the mistakes of others and benefit from the continued growth of the rich ones through spillover or trickle-down as well as generous economic aid.

Most of these assumptions have proved wrong. Indeed, the two so-called Development Decades have been described by K.K.S. Dadzie as "Decades of Disappointment." True, there has been growth in some areas in aggregate terms. As a whole, the Third World grew from 1950 through 1976 at an average rate of 5%, as against 4.2% for developed countries, and their aggregate manufactured exports increased at an impressive rate of 10%. Despite skyrocketing oil import bills, developing countries together managed to save and reinvest nearly a quarter of their national income. Agricultural production grew at a rate of 3.2% (2.8% for developed countries), manufacturing production 6.9% (4.0% for developed countries) and gross investment 8% (4.8% for developed countries). In terms of national well-being, their progress was equally striking. Life expectancy increased in the South in the past two decades by as much as it increased in the North in a century, and a number of diseases, such as malaria, were brought under control and others, such as smallpox, virtually eradicated. The Physical Quality of Life Index—a composite indicator of infant mortality, life expectancy and literacy—rose in the Third World from 39 in 1960 to 60 in the late 1982.

But what these accomplishments fail to reveal—and even, in some cases, mask—are the disparities that still persist. With a population growing by 2.2% annually, as against 0.7% for developed countries, much of the gains made in aggregate terms are lost in per capita terms. The North-South gap remains as substantial as ever. The South accounts for only 21% of the "gross global product" (GGP) of $8.8 trillion, 25% of the total world export earnings, 22% of the world military expenditures, 16% of the world's educational expenditures and 9% of the world's public health expenditures. Average life expectancy is still 16 years lower than in the North and infant mortality is five times as high. Some 800 million are living in absolute poverty and over 460 million (nearly half of them children) are malnourished. Only 52% of Third World residents can read and write, as compared with 99% in the developed world, and average educational expenditures are only $18 per capita, compared with $286 per capita in the developed world. About 850 million have no access to schools and rarely go beyond the primary grades. Less than half the people of the Third World have safe water supplies and only half of the urban households have minimally adequate housing. Most disastrous of all, development has been accompanied by a crushing burden of debt, which in 1983 amounted to $530 billion and is expected to triple in the next 10 years.

The past two decades have also introduced new inequalities and intensified the fissures between the developing countries themselves, making it necessary to introduce at least three new subcategories. The first subcategory comprises what are known as advanced developing countries (ADCs), or newly industrializing countries (NICs), and includes Brazil, Argentina and Mexico as well as the East Asian "Gang of Four": Singapore, Taiwan, Hong Kong and South Korea. Their economies enjoyed spectacular growth during the 1960s and 1970s. Their average annual per capital GNP growth rates from 1960 to 1977 were higher than that of the United States, even though their populations grew twice as fast. Their export performance was still more impressive, growing by 24%, as compared with 14% for the United States. The second subcategory consists of petroleum exporting countries (PECs), a disparate group with super-rich nations, such as Libya and Kuwait, at one end of the spectrum and lower-income nations, such as Nigeria and Indonesia, at the other. With a fifth of the Third World's population, PECs and ADCs account for 40% of its wealth. Another 40% is accounted for by the 45 middle-income countries (MICs), such as Thailand, Malaysia and the Philippines, with middling growth rates of 4 to 5% and 25% of the Third World's population. The remaining 35 countries, sometimes called the Fourth World, are the poorest in the world and their conditions have changed only for the worse during the past decade. Although they make up 35% of the developing world's population, they account for a mere 3% of the gross global product (GGP) and 5% of Third World exports. Their average per capita GNP was less than $230 in 1980.

Even in countries that have experienced relatively high growth rates, there have been no appreciable changes in the quality of life for the impoverished majority of their inhabitants. As economists have discovered, during transitional stages of development, wealth rarely trickles down but stays in puddles at the top. It requires active and deliberate government intervention to enable the benefits of development to reach lower-income groups. In fact, the divisions between the poor, the middle and the rich are sharper today in the developing world than they are in the developed world. The conclusion is that there is a Third World within every Third World country—a group that, in the words of the ILO, "has income insufficient to buy a basket of goods and services essential to a minimum level of welfare."

While economic development cannot be considered as an isolated phenomenon and is obviously related to numerous issues that do not yield to economic analysis, it may be simply stated that the heart of underdevelopment is overdependence. The institutions of the international economic system, particularly the key ones that control trade and credit, created during and in the immediate aftermath of World War II, are designed to function in such a way as to perpetuate the patron-client relationships of the colonial era. The developing countries have "milch cow economies"—*l'economie de trait,* as the French call it—producing for the needs of the North. In consequence, these economies are disarticulated and lack organic linkage between production and domestic demand. Tied to the coattails of richer economies, they are bereft of indigenous sources of dynamism. Despite all the power ascribed to producer cartels, the real economic decisions affecting the Third World are made in London, New York, Paris, Zurich and Tokyo.

During the past decade, Third World countries have pressed for reforms in international trade and monetary policies that they consider discriminatory. Their call for a New International Economic Order (NIEO) includes establishment of preferential treatment for their manufactured goods in the markets of industrialized countries, more stable and higher prices for their commodities, renegotiation of their external public debt, codes of conduct for the activities of multinational corporations, more transfer of technology to LDCs and a greater voice in the management of the world's monetary system. Simultaneously, developing countries have pursued the concept of "delinking," or loosening the historical connections between industrialized countries and former colonies and fostering greater economic cooperation among developing countries.

2. POLITICAL INSTABILITY

Next to poverty, the term most commonly associated with the Third World is political instability. Indeed, instability appears to be the concomitant of the process of modernization and part of the rites of passage as a developing country moves toward maturity. As a consequence of urbanization, industrialization, media and communications development and widespread rise in educational levels, the legitimacy that was once attached to traditional leadership erodes over a period of time. The spread of education creates significant changes in attitudes toward government and increasing demands for a share in its decision making and scrutiny of its performance. Modernization also produces new social structures and groupings and new leadership to articulate their aspirations. At first, these changes are rarely resisted openly by the powers that be. Even before independence, political elites in developing countries had come to accept the notion that they needed at least a facade of popular support to maintain their own edifices of power. They are also aware of the risk of violent revolution in postponing liberalization too long. Further, political structures in developing countries are often borrowed from developed nations or modeled on those of developed nations, and magic labels, such as "popular" and democratic," are sanctified by use in the media and indiscriminately appropriated by authoritarian regimes.

Paying only lip service to democratic ideals—with grandiloquent phrases embodied in their national constitutions—traditional power structures in developing countries managed to survive while circumventing the process of participatory democracy. One of the methods of survival used was to revert to a more primitive form, as in Iran, where the Pahlevi dictatorship gave way to the dictatorship of the mullahs under the guise of revolution. In some cases, the old leadership entrenched itself in a new network of patron-client groups, each dominating its political turf and excluding outsiders from the spoils of office. The patron—an important father figure in this stage of political evolution—acts as a mediator between the government on the one hand and his followers on the other. Another approach was for the old authority to cloak itself under some new but meaningless label, such as Marxism or Socialism, designed to mute any further demands for popular participation. If such devices failed, the army would step in and take over the state under the pretext of restoring law and order. The past two decades have thus witnessed a withering of democracy in the Third World. It is not surprising that three out of four Third World residents live under authoritarian regimes of one sort or another. As Samuel Huntington noted in *No Easy Choice,* the whiplash of illegitimate, authoritarian regimes is the price that many Third World countries have had to pay in their quest for quick modernization.

One contributory factor in this failure of democracy in the Third World is the prevalence of ethnic rivalries and conflicts. In fact, it is not possible to understand Third World politics without reference to its ethnic divisions and antagonisms. While many sociologists had expected such divisions to die out as a result of the cohesive and melting-pot pressures of modernization, the opposite has been the case. Particularly in Africa, ethnic loyalties override political loyalties and ethnic interests take precedence over national interests.

3. POPULATION

Rapid population growth continues to be the most formidable problem for developing countries as a whole. During the 1960s and 1970s, Third World population grew by 2.3% while the GNP increased by 4.5 to 5.0%. High fertility rates and reduced mortality rates thus combined to reduce the impact of what otherwise would have been a healthy growth rate for developing economies. Population explosion is a relatively recent phenomenon in the Third World. Until the 20th century, the real rate of population growth was held in check by a high mortality rate. With improved nutrition and medical services, death rates fell sharply without a corresponding reduction in birth rates and the problem became unmanageable and alarming. However, the birth rates peaked during the 1950s and then, to the amazement and relief of demographers, declined. This decline has been estimated at between 15 and 20% during the past 20 years and has been substantial in Asia, Latin America and the Pacific countries but less so in Africa. Even so, there is little room for optimism. It is important to recognize that the slowdown in population from 2.3 to 2.2% annually is not in itself large enough to have a significant impact on aggregate population figures. At the lower rate, the populations of developing countries will double every 30 years, rather than 31 years as before. If fertility rates continue to decline at the present rate, a global replacement level of reproduction (with the average of one surviving child for one parent) will be reached around 2020. Were this to happen, global population will eventually stabilize at about 11 billion.

This modest progress has been achieved as a result of the convergence of two factors: One is rapid urbanization, with urban couples generally having fewer children than their rural counterparts, and the other the improved availability of contraceptive devices. Between 1960 and 1975 more than 30 governments of developing countries adopted official policies and programs designed to encourage family planning and control.

4. FINANCE

1973 was a watershed year for the international monetary system; it marked not only the final collapse of the Bretton Woods system—which had been moribund for a number of years—but also the rise of OPEC as a kind of economic superpower, or more accurately, a monetary monster. It also added a new term to the vocabulary of international finance—petrodollar, a combination of two powerful words, petroleum and dollar. In fact, black gold became the de facto core of the monetary system.

Instability had been inherent in the international monetary system long before 1973. A few years earlier, the dollar had been displaced as the numeraire (the major currency for expressing the value of international transactions) and the principal intervention currency, and a floating system of exchange had been adopted. But the OPEC bombshell served to institutionalize this instability. The era immediately following the hike in oil prices was characterized by wild fluctuations in exchange rates, rapid swings in balances of payments and large accumulations of debt.

In the midst of these crises, the plight of the oil-importing developing countries (OIDC) went unnoticed. In just one year—1974 to 1975—their overall deficit went from $30 billion to $38 billion. They have also experienced average inflation rates of 25% or above since 1974. Unlike many developed countries that generated foreign reserves by receiving deposits from countries with surpluses or merely by printing money and receiving seigniorage rights, most developing countries had to earn their foreign reserves.

As a result, OIDCs have had to finance their debts through large-scale borrowing. The aggregate foreign debt of these countries exceeded $530 billion in 1983, $350 billion of it from private sources. Although statistics on short-term debt are not reliable, it is probably in the range of $170 billion. The bulk of this debt is managed by commercial banks, which provide almost two-thirds of the net external financial requirements of the OIDCs, as against only 3% supplied by the IMF. Commercial lending of recycled petrodollars increased by 11 times in real terms, swelling from one-fourteenth to one-fourth of the total flow of capital to developing countries. Developing countries preferred to deal with private lenders rather than the IMF, not only because the former had substantially larger assets—the eurocurrency market alone had 20 times the assets of the IMF—but because they considered the IMF's conditionality, or terms for standby lending, excessively stringent and an unwarranted interference in their domestic affairs. Moreover, most of the IMF credits are repayable in three to four years, a period economists generally consider too short a period for making the necessary economic adjustments.

The bulk of private-sector borrowing is concentrated in a small number of advanced developing countries (ADCs), which the commercial bankers consider as good risks because of their higher export potentials. By the end of the 1970s, four countries—Brazil, Mexico, Argentina and South Korea—accounted for 65% of all eurocurrency borrowings by developed countries. Other countries, especially the low-income ones, have had to rely on concessional assistance from multilateral aid agencies.

The financial plight of the OIDCs is likely to be even more serious in the 1980s than it was in the 1970s. Between 1980 and 1982, falling export income and rising debt service together had a negative impact of about $70 billion on the balance of payments of the developing countries. The proportion between payments on medium- and long-term debt and export income jumped from 18% in 1980 to 24% in 1982, and the ratio between debt outstanding and exports rose from 1:1 to 1:3. The record of the top 20 borrowers

—which are responsible for three-fourths of all Third World debt—was even worse. Their proportion between payments on medium- and long-term debt and export income reached 34%; the top four borrowers had debt service that exceeded 50% of their export income.

The sheer magnitude of this problem defies easy diagnosis. Obviously, its origins are in the worldwide recession of the late 1970s. The export sales of the developing countries were virtually stagnant in 1982, partially because of the protectionist measures adopted in developed countries. The terms of trade of the low-income countries have deteriorated by 30% between 1979 and 1982. In addition, about half the increase in Third World debt-service payments since 1980 has been due to higher interest rates. Real rates of interest averaged 2% in the 1960s, were negative in the mid-1970s and then jumped to 5% by 1981. A one-point increase in interest rates costs Mexico, Brazil and Argentina $1.2 billion a year.

Falling export sales and high interest rates have resulted in a rash of debt repayment problems. A number of countries—notably Zaire, Nicaragua, Turkey, Jamaica, Sudan and Mexico—have had to reschedule their outstanding debts, and four of the largest debtors—Mexico, Brazil, Argentina and Chile—have recently had to defer payments on the principals. Almost as many countries have had to reschedule loans in the past two years as in the previous 25 years. Eight of the 15 developing countries that rescheduled debt in 1981 and 1982 were low-income African countries, and seven of them had accumulated more debt than they could manage without disrupting their exports.

Commercial banks, especially the smaller ones, have understandably been sobered by these problems and have pulled back from lending to OIDCs. In the third quarter of 1982, the banks lent less to them than they took back in principal repayments. Nervousness about the capacity of borrowing countries to service existing debt has weakened the fabric of confidence on which all international economic transactions depend.

Nevertheless, there are at least three hopeful signs that indicate the current debt problem of the Third World can be brought under control. The first is that capital flows between developed and developing nations are not a recent phenomenon; they have been a normal feature of the international economy for over two centuries and have weathered wars, recessions, depressions, and near bankruptcies of nations. The second is that many developing countries have acquired, during the past two decades, a successful track record in managing economic stress and have demonstrated their ability to adjust to and survive adverse economic and political conditions. Essentially, their present problems are those of liquidity, not solvency. It is interesting to note that although many developing countries have defaulted on their debt, none has repudiated it, as the Soviet Union did not too many decades ago. The third is the resiliency and the robustness of the international banking system itself. The lending system is designed to absorb shocks when the going gets bumpy and has built-in corrective mechanisms.

Over the long haul, the financial surplus of OPEC coffers will continue to bring about a drastic shift in the patterns of resource transfers to and from the developing countries. Official development assistance will become much less important relative to private capital flows. Above all, the financial health of the developing countries will be a stabilizing element in the international monetary system.

5. TRADE

The one area where developing and developed countries clearly interact is that of trade. One-quarter of everything produced in the world is now traded across national borders, making it possible to speak of a global supply and a global demand. The South has learned to use trade as a developmental tool only within the past two decades. The basic strategy of Third World nations in the beginning was known as import substitution. It meant transfer of resources from agriculture to industry, and production for the internal market rather than for export. As a result, world primary exports grew very slowly, and the share of developing countries in this trade rapidly diminished. While their overall volume of exports grew in the 1950s and 1960s at a rate of 5%, their import purchasing power rose at a lower rate, 2%, because of deteriorating terms of trade.

During the 1970s, the demand for primary commodities increased more rapidly and the terms of trade stabilized. Many trade restrictions were phased out as liberalism came to be accepted as the standard official policy. International capital and technology transfers stimulated the expansion of trade. A few developing countries seized this opportunity to accelerate their exports and found a new niche in the South under the name advanced developing countries. The group included the so-called Gang of Four—Hong Kong, Singapore, Taiwan and South Korea—as well the South American giant, Brazil. These countries thus made trade itself an engine of growth. ADCs also found access to new sources of finance from international capital markets. At the same time, the expansion of trade created new fissures within the developing world as the low-income nations fell behind, their frail economies having little to contribute to the arena of trade. These economic basket cases became a Third World within the Third World.

A new factor entered into the picture with the 1973 oil embargo and the quantum jump in oil prices. While all OIDCs as a group have experienced consistent current account deficits since the first oil price shock, ADCs in particular have accumulated large deficits. Having to pay off their debts as well as their oil bills, these ADCs redoubled their efforts to export more goods despite less favorable opportunities for trade. For them exports became not merely an engine of growth but the very stuff of survival.

Thus the benefits of trade are heavily concentrated in a handful of Third World countries that can produce a diverse range of manufactured products at competitive prices. During the 1970s, they accounted for 98% of the gain in the export-derived purchasing power of the Third World. Seven countries are responsible for 75% of the manufactured exports of developing countries. However, by the end of the century, it is expected that the benefits of trade will become more widely diffused, enabling middle-income countries, such as Malaysia, Thailand, the Philippines, Colombia, Morocco and the Ivory Coast, to stake a presence in world markets. The poorer countries' share of world exports and their percentage of production exported will continue to fall in the remaining decades of this century because of uncertain and volatile market conditions in the industrialized world.

6. FOOD

The recent absence of food crises from the front pages of newspapers does not mean that food has ceased to be a critical issue for the

Third World. True, it is no longer the doomsday indicator that it once was and the crisis in the Sahel is now only a memory for those who do not live there. Since the early 1970s the world's food system has become more closely integrated than at any other time in human history. No longer a strictly national issue, food is now a global concern. Self-sufficiency in food is less urgent as a developmental imperative for the poorer nations when they have access to the overflowing silos of the richer countries. To rephrase the U.S. Presidential Commission on World Hunger, the war against famine in Africa is won on the farmlands of Kansas.

Yet surprisingly, the food beggars of the world are *not* the poorest nations but the relatively well-to-do, such as the Soviet Union, Japan, South Korea and Egypt. The typical customer in the global food market is not the destitute Djiboutian but the rotund Russian. The hungriest nations, in the starvation belt of Southeast Asia and the Sahel, have just barely increased their food imports over the past decade. India, for example, where half the world's undernourished people live, imported scarcely any grain between 1977 and 1981. Taiwan and South Korea, on the other hand, with a total population of 54 million, imported more grain (9.4 million tons in 1980) than all the low-income nations combined, with a total population 1.3 billion. An even greater irony is that the poorer nations use much of their scarce agricultural resources to produce coffee, cocoa, sugar, jute and bananas for the delectation of wealthy customers abroad. If land used to grow these products were given over to cereal production, then all Africa and Latin America would become truly self-sufficient in food.

Within a global context, food grain import costs still represent only a modest foreign exchange burden for most countries, averaging 20% of export earnings from agriculture and 5% of total export earnings. This share has remained fairly steady over the past 20 years.

Even though world food production has expanded steadily over the previous 30 years—by over 75% in developing countries—per capita production has only edged forward and in some cases declined. The problem lies not so much with the Third World farmer, who, as economist Theodore W. Schultz of the University of Chicago asserts, is "poor but efficient"; he responds to price incentives and has learned to maximize profits within available technology in much the same way as farmers in industrialized countries. The problem lies rather with official policies and external assistance programs that are targeted toward more visible and prestigious sectors, such as industry, to the exclusion of agriculture. The sector also suffers from price disincentives. Artificially low producer prices are, at least partially, the result of surplus disposal programs of richer countries. U.S. food aid, for example, has helped to depress agricultural prices in all countries to which it has been extended. National food policies also often distort market forces and frequently magnify the effect of short-term scarcities. In Egypt, official control over wheat, corn and rice led farmers to turn to fruits, vegetables and livestock (which were not price-controlled), with the result that Egypt now has to import six million tons of grain annually. Similarly, in India the production of rice lagged for years because it was relatively less profitable than wheat, which received government subsidies. It follows that official policies must reflect agricultural needs and allocate adequate resources to meet those needs.

7. EDUCATION

The 1948 U.N. *Universal Declaration of Human Rights* stated: "Everyone has the right to education. Education shall be free at least in the elementary and fundamental stages... Higher education shall be equally accessible to all on the basis of merit." Three decades later, this objective is far from reality. In the developing countries, less than 65% of children between the ages of 6 and 11 are enrolled in school and of them only about 50% reach the fourth grade. The enrollment rates of 12- to 17-year-olds and 18- to 23-year-olds are about 38% and 9% respectively. By 1985 UNESCO projects that the enrollment rates for these three age groups will be 68%, 42% and 12% respectively. The disparities in Africa and Asia will be even more striking. Twenty-eight of 46 African countries representing 77% of the continent's population and 14 of 27 Asian countries representing 88% of Asia's population will fall below the UNESCO projections. Youth not in school will increase by about 30 million. To maintain the current primary enrollment rate in the face of rapidly growing population, enrollment must increase by 30% over the next decade. Provision of basic education to the adult population is likewise inadequate. While the percentage of adult illiterates in developing countries declined by 12% between 1950 and 1975, it increased in absolute numbers to over 600 million by 1978 and is not expected to decrease before the year 2000.

In addition, there are unequal educational opportunities within countries based on sex, socioeconomic status, and differing rural, urban, regional and ethnic backgrounds. Of all these disparities, none is a greater hindrance to development than that based on sex. Aggregate data for developing countries as a whole show wide disparities between male and female enrollments, especially when compared with virtual parity in developed countries. In the primary age group the enrollment rate was 72% for boys and 56% for girls, in the secondary age group it was 44% for boys and 32% for girls and in the postsecondary age group it was 11% for boys and 6% for girls. The effect of other factors on enrollment is not always clearly distinguishable, but a few examples will illustrate conditions common throughout the developing world. The average enrollment rate for urban areas in Brazil is 92%, but the corresponding rate for the rural population is only 52%. The primary enrollment rate in the northern states of Nigeria is only 14%, compared with 76% in the southern states. In Indonesia, there is a gap of 15 percentage points between the enrollment rate for rural and urban children, increasing to about 40 percentage points by the last year of secondary school.

Educational programs in developing countries during the 1960s were aimed at expanding enrollment rather than changing the character of education. Although the newly independent countries replaced the foreign content in their school curricula with content related to national culture and traditions, these changes did not significantly alter other aspects of the educational system, such as the structure of cycles, the language of instruction, school calendars, or teaching and examination techniques. Nevertheless, a growing desire to assert national identity coupled with an urge to experiment with broader concepts of social development led to educational reforms, particularly in five areas: equality of educational opportunity, development of science teaching, improvement of the internal efficiencies of the school system, enhancement of the relevance of education to perceived national needs, and the indigenization of management and research. The new trends were most clearly defined in two areas: relevance and language. Relevance was identified as a function of education in the creation of an authentic national culture, especially one free of the vestiges of colonial rule. The quest for relevance also included efforts to establish, by official fiat, an indigenous national language as the medium of instruction. But the conflict proved to be not merely between the national and foreign languages but, even more so, between the national and local or ethnic languages. Linguistic chauvinism also served to sever the access that former colonies had hitherto enjoyed to the whole corpus of knowledge available only in Western languages as well as opportunities for higher education and training abroad. Confronted with such problems, few Third World countries have managed to evolve a clear and workable language policy. To nationalize the system of education, to make it relevant and to manage its growing complexities, many developing countries established units for planning and research. Unfortunately, these units have suffered from a lack of trained staff, sparseness of educational data, and a want of consensus regarding educational policies and programs.

Efforts to expand and equalize educational opportunities in developing countries face many constraints. The most obvious and frequent is the lack of resources—financial as well as human. Although during the past two decades developing countries have, on the average, steadily increased public expenditures for education as percentages of both their GNP and national budget, they are spending much less per student than developed countries and the gap is widening. Another major problem is that inefficiencies in the school system vitiate the quality of learning. Such inefficiencies are reflected in a high degree of waste—students dropping out and repeating, low student-teacher ratios and underused physical facilities. The relationship between education and work suffers from a shortage of training opportunities and work experiences, the discouraging prevalence of unemployment and the fact that even though education is considered primarily a passport to jobs, it is not always geared to employment opportunities in the economy. Finally, the development of national managerial and administrative as well as research capabilities lags behind the growth in size and complexity of the educational sector. Many school systems have poor management procedures, and decision-making responsibilities are distributed among numerous agencies without clear concomitant accountability.

8. HEALTH

Health problems in the South are very different from those in the North. In a typical developing country, more than 40% of the deaths are from infectious, parasitic and respiratory diseases (as against 10% in the North, where the major killers are cancer and heart and vascular diseases). One-half of the people, in middle-income countries and two-thirds of the residents of the world's poorest countries drink contaminated water. The most widespread diseases in developing countries are diarrheal ones transmitted by human fecal contamination of soil, food and water. The parasitic diseases are usually more chronic and debilitating than acute, and they flourish in the poorest areas, such as slums. Diseases transmitted by insects, such as malaria, remain widespread in certain areas years after WHO believed they would be wiped out. Some 850 million people live in areas where malaria has been only partially controlled. Schistosomiasis, caused by a snail-borne parasite, is endemic in some countries with a population of 200 million. Ironically, development projects have increased the incidence of schistosomiasis and onchocerciasis (or river blindness) in many parts of Africa; drainage and irrigation canals provide habitat for the snails, and the spillways of dams for blackfly larvae.

Disease must be regarded as not merely a personal but a national waste, just as health must be considered a fundamental right, not merely a by-product of development. In no area is the North-South gap so dramatic as in that of health. The average life expectancy of a Northerner is 15 years greater than that of a Southerner, and 100 to 180 more live-born infants die per 1,000 in the Third World than in the developed world. In a typical developing country a third of all deaths are among children under five. The extent of sickness and disability is harder to document, but some studies suggest that a tenth of the life of an average Third World resident is seriously disrupted by illness.

Health is one of the least controversial developmental goals and receives considerable vocal support from Third World politicians. But when it comes to actual allocation of funds for health care, their performance has been disappointing. Most underdeveloped countries spend less than 1% of their GNP on health, compared with 6 to 12% in developed countries; in other words, only a few pennies per day per person is expended in the former compared with several dollars in the latter. Worse, even these exiguous amounts are spent on the urban and the rich, with the result that health services are practically nonexistent at the lowest levels. Such demographic and geographic discrimination is often aggravated by wrong choices in the forms and techniques of health delivery services. Western-type medical education prepares Third World doctors to look at medical episodes rather than at individuals holistically and to look at clinical conditions rather than at health problems. Increasingly complex and expensive medical technology is oriented toward hospital care rather than outpatient and home care. The quality of medical care in the Third World thus suffers on many levels: its availability, its orientation, its costs. Since health is the key element determining the national quality of life, the implications of an ill-guided and underfunded health-care system can be disastrous.

9. ENERGY

The future pace of energy consumption growth in developing countries will be dramatically different from that in developed countries. Consumption is expected to rise 200 to 250% in the former over the next 20 years, compared with only 50% in the latter. The proportion of commercial energy consumed in the Third World will grow from 18% in 1976 to 25% in 1990 and 30% in the year 2000.

Rapid escalation of energy demand is a correlate of development, because in the initial or transitional stages traditional sources of energy are replaced with more efficient ones, such as oil. The shift from traditional energy to oil could put significant additional pressure on the world's dwindling supplies of oil by the end of the century. The energy strategy of developing countries therefore needs to be directed toward three goals: producing more oil and gas, reducing dependence on oil and substituting renewable energy resources for it, and conserving energy.

Although 40% of the world's prospective oil-bearing terrain is located in OIDCs, including China, their share of proven oil reserves is only 11.5% of the world total. But much of this terrain remains underexplored. The intensity of drilling in the United States, for example, is 800 times as great as in Africa.

A second key element in the transition to the post-oil era is the exploitation and deployment of renewable energy resources, such as the sun, as well as more plentiful resources, such as coal and hydroelectric power. Developing countries account for 10% of the world's reserves of coal, most of it in India. Nevertheless, some 20 countries have considerable potential coal resources. Hydroelectric energy is more promising. About 70% of the world's potential large-scale hydroelectric resources is in developing countries, yet it accounts for only 20% of Third World energy production. While nuclear energy is not a viable alternative for many developing countries (because nuclear generating units currently generate electricity in amounts too large for these countries' delivery grids), solar power is an ideal energy resource for low-income nations. Not only do many of them have more sunlight than industrialized countries, but producing units can be adapted to small-scale rural development. In addition, their climatic conditions often permit faster growth of vegetation for firewood and biogasification.

Meanwhile, along with developed nations, Third World countries are learning to conserve energy and thereby cut back on imports, which already cost them $60 to $70 billion annually. But further cutbacks of oil imports could take a toll on development programs.

10. EMPLOYMENT

The most striking feature of the employment situation in the Third World is that nearly one-third of the working-age population is seriously *under*employed. The problem is the absence of productive jobs at fair wages for those who are technically considered employed. Unemployment, such as is found in the United States affecting 10% of the work force, is rarer in the Third World than it is in the industrialized world. The ILO reported in the mid-1970s that some 250 million people (or 35.7% of the Third World workforce) were underemployed. Not surprisingly, this is the same percentage of Third World residents who are reported to be living in absolute poverty.

The World Bank estimates that between now and the year 2000 the Third World labor force will increase to 1.25 billion, necessitating the creation of an additional 500 to 850 million jobs to absorb the new entrants into the labor force. In order to do so, the South will have to industrialize three to five times as rapidly as it did during the 1960s and 1970s as well as grow at an average annual rate of 20 to 25% over the next 17 years. Both these alternatives are impossible given the other constraints on growth already at work in the Third World. But it is not merely the length of the unemployment line that concerns Third World planners, it is also the generally poor productivity and the depressed quality of working life. Since agriculture is the least productive of all sectors, there is a need to encourage the shift of labor from agriculture to other sectors. Such a shift—one of the most reliable indicators of development—is already evident on the statistical charts but is too slow to make any impact on actual demographics. Between 1950 and 1970, it is estimated that the share of agricultural employment in low-income countries fell by only 3%.

One result of the difficult employment picture in the South is the vastly increased movement of workers from poor to rich countries, believed to be one of the largest such migrations in human history for economic and not political reasons. One widely cited source estimates the number of people involved at over 20 million. In recent years, these workers have tended to move principally to one of three areas: Western Europe, where there are now 5 to 6 million resident aliens from Southern Europe, Turkey and North Africa; the Arabian Peninsula, with 2 to 3 million workers from the not-so-rich Arab states and the Indian subcontinent; and the United States and Canada, with over 12 million (legal and illegal) aliens from Mexico, the Caribbean, Central America and northern South America.

The magnitude of transnational labor flows from the developing countries is not large enough to make a dent in their overall employment picture or afford them any significant relief. Migrants constitute less than 5% of their total out-of-work force. For the receiving countries, however, the influx may cause a significant imbalance in their ethnic makeup. For example, foreign workers constitute 75% of Kuwait's workforce and 25% of the workforces of Switzerland and Luxembourg. Outweighing this disadvantage is the fact that migrants contribute less expensive labor, which helps to hold down labor costs (and thus benefits employers) and prices (and thus benefits consumers).

There is considerable disagreement about the benefits of the brain drain and brawn drain for the developing countries themselves. The size of the annual remittances from migrant workers is at least one benefit. But more often than not, the people who migrate are professionals, skilled workers and entrepreneurs, whose talents are needed in their own societies. The prolonged absence of the predominantly male migrants may cause hardships, psychological and otherwise, to the mainly female dependents they leave behind. The remittances, therefore, are not always unmixed blessings for the sending nations.

11. INTERDEPENDENCE

Interdependence between developed and developing societies is not a new concept. But it has gained new urgency as a result of the events of the past two decades. It now defines not so much a passive state of awareness but an active resource energizing international transactions and helping to curb the excesses of short-sighted nationalism. It is also becoming an imperative in promoting a sustainable growth in world economy. The poor nations can no longer be dismissed as stragglers and basket cases; there is sound economic wisdom in any alliance between rich and poor nations because their ultimate interests coincide.

Increasingly, the developing countries are acting as engines of progress for the rest of the world. While the main transmission of economic activity is from the North to the South, the reverse effects are not negligible. Some estimates suggest that an extra percentage point in the growth rate of developing countries would add another 0.1 to 0.2% to the growth rate of developed nations. Another study calculatedthat by sustaining their imports during the mid-1970s while the rest of the world's slowed down, the middle-income countries had an impact on the industrialized countries equivalent to a signficant reflation of the economy of West Germany. They prevented the recession in the North from becoming even worse than it was.

The developing countries also play an increasingly important role in world trade. They will account for nearly 30% of the increase in world trade between 1980 and 1990. The OIDCs alone purhased 19% of EEC exports, 24% of U.S. exports and 32% of Japanese exports. In the trade in manufactured goods as a whole, industrial market economies enjoyed a surplus of $34.5 billion with the developing countries in 1978.

For Third World countries, the concept of interdependence has a particular significance because it is the most powerful argument they can advance for the greater involvement of the industrialized world in their development. In one sense, all countries in the world are developing countries, just as all are dependent countries; it is this web of dependence and development that will sustain the continuing dialogue between North and South on the basis of equality and mutual respect.

A NOTE ON READING CHARTS

Charts presented in this book are based on basic data (frequency counts of persons, events etc.) or derived statistics (summary measures, such as averages, rates, ratios, proportions and percentage distributions). These data are often of uneven quality because data collection operations may not adhere to uniform standards. All data, however collected, are subject to some risk of inaccuracy or error. Even population figures, the most reliable of all, may vary by as much as 2%.

Two types of charts appear most often: bar charts, where the heights of vertical bars or the lengths of horizontal bars indicate magnitude, and line charts, whose connected points denote successive magnitudes or trends over time. The labels of the axes identify the variables and scales of measurement, which denote the values of the variables. At times, a break may appear on a bar denoting a single value that exceeds the limits of the chart scale. On many line charts time is represented on the x axis and the values of the variable are shown along the y axis. The line does not necessarily represent the values for periods between observations.

The ATLAS OF THE THIRD WORLD, like the ENCYCLOPEDIA OF THE THIRD WORLD and other projects before it, has been fortunate in that it had the steady skipper's hand of Edward W. Knappman, Executive Vice President of Facts On File, to guide it through the two years it was in gestation. I am completing this project with a large debt of gratitude for his patience and encouragement. The art department of Facts On File has done a magnificent job on the maps and charts within record time. My thanks are particularly due to Andrew Elias, the cartographer and graphic artist in charge of the project. Andrew's comment that he had learned to understand the Third World more after working on the ATLAS is one that I hope every reader can make. This work can have no better purpose. My thanks are also due to my daughter, Sarah Claudine Kurian, who has helped me out on more occasions than I can count with her usual cheerfulness.

April 27, 1983   GEORGE THOMAS KURIAN

SOURCES: COUNTRY PROFILES

Population Growth: *The World Factbook 1990* (Washington, D.C.: CIA, 1990).
Gross Natonal Product: *World Bank Atlas 1990* (Washington, D.C.: World Bank, 1990).
Central Government Revenues and Expenditures: *Government Finance Statistics Yearbook 1990* (Washington, D.C.: IMF, 1990).
Exchange Rate: *International Financial Statistics 1990* (Washington, D.C.: IMF, 1990).
Total Reserve: *International Financial Statistics 1990* (Washington, D.C.: IMF, 1990).
Reserve Money: *International Financial Statistics 1990* (Washington, D.C.: IMF, 1990).
Money: *International Financial Statistics 1990* (Washington, D.C.: IMF, 1990).
Consumer Prices: *International Financial Statistics 1990* (Washington, D.C.: IMF, 1990).
International Transactions: *International Financial Statistics 1990* (Washington, D.C.: IMF, 1990).
Land Use: *Britannica World Data 1991* (Chicago: Encyclopaedia Britannica, 1991).
Labor Force: *Britannica World Data 1991* (Chicago: Encyclopaedia Britannica, 1991).
Budget Expenditures: *International Financial Statistics 1990* (Washington, D.C.: IMF, 1990).
Imports: *Britannica World Data 1991* (Chicago: Encyclopaedia Britannica, 1991).
Exports: *Britannica World Data 1991* (Chicago: Encyclopaedia Britannica, 1991).
GDP by Economic Activity: *Britannica World Data 1991* (Chicago: Encyclopaedia Britannica, 1991).
Educational Enrollment: *Statistical Yearbook 1990* (Paris: Unesco 1990).
Defense Budget: *Government Finance Statistics Yearbook 1990* (Washington, D.C.: IMF, 1990).
Sectoral Growth: *World Development Report 1988* (Washington, D.C.: World Bank, 1988).
Foregin Aid: *The World Factbook 1989* (Washington, D.C.: CIA, 1989).

PART I:
THEMATIC PROFILES

PROLOGUE:
DEVELOPED AND DEVELOPING NATIONS

POPULATION 1990

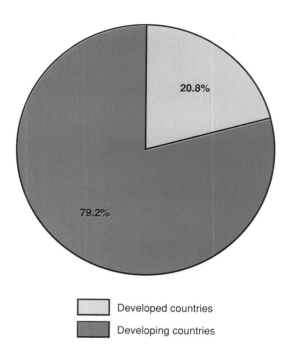

Source: Overseas Development Council

POPULATION GROWTH RATE 1985-90

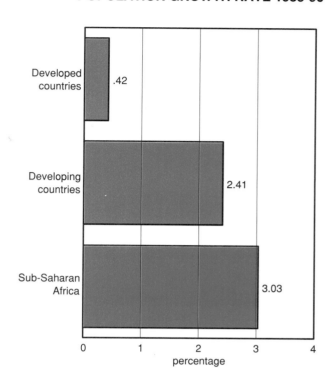

Source: World Resources 1990-91
(New York: Oxford University Press, 1990)

POPULATION "DOUBLING TIME" IN YEARS
(at current rate)

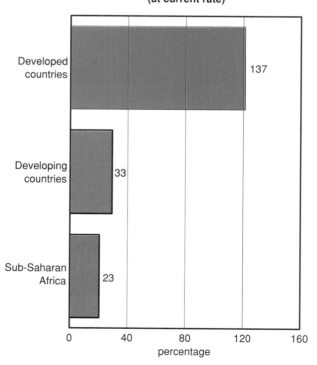

Source: 1991 World Population Data Sheet
(Washington, D.C.: Population Reference Bureau, 1991)

BIRTH RATE
(per 1,000 population)

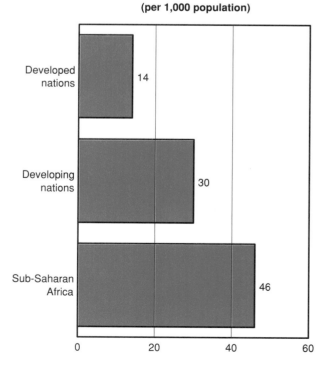

Source: 1991 World Population Data Sheet
(Washington, D.C.: Population Reference Bureau, 1991)

LIFE EXPECTANCY AT BIRTH

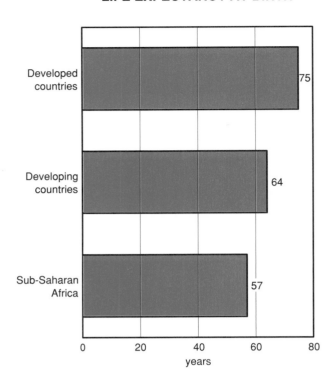

Source: World Development Report 1990
(New York: World Bank, 1990)

FEMALE LIFE EXPECTANCY

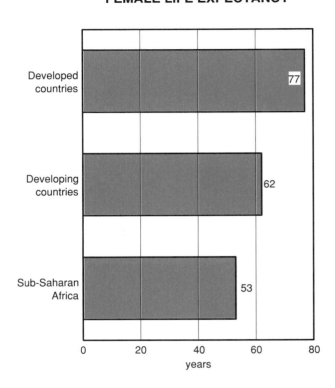

Source: Ruth Leger Sivard, Women... a World Survey
(Washington, D.C.: World Priorities, 1985)

DAILY CALORIE SUPPLY PER CAPITA

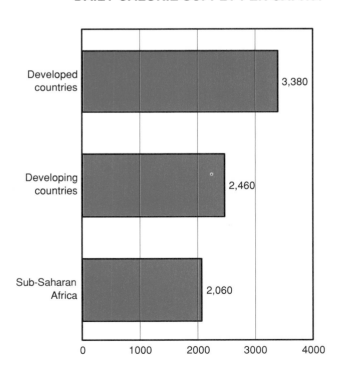

Source: World Resources 1990-91
(New York: Oxford University Press, 1990)

INFANT MORTALITY RATE
(per 1,000 population)

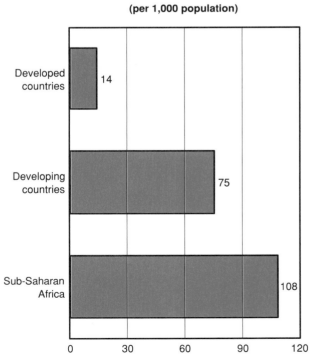

Source: 1991 World Population Data Sheet
(Washington, D.C.: Population Reference Bureau, 1991)

ADULT ILLITERACY RATE

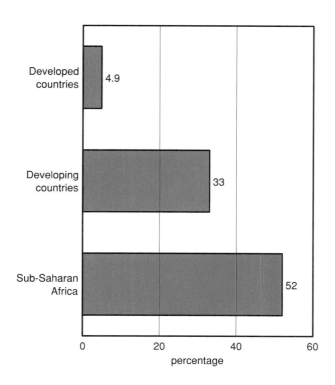

Source: *World Development Report 1990*
(New York: World Bank, 1990)

FEMALE ILLITERACY RATE

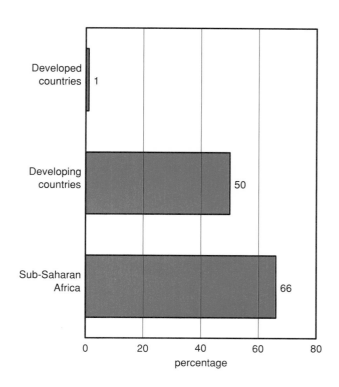

Source: Ruth Leger Sivard, *Women... a World Survey*
(Washington, D.C.: World Priorities, 1985)

PER CAPITA PUBLIC SPENDING ON EDUCATION

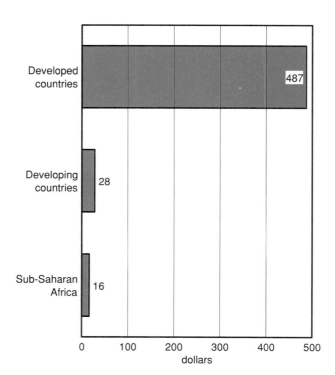

Source: John W. Sewell, Stuart K. Tucker et al,
Growth, Exports, and Jobs in a Changing World Economy, Agenda 1988
(New Brunswick: Transaction Books, 1988)

PHYSICAL QUALITY OF LIFE INDEX

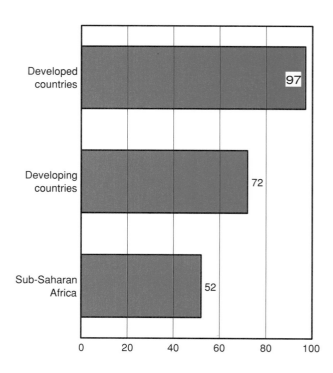

Source: *Overseas Development Council*

WORLD GNP 1989

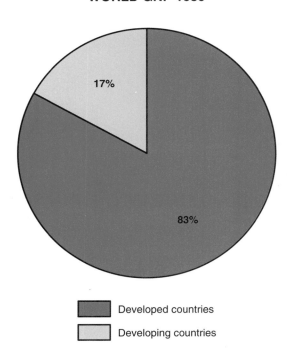

17%

83%

■ Developed countries

□ Developing countries

Source: World Bank Atlas 1990
(Washington, D.C.: World Bank, 1990)

PER CAPITA GNP 1989

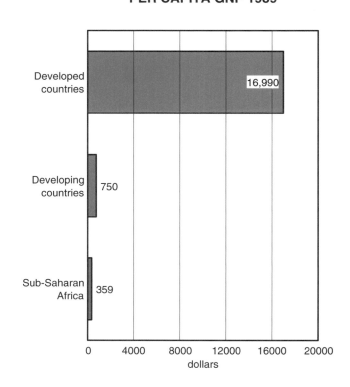

Developed countries — 16,990

Developing countries — 750

Sub-Saharan Africa — 359

0   4000   8000   12000   16000   20000
dollars

Source: 1991 World Population Data Sheet
(Washington, D.C.: Population Reference Bureau, 1991)

ENERGY CONSUMPTION PER CAPITA 1988
(kilograms of oil equivalent)

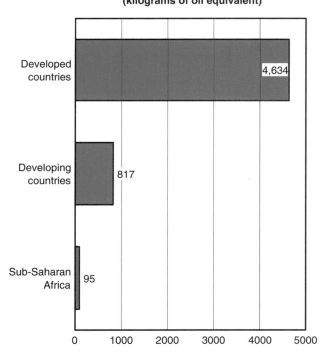

Developed countries — 4,634

Developing countries — 817

Sub-Saharan Africa — 95

0   1000   2000   3000   4000   5000

Source: World Development Report 1990
(New York: World Bank, 1990)

SHARE OF AGRICULTURE IN GDP 1988

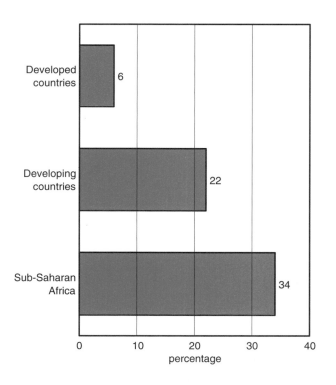

Developed countries — 6

Developing countries — 22

Sub-Saharan Africa — 34

0   10   20   30   40
percentage

Source: World Development Report 1990
(New York: World Bank, 1990)

1: POLITICAL DIVISIONS

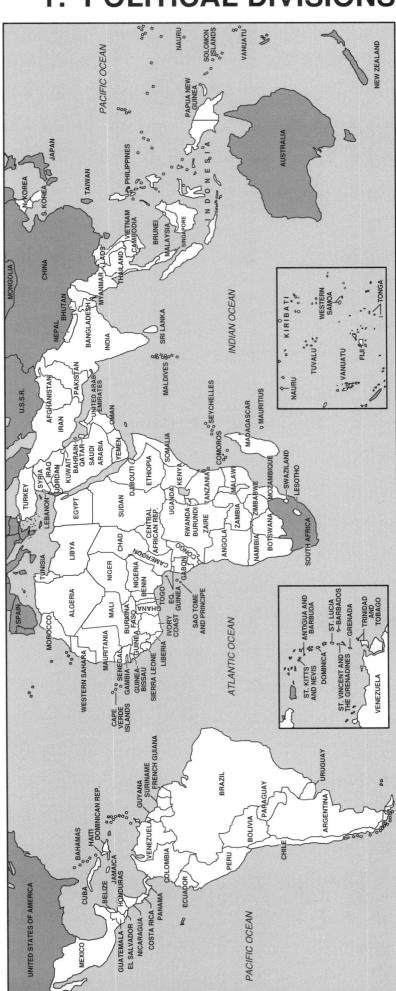

FIGURE 1-1
POLITICAL DIVISIONS

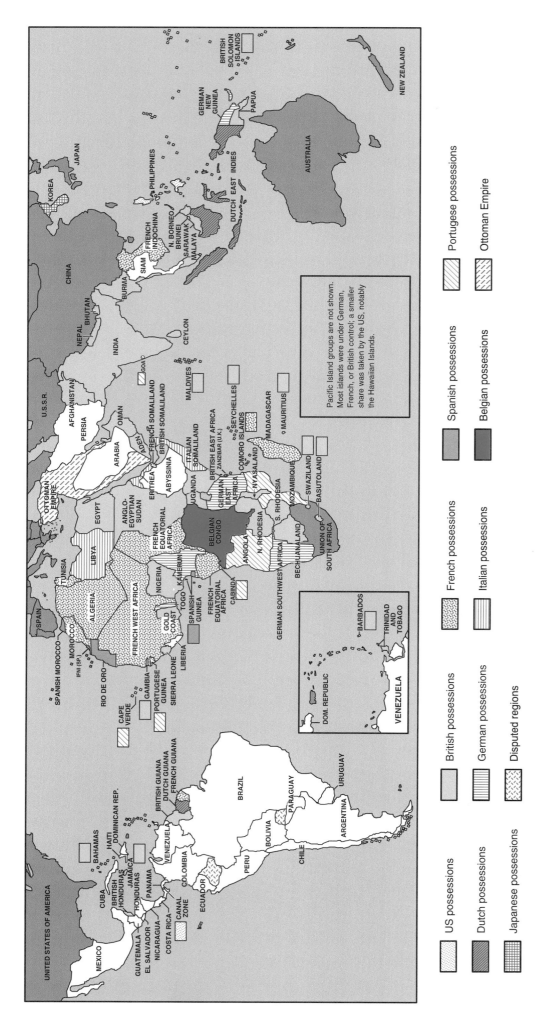

FIGURE 1-2
THE THIRD WORLD IN 1914

US possessions

Dutch possessions

Japanese possessions

British possessions

German possessions

Disputed regions

French possessions

Italian possessions

Spanish possessions

Belgian possessions

Portugese possessions

Ottoman Empire

Pacific Island groups are not shown. Most islands were under German, French, or British control; a smaller share was taken by the US, notably the Hawaiian Islands.

Source: Africa South of the Sahara 1991
(London: Europa Publications Limited, 1991)

FIGURE 1-3
POLITICAL INDEPENDENCE

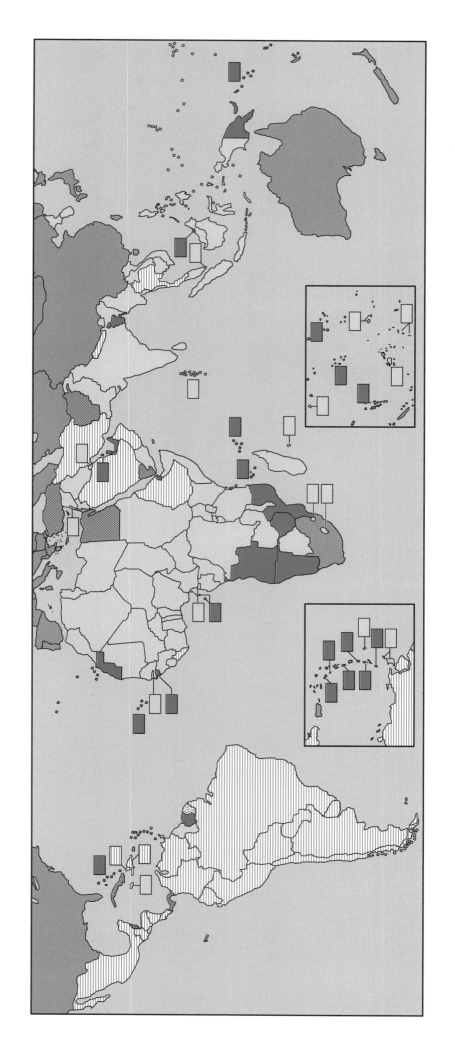

Independent by 1900

Gained independence after 1970

Gained independence 1900-1930

Dependent territory

Gained independence 1931-1970

Sources: George Kurian, *Encyclopedia of the Third World, 4th ed.* (New York: Facts On File, 1992)
The World Factbook 1990. (Washington, D.C.: CIA, 1991)

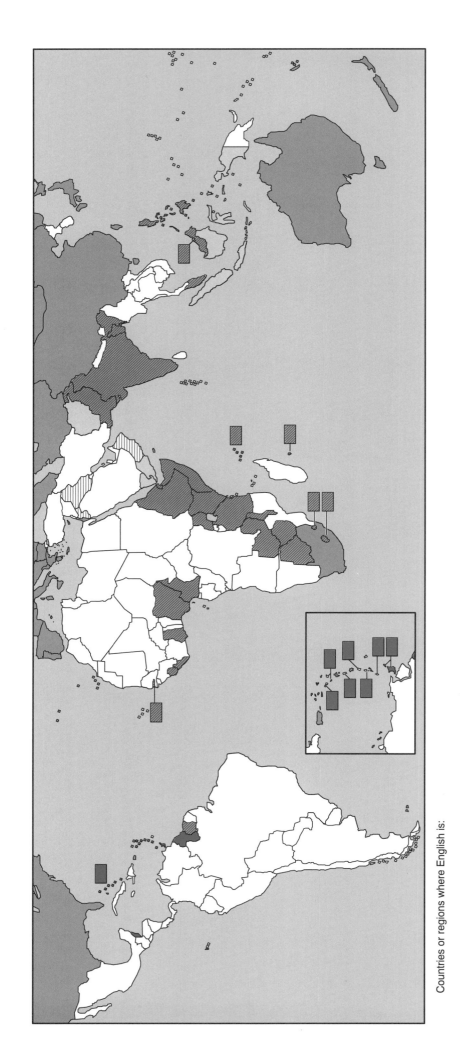

FIGURE 1-4
ENGLISH IN THE THIRD WORLD

Countries or regions where English is:

▪ Dominant native language

▨ Introduced as compulsory subject on primary level (as of 1979)

▨ Official language or widely used in public administration or instruction

☐ Officially recognized as first foreign language (as of 1979)

Source: Atlas of U.S. Foreign Relations
(Washington, D.C.: U.S. State Department, 1985)

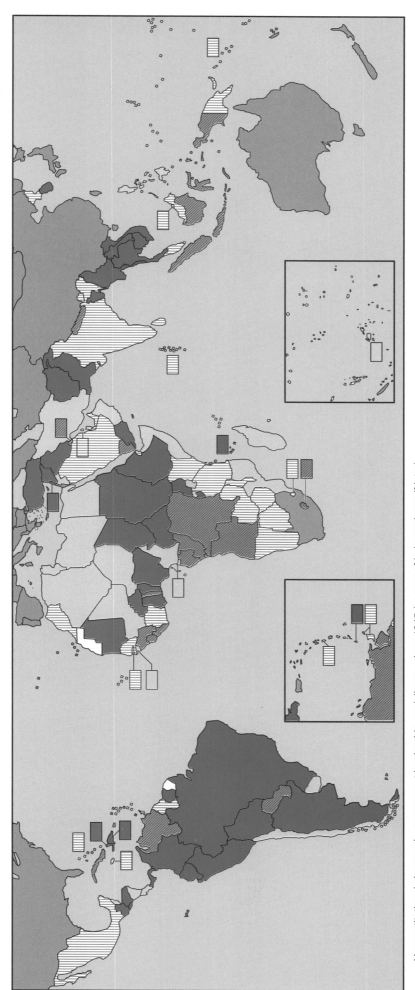

FIGURE 1-5
POLITICAL INSTABILITY
(1945-87)

Unconstitutional changes in government leadership or civil wars since 1945 (or year of independence if later)

None

Three or more

One

Data not available

Two

Source: George Kurian, *Encyclopedia of the Third World 4th ed.,* (New York: Facts On File, 1992)
Roger East, ed., *World Fact File 1990,* (New York: Facts On File, 1990)
New York Times, 5/2/91

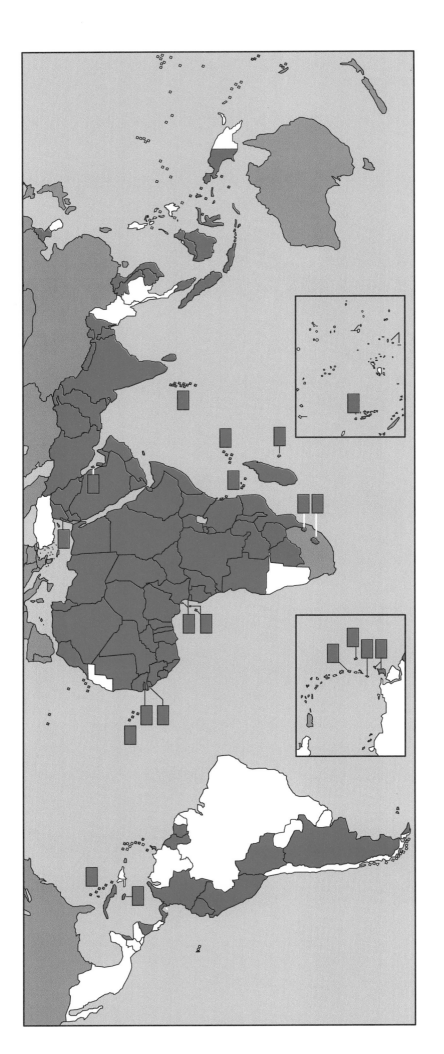

FIGURE 1-6
NONALIGNED MOVEMENT

■ Nonaligned Movement member countries

Source: Atlas of U.S. Foreign Relations
(Washington, D.C.: U.S. State Department, 1985)

2: POPULATION

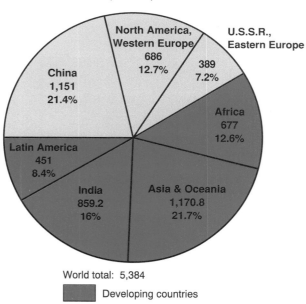

FIGURE 2-1
POPULATION 1991
(millions)

China
1,151
21.4%

North America,
Western Europe
686
12.7%

U.S.S.R.,
Eastern Europe
389
7.2%

Africa
677
12.6%

Latin America
451
8.4%

India
859.2
16%

Asia & Oceania
1,170.8
21.7%

World total: 5,384

■ Developing countries

Source: 1991 World Population Data Sheet
(Washington, D.C.: Population Reference Bureau, 1991)

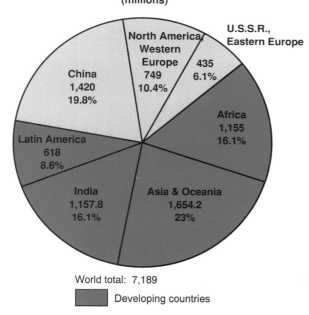

FIGURE 2-2
PROJECTED POPULATION 2010
(millions)

China
1,420
19.8%

North America,
Western
Europe
749
10.4%

U.S.S.R.,
Eastern Europe
435
6.1%

Africa
1,155
16.1%

Latin America
618
8.6%

India
1,157.8
16.1%

Asia & Oceania
1,654.2
23%

World total: 7,189

■ Developing countries

Source: 1991 World Population Data Sheet
(Washington, D.C.: Population Reference Bureau, 1991)

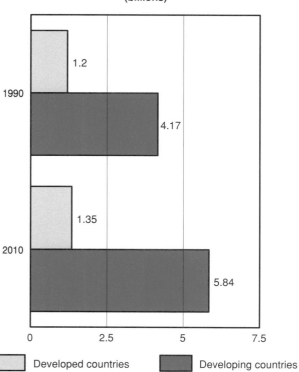

FIGURE 2-3
COMPARATIVE POPULATIONS
(billions)

1990
1.2
4.17

2010
1.35
5.84

0   2.5   5   7.5

□ Developed countries   ■ Developing countries

Source: 1991 World Population Data Sheet
(Washington, D.C.: Population Reference Bureau, 1991)

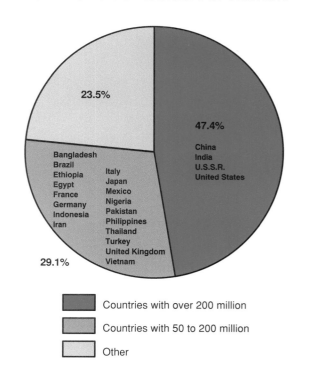

FIGURE 2-4
DISTRIBUTION OF WORLD POPULATION

23.5%

47.4%

China
India
U.S.S.R.
United States

Bangladesh
Brazil
Ethiopia
Egypt
France
Germany
Indonesia
Iran

Italy
Japan
Mexico
Nigeria
Pakistan
Philippines
Thailand
Turkey
United Kingdom
Vietnam

29.1%

■ Countries with over 200 million

▨ Countries with 50 to 200 million

□ Other

Source: 1991 World Population Data Sheet
(Washington, D.C.: Population Reference Bureau, 1991)

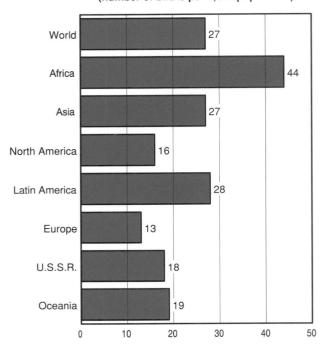

FIGURE 2-5
BIRTH RATE 1991
(number of births per 1,000 population)

Source: 1991 World Population Data Sheet
(Washington, D.C.: Population Reference Bureau, 1991)

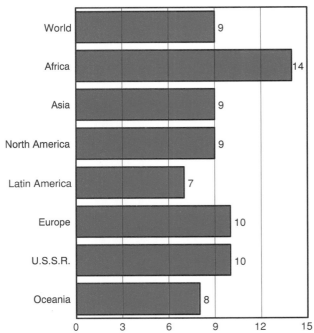

FIGURE 2-6
DEATH RATE 1991
(number of births per 1,000 population)

Source: 1991 World Population Data Sheet
(Washington, D.C.: Population Reference Bureau, 1991)

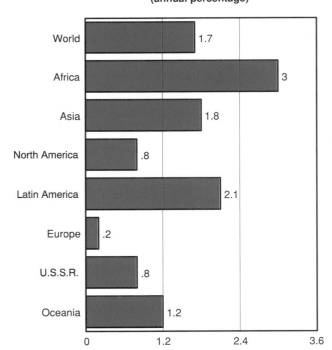

FIGURE 2-7
NATURAL INCREASE
(annual percentage)

Source: 1991 World Population Data Sheet
(Washington, D.C.: Population Reference Bureau, 1991)

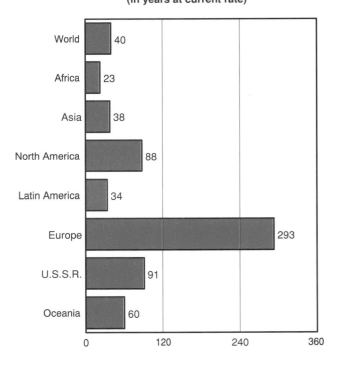

FIGURE 2-8
POPULATION DOUBLING TIME
(in years at current rate)

Source: 1991 World Population Data Sheet
(Washington, D.C.: Population Reference Bureau, 1991)

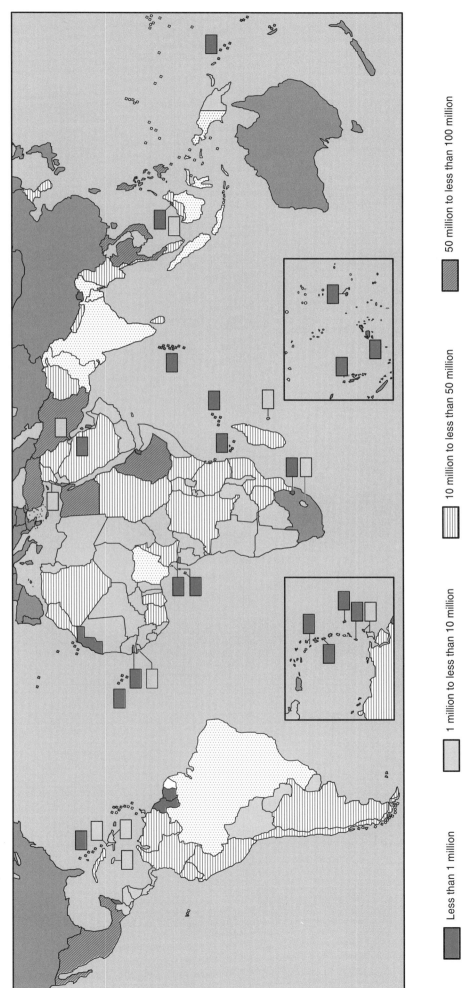

FIGURE 2-9
POPULATION 1991
(Estimated)

50 million to less than 100 million

10 million to less than 50 million

1 million to less than 10 million

Data not available

Less than 1 million

100 million and more

Source: 1991 World Population Data Sheet
(Washington, D.C.: Population Reference Bureau, 1991)

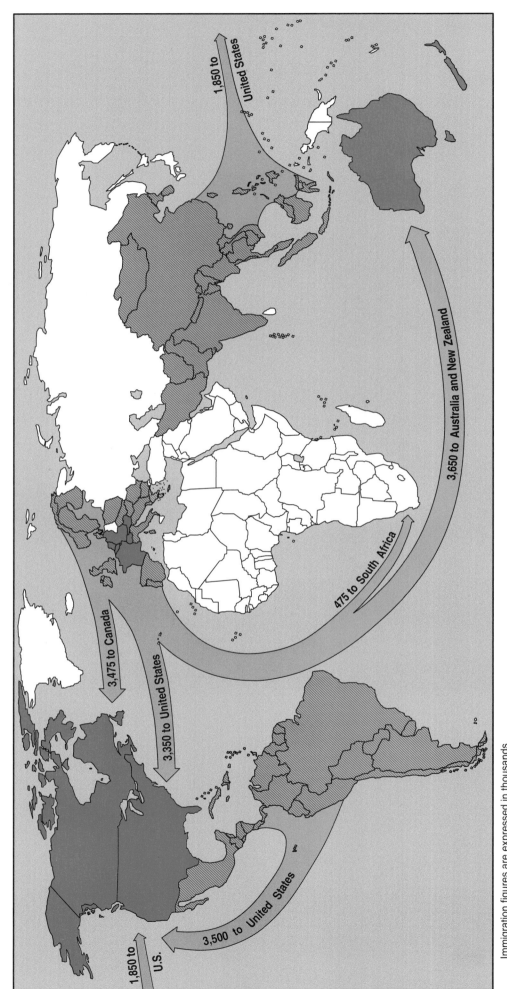

FIGURE 2-10
WORLD IMMIGRATION SINCE
WORLD WAR II

1,850 to
United States

3,650 to Australia and New Zealand

475 to South Africa

3,475 to Canada

3,350 to United States

3,500 to United States

1,850 to
U.S.

Immigration figures are expressed in thousands

Regions with net migration surplus

Regions with net migration deficit

Source: Atlas of U.S. Foreign Relations
(Washington, D.C.: U.S. State Department, 1985)

FIGURE 2-11
FAMILY PLANNING

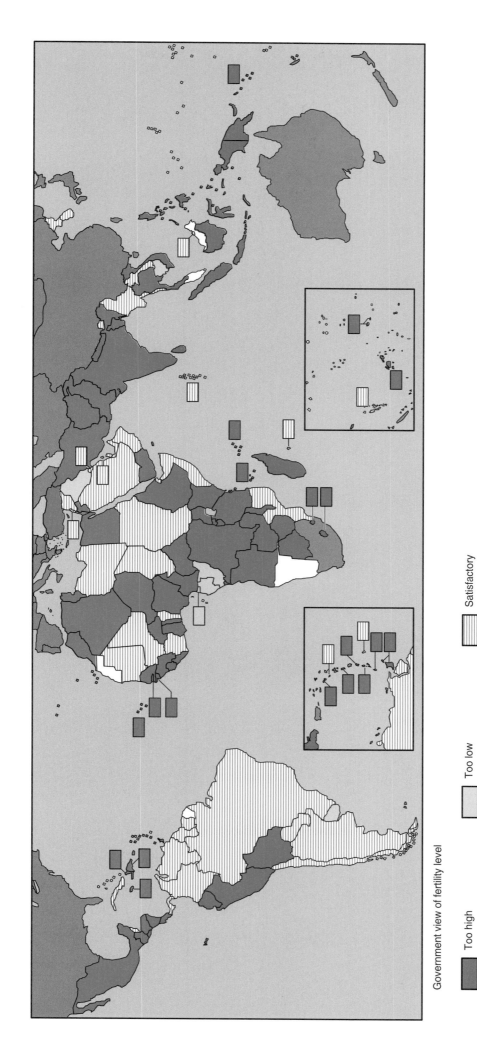

Government view of fertility level

Too high

Too low

Data not available

Satisfactory

Source: 1991 World Population Data Sheet
(Washington, D.C.: Population Reference Bureau, 1991)

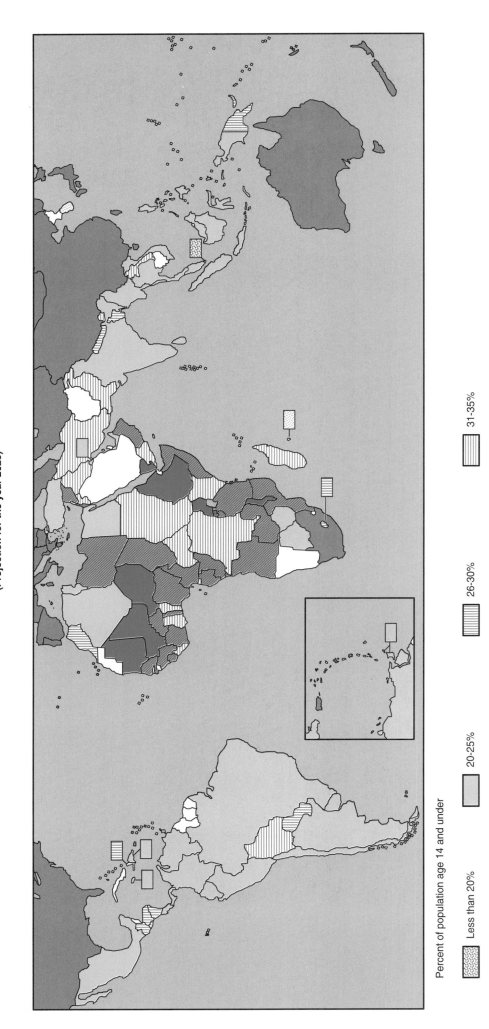

FIGURE 2-12
PERCENTAGE OF POPULATION AGES 0-14
(Projection for the year 2025)

Percent of population age 14 and under

Less than 20%   20-25%   26-30%   31-35%

36-40%   41-45%   Data not available

Source: *World Development Report 1990*
(New York: Oxford University Press, 1990)

FIGURE 2-13
CONTRACEPTIVE USE

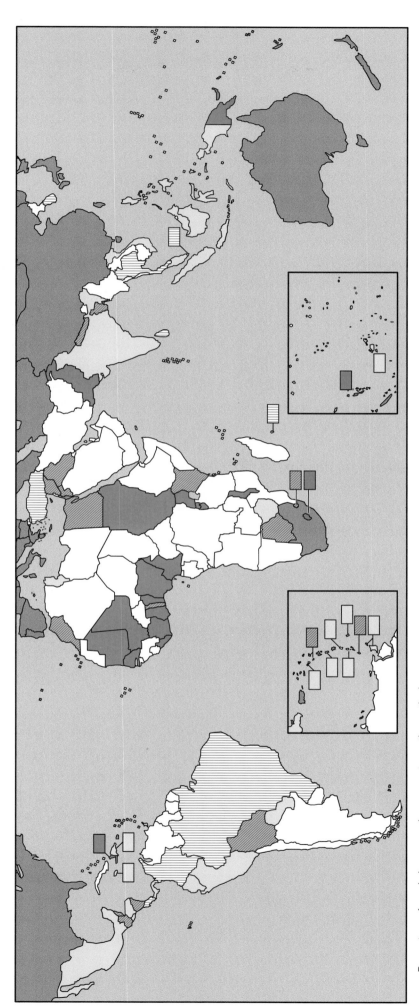

Percentage of married women using any contraceptive method

Less than 15%   15-39%   40-59%

60% and over   Data not available

Source: 1991 World Population Data Sheet
(Washington, D.C.: Population Reference Bureau, 1991)

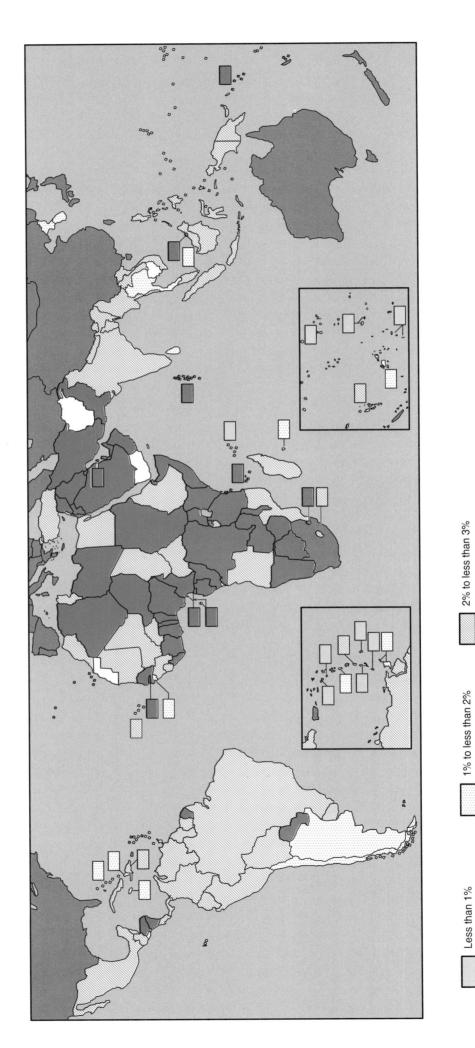

FIGURE 2-14
POPULATION GROWTH RATE
(1980-89)

Less than 1%

3% and more

1% to less than 2%

Data not available

2% to less than 3%

Source: World Bank Atlas, 1990
(Washington, D.C.: World Bank, 1990)

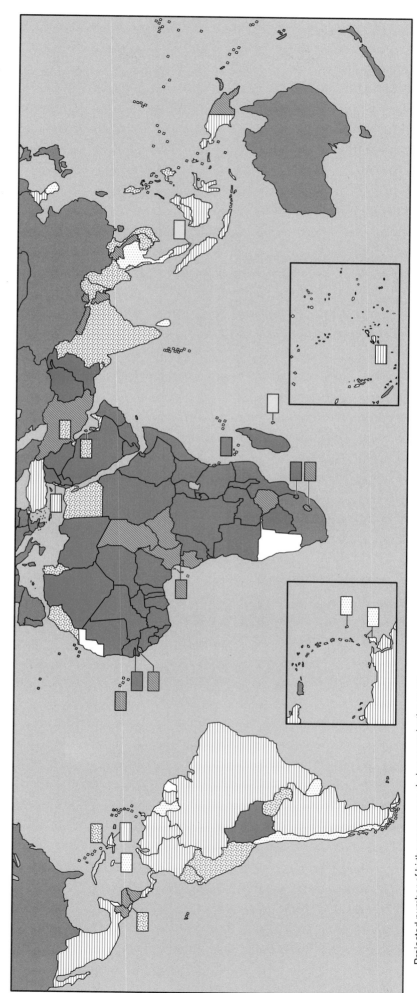

FIGURE 2-15
TOTAL FERTILITY RATE
(1985-90)

Projected number of births per woman during reproductive years

Less than 2

2 to less than 3

3 to less than 4

4 to less than 5

5 to less than 6

6 or more

Data not available

Source: World Resources 1990-91
(New York: Oxford University Press, 1990)

FIGURE 2-16
DEPENDENCY RATIO*
(1985)

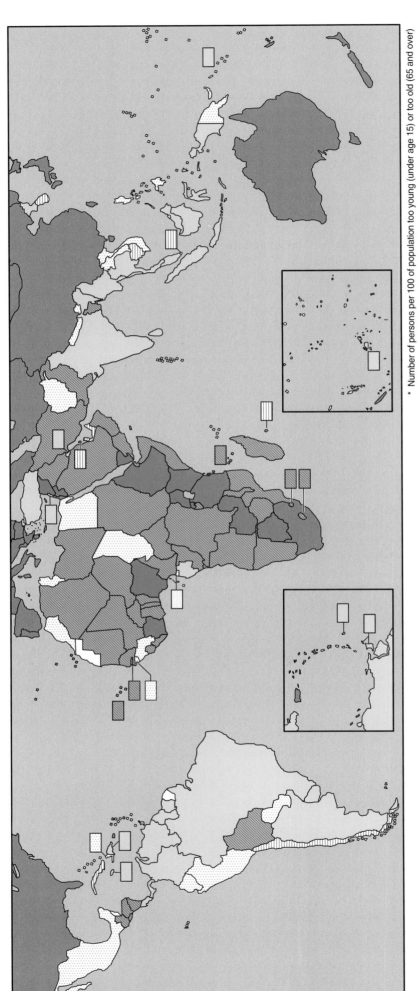

* Number of persons per 100 of population too young (under age 15) or too old (65 and over) to be economically self-sustaining.

Less than 60

60-75.9

76-85.9

86-100

Above 100

Data not available

Source: World Population Prospects 1988
(Rome: United Nations, 1989)

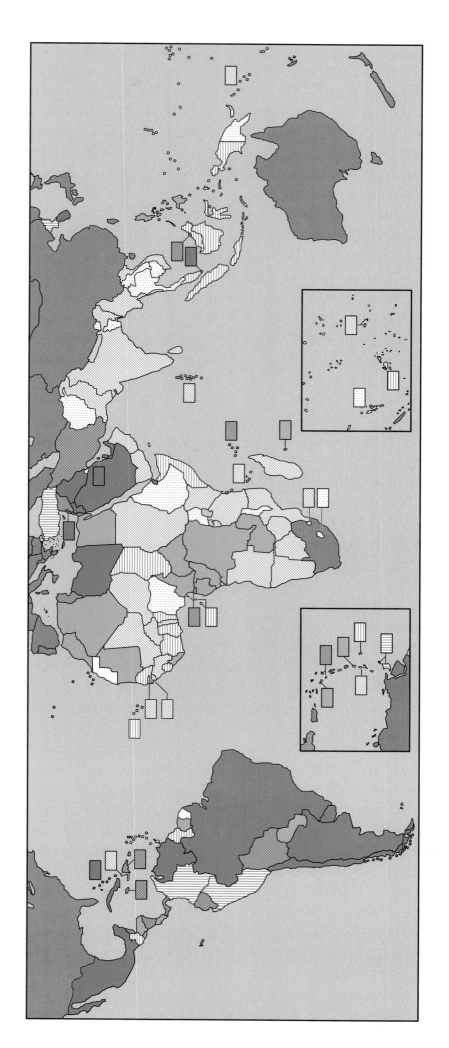

FIGURE 2-17
URBAN POPULATION
(1991)

Less than 10%

10-19%

20-29%

30-39%

40-49%

50-59%

60-69%

70% and over

Data not available

Source: 1991 World Population Data Sheet
(Washington, D.C.: Population Reference Bureau, 1991)

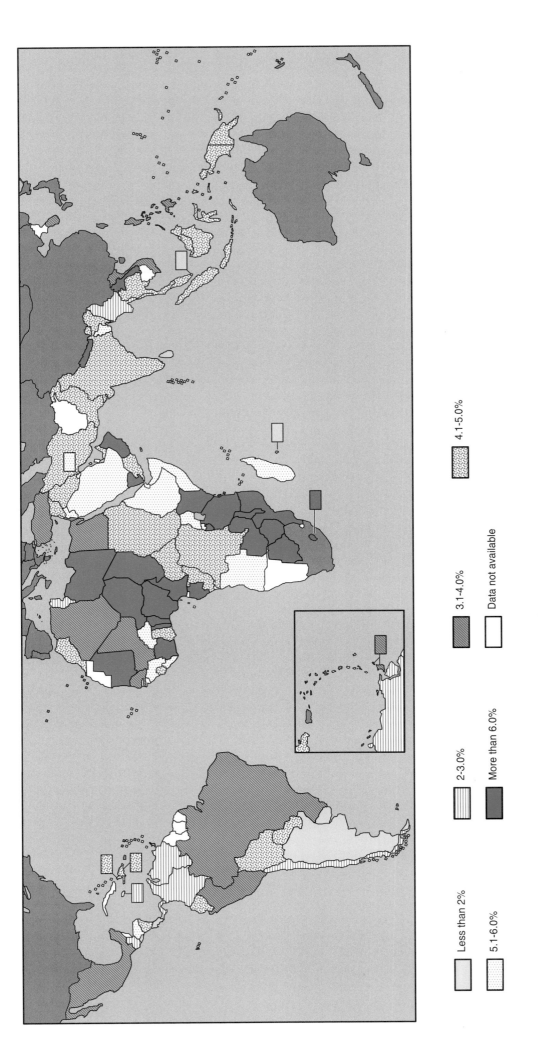

FIGURE 2-18
URBAN GROWTH RATE
(1980-88)

Less than 2%

5.1-6.0%

2-3.0%

More than 6.0%

3.1-4.0%

4.1-5.0%

Data not available

Source: World Development Report 1990
(New York: Oxford University Press, 1990)

3: ECONOMIC CONDITIONS

FIGURE 3-1
GNP AT CURRENT PRICES 1987
($ billions)

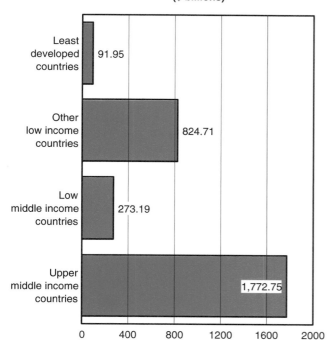

Source: *Geographical Distribution of Financial Flows to Developing Countries*
(Paris: OECD, 1991)

FIGURE 3-2
SHARE OF WORLD EXPORTS 1988
($ billions)

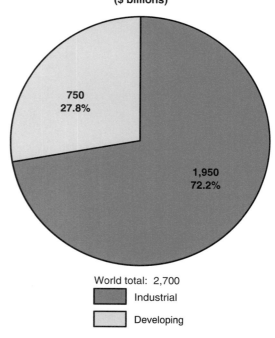

World total: 2,700

■ Industrial

□ Developing

Source: *International Financial Statistics*
(Washington, D.C.: IMF, 1990)

FIGURE 3-3
SHARE OF WORLD IMPORTS 1988
($ billions)

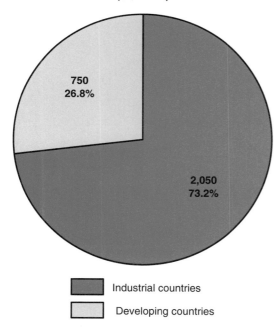

■ Industrial countries

□ Developing countries

Source: *International Financial Statistics*
(Washington, D.C.: IMF, 1990)

FIGURE 3-4
AVERAGE ANNUAL GDP GROWTH RATE 1980-88
(percentage)

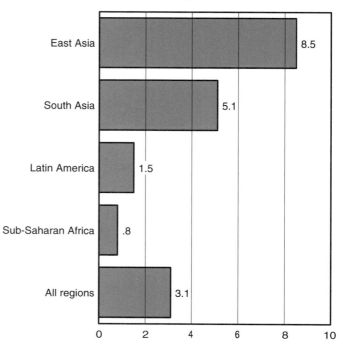

Source: *World Development Report 1990*
(New York: World Bank, 1990)

FIGURE 3-5
COMPARATIVE REAL GDP GROWTH 1965-88

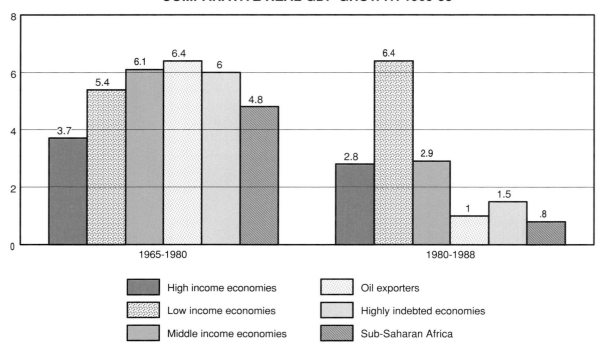

Source: World Development Report 1990
(New York: World Bank, 1990)

FIGURE 3-6
CONSUMER PRICES 1985 AND 1989
(annual percentage increase)

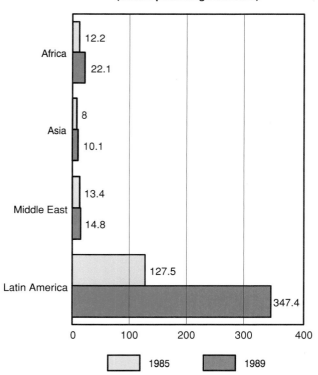

Source: International Financial Statistics
(Washington, D.C.: IMF, 1990)

FIGURE 3-7
ANNUAL PERCENTAGE CHANGE
IN CONSUMER PRICES 1980-89

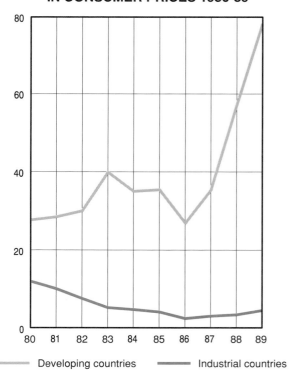

Source: International Financial Statistics
(Washington, D.C.: IMF, 1990)

FIGURE 3-8
SECTORAL SHARES OF GDP
($ millions)

A. LOW INCOME COUNTRIES

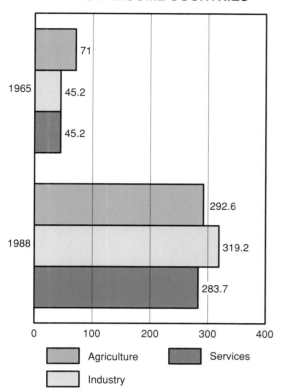

Source: *World Development Report 1990*
(New York: World Bank, 1990)

B. MIDDLE INCOME COUNTRIES

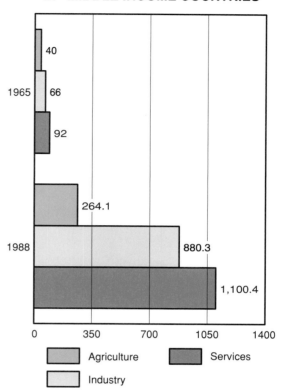

Source: *World Development Report 1990*
(New York: World Bank, 1990)

C. HIGH INCOME OIL EXPORTERS

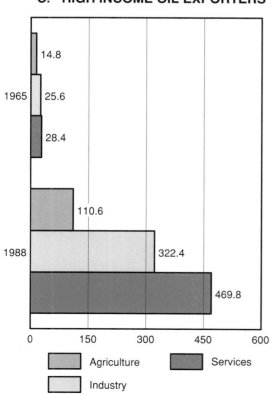

Source: *World Development Report 1990*
(New York: World Bank, 1990)

D. OTHER HIGH INCOME COUNTRIES

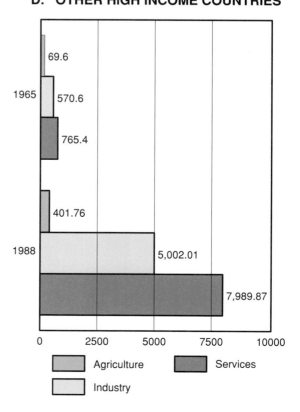

Source: *World Development Report 1990*
(New York: World Bank, 1990)

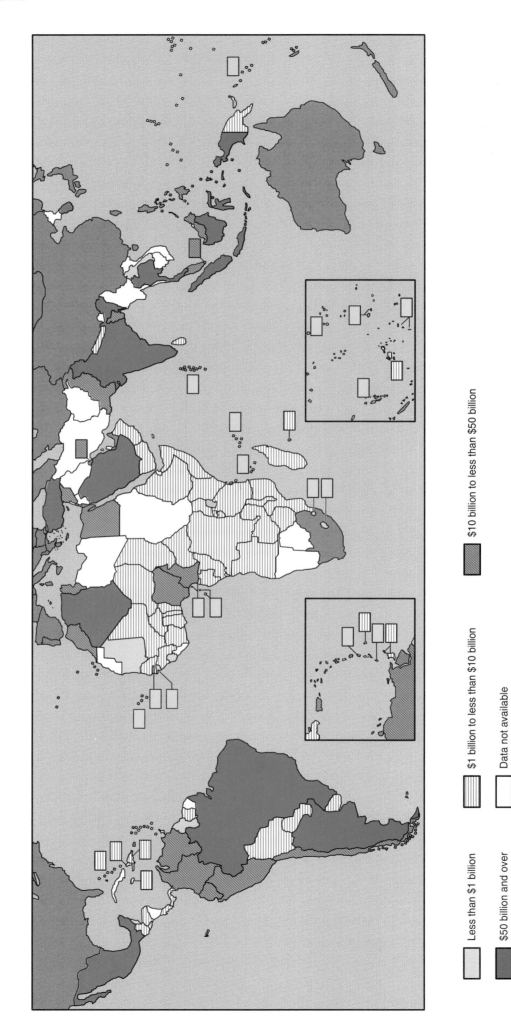

FIGURE 3-9
GROSS NATIONAL PRODUCT 1989
(in $U.S.)

Less than $1 billion

$50 billion and over

$1 billion to less than $10 billion

Data not available

$10 billion to less than $50 billion

Source: World Bank Atlas 1990
(Washington, D.C.: World Bank, 1990)

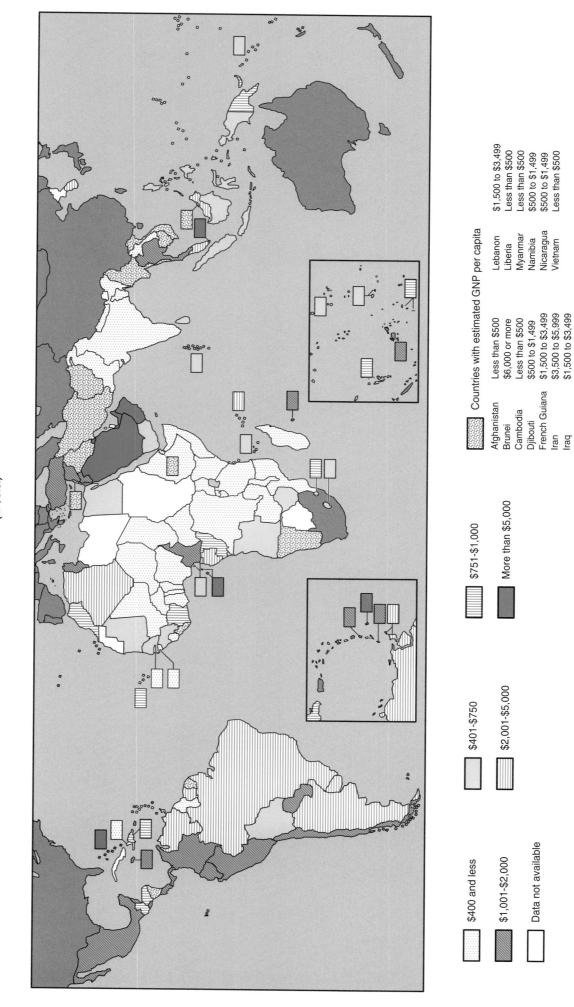

FIGURE 3-10
GROSS NATIONAL PRODUCT PER CAPITA 1989
(in $U.S.)

$400 and less

$1,001-$2,000

Data not available

$751-$1,000

$2,001-$5,000

More than $5,000

Countries with estimated GNP per capita

Afghanistan	Less than $500	Lebanon	$1,500 to $3,499
Brunei	$6,000 or more	Liberia	Less than $500
Cambodia	Less than $500	Myanmar	Less than $500
Djibouti	$500 to $1,499	Namibia	$500 to $1,499
French Guiana	$1,500 to $3,499	Nicaragua	$500 to $1,499
Iran	$3,500 to $5,999	Vietnam	Less than $500
Iraq	$1,500 to $3,499		

Source: World Bank Atlas 1990
(Washington, D.C.: World Bank, 1990)

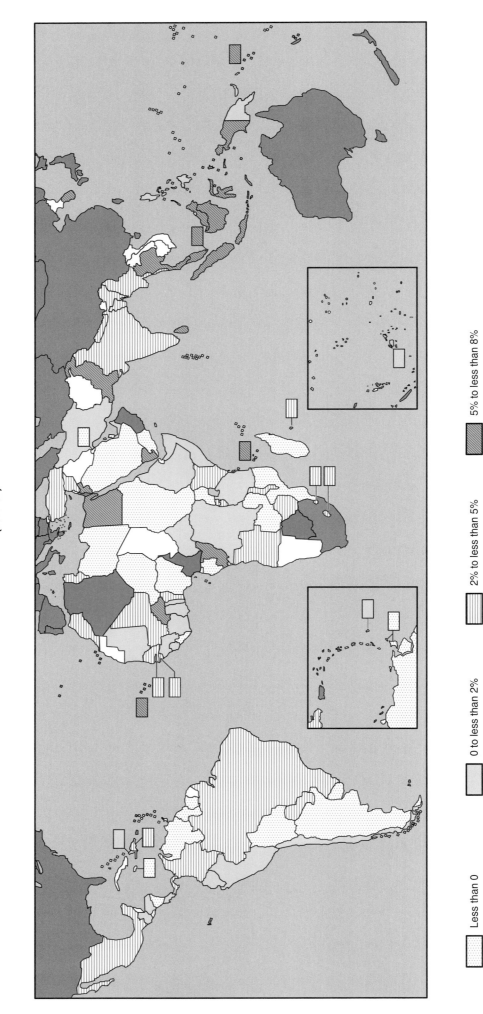

FIGURE 3-11
AVERAGE ANNUAL REAL GNP GROWTH RATE
(1977-87)

Less than 0

8% and more

0 to less than 2%

Data not available

2% to less than 5%

5% to less than 8%

Source: *World Resources 1990-91*
(New York: Oxford University Press, 1990)

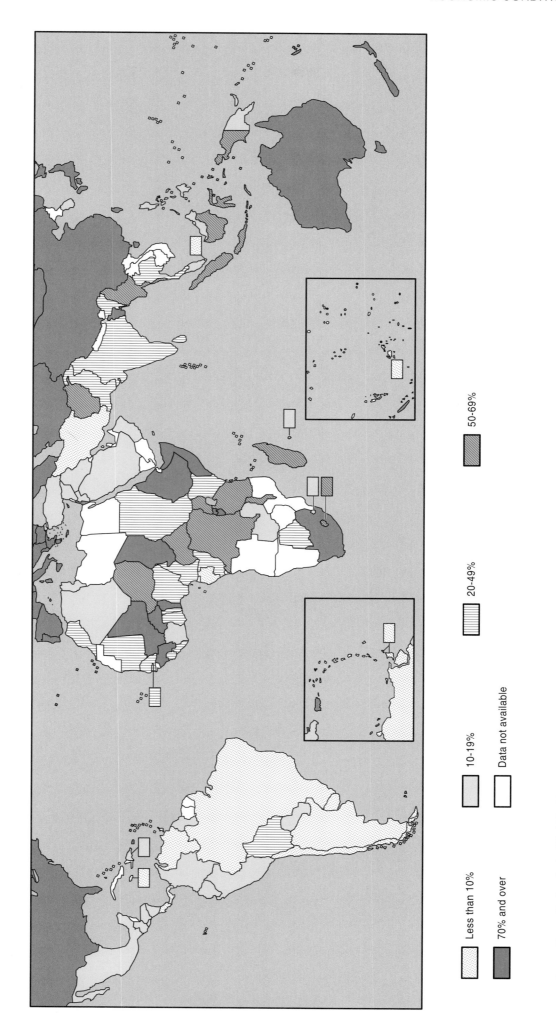

FIGURE 3-12
POPULATION IN ABSOLUTE POVERTY

Less than 10%

70% and over

10-19%

Data not available

20-49%

50-69%

Source: George Kurian, *Book of World Rankings, 3rd ed.*
(New York: Facts On File, 1990)

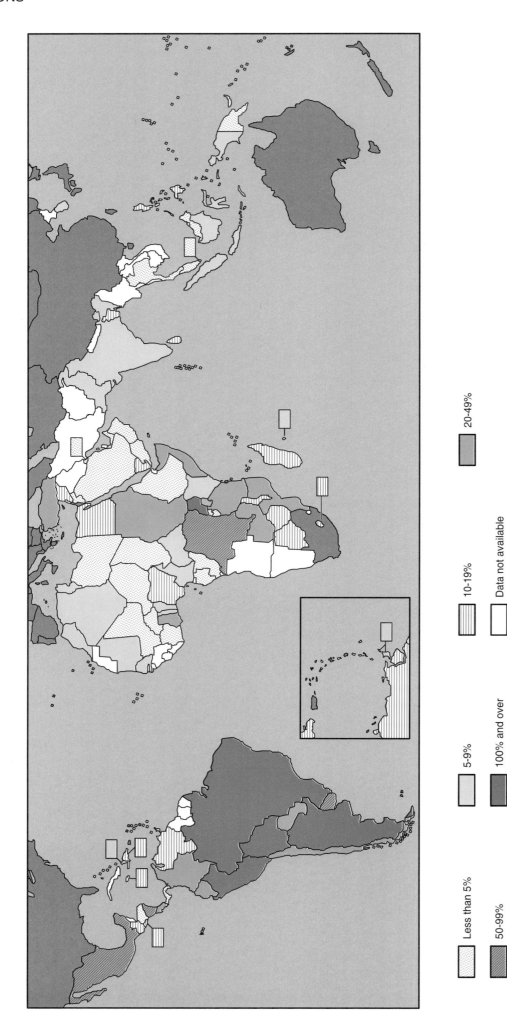

FIGURE 3-13
AVERAGE ANNUAL INFLATION RATE
(1980–88)

Less than 5%

5–9%

10–19%

20–49%

50–99%

100% and over

Data not available

Source: *World Development Report 1990*
(New York: Oxford University Press, 1990)

4: THE BURDEN OF DEBT

FIGURE 4-1

THE BURDEN OF DEBT 1988
(As a percentage of GNP)

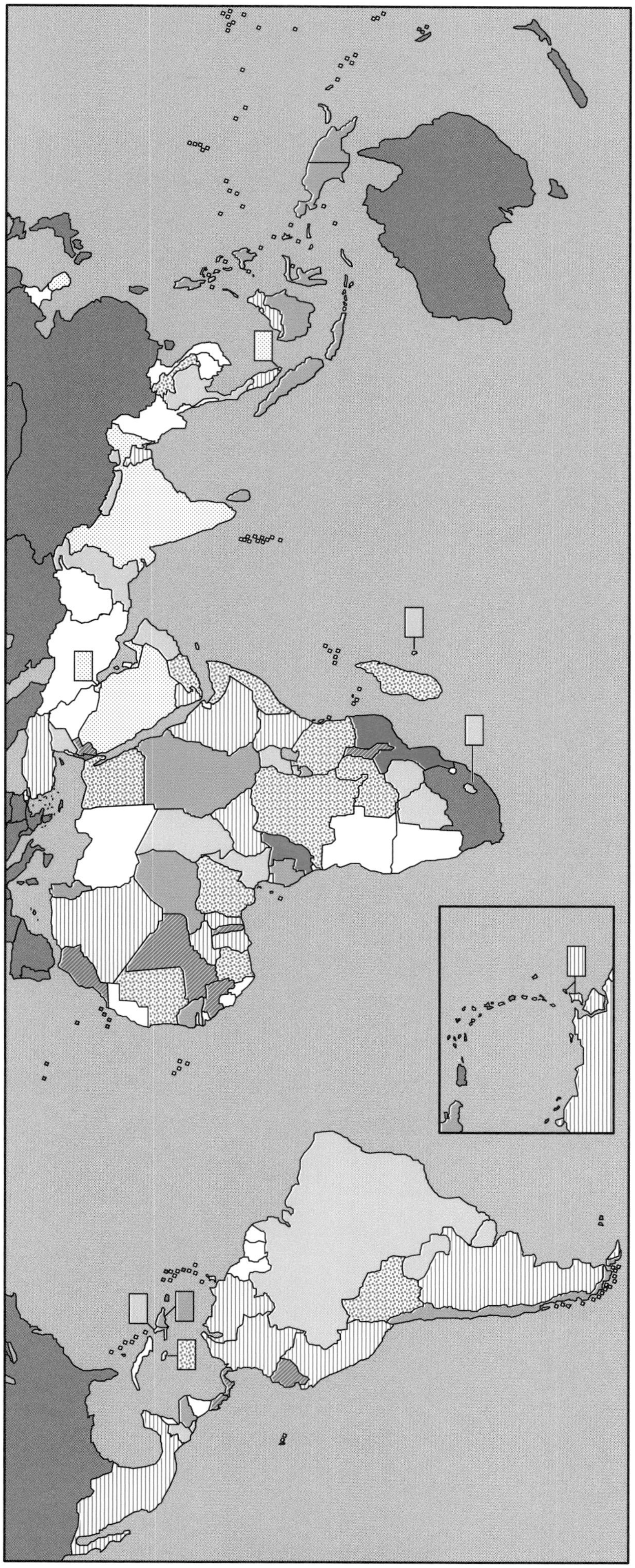

Total external public and private debt as a percentage of GNP

20% and below	21-40%	41-60%	61-80%
81-100%	101-200%	More than 200%	Data not available

Source: *World Development Report 1990*
(New York: Oxford University Press, 1990)

FIGURE 4-2
CAPITAL-IMPORTING DEVELOPING COUNTRIES' GROSS FOREIGN DEBT 1980-86

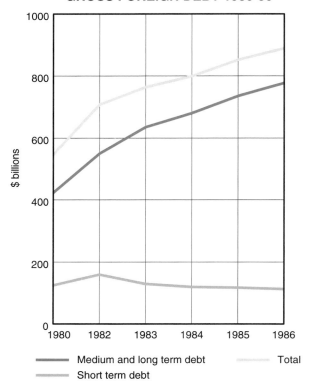

Medium and long term debt   Total
Short term debt

Source: World Economic Survey 1987
(New York: UN, 1987)

FIGURE 4-3
TOTAL EXTERNAL DEBT
($ billions)

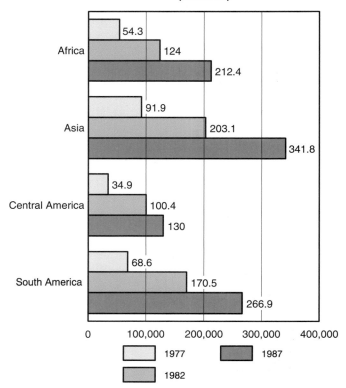

☐ 1977   ■ 1987
☐ 1982

Source: World Resources 1990-91
(New York: Oxford University Press, 1990)

FIGURE 4-4
EXTERNAL PUBLIC DEBT OUTSTANDING AS A PERCENTAGE OF GNP 1970 AND 1988

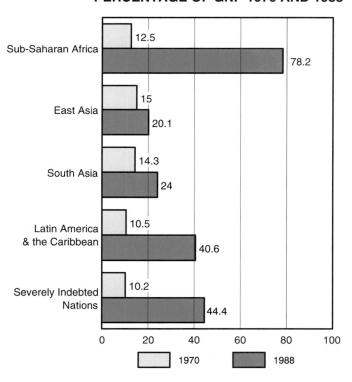

☐ 1970   ■ 1988

Source: World Development Report 1990
(New York: World Bank, 1990)

FIGURE 4-5
DEBT SERVICE AS A PERCENTAGE OF GNP 1970 AND 1988

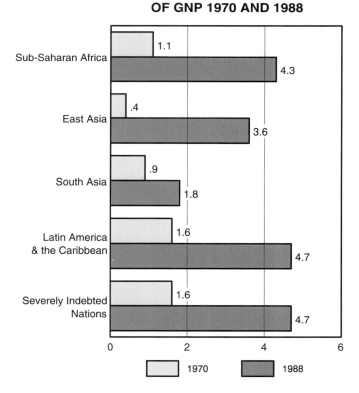

☐ 1970   ■ 1988

Source: World Development Report 1990
(New York: World Bank, 1990)

FIGURE 4-6
MAJOR THIRD WORLD DEBTOR COUNTRIES 1980 AND 1985

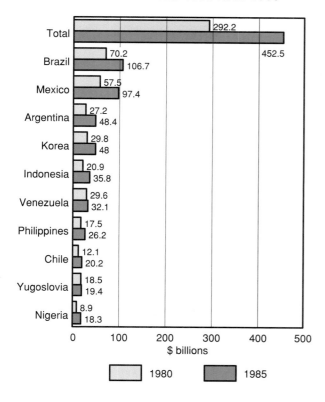

Source: John W. Sewell, Stuart K. Tucker et al,
Growth, Exports, and Jobs in a Changing World Economy, Agenda 1988
(New Brunswick: Transaction Books, 1988)

FIGURE 4-7
NET ODA FLOWS TO DEVELOPING COUNTRIES 1989
($ millions)

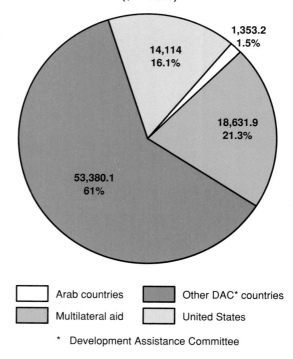

Source: Geographical Distribution of Financial Flows to Developing Countries
(Paris: OECD, 1991)

FIGURE 4-8
COMPOSITION OF DAC* TRANSFERS TO DEVELOPING COUNTRIES

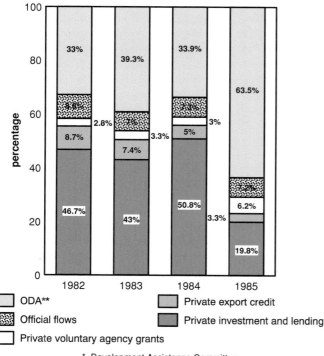

* Development Assistance Committee
** Official Development Assistance

Source: John W. Sewell, Stuart K. Tucker et al,
Growth, Exports, and Jobs in a Changing World Economy, Agenda 1988
(New Brunswick: Transaction Books, 1988)

FIGURE 4-9
NET FLOW OF MULTILATERAL INSTITUTIONAL RESOURCES 1986-89

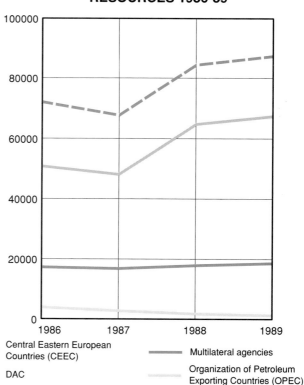

Source: Geographical Distribution of Financial Flows to Developing Countries
(Paris: OECD, 1991)

FIGURE 4-10
COMPARATIVE IMF LENDING TO DEVELOPING COUNTRIES 1977-89

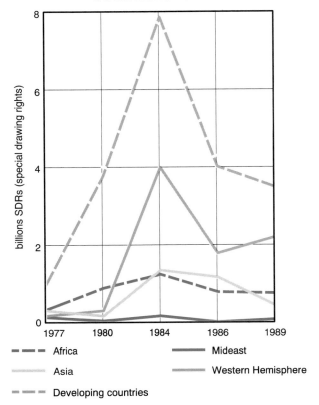

━ ━ ━ Africa	━━━ Mideast
━━━ Asia	▦▦▦ Western Hemisphere
━ ━ ━ Developing countries	

Source: International Financial Statistics
(Washington, D.C.: IMF, 1990)

FIGURE 4-11
INTERNATIONAL COMMERCIAL BANKS' NET LENDING TO DEVELOPING COUNTRIES 1981-86

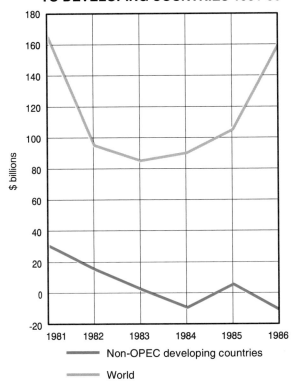

━━━ Non-OPEC developing countries	
━━━ World	

Source: John W. Sewell, Stuart K. Tucker et al,
Growth, Exports, and Jobs in a Changing World Economy, Agenda 1988
(New Brunswick: Transaction Books, 1988)

FIGURE 4-12
U.S. BANKS' LENDING TO DEVELOPING COUNTRIES 1980-86

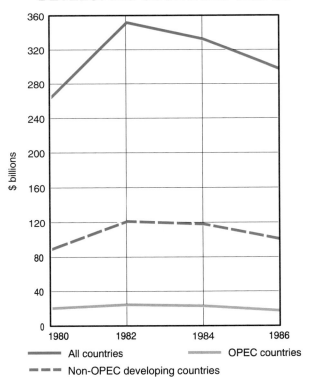

━━━ All countries	━━━ OPEC countries
━ ━ ━ Non-OPEC developing countries	

Source: John W. Sewell, Stuart K. Tucker et al,
Growth, Exports, and Jobs in a Changing World Economy, Agenda 1988
(New Brunswick: Transaction Books, 1988)

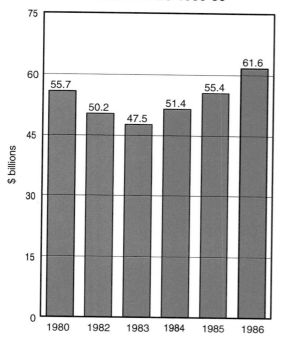

FIGURE 4-13
U.S. DIRECT INVESTMENT IN DEVELOPING COUNTRIES 1980-86

Source: John W. Sewell, Stuart K. Tucker et al,
Growth, Exports, and Jobs in a Changing World Economy, Agenda 1988
(New Brunswick: Transaction Books, 1988)

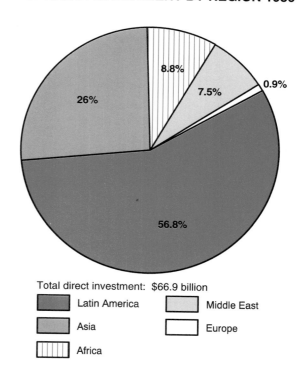

FIGURE 4-14
U.S. DIRECT INVESTMENT BY REGION 1986

Total direct investment: $66.9 billion

- Latin America
- Asia
- Africa
- Middle East
- Europe

Source: John W. Sewell, Stuart K. Tucker et al,
Growth, Exports, and Jobs in a Changing World Economy, Agenda 1988
(New Brunswick: Transaction Books, 1988)

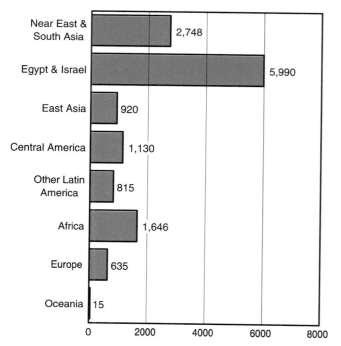

FIGURE 4-15
U.S. BILATERAL AID 1985-86
($ millions)

Source: John W. Sewell, Stuart K. Tucker et al,
Growth, Exports, and Jobs in a Changing World Economy, Agenda 1988
(New Brunswick: Transaction Books, 1988)

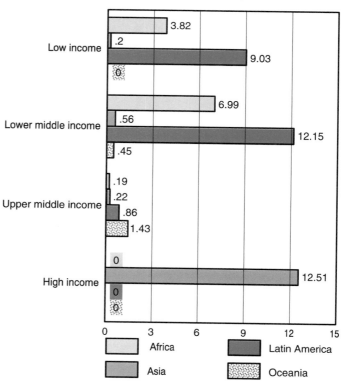

FIGURE 4-16
U.S. BILATERAL AID PER CAPITA 1985
(dollars)

- Africa
- Asia
- Latin America
- Oceania

Source: John W. Sewell, Stuart K. Tucker et al,
Growth, Exports, and Jobs in a Changing World Economy, Agenda 1988
(New Brunswick: Transaction Books, 1988)

FIGURE 4-17a
DEBT SERVICE AS A PERCENTAGE
OF CURRENT BORROWING

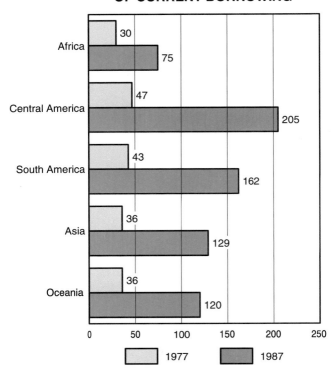

Source: World Resources 1990-91
(New York: Oxford University Press, 1990)

FIGURE 4-17b
CURRENT BORROWING PER CAPITA 1987
($ U.S.)

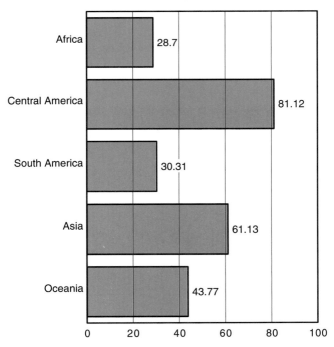

Source: World Resources 1990-91
(New York: Oxford University Press, 1990)

FIGURE 4-18
U.S. ECONOMIC AID 1970-88*
(in $U.S.)

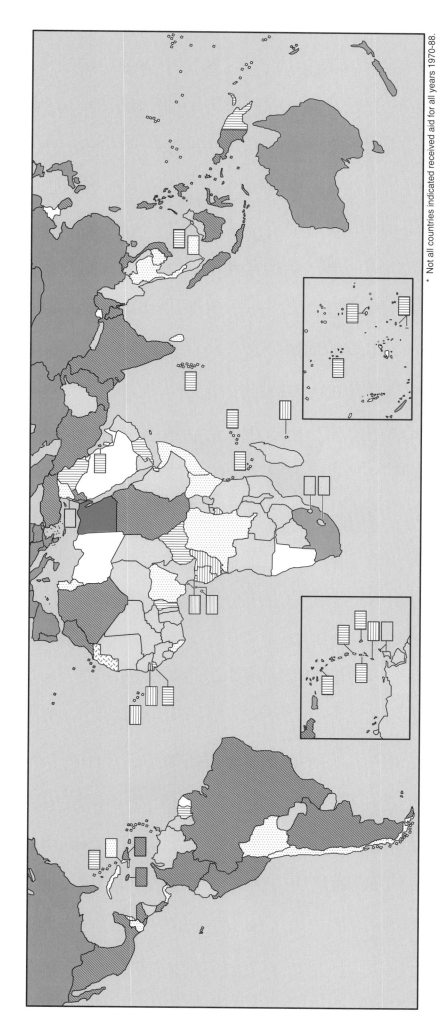

* Not all countries indicated received aid for all years 1970-88.

Less than 50 million

50 million to less than 100 million

100 million to less than 500 million

500 million to less than 1 billion

1 to 5 billion

More than 5 billion

None

Data not available

Source: The World Factbook 1990
(Washington, D.C.: CIA, 1990)

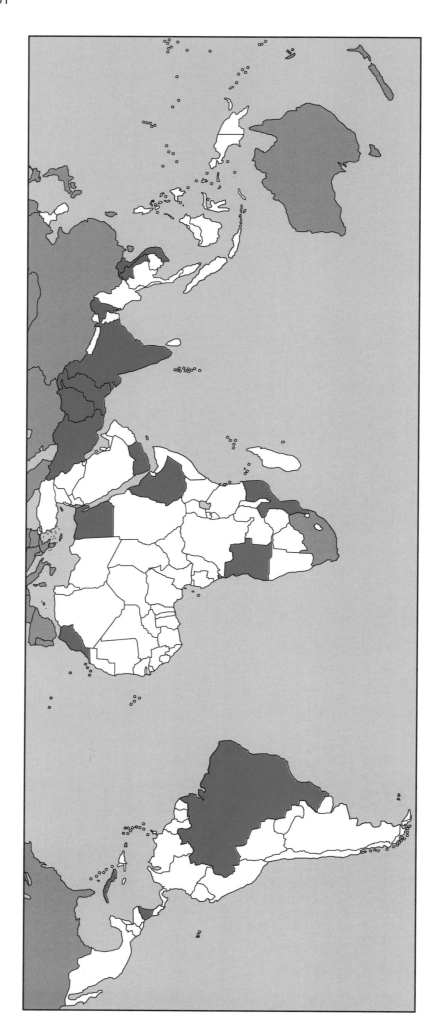

FIGURE 4-19
EASTERN EUROPEAN AID
(1989)

Nations received aid from Central Eastern European countries (Bulgaria, Czechoslovakia, Hungary, Poland, Romania, and the U.S.S.R.)

Source: Organization for Economic Co-operation and Development. *Geographical Distribution of Financial Flows to Developing Countries* (Paris: OECD, 1991)

5: FOOD AND AGRICULTURE

FIGURE 5-1
TRENDS IN TOTAL AGRICULTURAL AND FOOD PRODUCTION 1982-88

A. Agricultural production (index: 1979-81 = 100%)

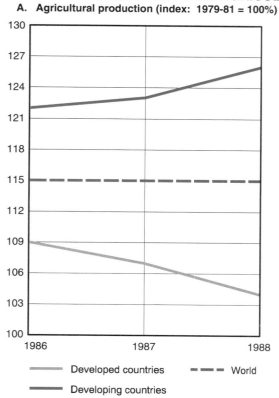

B. Food production (index: 1979-81 = 100%)

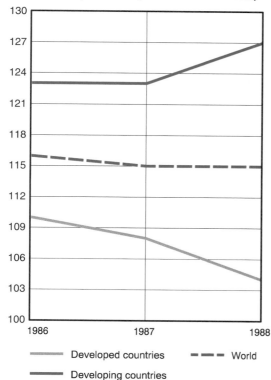

Developed countries — — — World
Developing countries

Source: The State of Food and Agriculture 1989
(Rome: FAO, 1989)

Developed countries — — — World
Developing countries

Source: The State of Food and Agriculture 1989
(Rome: FAO, 1989)

FIGURE 5-2
AVERAGE AGRICULTURAL GDP PER TOTAL GDP 1987

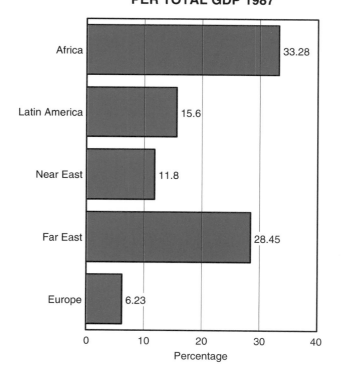

Source: The State of Food and Agriculture 1989
(Rome: FAO, 1989)

FIGURE 5-3
AGRICULTURAL EXPORTS PER TOTAL THIRD WORLD EXPORTS 1985

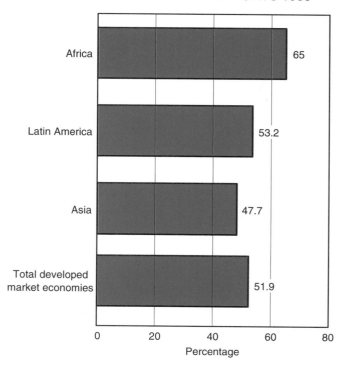

Source: The State of Food and Agriculture 1989
(Rome: FAO, 1989)

FIGURE 5-4
GROSS VALUE ADDED IN AGRICULTURE 1988
($ billions)

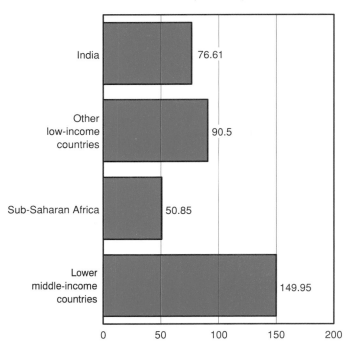

Source: World Development Report 1990
(New York: World Bank, 1990)

FIGURE 5-5
AGRICULTURAL CONTRIBUTION TO GROWTH OF GDP

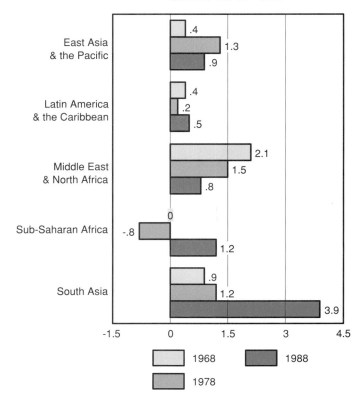

	1968		1988
	1978		

Source: World Tables, 1989-90
(Washington D.C.: World Bank, 1990)

FIGURE 5-6
PERCENTAGE DISTRIBUTION OF OFFICIAL COMMITMENTS TO AGRICULTURE (OCA) 1987

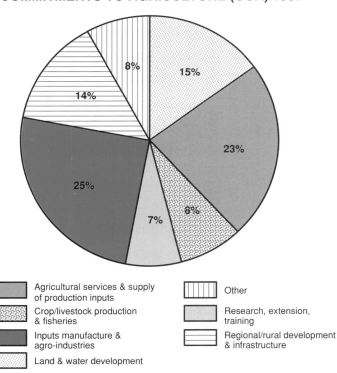

Agricultural services & supply of production inputs

Crop/livestock production & fisheries

Inputs manufacture & agro-industries

Land & water development

Other

Research, extension, training

Regional/rural development & infrastructure

Source: The State of Food and Agriculture 1989
(Rome: FAO, 1989)

FIGURE 5-7
REGIONAL SHARES OF OCA 1987

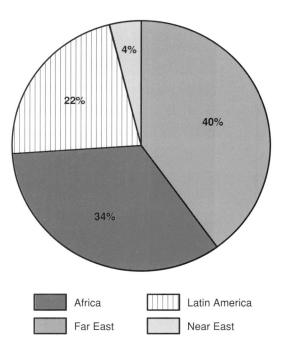

Africa   Latin America

Far East   Near East

Source: The State of Food and Agriculture 1989
(Rome: FAO, 1989)

FIGURE 5-8
MAJOR FOOD-PRODUCING AREAS

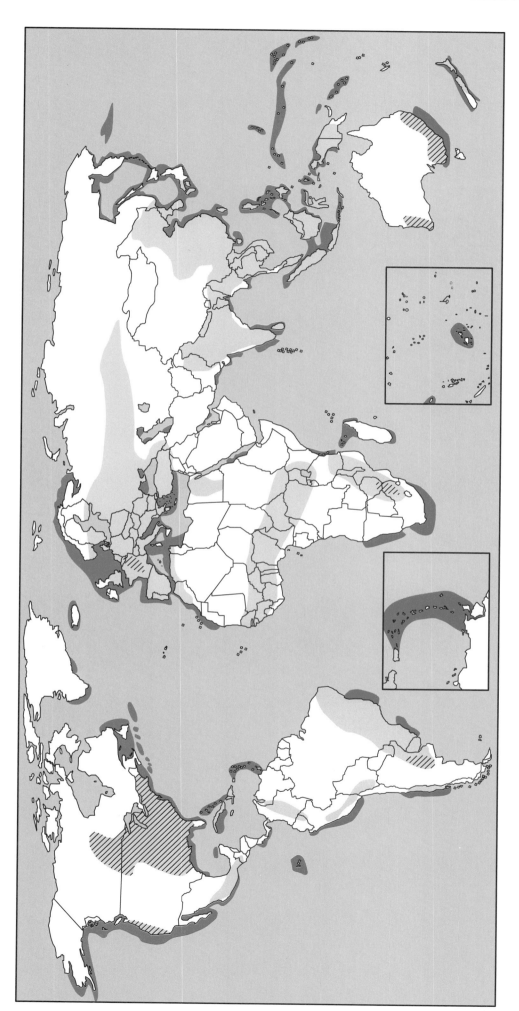

Major crop and meat
producing areas

Areas with significant
exportable crop surplus

Significant fisheries

Source: Atlas of U.S. Foreign Relations
(Washington, D.C.: U.S. State Department, 1985)

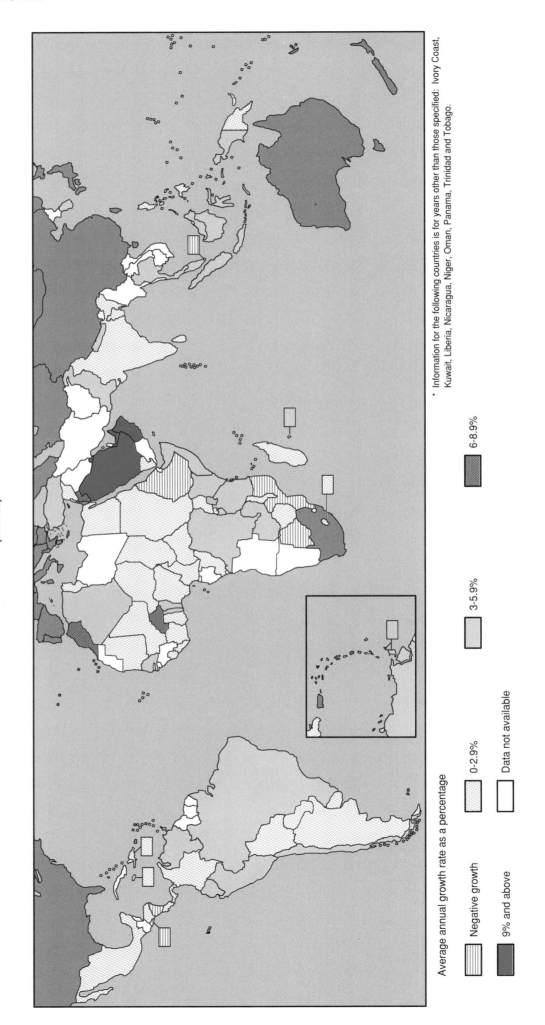

FIGURE 5-9
AGRICULTURAL DEVELOPMENT
(1980-88)*

Average annual growth rate as a percentage

Negative growth

0-2.9%

3-5.9%

6-8.9%

9% and above

Data not available

* Information for the following countries is for years other than those specified: Ivory Coast, Kuwait, Liberia, Nicaragua, Niger, Oman, Panama, Trinidad and Tobago.

Source: World Development Report 1990 (New York: Oxford University Press, 1990)

FIGURE 5-10
SHARE OF AGRICULTURE IN GDP

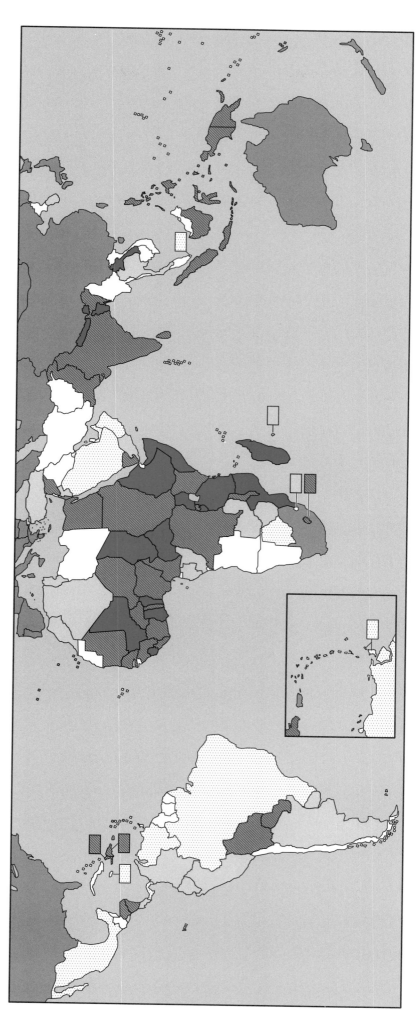

0-9%

10-19%

20-39%

More than 40%

Data not available

Source: World Development Report 1990
(New York: Oxford University Press, 1990)

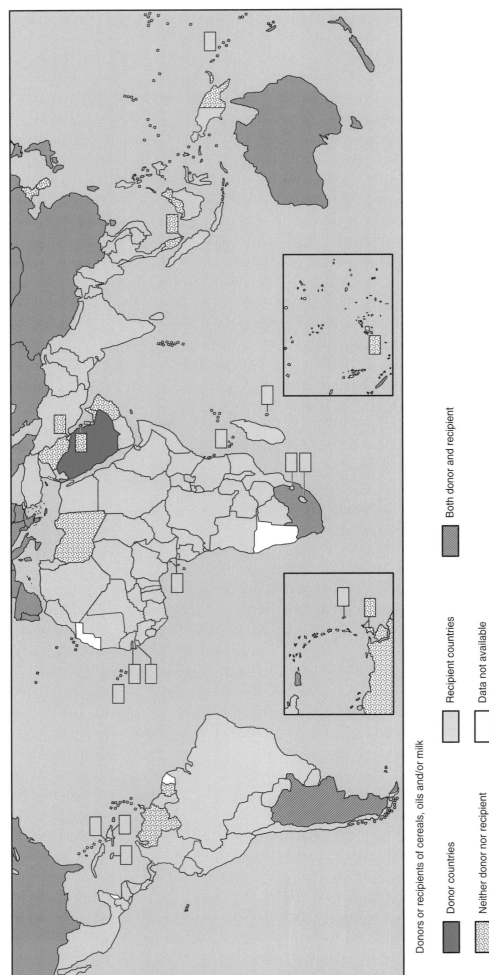

FIGURE 5-11
WORLD FOOD AID
(1985-87)

Donors or recipients of cereals, oils and/or milk

Donor countries

Neither donor nor recipient

Recipient countries

Data not available

Both donor and recipient

Source: World Resources 1990-91
(New York: Oxford University Press, 1990)

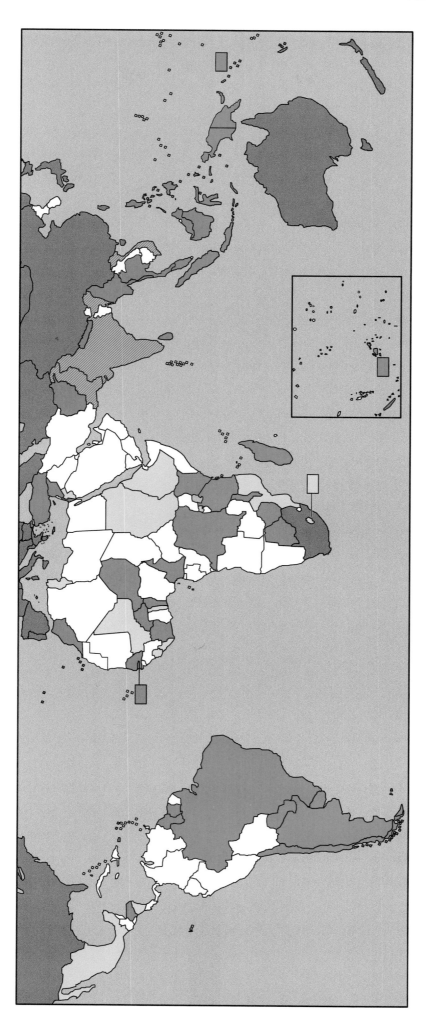

FIGURE 5-12
FOOD EXPORTERS

1975-77

1985-87

Both 1975-77 and 1985-87

Source: World Resources 1990-91
(New York: Oxford University Press, 1991)

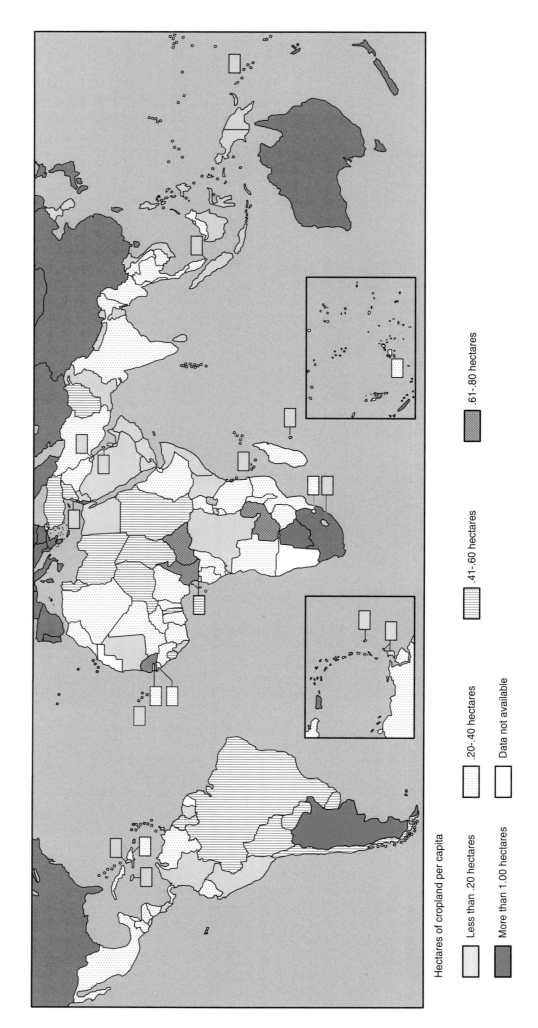

FIGURE 5-13
CROPLAND PER CAPITA
(1989)

Hectares of cropland per capita

Less than .20 hectares

More than 1.00 hectares

.20-.40 hectares

Data not available

.41-.60 hectares

.61-.80 hectares

Source: *World Resources 1990-91*
(New York: Oxford University Press, 1990)

FIGURE 5-14
WORLD INCREASES IN CROP AREA
(1975-77 to 1985-87)

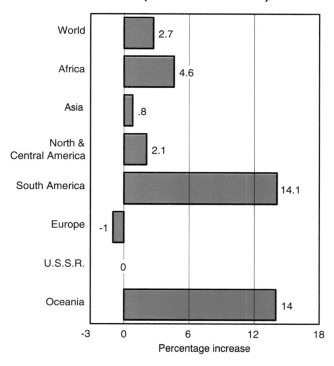

Source: *World Resources 1990-91*
(New York: Oxford University Press, 1990)

FIGURE 5-15
CHANGE IN CROP YIELDS
(1976-78 to 1986-88)

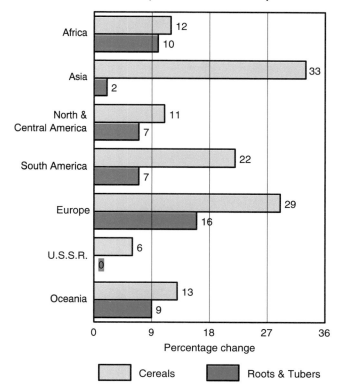

Source: *World Resources 1990-91*
(New York: Oxford University Press, 1990)

FIGURE 5-16
REGIONAL SHARES OF AGRICULTURAL
POPULATION 1985
(millions)

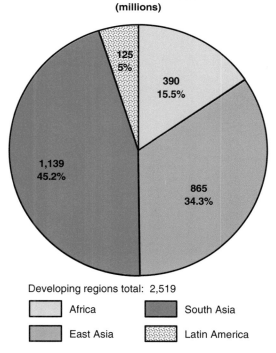

Developing regions total: 2,519

Source: *The State of Food and Agriculture 1989*
(Rome: FAO, 1989)

FIGURE 5-17
DAILY CALORIES PER CAPITA
1964-66 AND 1986-88

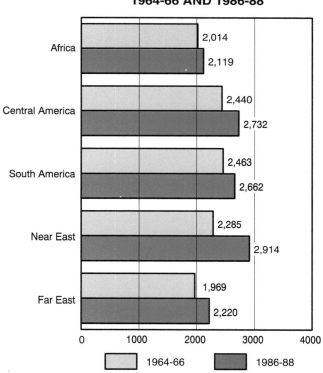

Source: *Quarterly Bulletin of Statistics*
(Rome: FAO, 1990)

FIGURE 5-18
CEREAL PRODUCTION 1986-88
(million metric tons)

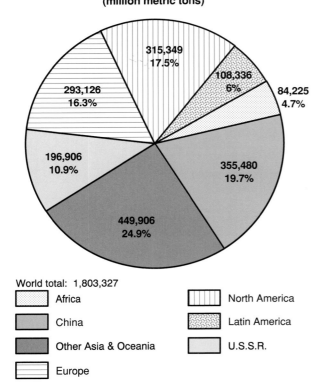

World total: 1,803,327

Africa	North America
China	Latin America
Other Asia & Oceania	U.S.S.R.
Europe	

Source: World Resources 1990-91
(New York: Oxford University Press, 1990)

FIGURE 5-19
RICE PRODUCTION 1981-83
(million metric tons)

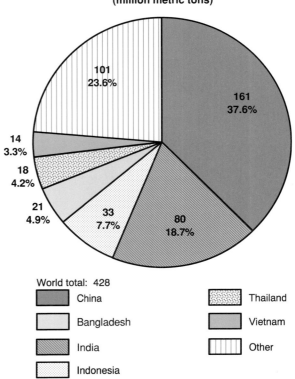

World total: 428

China	Thailand
Bangladesh	Vietnam
India	Other
Indonesia	

Source: Atlas of U.S. Foreign Relations
(Washington D.C.: U.S. State Department, 1985)

FIGURE 5-20
ROOT CROPS 1988
(thousand metric tons)

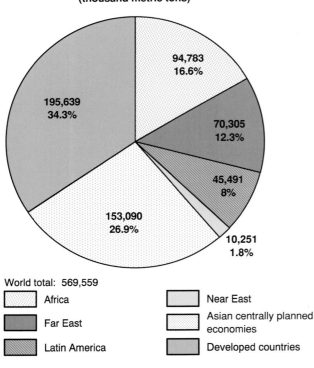

World total: 569,559

Africa	Near East
Far East	Asian centrally planned economies
Latin America	Developed countries

Source: World Resources 1990-91
(New York: Oxford University Press, 1990)

FIGURE 5-21
CATTLE 1986-88
(thousands of head)

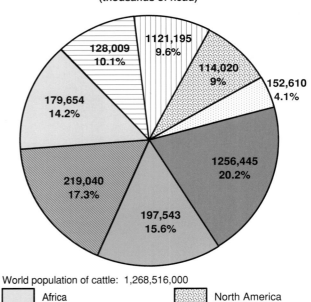

World population of cattle: 1,268,516,000

Africa	North America
Central America	Asia and Oceania (excluding India)
Europe	South America
India	U.S.S.R.

Source: World Resources 1990-91
(New York: Oxford University Press, 1990)

FIGURE 5-22
CATCH OF FISH 1987
(millions of tons)

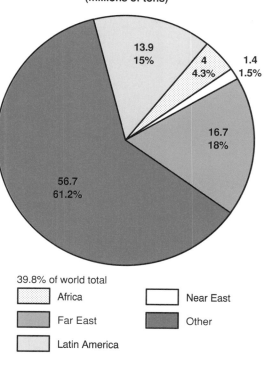

39.8% of world total

- Africa
- Far East
- Latin America
- Near East
- Other

Source: The State of Food and Agriculture 1989
(Rome: FAO, 1989)

FIGURE 5-23
ROUNDWOOD PRODUCTION 1987
(million cubic meters)

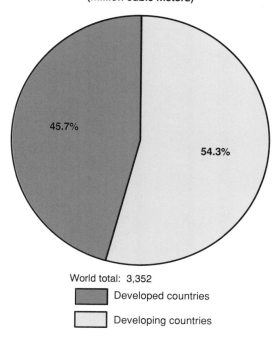

World total: 3,352

- Developed countries
- Developing countries

Source: The State of Food and Agriculture 1989
(Rome: FAO, 1989)

FIGURE 5-24
FERTILIZER CONSUMPTION 1988-1989
(million metric tons)

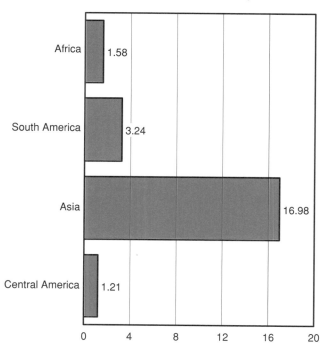

Source: The State of Food and Agriculture 1989
(Rome: FAO, 1989)

FIGURE 5-25
IRRIGATED LAND 1985-87
(as % of arable and permanent cropland)

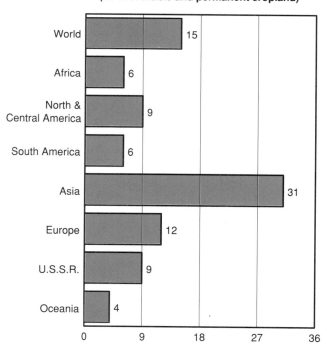

Source: World Resources 1990-91
(New York: Oxford University Press, 1990)

FIGURE 5-26

DOMINANT STAPLE CROPS OF THE THIRD WORLD

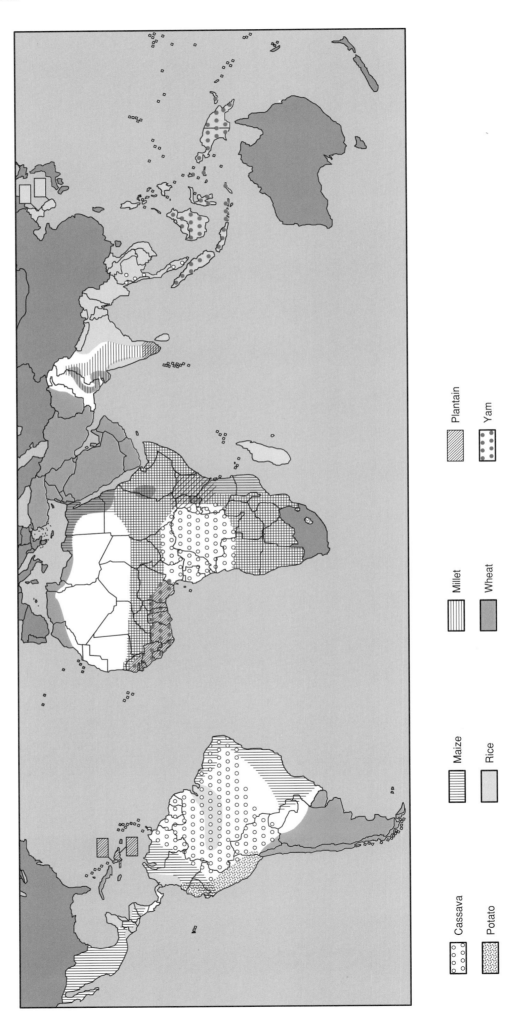

Cassava

Potato

Maize

Rice

Millet

Wheat

Plantain

Yam

Source: *State of Food and Agriculture, 1989*
(Rome: FAO, 1989)

FIGURE 5-27
DAILY CALORIE SUPPLY

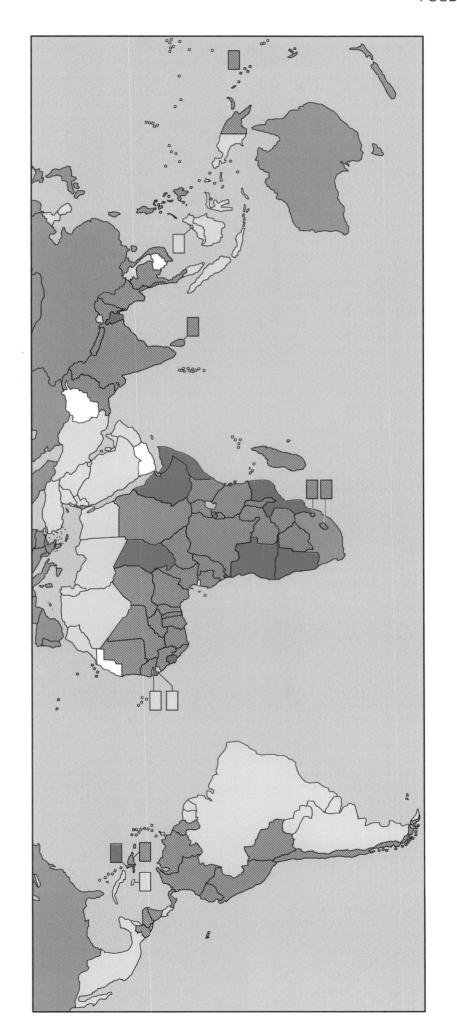

Less than 2,600 calories
per capita, per day

Data not available

2,600 or more calories
per capita, per day

Countries with calorie supply more than
25% below recommended daily intake

Source: The World Bank Atlas 1990
(Washington, D.C.: The World Bank, 1990)

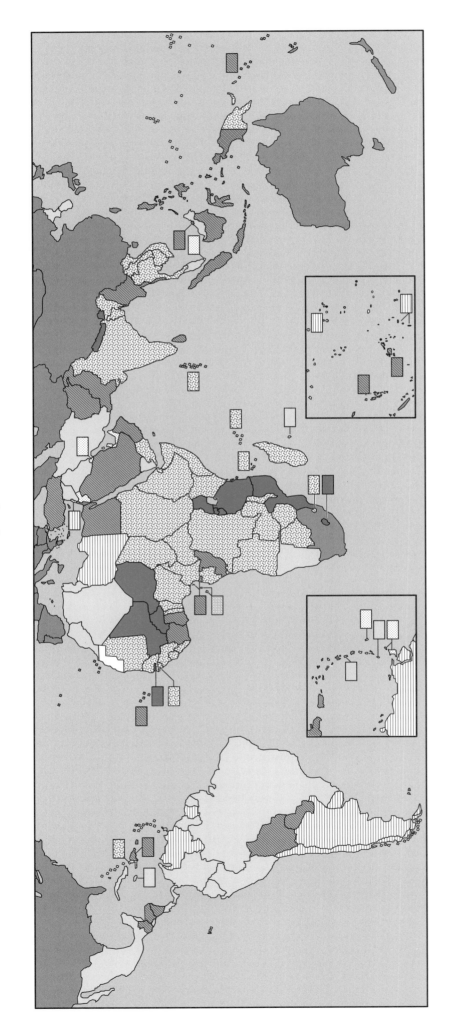

FIGURE 5-28
**PERCENTAGE OF THIRD WORLD POPULATION
DEPENDENT ON AGRICULTURE**
(1987)

Less than 10%

10-20%

21-40%

41-60%

61-80%

81-100%

Data not available

Source: World Development Report 1990
(New York: Oxford University Press, 1990)

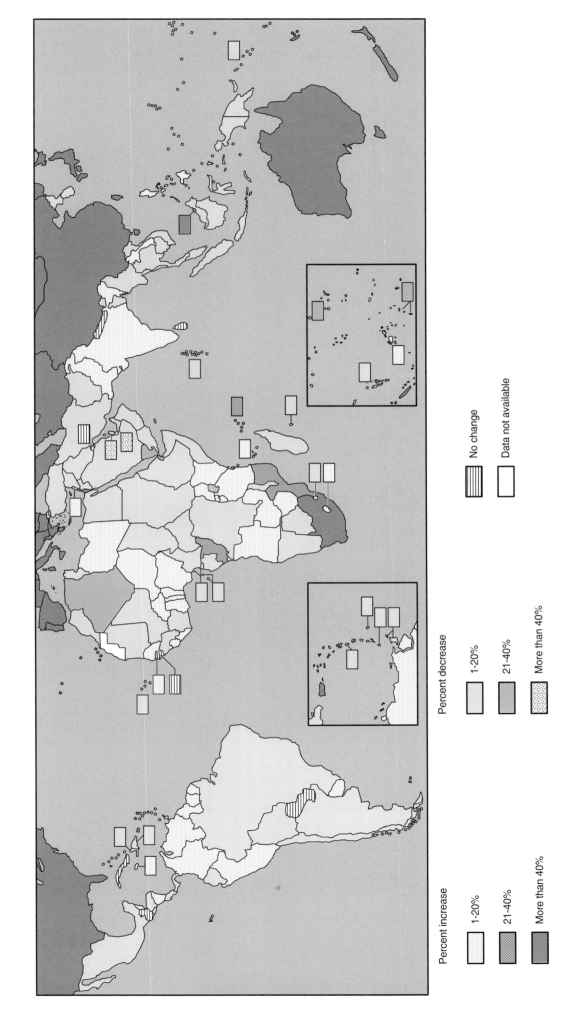

FIGURE 5-29

**PERCENTAGE CHANGE IN THIRD WORLD POPULATION
DEPENDENT ON AGRICULTURE**

(1983-87)

Percent increase

	1-20%
	21-40%
	More than 40%

Percent decrease

	1-20%
	21-40%
	More than 40%

	No change
	Data not available

Source: World Development Report 1990
(New York: Oxford University Press, 1990)

6: INDUSTRY

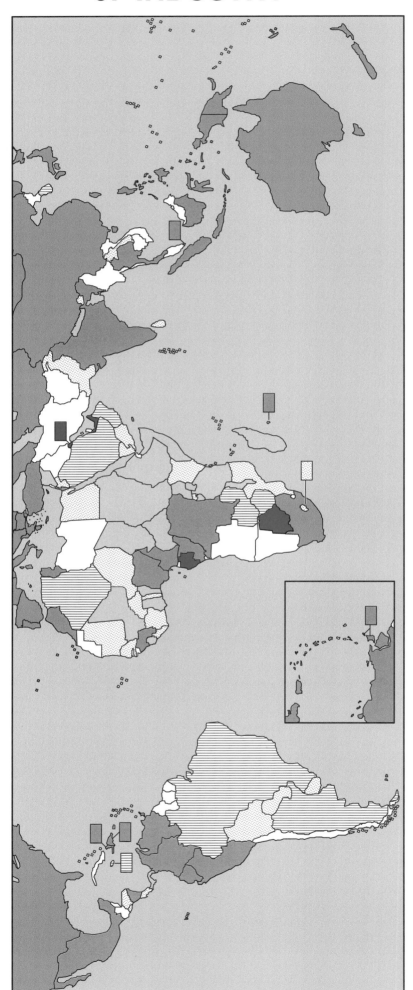

FIGURE 6-1
INDUSTRY'S SHARE OF GDP
(1988)

Less than 20%

50% and more

20% to less than 30%

Data not available

30% to less than 40%

40% to less than 50%

Source: George Kurian, *Book of World Rankings, 3rd ed.*
(New York: Facts on File, 1991)

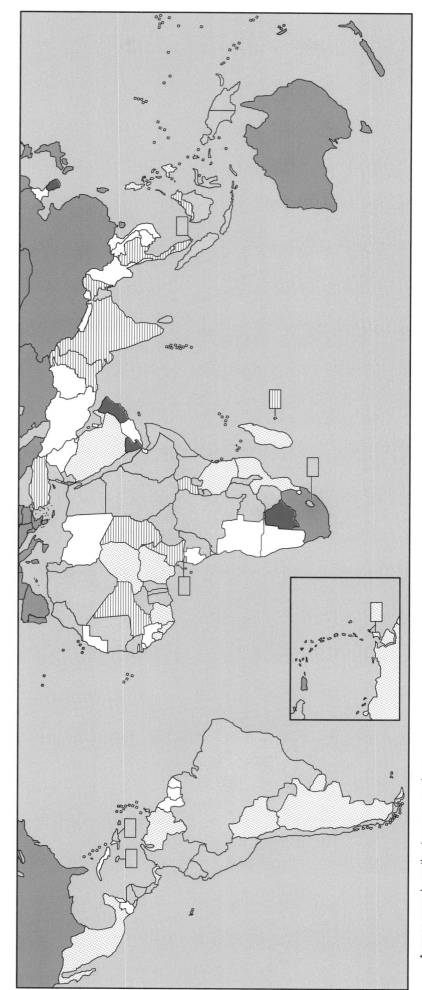

FIGURE 6-2
INDUSTRIAL DEVELOPMENT
(1980-88)

Average annual growth rate as a percentage

Negative growth

0-5%

6-10%

11% and over

Data not available

Source: World Development Report 1990
(New York: Oxford University Press, 1990)

FIGURE 6-3
ANNUAL PERCENTAGE CHANGE IN ECONOMIC OUTPUT 1980-88

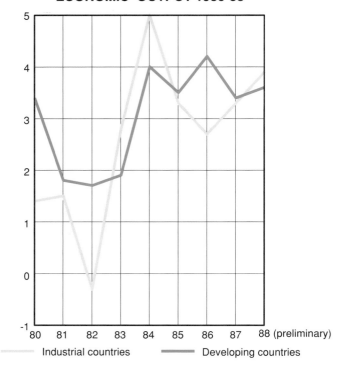

Source: *The State of Food and Agriculture 1989*
(Rome: FAO, 1989)

FIGURE 6-4
THIRD WORLD OUTPUT OF GOODS AND SERVICES 1985 AND 1988
(annual percentage change)

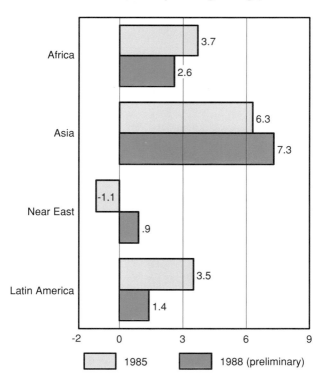

Source: *The State of Food and Agriculture 1989*
(Rome: FAO, 1989)

7: ENERGY

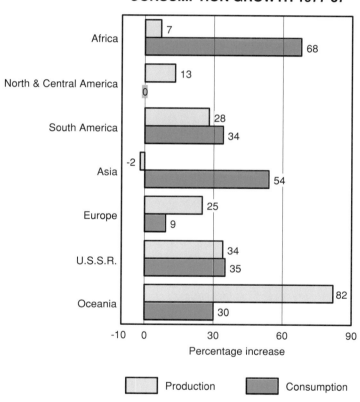

FIGURE 7-1
**ENERGY PRODUCTION AND
CONSUMPTION GROWTH 1977-87**

Africa
7
68

North & Central America
13
0

South America
28
34

Asia
-2
54

Europe
25
9

U.S.S.R.
34
35

Oceania
82
30

-10   0   30   60   90
Percentage increase

Production   Consumption

Source: *World Resources 1990-91*
(New York: Oxford University Press, 1990)

FIGURE 7-2

**SHARE OF ENERGY IMPORTS IN
TOTAL MERCHADISE IMPORTS**

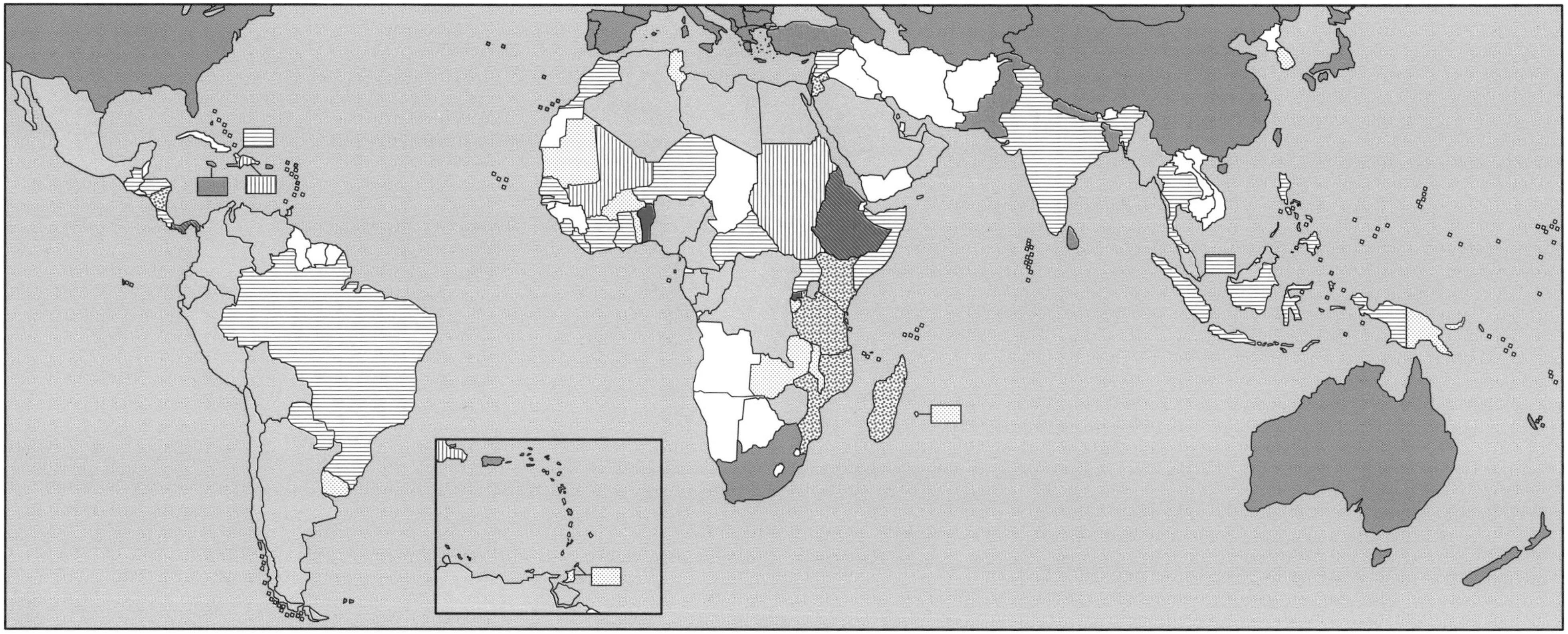

0-5%

6-10%

11-20%

21-30%

31-40%

41-50%

51-60%

More than 60%

Data not available

Source: *World Development Report 1990*
(New York: Oxford University Press, 1990)

FIGURE 7-3
PER CAPITA ENERGY CONSUMPTION
(1988)

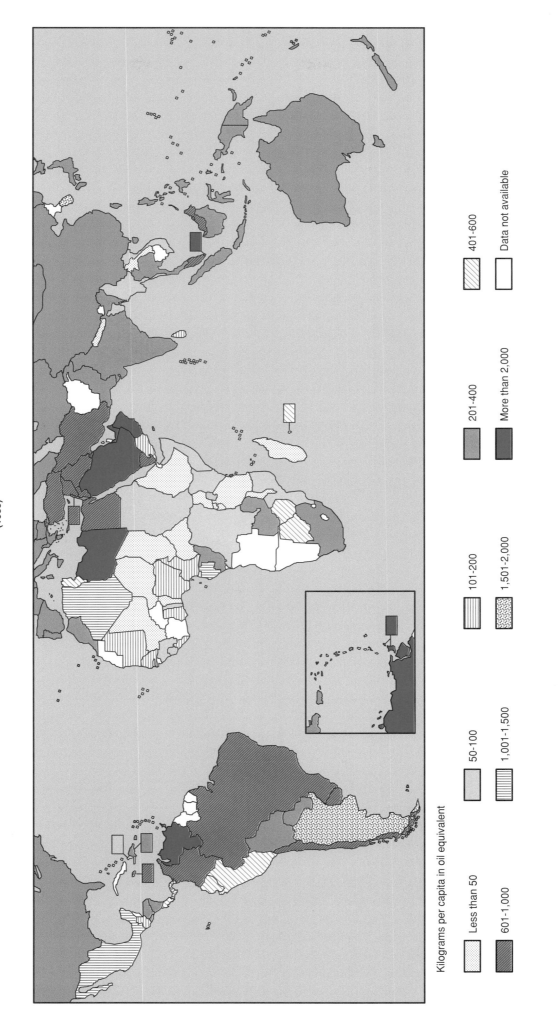

Kilograms per capita in oil equivalent

| | Less than 50 | | 50-100 | | 101-200 | | 201-400 | | 401-600 |
| | 601-1,000 | | 1,001-1,500 | | 1,501-2,000 | | More than 2,000 | | Data not available |

Source: World Development Report 1990
(New York: Oxford University Press, 1990)

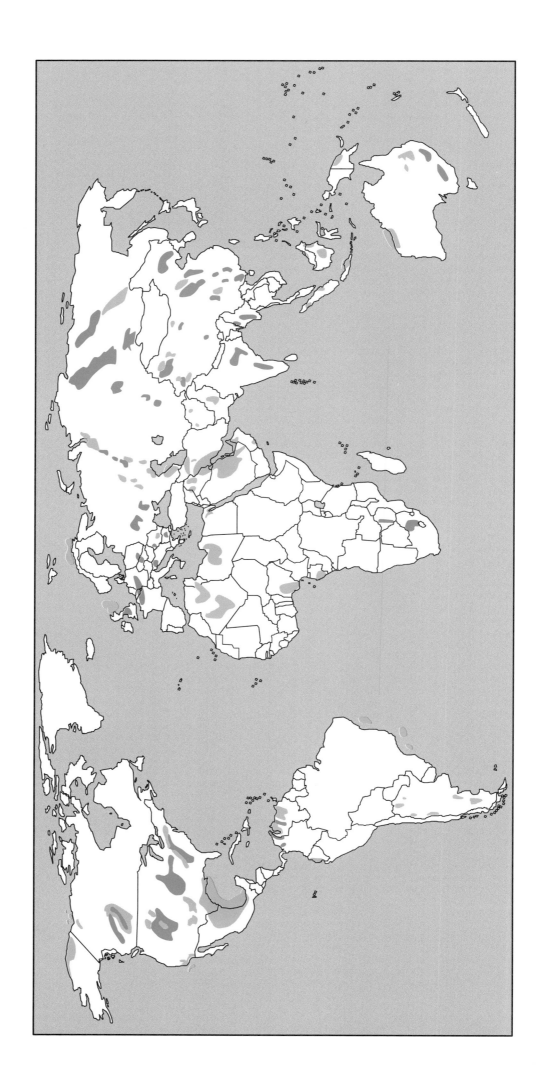

FIGURE 7-4
WORLD FOSSIL FUEL DEPOSITS

Coal

Oil and natural gas

Source: Atlas of U.S. Foreign Relations
(Washington, D.C.: U.S. Department of State, 1985)

FIGURE 7-5
OIL RESERVES 1987
(million metric tons)

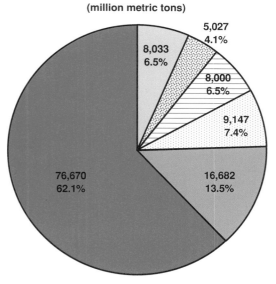

World total: 123,559 million tons

	Africa		Middle East*
	Asia and Oceania		U.S.S.R.
	Latin America		Other

* Middle East consists of the Arabian Penninsula,
Jordan, Lebanon, Iran, Iraq, Israel, Syria, Turkey

Source: World Resources 1990-91
(New York: Oxford University Press, 1990)

FIGURE 7-6
NATURAL GAS RESERVES 1987
(billion cubic meters)

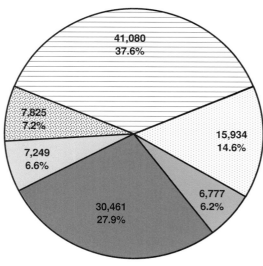

World total:109,326 billion cubic meters

	Africa		Middle East*
	Asia and Oceania		U.S.S.R.
	Latin America		Other

* Middle East consists of the Arabian Penninsula,
Jordan, Lebanon, Iran, Iraq, Israel, Syria, Turkey

Source: World Resources 1990-91
(New York: Oxford University Press, 1990)

FIGURE 7-7
BITUMINOUS COAL RESERVES 1987
(million metric tons)

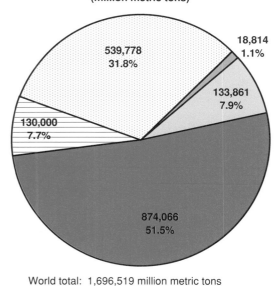

World total: 1,696,519 million metric tons

	Africa		U.S.S.R.
	Asia* and Oceania		Other
	Latin America		

* Middle East inclusive

Source: World Resources 1990-91
(New York: Oxford University Press, 1990)

FIGURE 7-8
TOTAL ENERGY RESERVES 1988
(in petajoules)

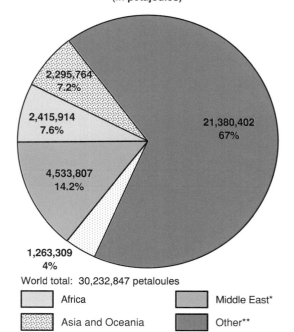

World total: 30,232,847 petaloules

	Africa		Middle East*
	Asia and Oceania		Other**
	Latin America		

* Middle East consists of the Arabian Penninsula,
Jordan, Lebanon, Iran, Iraq, Israel, Turkey

** Centrally planned economies inclusive

Source: World Resources 1990-91
(New York: Oxford University Press, 1990)

8: LABOR

FIGURE 8-1a
LABOR FORCE 1985
(thousands)

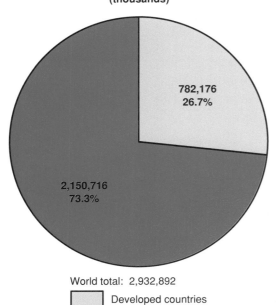

World total: 2,932,892

☐ Developed countries

☐ Developing countries

Source: World Population Prospects 1988
(New York: UN, 1989)

FIGURE 8-1b
LABOR FORCE 2025
(thousands)

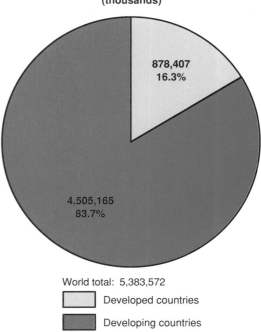

World total: 5,383,572

☐ Developed countries

☐ Developing countries

Source: World Population Prospects 1988
(New York: UN, 1989)

FIGURE 8-2a
YOUTH POPULATION 1990
(age 15-24, thousands)

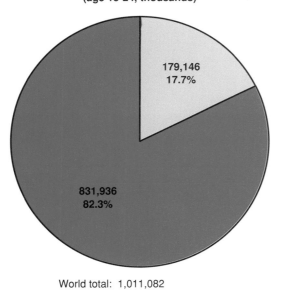

World total: 1,011,082

☐ More developed countries

☐ Less developed countries

Source: World Population Prospects 1988
(New York: UN, 1989)

FIGURE 8-2b
YOUTH POPULATION 2025
(age 15-24, thousands)

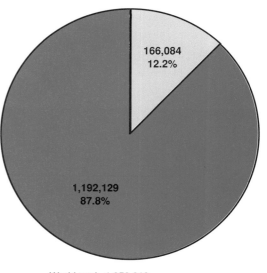

World total: 1,358,213

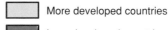

☐ More developed countries

☐ Less developed countries

Source: World Population Prospects 1988
(New York: UN, 1989)

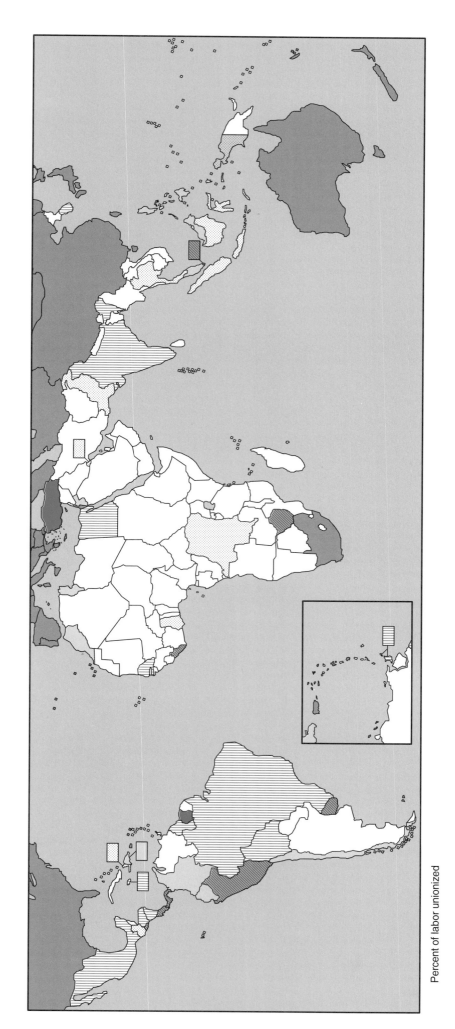

FIGURE 8-3
UNIONIZATION
(1984-89)

Percent of labor unionized

Less than 10%

10-14.9%

15-19.9%

20-30%

More than 30%

Data not available

Source: Foreign Labor Trends
(Washington, D.C.: U.S. Department of Labor, 1989)

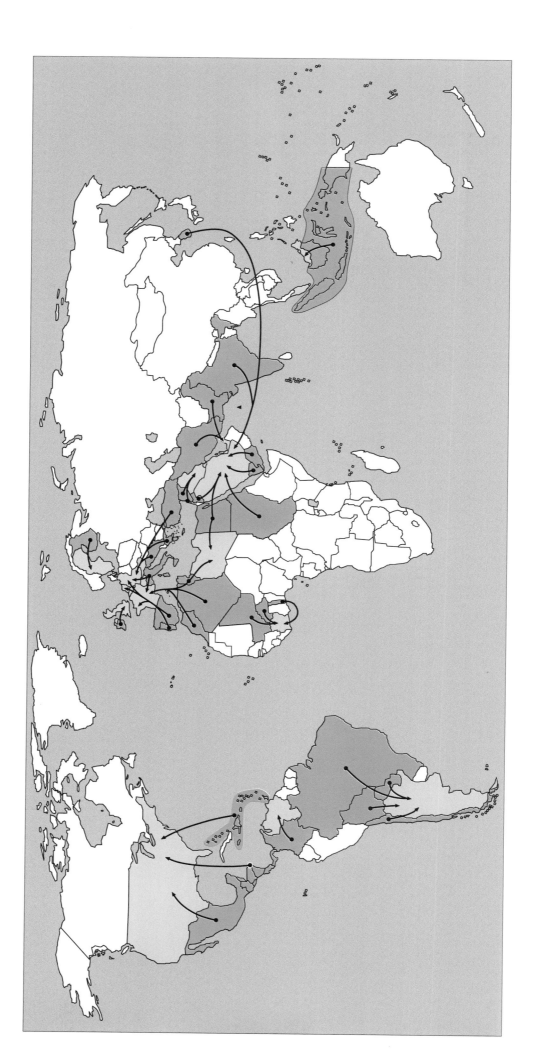

FIGURE 8-4
MIGRANT LABOR
(Since 1945)

Chief sources of international
migrant labor

Main countries or regions
employing foreign migrant labor

Source: Atlas of U.S. Foreign Relations
(Washington, D.C.: U.S. State Department, 1985)

FIGURE 8-5
**PERCENTAGE OF WOMEN IN
THE LABOR FORCE**

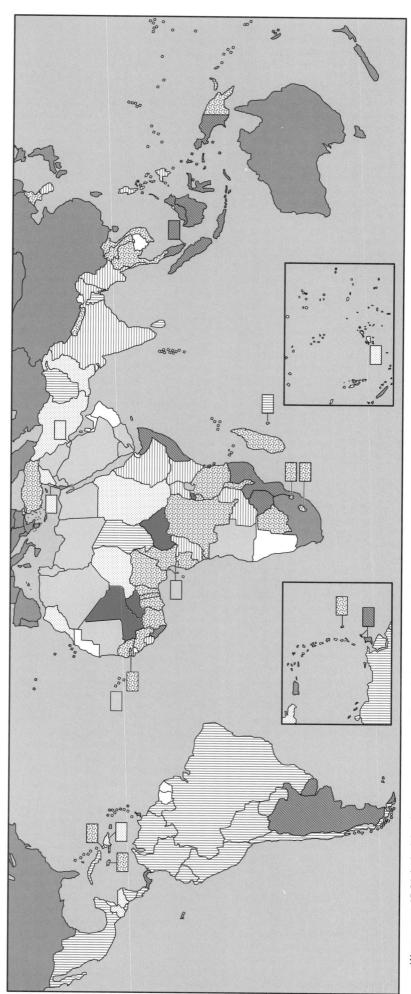

Women, age 15-64, in the labor force as a percentage of population of women, age 15-64

Less than 10%   10-19%   20-29%   30-39%

40-49%   50-75%   More than 75%   Data not available

Source: Ruth Leger Sivard, *Women: A World Survey*
(Washington, D.C.: World Priorities, 1985)

9: ENVIRONMENT

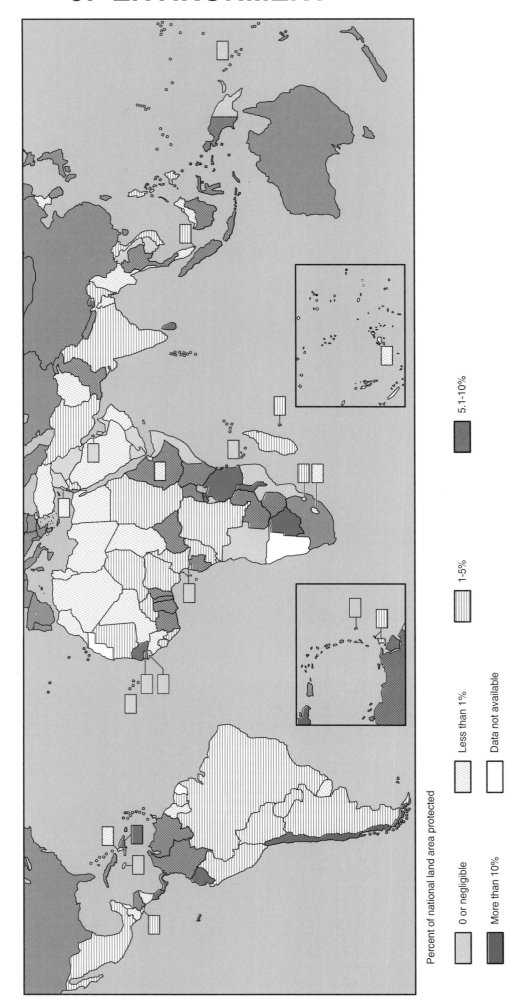

FIGURE 9-1
NATIONALLY PROTECTED NATURAL AREAS
(1989)

Percent of national land area protected

- 0 or negligible
- Less than 1%
- 1-5%
- 5.1-10%
- More than 10%
- Data not available

Source: *World Resources 1990-91*
(New York: Oxford University Press, 1990)

FIGURE 9-2
PER CAPITA WATER AVAILABILITY
(Projection for the year 2000)

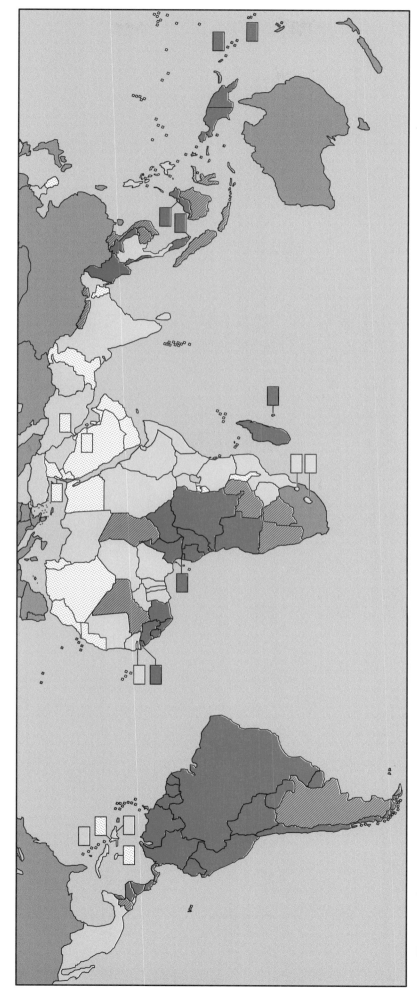

Thousands of cubic meters of water per person per year

Very low (1 or less)

Low (1-5)

Data not available

High (more than10)

Medium (5-10)

Source: *The Global 2000 Report to the President--Entering the Twenty-first Century: A Report
Prepared by the Council on Environmental Quality and the Department of State*
(Washington, D.C.: The U.S. Govt. Printing Office, 1980-81)

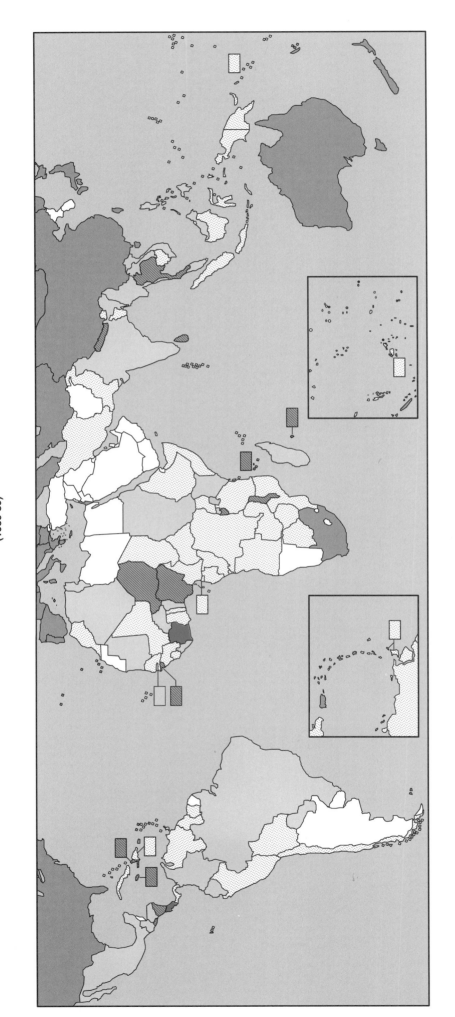

FIGURE 9-3
DEFORESTATION - AVERAGE ANNUAL PERCENTAGE RATE
(1980-89)

Less than 1%

5% and over

1% to under 2.5%

Data not available

2.5% to under 5%

Source: *World Resources 1990-91*
(New York: Oxford University Press, 1990)

FIGURE 9-4
DESERTIFICATION

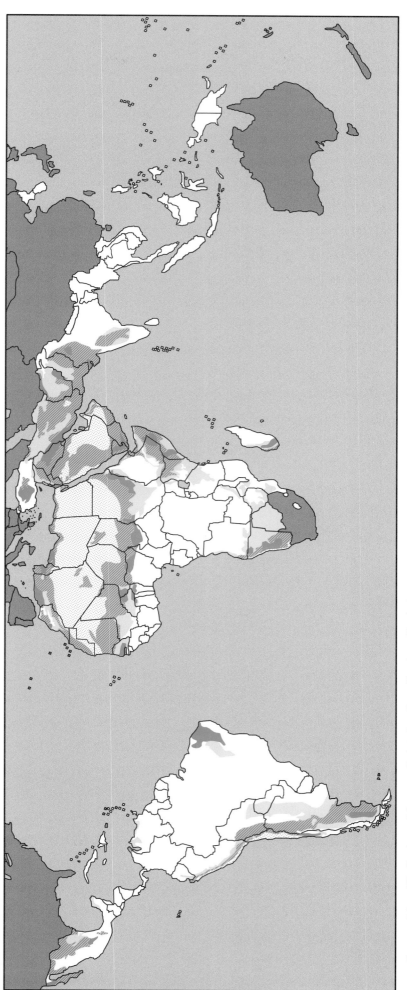

Degree of desertification hazard (in zones likely to be affected by desertification)

Very high

High

Existing deserts

Moderate

Source: U.N. Conference on Desertification 1977

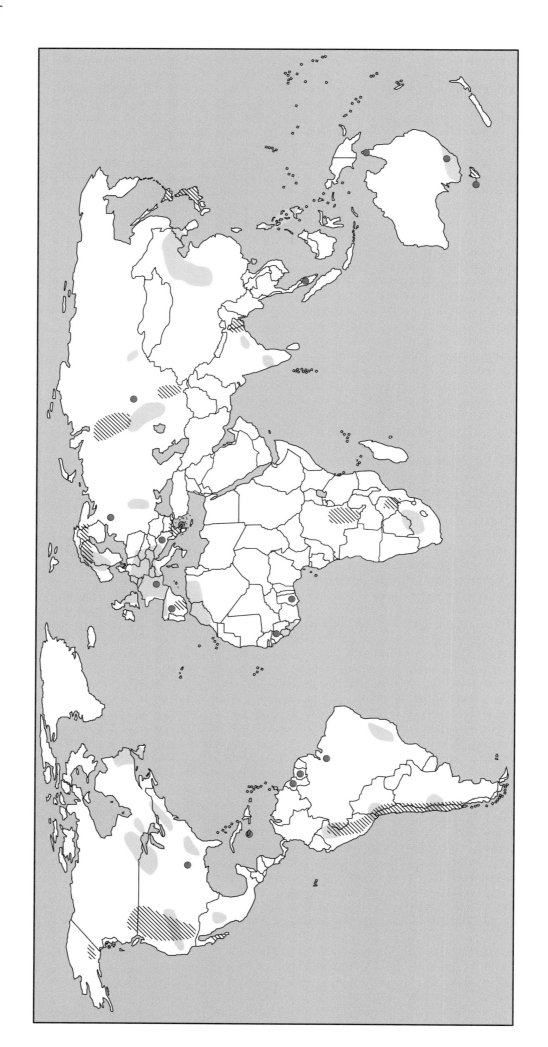

FIGURE 9-5
WORLD MINERAL DEPOSITS

Copper

Iron ore

Bauxite

Source: *Atlas of U.S. Foreign Relations*
(Washington, D.C.: U.S. Department of State, 1985)

10: TRADE

FIGURE 10-1
CURRENT ACCOUNT BALANCE 1983-88

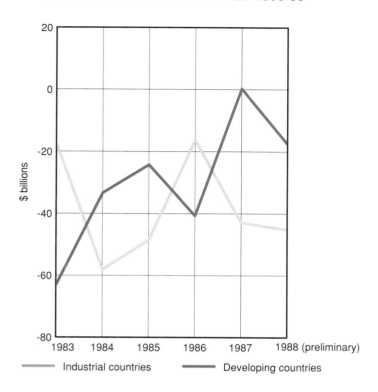

Industrial countries   Developing countries

Source: The State of Food and Agriculture 1989
(Rome: FAO, 1989)

FIGURE 10-2
CURRENT ACCOUNT BALANCE FOR DEVELOPING COUNTRIES 1983-88

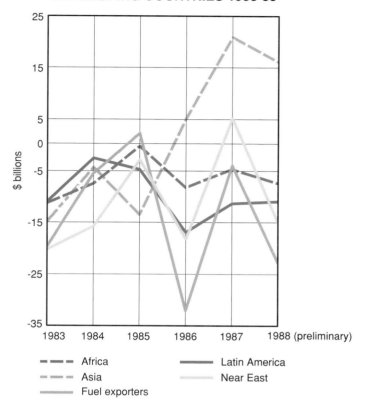

Africa   Latin America
Asia   Near East
Fuel exporters

Source: International Financial Statistics
(Washington, D.C.: IMF, 1990)

FIGURE 10-3
ANNUAL PERCENT CHANGE IN TERMS OF TRADE 1980-88

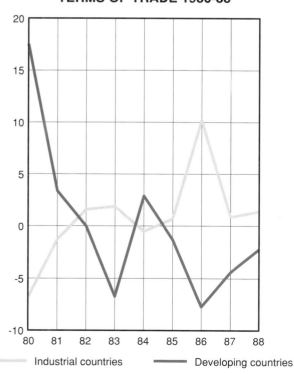

Industrial countries   Developing countries

Source: International Financial Statistics
(Washington, D.C.: IMF, 1990)

FIGURE 10-4
TERMS OF TRADE 1980 AND 1987
(annual percent change)

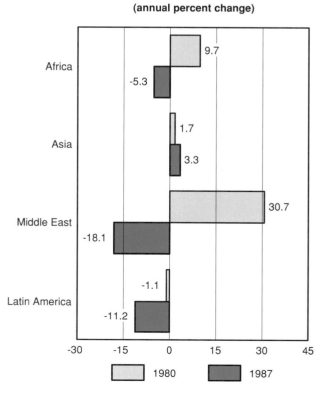

1980   1987

Source: International Financial Statistics
(Washington, D.C.: IMF, 1990)

FIGURE 10-5
ANNUAL PERCENTAGE CHANGE IN EXPORT VOLUMES 1980-88

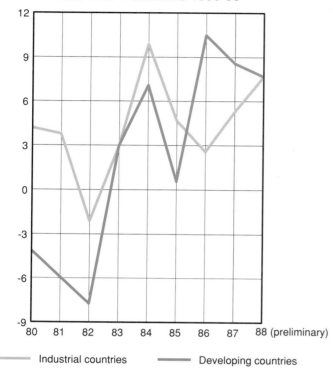

Industrial countries   Developing countries

Source: *The State of Food and Agriculture 1989*
(Rome: FAO, 1989)

FIGURE 10-6
THIRD WORLD EXPORT VOLUMES 1980 AND 1987

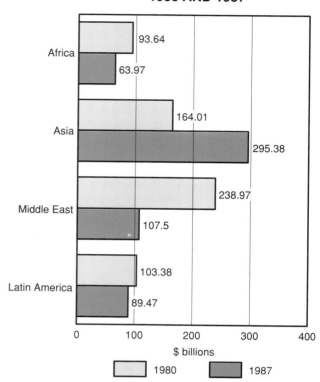

$ billions

1980   1987

Source: *International Financial Statistics*
(Washington, D.C.: IMF, 1990)

FIGURE 10-7
ANNUAL PERCENTAGE CHANGE IN IMPORT VOLUMES 1980-88

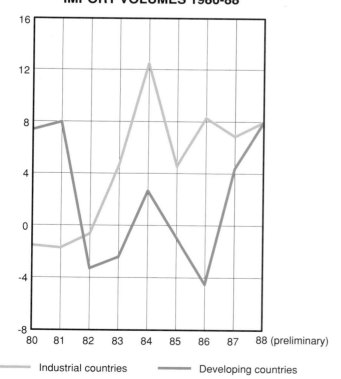

Industrial countries   Developing countries

Source: *The State of Food and Agriculture 1989*
(Rome: FAO, 1989)

FIGURE 10-8
THIRD WORLD IMPORT VOLUMES 1980 AND 1988

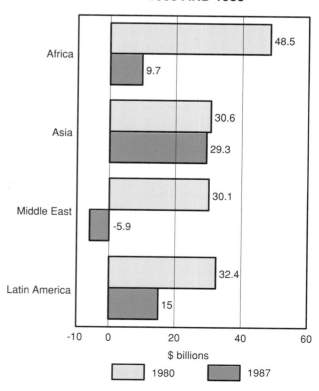

$ billions

1980   1987

Source: *International Financial Statistics*
(Washington, D.C.: IMF, 1990)

FIGURE 10-9
DEVELOPING COUNTRY EXPORTS 1983
($ billions)

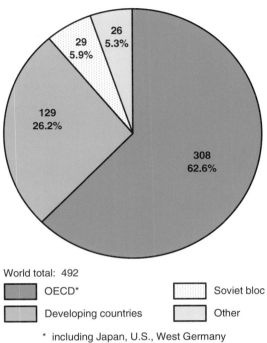

World total: 492

■ OECD*	▨ Soviet bloc
▨ Developing countries	□ Other

* including Japan, U.S., West Germany

Source: Atlas of U.S. Foreign Relations
(Washington D.C.: U.S. State Department, 1985)

FIGURE 10-10
AVERAGE ANNUAL PERCENTAGE
GROWTH RATE OF EXPORTS

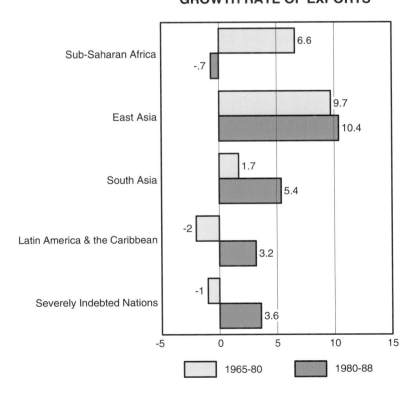

Source: World Development Report 1990
(New York: World Bank, 1990)

FIGURE 10-11
THIRD WORLD SHARE OF U.S. MERCHANDISE EXPORTS 1984
($ billions)

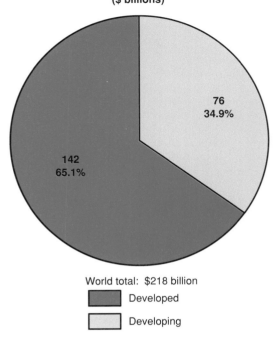

76
34.9%

142
65.1%

World total: $218 billion

■ Developed

□ Developing

Source: Atlas of U.S. Foreign Relations
(Washington D.C.: U.S. State Department, 1985)

FIGURE 10-12
THIRD WORLD CONTRIBUTION TO U.S. MERCHANDISE IMPORTS 1984
($ billions)

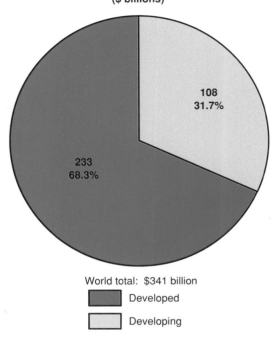

108
31.7%

233
68.3%

World total: $341 billion

■ Developed

□ Developing

Source: Atlas of U.S. Foreign Relations
(Washington D.C.: U.S. State Department, 1985)

FIGURE 10-13
THIRD WORLD SHARE OF U.S. MANUFACTURED EXPORTS 1984
($ billions)

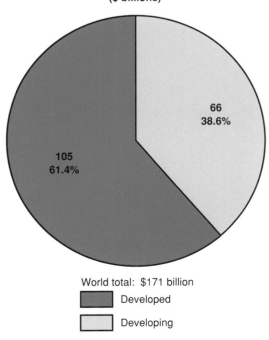

66
38.6%

105
61.4%

World total: $171 billion

■ Developed

□ Developing

Source: Atlas of U.S. Foreign Relations
(Washington D.C.: U.S. State Department, 1985)

FIGURE 10-14
THIRD WORLD CONTRIBUTION TO U.S. MANUFACTURED IMPORTS 1984
($ billions)

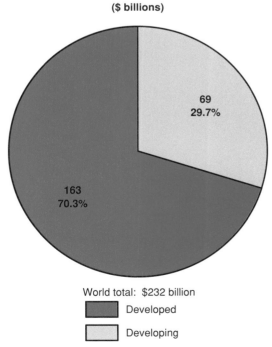

69
29.7%

163
70.3%

World total: $232 billion

■ Developed

□ Developing

Source: Atlas of U.S. Foreign Relations
(Washington D.C.: U.S. State Department, 1985)

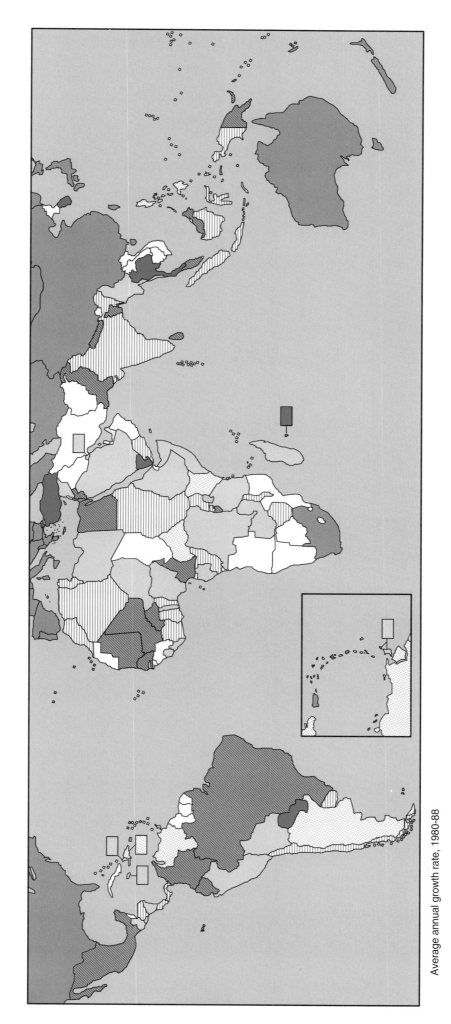

FIGURE 10-15
AVERAGE ANNUAL EXPORT GROWTH
(1980-88)

Average annual growth rate, 1980-88

Negative growth

More than 10%

Less than 1%

Data not available

1-5%

5.1-10%

Source: World Development Report, 1990
(New York: Oxford University Press, 1990)

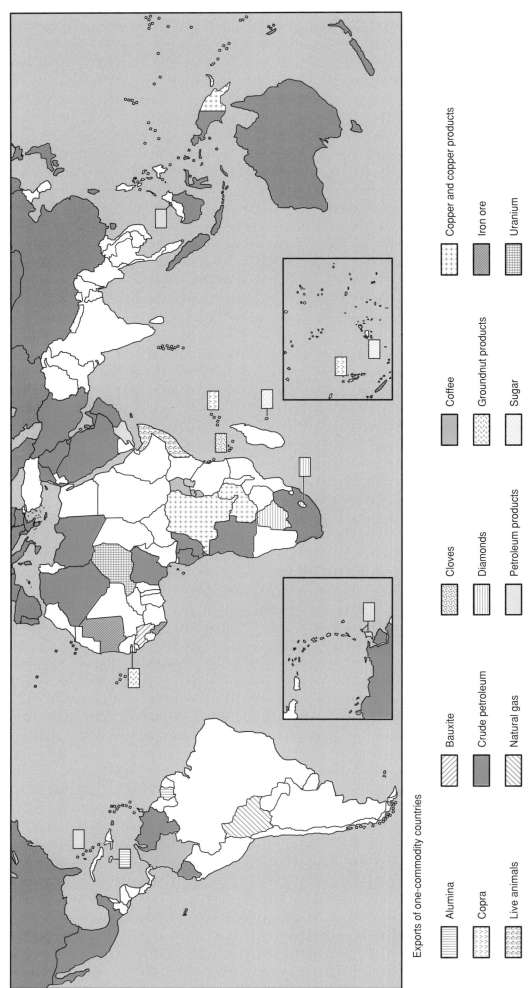

FIGURE 10-16
ONE-COMMODITY COUNTRIES
(One commodity provides more than 50% of export earnings)

Exports of one-commodity countries

Alumina	Bauxite	Cloves	Coffee	Copper and copper products
Copra	Crude petroleum	Diamonds	Groundnut products	Iron ore
Live animals	Natural gas	Petroleum products	Sugar	Uranium

Source: Atlas of U.S. Foreign Relations
(Washington, D.C.: U.S. State Department, 1985)

11: DEFENSE

FIGURE 11-1
WORLD MILITARY EXPENDITURES 1988
($ billions)

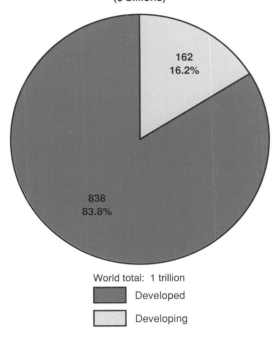

162
16.2%

838
83.8%

World total: 1 trillion

Developed

Developing

Source: World Military Expenditures and Arms Transfers (Washington, D.C.: U.S. Arms Control and Disarmament Agency, 1988)

FIGURE 11-2
REGIONAL SHARES OF MILITARY EXPENDITURES 1987

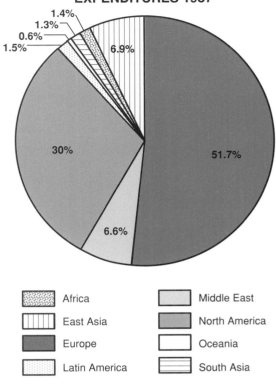

1.4%
1.3%
0.6%
1.5%
6.9%
30%
51.7%
6.6%

Africa   Middle East

East Asia   North America

Europe   Oceania

Latin America   South Asia

Source: World Military Expenditures and Arms Transfers (Washington, D.C.: U.S. Arms Control and Disarmament Agency, 1988)

FIGURE 11-3
MILITARY EXPENDITURES AS PERCENTAGE OF GNP 1987

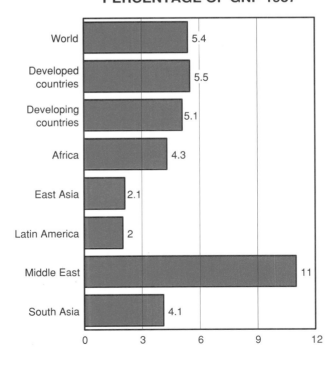

World	5.4
Developed countries	5.5
Developing countries	5.1
Africa	4.3
East Asia	2.1
Latin America	2
Middle East	11
South Asia	4.1

Source: World Military Expenditures and Arms Transfers (Washington, D.C.: U.S. Arms Control and Disarmament Agency, 1988)

FIGURE 11-4
WORLD ARMS IMPORTS 1977-87
(billions of constant 1987 dollars)

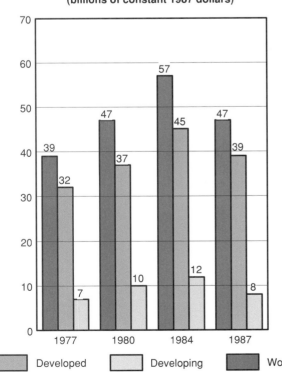

	1977	1980	1984	1987
Developed	39	47	57	47
Developing	32	37	45	39
World	7	10	12	8

Developed   Developing   World

Source: World Military Expenditures and Arms Transfers (Washington, D.C.: U.S. Arms Control and Disarmament Agency, 1988)

FIGURE 11-5
REGIONAL SHARES OF WORLD ARMS IMPORTS 1987

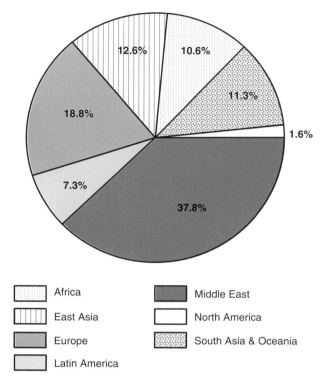

Africa — East Asia — Europe — Latin America — Middle East — North America — South Asia & Oceania

Source: *World Military Expenditures and Arms Transfers* (Washington, D.C.: U.S. Arms Control and Disarmament Agency, 1988)

FIGURE 11-6
ARMS TRADE AS PERCENTAGE OF TOTAL TRADE 1987

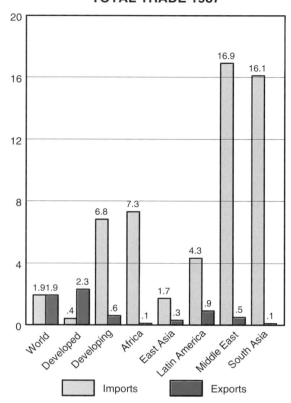

Imports — Exports

Source: *World Military Expenditures and Arms Transfers* (Washington, D.C.: U.S. Arms Control and Disarmament Agency, 1988)

FIGURE 11-7
ARMED FORCES 1987
(millions)

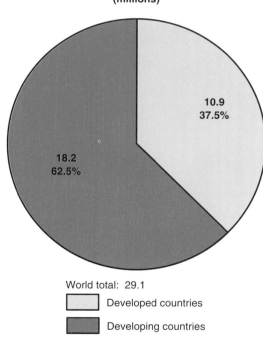

World total: 29.1

Developed countries — Developing countries

Source: *World Military Expenditures and Arms Transfers* (Washington, D.C.: U.S. Arms Control and Disarmament Agency, 1988)

FIGURE 11-8
ARMED FORCES PER 1,000 POPULATION

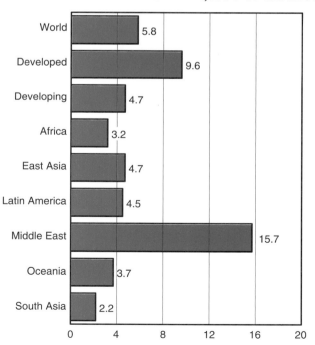

Source: *World Military Expenditures and Arms Transfers* (Washington, D.C.: U.S. Arms Control and Disarmament Agency, 1988)

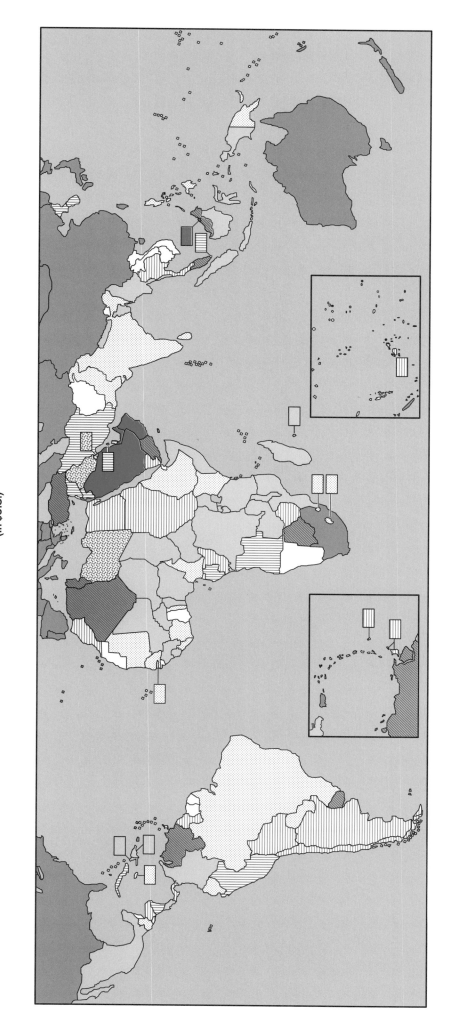

FIGURE 11-9
MILITARY EXPENDITURES PER CAPITA 1987
(in $U.S.)

Less than 10

101-500

10-25

501-1,000

26-50

1,001-1,400

51-100

Data not available

Source: Ruth Leger Sivard, *World Military and Social Expenditures 1991* (Washington, D.C.: World Priorities, 1991)

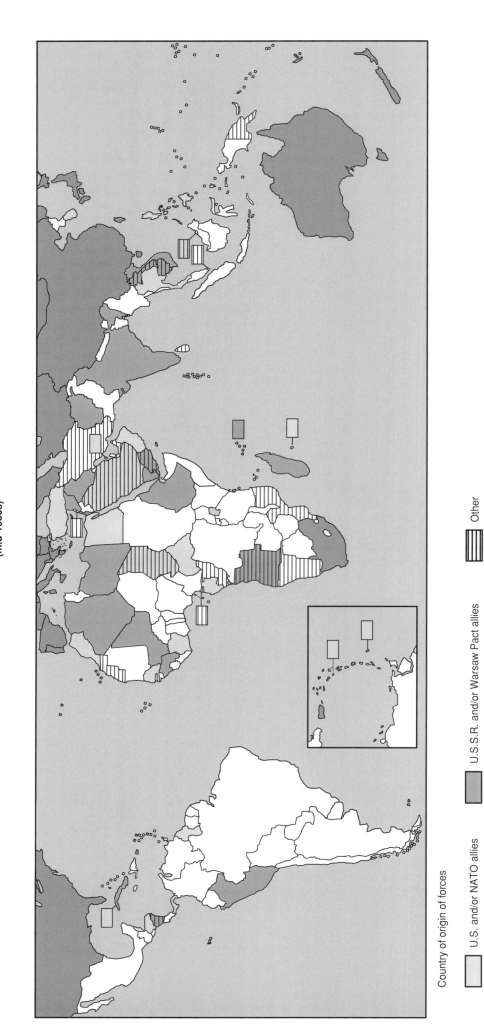

FIGURE 11-10
FOREIGN MILITARY PRESENCE
(mid-1980s)

Country of origin of forces

U.S. and/or NATO allies

U.S.S.R. and/or Warsaw Pact allies

Other

Source: Ruth Leger Sivard, *World Military and Social Expenditures 1987-88* (Washington, D.C.: World Priorities, 1988)

FIGURE 11-11
ARMS SUPPLIERS TO THE THIRD WORLD
(mid-1980s)

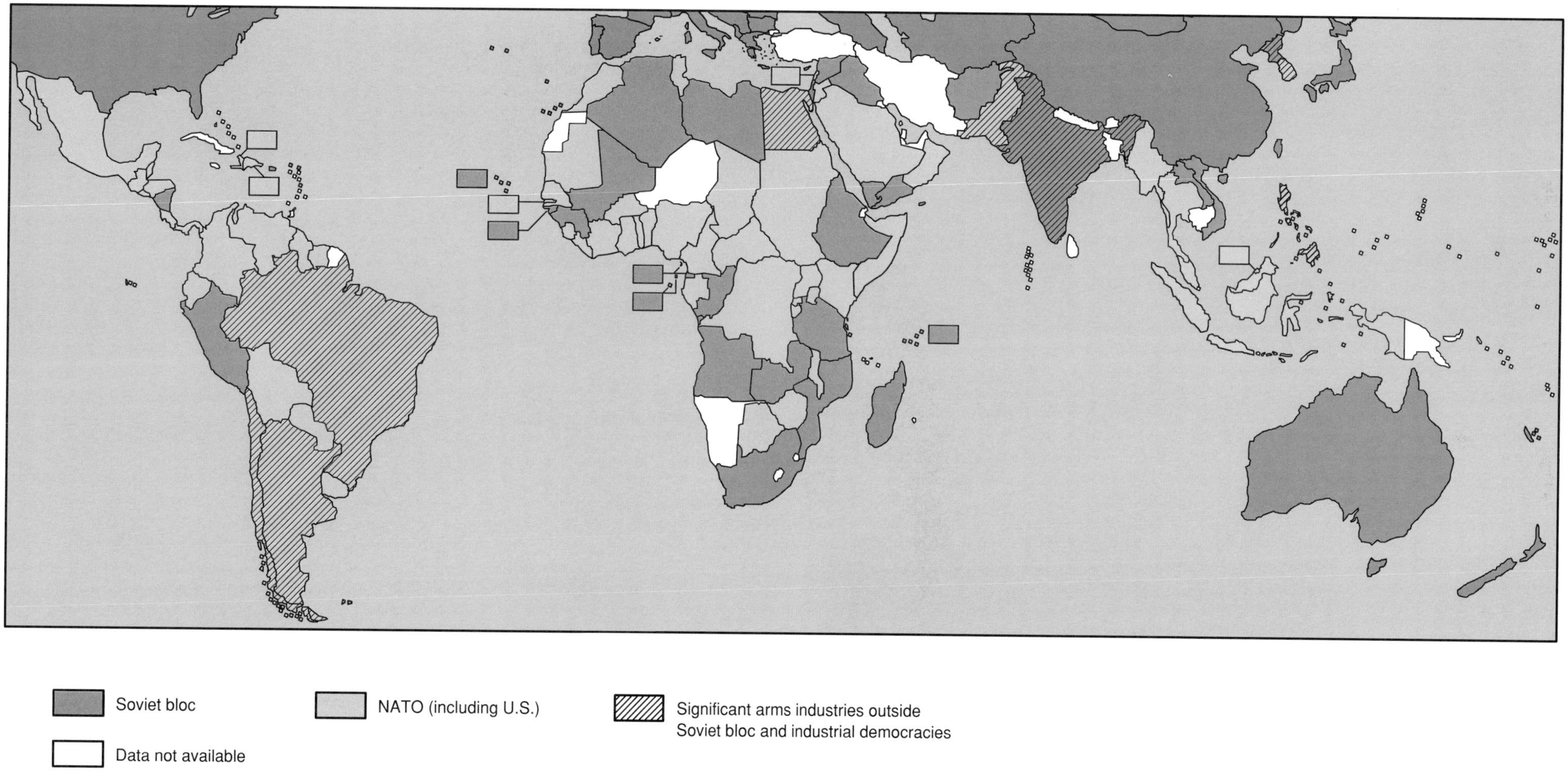

Soviet bloc

Data not available

NATO (including U.S.)

Significant arms industries outside
Soviet bloc and industrial democracies

Source: Atlas of U.S. Foreign Relations
(Washington, D.C.: U.S. State Department, 1985)

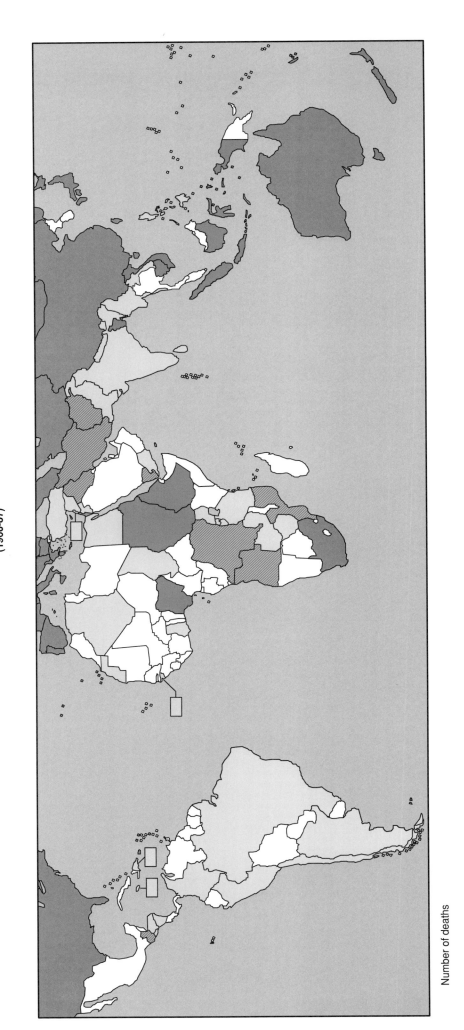

FIGURE 11-12
WAR DEATHS
(1960-87)

Number of deaths

1,000-99,999

100,000-499,999

500,000 or more

Source: Ruth Leger Sivard, *World Military and Social Expenditures 1987-88* (Washington, D.C.: World Priorities, 1987)

12: EDUCATION

FIGURE 12-1
ILLITERACY

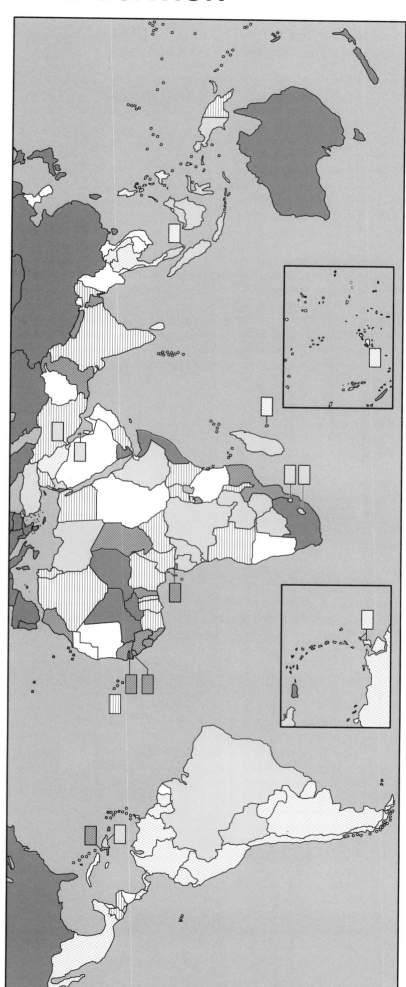

0-20%

81-100%

21-40%

Data not available

41-60%

61-80%

Source: *World Development Report 1990*
(New York: Oxford University Press, 1990)

FIGURE 12-2
FEMALE ILLITERACY
(1985)

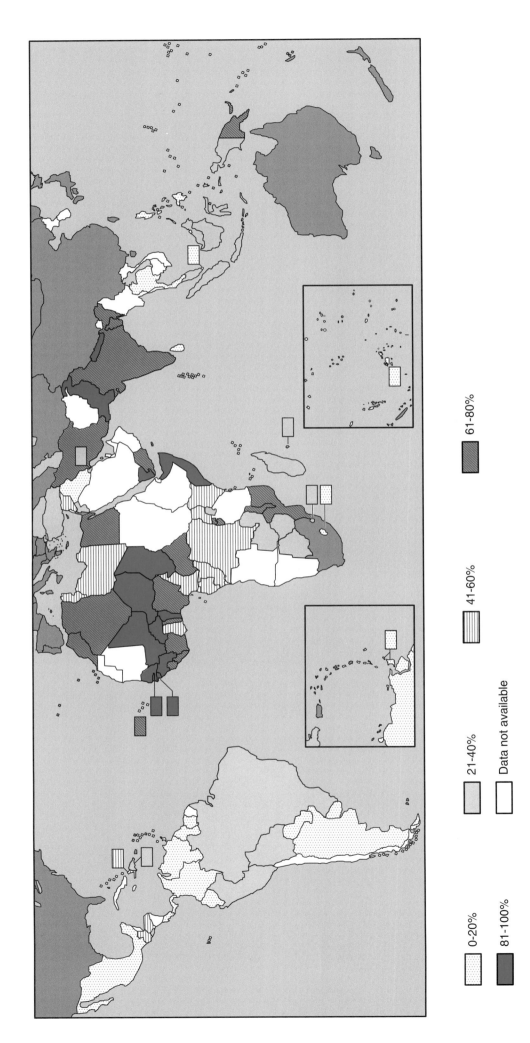

0-20%

81-100%

21-40%

Data not available

41-60%

61-80%

Source: World Development Report 1990
(New York: Oxford University Press, 1990)

FIGURE 12-3
EDUCATIONAL EXPENDITURES

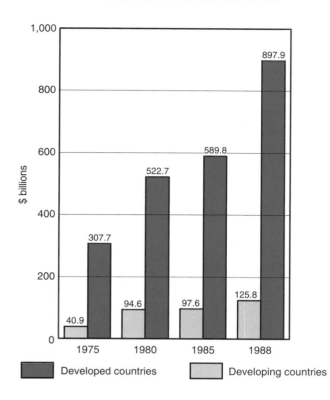

Developed countries   Developing countries

Source: *1990 Statistical Yearbook*
(Paris: UNESCO, 1990)

FIGURE 12-4
EDUCATIONAL EXPENDITURES AS PERCENTAGE OF GNP

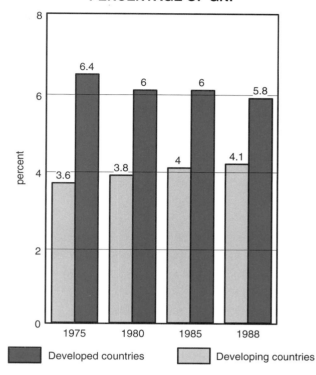

Developed countries   Developing countries

Source: *1990 Statistical Yearbook*
(Paris: UNESCO, 1990)

FIGURE 12-5
EDUCATIONAL EXPENDITURES PER CAPITA

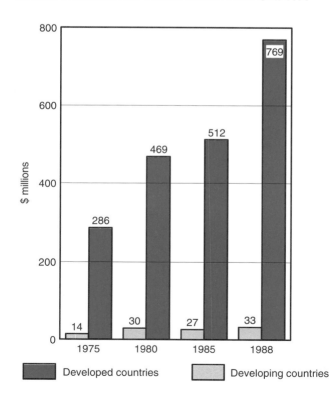

Developed countries   Developing countries

Source: *1990 Statistical Yearbook*
(Paris: UNESCO, 1990)

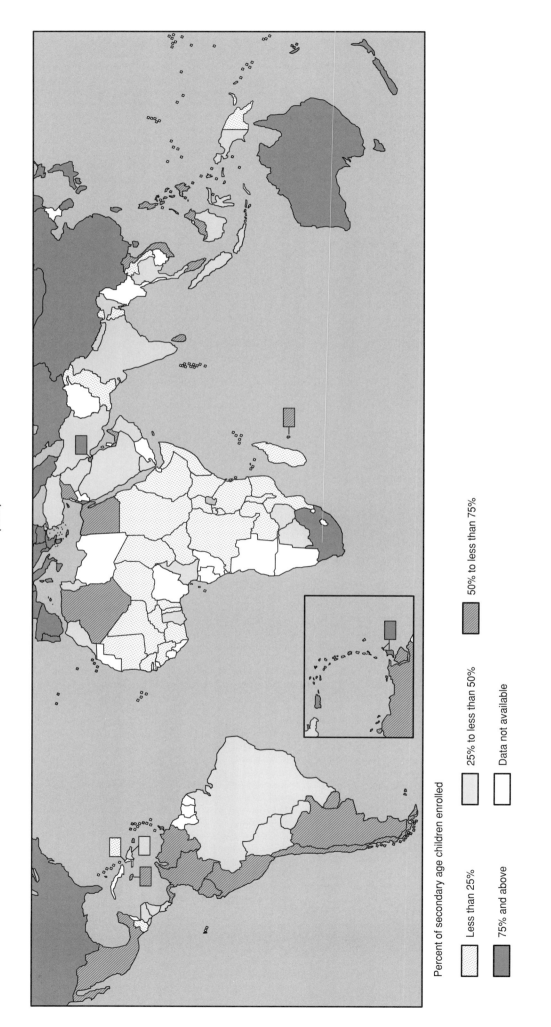

FIGURE 12-6
SECONDARY SCHOOL ENROLLMENT
(1987)

Percent of secondary age children enrolled

Less than 25%

25% to less than 50%

50% to less than 75%

75% and above

Data not available

Source: World Development Report 1990
(New York: Oxford University Press, 1990)

13: HEALTH

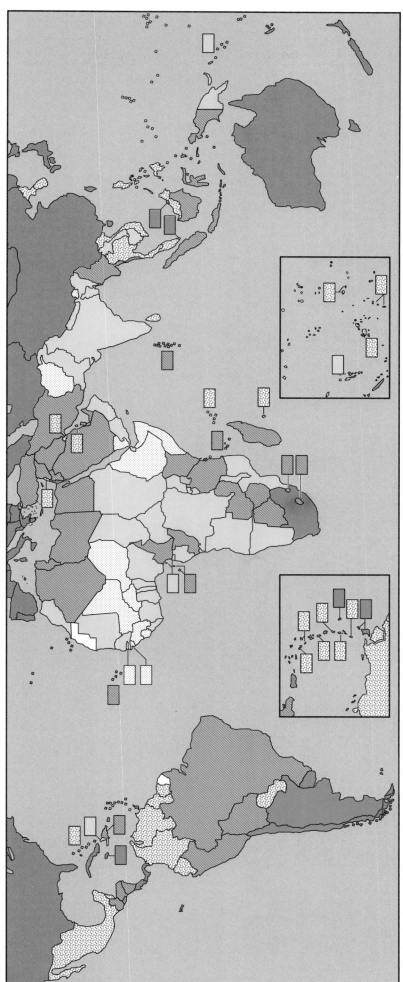

FIGURE 13-1
PHYSICAL QUALITY OF LIFE INDEX*
(PQLI)

PQLI of 30 or below

PQLI of 78-89

PQLI of 31-55

PQLI of 90 or above

PQLI of 5-77

Data not available

* The index is calculated by averaging child mortality, literacy and life expectancy, giving equal weight to each factor.

Source: George Kurian, *The New Book of World Rankings, 3rd ed.* (New York: Facts On File, 1991)

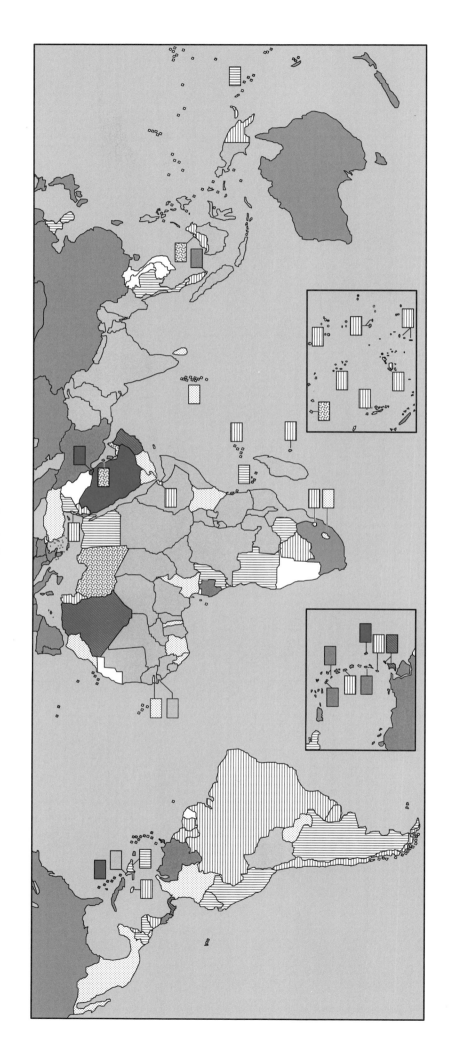

FIGURE 13-2
ANNUAL PUBLIC HEALTH EXPENDITURES PER CAPITA
(in $U.S.)

Less than $5

$5-$10

$10.01-$20

$20.01-$50

$50.01-$100

$100.01-$150

$150.01-$200

More than $200

Data not available

Source: *1991 Britannica Book of the Year*
(Chicago: Encyclopedia Britannica, 1991)

FIGURE 13-3
ACCESS TO SAFE WATER
(Rural)

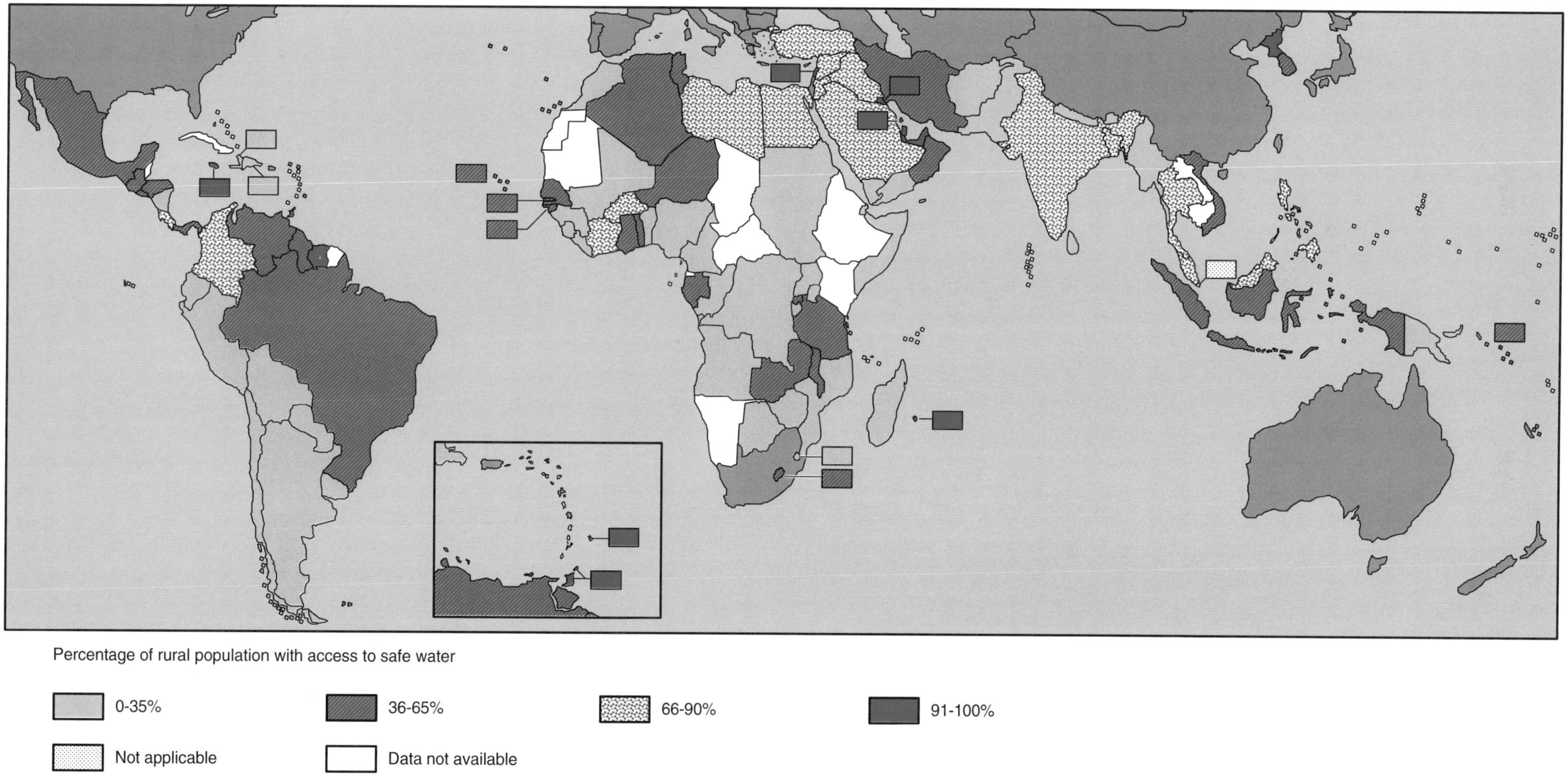

Percentage of rural population with access to safe water

0-35%   36-65%   66-90%   91-100%

Not applicable   Data not available

Source: *World Resources 1990-91*
(New York: Oxford University Press, 1990)

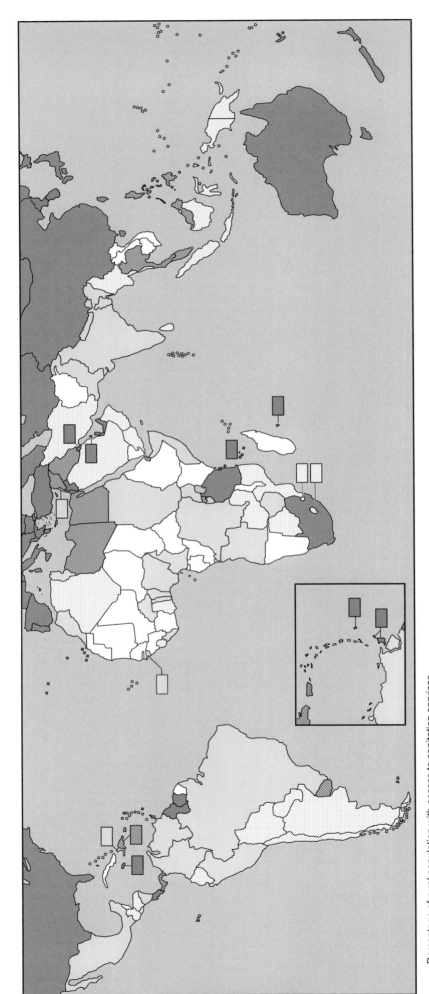

FIGURE 13-4
ACCESS TO SANITATION SERVICES
(Rural)

Percentage of rural population with access to sanitation services

Less than 20%

20% to less than 50%

50% to less than 75%

75% and over

Data not available

Source: World Resources 1990-91
(New York: Oxford University Press, 1990)

FIGURE 13-5
IMMUNIZATION

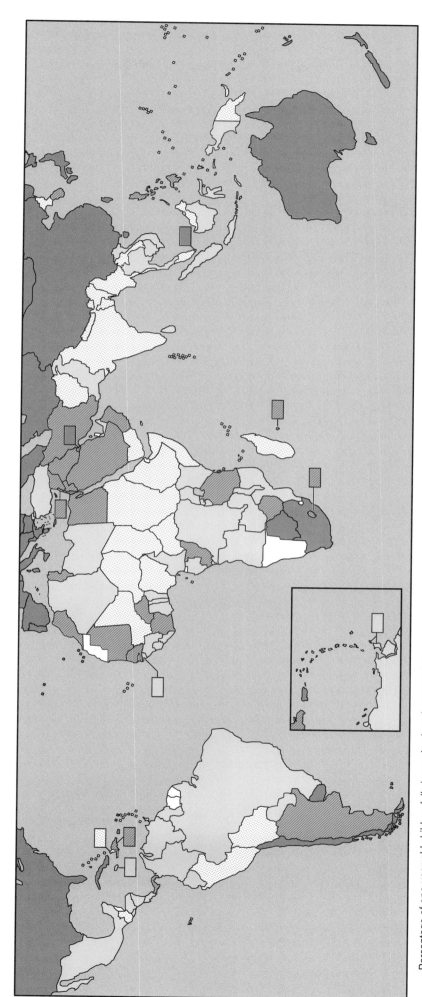

Percentage of one-year-old children fully immunized against measles

0-35%

91-100%

36-65%

Data not available

66-90%

Source: World Resources 1990-91
(New York: Oxford University Press, 1990)

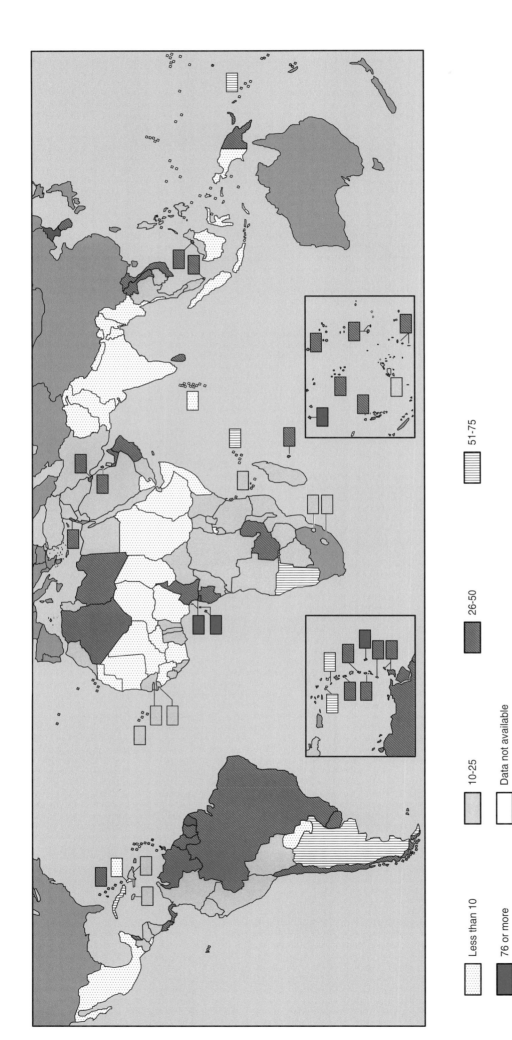

FIGURE 13-6
HOSPITAL BEDS
(Per 10,000 population)

Less than 10

10-25

26-50

51-75

76 or more

Data not available

Source: 1991 Britannica Book of the Year
(Chicago: Encyclopedia Britannica, 1991)

FIGURE 13-7
POPULATION PER PHYSICIAN

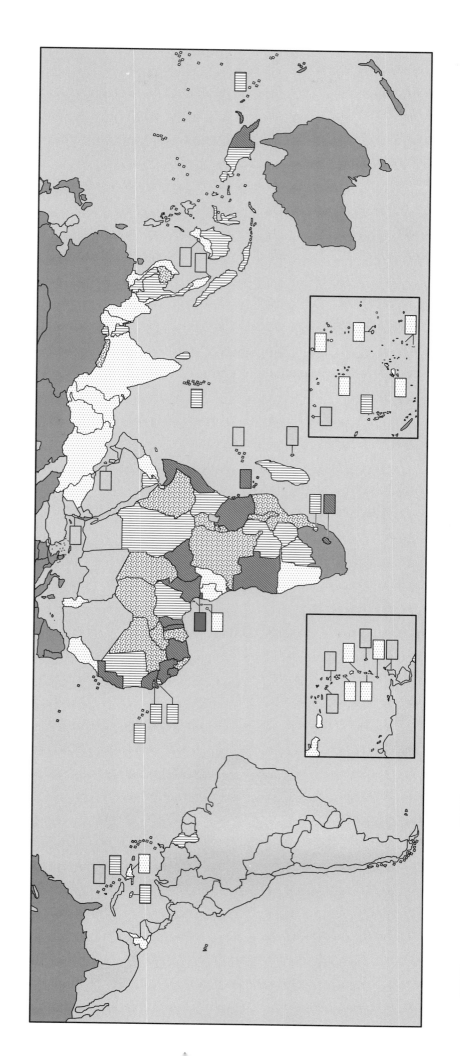

Less than 2,000

20,001-50,000

2,000-5,000

More than 50,000

5,001-10,000

Data not available

10,001-20,000

Source: *1991 Britannica Book of the Year*
(Chicago: Encyclopedia Britannica, 1991)

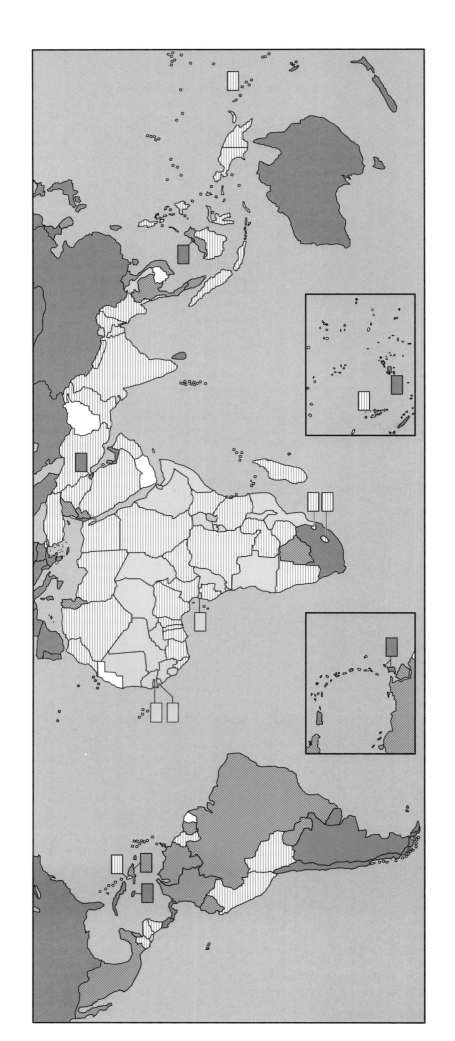

FIGURE 13-8
LIFE EXPECTANCY AT BIRTH
(1989)

Less than 50

70 or more

50-64.9

Data not available

65-69.9

Source: *World Bank Atlas 1990*
(Washington, D.C.; World Bank, 1990)

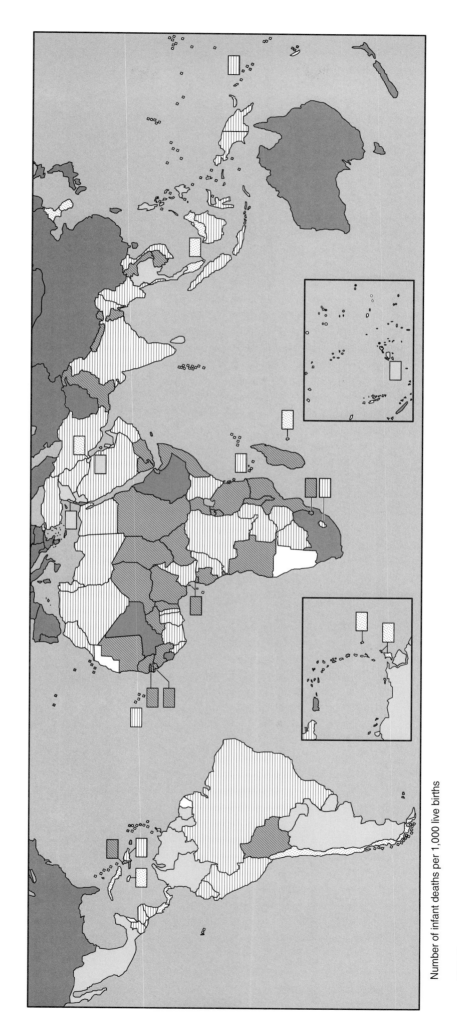

FIGURE 13-9
INFANT MORTALITY RATE
(1985-90)

Number of infant deaths per 1,000 live births

25 and under

More than 150

26-50

Data not available

51-100

101-150

Source: World Resources 1990-91
(New York: Oxford University Press, 1990)

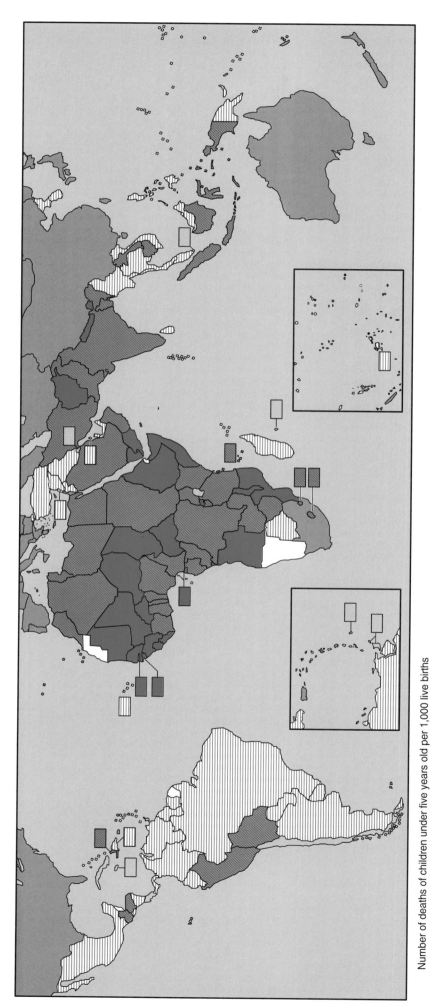

FIGURE 13-10
UNDER-FIVE MORTALITY RATE
(1985-90)

Number of deaths of children under five years old per 1,000 live births

Low (under 30)

High (95-194)

Extremely high (195 or more)

Middle (30-94)

Data not available

Source: World Resources 1990-91
(New York: Oxford University Press, 1990)

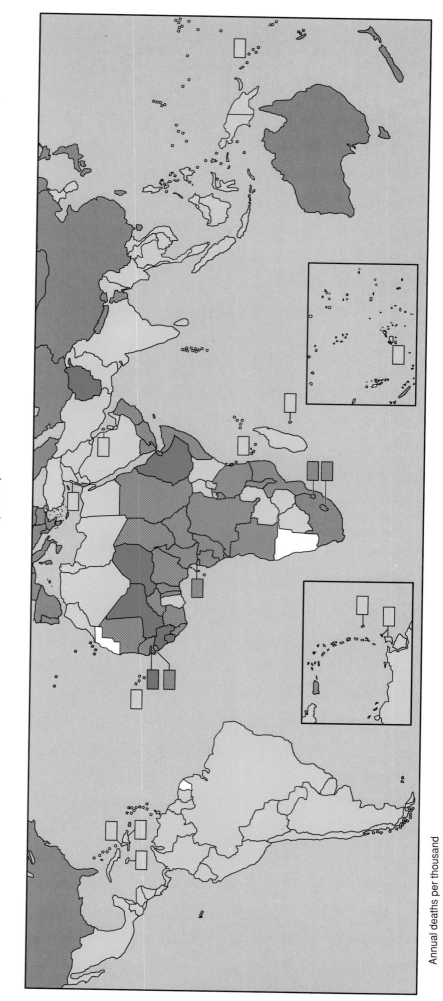

FIGURE 13-11
**DEATH RATE REDUCTION IN
DEVELOPING COUNTRIES**
(1970-90)

Annual deaths per thousand

20 and below by 1970

Data not available

20 and below by 1990

More than 20 as of 1990

Source: World Resources 1990-91
(New York: Oxford University Press, 1990)

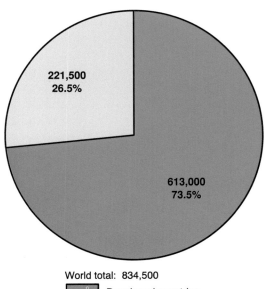

FIGURE 14-1
BOOKS PUBLISHED 1988
(number of titles)

221,500
26.5%

613,000
73.5%

World total: 834,500

◼ Developed countries

◻ Developing countries

Source: 1990 Statistical Yearbook
(Paris: UNESCO,1990)

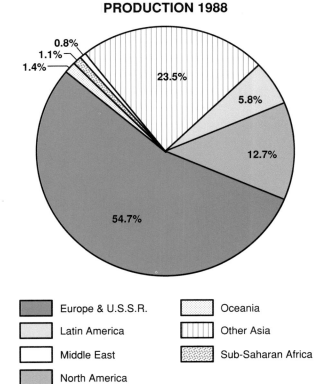

FIGURE 14-2
**DISTRIBUTION OF BOOK
PRODUCTION 1988**

0.8%
1.1%
1.4%
23.5%
5.8%
12.7%
54.7%

◼ Europe & U.S.S.R.   ▦ Oceania

◻ Latin America   ▥ Other Asia

◻ Middle East   ▦ Sub-Saharan Africa

◼ North America

Source: 1990 Statistical Yearbook
(Paris: UNESCO,1990)

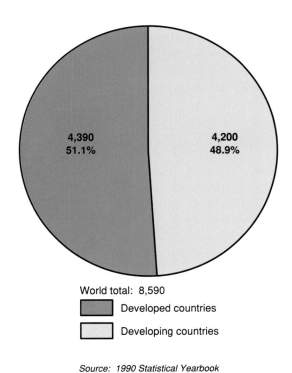

FIGURE 14-3
DAILY NEWSPAPERS 1988

4,390
51.1%

4,200
48.9%

World total: 8,590

◼ Developed countries

◻ Developing countries

Source: 1990 Statistical Yearbook
(Paris: UNESCO,1990)

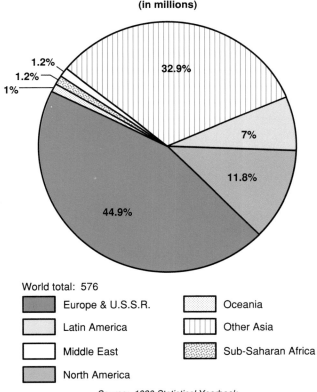

FIGURE 14-4
**DISTRIBUTION OF DAILY NEWSPAPER
CIRCULATION 1988**
(in millions)

1.2%
1.2%
1%
32.9%
7%
11.8%
44.9%

World total: 576

◼ Europe & U.S.S.R.   ▦ Oceania

◻ Latin America   ▥ Other Asia

◻ Middle East   ▦ Sub-Saharan Africa

◼ North America

Source: 1990 Statistical Yearbook
(Paris: UNESCO,1990)

FIGURE 14-5
DISTRIBUTION OF NEWSPRINT
CONSUMPTION 1988
(million metric tons)

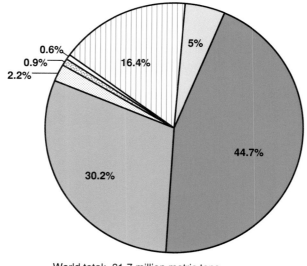

World total: 31.7 million metric tons

Europe & U.S.S.R.		Oceania	
Latin America		Other Asia	
Middle East		Sub-Saharan Africa	
North America			

Source: 1990 Statistical Yearbook
(Paris: UNESCO,1990)

FIGURE 14-6
DISTRIBUTION OF TELEVISION
RECEIVERS 1988

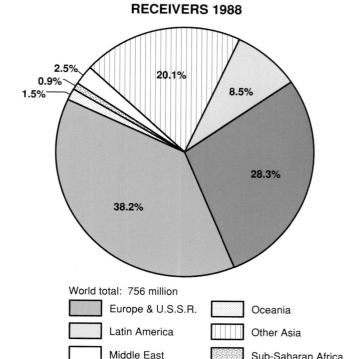

World total: 756 million

Europe & U.S.S.R.		Oceania	
Latin America		Other Asia	
Middle East		Sub-Saharan Africa	
North America			

Source: 1990 Statistical Yearbook
(Paris: UNESCO,1990)

FIGURE 14-7
DISTRIBUTION OF RADIO
RECEIVERS 1988

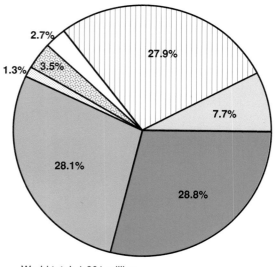

World total: 1,891 million

Europe & U.S.S.R.		Oceania	
Latin America		Other Asia	
Middle East		Sub-Saharan Africa	
North America			

Source: 1990 Statistical Yearbook
(Paris: UNESCO,1990)

FIGURE 14-8
DISTRIBUTION OF LONG FILM PRODUCTION 1987
(based on annual estimated production)

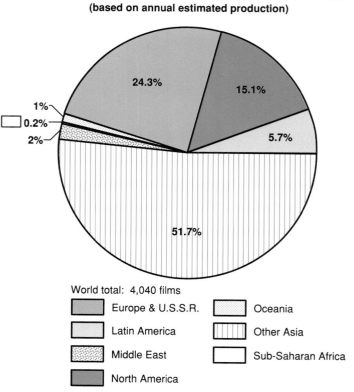

World total: 4,040 films

Europe & U.S.S.R.		Oceania	
Latin America		Other Asia	
Middle East		Sub-Saharan Africa	
North America			

Source: 1990 Statistical Yearbook
(Paris: UNESCO,1990)

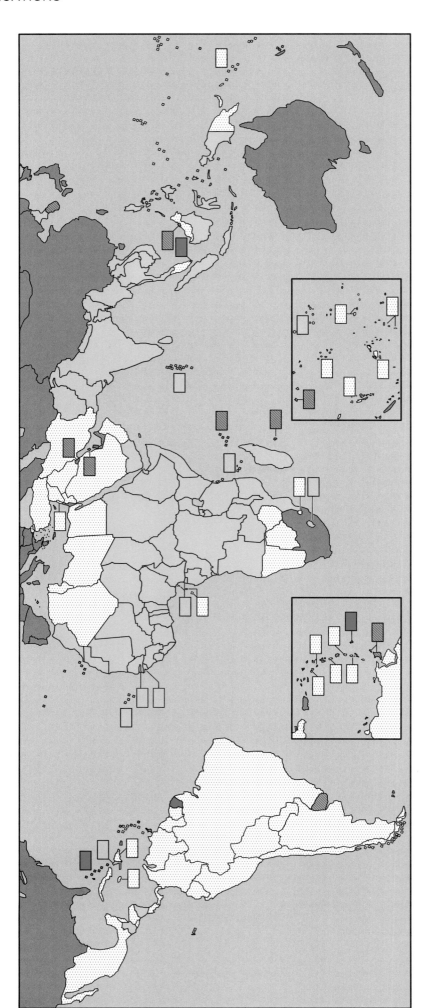

FIGURE 14-9
TELEPHONES IN USE
(Per 100 inhabitants)

Less than 2

30-50

2-14.99

Data not available

15-29.99

Source: *1991 Britannica Book of the Year*
(Chicago: Encyclopedia Britannica, 1991)

FIGURE 14-10
RADIOS IN USE PER 1,000 INHABITANTS
(1988)

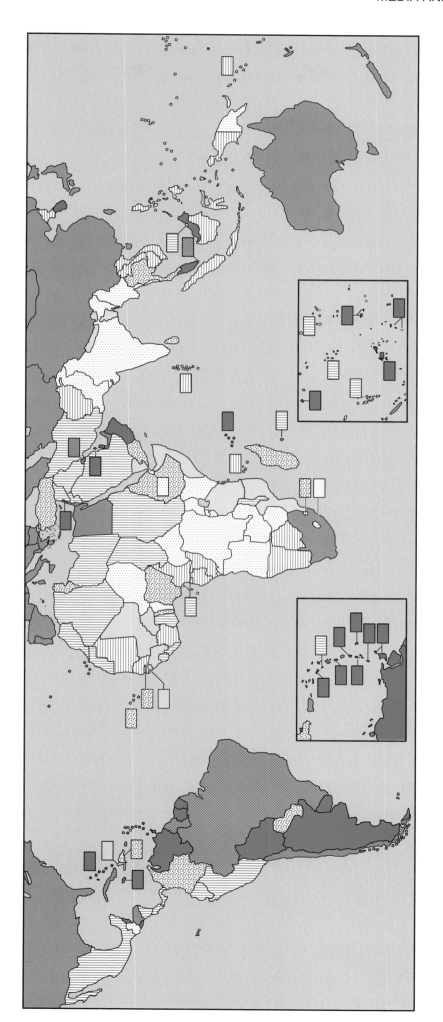

Less than 50

50-99

100-149

150-199

200-299

300-399

400 and over

Data not available

Source: *1990 Statistical Yearbook* (Paris: UNESCO, 1990)

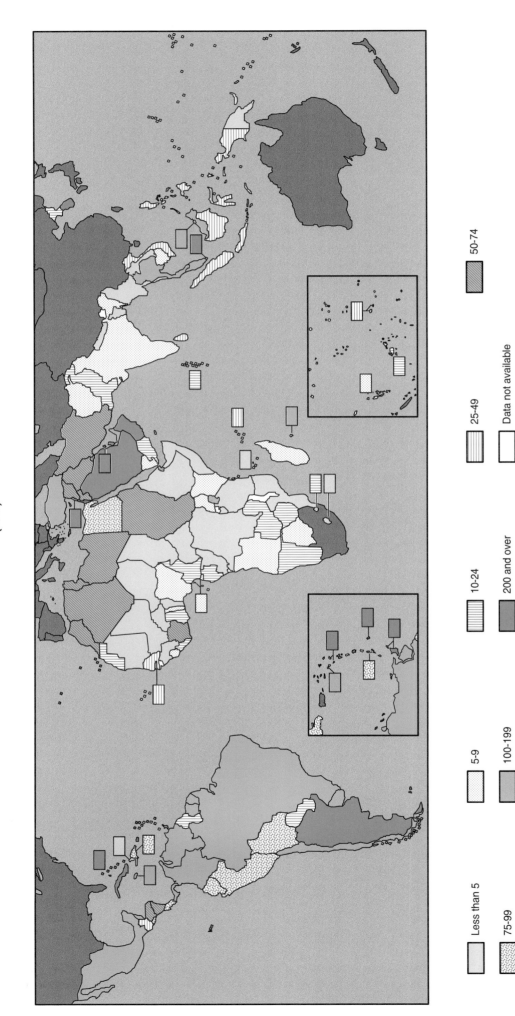

FIGURE 14-11
TELEVISIONS IN USE PER 1,000 INHABITANTS
(1988)

Less than 5

5-9

10-24

25-49

50-74

75-99

100-199

200 and over

Data not available

Source: 1990 Statistical Yearbook
(Paris: UNESCO, 1990)

PART II:
COUNTRY PROFILES

Educational enrollment figures are taken from UNESCO where, in some cases, they are shown as over 100%, especially at the primary level. Since enrollment figures are age-specific, the presence of children outside the age limits at any level would also have the same effect.

Foreign aid figures are sometimes shown as negative. This happens in situations where either the repayments of certain forms of foreign aid exceed receipts or where the receiving country itself extends foreign aid to other countries over and above its receipts.

Charts based on IMF data may sometimes have breaks in them reflecting any one of several causes, such as the changes in base indexes, changes in currency, etc.

AFGHANISTAN

Afghanistan, a landlocked country in central Asia, ranks 40th in the world in land area and 54th in population. (Because a proper census has never been held, estimates of the country's population vary widely.) Although one of the least developed nations in the Third World, Afghanistan has substantial natural gas resources as well as reserves of high-quality iron ore in Bamiyam province and Hajigak. The country's recent economic development plans have been crippled by the Soviet occupation of 1979 and subsequent guerrilla warfare. As a Soviet satellite, Afghanistan received massive loans and grants from the USSR, representing over 30% of government revenues, and continued to receive substantial aid from the Soviet Union after the departure of Soviet troops in 1989. Although the US and the USSR agreed to end aid to the struggling sides in Afghanistan's civil war, fighting continued between government troops and guerrillas throughout 1990.

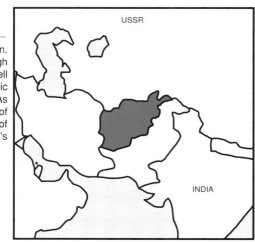

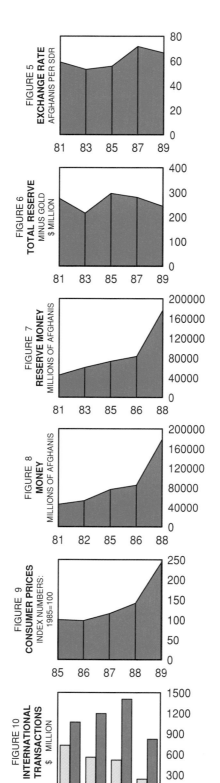

FIGURE 5 EXCHANGE RATE AFGHANIS PER SDR

FIGURE 6 TOTAL RESERVE MINUS GOLD $ MILLION

FIGURE 7 RESERVE MONEY MILLIONS OF AFGHANIS

FIGURE 8 MONEY MILLIONS OF AFGHANIS

FIGURE 9 CONSUMER PRICES INDEX NUMBERS: 1985=100

FIGURE 10 INTERNATIONAL TRANSACTIONS $ MILLION
Exports Imports

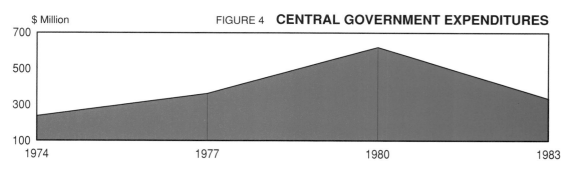

FIGURE 1 **POPULATION GROWTH**

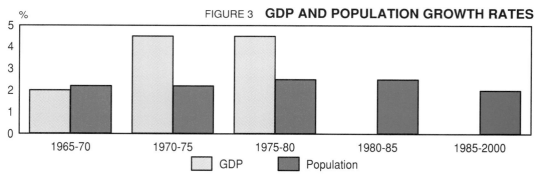

FIGURE 2 **GROSS NATIONAL PRODUCT**

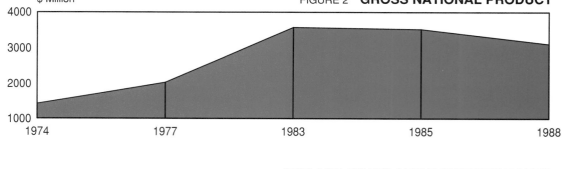

FIGURE 3 **GDP AND POPULATION GROWTH RATES**
GDP Population

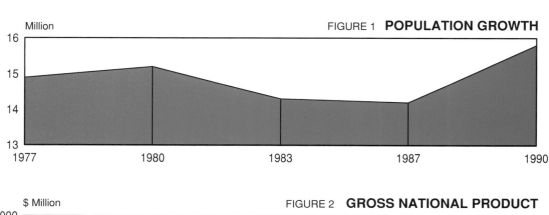

FIGURE 4 **CENTRAL GOVERNMENT EXPENDITURES**

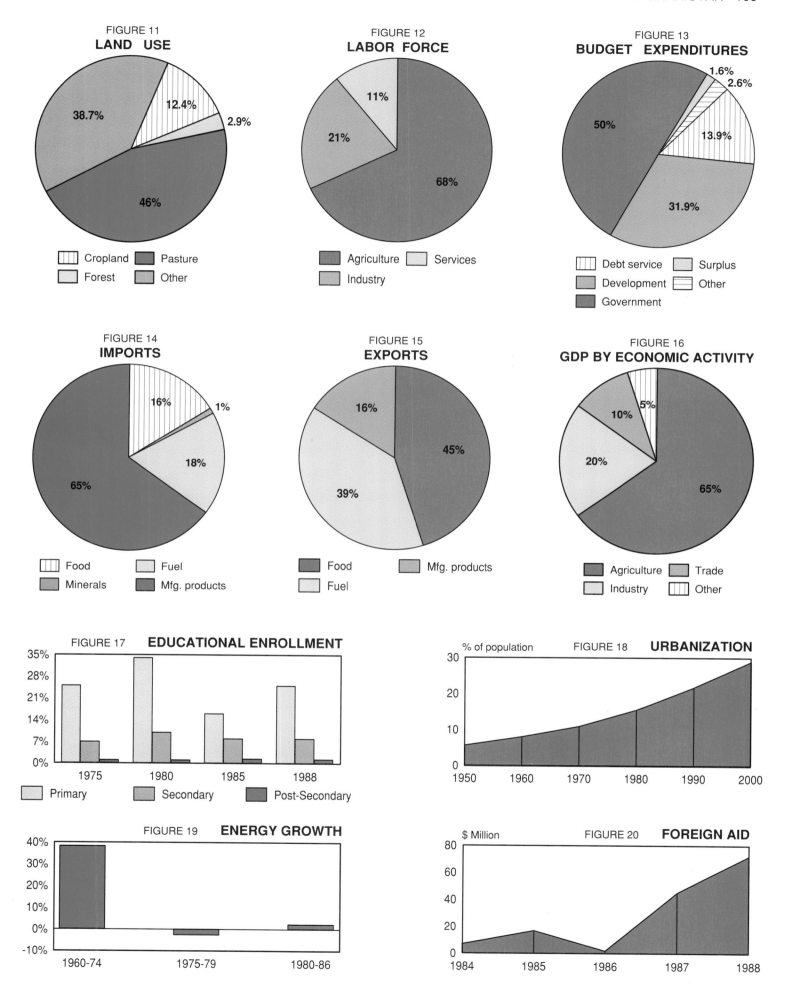

FIGURE 11
LAND USE

38.7%
12.4%
2.9%
46%

Cropland   Pasture
Forest   Other

FIGURE 12
LABOR FORCE

11%
21%
68%

Agriculture   Services
Industry

FIGURE 13
BUDGET EXPENDITURES

1.6%
2.6%
50%
13.9%
31.9%

Debt service   Surplus
Development   Other
Government

FIGURE 14
IMPORTS

16%
1%
18%
65%

Food   Fuel
Minerals   Mfg. products

FIGURE 15
EXPORTS

16%
45%
39%

Food   Mfg. products
Fuel

FIGURE 16
GDP BY ECONOMIC ACTIVITY

5%
10%
20%
65%

Agriculture   Trade
Industry   Other

FIGURE 17 **EDUCATIONAL ENROLLMENT**

35%
28%
21%
14%
7%
0%
1975   1980   1985   1988

Primary   Secondary   Post-Secondary

% of population   FIGURE 18   **URBANIZATION**

30
20
10
0
1950   1960   1970   1980   1990   2000

FIGURE 19   **ENERGY GROWTH**

40%
30%
20%
10%
0%
-10%
1960-74   1975-79   1980-86

$ Million   FIGURE 20   **FOREIGN AID**

80
60
40
20
0
1984   1985   1986   1987   1988

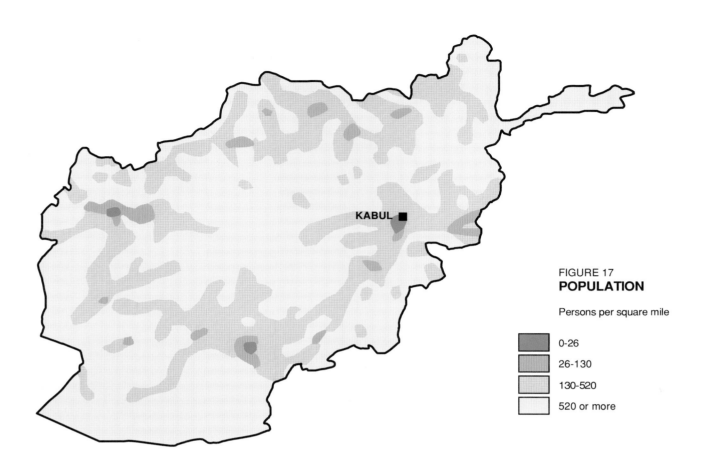

FIGURE 17
POPULATION

Persons per square mile

- 0-26
- 26-130
- 130-520
- 520 or more

KABUL

FIGURE 18
ETHNOLINGUISTIC GROUPS

- Pushtun
- Hazara
- Chahar Aimak
- Tajik
- Other

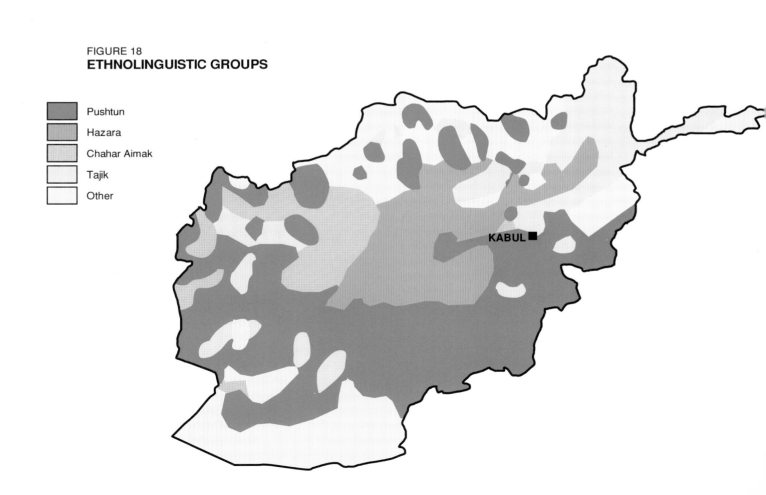

KABUL

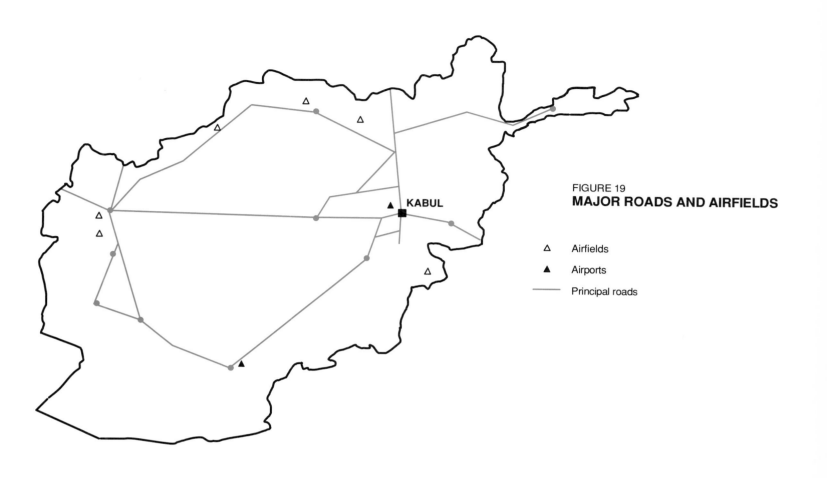

FIGURE 19
MAJOR ROADS AND AIRFIELDS

△   Airfields

▲   Airports

—   Principal roads

KABUL

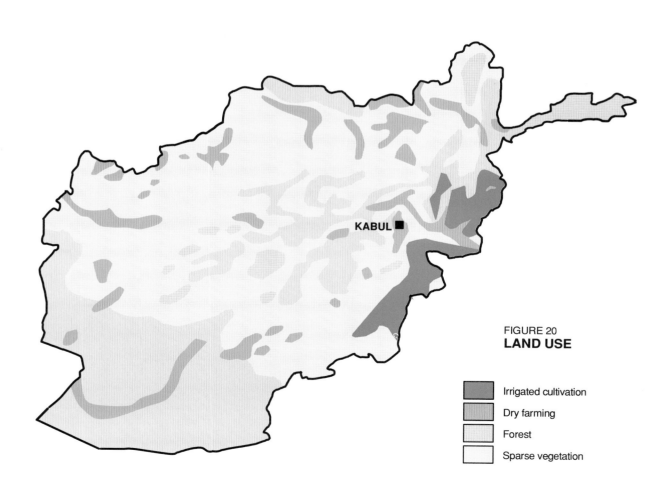

FIGURE 20
LAND USE

KABUL

Irrigated cultivation

Dry farming

Forest

Sparse vegetation

ALGERIA

Located midway along the Maghrebian littoral, and extending southward into the heart of the Sahara, Algeria is the 10th largest country in the world but ranks only 35th in population. Despite its Islamic and Arabic orientation, Algeria is still part of the French cultural bloc. With a socialistic economy, the government dominates all sectors of national life. Its GNP is growing at a faster rate than its population. At the current rate of growth, Algeria has the potential to develop into a modern industrial state. Petroleum revenues have enabled Algeria to embark on a massive and ambitious program of industrialization. Algeria is one of the leading exporters of natural gas. After nationwide riots in 1988, the democratization process in Algeria began. Political parties were allowed to form and in 1990 the first democratic elections were held for local representatives.

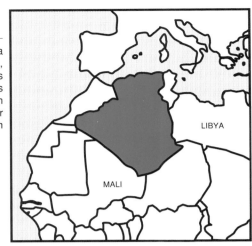

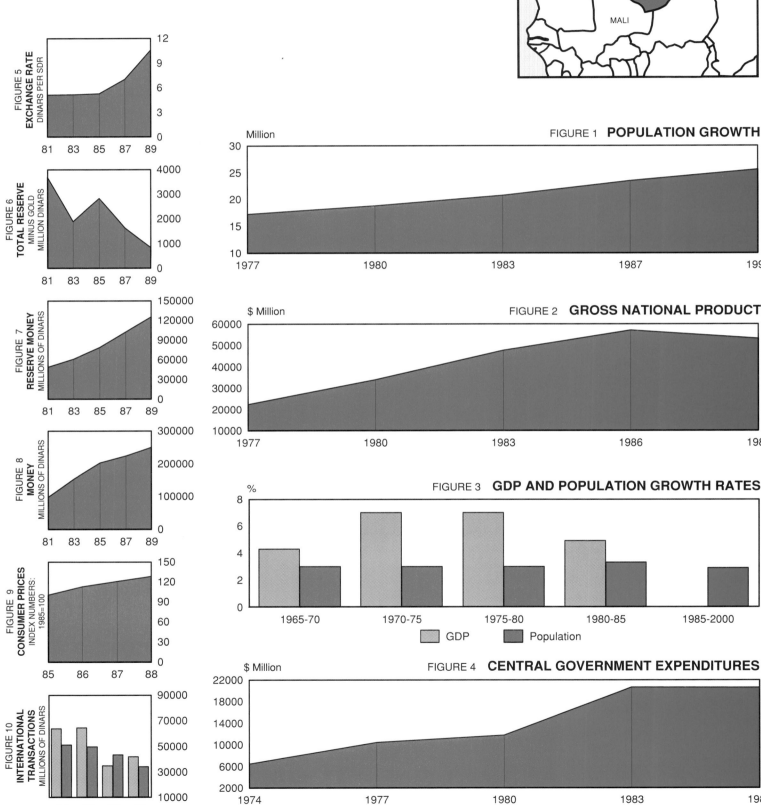

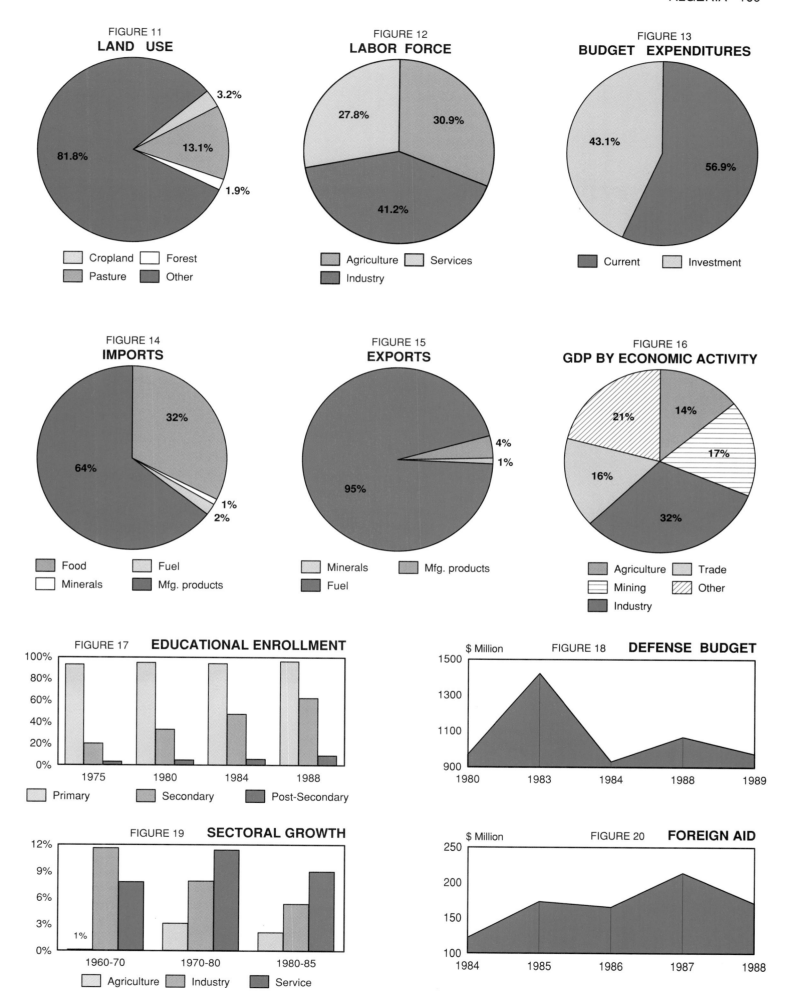

FIGURE 11
LAND USE

3.2%
81.8%
13.1%
1.9%

Cropland Forest
Pasture Other

FIGURE 12
LABOR FORCE

27.8% 30.9%
41.2%

Agriculture Services
Industry

FIGURE 13
BUDGET EXPENDITURES

43.1% 56.9%

Current Investment

FIGURE 14
IMPORTS

32%
64%
1%
2%

Food Fuel
Minerals Mfg. products

FIGURE 15
EXPORTS

4%
1%
95%

Minerals Mfg. products
Fuel

FIGURE 16
GDP BY ECONOMIC ACTIVITY

21% 14%
17%
16%
32%

Agriculture Trade
Mining Other
Industry

FIGURE 17 EDUCATIONAL ENROLLMENT

1975 1980 1984 1988

Primary Secondary Post-Secondary

FIGURE 18 DEFENSE BUDGET

$ Million
1500
1300
1100
900
1980 1983 1984 1988 1989

FIGURE 19 SECTORAL GROWTH

12%
9%
6%
3%
1%
0%
1960-70 1970-80 1980-85

Agriculture Industry Service

FIGURE 20 FOREIGN AID

$ Million
250
200
150
100
1984 1985 1986 1987 1988

ALGIERS

FIGURE 21
POPULATION

Persons per square mile

0-26

26-130

130-260

260 or more

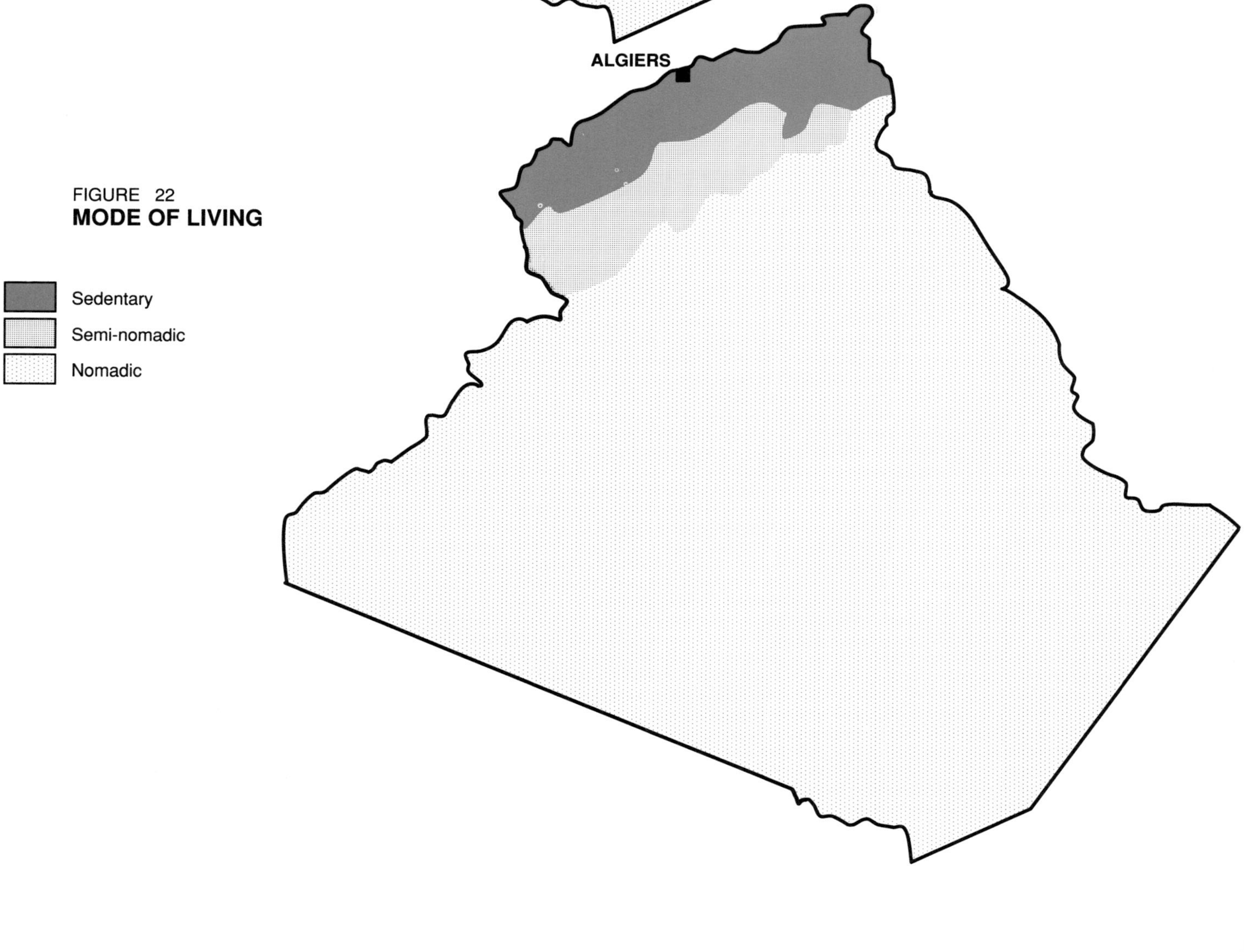

ALGIERS

FIGURE 22
MODE OF LIVING

Sedentary

Semi-nomadic

Nomadic

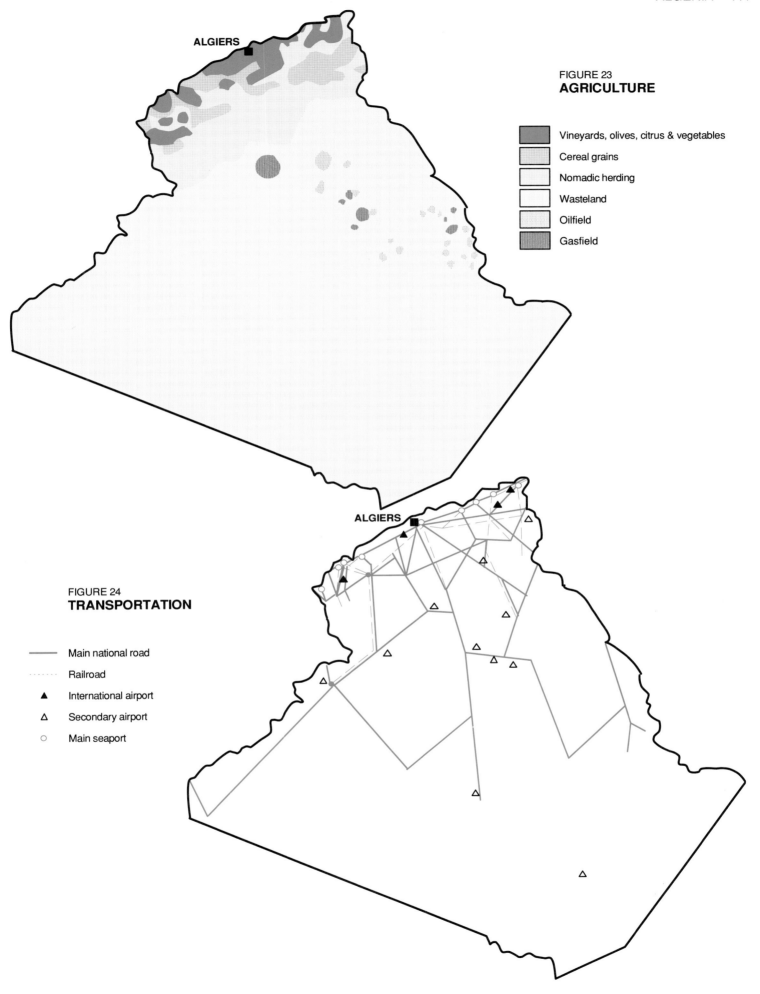

ALGIERS

FIGURE 23
AGRICULTURE

Vineyards, olives, citrus & vegetables
Cereal grains
Nomadic herding
Wasteland
Oilfield
Gasfield

FIGURE 24
TRANSPORTATION

—— Main national road
········· Railroad
▲ International airport
△ Secondary airport
○ Main seaport

ALGIERS

ANGOLA

Located on the west coast of southern Africa, Angola ranks 21st in the world in land area and 73rd in population. It is one of the richest countries on the continent in mineral resources, notably diamonds, iron ore and copper. Nevertheless, the civil war that followed the departure of the Portuguese posed enormous barriers in achieving this potential. Although oil production returned to near pre-war levels, other areas of the economy experienced varying degrees of stagnation. Many of the stores and shops owned by the Portuguese before independence were not reopened. In an effort to offset the gap in skilled workers, Cuba sent 5,000 technicians and helped to train Angolan workers in Cuba. Under President Agostino Neto, Angola moved toward complete state control of the economy, including petroleum production and distribution. These policies were continued by his successor, Jose Eduardo dos Santos. In December 1990 an agreement was reached between the government and rebels that included setting a date for free elections, an internationally guaranteed cease-fire, and end to outside arms shipments.

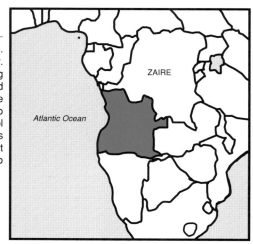

**I.M.F.
INFORMATION
NOT
AVAILABLE**

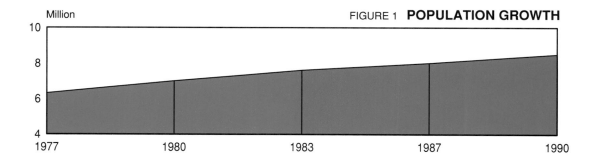

FIGURE 1 **POPULATION GROWTH**

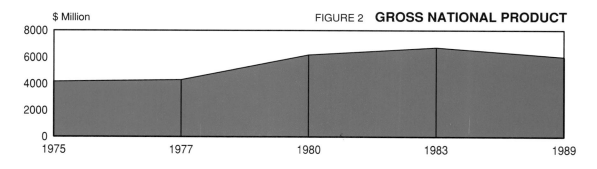

FIGURE 2 **GROSS NATIONAL PRODUCT**

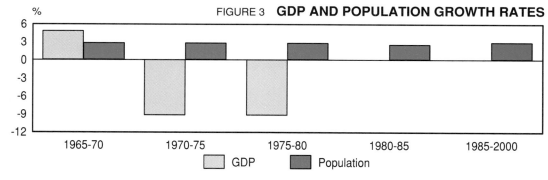

FIGURE 3 **GDP AND POPULATION GROWTH RATES**

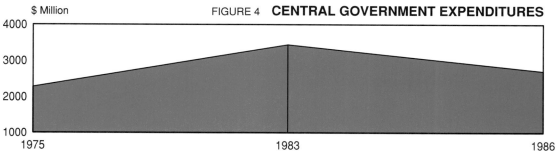

FIGURE 4 **CENTRAL GOVERNMENT EXPENDITURES**

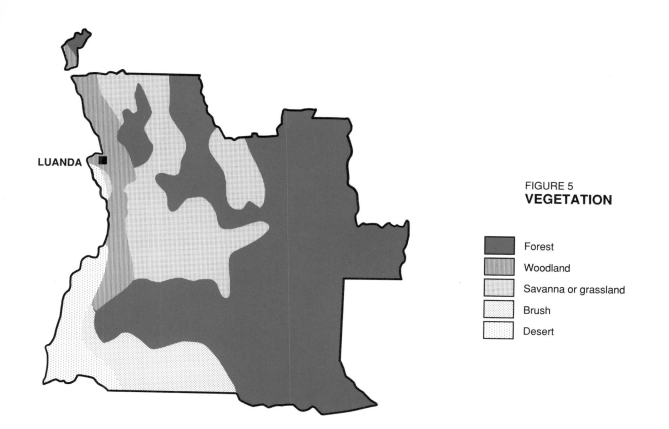

FIGURE 5
VEGETATION

Forest

Woodland

Savanna or grassland

Brush

Desert

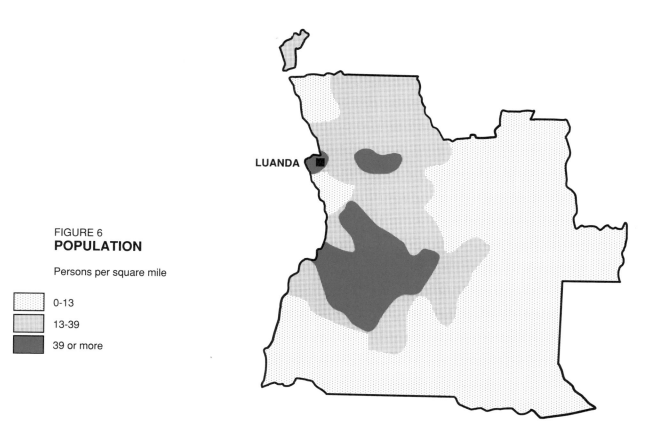

FIGURE 6
POPULATION

Persons per square mile

0-13

13-39

39 or more

ARGENTINA

The 2nd largest country in Latin America and the 8th largest in the world, Argentina ranks only 29th in size of population because of low population density. Classified as an upper middle-income country, it has one of the highest per capita incomes in Latin America and its GNP growth rate is more than double the population growth rate. Despite having one of the highest inflation rates in the world, the Argentines enjoy a better standard of living than most other Latin Americans. The bulwark of such economic well-being is the pampa, which, with its deep rich soil, is the granary of South America. The Argentine cattle herds are among the world's finest and the country is among the world's largest exporters of livestock products. Despite such immense resources, Argentina has never achieved its full potential because its economy is constantly muddied by labor and political unrest and violence, misguided military ambitions, lack of a coherent fiscal or industrial policy, high inflation, and a weak currency.

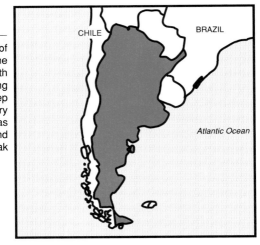

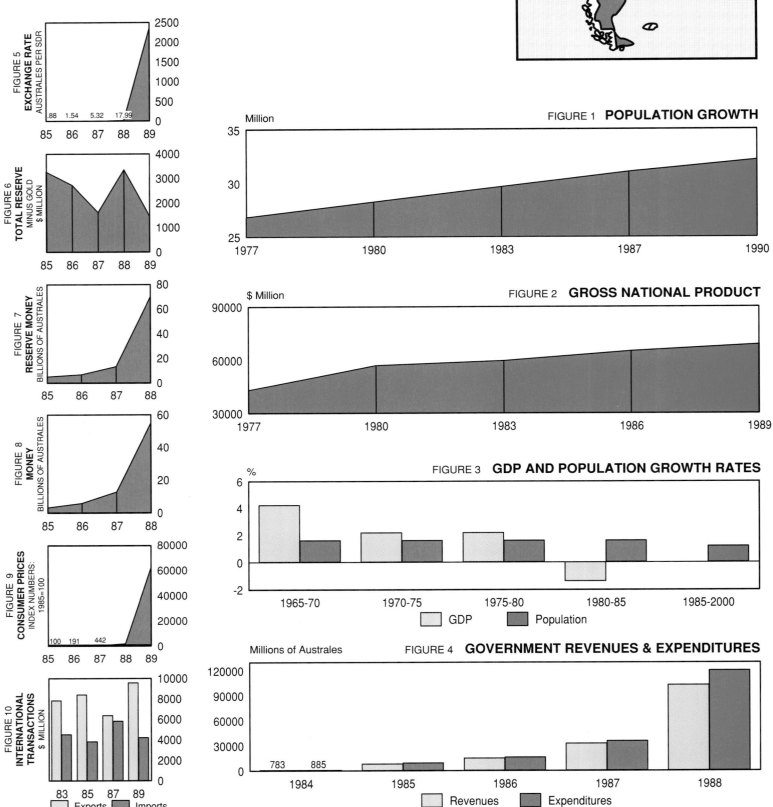

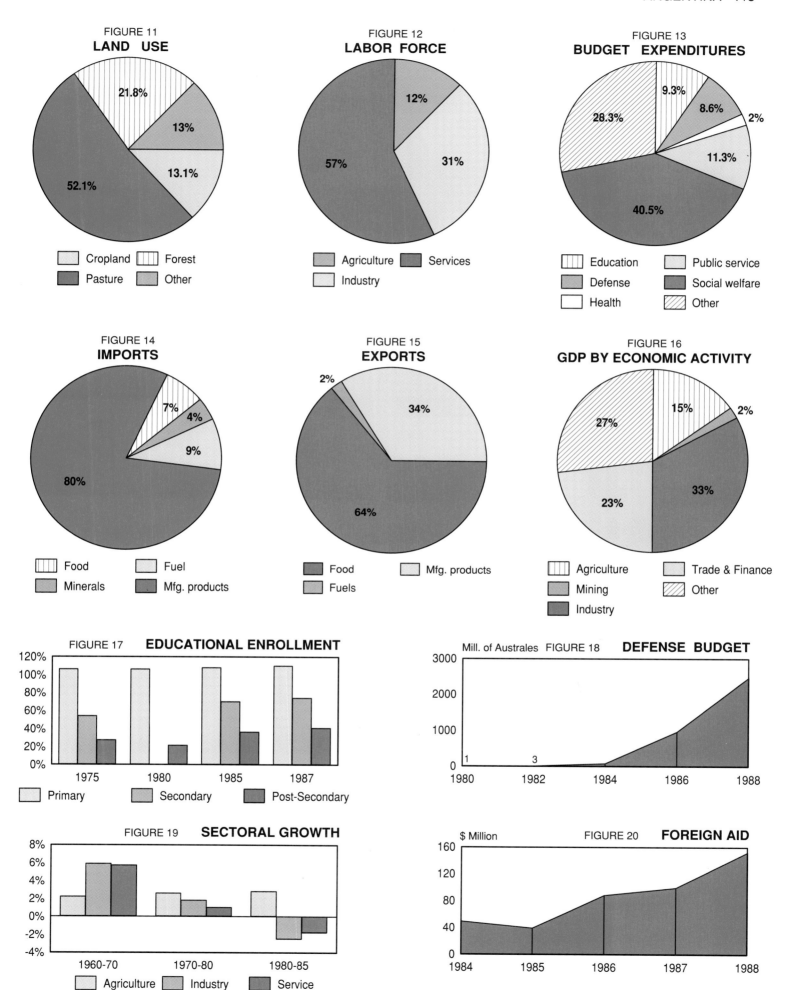

FIGURE 11
LAND USE

21.8%
13%
13.1%
52.1%

Cropland | Forest
Pasture | Other

FIGURE 12
LABOR FORCE

12%
31%
57%

Agriculture | Services
Industry

FIGURE 13
BUDGET EXPENDITURES

9.3%
8.6%
2%
28.3%
11.3%
40.5%

Education | Public service
Defense | Social welfare
Health | Other

FIGURE 14
IMPORTS

7%
4%
9%
80%

Food | Fuel
Minerals | Mfg. products

FIGURE 15
EXPORTS

2%
34%
64%

Food | Mfg. products
Fuels

FIGURE 16
GDP BY ECONOMIC ACTIVITY

15%
2%
27%
23%
33%

Agriculture | Trade & Finance
Mining | Other
Industry

FIGURE 17 **EDUCATIONAL ENROLLMENT**

120%
100%
80%
60%
40%
20%
0%
1975   1980   1985   1987

Primary | Secondary | Post-Secondary

Mill. of Australes FIGURE 18 **DEFENSE BUDGET**

3000
2000
1000
0
1   3
1980   1982   1984   1986   1988

FIGURE 19 **SECTORAL GROWTH**

8%
6%
4%
2%
0%
-2%
-4%
1960-70   1970-80   1980-85

Agriculture | Industry | Service

$ Million   FIGURE 20   **FOREIGN AID**

160
120
80
40
0
1984   1985   1986   1987   1988

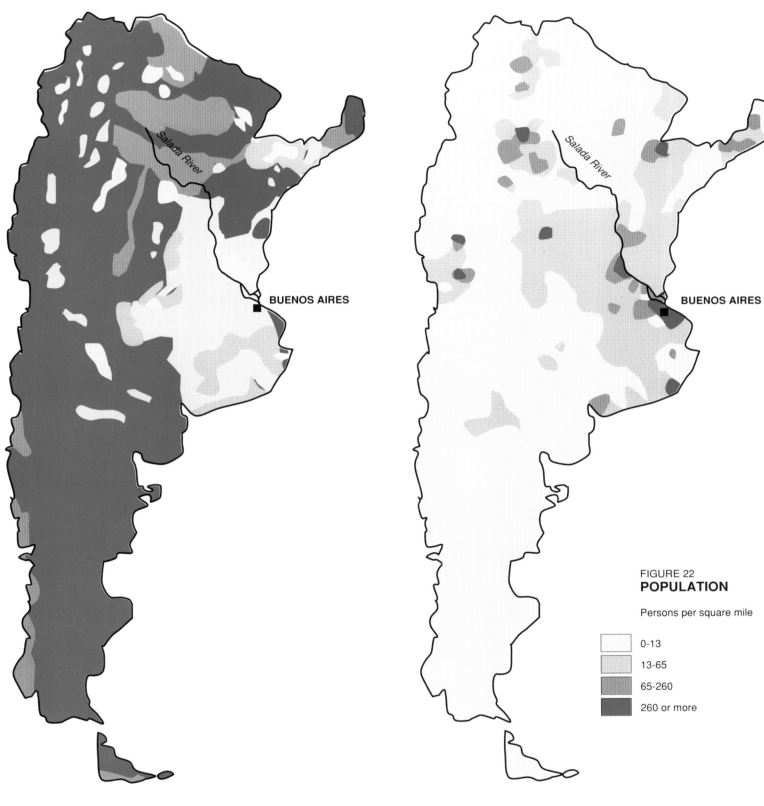

FIGURE 22
POPULATION

Persons per square mile

0-13

13-65

65-260

260 or more

FIGURE 21
VEGETATION

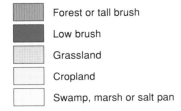

Forest or tall brush

Low brush

Grassland

Cropland

Swamp, marsh or salt pan

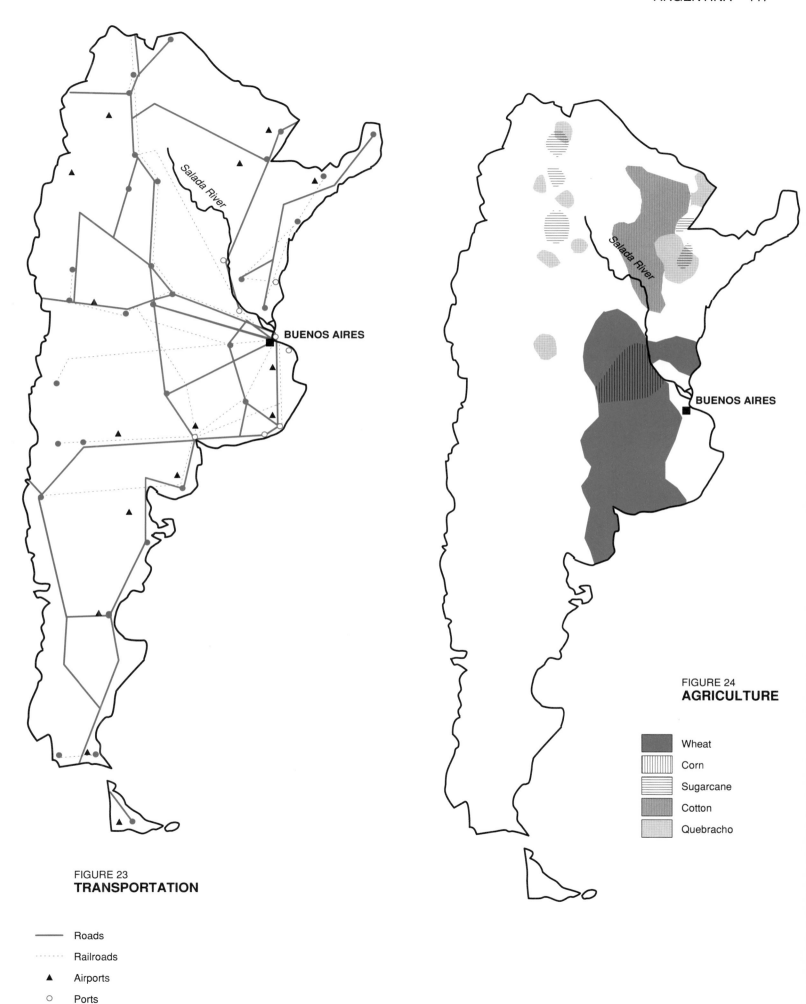

Salada River

BUENOS AIRES

FIGURE 23
TRANSPORTATION

——— Roads

········ Railroads

▲ Airports

○ Ports

Salada River

BUENOS AIRES

FIGURE 24
AGRICULTURE

Wheat

Corn

Sugarcane

Cotton

Quebracho

BANGLADESH

Located on the Indian subcontinent in the great combined delta of the Ganges, the Brahmaputra and the Meghna Rivers, Bangladesh ranks 90th in land area but 9th in size of population. The result is that Bangladesh has the highest density of population of any nation on earth other than small city states. Its birth rate, fertility rate and death rate are among the highest in the world. An economic basket case, Bangladesh has learned to live on the brink of disaster, while surviving on its exiguous natural resources as well as handouts from the richer nations. Agriculture, on which 90% of Bangladeshis depend for their livelihood, remains the key to the continued survival of the country. However, it has few mineral resources, and its industrial sector is small and inefficient, making Bangladesh a classic textbook case of the underdevelopment-overpopulation-resourcelessness syndrome that afflicts most Third World nations. In 1991 Bangladesh suffered one of the worst floods in its history.

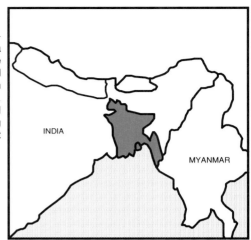

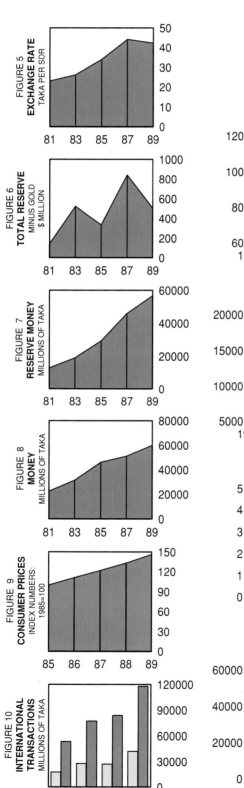

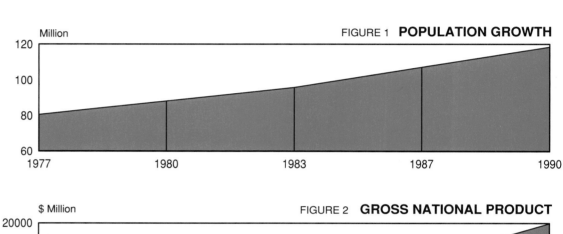

FIGURE 1 **POPULATION GROWTH**

FIGURE 2 **GROSS NATIONAL PRODUCT**

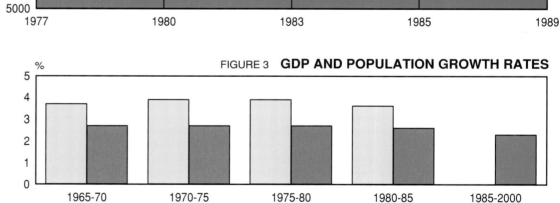

FIGURE 3 **GDP AND POPULATION GROWTH RATES**

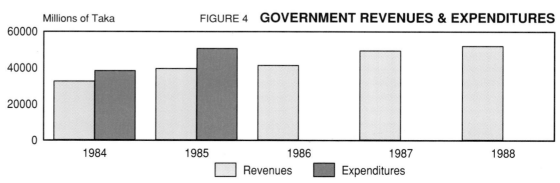

FIGURE 4 **GOVERNMENT REVENUES & EXPENDITURES**

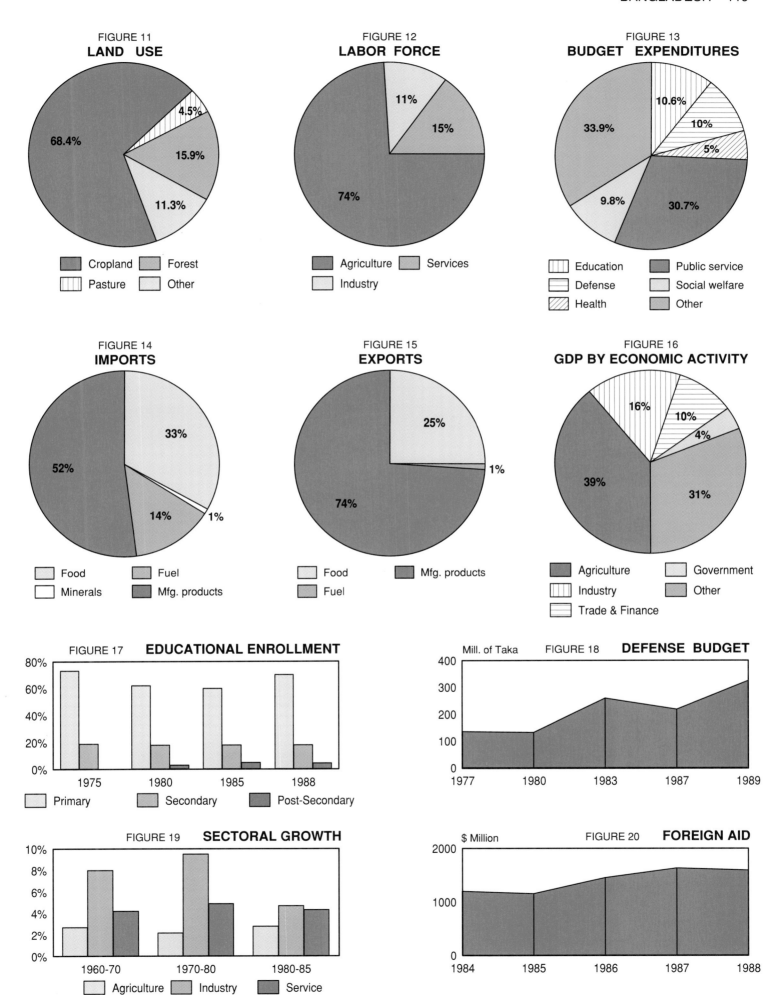

FIGURE 11
LAND USE

68.4% Cropland
4.5%
15.9%
11.3%

Cropland   Forest
Pasture   Other

FIGURE 12
LABOR FORCE

11%
15%
74%

Agriculture   Services
Industry

FIGURE 13
BUDGET EXPENDITURES

33.9%
10.6%
10%
5%
9.8%
30.7%

Education   Public service
Defense   Social welfare
Health   Other

FIGURE 14
IMPORTS

33%
52%
14%
1%

Food   Fuel
Minerals Mfg. products

FIGURE 15
EXPORTS

25%
1%
74%

Food   Mfg. products
Fuel

FIGURE 16
GDP BY ECONOMIC ACTIVITY

16%
10%
4%
39%
31%

Agriculture   Government
Industry   Other
Trade & Finance

FIGURE 17   **EDUCATIONAL ENROLLMENT**

80%
60%
40%
20%
0%
1975   1980   1985   1988

Primary   Secondary   Post-Secondary

Mill. of Taka   FIGURE 18   **DEFENSE BUDGET**

400
300
200
100
0
1977   1980   1983   1987   1989

FIGURE 19   **SECTORAL GROWTH**

10%
8%
6%
4%
2%
0%
1960-70   1970-80   1980-85

Agriculture   Industry   Service

$ Million   FIGURE 20   **FOREIGN AID**

2000
1000
0
1984   1985   1986   1987   1988

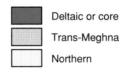

FIGURE 21
CULTURAL REGIONS

- Deltaic or core
- Trans-Meghna
- Northern

FIGURE 22
PRINCIPAL REGIONS

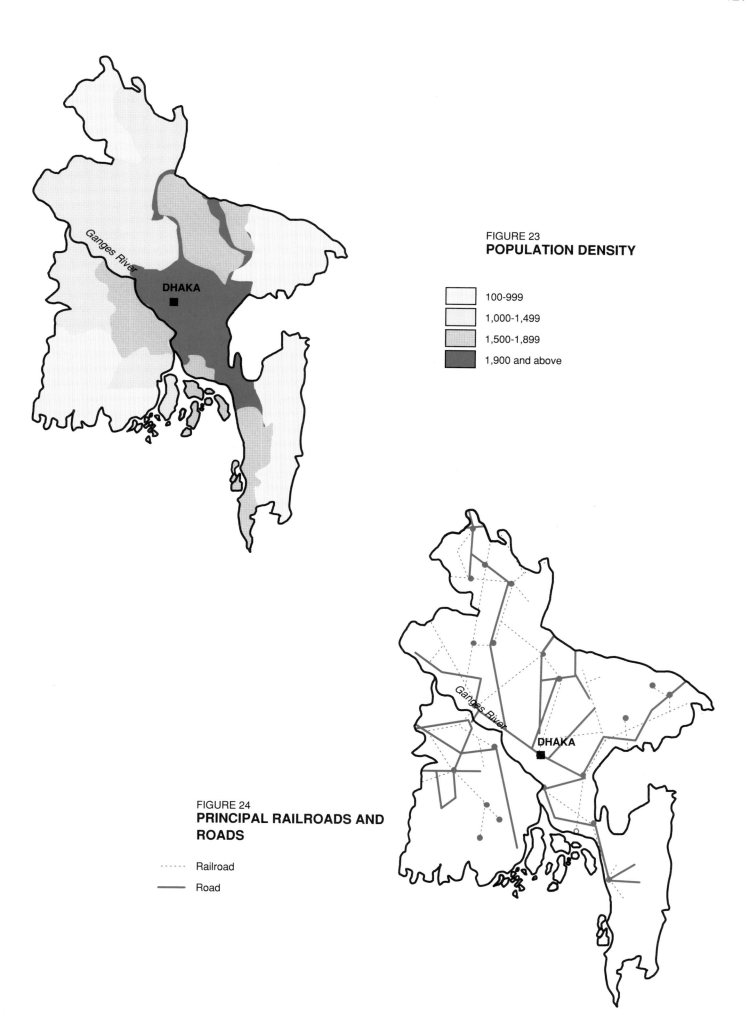

FIGURE 23
POPULATION DENSITY

100-999
1,000-1,499
1,500-1,899
1,900 and above

FIGURE 24
**PRINCIPAL RAILROADS AND
ROADS**

- - - - Railroad
──── Road

BENIN

Sandwiched between Nigeria and Togo, on the western coast of Africa, Benin ranks 96th in both land area and in population. It is one of the least developed countries in Africa. The economy is highly dependent on agriculture which provides 49% of the GDP and employs nearly 70% of the population. Government finances are sustained only through foreign aid, especially from France. In 1974 the government of President Mathieu Kerekou declared Benin a Marxist-Leninist state and launched a program of nationalization that virtually eliminated foreign investment from the economy. A series of three-year plans were launched in 1977 with only mixed results, and the country's agricultural exports, rather than increasing, have continued to decline. The most hopeful feature is the transportation sector which produces one-fourth of the nation's GDP and is rapidly growing because of Benin's key position as a transit point for Niger. In 1989 Benin abandoned Marxism-Leninism in the wake of the collapse of Communism in Eastern Europe, and in 1990, a national referendum approved a new constitution which provided for a multi-party system and a free market economy.

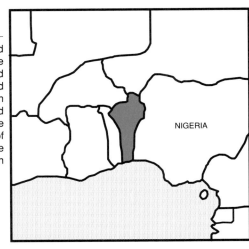

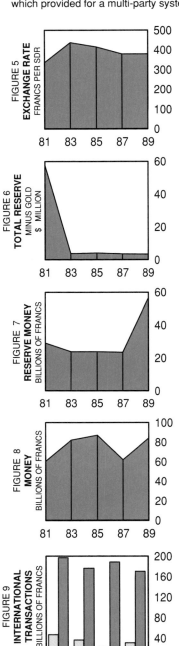

FIGURE 5 **EXCHANGE RATE** FRANCS PER SDR

FIGURE 6 **TOTAL RESERVE** MINUS GOLD $ MILLION

FIGURE 7 **RESERVE MONEY** BILLIONS OF FRANCS

FIGURE 8 **MONEY** BILLIONS OF FRANCS

FIGURE 9 **INTERNATIONAL TRANSACTIONS** BILLIONS OF FRANCS

Exports Imports

Million   FIGURE 1 **POPULATION GROWTH**

$ Million   FIGURE 2 **GROSS NATIONAL PRODUCT**

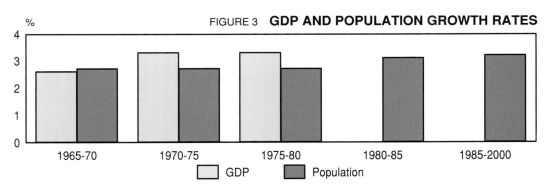

%   FIGURE 3 **GDP AND POPULATION GROWTH RATES**

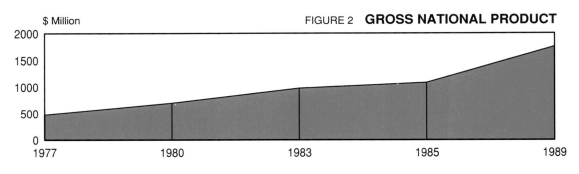

GDP   Population

$ Million   FIGURE 4 **GOVERNMENT REVENUES & EXPENDITURES**

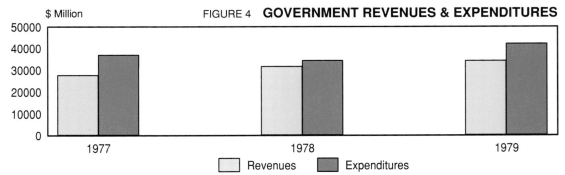

Revenues   Expenditures

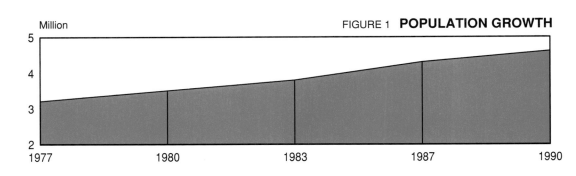

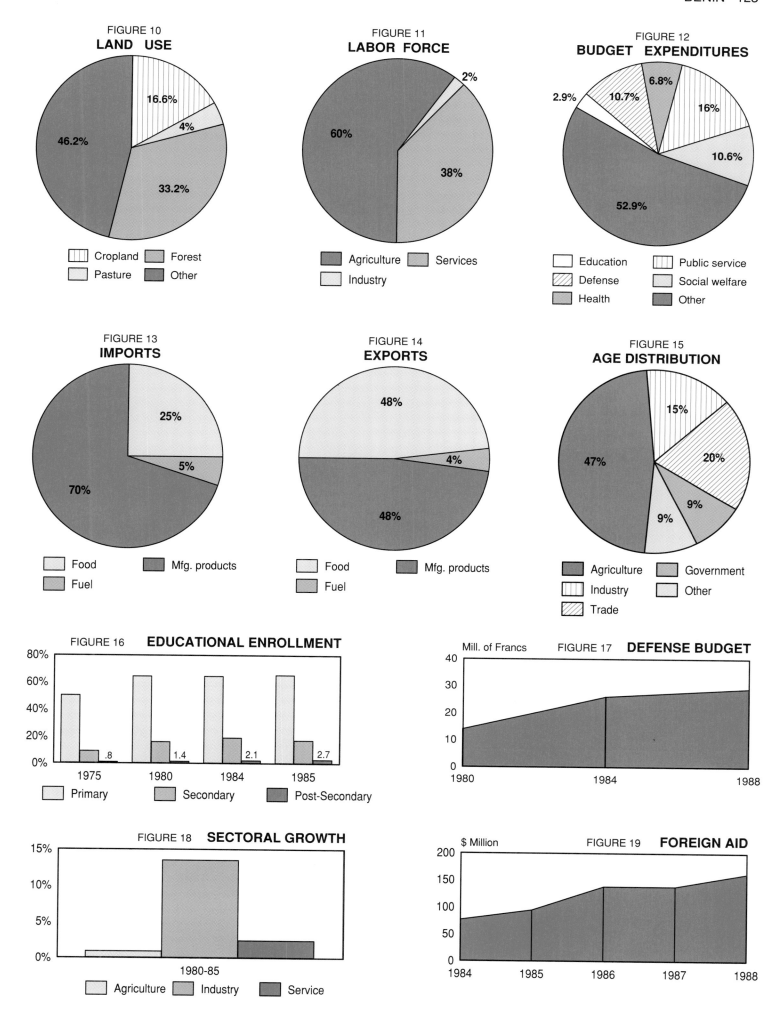

FIGURE 10
LAND USE

16.6%
4%
46.2%
33.2%

Cropland   Forest
Pasture   Other

FIGURE 11
LABOR FORCE

2%
60%
38%

Agriculture   Services
Industry

FIGURE 12
BUDGET EXPENDITURES

2.9%   10.7%   6.8%
16%
10.6%
52.9%

Education   Public service
Defense   Social welfare
Health   Other

FIGURE 13
IMPORTS

25%
5%
70%

Food   Mfg. products
Fuel

FIGURE 14
EXPORTS

48%
4%
48%

Food   Mfg. products
Fuel

FIGURE 15
AGE DISTRIBUTION

15%
20%
47%
9%   9%

Agriculture   Government
Industry   Other
Trade

FIGURE 16   **EDUCATIONAL ENROLLMENT**

80%
60%
40%
20%
0%
.8   1.4   2.1   2.7
1975   1980   1984   1985

Primary   Secondary   Post-Secondary

FIGURE 17   **DEFENSE BUDGET**
Mill. of Francs

40
30
20
10
0
1980   1984   1988

FIGURE 18   **SECTORAL GROWTH**

15%
10%
5%
0%
1980-85

Agriculture   Industry   Service

FIGURE 19   **FOREIGN AID**
$ Million

200
150
100
50
0
1984   1985   1986   1987   1988

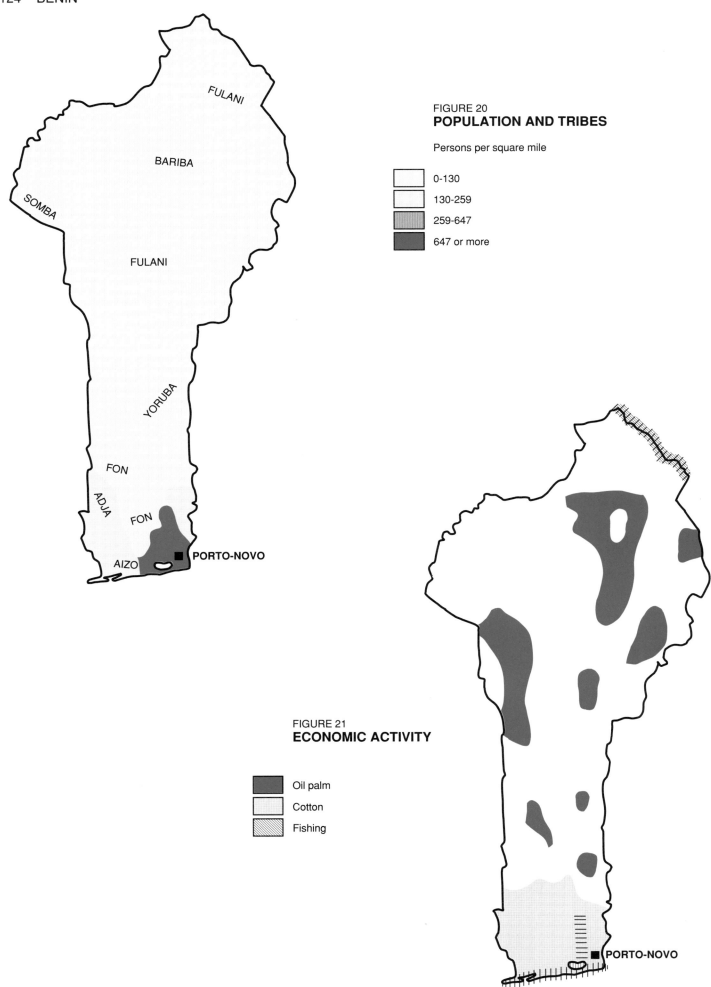

FIGURE 20
POPULATION AND TRIBES

Persons per square mile

0-130
130-259
259-647
647 or more

FULANI

BARIBA

SOMBA

FULANI

YORUBA

FON

ADJA

FON

AIZO

PORTO-NOVO

FIGURE 21
ECONOMIC ACTIVITY

Oil palm
Cotton
Fishing

PORTO-NOVO

FIGURE 22
VEGETATION

Evergreen forest

Forest, brush & cultivated

Tall grass savanna, brush & cultivated

Short grass savanna

Marsh, mangrove & cultivated

PORTO-NOVO

FIGURE 23
RAILROADS

- - - - - - Railroad

PORTO-NOVO

BOLIVIA

One of the two landlocked countries in South America, Bolivia ranks 27th in land area and 87th in population. It also has one of the highest concentrations of native Indians in Latin America, with Indians constituting 55% of the population. Bolivia has immense mineral resources, remarkable both for the size of the deposits and the variety of the ores. It is the largest tin producer in the Western Hemisphere and the second largest in the world. It is also the world's largest producer of bismuth and the second largest producer of antimony. At the same time, it is officially classified as a low-income country and the agricultural sector, which employs about two-thirds of the population, is mostly on the subsistence level. In 1952 Bolivia experienced a popular revolution which changed the social and political structure of the country. Since that time, the state has played a large role in the economy. However, the main thrust of economic policy in 1990 was to increase investment in the private sector.

BRAZIL

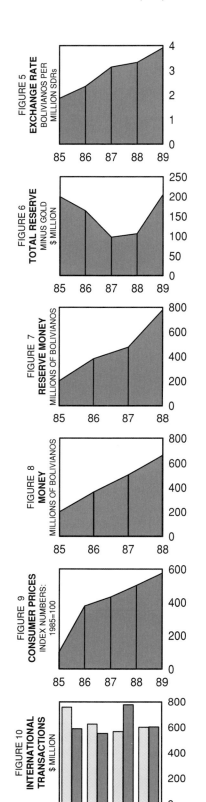

FIGURE 5 EXCHANGE RATE BOLIVIANOS PER MILLION SDRs

FIGURE 6 TOTAL RESERVE MINUS GOLD $ MILLION

FIGURE 7 RESERVE MONEY MILLIONS OF BOLIVIANOS

FIGURE 8 MONEY MILLIONS OF BOLIVIANOS

FIGURE 9 CONSUMER PRICES INDEX NUMBERS: 1985=100

FIGURE 10 INTERNATIONAL TRANSACTIONS $ MILLION
Exports   Imports

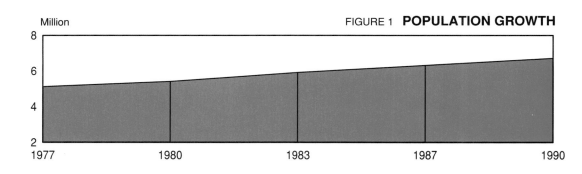

Million   FIGURE 1 **POPULATION GROWTH**

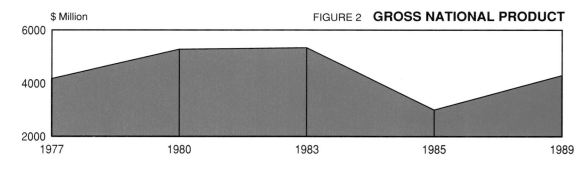

$ Million   FIGURE 2 **GROSS NATIONAL PRODUCT**

FIGURE 3 **GDP AND POPULATION GROWTH RATES**
%
GDP   Population

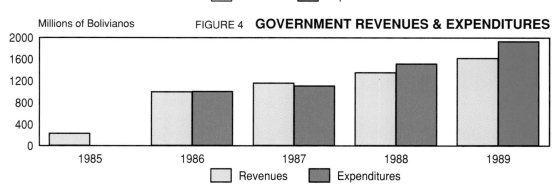

Millions of Bolivianos   FIGURE 4 **GOVERNMENT REVENUES & EXPENDITURES**
Revenues   Expenditures

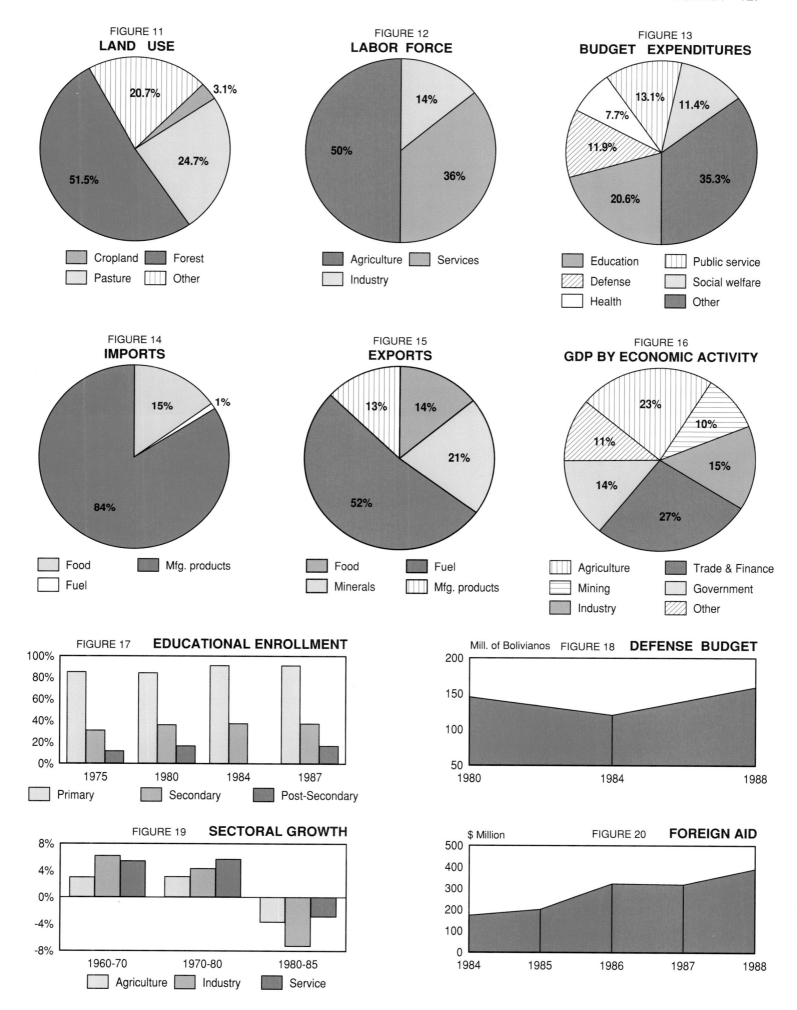

FIGURE 11
LAND USE

20.7%   3.1%
24.7%
51.5%

Cropland   Forest
Pasture   Other

FIGURE 12
LABOR FORCE

14%
50%
36%

Agriculture   Services
Industry

FIGURE 13
BUDGET EXPENDITURES

13.1%   11.4%
7.7%
11.9%
35.3%
20.6%

Education   Public service
Defense   Social welfare
Health   Other

FIGURE 14
IMPORTS

15%   1%
84%

Food   Mfg. products
Fuel

FIGURE 15
EXPORTS

13%   14%
21%
52%

Food   Fuel
Minerals   Mfg. products

FIGURE 16
GDP BY ECONOMIC ACTIVITY

23%
10%
11%
15%
14%
27%

Agriculture   Trade & Finance
Mining   Government
Industry   Other

FIGURE 17   **EDUCATIONAL ENROLLMENT**

100%
80%
60%
40%
20%
0%
1975   1980   1984   1987

Primary   Secondary   Post-Secondary

Mill. of Bolivianos   FIGURE 18   **DEFENSE BUDGET**

200
150
100
50
1980   1984   1988

FIGURE 19   **SECTORAL GROWTH**

8%
4%
0%
-4%
-8%
1960-70   1970-80   1980-85

Agriculture   Industry   Service

$ Million   FIGURE 20   **FOREIGN AID**

500
400
300
200
100
0
1984   1985   1986   1987   1988

BRAZIL

The 5th largest country in the world and 6th in population, Brazil covers approximately one-half of the South American continent and also accounts for half of its population. Its international borders, the third longest in the world, touch every South American country except Ecuador and Chile. Brazil is officially classified as an upper middle-income country. Brazil's GNP has grown steadily since 1968, but its prosperity is being eroded by one of the highest rates of inflation in the world. The economy is in a transitional phase moving from an agricultural to an industrial base. Brazil is burdened with one of the largest external debts in the world. Democracy was restored in the 1980s, albeit in a muted form. The country fell into recession in 1990, with all sectors of the economy being affected, the most pronounced impact taking place in manufacturing.

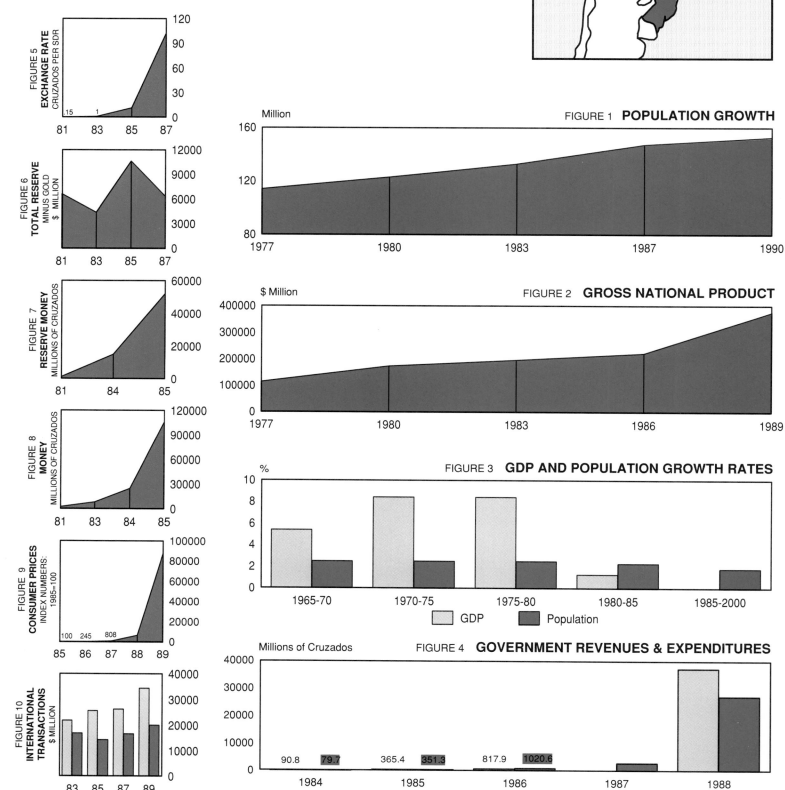

FIGURE 5 **EXCHANGE RATE** CRUZADOS PER SDR

FIGURE 6 **TOTAL RESERVE** MINUS GOLD $ MILLION

FIGURE 7 **RESERVE MONEY** MILLIONS OF CRUZADOS

FIGURE 8 **MONEY** MILLIONS OF CRUZADOS

FIGURE 9 **CONSUMER PRICES** INDEX NUMBERS: 1985=100

FIGURE 10 **INTERNATIONAL TRANSACTIONS** $ MILLION
Exports Imports

FIGURE 1 **POPULATION GROWTH**
Million

FIGURE 2 **GROSS NATIONAL PRODUCT**
$ Million

FIGURE 3 **GDP AND POPULATION GROWTH RATES**
%
GDP Population

FIGURE 4 **GOVERNMENT REVENUES & EXPENDITURES**
Millions of Cruzados
Revenues Expenditures

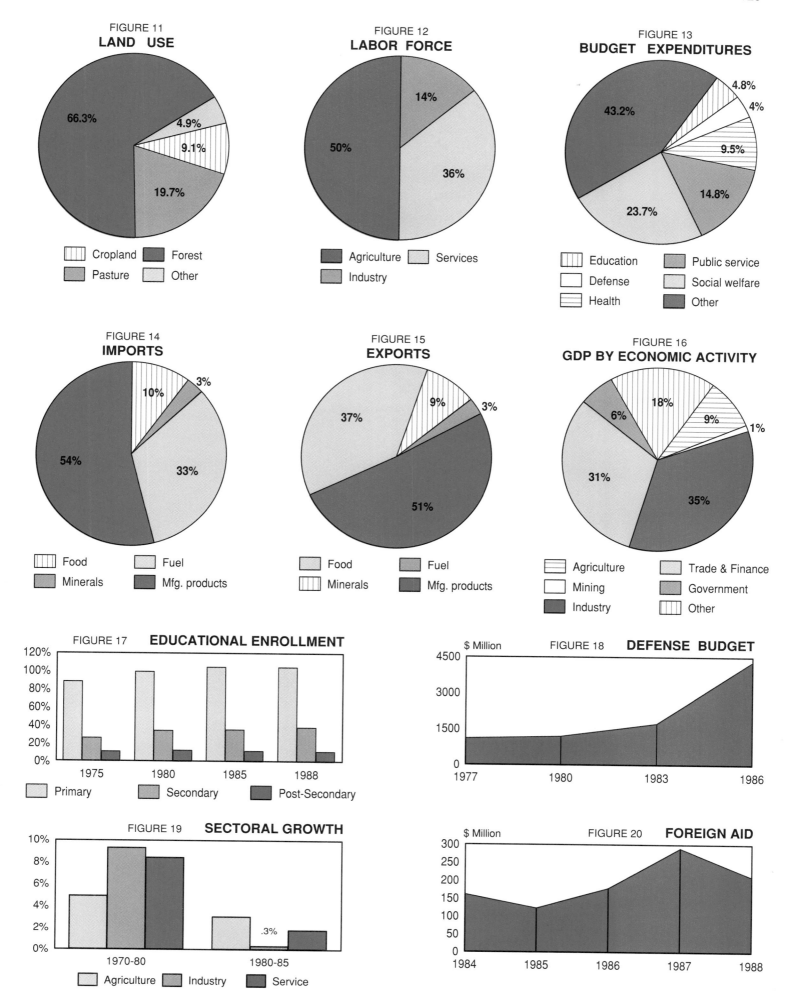

FIGURE 11
LAND USE

66.3%
4.9%
9.1%
19.7%

Cropland | Forest
Pasture | Other

FIGURE 12
LABOR FORCE

14%
50%
36%

Agriculture | Services
Industry

FIGURE 13
BUDGET EXPENDITURES

43.2%
4.8%
4%
9.5%
14.8%
23.7%

Education | Public service
Defense | Social welfare
Health | Other

FIGURE 14
IMPORTS

10%
3%
54%
33%

Food | Fuel
Minerals | Mfg. products

FIGURE 15
EXPORTS

37%
9%
3%
51%

Food | Fuel
Minerals | Mfg. products

FIGURE 16
GDP BY ECONOMIC ACTIVITY

18%
6%
9%
1%
31%
35%

Agriculture | Trade & Finance
Mining | Government
Industry | Other

FIGURE 17 **EDUCATIONAL ENROLLMENT**

120%
100%
80%
60%
40%
20%
0%
1975 1980 1985 1988

Primary | Secondary | Post-Secondary

$ Million FIGURE 18 **DEFENSE BUDGET**

4500
3000
1500
0
1977 1980 1983 1986

FIGURE 19 **SECTORAL GROWTH**

10%
8%
6%
4%
2%
.3%
0%
1970-80 1980-85

Agriculture | Industry | Service

$ Million FIGURE 20 **FOREIGN AID**

300
250
200
150
100
50
0
1984 1985 1986 1987 1988

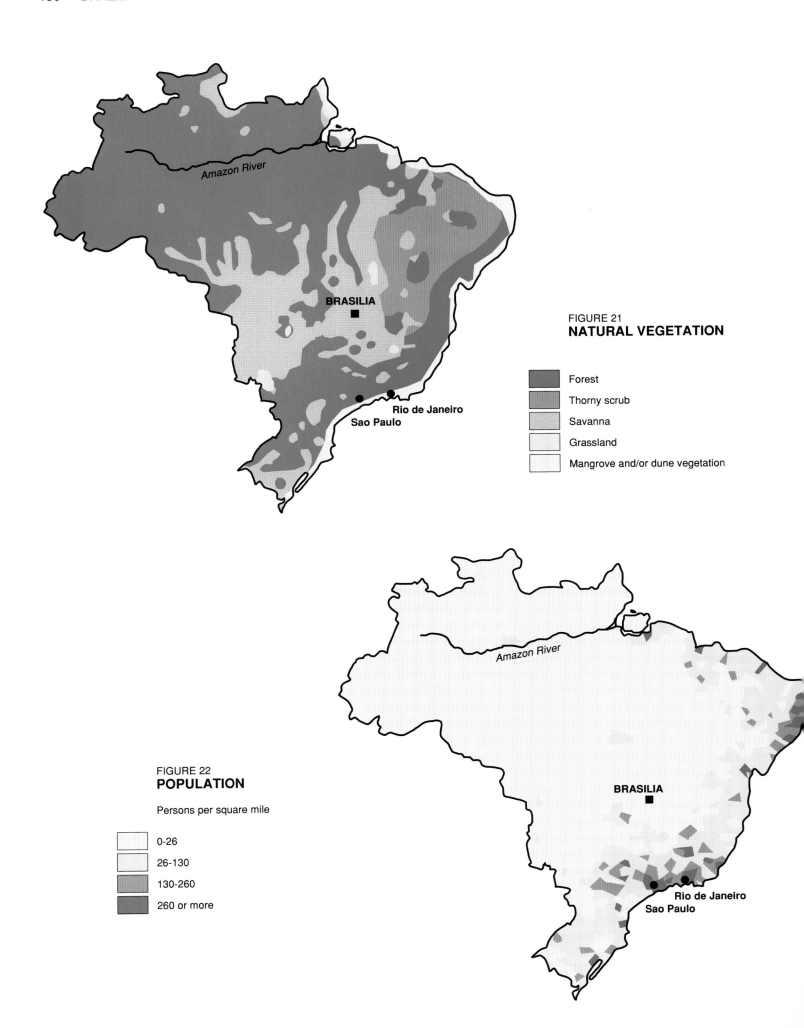

FIGURE 21
NATURAL VEGETATION

Amazon River

BRASILIA

Rio de Janeiro
Sao Paulo

Forest
Thorny scrub
Savanna
Grassland
Mangrove and/or dune vegetation

FIGURE 22
POPULATION

Persons per square mile

0-26
26-130
130-260
260 or more

Amazon River

BRASILIA

Rio de Janeiro
Sao Paulo

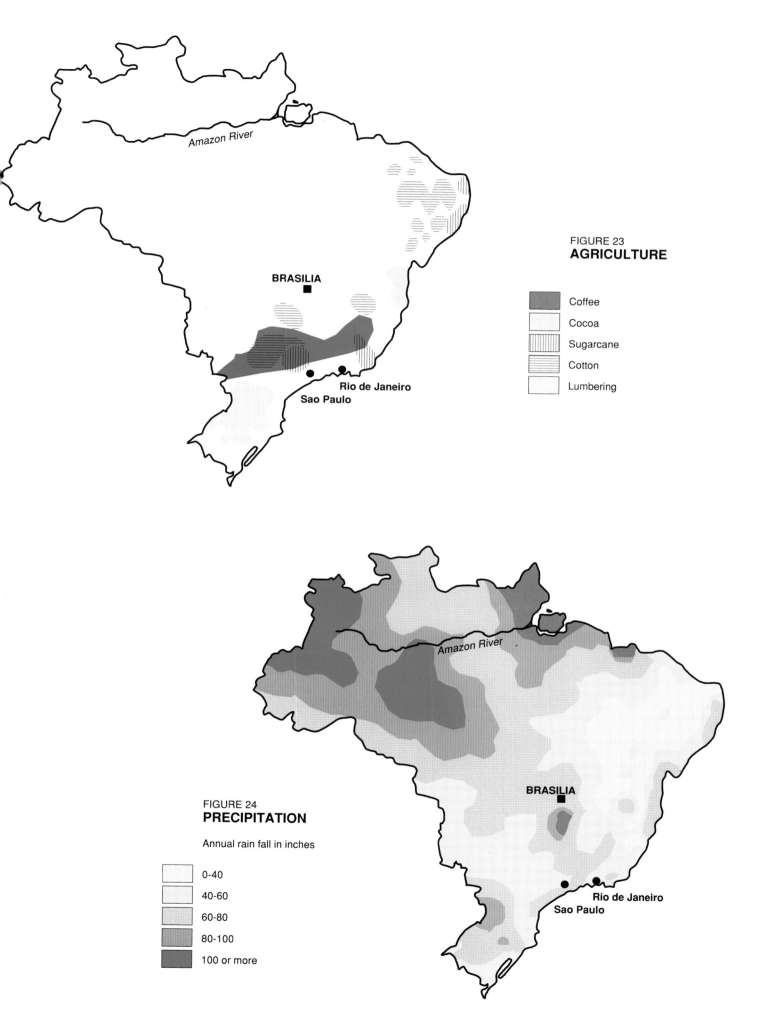

FIGURE 23
AGRICULTURE

BRASILIA

Rio de Janeiro
Sao Paulo

Amazon River

Coffee
Cocoa
Sugarcane
Cotton
Lumbering

FIGURE 24
PRECIPITATION

Annual rain fall in inches

0-40
40-60
60-80
80-100
100 or more

Amazon River

BRASILIA

Rio de Janeiro
Sao Paulo

BURKINA FASO

A landlocked country in West Africa, Burkina Faso ranks 68th in land area and 72nd in population. Burkina Faso is classified as among the least developed of the low-income countries. Over 75% of the population subsists in absolute poverty. Agricultural production has not yet completely recovered from the periodic droughts of the 1970s and 1980s that decimated the livestock and laid waste most areas of the country. Even the limited mineral resources that the country possesses, mostly gold deposits at Poura, manganese deposits at Tambao, and lesser deposits of vanadium, nickel, lead, zinc and bauxite, cannot be properly exploited for lack of transportation facilities. Manufacturing is rudimentary and is concentrated in urban centers along the Abidjan-Niger railway. The country is a prime target for developmental aid, especially from France and the World Bank. A new constitution, calling for democratization and multiparty elections, was approved in 1991.

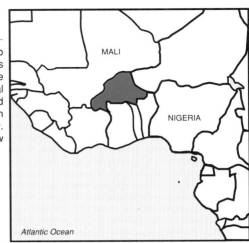

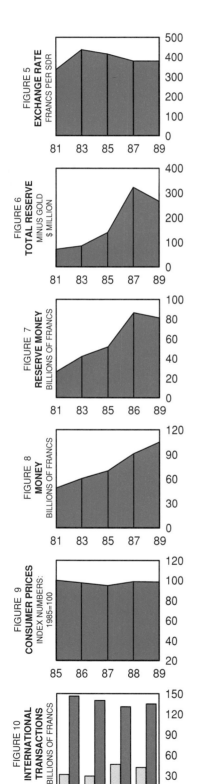

FIGURE 5 **EXCHANGE RATE** FRANCS PER SDR

FIGURE 6 **TOTAL RESERVE** MINUS GOLD $ MILLION

FIGURE 7 **RESERVE MONEY** BILLIONS OF FRANCS

FIGURE 8 **MONEY** BILLIONS OF FRANCS

FIGURE 9 **CONSUMER PRICES** INDEX NUMBERS: 1985=100

FIGURE 10 **INTERNATIONAL TRANSACTIONS** BILLIONS OF FRANCS
Exports   Imports

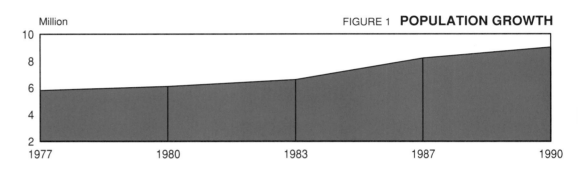

Million   FIGURE 1 **POPULATION GROWTH**

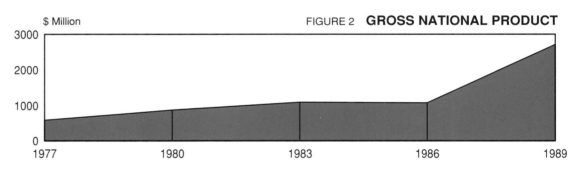

$ Million   FIGURE 2 **GROSS NATIONAL PRODUCT**

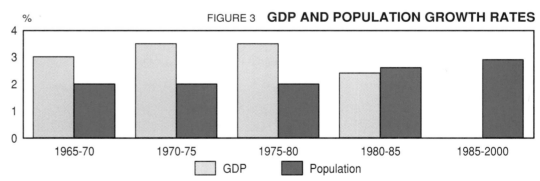

%   FIGURE 3 **GDP AND POPULATION GROWTH RATES**
GDP   Population

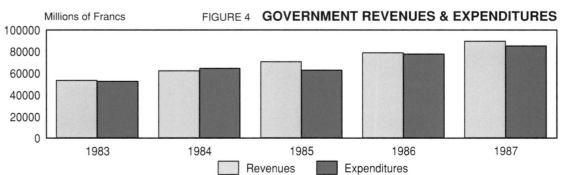

Millions of Francs   FIGURE 4 **GOVERNMENT REVENUES & EXPENDITURES**
Revenues   Expenditures

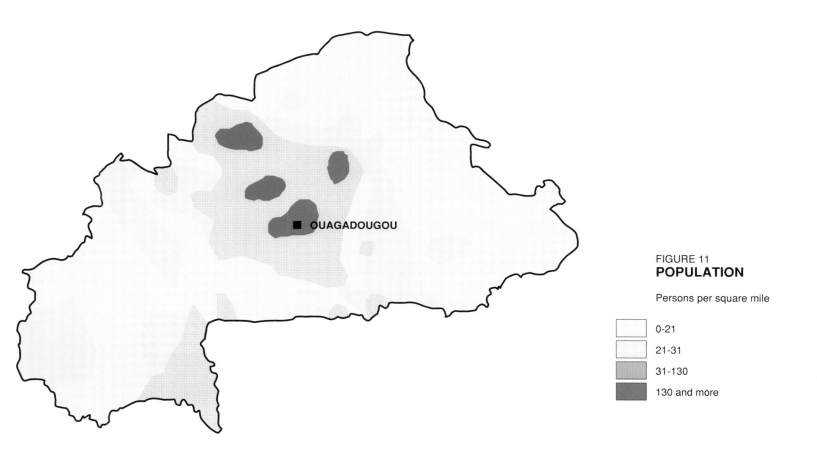

FIGURE 11
POPULATION

Persons per square mile

0-21
21-31
31-130
130 and more

OUAGADOUGOU

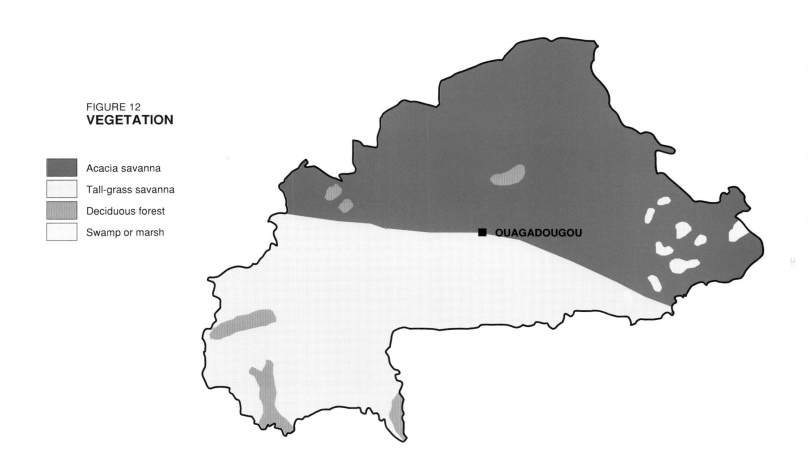

FIGURE 12
VEGETATION

Acacia savanna
Tall-grass savanna
Deciduous forest
Swamp or marsh

OUAGADOUGOU

CAMBODIA

Cambodia, the smallest state in Southeast Asia, ranks 85th in both land area and in population. The severe disruptions following the Vietnamese takeover of the country dried up even the small trickle of information that reached the West through unofficial channels. Its annual population growth rate is modest compared to other countries of similar size in the developing world but this could be attributed to the decimation of the population through politically motivated massacres and forced relocation of urban populations and resulting starvation-deaths. A series of natural disasters (including flooding in the Mekong Valley) and intensified internal insurgency combined to wipe out the economy. An end to Cambodia's civil war looked hopeful when, in June 1991, the Vietnam-backed government signed a cease-fire with warring factions and agreed to implement a plan for free elections.

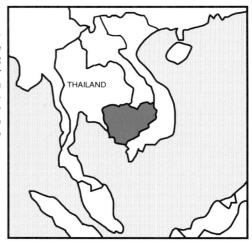

I.M.F.
INFORMATION
NOT
AVAILABLE

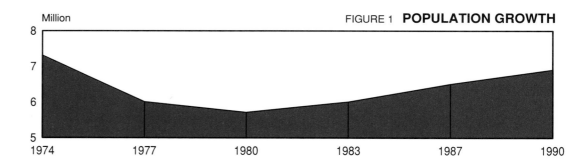

FIGURE 1 **POPULATION GROWTH**

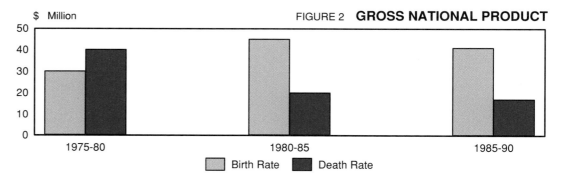

FIGURE 2 **GROSS NATIONAL PRODUCT**

Birth Rate   Death Rate

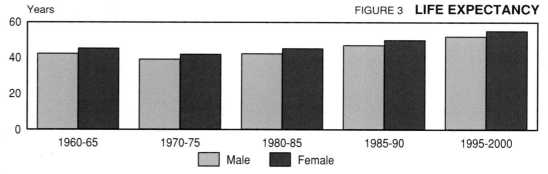

FIGURE 3 **LIFE EXPECTANCY**

Male   Female

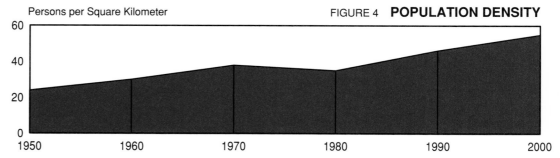

FIGURE 4 **POPULATION DENSITY**

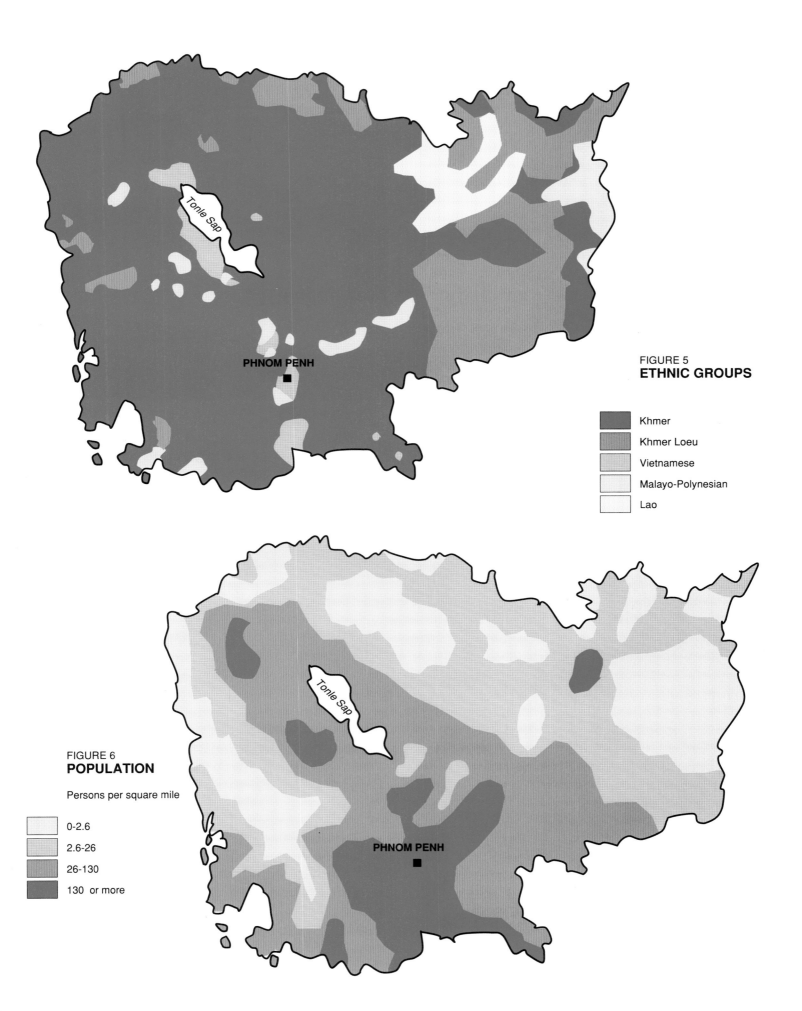

FIGURE 5
ETHNIC GROUPS

Khmer
Khmer Loeu
Vietnamese
Malayo-Polynesian
Lao

Tonle Sap

PHNOM PENH

FIGURE 6
POPULATION

Persons per square mile

0-2.6
2.6-26
26-130
130 or more

Tonle Sap

PHNOM PENH

CAMEROON

Located on the western part of the waist of the African continent, Cameroon ranks 49th in land area and 63rd in population. The country's main distinctions are its political stability (since independence it has had only two presidents and its history is unmarred by coups or rebellions) and the fact that it is the only African country where both French and English are accorded official status. However, numerous demonstrations and strikes calling for democratic reform forced the president in 1990 to endorse a multiparty system, free political prisoners, and legalize opposition parties. Cameroon has a very diverse ethnic configuration even by African standards, with over 200 tribes speaking 24 major African languages. The mainstay of the economy is agriculture, which employs 70% of the labor force and accounts for 70% of export earnings. The main cash crop is cocoa. Other major exports include coffee, timber, wood, aluminum ingots, cotton, rubber, peanuts, tobacco and tea.

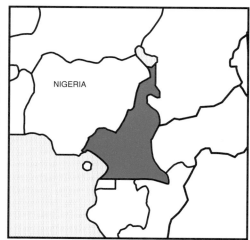

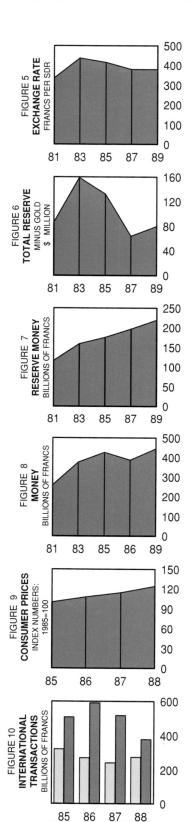

FIGURE 5 EXCHANGE RATE — FRANCS PER SDR

FIGURE 6 TOTAL RESERVE — MINUS GOLD $ MILLION

FIGURE 7 RESERVE MONEY — BILLIONS OF FRANCS

FIGURE 8 MONEY — BILLIONS OF FRANCS

FIGURE 9 CONSUMER PRICES — INDEX NUMBERS: 1985=100

FIGURE 10 INTERNATIONAL TRANSACTIONS — BILLIONS OF FRANCS
Exports   Imports

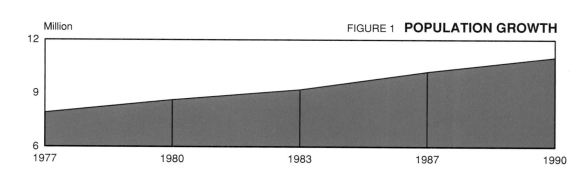

FIGURE 1 **POPULATION GROWTH**
Million

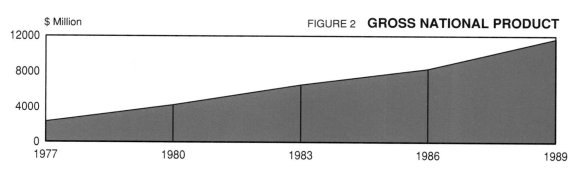

FIGURE 2 **GROSS NATIONAL PRODUCT**
$ Million

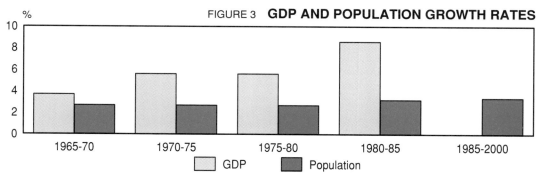

FIGURE 3 **GDP AND POPULATION GROWTH RATES**
%
GDP   Population

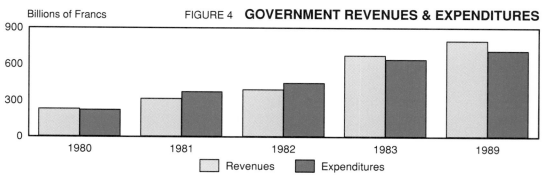

FIGURE 4 **GOVERNMENT REVENUES & EXPENDITURES**
Billions of Francs
Revenues   Expenditures

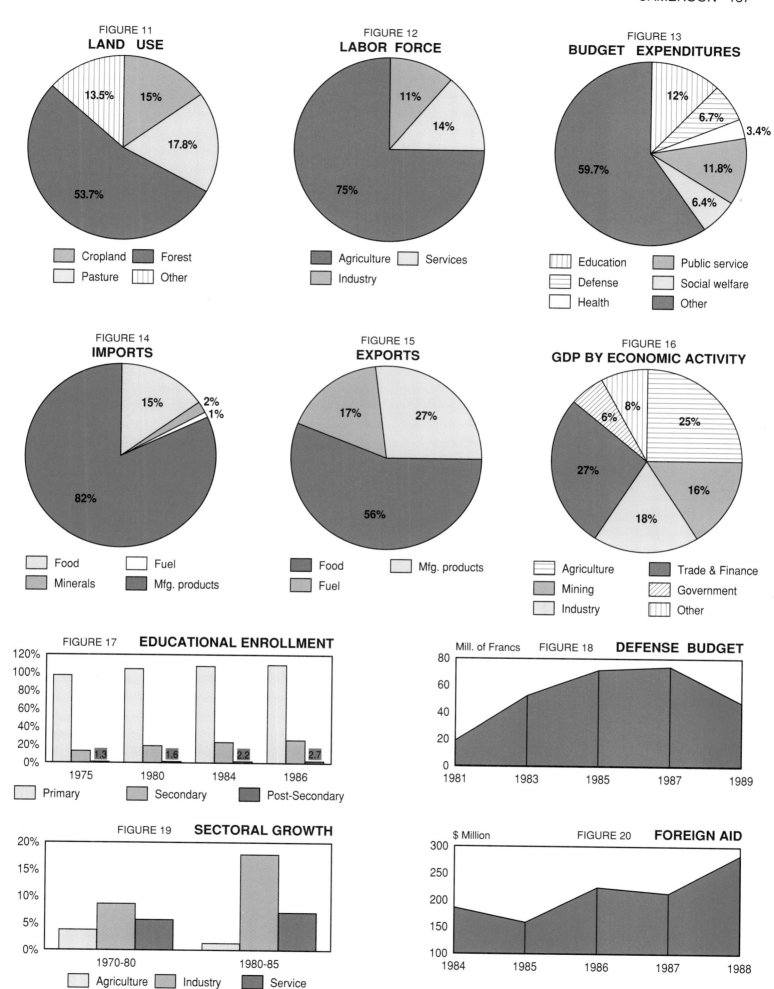

FIGURE 11
LAND USE

13.5% 15%
17.8%
53.7%

Cropland · Forest
Pasture · Other

FIGURE 12
LABOR FORCE

11%
14%
75%

Agriculture · Services
Industry

FIGURE 13
BUDGET EXPENDITURES

12%
6.7%
3.4%
59.7%
11.8%
6.4%

Education · Public service
Defense · Social welfare
Health · Other

FIGURE 14
IMPORTS

15% 2%
1%
82%

Food · Fuel
Minerals · Mfg. products

FIGURE 15
EXPORTS

17% 27%
56%

Food · Mfg. products
Fuel

FIGURE 16
GDP BY ECONOMIC ACTIVITY

8% 25%
6%
27% 16%
18%

Agriculture · Trade & Finance
Mining · Government
Industry · Other

FIGURE 17 **EDUCATIONAL ENROLLMENT**

1.3 1.6 2.2 2.7
1975 1980 1984 1986

Primary · Secondary · Post-Secondary

FIGURE 18 **DEFENSE BUDGET**
Mill. of Francs

1981 1983 1985 1987 1989

FIGURE 19 **SECTORAL GROWTH**

1970-80 1980-85

Agriculture · Industry · Service

FIGURE 20 **FOREIGN AID**
$ Million

1984 1985 1986 1987 1988

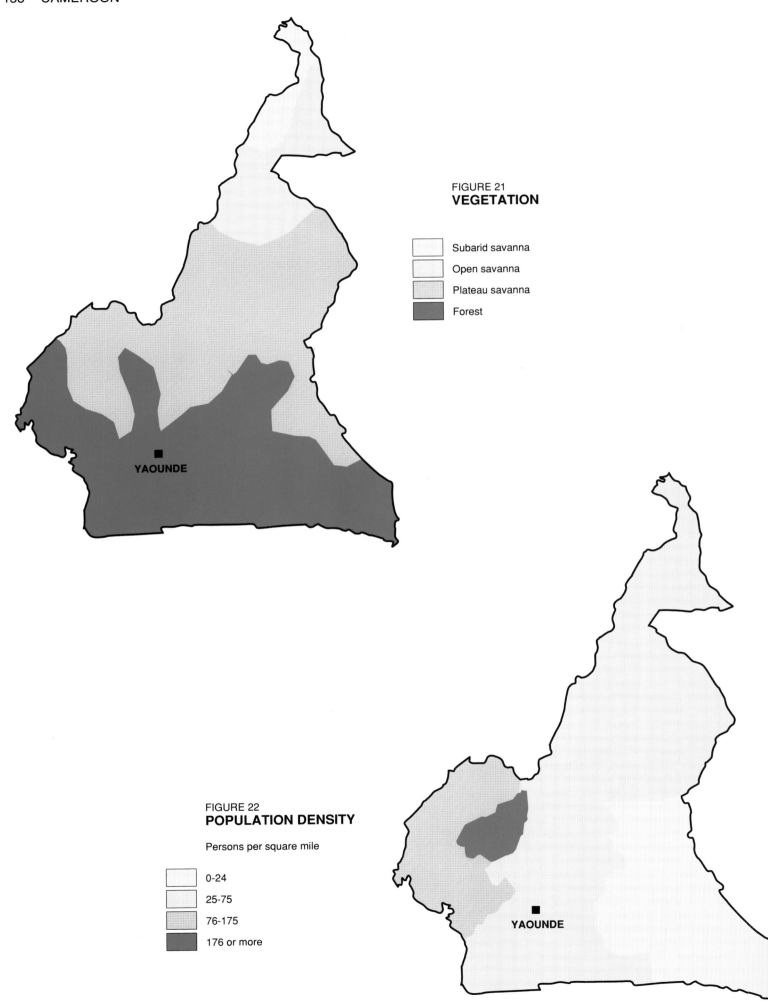

FIGURE 21
VEGETATION

Subarid savanna
Open savanna
Plateau savanna
Forest

YAOUNDE

FIGURE 22
POPULATION DENSITY

Persons per square mile

0-24
25-75
76-175
176 or more

YAOUNDE

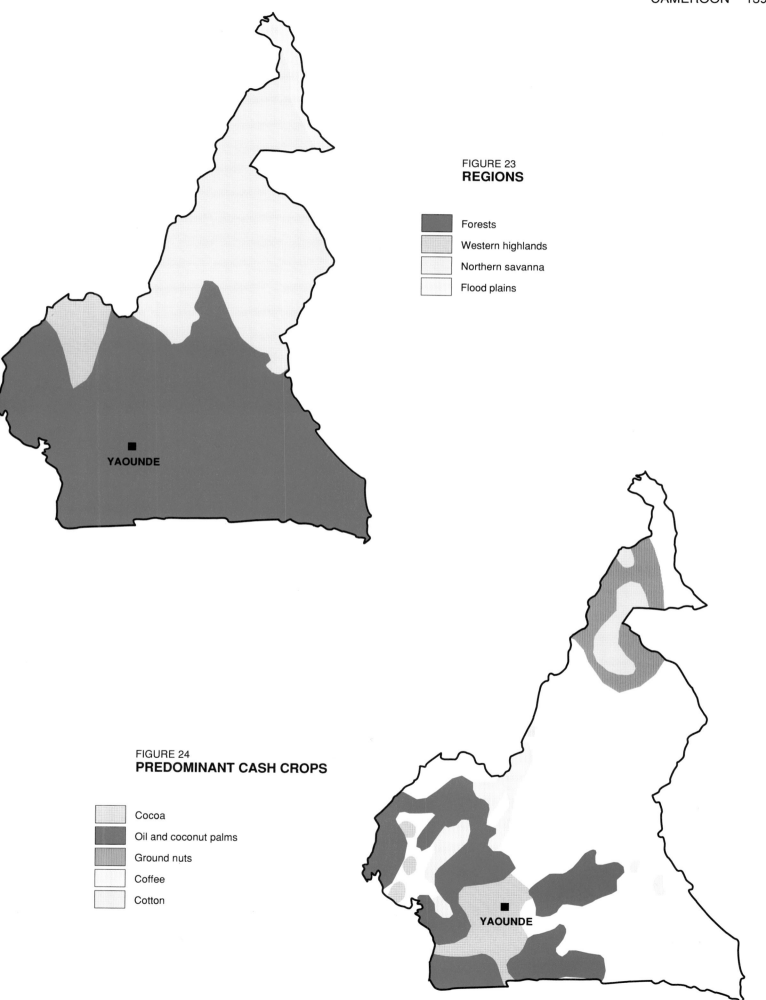

FIGURE 23
REGIONS

Forests
Western highlands
Northern savanna
Flood plains

YAOUNDE

FIGURE 24
PREDOMINANT CASH CROPS

Cocoa
Oil and coconut palms
Ground nuts
Coffee
Cotton

YAOUNDE

CHAD

Chad, the largest among the countries of former French Equatorial Africa, ranks 20th inland area and 95th in population. The civil war and subsequent Libyan occupation of the country retarded its economic and political growth to the point where conditions of anarchy and chaos prevailed in many areas. Once the leading cotton producer in francophone Africa, its output has steadily dropped since 1975-76 when it produced a record high of 174,000 tons. The central government has only nominal control over the northern zone, an extension of the Sahara Desert, whose nomadic people consider themselves as having nothing in common with the southerners. In addition to political instability, Chad has substantial barriers to economic growth, not the least of which is its total lack of transportation facilities. It has no outlet to the sea, no railroads, little paved road mileage (what roads exist are nearly impassable in the rainy season) and little river shipping. Chad's long civil war came to an end in 1988 with the defeat of Libyan invaders. In December 1990, General Idriss Deby overthrew the government, freeing Libyan prisoners and suspending the constitution, but also promising multiparty democracy.

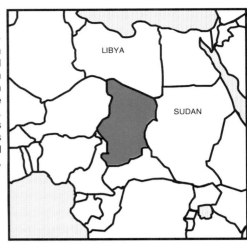

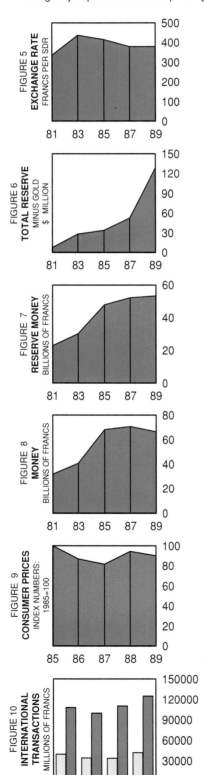

FIGURE 5 **EXCHANGE RATE** FRANCS PER SDR

FIGURE 6 **TOTAL RESERVE** MINUS GOLD $ MILLION

FIGURE 7 **RESERVE MONEY** BILLIONS OF FRANCS

FIGURE 8 **MONEY** BILLIONS OF FRANCS

FIGURE 9 **CONSUMER PRICES** INDEX NUMBERS: 1985=100

FIGURE 10 **INTERNATIONAL TRANSACTIONS** MILLIONS OF FRANCS
Exports   Imports

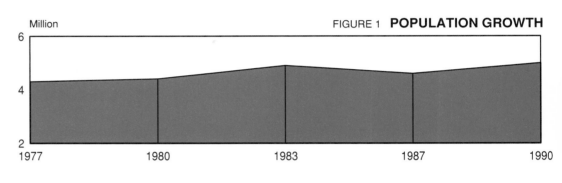

FIGURE 1 **POPULATION GROWTH**

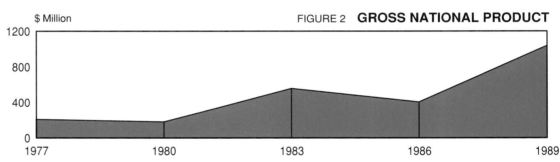

FIGURE 2 **GROSS NATIONAL PRODUCT**

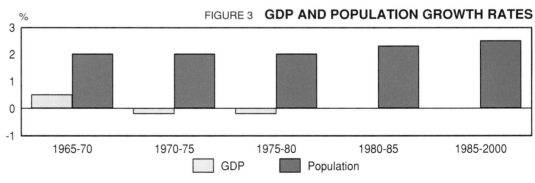

FIGURE 3 **GDP AND POPULATION GROWTH RATES**
GDP   Population

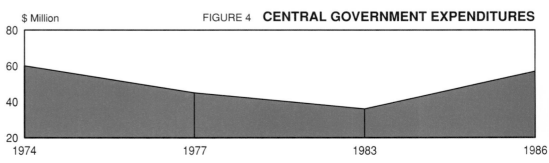

FIGURE 4 **CENTRAL GOVERNMENT EXPENDITURES**

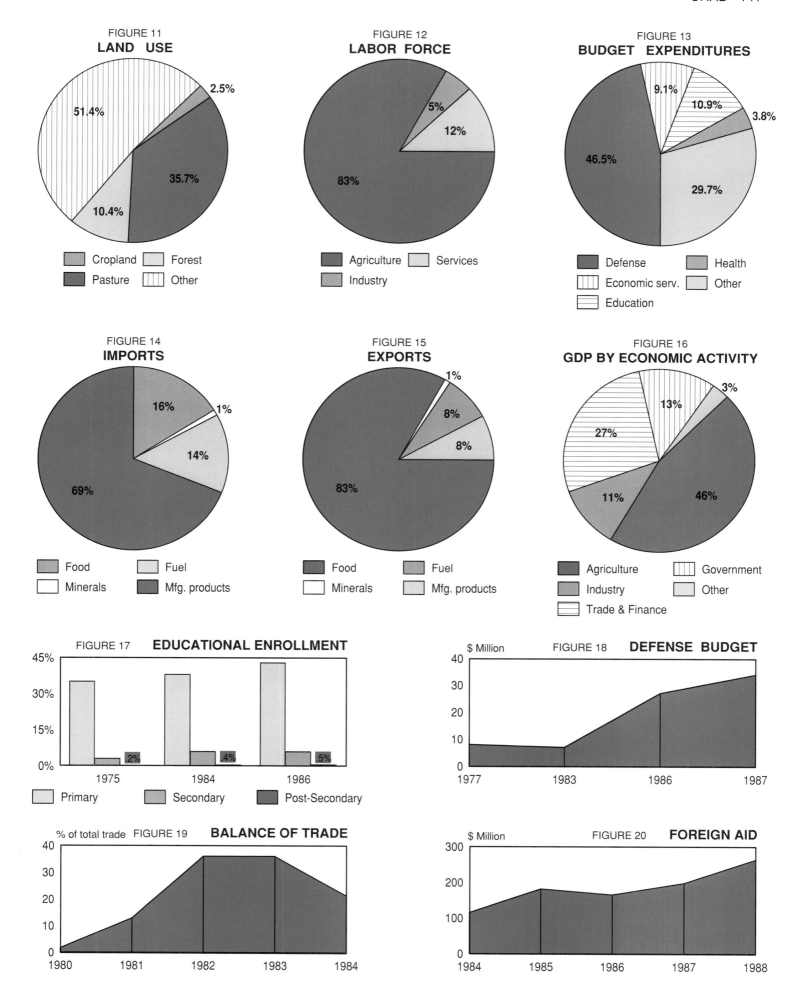

FIGURE 11
LAND USE

51.4%
2.5%
35.7%
10.4%

Cropland Forest
Pasture Other

FIGURE 12
LABOR FORCE

5%
12%
83%

Agriculture Services
Industry

FIGURE 13
BUDGET EXPENDITURES

9.1%
10.9%
3.8%
46.5%
29.7%

Defense Health
Economic serv. Other
Education

FIGURE 14
IMPORTS

16%
1%
14%
69%

Food Fuel
Minerals Mfg. products

FIGURE 15
EXPORTS

1%
8%
8%
83%

Food Fuel
Minerals Mfg. products

FIGURE 16
GDP BY ECONOMIC ACTIVITY

3%
13%
27%
11%
46%

Agriculture Government
Industry Other
Trade & Finance

FIGURE 17 EDUCATIONAL ENROLLMENT

45%
30%
15%
0%
.2% .4% .5%
1975 1984 1986

Primary Secondary Post-Secondary

$ Million FIGURE 18 DEFENSE BUDGET

40
30
20
10
0
1977 1983 1986 1987

% of total trade FIGURE 19 BALANCE OF TRADE

40
30
20
10
0
1980 1981 1982 1983 1984

$ Million FIGURE 20 FOREIGN AID

300
200
100
0
1984 1985 1986 1987 1988

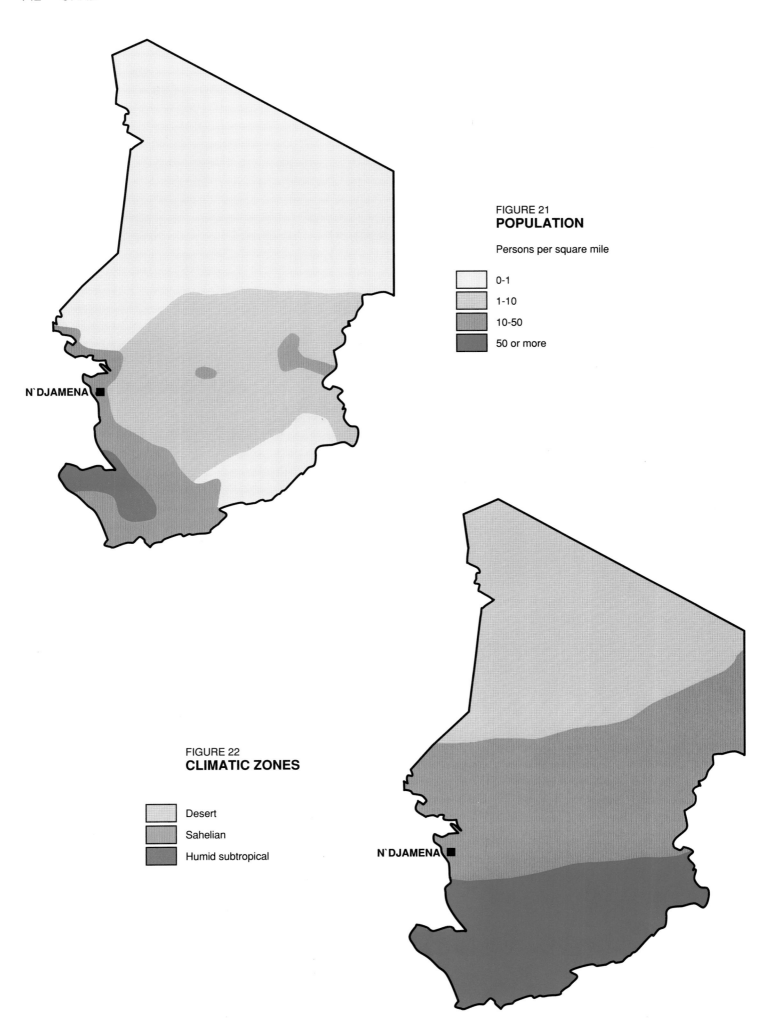

FIGURE 21
POPULATION

Persons per square mile

0-1

1-10

10-50

50 or more

N`DJAMENA ■

FIGURE 22
CLIMATIC ZONES

Desert

Sahelian

Humid subtropical

N`DJAMENA ■

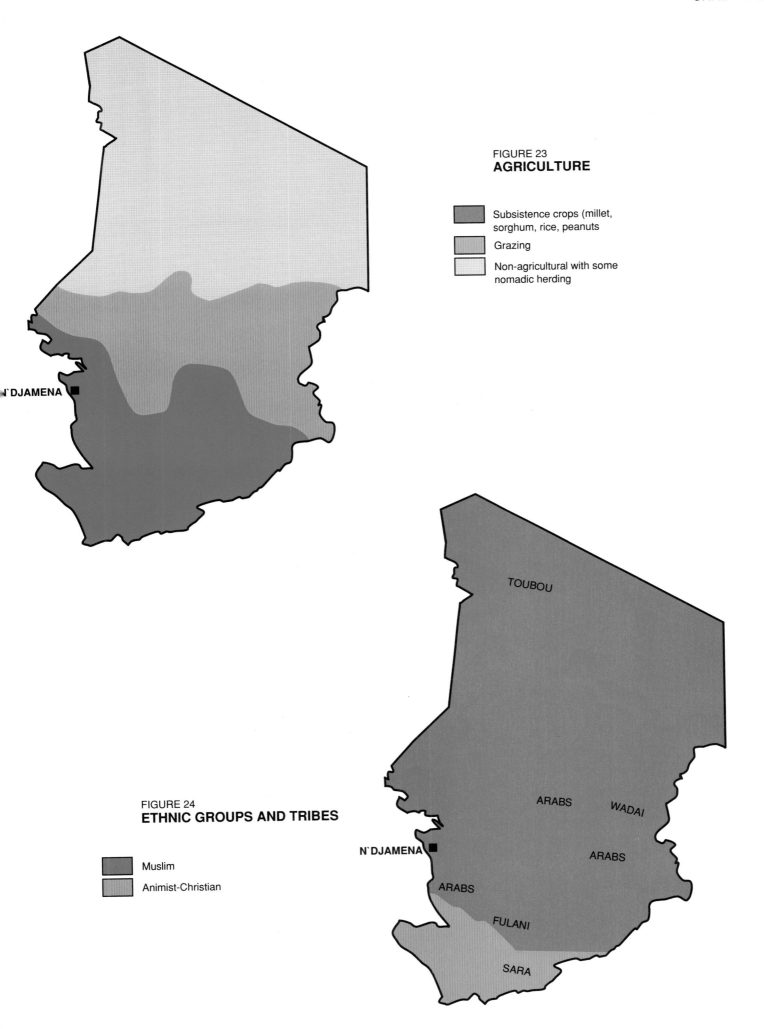

FIGURE 23
AGRICULTURE

- Subsistence crops (millet, sorghum, rice, peanuts
- Grazing
- Non-agricultural with some nomadic herding

N`DJAMENA

FIGURE 24
ETHNIC GROUPS AND TRIBES

- Muslim
- Animist-Christian

TOUBOU

ARABS   WADAI

N`DJAMENA

ARABS

ARABS

FULANI

SARA

CHILE

A country that is shaped like a narrow, pointed stake, extending 2,700 miles along the southwest coast of South America, Chile ranks 37th in land area and 56th in population. Over 70% of the population live in urban centers and more than one-third of the inhabitants are concentrated in and around Santiago and Valparaiso. Compared to other Latin American countries, Chile enjoys many significant advantages. Because of its geographical and cultural isolation, the population is extremely homogeneous. The country also has one of the highest literacy rates in Latin America. Despite these advantages the Chilean economy has been reeling for years under one of the highest inflation rates in the world. The reason for Chile's poor economic performance is partly the decline in agricultural output and partly the disastrous price controls and redistributive programs of the Salvador Allende regime. Under General Augusto Pinochet Ugarte, Chile's economy recovered in the 1980s but the country continued to be plagued by political unrest. In 1989 Chile returned to a democratic form of government, and in 1990 Patricio Aylwin Azocar took office as president, ending 17 years of military rule.

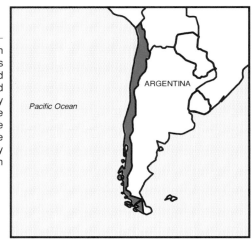

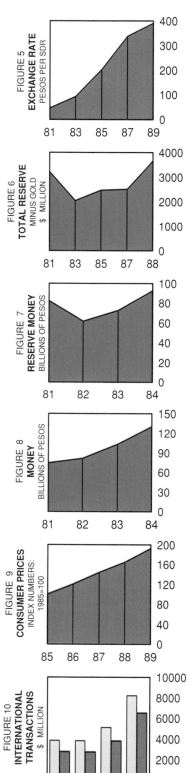

FIGURE 5 **EXCHANGE RATE** PESOS PER SDR

FIGURE 6 **TOTAL RESERVE** MINUS GOLD $ MILLION

FIGURE 7 **RESERVE MONEY** BILLIONS OF PESOS

FIGURE 8 **MONEY** BILLIONS OF PESOS

FIGURE 9 **CONSUMER PRICES** INDEX NUMBERS: 1985=100

FIGURE 10 **INTERNATIONAL TRANSACTIONS** $ MILLION

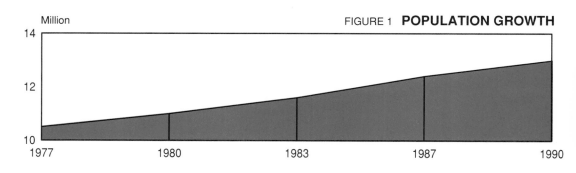

FIGURE 1 **POPULATION GROWTH**

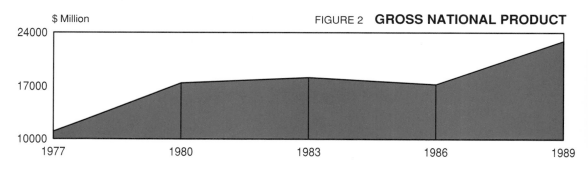

FIGURE 2 **GROSS NATIONAL PRODUCT**

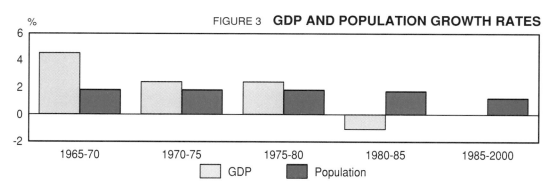

FIGURE 3 **GDP AND POPULATION GROWTH RATES**

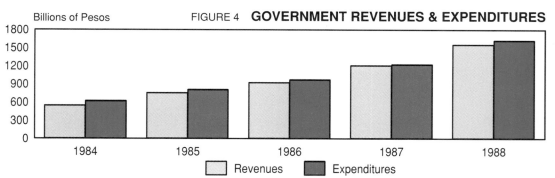

FIGURE 4 **GOVERNMENT REVENUES & EXPENDITURES**

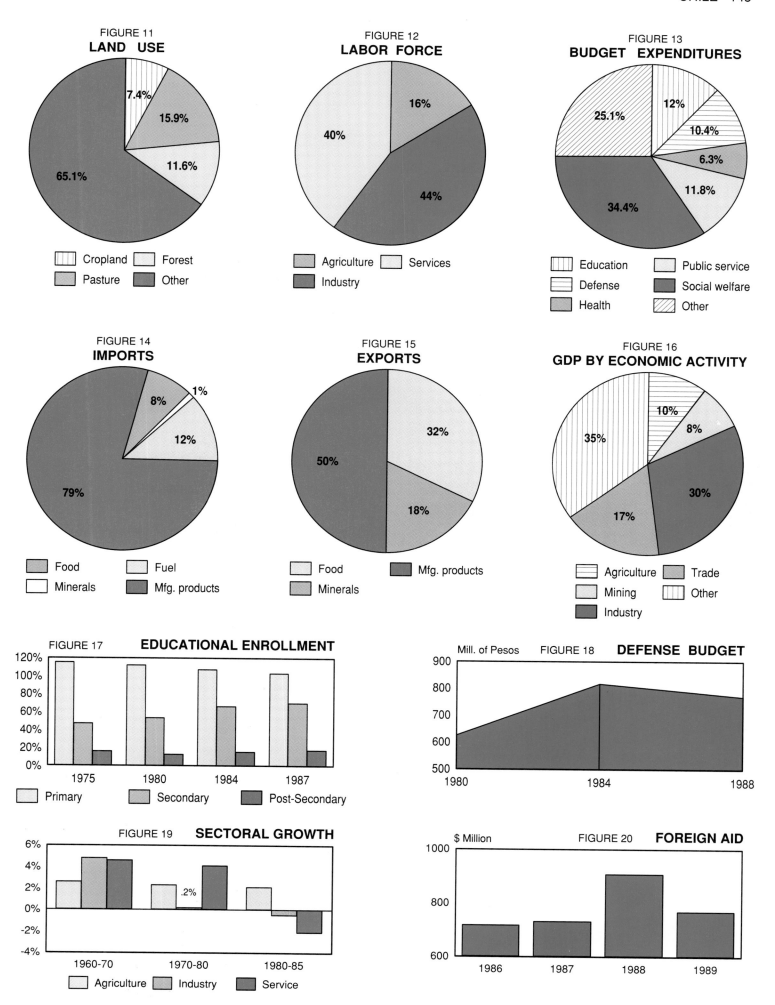

FIGURE 11
LAND USE
7.4%
15.9%
11.6%
65.1%

Cropland Forest
Pasture Other

FIGURE 12
LABOR FORCE
16%
40%
44%

Agriculture Services
Industry

FIGURE 13
BUDGET EXPENDITURES
25.1% 12%
10.4%
6.3%
11.8%
34.4%

Education Public service
Defense Social welfare
Health Other

FIGURE 14
IMPORTS
8% 1%
12%
79%

Food Fuel
Minerals Mfg. products

FIGURE 15
EXPORTS
32%
50%
18%

Food Mfg. products
Minerals

FIGURE 16
GDP BY ECONOMIC ACTIVITY
10%
35% 8%
30%
17%

Agriculture Trade
Mining Other
Industry

FIGURE 17 **EDUCATIONAL ENROLLMENT**
120%
100%
80%
60%
40%
20%
0%
1975 1980 1984 1987
Primary Secondary Post-Secondary

Mill. of Pesos FIGURE 18 **DEFENSE BUDGET**
900
800
700
600
500
1980 1984 1988

FIGURE 19 **SECTORAL GROWTH**
6%
4%
2% .2%
0%
-2%
-4%
1960-70 1970-80 1980-85
Agriculture Industry Service

$ Million FIGURE 20 **FOREIGN AID**
1000
800
600
1986 1987 1988 1989

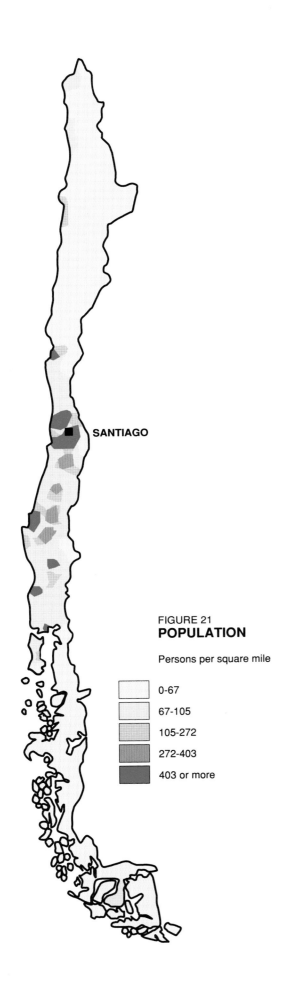

FIGURE 21
POPULATION

Persons per square mile

0-67
67-105
105-272
272-403
403 or more

SANTIAGO

FIGURE 22
VEGETATION

Mostly forest
Mostly scrub
Mostly grass
Cultivated and pastureland
Desert or alpine barrens

FIGURE 23
MINING

△   Copper

□   Iron

▲   Manganese

○   Nitrates

●   Petroleum

SANTIAGO

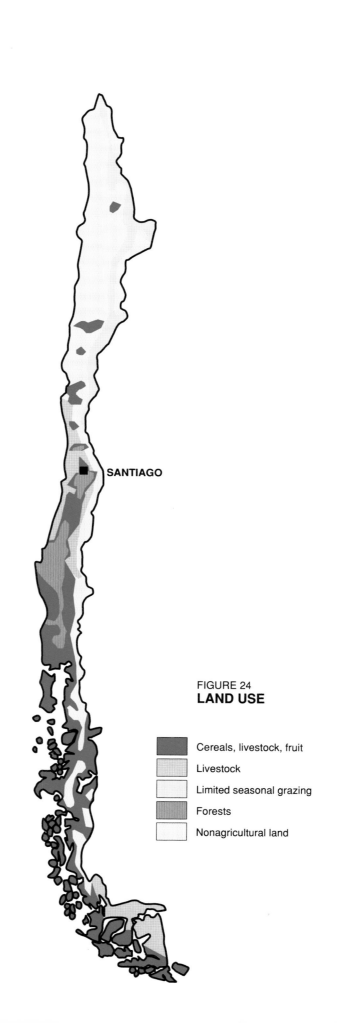

SANTIAGO

FIGURE 24
LAND USE

Cereals, livestock, fruit

Livestock

Limited seasonal grazing

Forests

Nonagricultural land

COLOMBIA

The fourth most populous as well as the fourth largest country in South America, Colombia ranks 26th in land area and 30th in population in the world. As all coffee lovers know, Colombia is the world's second largest producer and exporter of coffee and coffee earnings constitute almost one third of the GDP. The economy is predominantly agricultural. Colombia is also an important producer of cocoa. The country is rich in minerals and its 18 million tons of known coal reserves are the largest in Latin America. It is also the source of 90% of the world's emeralds. More recently, the country has gained some notoriety as the source of 70% of illegal drugs consumed in North America; drug-related income is estimated at several billions of dollars annually. Despite a high rate of inflation and a 30% growth in money supply, the Colombian economy has maintained a steady rate of expansion.

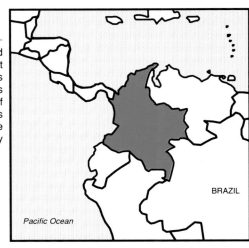

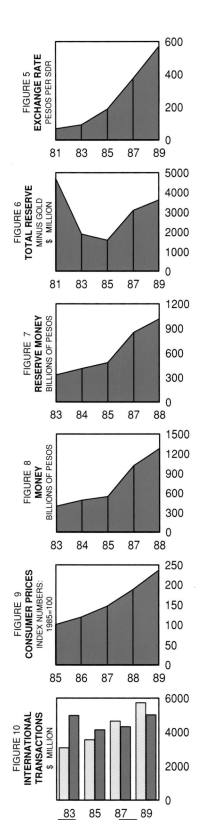

FIGURE 5 EXCHANGE RATE PESOS PER SDR

FIGURE 6 TOTAL RESERVE MINUS GOLD $ MILLION

FIGURE 7 RESERVE MONEY BILLIONS OF PESOS

FIGURE 8 MONEY BILLIONS OF PESOS

FIGURE 9 CONSUMER PRICES INDEX NUMBERS: 1985=100

FIGURE 10 INTERNATIONAL TRANSACTIONS $ MILLION — Exports Imports

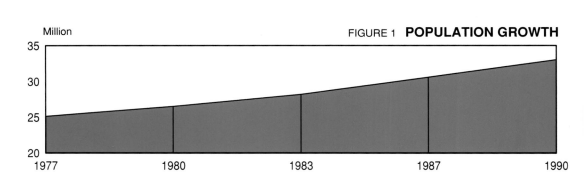

FIGURE 1 **POPULATION GROWTH**

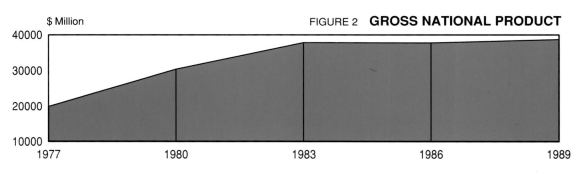

FIGURE 2 **GROSS NATIONAL PRODUCT**

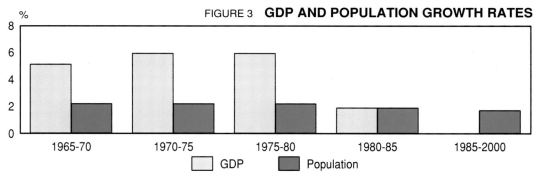

FIGURE 3 **GDP AND POPULATION GROWTH RATES**

GDP   Population

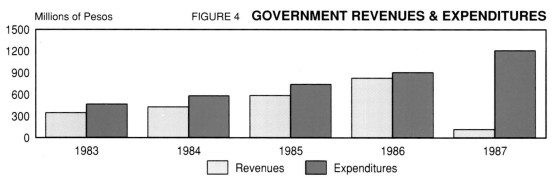

FIGURE 4 **GOVERNMENT REVENUES & EXPENDITURES**

Revenues   Expenditures

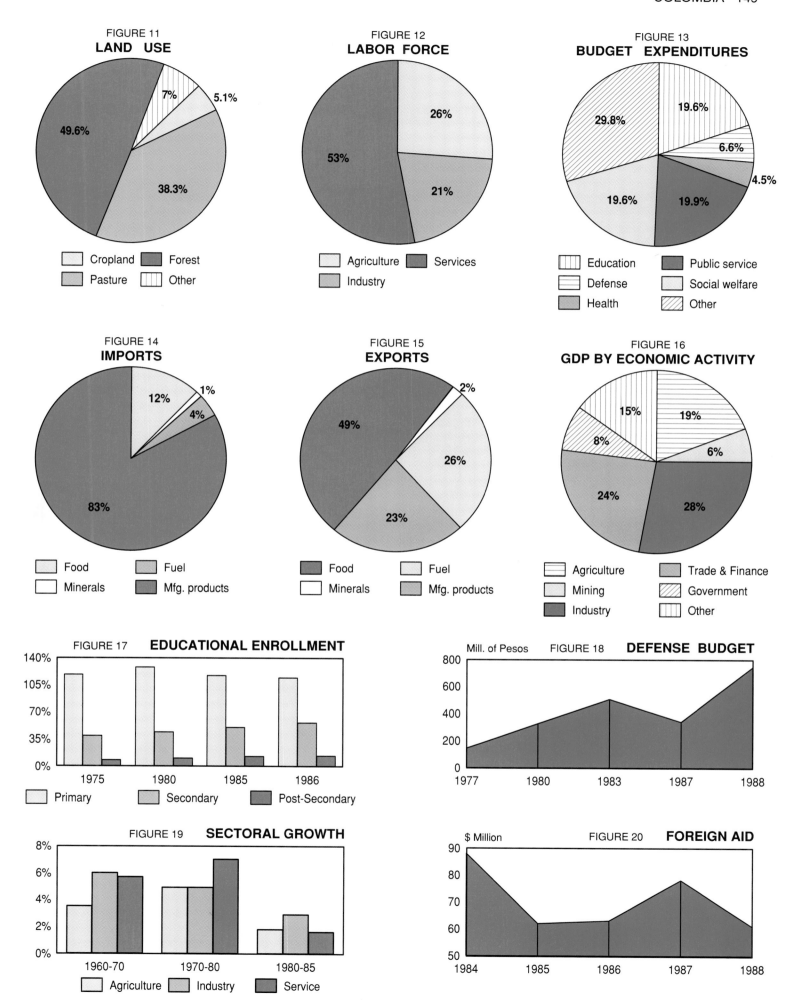

FIGURE 11
LAND USE

7%
5.1%
49.6%
38.3%

Cropland   Forest
Pasture   Other

FIGURE 12
LABOR FORCE

26%
53%
21%

Agriculture   Services
Industry

FIGURE 13
BUDGET EXPENDITURES

29.8%   19.6%
6.6%
19.6%   19.9%   4.5%

Education   Public service
Defense   Social welfare
Health   Other

FIGURE 14
IMPORTS

12%   1%
4%
83%

Food   Fuel
Minerals   Mfg. products

FIGURE 15
EXPORTS

2%
49%   26%
23%

Food   Fuel
Minerals   Mfg. products

FIGURE 16
GDP BY ECONOMIC ACTIVITY

15%   19%
8%
6%
24%   28%

Agriculture   Trade & Finance
Mining   Government
Industry   Other

FIGURE 17   **EDUCATIONAL ENROLLMENT**

140%
105%
70%
35%
0%
1975   1980   1985   1986

Primary   Secondary   Post-Secondary

Mill. of Pesos   FIGURE 18   **DEFENSE BUDGET**

800
600
400
200
0
1977   1980   1983   1987   1988

FIGURE 19   **SECTORAL GROWTH**

8%
6%
4%
2%
0%
1960-70   1970-80   1980-85

Agriculture   Industry   Service

$ Million   FIGURE 20   **FOREIGN AID**

90
80
70
60
50
1984   1985   1986   1987   1988

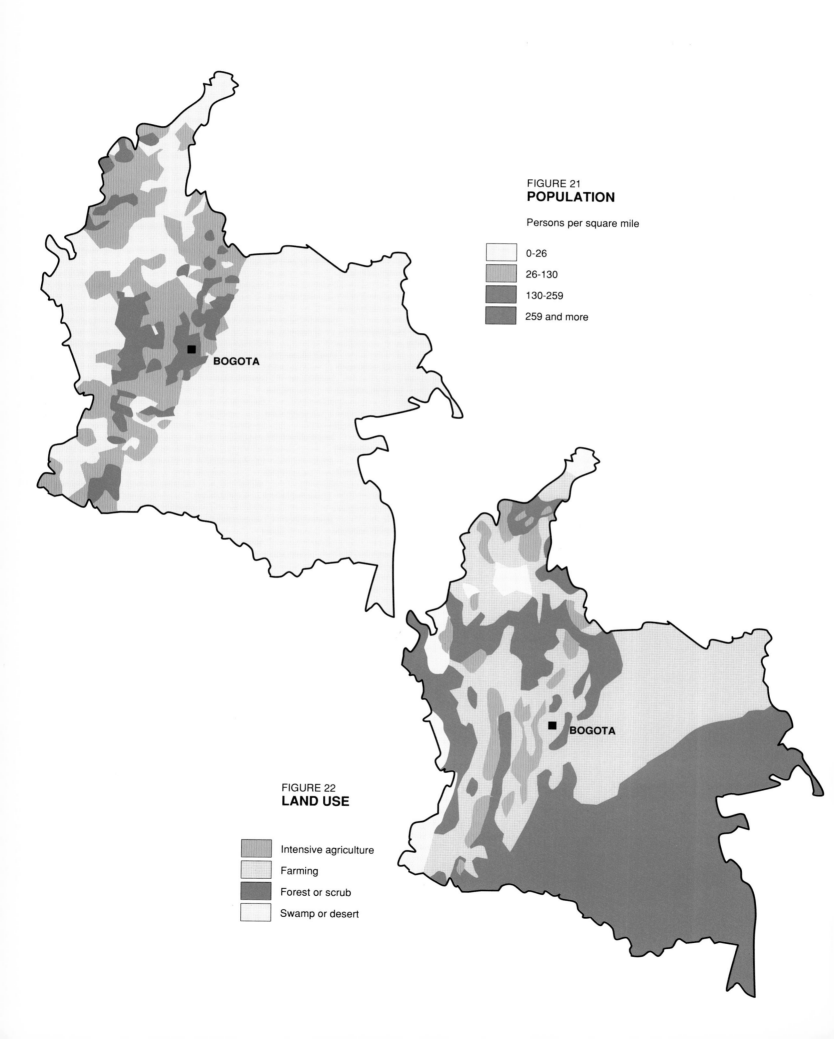

FIGURE 21
POPULATION

Persons per square mile

0-26

26-130

130-259

259 and more

BOGOTA

FIGURE 22
LAND USE

Intensive agriculture

Farming

Forest or scrub

Swamp or desert

BOGOTA

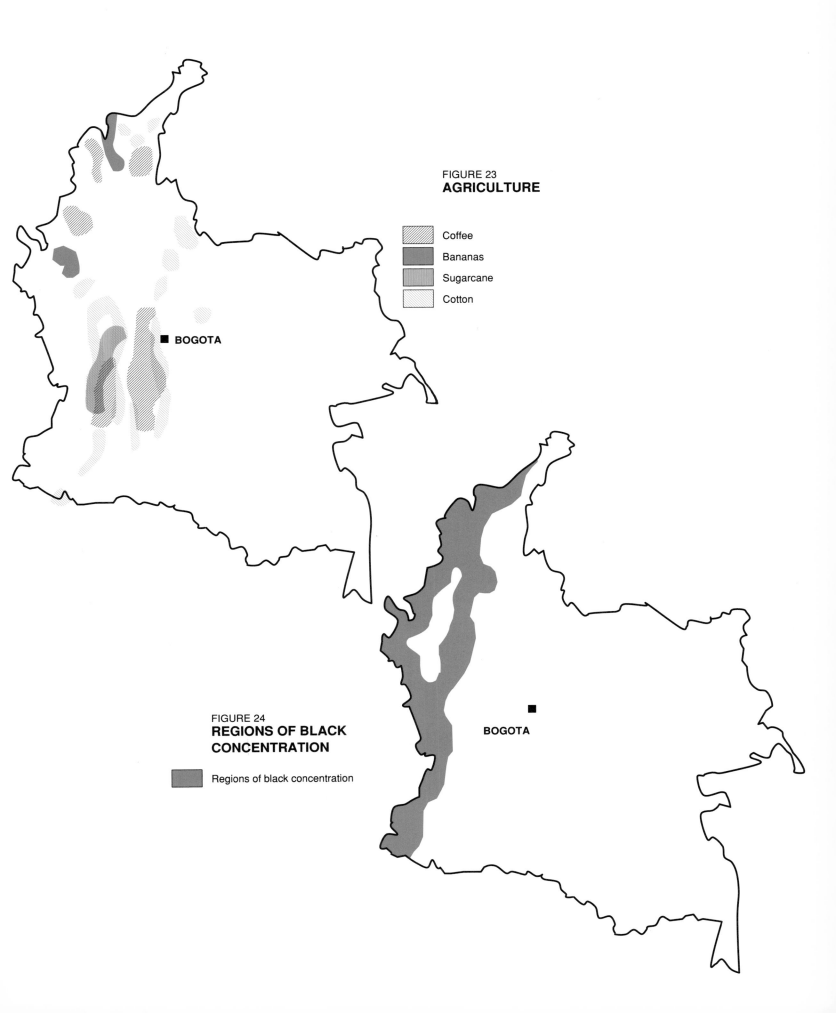

FIGURE 23
AGRICULTURE

Coffee
Bananas
Sugarcane
Cotton

■ **BOGOTA**

FIGURE 24
REGIONS OF BLACK CONCENTRATION

Regions of black concentration

BOGOTA

CONGO

Located on the Equator in west-central Africa, Congo ranks 57th in land area and 120th in population. Congo is one of the few African countries that has managed to reach the lower middle-income level, perhaps because of its rich natural resources, low population density, high degree of urbanization, and high literacy. It was also the first Marxist African republic and in accordance with its official ideology state-owned enterprises played a major part in the economy. However, in 1990, the congress renounced Marxism and adopted a social democratic platform; the president announced that opposition parties would become legal in 1991. Congo is also a major transportation hub for western Africa with the Zaire and Ubangi rivers as key waterways serving the Brazzaville port. In addition, a railroad links the port of Point-Noire on the Atlantic with Brazzaville and Gabon. As a result of falling demand for oil and wood, the economy suffered severe reverses during the 1980s. Recovery has been slow and erratic and many capital projects have been curtailed or abandoned as a result.

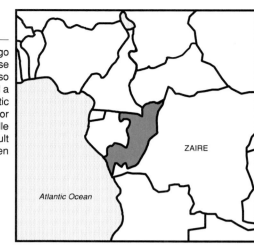

ZAIRE

Atlantic Ocean

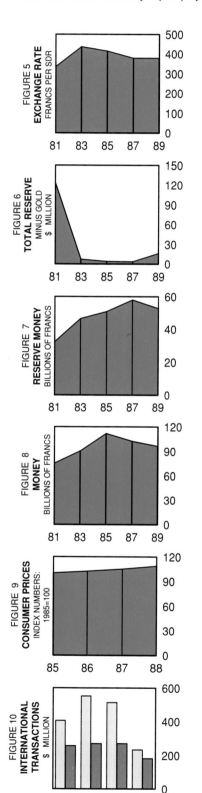

FIGURE 5 EXCHANGE RATE — FRANCS PER SDR

FIGURE 6 TOTAL RESERVE — MINUS GOLD $ MILLION

FIGURE 7 RESERVE MONEY — BILLIONS OF FRANCS

FIGURE 8 MONEY — BILLIONS OF FRANCS

FIGURE 9 CONSUMER PRICES — INDEX NUMBERS: 1985=100

FIGURE 10 INTERNATIONAL TRANSACTIONS — $ MILLION
Exports   Imports

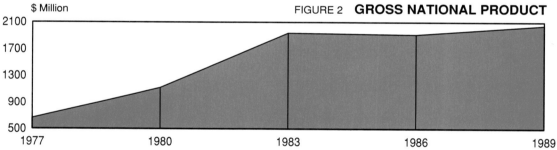

FIGURE 1 **POPULATION GROWTH**

Million

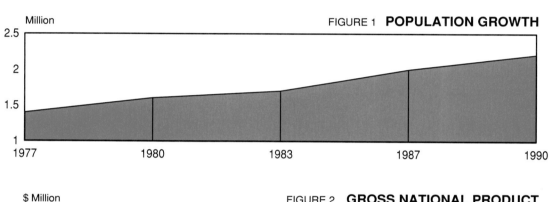

FIGURE 2 **GROSS NATIONAL PRODUCT**

$ Million

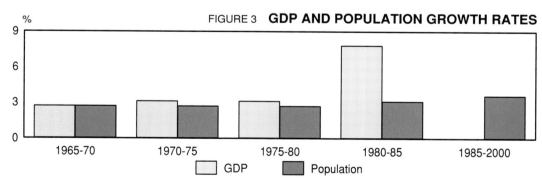

FIGURE 3 **GDP AND POPULATION GROWTH RATES**

%

GDP   Population

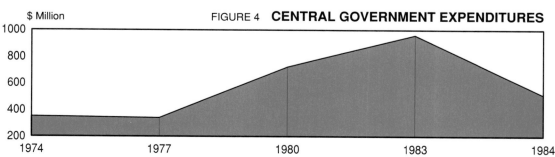

FIGURE 4 **CENTRAL GOVERNMENT EXPENDITURES**

$ Million

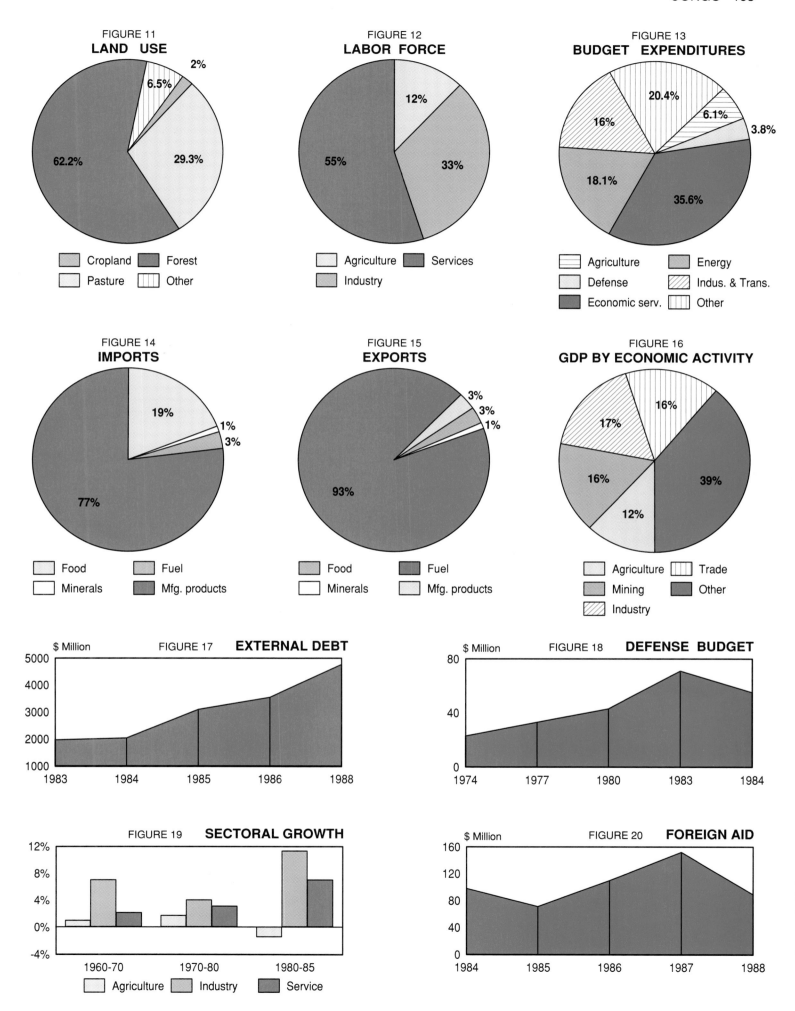

FIGURE 11
LAND   USE

2%
6.5%
62.2%
29.3%

Cropland   Forest
Pasture   Other

FIGURE 12
LABOR FORCE

12%
55%
33%

Agriculture   Services
Industry

FIGURE 13
BUDGET   EXPENDITURES

20.4%
16%
6.1%
3.8%
18.1%
35.6%

Agriculture   Energy
Defense   Indus. & Trans.
Economic serv.   Other

FIGURE 14
IMPORTS

19%
1%
3%
77%

Food   Fuel
Minerals   Mfg. products

FIGURE 15
EXPORTS

3%
3%
1%
93%

Food   Fuel
Minerals   Mfg. products

FIGURE 16
GDP BY ECONOMIC ACTIVITY

16%
17%
16%
12%
39%

Agriculture   Trade
Mining   Other
Industry

$ Million   FIGURE 17   **EXTERNAL DEBT**
5000
4000
3000
2000
1000
1983   1984   1985   1986   1988

$ Million   FIGURE 18   **DEFENSE BUDGET**
80
40
0
1974   1977   1980   1983   1984

FIGURE 19   **SECTORAL GROWTH**
12%
8%
4%
0%
-4%
1960-70   1970-80   1980-85
Agriculture   Industry   Service

$ Million   FIGURE 20   **FOREIGN AID**
160
120
80
40
0
1984   1985   1986   1987   1988

COSTA RICA

The second smallest Central American republic, Costa Rica ranks 116th in land area and 112th in population. With a per capita income of $1,420 it is one of the 35 upper middle-income countries. Its main distinctions are that it is politically one of the most stable countries in Latin America, that it does not maintain a standing army and that it has a literacy rate of over 90%. Not only does Costa Rica have the highest per capita GNP in the region, but the national income is more evenly distributed than among its neighbors. This relatively equitable income distribution is one of the durable results of the Revolution of 1948 when the state became the dominant economic force. By the late 1970s industry and commerce had surpassed agriculture in their contribution to the GDP. At the same time, spiraling inflation and resulting demands for substantial wage increases by workers forced the government to adopt a broad stabilization program emphasizing monetary and fiscal restraint.

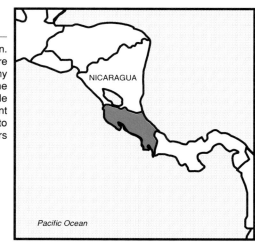

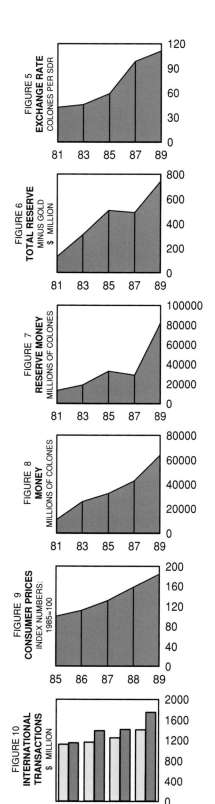

FIGURE 5 **EXCHANGE RATE** COLONES PER SDR

FIGURE 6 **TOTAL RESERVE** MINUS GOLD $ MILLION

FIGURE 7 **RESERVE MONEY** MILLIONS OF COLONES

FIGURE 8 **MONEY** MILLIONS OF COLONES

FIGURE 9 **CONSUMER PRICES** INDEX NUMBERS: 1985=100

FIGURE 10 **INTERNATIONAL TRANSACTIONS** $ MILLION

□ Exports ■ Imports

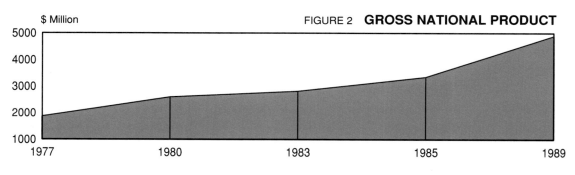

FIGURE 1 **POPULATION GROWTH**

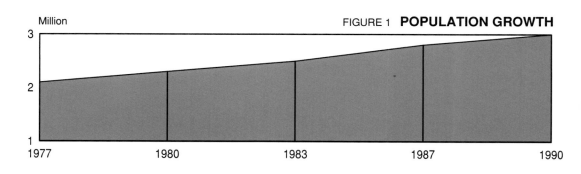

FIGURE 2 **GROSS NATIONAL PRODUCT**

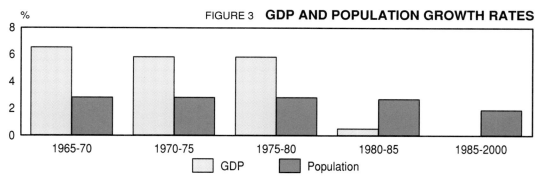

FIGURE 3 **GDP AND POPULATION GROWTH RATES**

□ GDP ■ Population

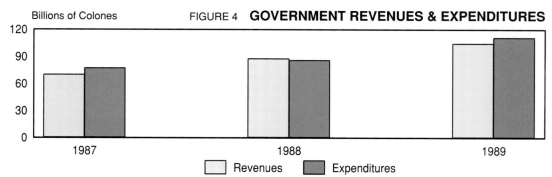

FIGURE 4 **GOVERNMENT REVENUES & EXPENDITURES**

□ Revenues ■ Expenditures

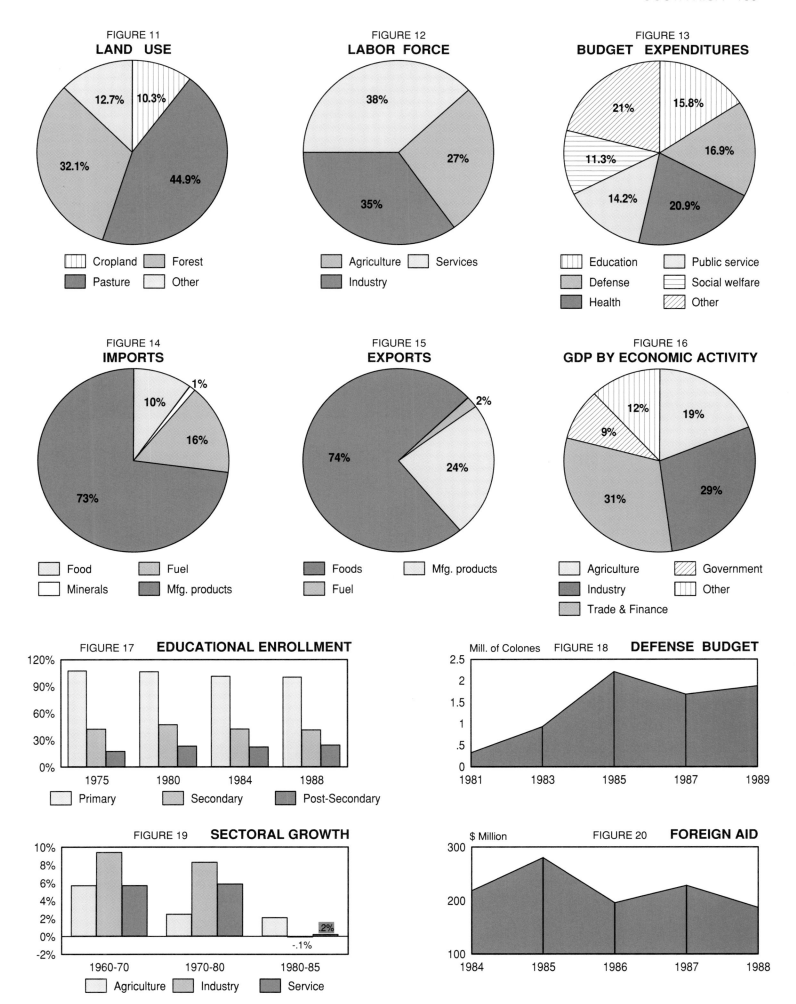

FIGURE 11
LAND USE

12.7% 10.3%
32.1%
44.9%

Cropland   Forest
Pasture   Other

FIGURE 12
LABOR FORCE

38%
27%
35%

Agriculture   Services
Industry

FIGURE 13
BUDGET EXPENDITURES

21%   15.8%
11.3%   16.9%
14.2%   20.9%

Education   Public service
Defense   Social welfare
Health   Other

FIGURE 14
IMPORTS

1%
10%
16%
73%

Food   Fuel
Minerals Mfg. products

FIGURE 15
EXPORTS

2%
74%   24%

Foods   Mfg. products
Fuel

FIGURE 16
GDP BY ECONOMIC ACTIVITY

12%   19%
9%
31%   29%

Agriculture   Government
Industry   Other
Trade & Finance

FIGURE 17   **EDUCATIONAL ENROLLMENT**

120%
90%
60%
30%
0%
1975   1980   1984   1988

Primary   Secondary   Post-Secondary

Mill. of Colones   FIGURE 18   **DEFENSE BUDGET**

2.5
2
1.5
1
.5
0
1981   1983   1985   1987   1989

FIGURE 19   **SECTORAL GROWTH**

10%
8%
6%
4%
2%
0%
-2%
.2%
-.1%
1960-70   1970-80   1980-85

Agriculture   Industry   Service

$ Million   FIGURE 20   **FOREIGN AID**

300
200
100
1984   1985   1986   1987   1988

CUBA

The largest and western-most island in the West Indies, Cuba ranks 99th in land area and 62nd in population. The Cuban economy is dominated by four factors; a heavy commodity concentration in the production and export of sugar; a loosely defined Communist ideology governing policy decisions; hostility toward the United States which reciprocates in kind; and a corresponding dependence on the Soviet bloc, especially Soviet subsidies, grants and technical assistance. In 1972 Cuba bowed to Soviet pressure to join the Council for Mutual Economic Assistance (CMEA) as a full member, receiving in return preferential trade terms and expanded technical assistance. Although Cuba's nickel deposits are among the largest in the world, extraction presents serious technical problems; however, production has increased substantially and nickel is now the country's second most valuable export item. The Soviet Union curtailed aid in the late 1980s, weakening the Cuban economy further.

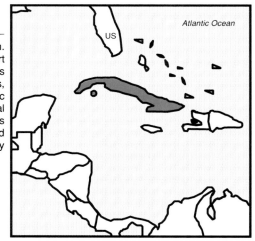

**I.M.F.
INFORMATION
NOT
AVAILABLE**

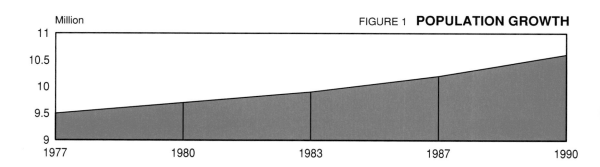

FIGURE 1 **POPULATION GROWTH**

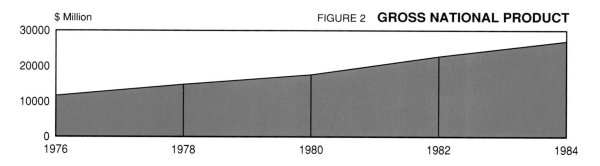

FIGURE 2 **GROSS NATIONAL PRODUCT**

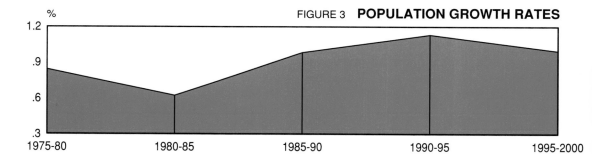

FIGURE 3 **POPULATION GROWTH RATES**

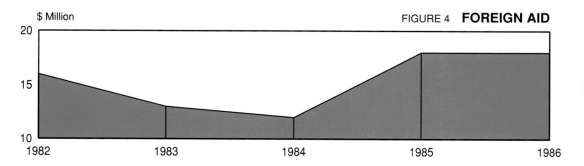

FIGURE 4 **FOREIGN AID**

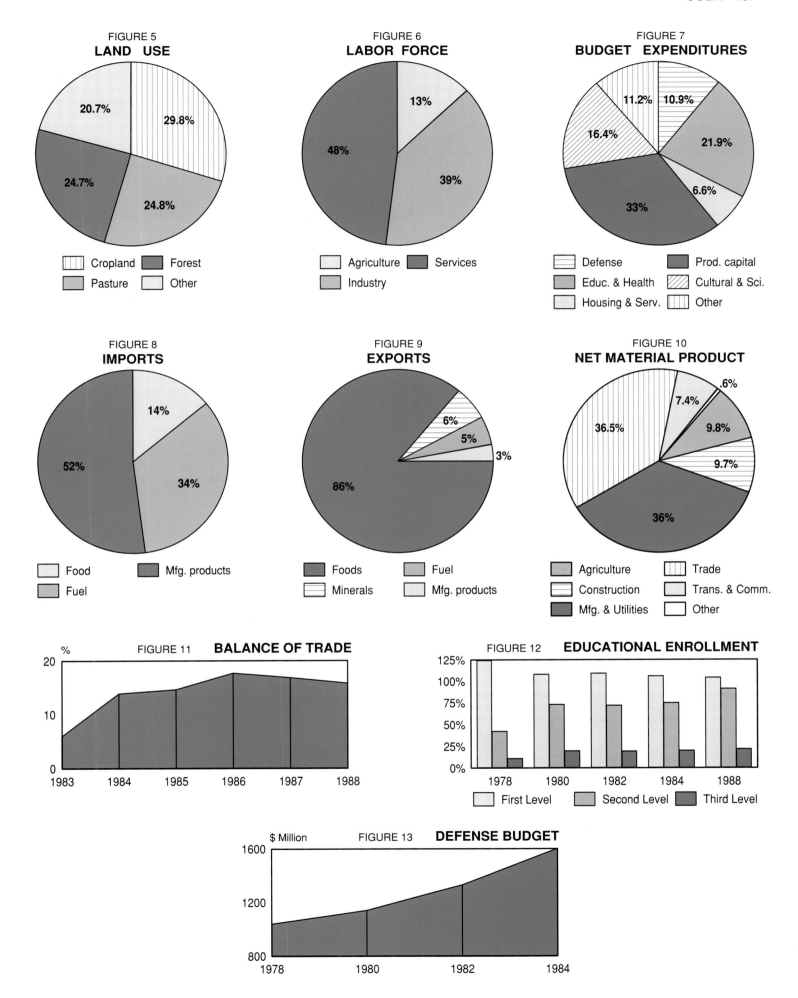

FIGURE 5
LAND USE

20.7%
29.8%
24.7%
24.8%

Cropland   Forest
Pasture   Other

FIGURE 6
LABOR FORCE

13%
48%
39%

Agriculture   Services
Industry

FIGURE 7
BUDGET EXPENDITURES

11.2%   10.9%
16.4%
21.9%
6.6%
33%

Defense   Prod. capital
Educ. & Health Cultural & Sci.
Housing & Serv. Other

FIGURE 8
IMPORTS

14%
52%
34%

Food   Mfg. products
Fuel

FIGURE 9
EXPORTS

6%
5%
3%
86%

Foods   Fuel
Minerals   Mfg. products

FIGURE 10
NET MATERIAL PRODUCT

.6%
7.4%
36.5%
9.8%
9.7%
36%

Agriculture   Trade
Construction   Trans. & Comm.
Mfg. & Utilities Other

FIGURE 11   BALANCE OF TRADE

%
20
10
0
1983 1984 1985 1986 1987 1988

FIGURE 12   EDUCATIONAL ENROLLMENT

125%
100%
75%
50%
25%
0%
1978 1980 1982 1984 1988

First Level   Second Level   Third Level

FIGURE 13   DEFENSE BUDGET

$ Million
1600
1200
800
1978 1980 1982 1984

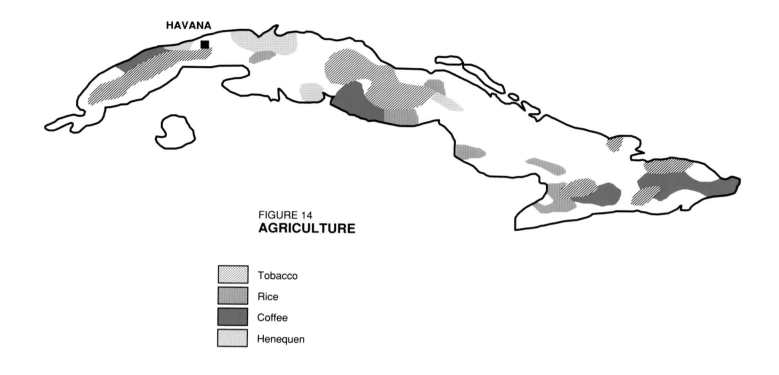

FIGURE 14
AGRICULTURE

Tobacco

Rice

Coffee

Henequen

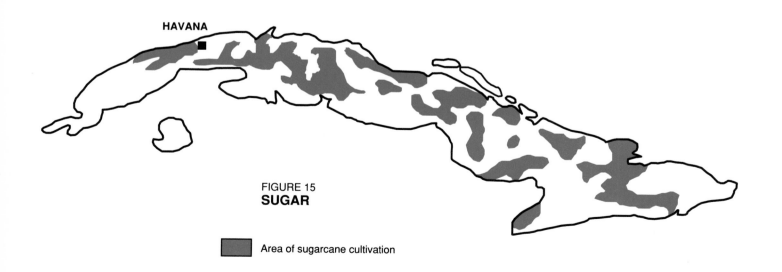

FIGURE 15
SUGAR

Area of sugarcane cultivation

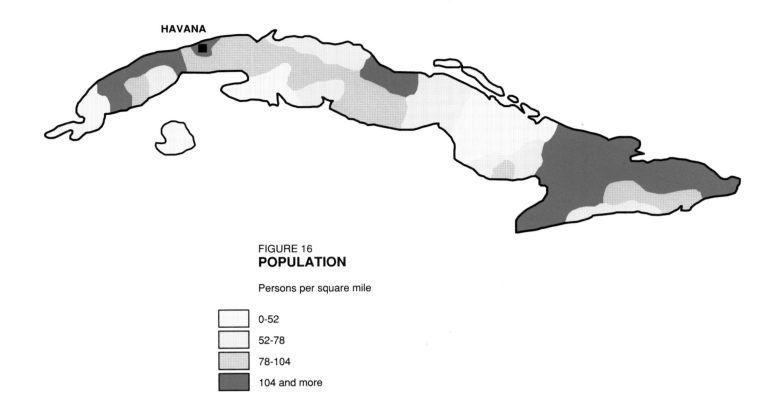

HAVANA

FIGURE 16
POPULATION

Persons per square mile

0-52

52-78

78-104

104 and more

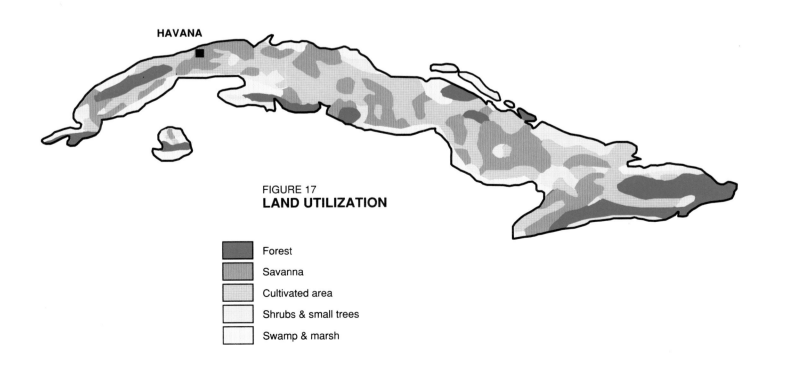

HAVANA

FIGURE 17
LAND UTILIZATION

Forest

Savanna

Cultivated area

Shrubs & small trees

Swamp & marsh

DOMINICAN REPUBLIC

Occupying the eastern two-thirds of the island of Hispaniola in the Caribbean Sea, the Dominican Republic ranks 117th in land area and 81st in size of population. During the period 1968 to 1974 the country's GDP expanded at an annual rate of about 11%, one of the highest rates in the world. However, spiraling oil prices and the devastation caused by Hurricane David and the tropical storm Frederick reduced this growth rate to 3.2% from 1974 to 1986. Agriculture accounts for well over half the country's foreign exchange earnings, although industry surpassed it some time ago in terms of contribution to the GDP. It has been estimated that, when properly developed, mineral resources alone could earn the Dominican Republic more than $1 billion in foreign exchange. Since the fall of dictator Rafael Leonidas Trujillo Molina in 1961, the state has been an active participant in the economy, especially through the Corporacion Dominicana de Empresas Estatales (Corde), which administers some 26 enterprises.

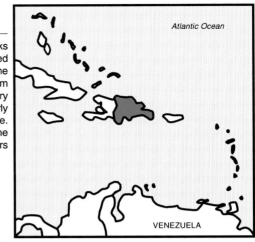

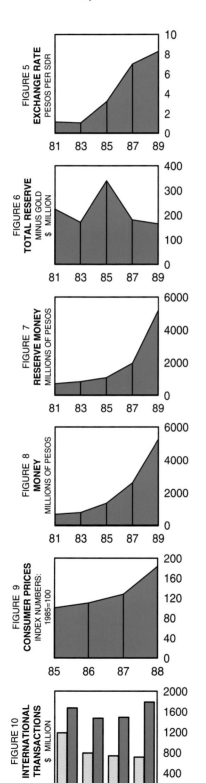

FIGURE 5 EXCHANGE RATE PESOS PER SDR

FIGURE 6 TOTAL RESERVE MINUS GOLD $ MILLION

FIGURE 7 RESERVE MONEY MILLIONS OF PESOS

FIGURE 8 MONEY MILLIONS OF PESOS

FIGURE 9 CONSUMER PRICES INDEX NUMBERS: 1985=100

FIGURE 10 INTERNATIONAL TRANSACTIONS $ MILLION
Exports   Imports

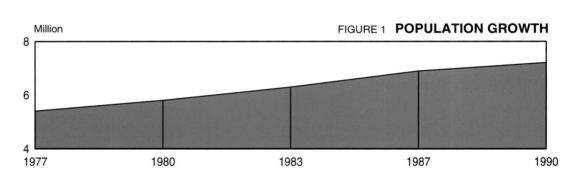

FIGURE 1 **POPULATION GROWTH**
Million

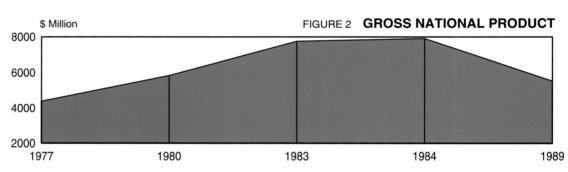

FIGURE 2 **GROSS NATIONAL PRODUCT**
$ Million

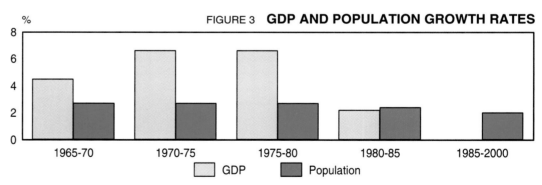

FIGURE 3 **GDP AND POPULATION GROWTH RATES**
%
GDP   Population

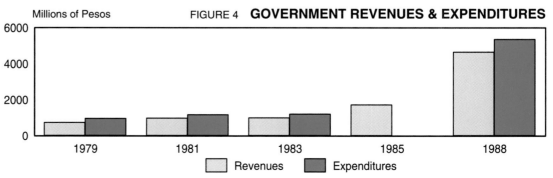

FIGURE 4 **GOVERNMENT REVENUES & EXPENDITURES**
Millions of Pesos
Revenues   Expenditures

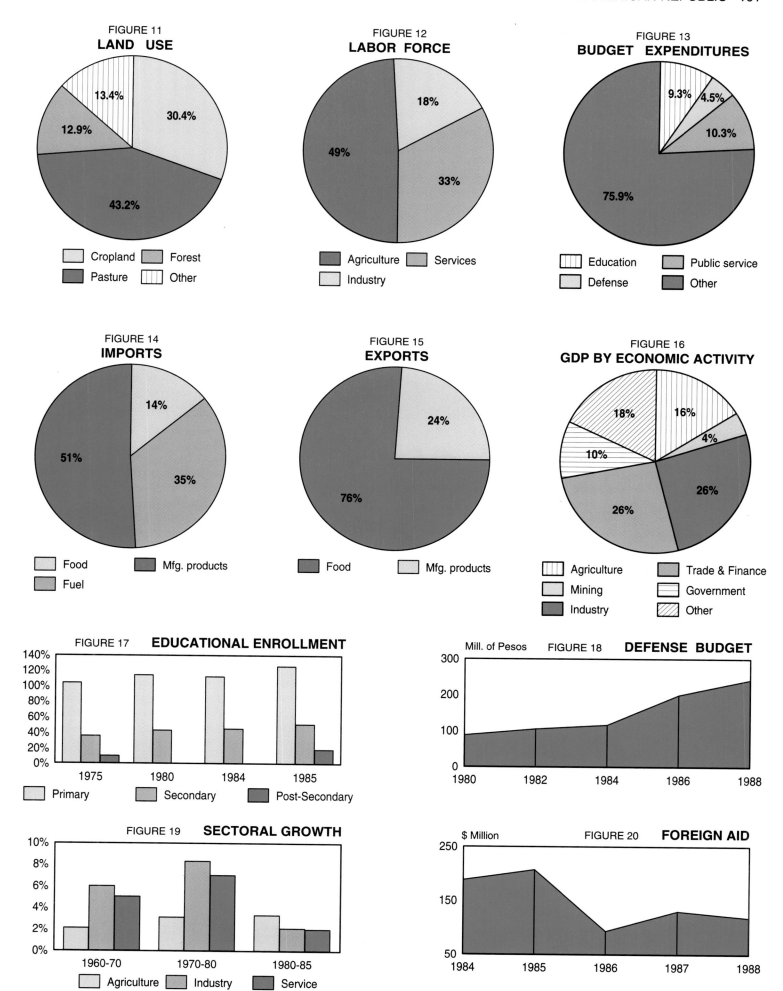

FIGURE 11
LAND USE

13.4%
30.4%
12.9%
43.2%

Cropland Forest
Pasture Other

FIGURE 12
LABOR FORCE

18%
49%
33%

Agriculture Services
Industry

FIGURE 13
BUDGET EXPENDITURES

9.3% 4.5%
10.3%
75.9%

Education Public service
Defense Other

FIGURE 14
IMPORTS

14%
51%
35%

Food Mfg. products
Fuel

FIGURE 15
EXPORTS

24%
76%

Food Mfg. products

FIGURE 16
GDP BY ECONOMIC ACTIVITY

18% 16%
4%
10%
26% 26%

Agriculture Trade & Finance
Mining Government
Industry Other

FIGURE 17 **EDUCATIONAL ENROLLMENT**

140%
120%
100%
80%
60%
40%
20%
0%
1975 1980 1984 1985

Primary Secondary Post-Secondary

Mill. of Pesos FIGURE 18 **DEFENSE BUDGET**

300
200
100
0
1980 1982 1984 1986 1988

FIGURE 19 **SECTORAL GROWTH**

10%
8%
6%
4%
2%
0%
1960-70 1970-80 1980-85

Agriculture Industry Service

$ Million FIGURE 20 **FOREIGN AID**

250
150
50
1984 1985 1986 1987 1988

ECUADOR

Straddling the Equator (after which it is named) on the Pacific coast of South America, Ecuador is the third smallest South American country, the worlds 69th largest and the 65th most populous. The fall in oil production during the early 1980s, reduced per capita annual GNP growth rate to 1% while the population growth rate was almost 3%. Currently, the petroleum industry accounts for over one-half of national export earnings and most of the foreign capital invested in the country. However, if significant new reserves are not found, Ecuador may cease to be a net exporter of petroleum. Next to oil, agriculture is the mainstay of the economy, employing over one-half of the labor force and contributing over one-quarter of the GNP. Since the liberalization of the Andean Foreign Investment Code in 1976, Ecuador has gone further than other members of the Andean Common Market to open its doors to foreign investment. The United States accounts for two-thirds of total foreign investment.

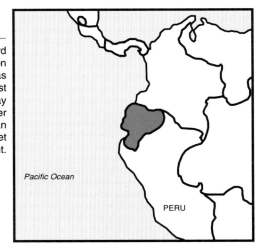

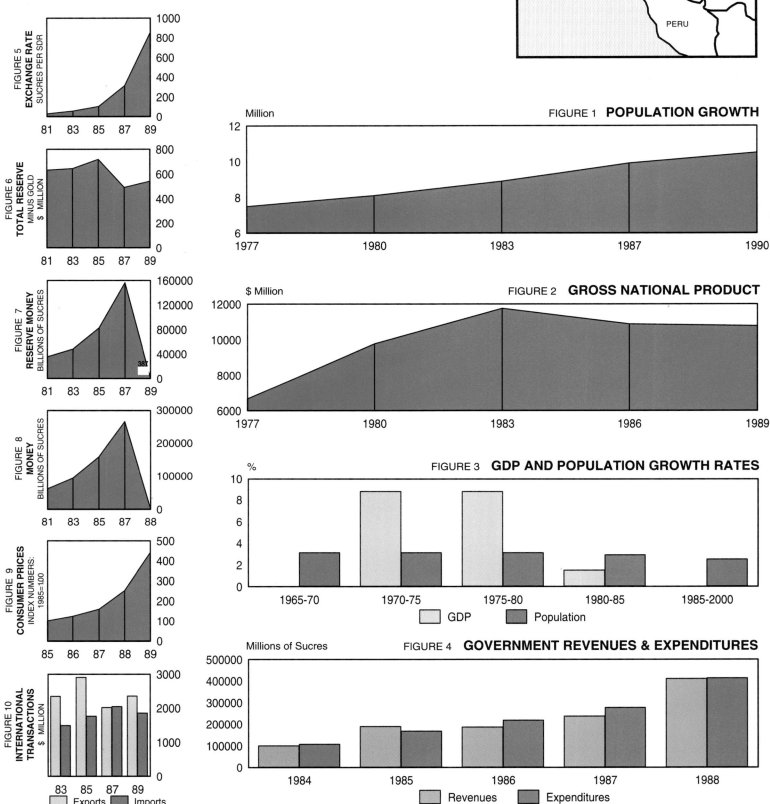

FIGURE 5 EXCHANGE RATE — SUCRES PER SDR

FIGURE 6 TOTAL RESERVE — MINUS GOLD — $ MILLION

FIGURE 7 RESERVE MONEY — BILLIONS OF SUCRES

FIGURE 8 MONEY — BILLIONS OF SUCRES

FIGURE 9 CONSUMER PRICES — INDEX NUMBERS: 1985=100

FIGURE 10 INTERNATIONAL TRANSACTIONS — $ MILLION — Exports — Imports

FIGURE 1 **POPULATION GROWTH**

FIGURE 2 **GROSS NATIONAL PRODUCT**

FIGURE 3 **GDP AND POPULATION GROWTH RATES** — GDP — Population

FIGURE 4 **GOVERNMENT REVENUES & EXPENDITURES** — Revenues — Expenditures

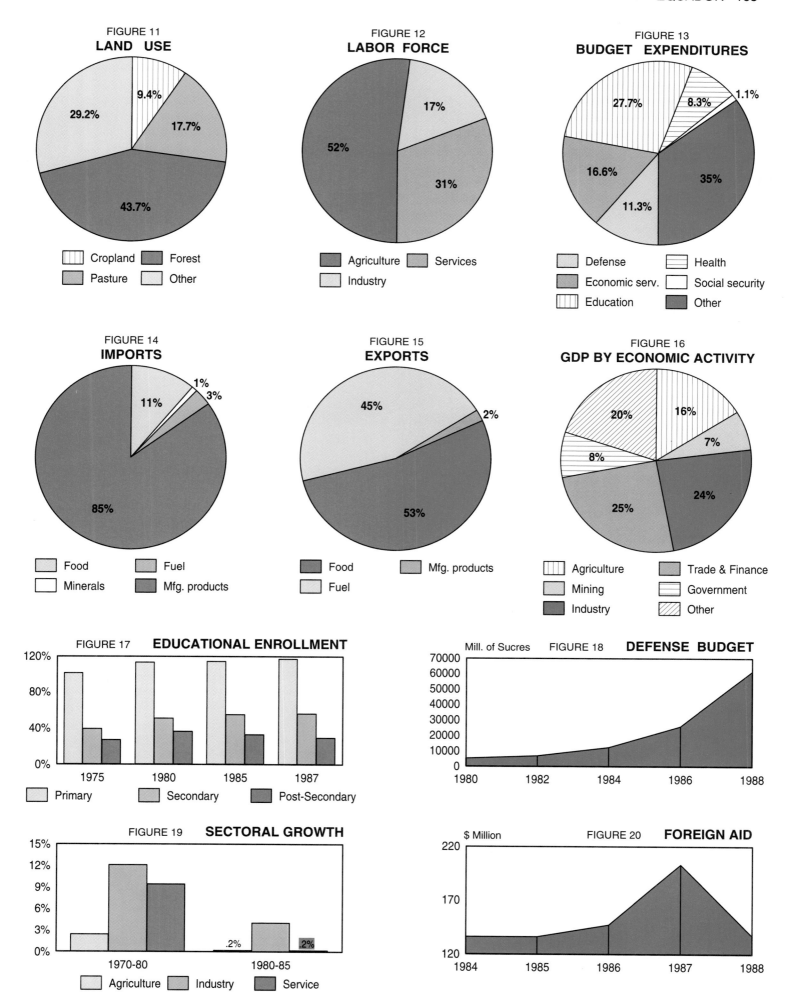

FIGURE 11
LAND USE

9.4%
29.2%
17.7%
43.7%

Cropland ▊ Forest
Pasture ▢ Other

FIGURE 12
LABOR FORCE

17%
52%
31%

▊ Agriculture ▊ Services
▢ Industry

FIGURE 13
BUDGET EXPENDITURES

27.7% 8.3% 1.1%
16.6% 35%
11.3%

Defense Health
Economic serv. Social security
Education ▊ Other

FIGURE 14
IMPORTS

11% 1% 3%
85%

Food Fuel
Minerals ▊ Mfg. products

FIGURE 15
EXPORTS

45% 2%
53%

▊ Food Mfg. products
Fuel

FIGURE 16
GDP BY ECONOMIC ACTIVITY

20% 16%
8% 7%
25% 24%

Agriculture Trade & Finance
Mining Government
▊ Industry Other

FIGURE 17 **EDUCATIONAL ENROLLMENT**

120%
80%
40%
0%
        1975   1980   1985   1987

▢ Primary ▊ Secondary ▊ Post-Secondary

Mill. of Sucres   FIGURE 18   **DEFENSE BUDGET**

70000
60000
50000
40000
30000
20000
10000
0
    1980   1982   1984   1986   1988

FIGURE 19 **SECTORAL GROWTH**

15%
12%
9%
6%
3%
0%
        1970-80   .2%   1980-85   .2%

▢ Agriculture ▊ Industry ▊ Service

$ Million   FIGURE 20   **FOREIGN AID**

220

170

120
    1984   1985   1986   1987   1988

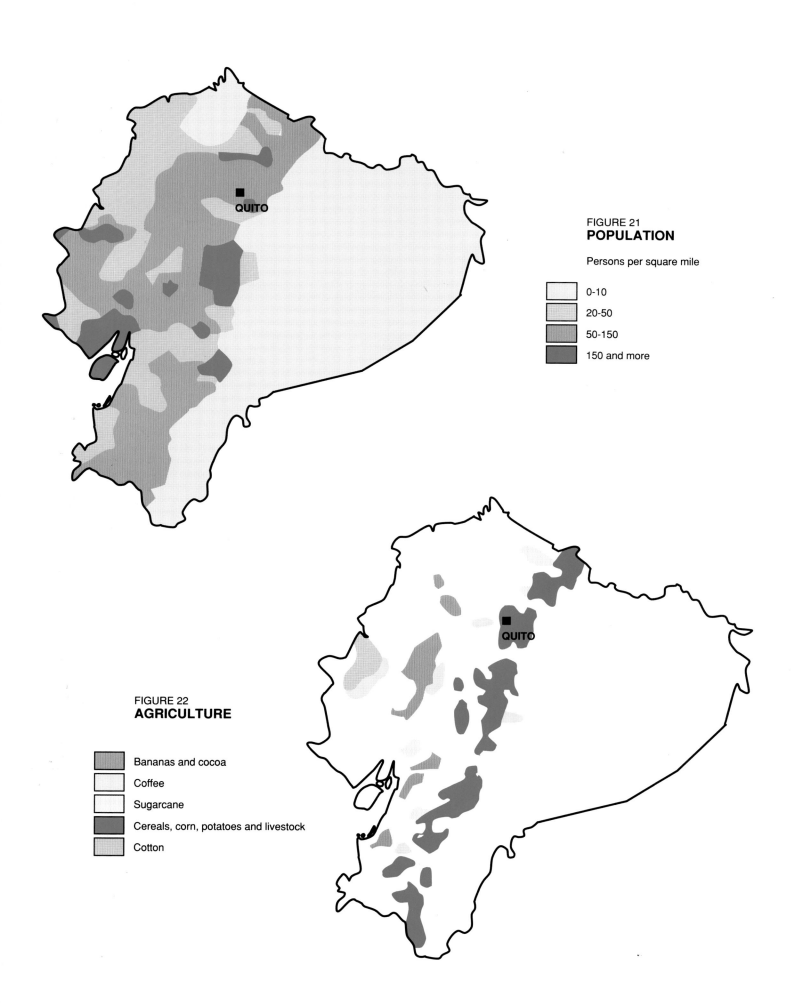

FIGURE 21
POPULATION

Persons per square mile

0-10

20-50

50-150

150 and more

QUITO

FIGURE 22
AGRICULTURE

Bananas and cocoa

Coffee

Sugarcane

Cereals, corn, potatoes and livestock

Cotton

QUITO

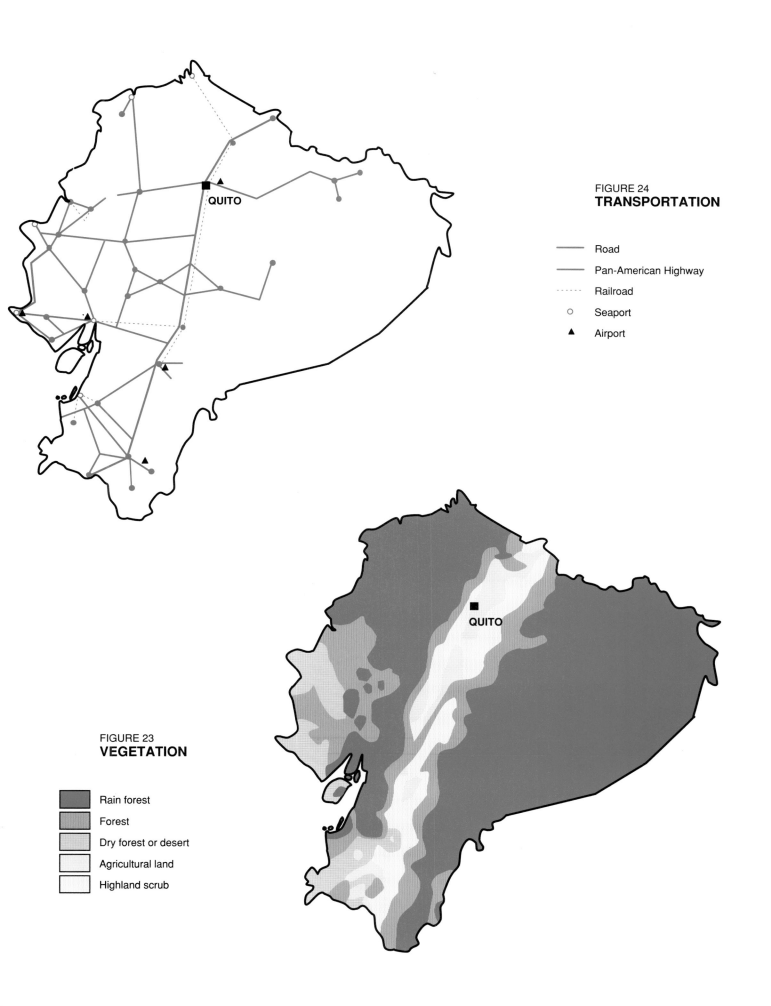

FIGURE 24
TRANSPORTATION

——— Road

——— Pan-American Highway

········· Railroad

○ Seaport

▲ Airport

QUITO

FIGURE 23
VEGETATION

Rain forest

Forest

Dry forest or desert

Agricultural land

Highland scrub

QUITO

EGYPT

Its territory straddling Africa and Asia, Egypt is the most populous Arab country, the second most populous in Africa and the 20th most populous in the world. It ranks 29th in land area. Nearly 99% of its population is compressed into 3.5% of the land area, one of the most skewed population distributions in the world. In the valley of the Nile, the population density is the fifth highest in the world. The Egyptian economy is still predominantly agrarian, and the country's farmland is intensively cultivated, with two and sometimes three crops annually and extremely high per-hectare yields. Virtually 100% of the cultivated area is irrigated. Nevertheless, Egypt is not self-sufficient in food, because much of the arable area is devoted to cash crops, such as cotton, of which Egypt has long been one of the world's leading producers. Peace with Israel has been beneficial for Egypt because it has enabled it to divert funds to economic development and to receive more favorable trade terms and investment capital from the West.

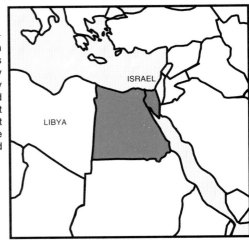

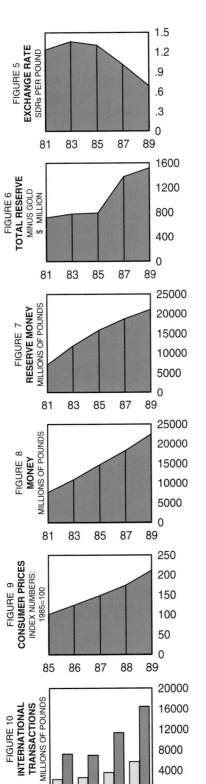

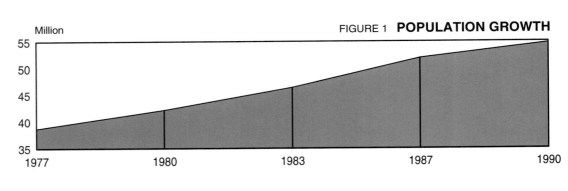

FIGURE 1 **POPULATION GROWTH**

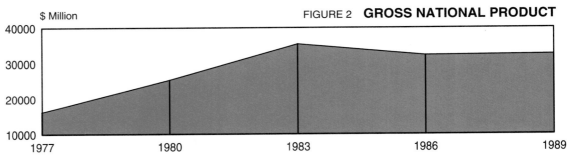

FIGURE 2 **GROSS NATIONAL PRODUCT**

FIGURE 3 **GDP AND POPULATION GROWTH RATES**

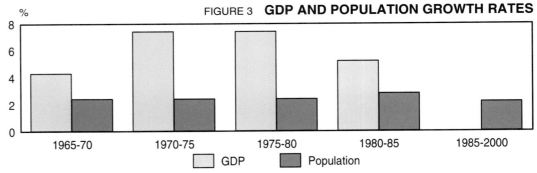

FIGURE 4 **GOVERNMENT REVENUES & EXPENDITURES**

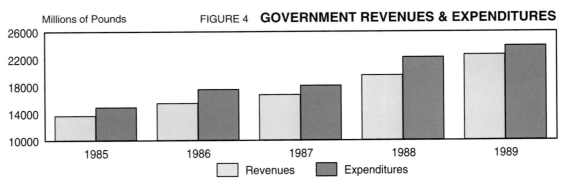

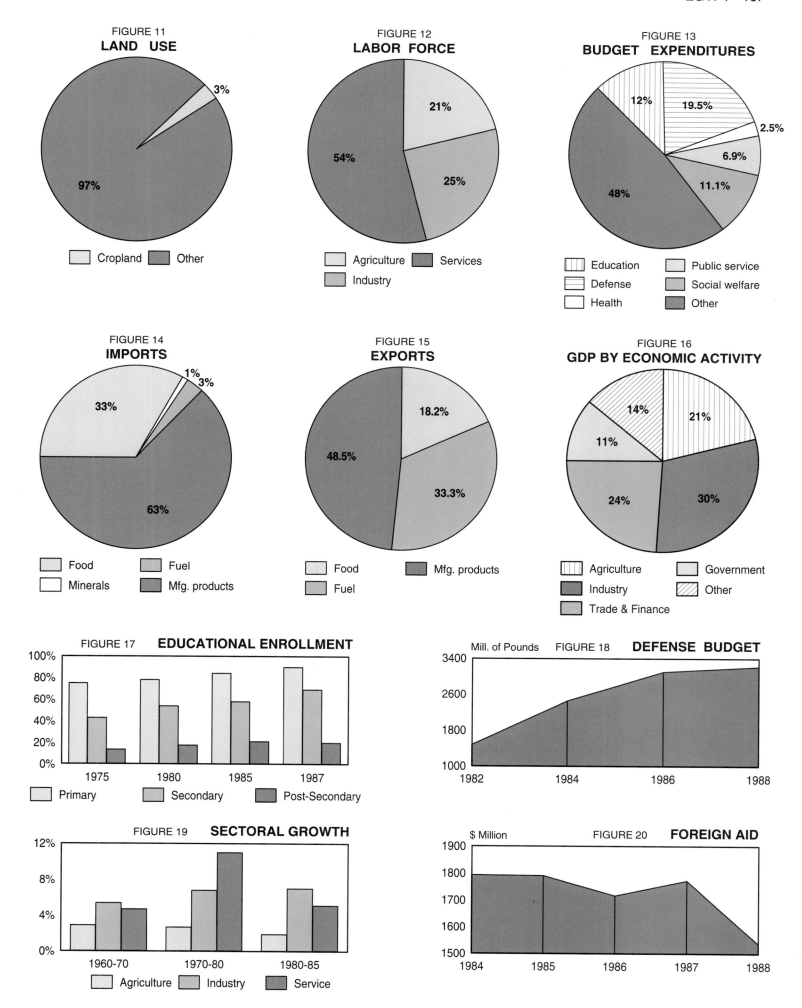

FIGURE 11
LAND USE

3%
97%

Cropland   Other

FIGURE 12
LABOR FORCE

21%
54%
25%

Agriculture   Services
Industry

FIGURE 13
BUDGET EXPENDITURES

12%   19.5%
2.5%
6.9%
48%   11.1%

Education   Public service
Defense   Social welfare
Health   Other

FIGURE 14
IMPORTS

1% 3%
33%
63%

Food   Fuel
Minerals   Mfg. products

FIGURE 15
EXPORTS

18.2%
48.5%
33.3%

Food   Mfg. products
Fuel

FIGURE 16
GDP BY ECONOMIC ACTIVITY

14%   21%
11%
24%   30%

Agriculture   Government
Industry   Other
Trade & Finance

FIGURE 17 EDUCATIONAL ENROLLMENT

Primary   Secondary   Post-Secondary

FIGURE 18 DEFENSE BUDGET
Mill. of Pounds

FIGURE 19 SECTORAL GROWTH

Agriculture   Industry   Service

FIGURE 20 FOREIGN AID
$ Million

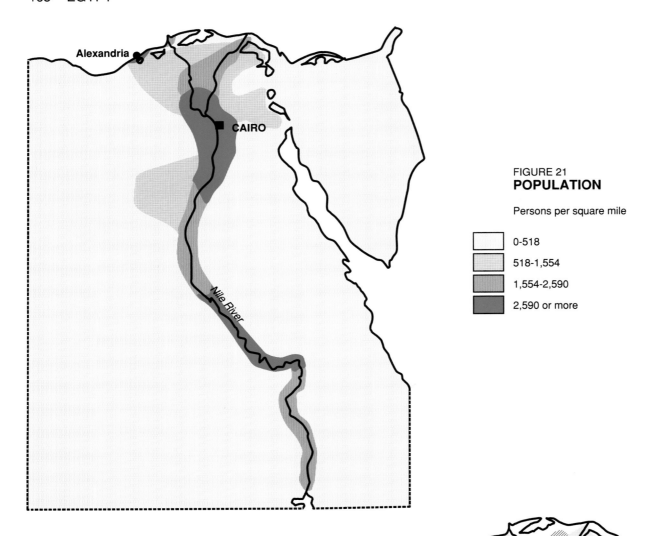

FIGURE 21
POPULATION

Persons per square mile

	0-518
	518-1,554
	1,554-2,590
	2,590 or more

FIGURE 22
ECONOMIC ACTIVITY

	Areas of cultivation
	Oilfield
	Gasfield
.....	Principal oil pipeline

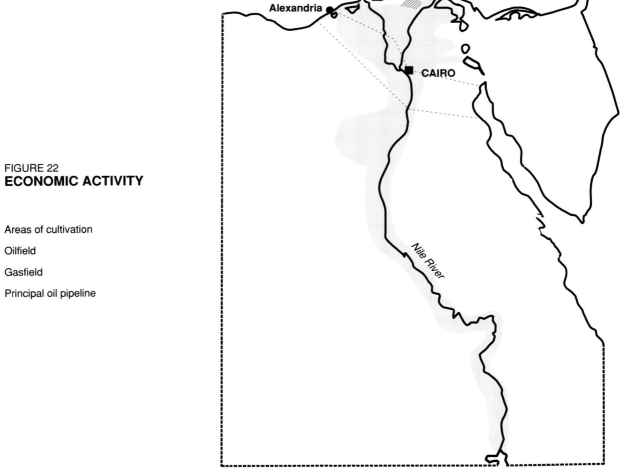

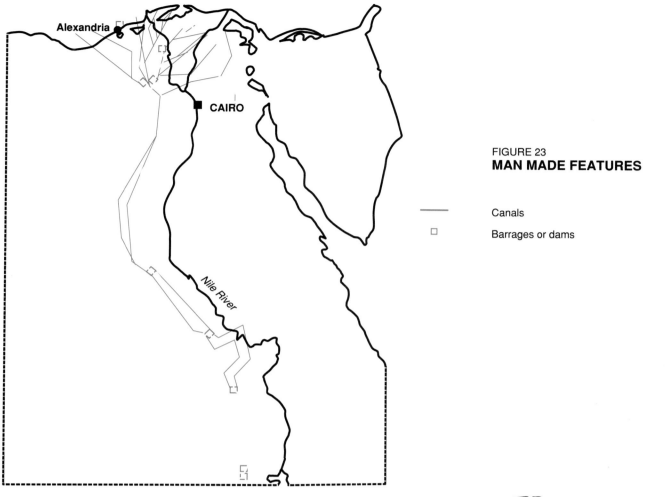

Alexandria

CAIRO

Nile River

FIGURE 23
MAN MADE FEATURES

—————— Canals

☐ Barrages or dams

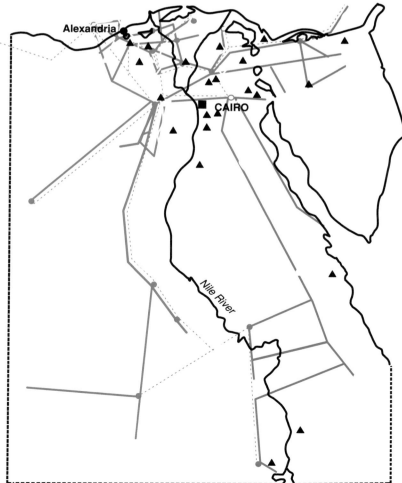

Alexandria

CAIRO

Nile River

FIGURE 24
TRANSPORTATION

○ Port

▲ Airport

········· Railroad

—————— Road

EL SALVADOR

The smallest mainland American republic, El Salvador ranks 134th in land area and 90th in size of population. Its per capita GNP growth rate trails behind the annual population growth rate. The country's basic problems include heavy pressure on available land and a very uneven distribution of income. Although more industrialized than its neighbors, the Salvadoran economy is still agricultural but this sector has been dominated historically by the "14 families," a group of wealthy landowners and business men. Until 1980 when the ruling junta launched the country's first major land reforms, the richest 5% of Salvadorans controlled 40% of the national wealth while the poorest 20% received only 2%. The same 14 families also control the industrial sector. The current political turmoil has only served to intensify the country's economic problems and during 1973-86 the GNP growth rate declined to -0.7% and nearly $1 billion in foreign investment is reported to have fled the country. Attempts to end the country's 11-year old civil war continued into 1991, but the government and rebels were unable to agree on conditions for a cease-fire.

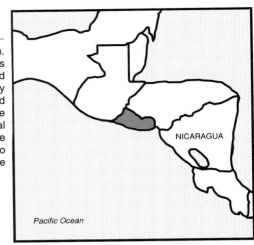

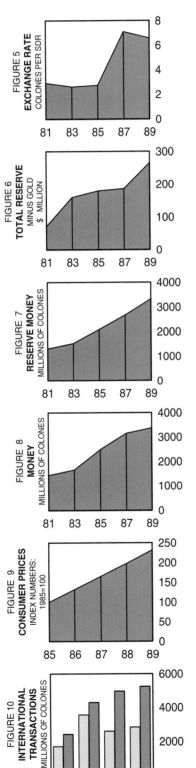

FIGURE 5 EXCHANGE RATE COLONES PER SDR

FIGURE 6 TOTAL RESERVE MINUS GOLD $ MILLION

FIGURE 7 RESERVE MONEY MILLIONS OF COLONES

FIGURE 8 MONEY MILLIONS OF COLONES

FIGURE 9 CONSUMER PRICES INDEX NUMBERS: 1985=100

FIGURE 10 INTERNATIONAL TRANSACTIONS MILLIONS OF COLONES

Exports Imports

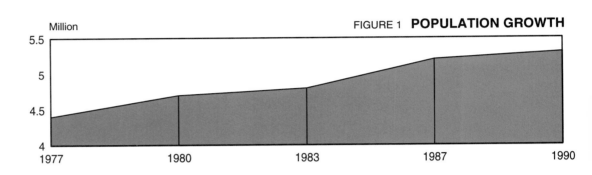

FIGURE 1 **POPULATION GROWTH**

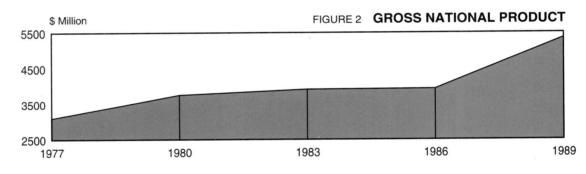

FIGURE 2 **GROSS NATIONAL PRODUCT**

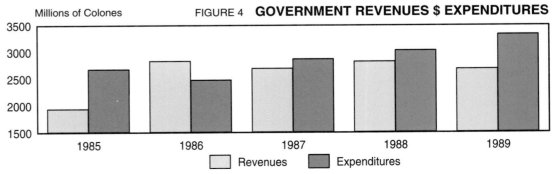

FIGURE 3 **GDP AND POPULATION GROWTH RATES**

GDP Population

FIGURE 4 **GOVERNMENT REVENUES $ EXPENDITURES**

Revenues Expenditures

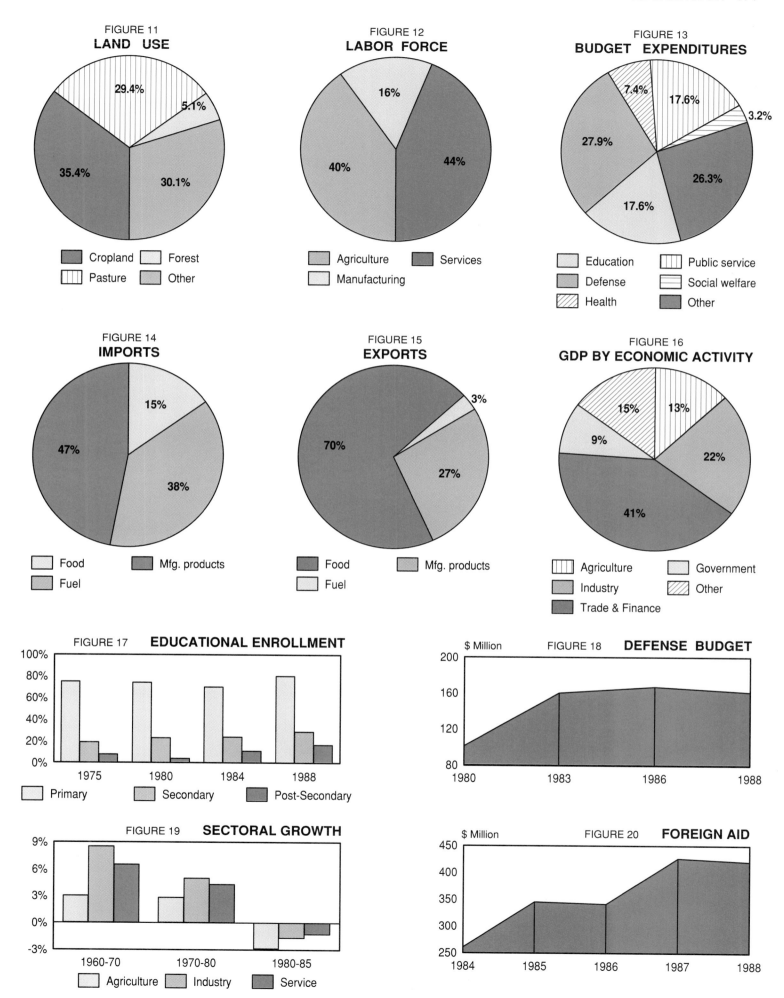

FIGURE 11
LAND USE

29.4%
5.1%
35.4%
30.1%

Cropland □ Forest
Pasture □ Other

FIGURE 12
LABOR FORCE

16%
40%
44%

Agriculture □ Services
Manufacturing

FIGURE 13
BUDGET EXPENDITURES

7.4%
17.6%
3.2%
27.9%
26.3%
17.6%

Education □ Public service
Defense □ Social welfare
Health □ Other

FIGURE 14
IMPORTS

15%
47%
38%

Food □ Mfg. products
Fuel

FIGURE 15
EXPORTS

3%
70%
27%

Food □ Mfg. products
Fuel

FIGURE 16
GDP BY ECONOMIC ACTIVITY

15%   13%
9%
22%
41%

Agriculture □ Government
Industry □ Other
Trade & Finance

FIGURE 17 **EDUCATIONAL ENROLLMENT**

100%
80%
60%
40%
20%
0%
1975   1980   1984   1988

Primary   Secondary   Post-Secondary

$ Million   FIGURE 18   **DEFENSE BUDGET**

200
160
120
80
1980   1983   1986   1988

FIGURE 19   **SECTORAL GROWTH**

9%
6%
3%
0%
-3%
1960-70   1970-80   1980-85

Agriculture   Industry   Service

$ Million   FIGURE 20   **FOREIGN AID**

450
400
350
300
250
1984   1985   1986   1987   1988

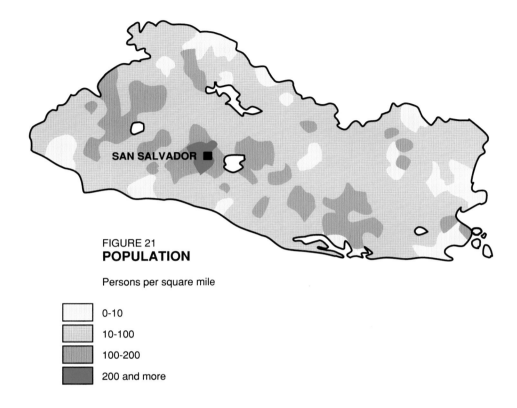

FIGURE 21
POPULATION

Persons per square mile

	0-10
	10-100
	100-200
	200 and more

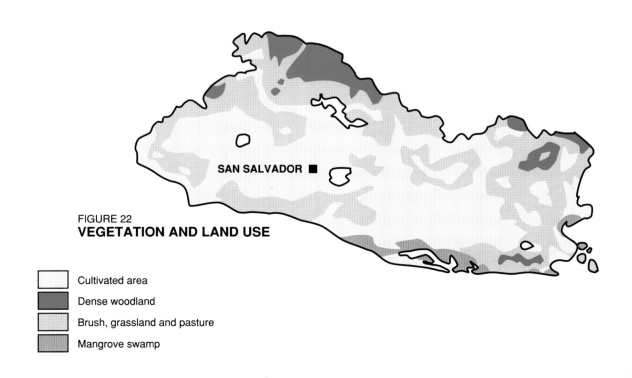

FIGURE 22
VEGETATION AND LAND USE

	Cultivated area
	Dense woodland
	Brush, grassland and pasture
	Mangrove swamp

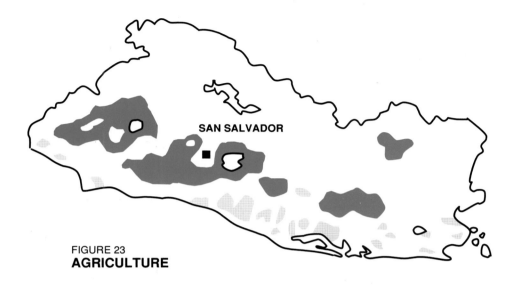

FIGURE 23
AGRICULTURE

Coffee

Cotton

FIGURE 24
TRANSPORTATION

Railroad

Road

ETHIOPIA

One of the oldest nations of the world, the home of the now-forgotten Lion of Judah, Ethiopia ranks 23th in land area and 22th in population. With a per capita GNP of $120 annually (among the lowest in the world), Ethiopia is acknowledged to be among the poorest of the poor nations of the world. More than 75% of its population subsist in absolute poverty. Despite such destitution, Ethiopia in recent years has undergone a political transformation and consolidation that has made it a power to be reckoned with in the Horn of Africa. After nearly 30 years of civil war, which began in 1962 with Eritrea's fight for independence, the fighting in Ethiopia came to an end in May 1991. A single-party socialist state since 1974, Ethiopia prepared for free, multiparty elections in its move towards democracy. A transitional government, representing Ethiopia's many political and ethnic groups, presented a charter in July 1991 which endorsed basic human rights, proposed national elections for a permanent government, and affirmed the right of Eritrea to seek independence.

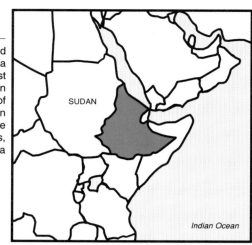

SUDAN

Indian Ocean

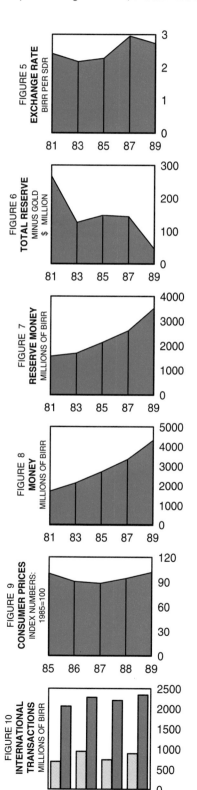

FIGURE 5 **EXCHANGE RATE** — BIRR PER SDR

FIGURE 6 **TOTAL RESERVE** — MINUS GOLD, $ MILLION

FIGURE 7 **RESERVE MONEY** — MILLIONS OF BIRR

FIGURE 8 **MONEY** — MILLIONS OF BIRR

FIGURE 9 **CONSUMER PRICES** — INDEX NUMBERS: 1985=100

FIGURE 10 **INTERNATIONAL TRANSACTIONS** — MILLIONS OF BIRR

Exports   Imports

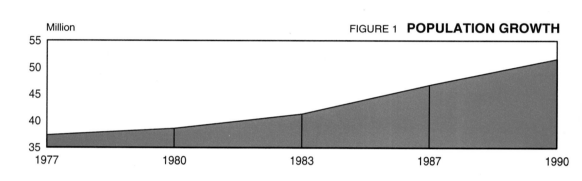

Million

FIGURE 1 **POPULATION GROWTH**

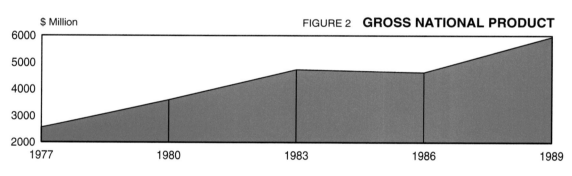

$ Million

FIGURE 2 **GROSS NATIONAL PRODUCT**

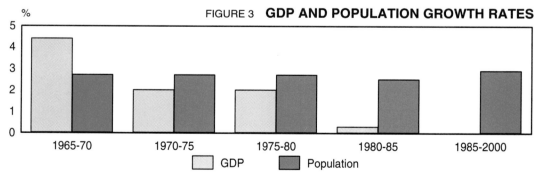

%

FIGURE 3 **GDP AND POPULATION GROWTH RATES**

GDP   Population

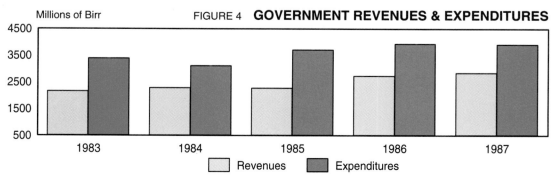

Millions of Birr

FIGURE 4 **GOVERNMENT REVENUES & EXPENDITURES**

Revenues   Expenditures

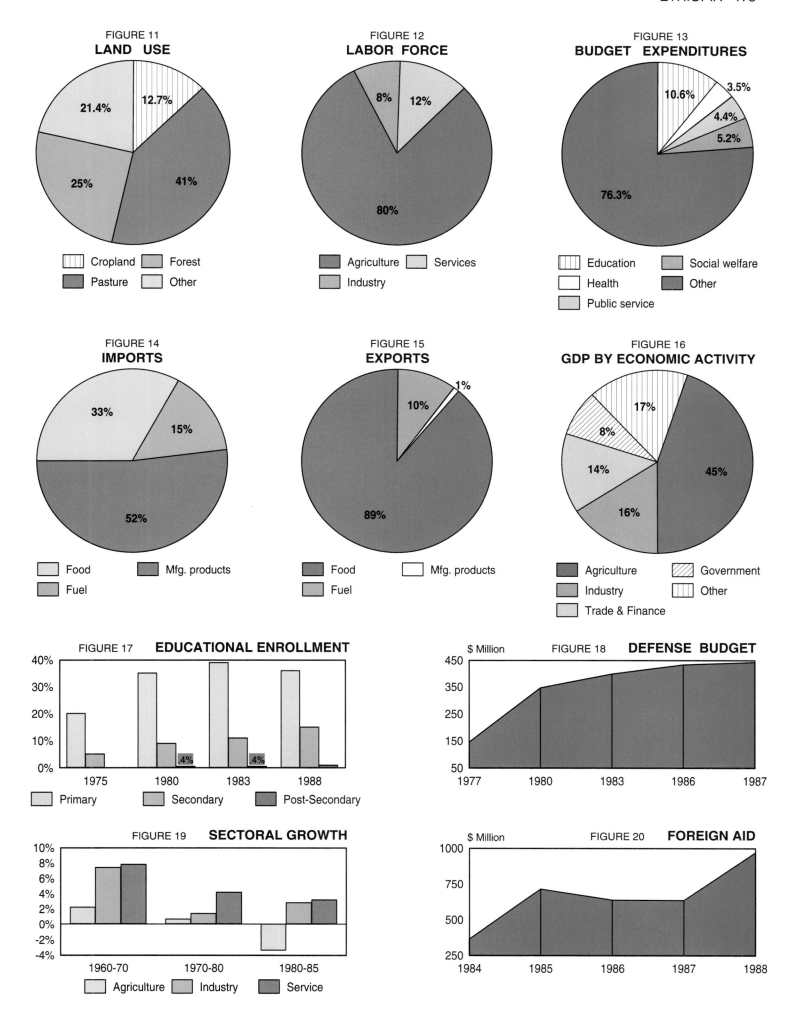

FIGURE 11
LAND   USE

12.7%
21.4%
25%
41%

Cropland   Forest
Pasture   Other

FIGURE 12
LABOR   FORCE

8%   12%
80%

Agriculture   Services
Industry

FIGURE 13
BUDGET   EXPENDITURES

10.6%   3.5%
4.4%
5.2%
76.3%

Education   Social welfare
Health   Other
Public service

FIGURE 14
IMPORTS

33%   15%
52%

Food   Mfg. products
Fuel

FIGURE 15
EXPORTS

1%
10%
89%

Food   Mfg. products
Fuel

FIGURE 16
GDP BY ECONOMIC ACTIVITY

17%
8%
14%   45%
16%

Agriculture   Government
Industry   Other
Trade & Finance

FIGURE 17   **EDUCATIONAL ENROLLMENT**

40%
30%
20%
10%
0%
.4%   .4%
1975   1980   1983   1988

Primary   Secondary   Post-Secondary

$ Million   FIGURE 18   **DEFENSE BUDGET**

450
350
250
150
50
1977   1980   1983   1986   1987

FIGURE 19   **SECTORAL GROWTH**

10%
8%
6%
4%
2%
0%
-2%
-4%
1960-70   1970-80   1980-85

Agriculture   Industry   Service

$ Million   FIGURE 20   **FOREIGN AID**

1000
750
500
250
1984   1985   1986   1987   1988

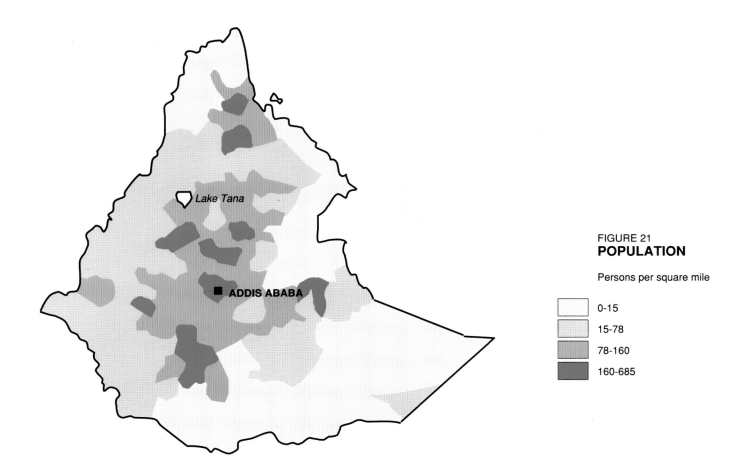

FIGURE 21
POPULATION

Persons per square mile

- 0-15
- 15-78
- 78-160
- 160-685

Lake Tana

■ ADDIS ABABA

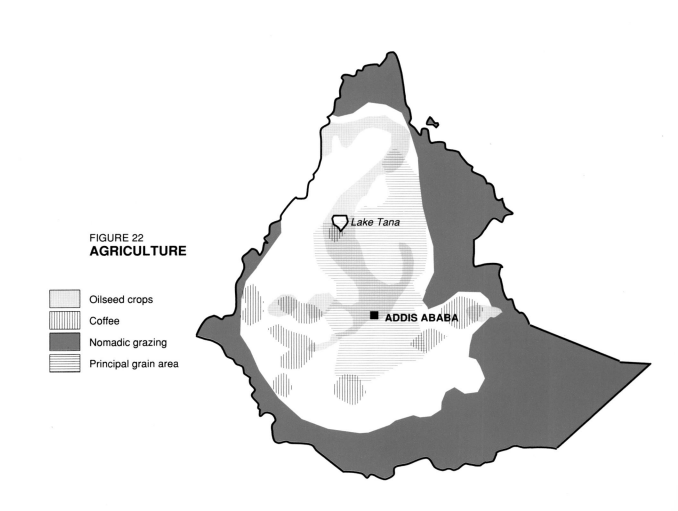

FIGURE 22
AGRICULTURE

- Oilseed crops
- Coffee
- Nomadic grazing
- Principal grain area

Lake Tana

■ ADDIS ABABA

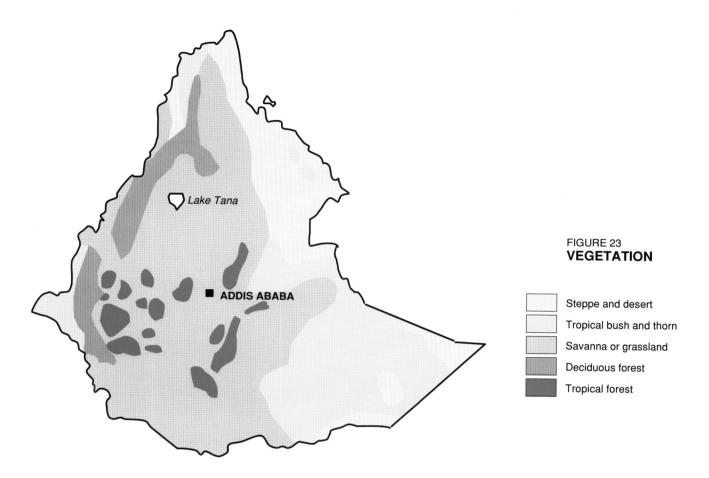

FIGURE 23
VEGETATION

Steppe and desert

Tropical bush and thorn

Savanna or grassland

Deciduous forest

Tropical forest

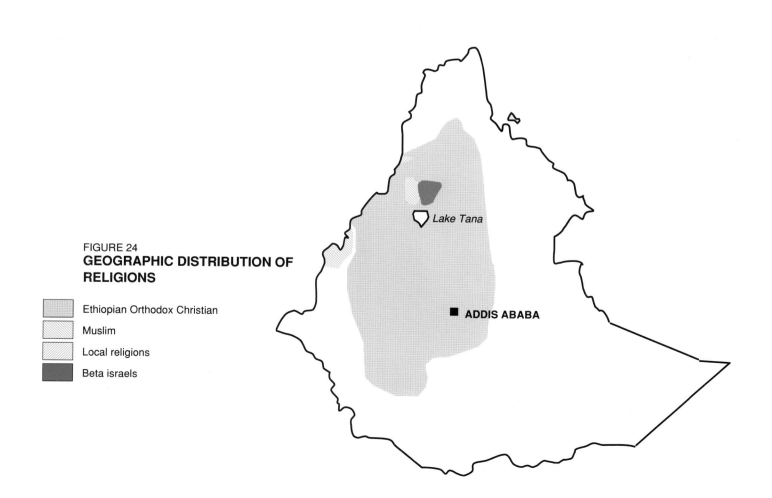

FIGURE 24
GEOGRAPHIC DISTRIBUTION OF RELIGIONS

Ethiopian Orthodox Christian

Muslim

Local religions

Beta israels

GABON

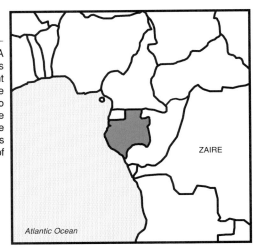

ZAIRE

Atlantic Ocean

Spanning the Equator on the west coast of Africa, Gabon ranks 70th in land area and 132nd in population. A small population and enormous mineral resources have combined to make Gabon one of the wealthiest nations in black Africa, one of the four African nations in the upper middle-income group. Despite this apparent prosperity, the benefits of national wealth have not trickled down to the lower classes. Although agriculture employs more than half the labor force, less than 1% of the land is cultivated and agricultural contributions to the GDP are negligible. Manufacturing is also a relatively small sector. On the other hand, petroleum, the country's most valuable export, accounts for more than one-half the government revenues. The output of the offshore wells may be exhausted by 2000 and vigorous efforts are being made to find new sources. If oil does run out, Gabon has other mineral resources to bank on, including 1 billion tons of iron ore and 20,000 tons of uranium.

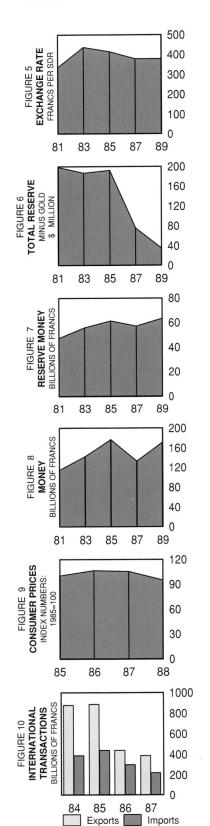

FIGURE 5 EXCHANGE RATE FRANCS PER SDR

FIGURE 6 TOTAL RESERVE MINUS GOLD $ MILLION

FIGURE 7 RESERVE MONEY BILLIONS OF FRANCS

FIGURE 8 MONEY BILLIONS OF FRANCS

FIGURE 9 CONSUMER PRICES INDEX NUMBERS: 1985=100

FIGURE 10 INTERNATIONAL TRANSACTIONS BILLIONS OF FRANCS
Exports Imports

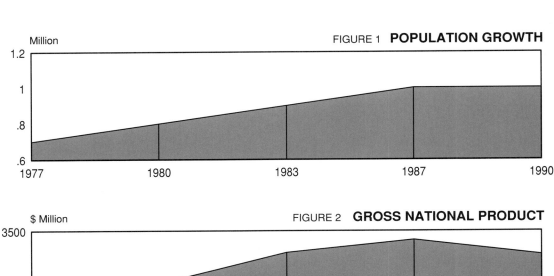

FIGURE 1 **POPULATION GROWTH**

Million

FIGURE 2 **GROSS NATIONAL PRODUCT**

$ Million

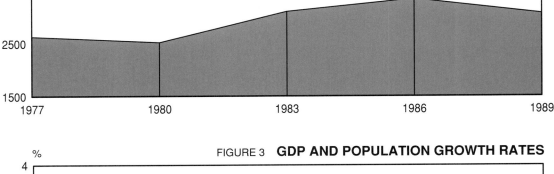

FIGURE 3 **GDP AND POPULATION GROWTH RATES**

%

GDP Population

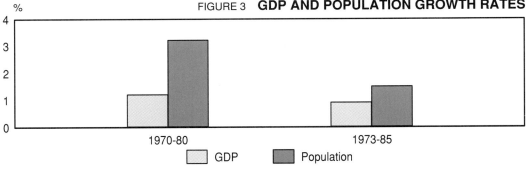

FIGURE 4 **GOVERNMENT REVENUES & EXPENDITURES**

$ Million

Revenues Expenditures

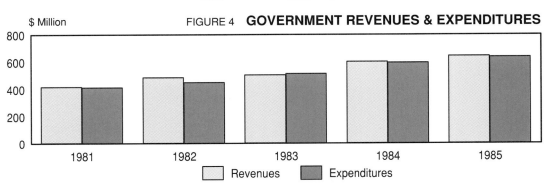

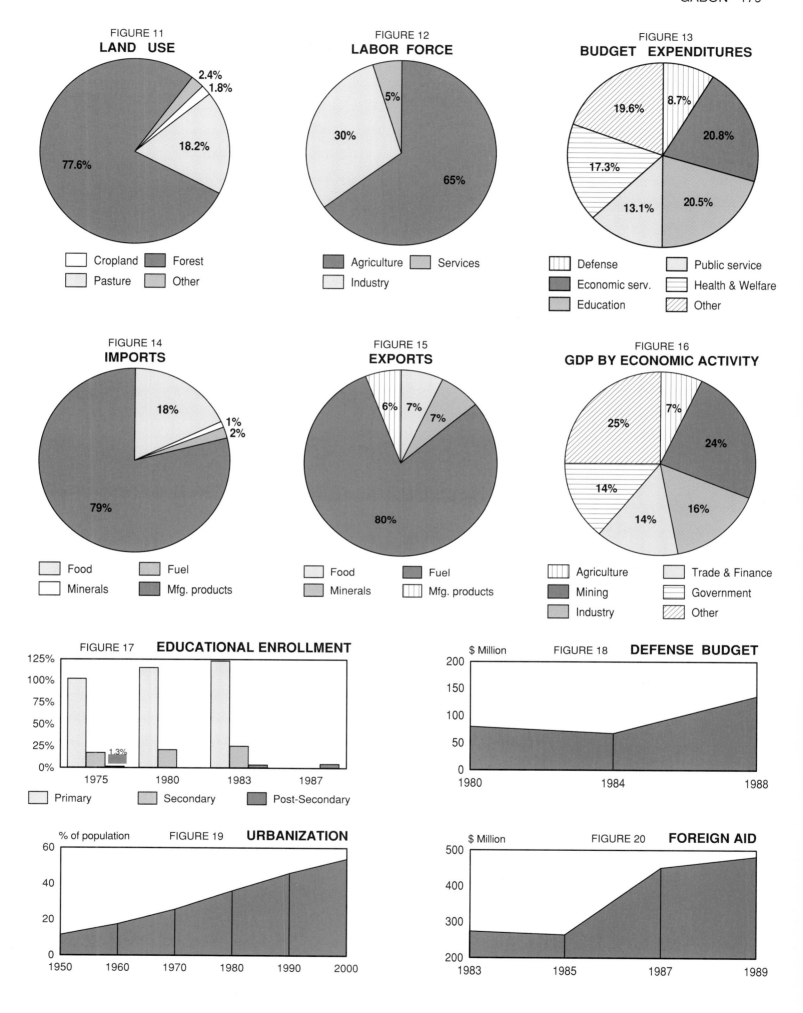

FIGURE 11
LAND   USE

2.4%
1.8%
18.2%
77.6%

Cropland Forest
Pasture   Other

FIGURE 12
LABOR   FORCE

5%
30%
65%

Agriculture   Services
Industry

FIGURE 13
BUDGET   EXPENDITURES

19.6%   8.7%
17.3%   20.8%
13.1%   20.5%

Defense   Public service
Economic serv.   Health & Welfare
Education   Other

FIGURE 14
IMPORTS

18%
1%
2%
79%

Food   Fuel
Minerals   Mfg. products

FIGURE 15
EXPORTS

6% 7% 7%
80%

Food   Fuel
Minerals   Mfg. products

FIGURE 16
GDP BY ECONOMIC ACTIVITY

25%   7%
24%
14%   16%
14%

Agriculture   Trade & Finance
Mining   Government
Industry   Other

FIGURE 17   **EDUCATIONAL ENROLLMENT**

125%
100%
75%
50%
25%   1.3%
0%
1975   1980   1983   1987

Primary   Secondary   Post-Secondary

$ Million   FIGURE 18   **DEFENSE BUDGET**

200
150
100
50
0
1980   1984   1988

% of population   FIGURE 19   **URBANIZATION**

60
40
20
0
1950   1960   1970   1980   1990   2000

$ Million   FIGURE 20   **FOREIGN AID**

500
400
300
200
1983   1985   1987   1989

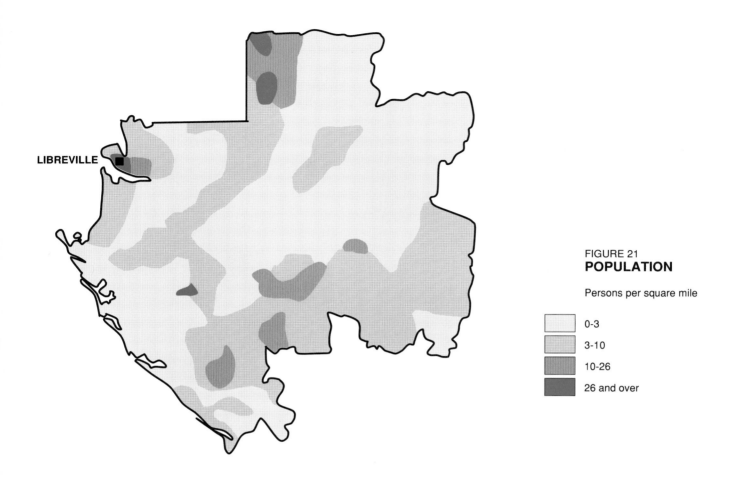

FIGURE 21
POPULATION

Persons per square mile

- 0-3
- 3-10
- 10-26
- 26 and over

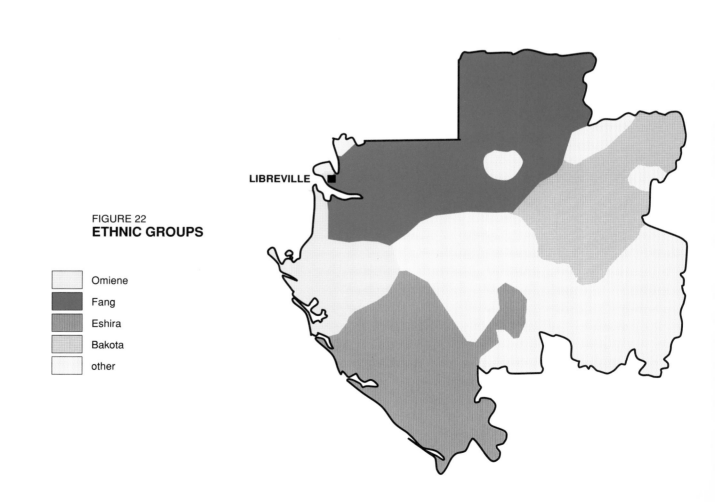

FIGURE 22
ETHNIC GROUPS

- Omiene
- Fang
- Eshira
- Bakota
- other

FIGURE 23
VEGETATION

Tropical rain forest

Wooded savanna

Swamp or marsh

LIBREVILLE

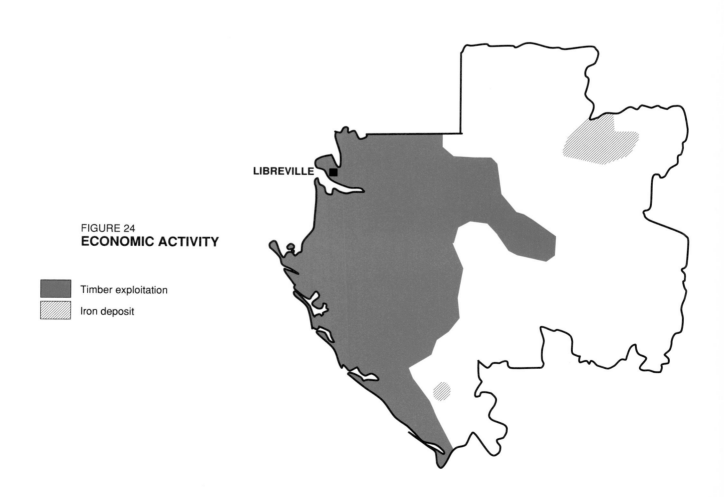

FIGURE 24
ECONOMIC ACTIVITY

Timber exploitation

Iron deposit

LIBREVILLE

GHANA

Located on the west coast of Africa and known as the Gold Coast before independence, Ghana ranks 78th in land area and 55th in population. Once a prosperous country and the world's leading cocoa producer, Ghana was one of the first Anglophone countries to gain independence and for a while served as a model and mentor for its neighbors. But Kwame Nkrumah's disastrous political and economic experiments set the country on a bumpy road leading to what the Economist once described as an "abysmal chaos," characterized by chronic instability, inefficiency, corruption, mismanagement and shortages of almost everything. Succeeding governments have tried to remedy the situation but ended up making it worse. The inflation rate stood at 50.8% during 1980-1986, industry was operating at 30% of capacity because of shortages of raw materials and the GDP declined by 5%. The return of Lt. Jerry Rawlings to power has brought some positive signs for the immediate future but economic recovery is still not in sight.

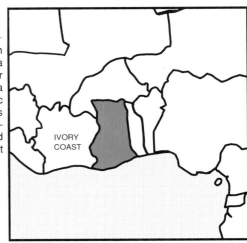

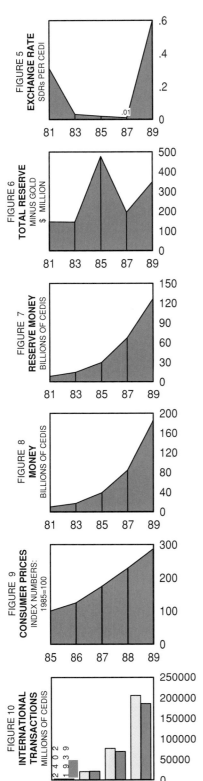

FIGURE 5 EXCHANGE RATE — SDRs PER CEDI

FIGURE 6 TOTAL RESERVE — MINUS GOLD $ MILLION

FIGURE 7 RESERVE MONEY — BILLIONS OF CEDIS

FIGURE 8 MONEY — BILLIONS OF CEDIS

FIGURE 9 CONSUMER PRICES — INDEX NUMBERS: 1985=100

FIGURE 10 INTERNATIONAL TRANSACTIONS — MILLIONS OF CEDIS — Exports / Imports

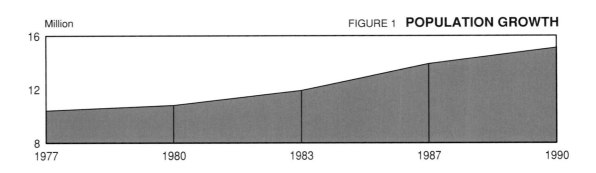

Million

FIGURE 1 **POPULATION GROWTH**

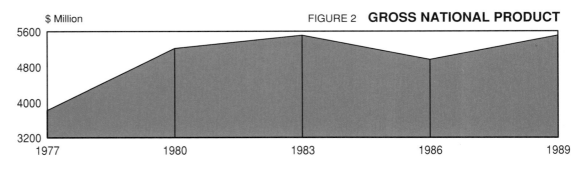

$ Million

FIGURE 2 **GROSS NATIONAL PRODUCT**

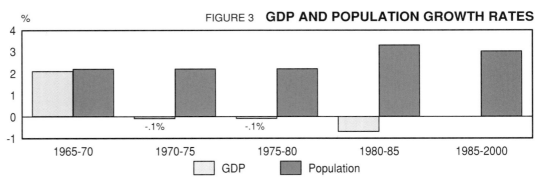

%

FIGURE 3 **GDP AND POPULATION GROWTH RATES**

GDP   Population

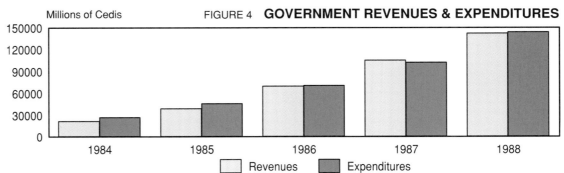

Millions of Cedis

FIGURE 4 **GOVERNMENT REVENUES & EXPENDITURES**

Revenues   Expenditures

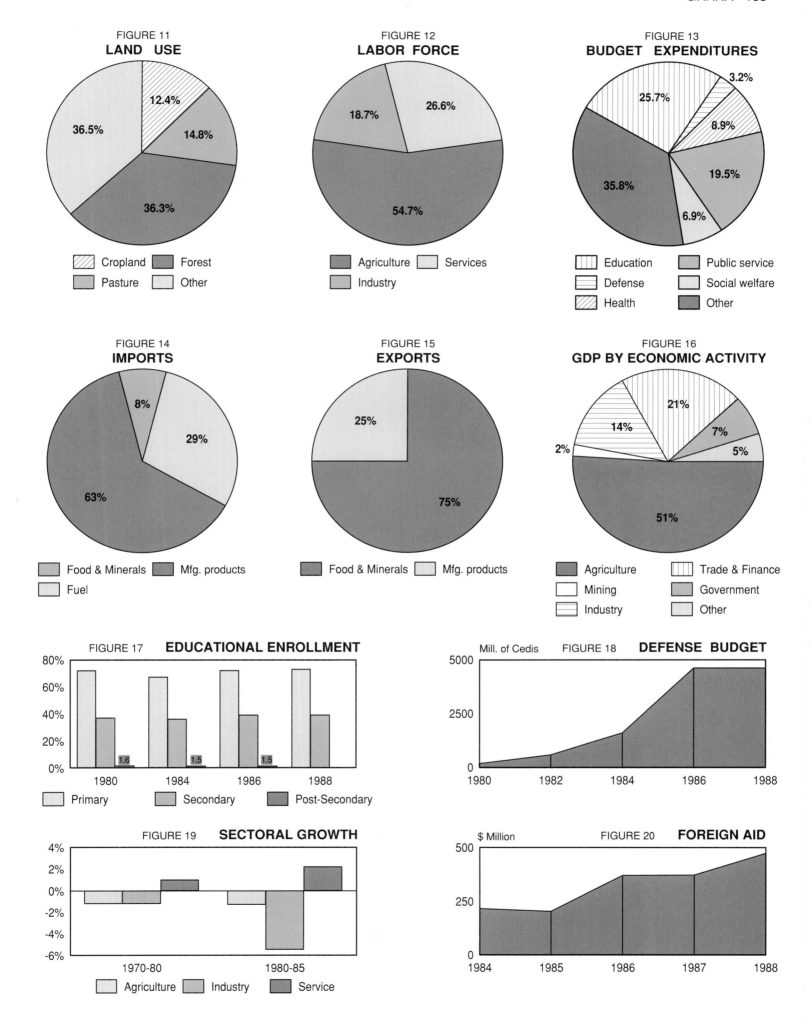

FIGURE 11
LAND USE

12.4%
36.5%
14.8%
36.3%

Cropland · Forest
Pasture · Other

FIGURE 12
LABOR FORCE

26.6%
18.7%
54.7%

Agriculture · Services
Industry

FIGURE 13
BUDGET EXPENDITURES

3.2%
25.7%
8.9%
19.5%
35.8%
6.9%

Education · Public service
Defense · Social welfare
Health · Other

FIGURE 14
IMPORTS

8%
29%
63%

Food & Minerals · Mfg. products
Fuel

FIGURE 15
EXPORTS

25%
75%

Food & Minerals · Mfg. products

FIGURE 16
GDP BY ECONOMIC ACTIVITY

21%
14%
7%
2%
5%
51%

Agriculture · Trade & Finance
Mining · Government
Industry · Other

FIGURE 17 EDUCATIONAL ENROLLMENT

1980 1984 1986 1988
1.6 1.5 1.5

Primary · Secondary · Post-Secondary

Mill. of Cedis FIGURE 18 DEFENSE BUDGET
5000 2500 0
1980 1982 1984 1986 1988

FIGURE 19 SECTORAL GROWTH
4% 2% 0% -2% -4% -6%
1970-80 1980-85
Agriculture · Industry · Service

$ Million FIGURE 20 FOREIGN AID
500 250 0
1984 1985 1986 1987 1988

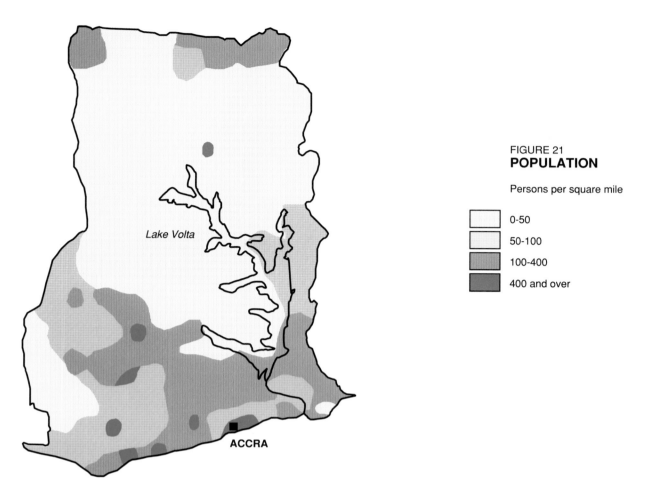

FIGURE 21
POPULATION

Persons per square mile

0-50
50-100
100-400
400 and over

Lake Volta

ACCRA

FIGURE 22
ETHNIC GROUPS

Akan
Ewe
Guan
Gub subfamily
Ga-Adangbe

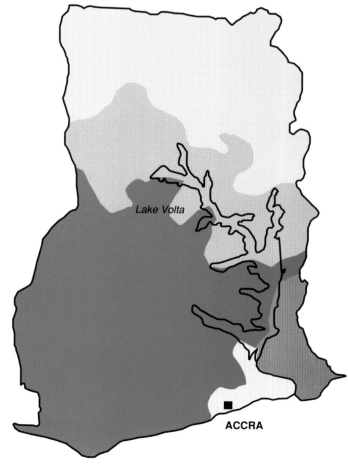

Lake Volta

ACCRA

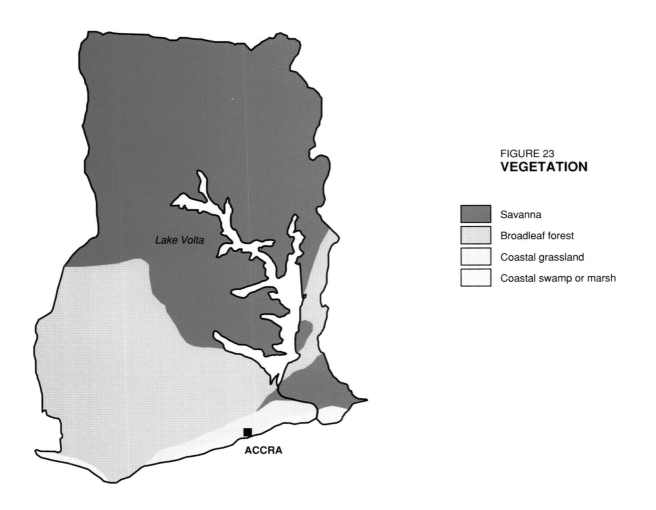

FIGURE 23
VEGETATION

Savanna
Broadleaf forest
Coastal grassland
Coastal swamp or marsh

FIGURE 24
ECONOMIC ACTIVITY

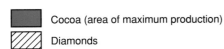

Cocoa (area of maximum production)
Diamonds

GUATEMALA

The northernmost and the most populous of the Central American republics, Guatemala ranks 99th in land area and 69th in population. As in other countries of the region, the economy is characterized by extreme disparities in the distribution of income and this has produced social tensions spilling over into the political sphere in the form of sporadic insurgences. The agricultural sector accounts for over one-quarter of the GDP and two-thirds of export earnings, the principal products being coffee, sugar and bananas. The country's agricultural wealth is concentrated in the hands of a small group of ladinos and foreigners (although the legendary United Fruit—later United Brands—has sold out its interests in Guatemala, U.S. interests are still substantial) who also control the larger manufacturing industries as well as trade and finance. The richest 2% are believed to control between 50% and 80% of the cultivable land, and the government's halfhearted land reform efforts have proved ineffective.

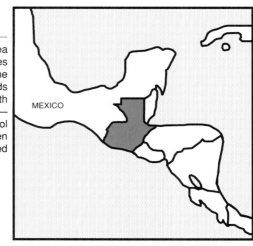

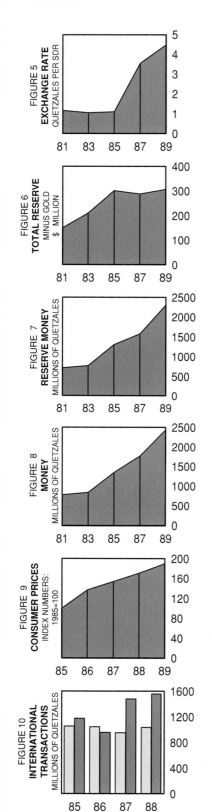

FIGURE 5 **EXCHANGE RATE** QUETZALES PER SDR

FIGURE 6 **TOTAL RESERVE** MINUS GOLD $ MILLION

FIGURE 7 **RESERVE MONEY** MILLIONS OF QUETZALES

FIGURE 8 **MONEY** MILLIONS OF QUETZALES

FIGURE 9 **CONSUMER PRICES** INDEX NUMBERS: 1985=100

FIGURE 10 **INTERNATIONAL TRANSACTIONS** MILLIONS OF QUETZALES
Exports Imports

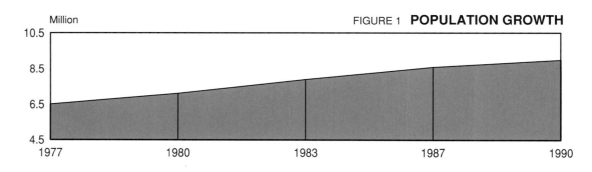

FIGURE 1 **POPULATION GROWTH**
Million

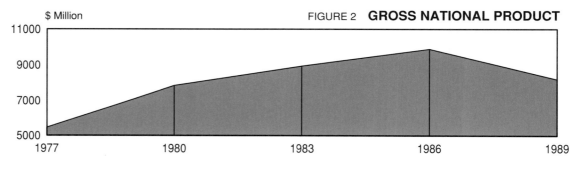

FIGURE 2 **GROSS NATIONAL PRODUCT**
$ Million

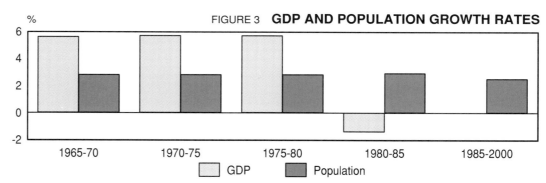

FIGURE 3 **GDP AND POPULATION GROWTH RATES**
%
GDP Population

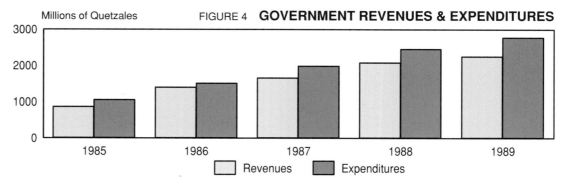

FIGURE 4 **GOVERNMENT REVENUES & EXPENDITURES**
Millions of Quetzales
Revenues Expenditures

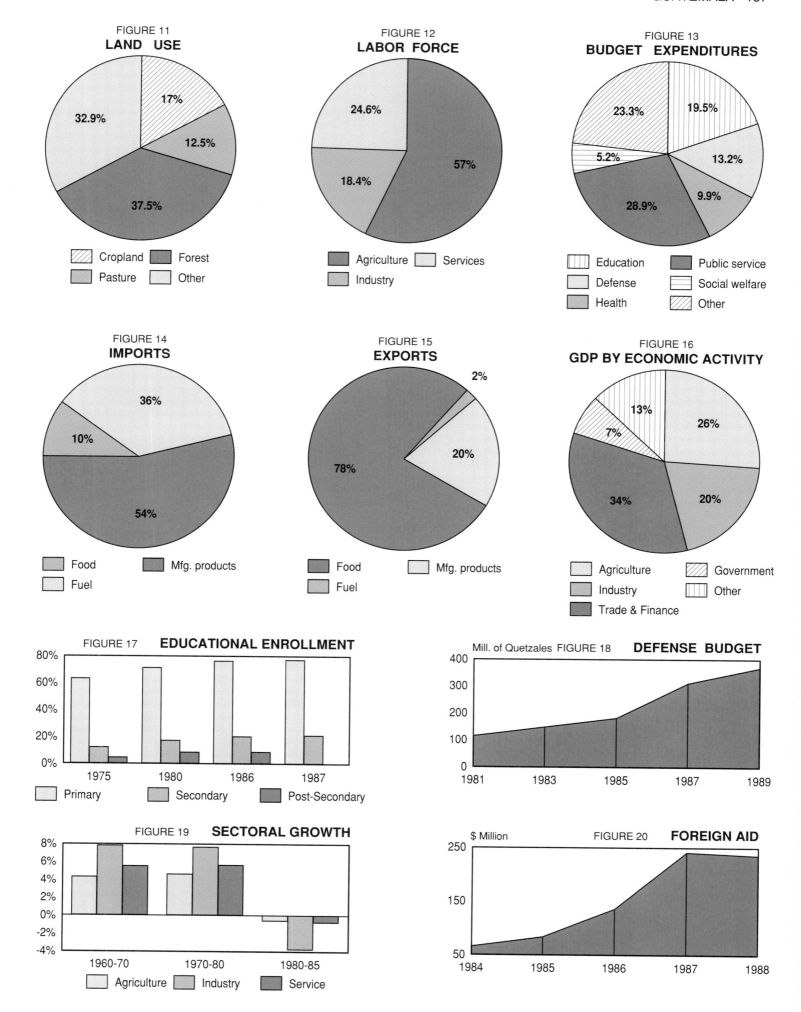

FIGURE 11
LAND USE

17%
32.9%
12.5%
37.5%

Cropland
Pasture
Forest
Other

FIGURE 12
LABOR FORCE

24.6%
18.4%
57%

Agriculture
Industry
Services

FIGURE 13
BUDGET EXPENDITURES

23.3%
19.5%
5.2%
13.2%
28.9%
9.9%

Education
Defense
Health
Public service
Social welfare
Other

FIGURE 14
IMPORTS

36%
10%
54%

Food
Fuel
Mfg. products

FIGURE 15
EXPORTS

2%
78%
20%

Food
Fuel
Mfg. products

FIGURE 16
GDP BY ECONOMIC ACTIVITY

13%
7%
26%
34%
20%

Agriculture
Industry
Trade & Finance
Government
Other

FIGURE 17 **EDUCATIONAL ENROLLMENT**

80%
60%
40%
20%
0%

1975   1980   1986   1987

Primary   Secondary   Post-Secondary

Mill. of Quetzales FIGURE 18 **DEFENSE BUDGET**

400
300
200
100
0

1981   1983   1985   1987   1989

FIGURE 19 **SECTORAL GROWTH**

8%
6%
4%
2%
0%
-2%
-4%

1960-70   1970-80   1980-85

Agriculture   Industry   Service

$ Million   FIGURE 20   **FOREIGN AID**

250
150
50

1984   1985   1986   1987   1988

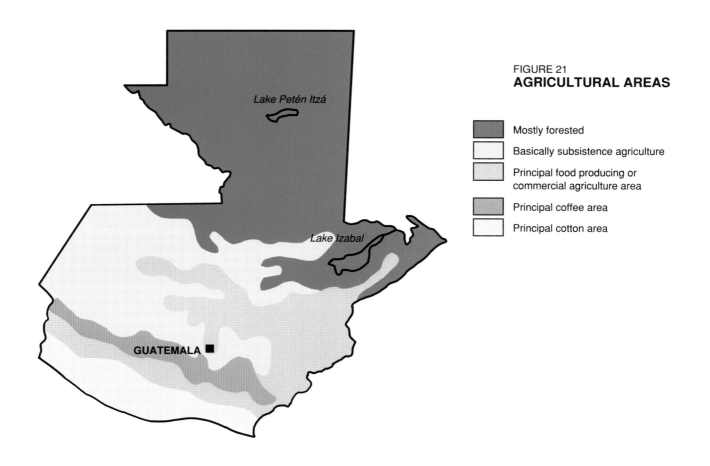

FIGURE 21
AGRICULTURAL AREAS

Mostly forested

Basically subsistence agriculture

Principal food producing or
commercial agriculture area

Principal coffee area

Principal cotton area

FIGURE 22
VEGETATION

Forest

Scrub

Thorn forest

Savanna and pasture

Swamp or marsh

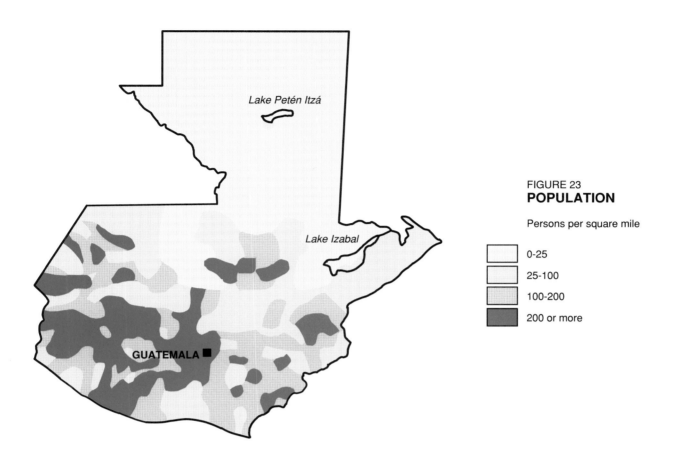

FIGURE 23
POPULATION

Persons per square mile

- 0-25
- 25-100
- 100-200
- 200 or more

Lake Petén Itzá

Lake Izabal

GUATEMALA ■

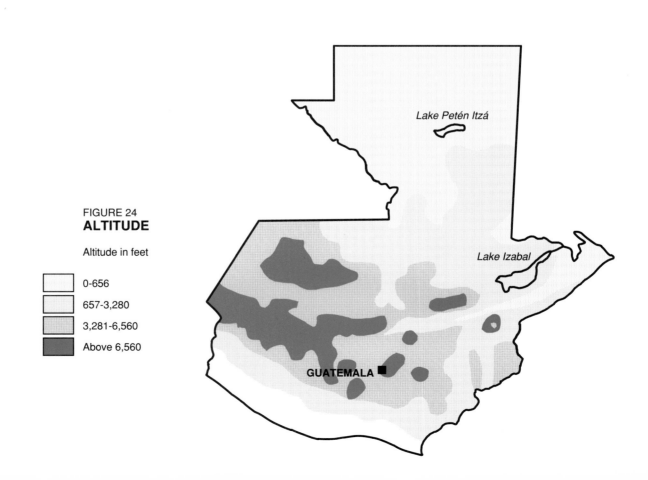

FIGURE 24
ALTITUDE

Altitude in feet

- 0-656
- 657-3,280
- 3,281-6,560
- Above 6,560

Lake Petén Itzá

Lake Izabal

GUATEMALA ■

GUINEA

Located on the bulge of West Africa, and one of the most politically stable countries in Africa, Guinea ranks 75th in land area and 83rd in population. Despite enormous mineral resources—its bauxite resources are reputed to be the third largest in the world—the Guinean economy has never really taken off and by all standard indicators it remains one of the poorest countries in the world, where 75% of the population subsists in absolute poverty. Many of the country's intractable problems could be traced to former President Ahmed Sekou Toure's unbending dedication to his concept of a centrally planned economy, especially as applied to agriculture, which employs 81% of the work force and contributes 40% of the GDP. After 30 years of independence, the collectivized economy has been a dismal failure resulting in the loss of the country's former self-sufficiency in food. More recently, however, the government has been restoring elements of private enterprise to all sectors and stepping up the exploitation of mineral resources to generate investment capital.

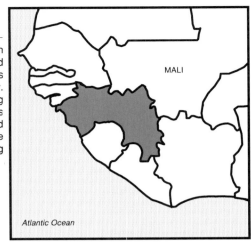

I.M.F.
INFORMATION
NOT
AVAILABLE

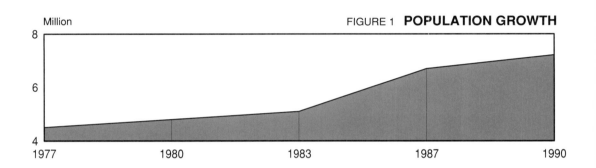

FIGURE 1 **POPULATION GROWTH**

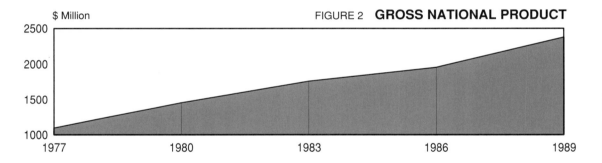

FIGURE 2 **GROSS NATIONAL PRODUCT**

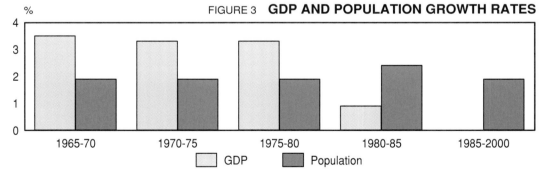

FIGURE 3 **GDP AND POPULATION GROWTH RATES**

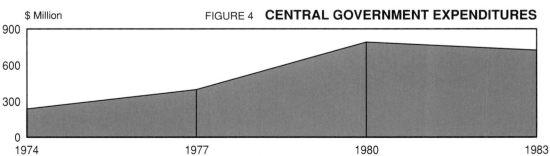

FIGURE 4 **CENTRAL GOVERNMENT EXPENDITURES**

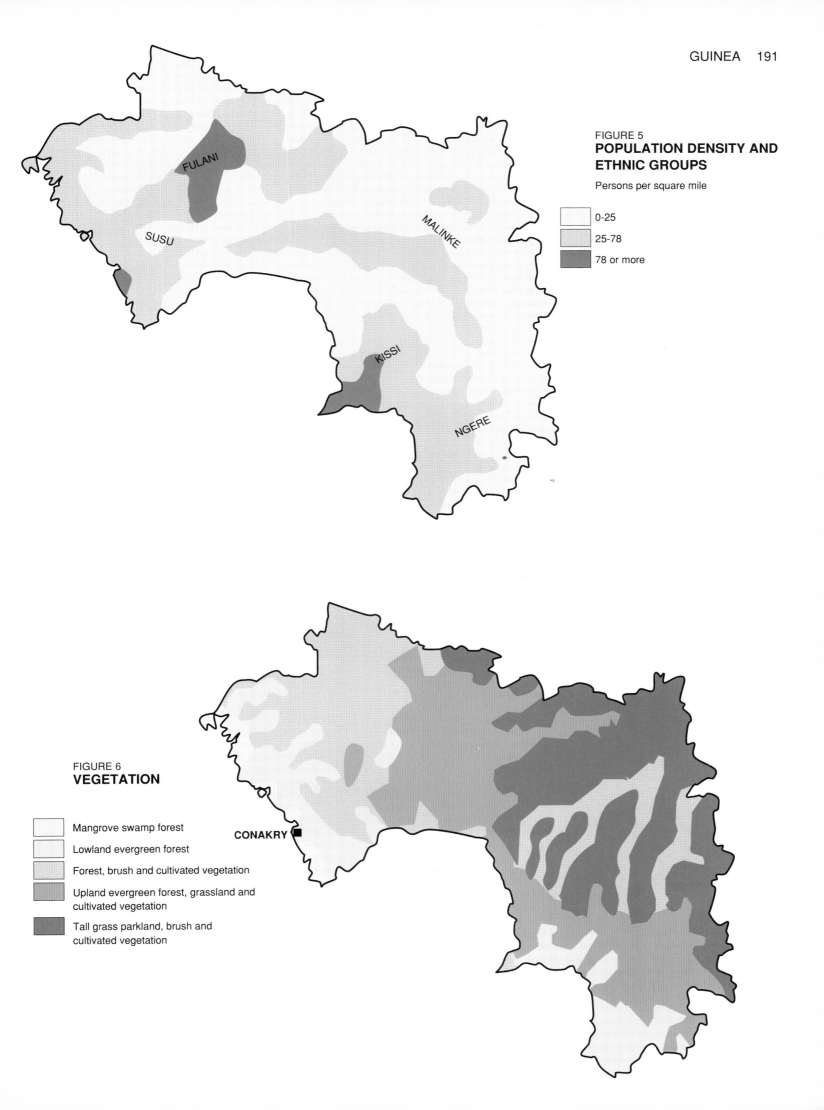

FIGURE 5
**POPULATION DENSITY AND
ETHNIC GROUPS**

Persons per square mile

0-25

25-78

78 or more

FULANI

SUSU

MALINKE

KISSI

NGERE

FIGURE 6
VEGETATION

Mangrove swamp forest

Lowland evergreen forest

Forest, brush and cultivated vegetation

Upland evergreen forest, grassland and
cultivated vegetation

Tall grass parkland, brush and
cultivated vegetation

CONAKRY

GUYANA

Located on the northern Atlantic coast of South America, Guyana ranks 81st in land area and 134th in population. A former British enclave, Guyana shares very little, culturally or politically, with its Luso-Hispanic neighbors. It has an ethnic and religious variety quite unknown in the larger countries of the South American continent and, in fact, has more in common with the former British West Indian territories. In 1980, it adopted a socialist constitution, the first state in South America to do so. In accordance with its socialist goals, the government has carried out a nationalization program affecting all large enterprises in agriculture, industry, and mining. Three commodities—bauxite, sugar and rice—account for over 80% of the country's foreign exchange earnings, bauxite alone accounting for half that figure.

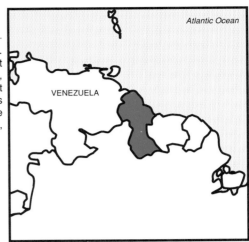

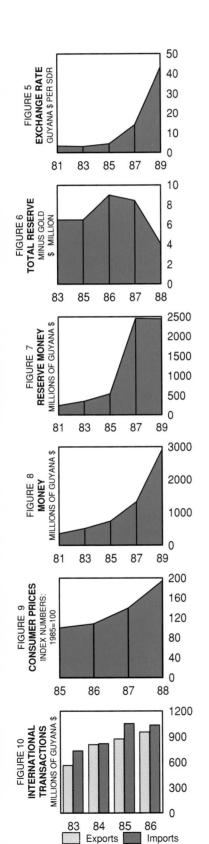

FIGURE 5 **EXCHANGE RATE** GUYANA $ PER SDR

FIGURE 6 **TOTAL RESERVE** MINUS GOLD $ MILLION

FIGURE 7 **RESERVE MONEY** MILLIONS OF GUYANA $

FIGURE 8 **MONEY** MILLIONS OF GUYANA $

FIGURE 9 **CONSUMER PRICES** INDEX NUMBERS: 1985=100

FIGURE 10 **INTERNATIONAL TRANSACTIONS** MILLIONS OF GUYANA $
Exports　Imports

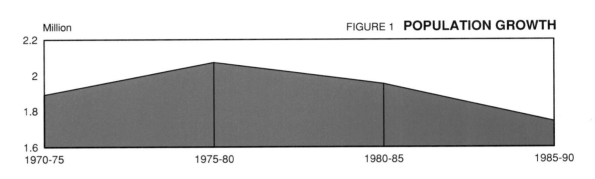

FIGURE 1 **POPULATION GROWTH**

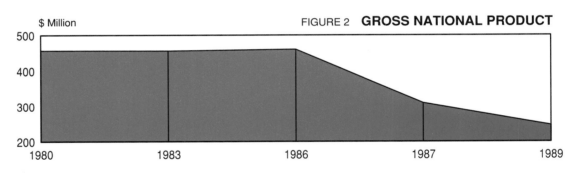

FIGURE 2 **GROSS NATIONAL PRODUCT**

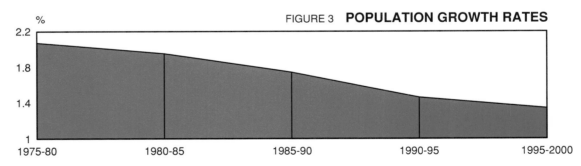

FIGURE 3 **POPULATION GROWTH RATES**

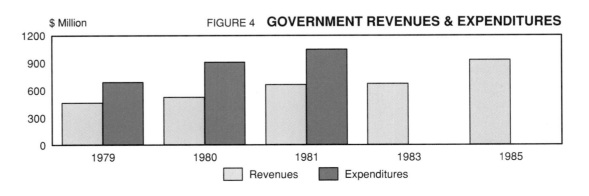

FIGURE 4 **GOVERNMENT REVENUES & EXPENDITURES**
Revenues　Expenditures

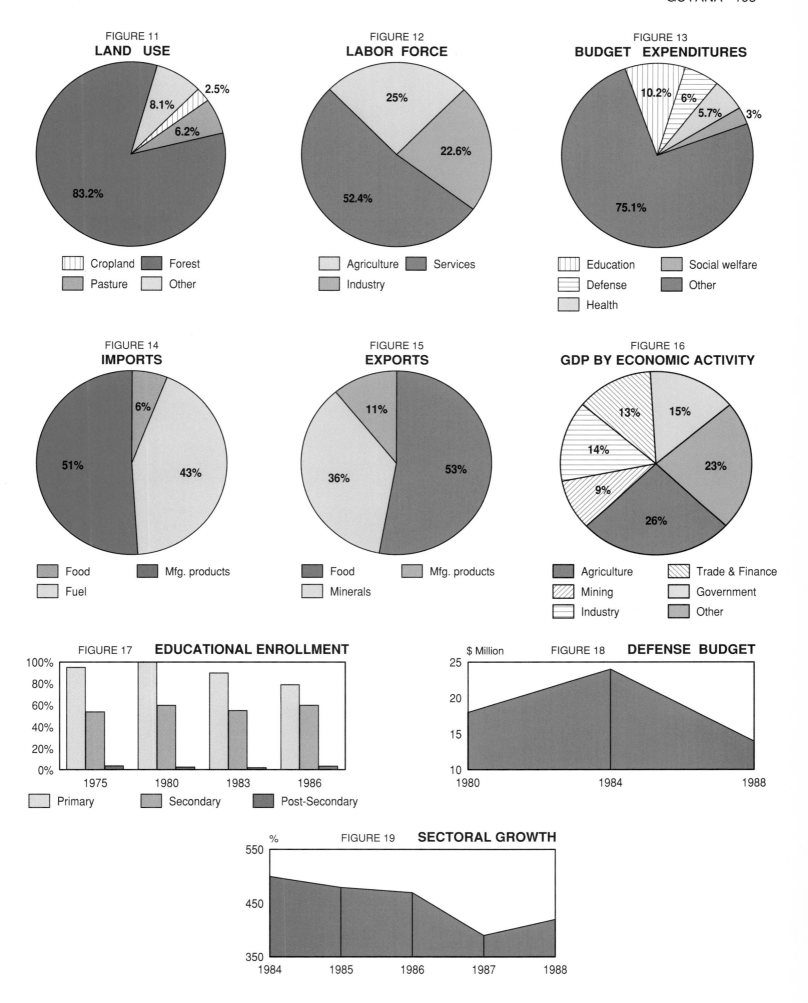

FIGURE 11
LAND USE

2.5%
8.1%
6.2%
83.2%

Cropland   Forest
Pasture   Other

FIGURE 12
LABOR FORCE

25%
22.6%
52.4%

Agriculture   Services
Industry

FIGURE 13
BUDGET EXPENDITURES

10.2%   6%
5.7%
3%
75.1%

Education   Social welfare
Defense   Other
Health

FIGURE 14
IMPORTS

6%
51%   43%

Food   Mfg. products
Fuel

FIGURE 15
EXPORTS

11%
36%   53%

Food   Mfg. products
Minerals

FIGURE 16
GDP BY ECONOMIC ACTIVITY

13%   15%
14%
23%
9%
26%

Agriculture   Trade & Finance
Mining   Government
Industry   Other

FIGURE 17   **EDUCATIONAL ENROLLMENT**

100%
80%
60%
40%
20%
0%
1975   1980   1983   1986

Primary   Secondary   Post-Secondary

$ Million   FIGURE 18   **DEFENSE BUDGET**

25
20
15
10
1980   1984   1988

%   FIGURE 19   **SECTORAL GROWTH**

550
450
350
1984   1985   1986   1987   1988

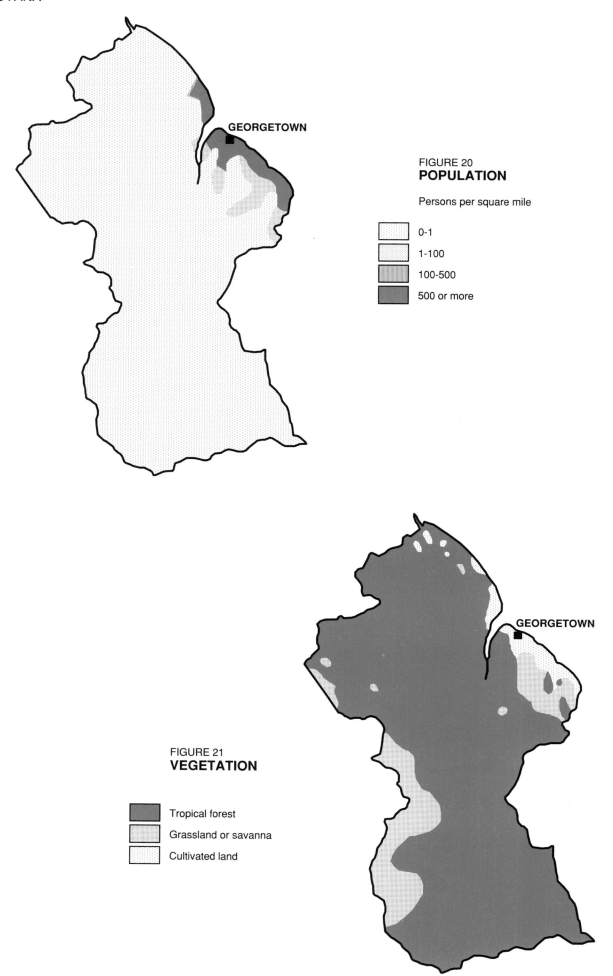

FIGURE 20
POPULATION

Persons per square mile

0-1
1-100
100-500
500 or more

GEORGETOWN

FIGURE 21
VEGETATION

Tropical forest
Grassland or savanna
Cultivated land

GEORGETOWN

FIGURE 22
AGRICULTURE

Sugar
Rice

FIGURE 23
ETHNIC GROUPS

Negro and mixed negro majority
Amerindian majority
East Indian majority
Presumably unpopulated

GEORGETOWN

GEORGETOWN

HAITI

Haiti occupies the western third of the islands of Hispaniola in the Caribbean and ranks 130th in land area and 88th in population. The sixth most densely populated country in the Western Hemisphere, Haiti is also one of the poorest with a per capita income of $330. Apart from its poverty and its voodoo practices, Haiti is best known as the only republic in the Western Hemisphere where French is the sole official language. Haiti ranks poorly in all physical quality of life indicators. Health conditions are substandard except in the capital, illiteracy approaches 80%, and nearly 25% are unemployed and 50% underemployed. While 90% of the population lives in absolute poverty, the riches 5% account for over half the national income. Agriculture employs 70% of the work force and contributes two-fifths of the GNP. Economic progress is also impeded by a lack of infrastructure. Apart from Port-au-Prince, the country is largely without electric power, telephone service, safe water supplies, paved roads, and rail transportation. In 1987 Jean-Claude (Baby Doc) Duvalier fled the country ending over half a century of Duvalier rule. Haiti's poverty has survived the Duvaliers. In 1991 Haiti's first freely-elected government was overthrown in a military coup.

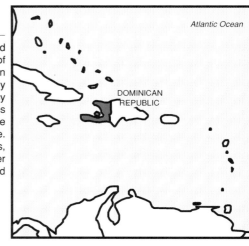

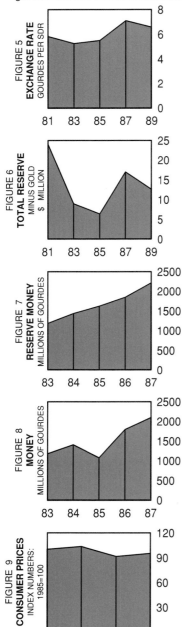

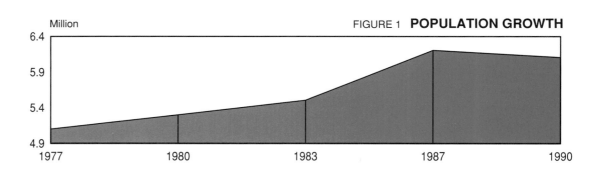

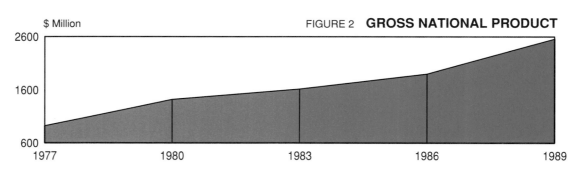

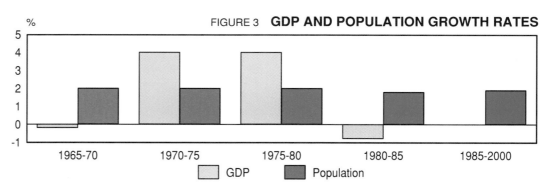

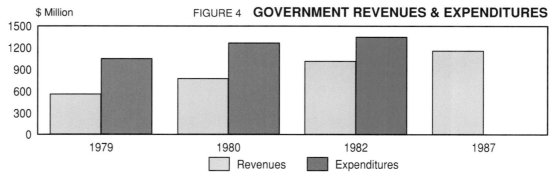

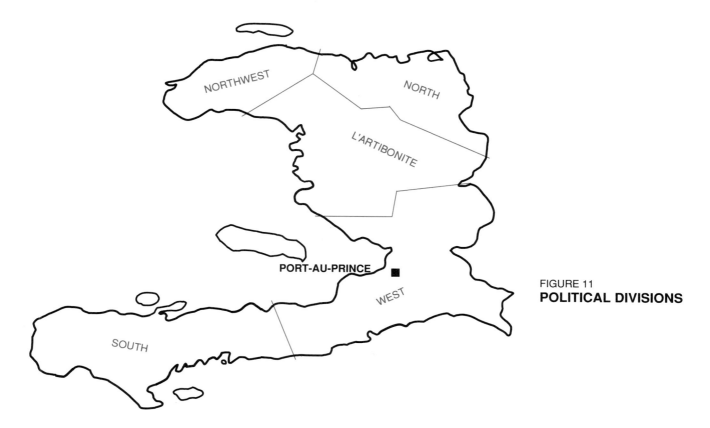

FIGURE 11
POLITICAL DIVISIONS

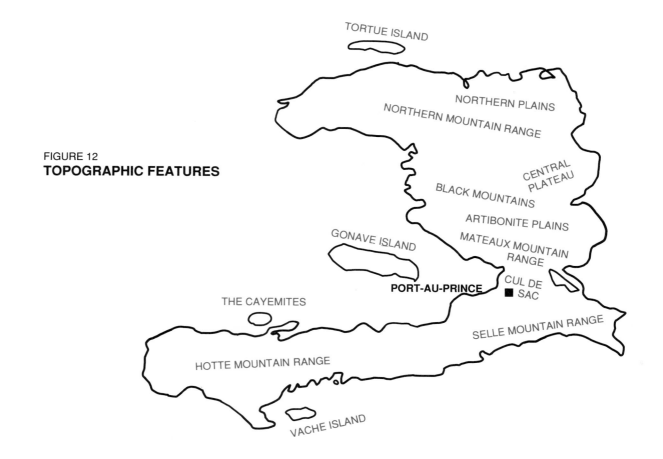

FIGURE 12
TOPOGRAPHIC FEATURES

HONDURAS

One of the banana republics of Central America, Honduras ranks 95th in land area and 94th in population. Although less adversely affected by the political unrest that has plagued its neighbors, Honduras still suffers from a population growth rate that is seven times higher than its GNP growth rate. Nevertheless, the economic prognosis is better for Honduras than for other Central American republics, and all sectors, particularly agriculture, industry, commerce, and tourism, have been expanding at impressive rates. Until 1976, bananas constituted the leading export crop but coffee has become the major foreign-exchange earner since then. Honduras has the most attractive investment climate in Central America, particularly because it has no restriction on the repatriation of dividends, interest or capital. Investors can also import basic materials and equipment duty free. Four of the five largest foreign corporate ventures are U.S.-owned, reflecting substantial U.S. involvement in the economy. In January 1990 Rafael Callejas took office as president in the first transition of elected power to an opposition party since 1932.

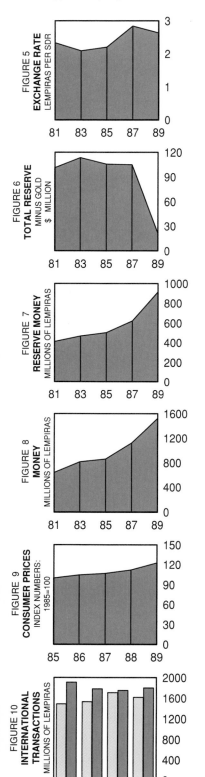

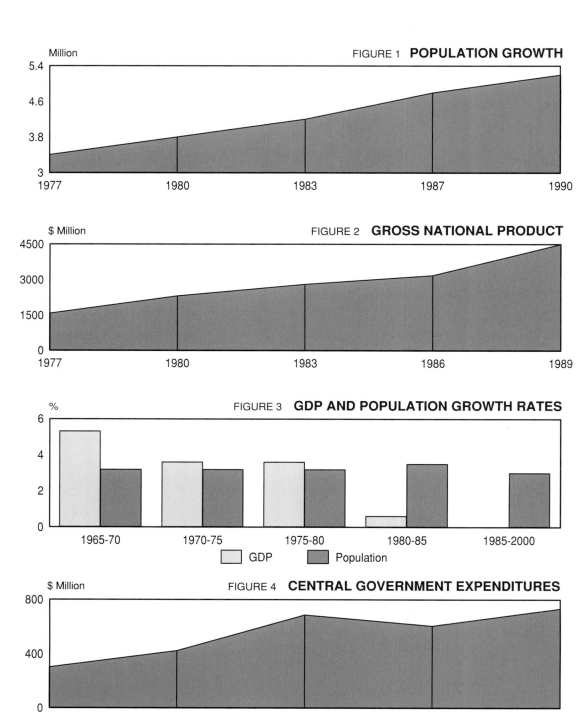

FIGURE 5 **EXCHANGE RATE** LEMPIRAS PER SDR

FIGURE 6 **TOTAL RESERVE** MINUS GOLD $ MILLION

FIGURE 7 **RESERVE MONEY** MILLIONS OF LEMPIRAS

FIGURE 8 **MONEY** MILLIONS OF LEMPIRAS

FIGURE 9 **CONSUMER PRICES** INDEX NUMBERS: 1985=100

FIGURE 10 **INTERNATIONAL TRANSACTIONS** MILLIONS OF LEMPIRAS

FIGURE 1 **POPULATION GROWTH**

FIGURE 2 **GROSS NATIONAL PRODUCT**

FIGURE 3 **GDP AND POPULATION GROWTH RATES**

FIGURE 4 **CENTRAL GOVERNMENT EXPENDITURES**

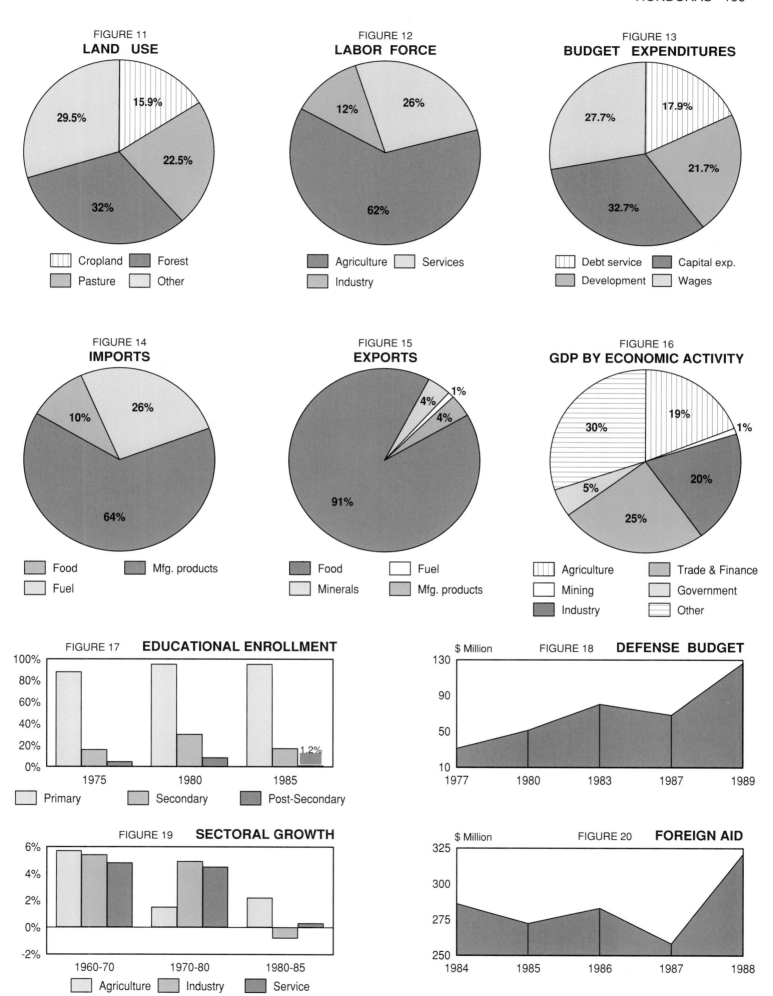

FIGURE 11
LAND USE

15.9%
29.5%
22.5%
32%

Cropland   Forest
Pasture   Other

FIGURE 12
LABOR FORCE

12%   26%
62%

Agriculture   Services
Industry

FIGURE 13
BUDGET EXPENDITURES

17.9%
27.7%
21.7%
32.7%

Debt service   Capital exp.
Development   Wages

FIGURE 14
IMPORTS

10%   26%
64%

Food   Mfg. products
Fuel

FIGURE 15
EXPORTS

1%
4%
4%
91%

Food   Fuel
Minerals Mfg. products

FIGURE 16
GDP BY ECONOMIC ACTIVITY

19%
30%
1%
20%
5%
25%

Agriculture   Trade & Finance
Mining   Government
Industry   Other

FIGURE 17   **EDUCATIONAL ENROLLMENT**

1.2%

1975   1980   1985

Primary   Secondary   Post-Secondary

$ Million   FIGURE 18   **DEFENSE BUDGET**

130
90
50
10

1977   1980   1983   1987   1989

FIGURE 19   **SECTORAL GROWTH**

6%
4%
2%
0%
-2%

1960-70   1970-80   1980-85

Agriculture   Industry   Service

$ Million   FIGURE 20   **FOREIGN AID**

325
300
275
250

1984   1985   1986   1987   1988

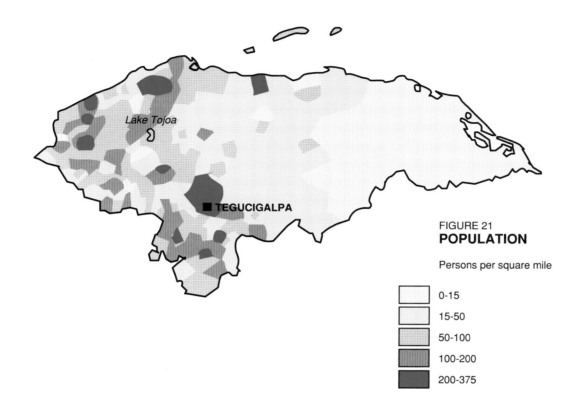

FIGURE 21
POPULATION

Persons per square mile

	0-15
	15-50
	50-100
	100-200
	200-375

FIGURE 22
LAND UTILIZATION

	Cultivated area
	Woodland
	Scrub woodland
	Savanna
	Marsh and swamp

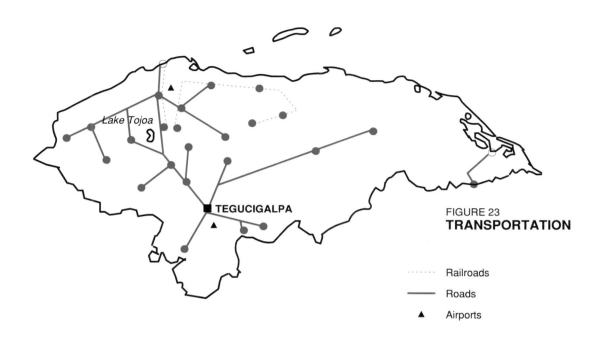

FIGURE 23
TRANSPORTATION

······· Railroads

——— Roads

▲ Airports

FIGURE 24
ALTITUDE

Altitude in feet

	0-656
	656-1,640
	1,640-3,280
	3,280 and above

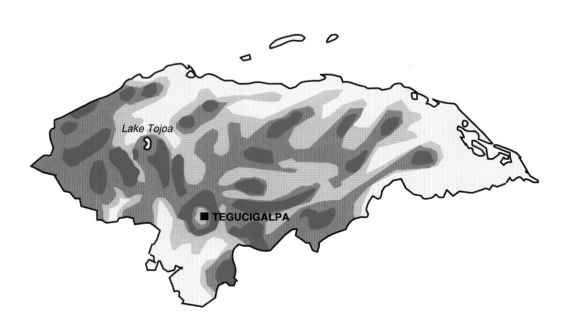

INDIA

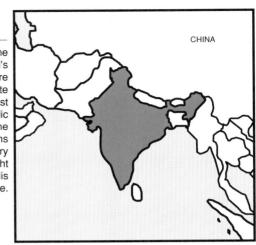

The largest country on the Indian subcontinent, India is the second most populous country in the world and the seventh largest. Although it occupies only 2.09% of the world's land surface, it supports 14% of the world's population and the latter percentage is growing at an alarming rate. More languages are spoken and more religions professed in India than in any other country in the world. Only 12 countries exceed India in aggregate GNP but, because of its high population, it ranks among the poorest in per capita income. Despite the socialist commitment of the Nehru and Gandhi governments, extremes of wealth and poverty continued. A sizable public sector exists cheek by jowl with a vigorous but shrinking private sector. Agriculture is the mainstay of the economy and one bad harvest usually sends shock waves through every sector. India's economy remains vulnerable and subject to many constraints; it has yet to reach the 5 to 6% aggregate growth rate necessary for a low-income country to escape the poverty cycle. During general elections in May 1991, and at the height of his campaign to regain the prime ministership, former Prime Minister Rajiv Gandhi was assassinated. His death cast uncertainty over the future of India, already wracked by separatist violence and economic decline.

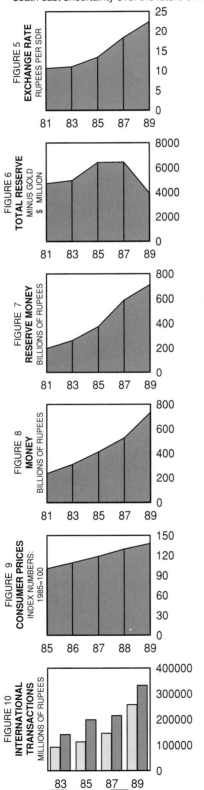

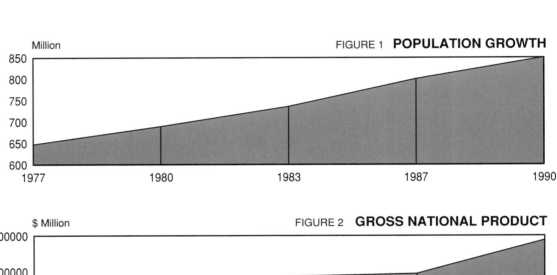

FIGURE 1 **POPULATION GROWTH**

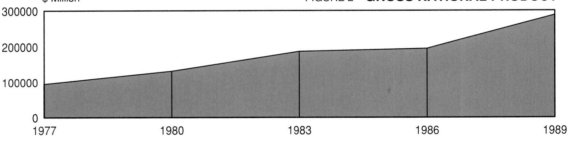

FIGURE 2 **GROSS NATIONAL PRODUCT**

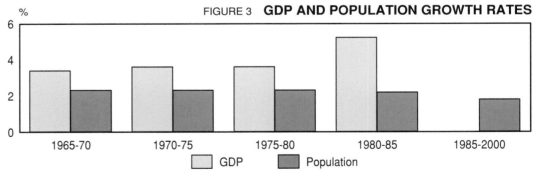

FIGURE 3 **GDP AND POPULATION GROWTH RATES**

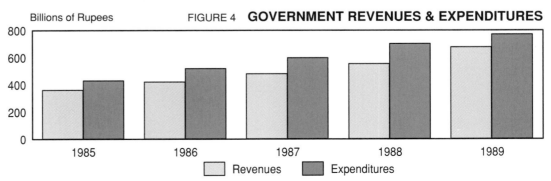

FIGURE 4 **GOVERNMENT REVENUES & EXPENDITURES**

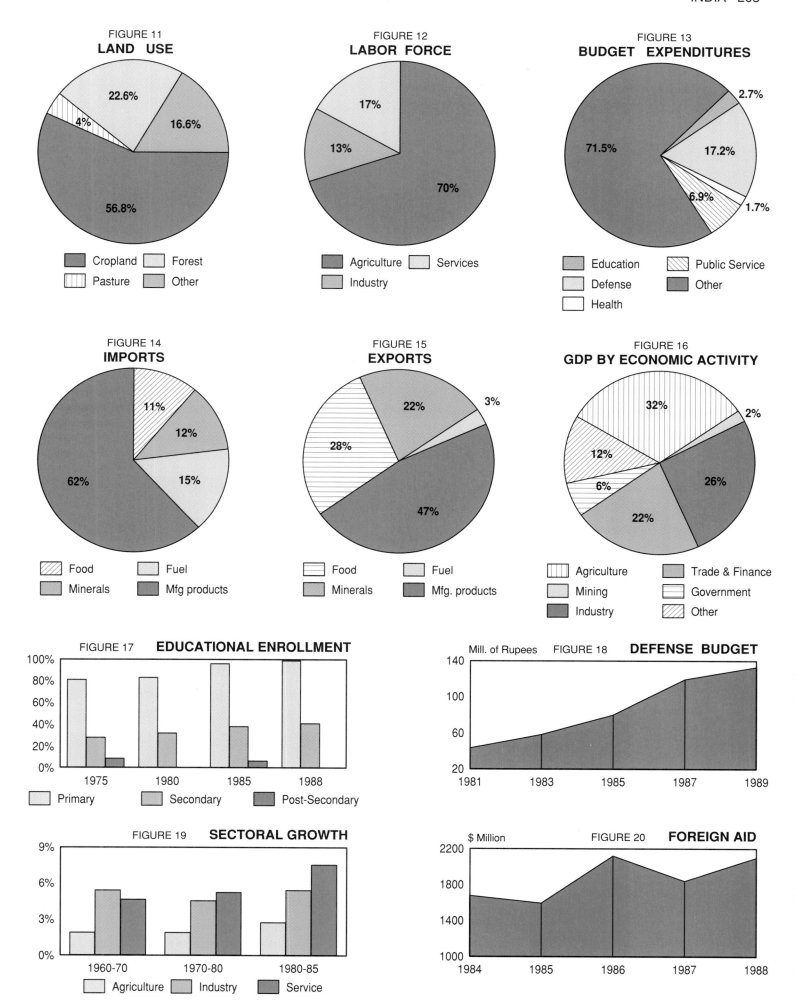

FIGURE 11
LAND USE

22.6%
4%
16.6%
56.8%

Cropland — Forest
Pasture — Other

FIGURE 12
LABOR FORCE

17%
13%
70%

Agriculture — Services
Industry

FIGURE 13
BUDGET EXPENDITURES

2.7%
71.5%
17.2%
6.9%
1.7%

Education — Public Service
Defense — Other
Health

FIGURE 14
IMPORTS

11%
12%
62%
15%

Food — Fuel
Minerals — Mfg products

FIGURE 15
EXPORTS

22%
3%
28%
47%

Food — Fuel
Minerals — Mfg. products

FIGURE 16
GDP BY ECONOMIC ACTIVITY

32%
2%
12%
26%
6%
22%

Agriculture — Trade & Finance
Mining — Government
Industry — Other

FIGURE 17 EDUCATIONAL ENROLLMENT

100%
80%
60%
40%
20%
0%
1975   1980   1985   1988

Primary — Secondary — Post-Secondary

FIGURE 18 DEFENSE BUDGET
Mill. of Rupees

140
100
60
20
1981   1983   1985   1987   1989

FIGURE 19 SECTORAL GROWTH

9%
6%
3%
0%
1960-70   1970-80   1980-85

Agriculture — Industry — Service

FIGURE 20 FOREIGN AID
$ Million

2200
1800
1400
1000
1984   1985   1986   1987   1988

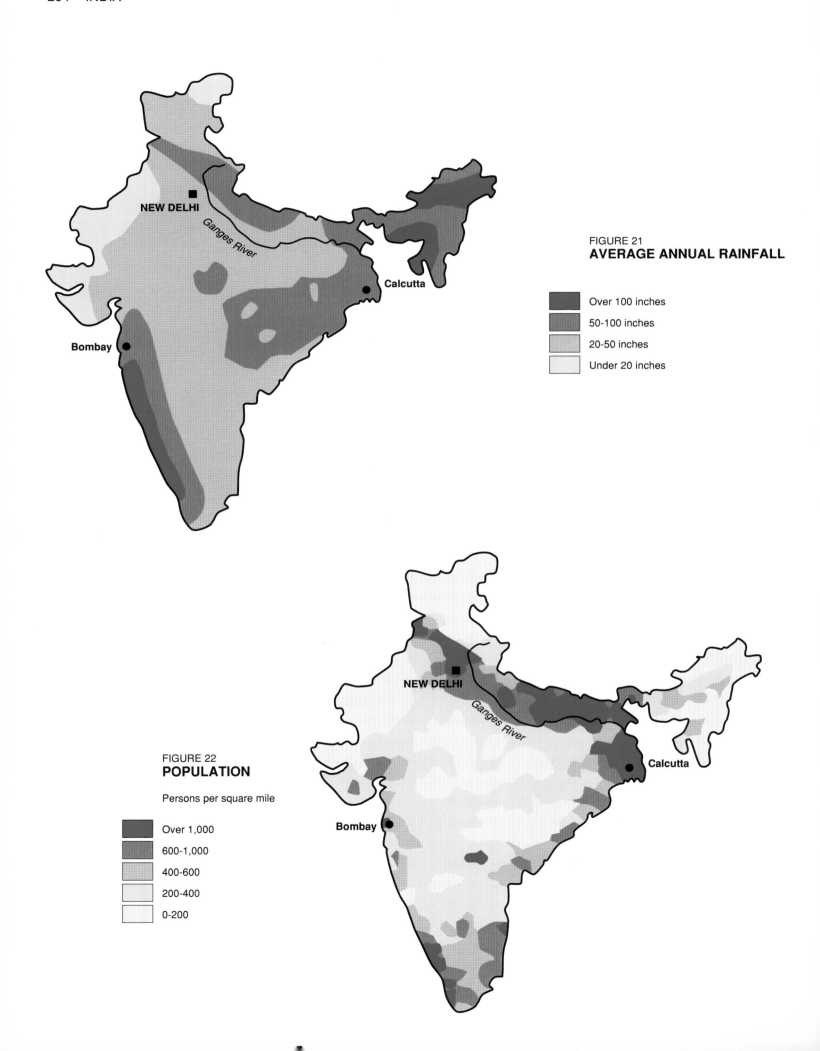

FIGURE 21
AVERAGE ANNUAL RAINFALL

	Over 100 inches
	50-100 inches
	20-50 inches
	Under 20 inches

FIGURE 22
POPULATION

Persons per square mile

	Over 1,000
	600-1,000
	400-600
	200-400
	0-200

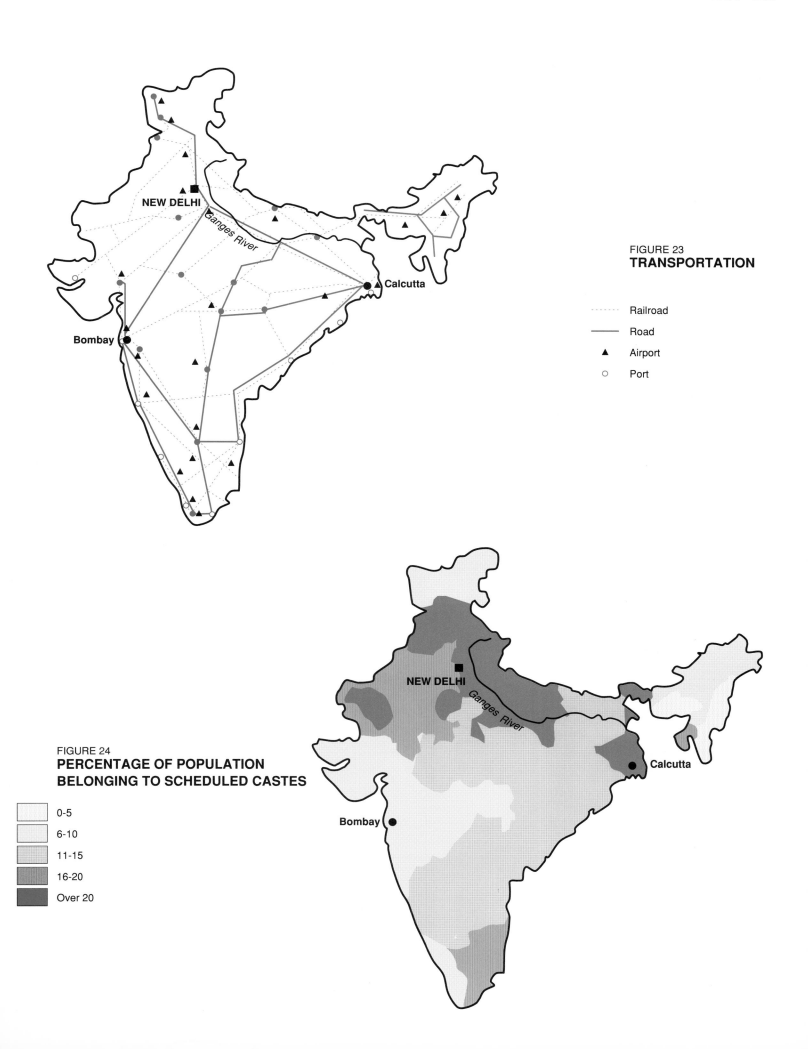

FIGURE 23
TRANSPORTATION

NEW DELHI

Ganges River

Calcutta

Bombay

- - - - - Railroad
───── Road
▲ Airport
○ Port

FIGURE 24
**PERCENTAGE OF POPULATION
BELONGING TO SCHEDULED CASTES**

	0-5
	6-10
	11-15
	16-20
	Over 20

NEW DELHI

Ganges River

Calcutta

Bombay

INDONESIA

An archipelago of some 13,500 islands extending along the Equator for over 3,000 miles, Indonesia is the fifth most populous nation in the world and the 15th largest in land size. Although overall density is moderate, Java is one of the most densely populated areas of the world with over 75 million inhabitants compressed into an area no larger than New York state. Despite its rich natural resources, Indonesia is classified as a low-income country and it is the only oil producer in this category. The economy is loosely divided between public and private sectors, the former dominated by the government and the latter by the Chinese. Agriculture employs approximately one half of the work force but contributes one fourth of the GDP. Although soil and climate favor multiple cropping and high yields, the country is not self-sufficient in rice. The five-year development plans known as Repelitas resulted in increasing the contribution of industry to GDP from one-seventh in 1960 to one-third in 1986. After 23 years of suspended diplomatic links, Indonesia and China normalized relations in August 1990.

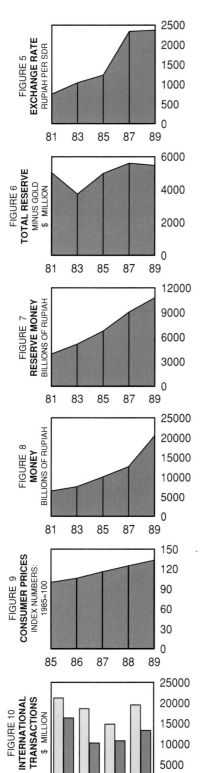

FIGURE 5 **EXCHANGE RATE** RUPIAH PER SDR

FIGURE 6 **TOTAL RESERVE** MINUS GOLD $ MILLION

FIGURE 7 **RESERVE MONEY** BILLIONS OF RUPIAH

FIGURE 8 **MONEY** BILLIONS OF RUPIAH

FIGURE 9 **CONSUMER PRICES** INDEX NUMBERS: 1985=100

FIGURE 10 **INTERNATIONAL TRANSACTIONS** $ MILLION

Exports   Imports

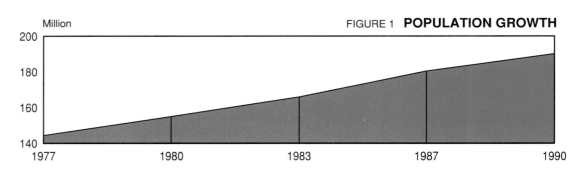

FIGURE 1 **POPULATION GROWTH**

Million

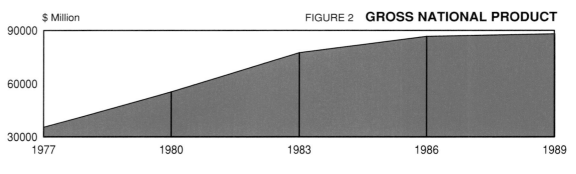

FIGURE 2 **GROSS NATIONAL PRODUCT**

$ Million

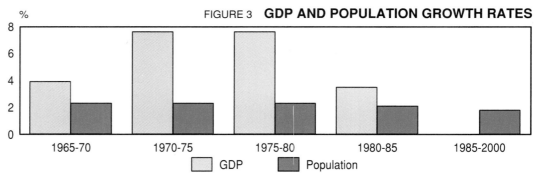

FIGURE 3 **GDP AND POPULATION GROWTH RATES**

%

GDP   Population

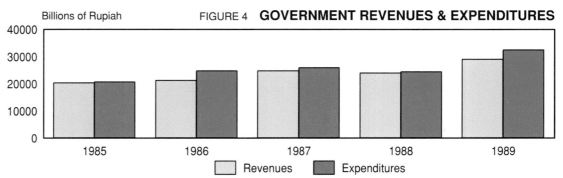

Billions of Rupiah   FIGURE 4 **GOVERNMENT REVENUES & EXPENDITURES**

Revenues   Expenditures

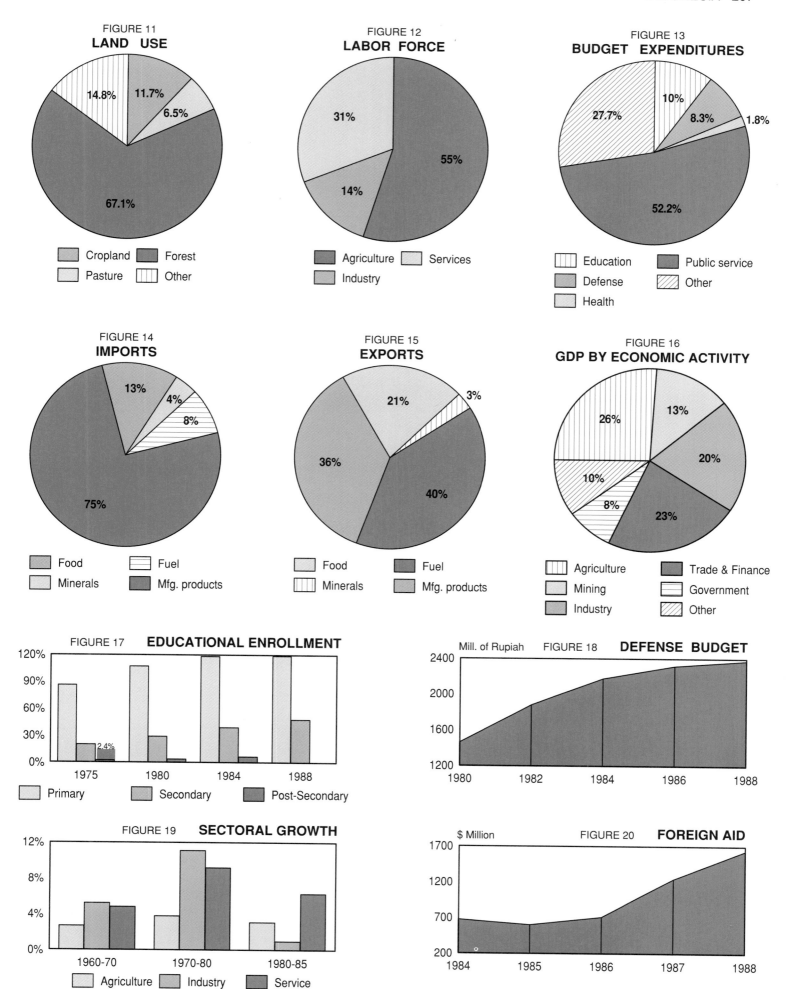

FIGURE 11
LAND USE

14.8% 11.7%
6.5%
67.1%

Cropland | Forest
Pasture | Other

FIGURE 12
LABOR FORCE

31%
55%
14%

Agriculture | Services
Industry

FIGURE 13
BUDGET EXPENDITURES

27.7% 10% 8.3% 1.8%
52.2%

Education | Public service
Defense | Other
Health

FIGURE 14
IMPORTS

13% 4%
8%
75%

Food | Fuel
Minerals | Mfg. products

FIGURE 15
EXPORTS

21% 3%
36%
40%

Food | Fuel
Minerals | Mfg. products

FIGURE 16
GDP BY ECONOMIC ACTIVITY

26% 13%
20%
10%
8% 23%

Agriculture | Trade & Finance
Mining | Government
Industry | Other

FIGURE 17 **EDUCATIONAL ENROLLMENT**

2.4%

Primary | Secondary | Post-Secondary

FIGURE 18 **DEFENSE BUDGET**

Mill. of Rupiah

1980 1982 1984 1986 1988

FIGURE 19 **SECTORAL GROWTH**

1960-70 1970-80 1980-85

Agriculture | Industry | Service

FIGURE 20 **FOREIGN AID**

$ Million

1984 1985 1986 1987 1988

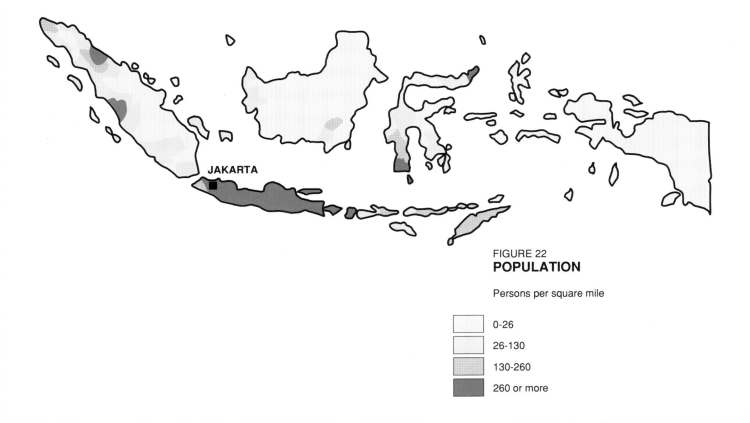

FIGURE 21
ETHNOLINGUISTIC DISTRIBUTION

Javanese

Coastal Malays

Balinese-Sasak

Papuan

Minangkabau

FIGURE 22
POPULATION

Persons per square mile

0-26

26-130

130-260

260 or more

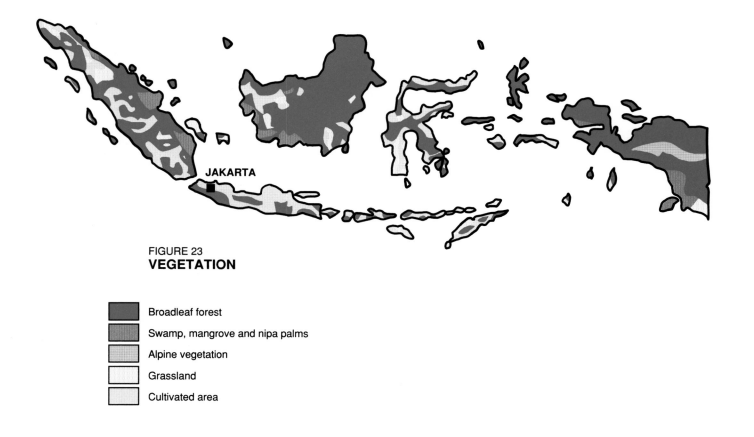

FIGURE 23
VEGETATION

Broadleaf forest

Swamp, mangrove and nipa palms

Alpine vegetation

Grassland

Cultivated area

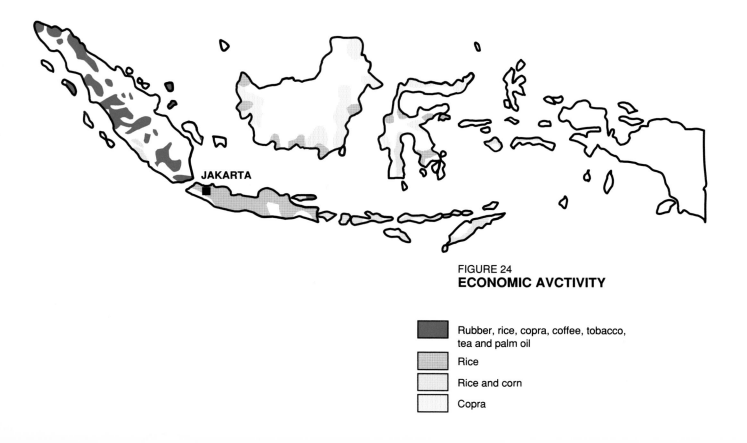

FIGURE 24
ECONOMIC AVCTIVITY

Rubber, rice, copra, coffee, tobacco, tea and palm oil

Rice

Rice and corn

Copra

IRAN

Located in southwestern Asia and larger than Alaska and Pennsylvania combined, Iran ranks 17th in land area and 21st in population. Iran is the only country in the world ruled by mullahs. Only Saudi Arabia among OPEC countries produces or exports more oil than Iran. Oil revenues have enabled Iran to survive the political crises that followed the ouster of the shah and the seizure and occupation of the U.S. embassy in Tehran, but if fared badly against Iraq in the Gulf War that ended in 1988, thus permanently damaging its long-term potential to become a first-rank industrial power. A severe earthquake in 1990 killed some 45,000 people; the government estimated the cost of rehabilitation at over $7 billion. Although Iran firmly opposed the 1990 Iraqi invasion of Kuwait, it refused to take part in the UN multinational force or to act in any military way against Iraq.

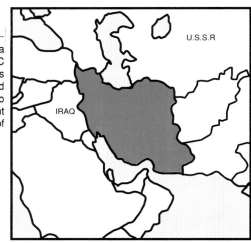

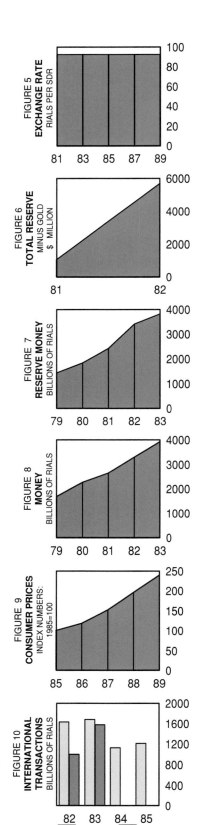

FIGURE 5 EXCHANGE RATE — RIALS PER SDR

FIGURE 6 TOTAL RESERVE — MINUS GOLD $ MILLION

FIGURE 7 RESERVE MONEY — BILLIONS OF RIALS

FIGURE 8 MONEY — BILLIONS OF RIALS

FIGURE 9 CONSUMER PRICES — INDEX NUMBERS: 1985=100

FIGURE 10 INTERNATIONAL TRANSACTIONS — BILLIONS OF RIALS — Exports — Imports

FIGURE 1 **POPULATION GROWTH**

Million

FIGURE 2 **GROSS NATIONAL PRODUCT**

$ Million

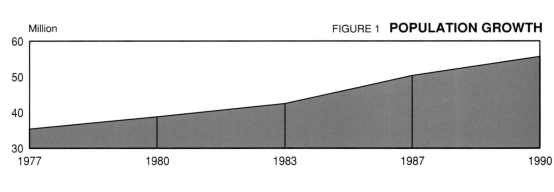

FIGURE 3 **GDP AND POPULATION GROWTH RATES**

%

GDP   Population

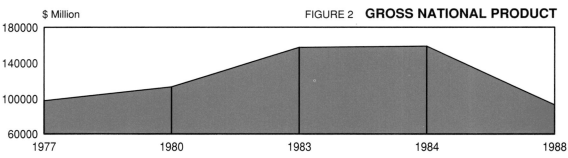

FIGURE 4 **GOVERNMENT REVENUES & EXPENDITURES**

Millions of Rials

Revenues   Expenditures

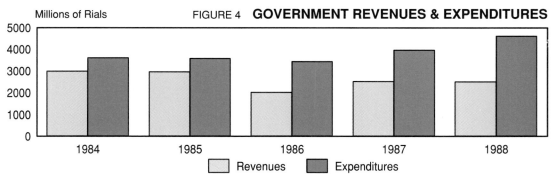

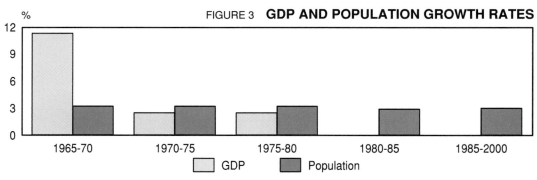

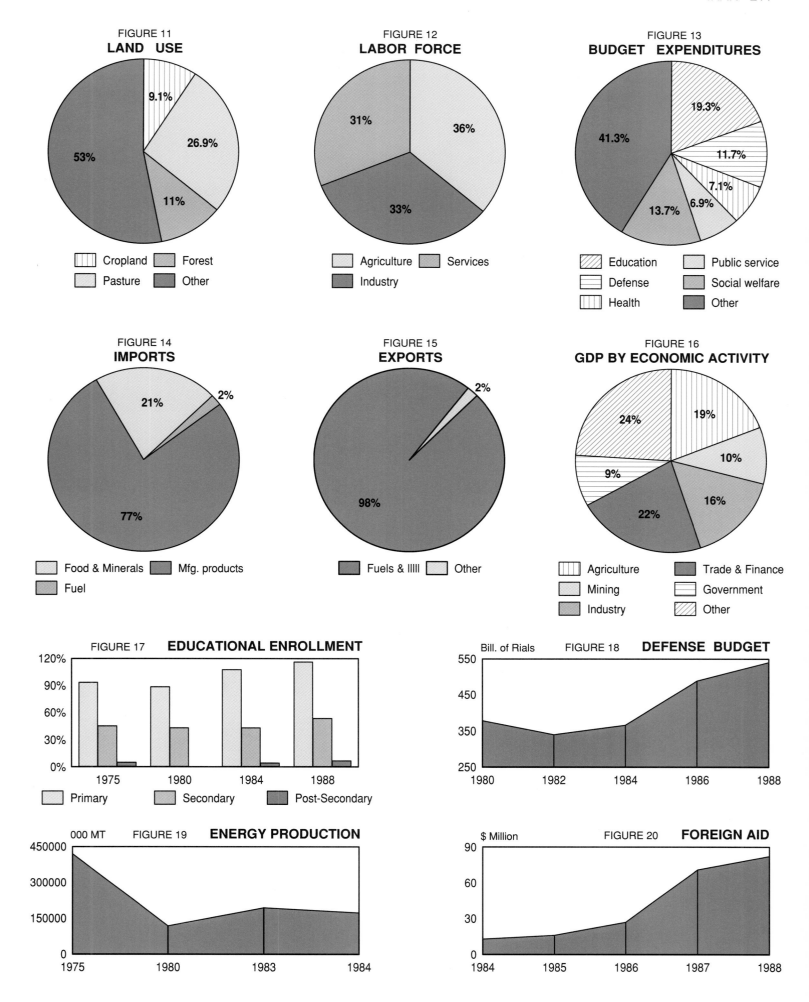

FIGURE 11
LAND USE

9.1%
26.9%
53%
11%

Cropland   Forest
Pasture   Other

FIGURE 12
LABOR FORCE

31%   36%
33%

Agriculture   Services
Industry

FIGURE 13
BUDGET   EXPENDITURES

19.3%
41.3%
11.7%
7.1%
6.9%
13.7%

Education   Public service
Defense   Social welfare
Health   Other

FIGURE 14
IMPORTS

21%   2%
77%

Food & Minerals   Mfg. products
Fuel

FIGURE 15
EXPORTS

2%
98%

Fuels & IIIII   Other

FIGURE 16
GDP BY ECONOMIC ACTIVITY

24%   19%
10%
9%
22%   16%

Agriculture   Trade & Finance
Mining   Government
Industry   Other

FIGURE 17 **EDUCATIONAL ENROLLMENT**

120%
90%
60%
30%
0%
1975   1980   1984   1988

Primary   Secondary   Post-Secondary

Bill. of Rials   FIGURE 18   **DEFENSE BUDGET**

550
450
350
250
1980   1982   1984   1986   1988

000 MT   FIGURE 19   **ENERGY PRODUCTION**

450000
300000
150000
0
1975   1980   1983   1984

$ Million   FIGURE 20   **FOREIGN AID**

90
60
30
0
1984   1985   1986   1987   1988

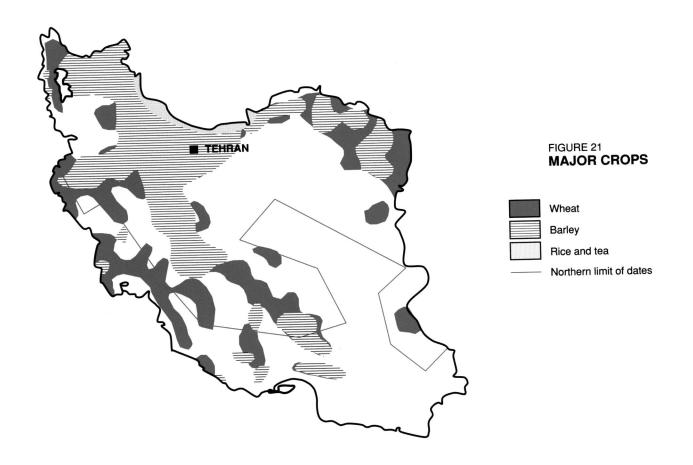

FIGURE 21
MAJOR CROPS

Wheat

Barley

Rice and tea

Northern limit of dates

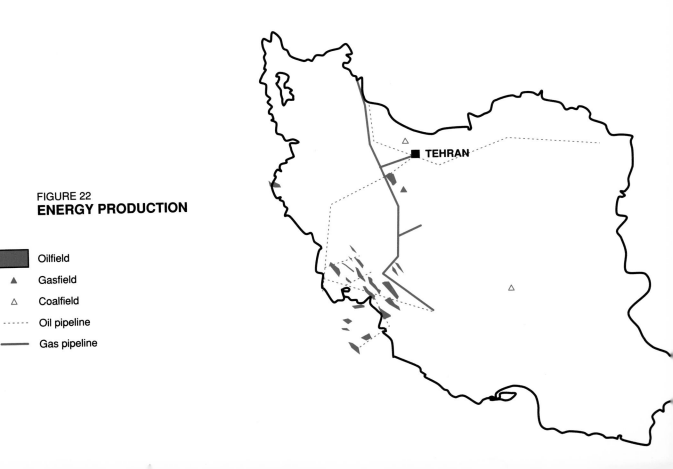

FIGURE 22
ENERGY PRODUCTION

Oilfield

▲ Gasfield

△ Coalfield

Oil pipeline

Gas pipeline

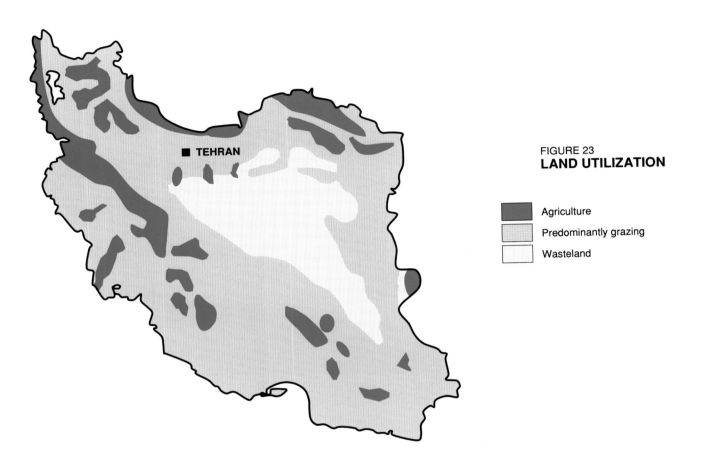

FIGURE 23
LAND UTILIZATION

■ TEHRAN

Agriculture

Predominantly grazing

Wasteland

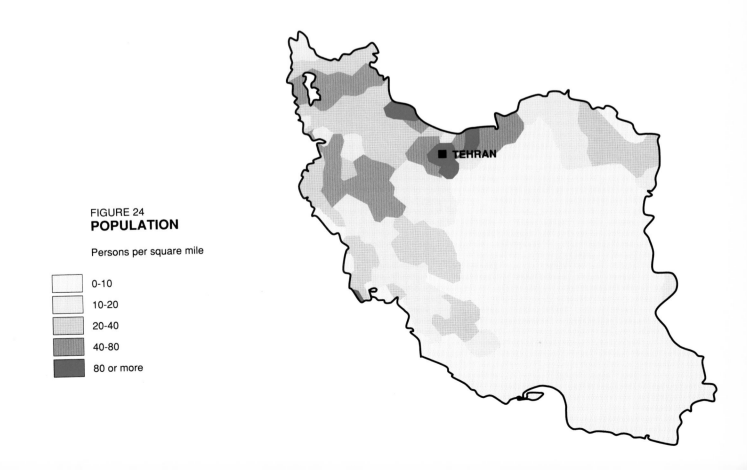

FIGURE 24
POPULATION

Persons per square mile

0-10

10-20

20-40

40-80

80 or more

■ TEHRAN

IRAQ

Known as Mesopotamia or the land between the rivers (i.e. the Tigris and the Euphrates), Iraq ranks 53rd in land area and 44th in population. Except for a short coastal strip on the Persian Gulf, Iraq is virtually a landlocked country, and one of its long held ambitions was to expand its coastline at the expense of Iran. Prior to the 1991 Persian Gulf War, Iraq was one of the largest oil producers in the world. Its potential reserves are considered second only to Saudi Arabia's. The oil industry was completely nationalized by 1977 as part of a program that brought under total state control the manufacturing and mining sectors. More recently, Iraq was forced to make substantial purchases of military equipment for its war against Iran; the economic effects of this war which ended in 1988 were severe. The Iraqi invasion and occupation of Kuwait in August 1990 temporarily provided Iraq with its long-desired access to the Persian Gulf as well as ownership of the disputed oil fields in Kuwait. The 1991 Persian Gulf War severely damaged its infrastructure and economy.

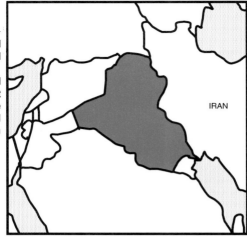

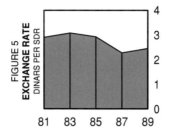

FIGURE 5
EXCHANGE RATE
DINARS PER SDR

ADDITIONAL
I.M.F.
INFORMATION
NOT
AVAILABLE

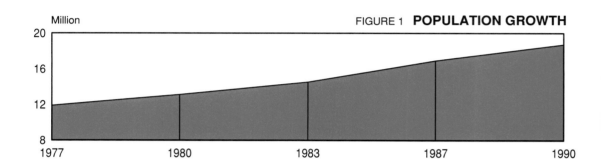

FIGURE 1 **POPULATION GROWTH**

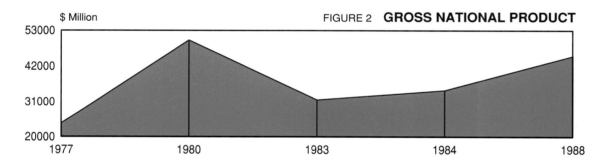

FIGURE 2 **GROSS NATIONAL PRODUCT**

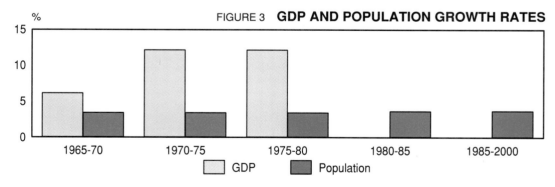

FIGURE 3 **GDP AND POPULATION GROWTH RATES**

GDP   Population

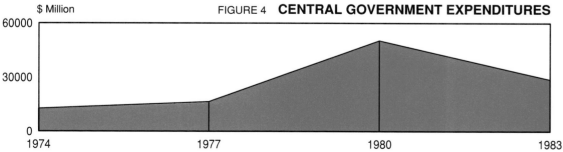

FIGURE 4 **CENTRAL GOVERNMENT EXPENDITURES**

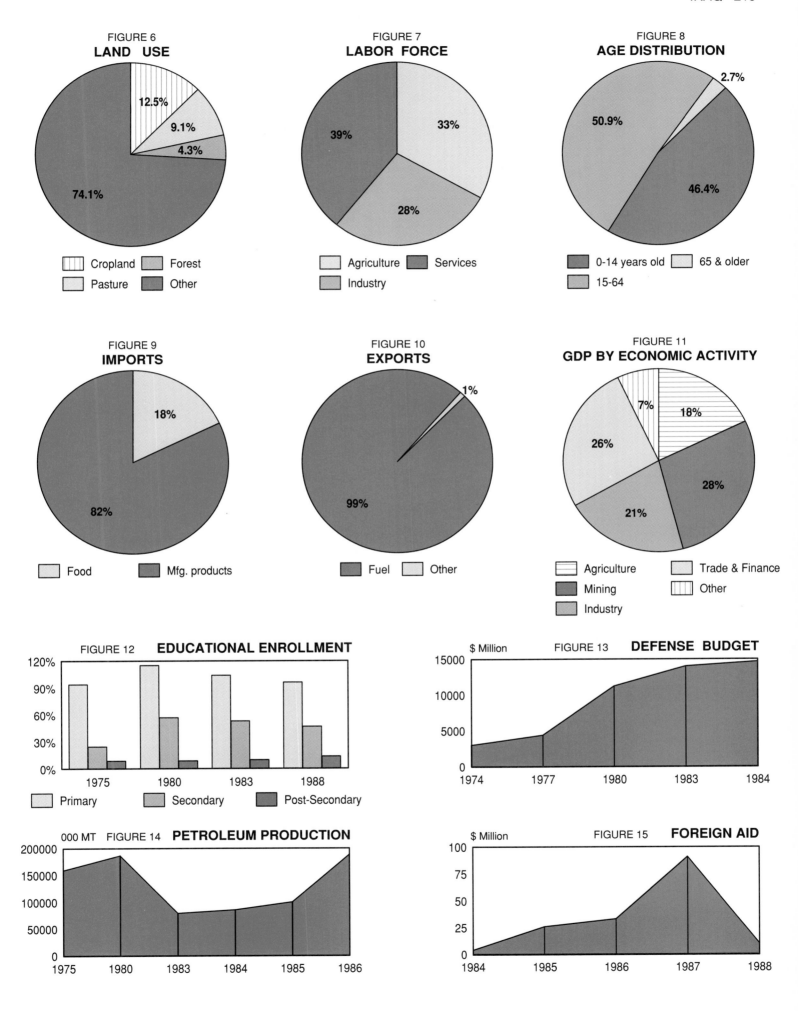

FIGURE 6
LAND USE

12.5%
9.1%
4.3%
74.1%

Cropland · Forest
Pasture · Other

FIGURE 7
LABOR FORCE

33%
39%
28%

Agriculture · Services
Industry

FIGURE 8
AGE DISTRIBUTION

2.7%
50.9%
46.4%

0-14 years old · 65 & older
15-64

FIGURE 9
IMPORTS

18%
82%

Food · Mfg. products

FIGURE 10
EXPORTS

1%
99%

Fuel · Other

FIGURE 11
GDP BY ECONOMIC ACTIVITY

7%
18%
26%
28%
21%

Agriculture · Trade & Finance
Mining · Other
Industry

FIGURE 12 EDUCATIONAL ENROLLMENT

120%
90%
60%
30%
0%
1975 1980 1983 1988

Primary · Secondary · Post-Secondary

$ Million FIGURE 13 DEFENSE BUDGET

15000
10000
5000
0
1974 1977 1980 1983 1984

000 MT FIGURE 14 PETROLEUM PRODUCTION

200000
150000
100000
50000
0
1975 1980 1983 1984 1985 1986

$ Million FIGURE 15 FOREIGN AID

100
75
50
25
0
1984 1985 1986 1987 1988

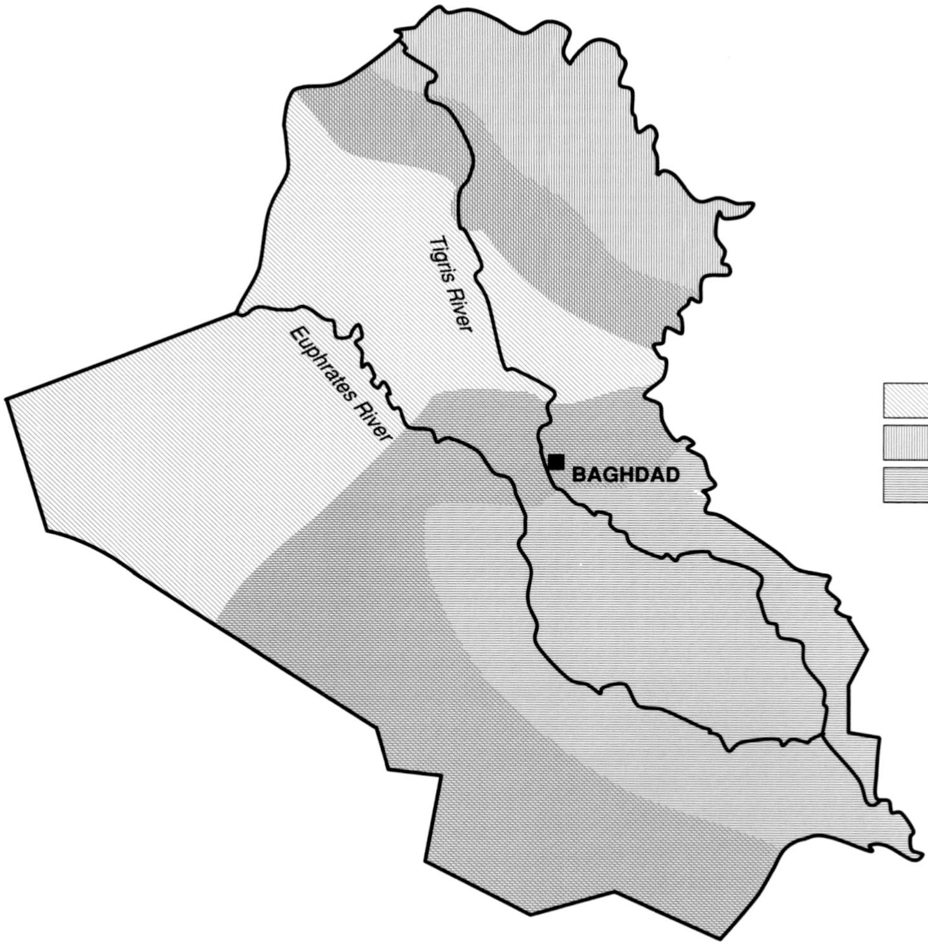

FIGURE 16
RELIGIOUS AND ETHNIC GROUPS

Sunni Arab
Sunni Kurd
Shia Arab

BAGHDAD

FIGURE 17
POPULATION

Persons per square mile

0-1
1-50
50-200
200-700
700 and more

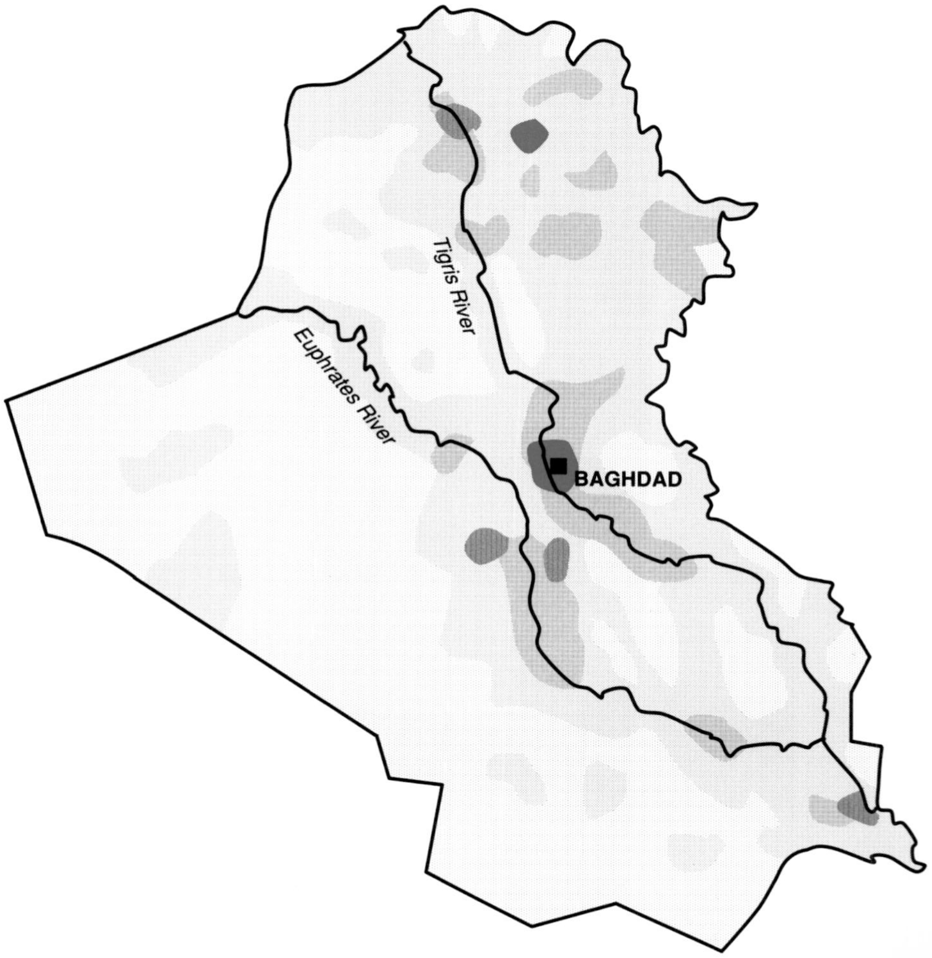

BAGHDAD

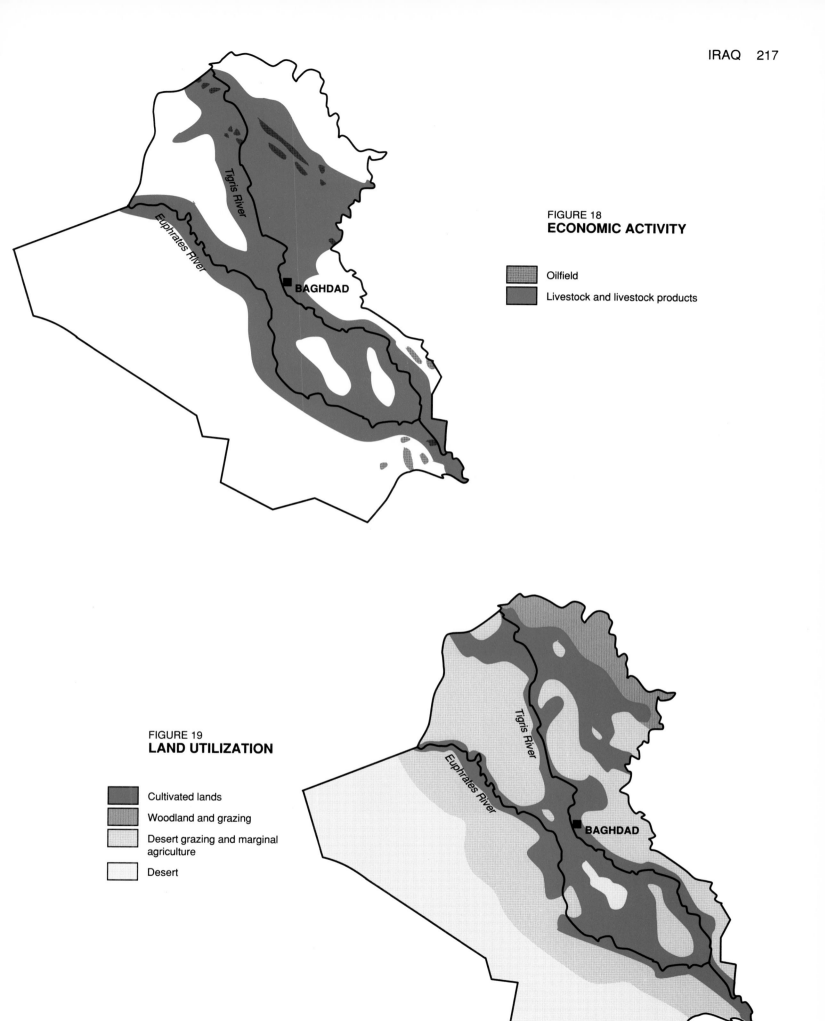

FIGURE 18
ECONOMIC ACTIVITY

Oilfield

Livestock and livestock products

BAGHDAD

FIGURE 19
LAND UTILIZATION

Cultivated lands

Woodland and grazing

Desert grazing and marginal agriculture

Desert

BAGHDAD

Tigris River

Euphrates River

IVORY COAST

One of the richest and most self-sufficient of African states, Ivory Coast ranks 63rd in land area and 58th in population. In the 23 years since independence, it has gained a reputation for political stability, moderation, and economic vitality. Such an extended period of growth was made possible by export earnings from the country's two principal commodities: coffee and cocoa. It ranks as Africa's major producer of both crops as well as the leading exporter of logs and lumber. The Houphouet-Boigny government has created the necessary climate for economic growth through liberal investment policies designed to encourage the inflow of foreign capital, technology, and management expertise. Although the government remains committed to Ivorianization, it has welcomed expatriate administrative and technical skills, with the result that the country has one of the largest non-national white populations in sub-Saharan Africa. Bowing to political pressure, Houphouet-Boigny was forced to legalize opposition parties in 1990 and run in the country's first contested election since independence.

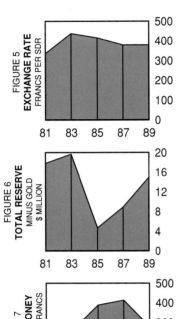

FIGURE 5 EXCHANGE RATE FRANCS PER SDR

FIGURE 6 TOTAL RESERVE MINUS GOLD $ MILLION

FIGURE 7 RESERVE MONEY BILLIONS OF FRANCS

FIGURE 8 MONEY BILLIONS OF FRANCS

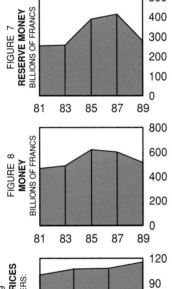

FIGURE 9 CONSUMER PRICES INDEX NUMBERS: 1985=100

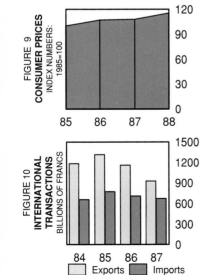

FIGURE 10 INTERNATIONAL TRANSACTIONS BILLIONS OF FRANCS

Exports   Imports

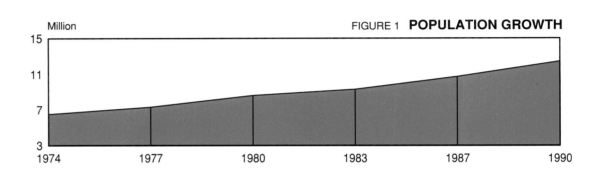

FIGURE 1 **POPULATION GROWTH**

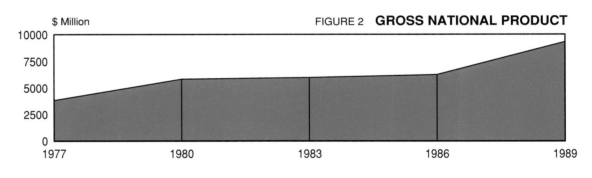

FIGURE 2 **GROSS NATIONAL PRODUCT**

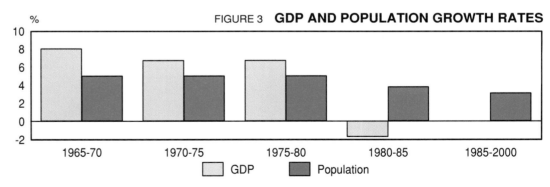

FIGURE 3 **GDP AND POPULATION GROWTH RATES**

GDP   Population

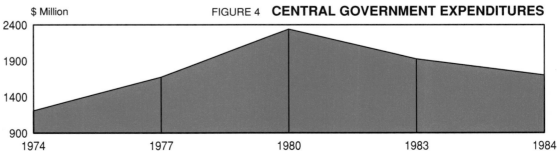

FIGURE 4 **CENTRAL GOVERNMENT EXPENDITURES**

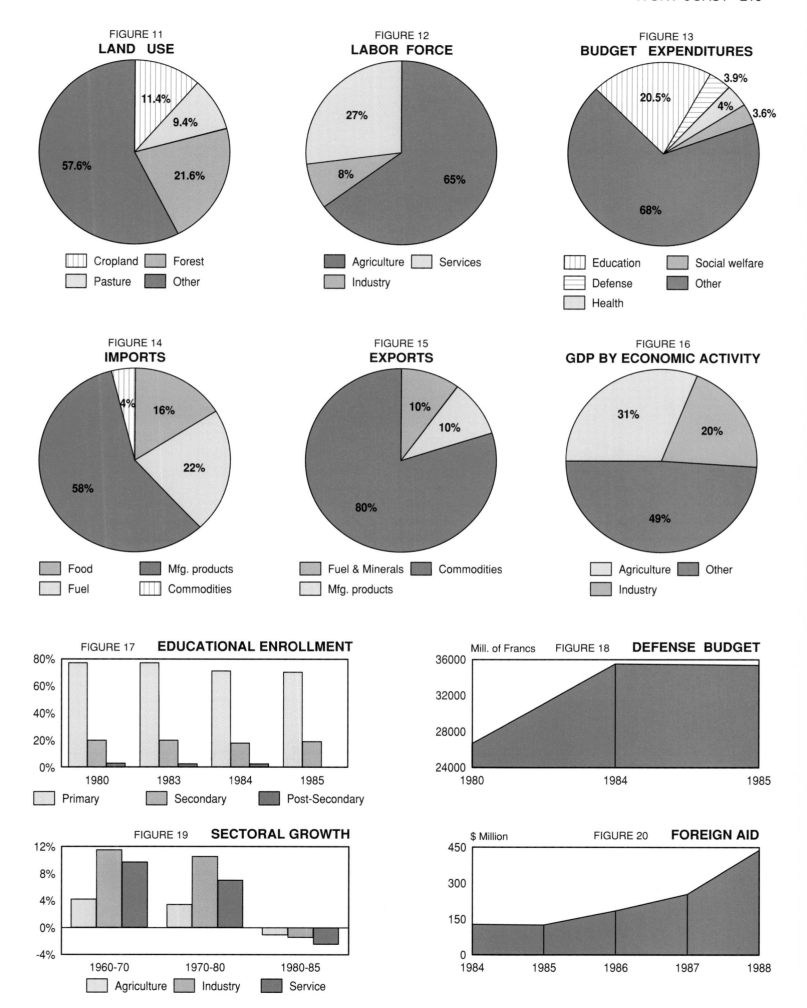

FIGURE 11
LAND USE
11.4%
9.4%
57.6%
21.6%

Cropland | Forest
Pasture | Other

FIGURE 12
LABOR FORCE
27%
8%
65%

Agriculture | Services
Industry

FIGURE 13
BUDGET EXPENDITURES
3.9%
20.5%
4%
3.6%
68%

Education | Social welfare
Defense | Other
Health

FIGURE 14
IMPORTS
4%
16%
22%
58%

Food | Mfg. products
Fuel | Commodities

FIGURE 15
EXPORTS
10%
10%
80%

Fuel & Minerals | Commodities
Mfg. products

FIGURE 16
GDP BY ECONOMIC ACTIVITY
31%
20%
49%

Agriculture | Other
Industry

FIGURE 17 **EDUCATIONAL ENROLLMENT**
80%
60%
40%
20%
0%
1980   1983   1984   1985

Primary | Secondary | Post-Secondary

Mill. of Francs   FIGURE 18   **DEFENSE BUDGET**
36000
32000
28000
24000
1980   1984   1985

FIGURE 19   **SECTORAL GROWTH**
12%
8%
4%
0%
-4%
1960-70   1970-80   1980-85

Agriculture | Industry | Service

$ Million   FIGURE 20   **FOREIGN AID**
450
300
150
0
1984   1985   1986   1987   1988

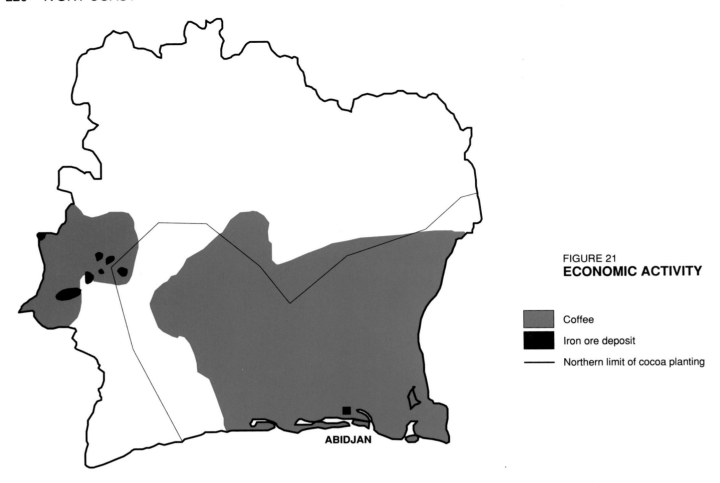

FIGURE 21
ECONOMIC ACTIVITY

Coffee

Iron ore deposit

Northern limit of cocoa planting

ABIDJAN

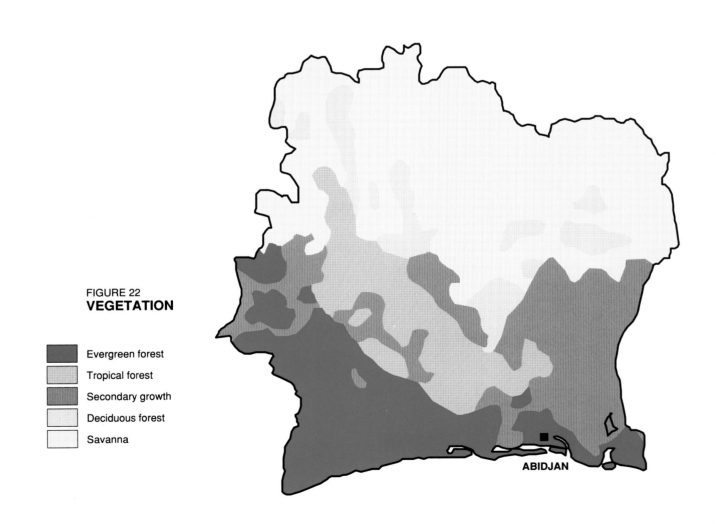

FIGURE 22
VEGETATION

Evergreen forest

Tropical forest

Secondary growth

Deciduous forest

Savanna

ABIDJAN

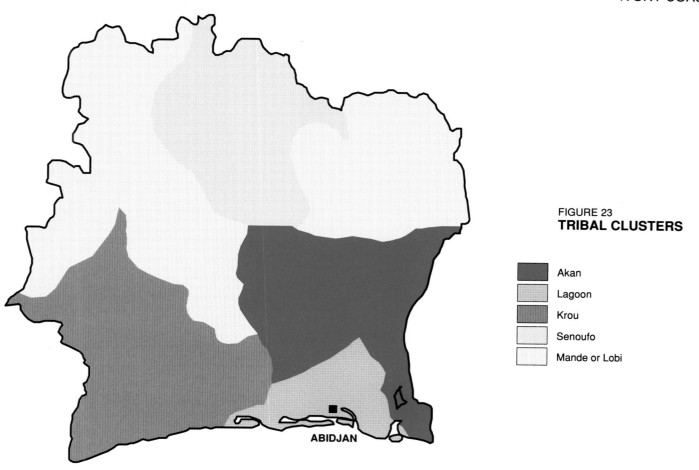

FIGURE 23
TRIBAL CLUSTERS

Akan

Lagoon

Krou

Senoufo

Mande or Lobi

ABIDJAN

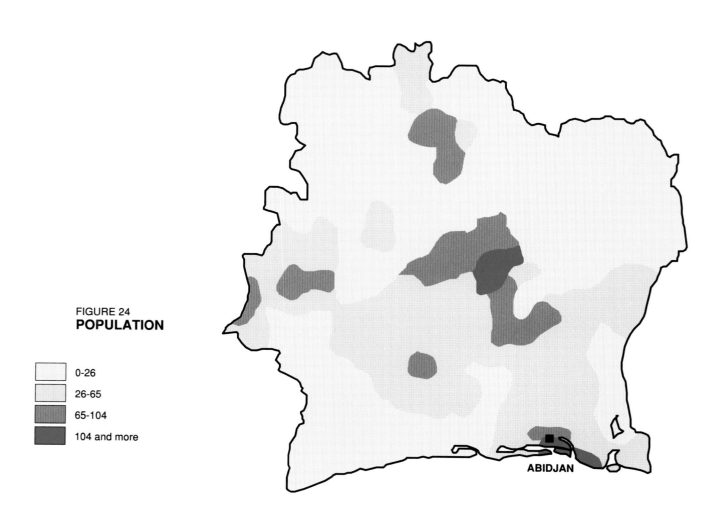

FIGURE 24
POPULATION

0-26

26-65

65-104

104 and more

ABIDJAN

JAMAICA

The third largest island in the Caribbean, Jamaica ranks 144th in size and 116th in population. Until the mid-1970s, it had a prosperous economy based partly on agricultural exports and partly on bauxite, of which it was the world's second largest producer. However, in the mid-1970s a number of circumstances combined to precipitate a downward spiral that brought the country to the brink of bankruptcy. The principal factor in this crisis was the Manley government's imposition of a levy on aluminum ingots, which led to a decline in their output from 15 million tons in 1974 to 10 million tons in 1976. Reduced production of bauxite combined with drastically increased energy costs caused a gap in the balance of payments that widened in the late 1980s. Tourism, Jamaica's second largest foreign exchange earner, has also faltered in recent years. Despite IMF credits totaling approximately $350 million, Jamaica has had negative economic growth for nearly every year during the past decade.

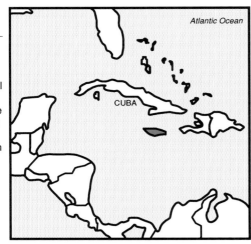

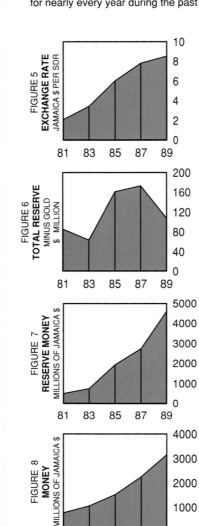

FIGURE 5 EXCHANGE RATE — JAMAICA $ PER SDR

FIGURE 6 TOTAL RESERVE MINUS GOLD — $ MILLION

FIGURE 7 RESERVE MONEY — MILLIONS OF JAMAICA $

FIGURE 8 MONEY — MILLIONS OF JAMAICA $

FIGURE 9 CONSUMER PRICES — INDEX NUMBERS: 1985=100

FIGURE 10 INTERNATIONAL TRANSACTIONS — MILLIONS OF JAMAICA $
Exports Imports

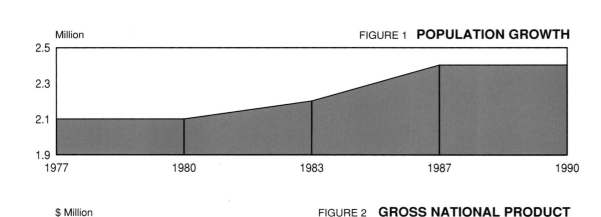

FIGURE 1 **POPULATION GROWTH**
Million

FIGURE 2 **GROSS NATIONAL PRODUCT**
$ Million

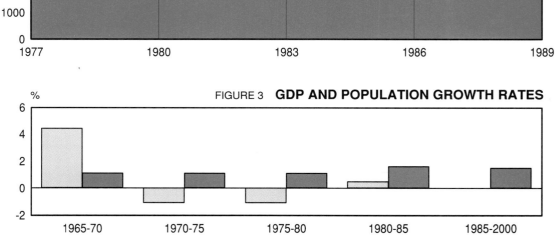

FIGURE 3 **GDP AND POPULATION GROWTH RATES**
%
GDP   Population

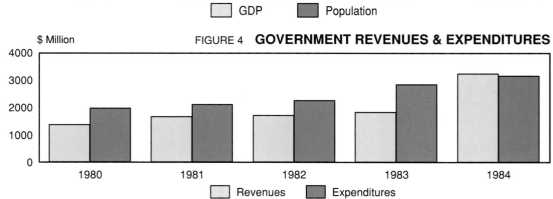

FIGURE 4 **GOVERNMENT REVENUES & EXPENDITURES**
$ Million
Revenues   Expenditures

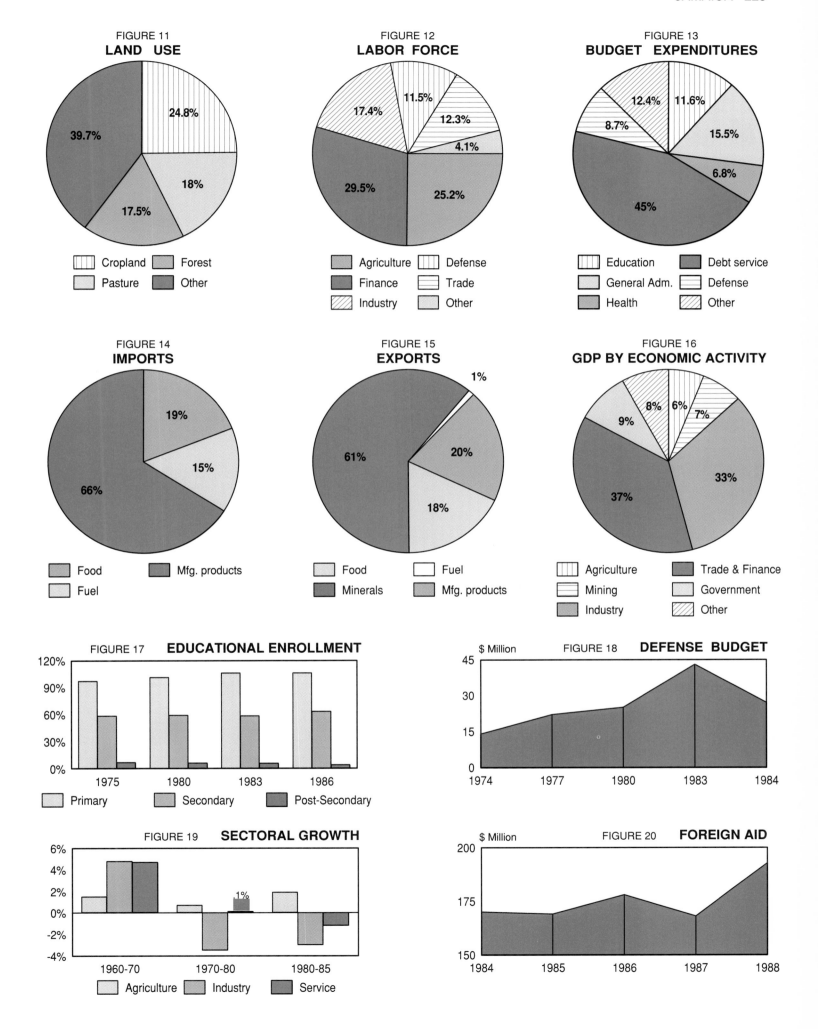

FIGURE 11
LAND USE

24.8%
39.7%
18%
17.5%

Cropland · Forest · Pasture · Other

FIGURE 12
LABOR FORCE

11.5%
17.4%
12.3%
4.1%
29.5%
25.2%

Agriculture · Defense · Finance · Trade · Industry · Other

FIGURE 13
BUDGET EXPENDITURES

12.4%
11.6%
8.7%
15.5%
6.8%
45%

Education · Debt service · General Adm. · Defense · Health · Other

FIGURE 14
IMPORTS

19%
15%
66%

Food · Mfg. products · Fuel

FIGURE 15
EXPORTS

1%
61%
20%
18%

Food · Fuel · Minerals · Mfg. products

FIGURE 16
GDP BY ECONOMIC ACTIVITY

8% 6%
9% 7%
37%
33%

Agriculture · Trade & Finance · Mining · Government · Industry · Other

FIGURE 17 **EDUCATIONAL ENROLLMENT**

120%
90%
60%
30%
0%
1975   1980   1983   1986

Primary · Secondary · Post-Secondary

$ Million FIGURE 18 **DEFENSE BUDGET**

45
30
15
0
1974   1977   1980   1983   1984

FIGURE 19 **SECTORAL GROWTH**

6%
4%
2%
1%
0%
-2%
-4%
1960-70   1970-80   1980-85

Agriculture · Industry · Service

$ Million FIGURE 20 **FOREIGN AID**

200
175
150
1984   1985   1986   1987   1988

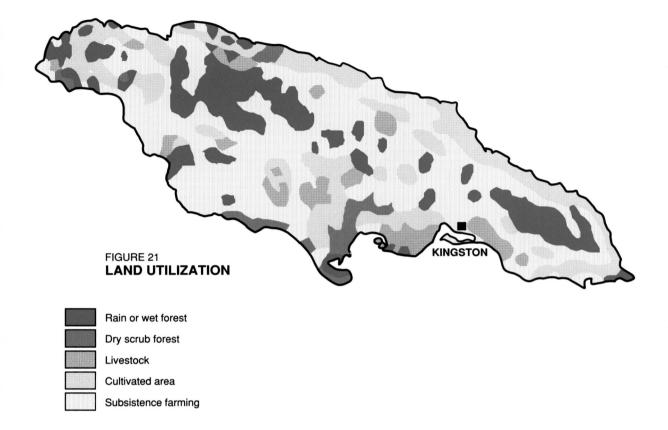

FIGURE 21
LAND UTILIZATION

Rain or wet forest

Dry scrub forest

Livestock

Cultivated area

Subsistence farming

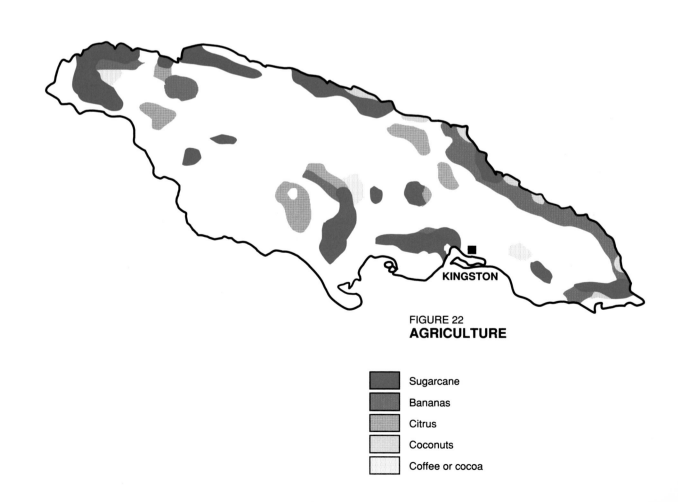

FIGURE 22
AGRICULTURE

Sugarcane

Bananas

Citrus

Coconuts

Coffee or cocoa

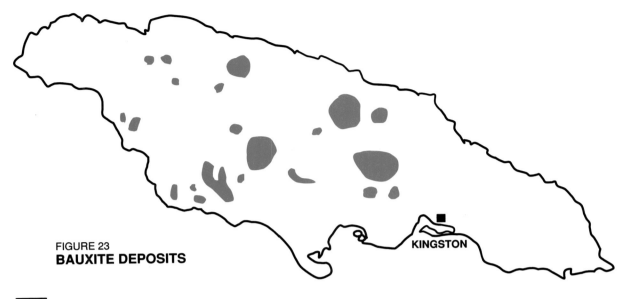

FIGURE 23
BAUXITE DEPOSITS

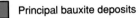

Principal bauxite deposits

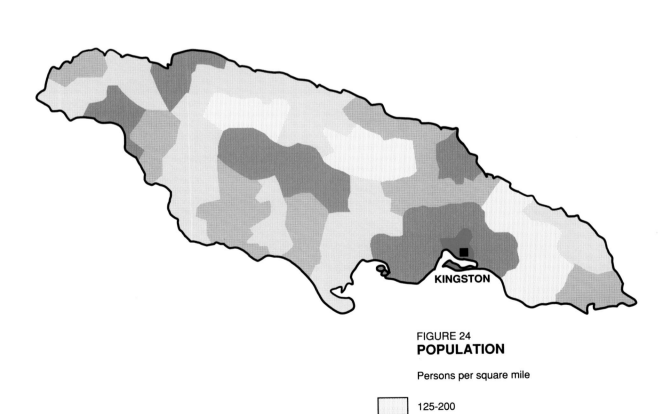

FIGURE 24
POPULATION

Persons per square mile

	125-200
	200-300
	300-400
	400-650
	5,000-40,000

JORDAN

A nearly landlocked nation in the heart of the Arab world, Jordan ranks 107th in land area and 113rd in population. While classified as a lower middle-income country, Jordan has many advantages over the other Middle Eastern countries: overall political and economic stability, dependable allies in the Arab world as well as in the West, and a liberal investment code. Barriers to growth are almost as numerous: a limited domestic market, lack of mineral resources other than phosphate, and a shortage of skilled labor aggravated by the flight of skilled labor to oil-rich Arab countries. The burden of hostilities with Israel (of which Jordan bore the brunt in the 1960s and 1970s) has been reduced following the no-war, no-peace stalemate of recent years while generous aid has been forthcoming from both the United States and Saudi Arabia. The economy has adjusted itself to the severe setbacks it sustained following the 1967 war, especially the loss of the agriculturally rich West Bank. However, the Iraqi invasion of Kuwait in 1990 and the ensuing flood of more than 650,000 refugees into Jordan threatened Jordan's fragile economy.

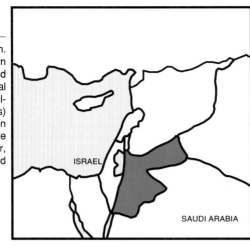

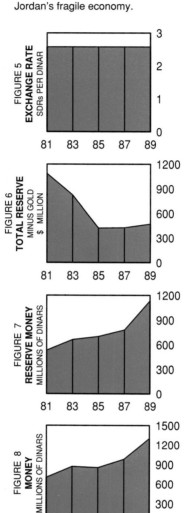

FIGURE 5 — EXCHANGE RATE — SDRs PER DINAR

FIGURE 6 — TOTAL RESERVE — MINUS GOLD — $ MILLION

FIGURE 7 — RESERVE MONEY — MILLIONS OF DINARS

FIGURE 8 — MONEY — MILLIONS OF DINARS

FIGURE 9 — CONSUMER PRICES — INDEX NUMBERS: 1985=100

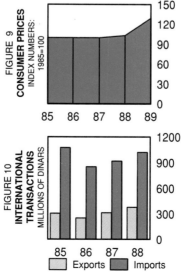

FIGURE 10 — INTERNATIONAL TRANSACTIONS — MILLIONS OF DINARS

Exports   Imports

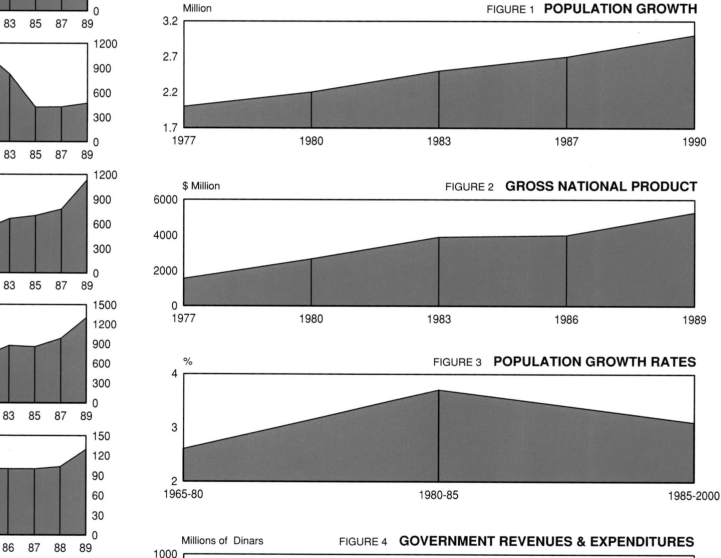

FIGURE 1 **POPULATION GROWTH**

FIGURE 2 **GROSS NATIONAL PRODUCT**

FIGURE 3 **POPULATION GROWTH RATES**

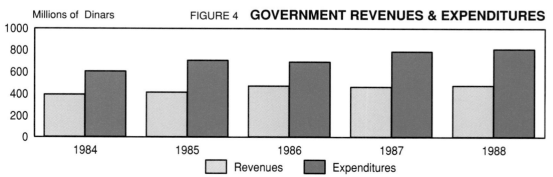

FIGURE 4 **GOVERNMENT REVENUES & EXPENDITURES**

Millions of Dinars

Revenues   Expenditures

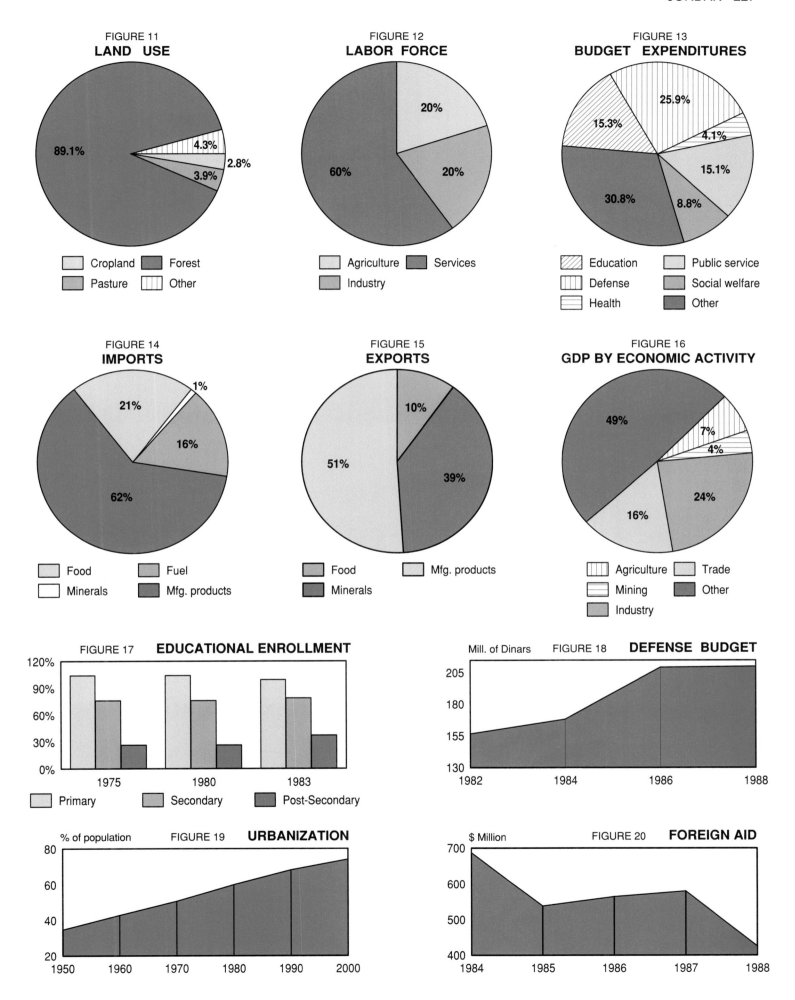

FIGURE 11
LAND USE

89.1%
4.3%
2.8%
3.9%

Cropland   Forest
Pasture   Other

FIGURE 12
LABOR FORCE

20%
20%
60%

Agriculture   Services
Industry

FIGURE 13
BUDGET EXPENDITURES

25.9%
15.3%
4.1%
15.1%
30.8%
8.8%

Education   Public service
Defense   Social welfare
Health   Other

FIGURE 14
IMPORTS

1%
21%
16%
62%

Food   Fuel
Minerals   Mfg. products

FIGURE 15
EXPORTS

10%
51%
39%

Food   Mfg. products
Minerals

FIGURE 16
GDP BY ECONOMIC ACTIVITY

49%
7%
4%
24%
16%

Agriculture   Trade
Mining   Other
Industry

FIGURE 17   EDUCATIONAL ENROLLMENT

120%
90%
60%
30%
0%
1975   1980   1983

Primary   Secondary   Post-Secondary

Mill. of Dinars   FIGURE 18   DEFENSE BUDGET

205
180
155
130
1982   1984   1986   1988

% of population   FIGURE 19   URBANIZATION

80
60
40
20
1950   1960   1970   1980   1990   2000

$ Million   FIGURE 20   FOREIGN AID

700
600
500
400
1984   1985   1986   1987   1988

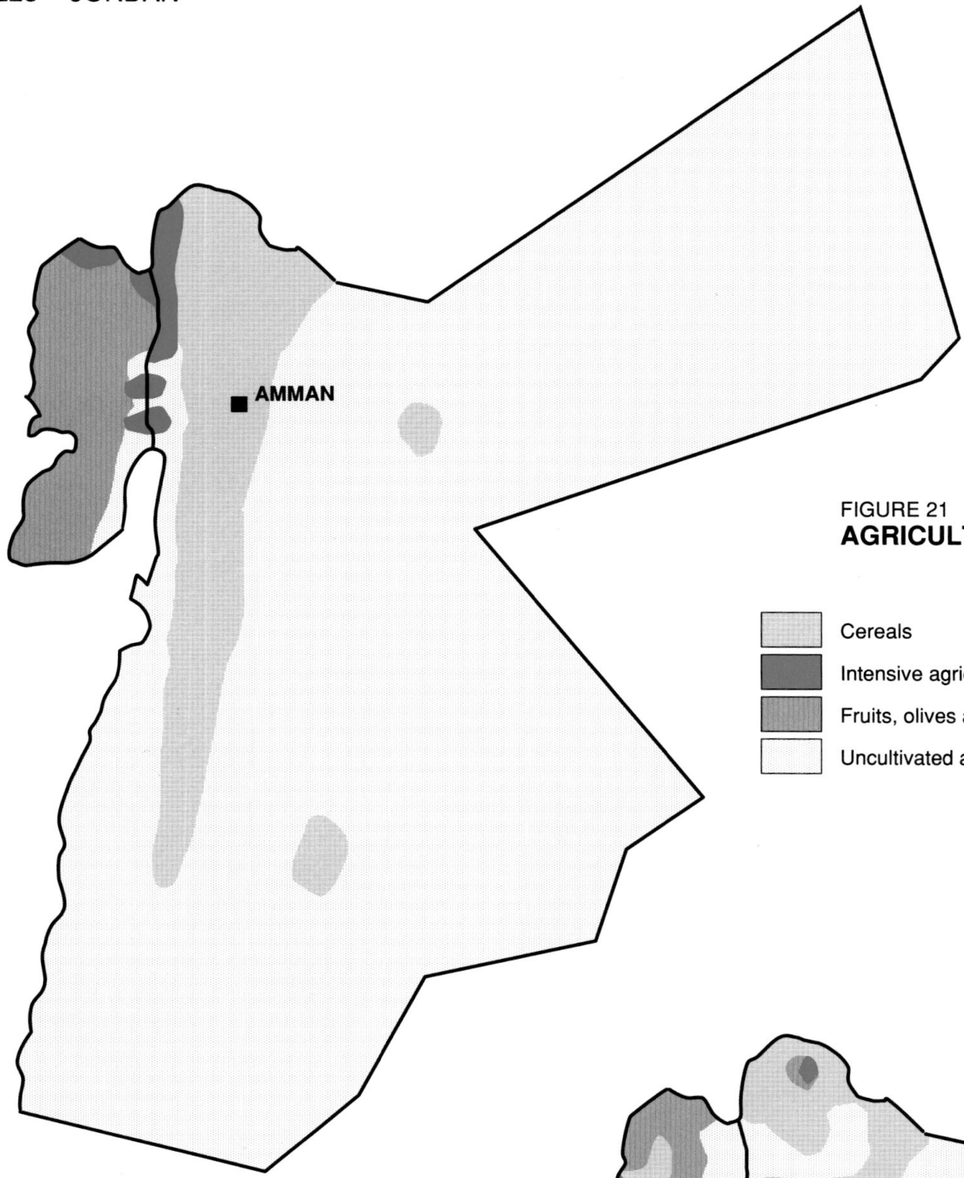

FIGURE 21
AGRICULTURE

Cereals

Intensive agriculture

Fruits, olives and grapes

Uncultivated arid region

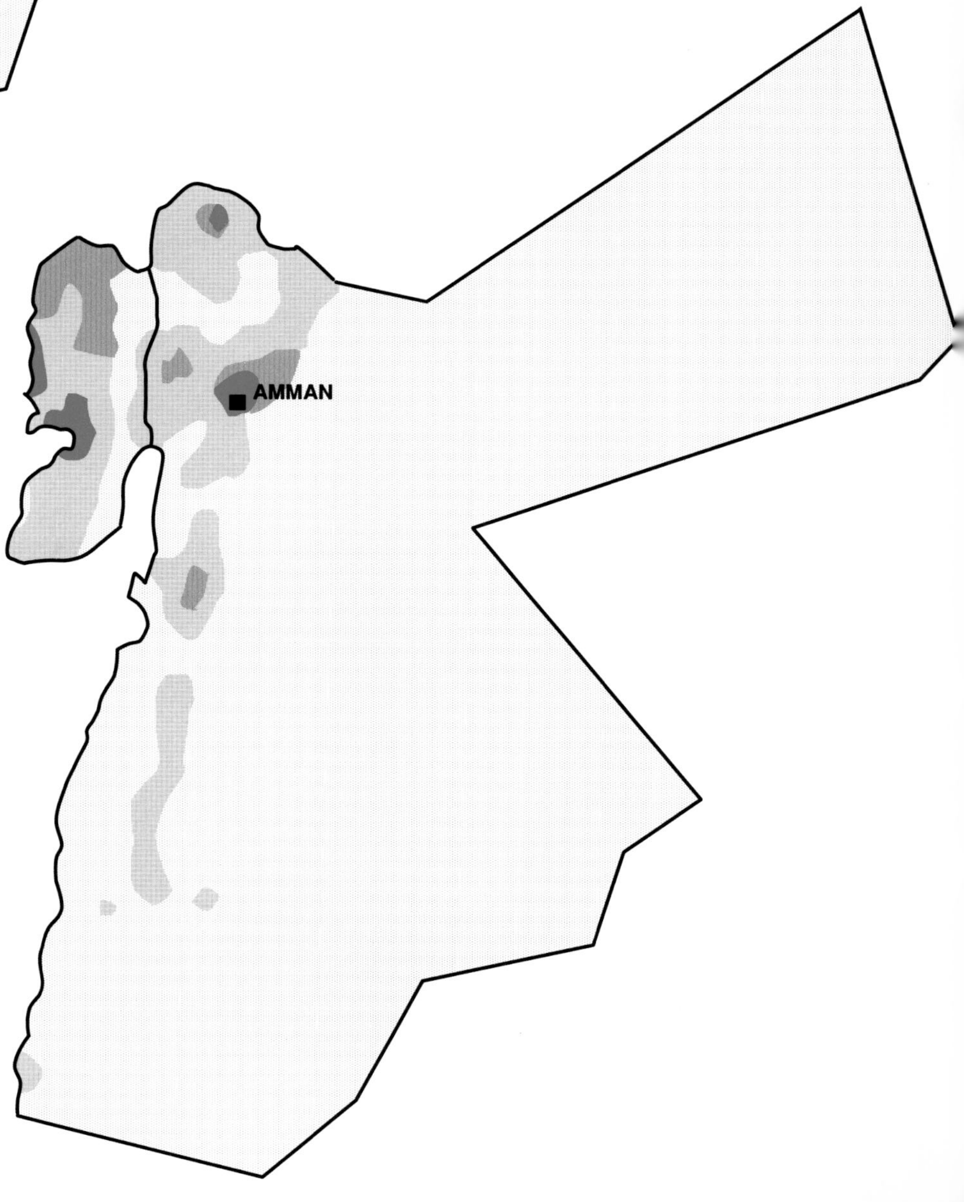

■ AMMAN

FIGURE 22
POPULATION

Persons per square mile

0-26

26-518

518-1,295

1,295-2,590

■ AMMAN

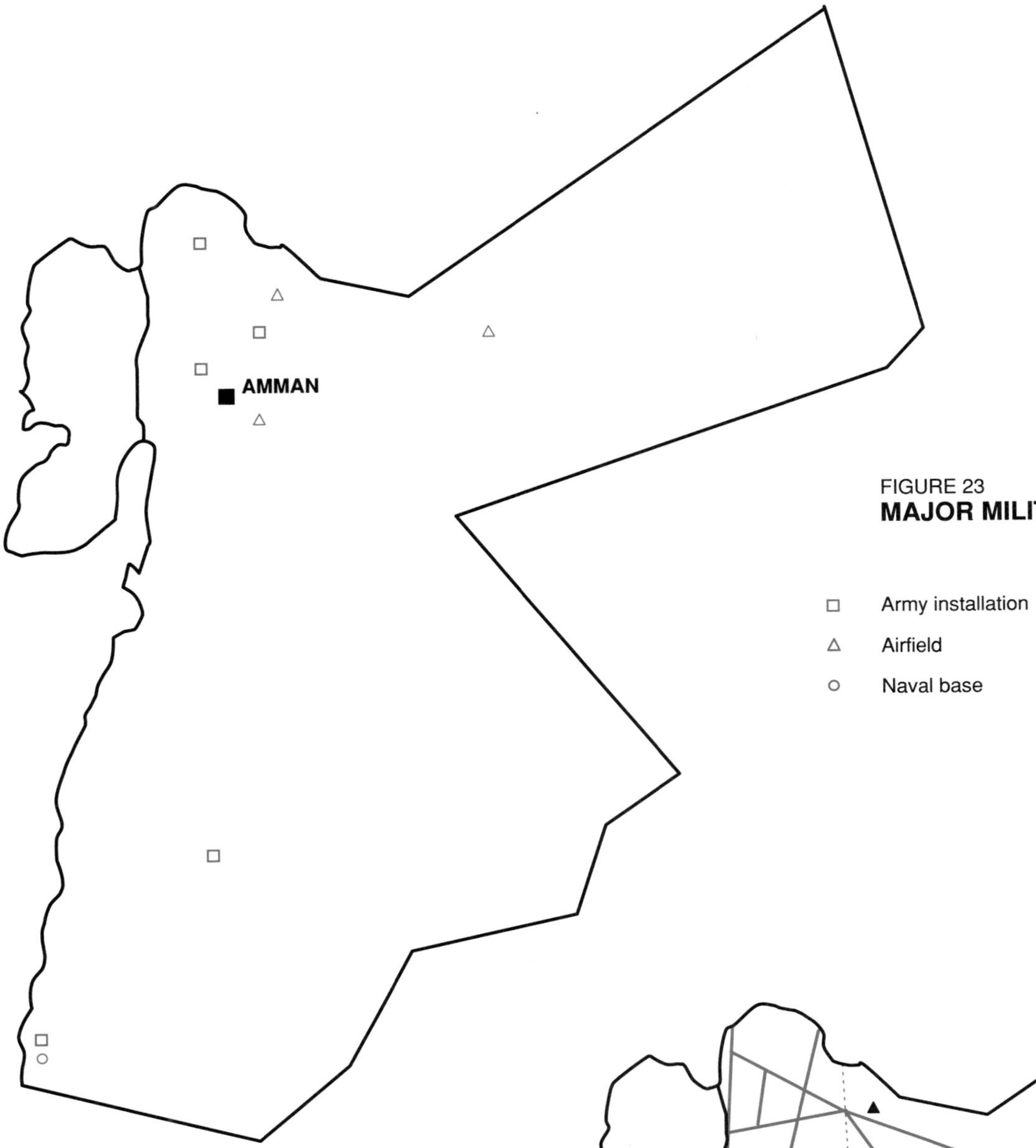

FIGURE 23
MAJOR MILITARY INSTALLATIONS

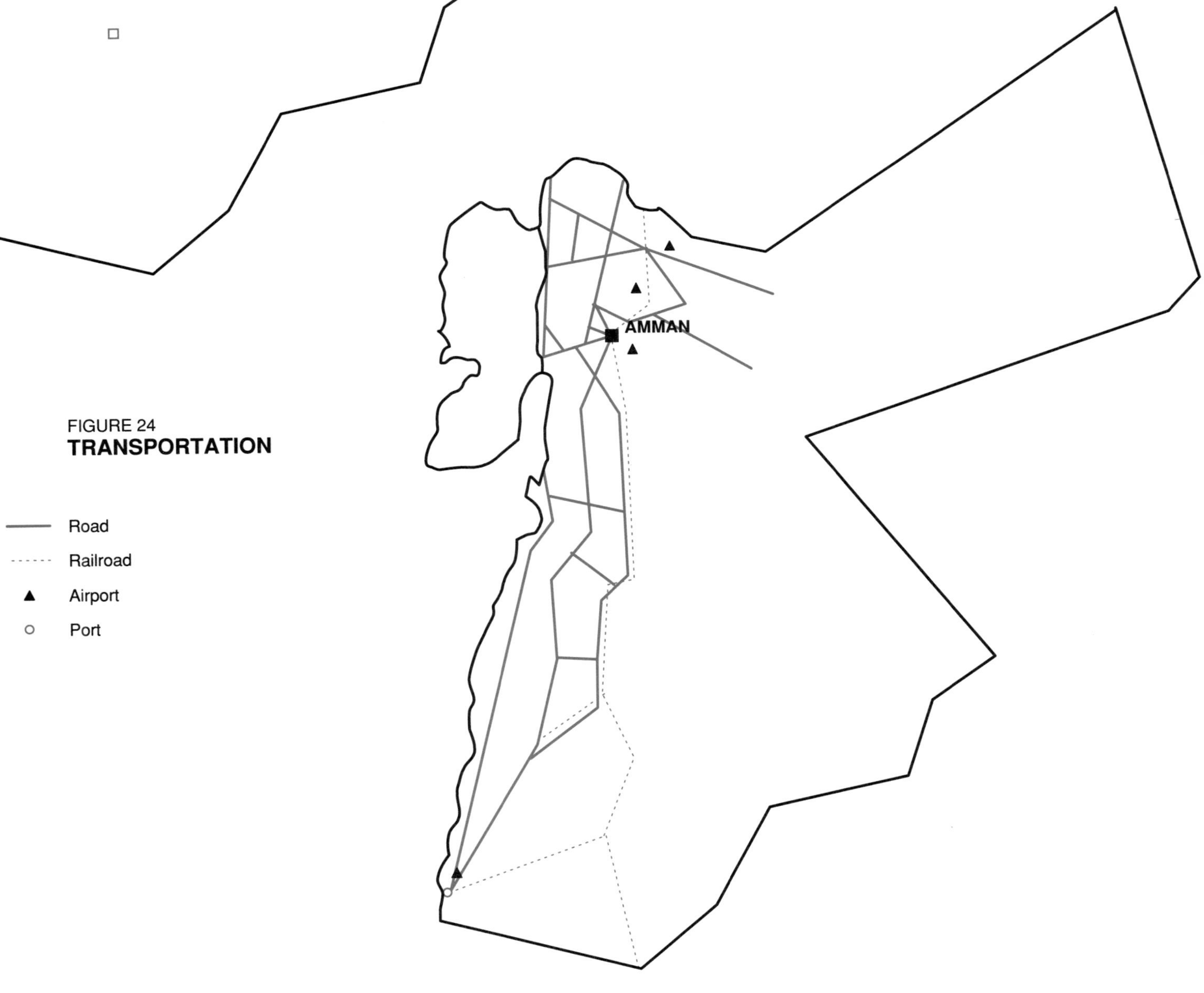

□ Army installation

△ Airfield

○ Naval base

FIGURE 24
TRANSPORTATION

——— Road

········· Railroad

▲ Airport

○ Port

AMMAN

KENYA

A country of striking topographical and climatic variety located on the Equator, Kenya ranks 44th in land area and 38th in population. It inherited from the British a strong agricultural and industrial base and was for long considered the bellwether of the East African economy. Kenya has not borne out its economic potential but, by the same token, it has been spared much of the political instability and economic disruptions suffered by some of its neighbors. Since independence some 20 years ago, it has launched development plans calling for a mixed economy. Despite impressive progress in certain areas, nearly a fifth of the GDP still originates outside the monetary economy and more than half the agricultural output consists of subsistence farming. President Daniel arap Moi has acknowledged corruption and smuggling as major problems facing the economy. However, in 1990 he continued to resist political pressure for a multiparty system and responded with increasingly repressive actions against his critics.

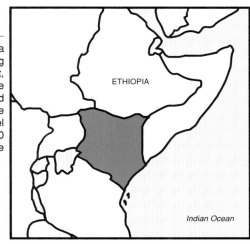

ETHIOPIA

Indian Ocean

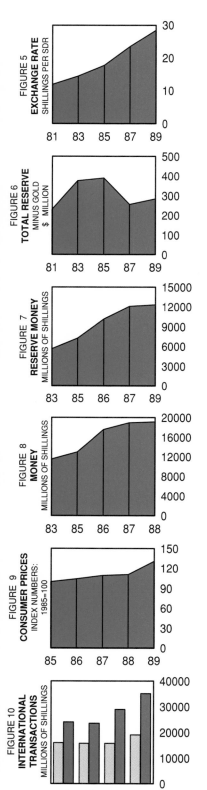

FIGURE 5 **EXCHANGE RATE** SHILLINGS PER SDR

FIGURE 6 **TOTAL RESERVE** MINUS GOLD $ MILLION

FIGURE 7 **RESERVE MONEY** MILLIONS OF SHILLINGS

FIGURE 8 **MONEY** MILLIONS OF SHILLINGS

FIGURE 9 **CONSUMER PRICES** INDEX NUMBERS: 1985=100

FIGURE 10 **INTERNATIONAL TRANSACTIONS** MILLIONS OF SHILLINGS

Exports Imports

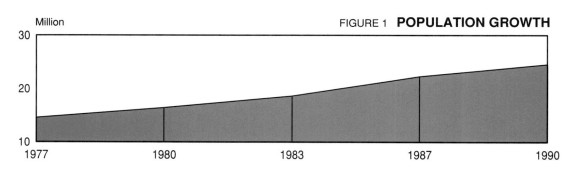

Million   FIGURE 1 **POPULATION GROWTH**

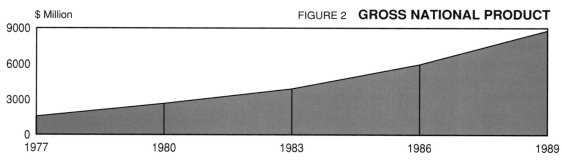

$ Million   FIGURE 2 **GROSS NATIONAL PRODUCT**

FIGURE 3 **GDP AND POPULATION GROWTH RATES**

%

GDP   Population

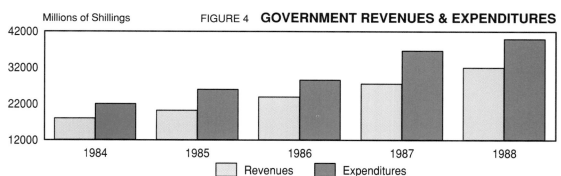

Millions of Shillings   FIGURE 4 **GOVERNMENT REVENUES & EXPENDITURES**

Revenues   Expenditures

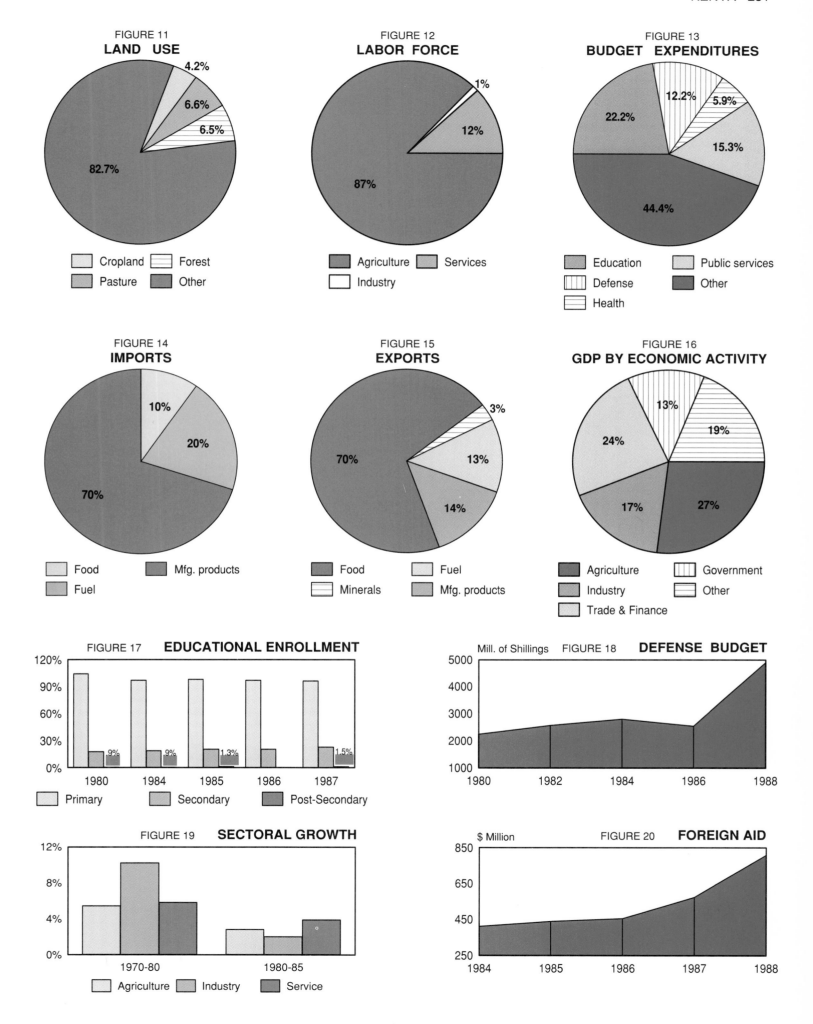

FIGURE 11
LAND USE

4.2%
6.6%
6.5%
82.7%

Cropland ▢ Forest ▤
Pasture ▢ Other ▢

FIGURE 12
LABOR FORCE

1%
12%
87%

Agriculture ▢ Services ▢
Industry ▢

FIGURE 13
BUDGET EXPENDITURES

12.2% 5.9%
22.2% 15.3%
44.4%

Education ▢ Public services ▢
Defense ▦ Other ▢
Health ▤

FIGURE 14
IMPORTS

10%
20%
70%

Food ▢ Mfg. products ▢
Fuel ▢

FIGURE 15
EXPORTS

3%
70% 13%
14%

Food ▢ Fuel ▢
Minerals ▤ Mfg. products ▢

FIGURE 16
GDP BY ECONOMIC ACTIVITY

13%
24% 19%
17% 27%

Agriculture ▢ Government ▦
Industry ▢ Other ▢
Trade & Finance ▢

FIGURE 17 **EDUCATIONAL ENROLLMENT**

120%
90%
60%
30%
0%
          1980   1984   1985   1986   1987
          .9%   .9%   1.3%   1.5%

Primary ▢ Secondary ▢ Post-Secondary ▢

Mill. of Shillings FIGURE 18 **DEFENSE BUDGET**

5000
4000
3000
2000
1000
     1980   1982   1984   1986   1988

FIGURE 19 **SECTORAL GROWTH**

12%
8%
4%
0%
          1970-80   1980-85

Agriculture ▢ Industry ▢ Service ▢

$ Million FIGURE 20 **FOREIGN AID**

850
650
450
250
     1984   1985   1986   1987   1988

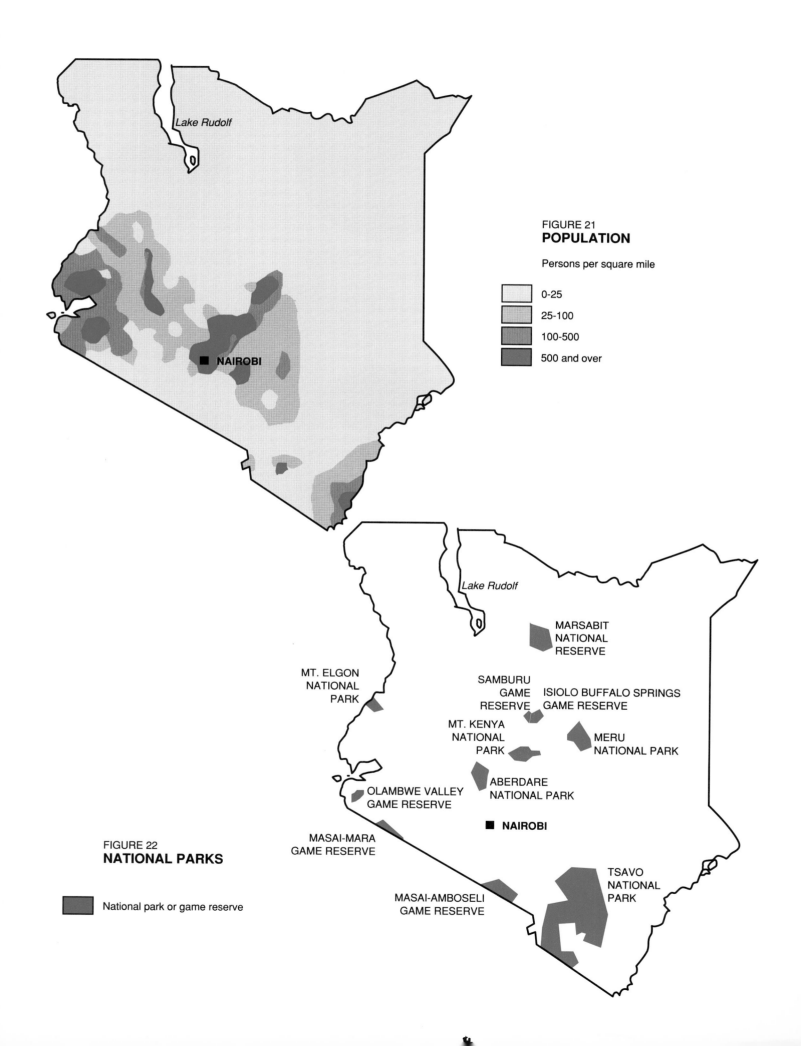

Lake Rudolf

FIGURE 21
POPULATION

Persons per square mile

0-25

25-100

100-500

500 and over

■ **NAIROBI**

Lake Rudolf

MARSABIT
NATIONAL
RESERVE

MT. ELGON
NATIONAL
PARK

SAMBURU
GAME
RESERVE

ISIOLO BUFFALO SPRINGS
GAME RESERVE

MT. KENYA
NATIONAL
PARK

MERU
NATIONAL PARK

ABERDARE
NATIONAL PARK

OLAMBWE VALLEY
GAME RESERVE

■ **NAIROBI**

FIGURE 22
NATIONAL PARKS

MASAI-MARA
GAME RESERVE

TSAVO
NATIONAL
PARK

National park or game reserve

MASAI-AMBOSELI
GAME RESERVE

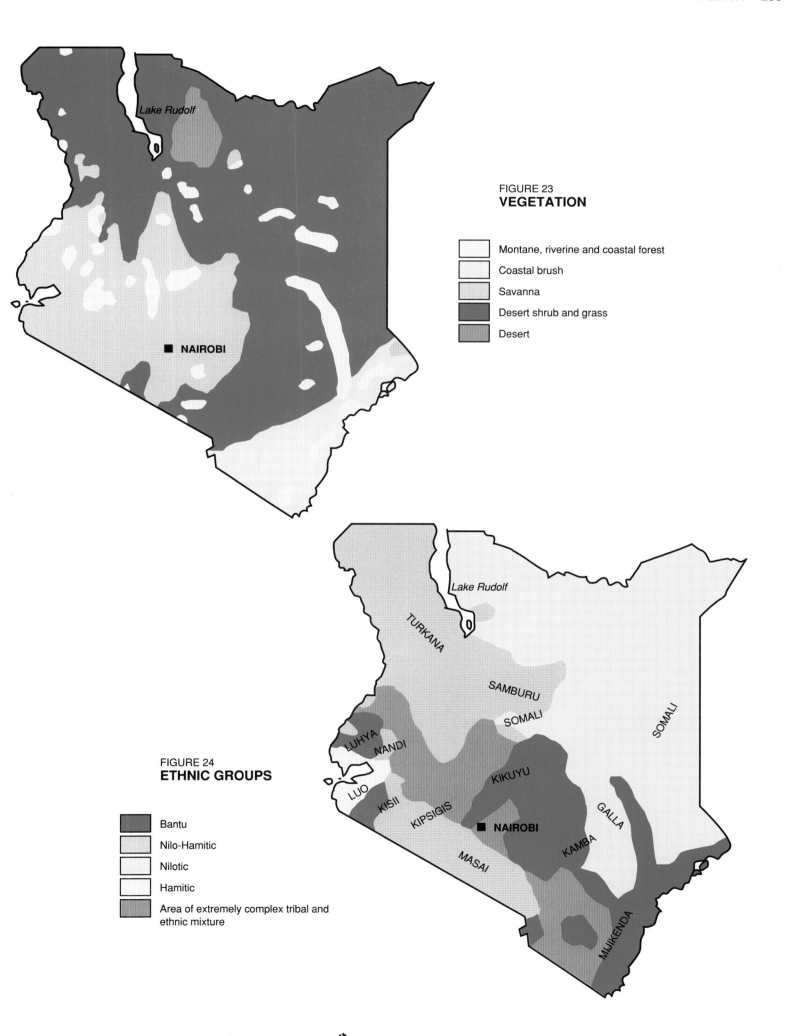

FIGURE 23
VEGETATION

Lake Rudolf

■ **NAIROBI**

Montane, riverine and coastal forest

Coastal brush

Savanna

Desert shrub and grass

Desert

FIGURE 24
ETHNIC GROUPS

Bantu

Nilo-Hamitic

Nilotic

Hamitic

Area of extremely complex tribal and
ethnic mixture

Lake Rudolf

TURKANA

SAMBURU

SOMALI

SOMALI

LUHYA

NANDI

LUO

KISII

KIPSIGIS

KIKUYU

GALLA

■ **NAIROBI**

KAMBA

MASAI

MIJIKENDA

NORTH KOREA

Located on the northern half of the Korean Peninsula, North Korea (or the Democratic People's Republic of Korea) ranks 94th in land area and 39th in population. On most indicators, it ranks poorly compared with South Korea. As a socialist, centrally planned, "command" economy, it has no market sector. Even agriculture is fully collectivized. Although heavy dependence on foreign aid (from the USSR as well as China) marked the early years of the republic, official emphasis is on chuch'e sasang, or self-reliance, elevated to the status of an ideology by Kim Il Sung, the only president the country has known since the end of World War II. The sparseness of official statistics makes it difficult to assess the current condition of the economy. However, travelers report that, while many consumer goods are not available, the standard of living is not much lower than that of South Korea, because most citizens receive free medical care, subsidized housing, and adequate food supplies.

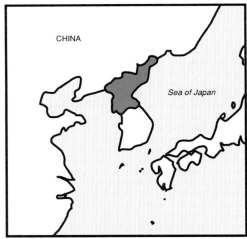

I.M.F.
INFORMATION
NOT
AVAILABLE

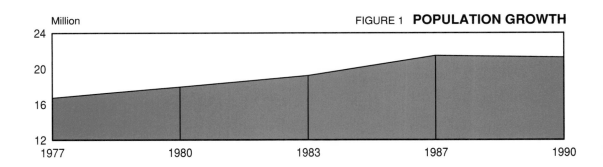

FIGURE 1 **POPULATION GROWTH**

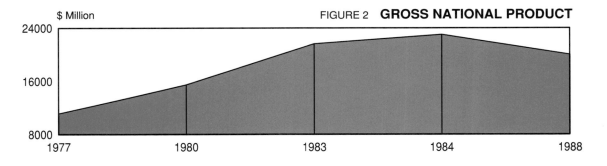

FIGURE 2 **GROSS NATIONAL PRODUCT**

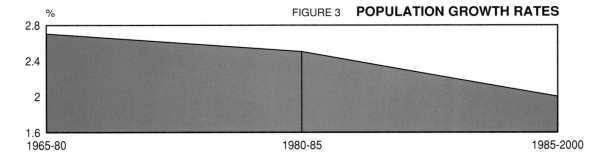

FIGURE 3 **POPULATION GROWTH RATES**

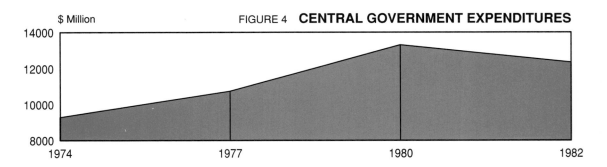

FIGURE 4 **CENTRAL GOVERNMENT EXPENDITURES**

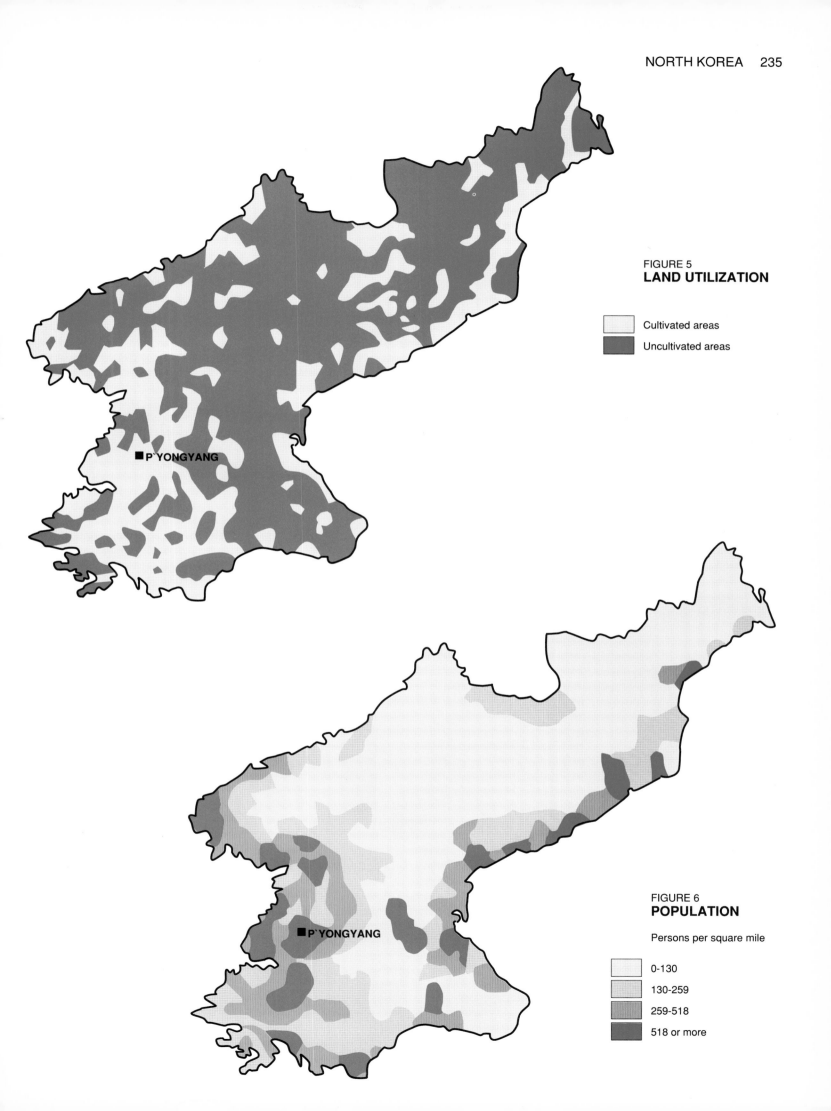

FIGURE 5
LAND UTILIZATION

Cultivated areas
Uncultivated areas

■ P'YONGYANG

FIGURE 6
POPULATION

Persons per square mile

0-130
130-259
259-518
518 or more

■ P'YONGYANG

SOUTH KOREA

Located on the southern half of the Korean Peninsula, South Korea ranks 103rd in land area and 23rd in population. Although it has fewer natural resources than its neighbor to the north, it outstrips North Korea on virtually all indicators. Its extraordinary economic growth during the 1960s and 1970s enabled it to join the ranks of the so-called ADCs (advanced developing countries) and to become one of the "Gang of Four," with Taiwan, Hong Kong, and Singapore. South Korea's economic miracle has been attributed to many factors, the most significant being strong central government intervention in the economy, incentives to private enterprise, constraints on unionization, and wage pauses. The entire industrial sector was geared for export rather than import-substitution. In the mid-1970s, South Korea began to diversify, moving into heavy capital goods, chemicals, and construction of industrial plants abroad. By the late 1980s South Korea's GNP was exceeded in Asia only by Japan, China, and India, although after three years of double-digit growth, the nation's GNP grew by only 6.7% in 1989. The growth rate for 1990 was expected to be just over 8%.

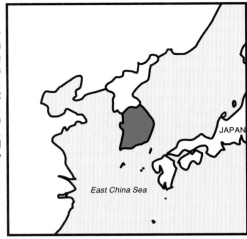

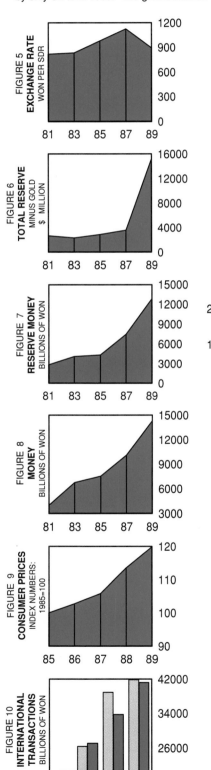

FIGURE 5 EXCHANGE RATE WON PER SDR

FIGURE 6 TOTAL RESERVE MINUS GOLD $ MILLION

FIGURE 7 RESERVE MONEY BILLIONS OF WON

FIGURE 8 MONEY BILLIONS OF WON

FIGURE 9 CONSUMER PRICES INDEX NUMBERS: 1985=100

FIGURE 10 INTERNATIONAL TRANSACTIONS BILLIONS OF WON — Exports / Imports

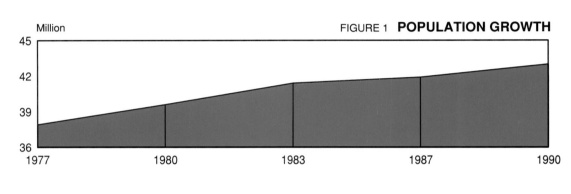

FIGURE 1 **POPULATION GROWTH**

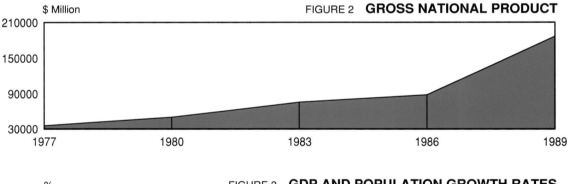

FIGURE 2 **GROSS NATIONAL PRODUCT**

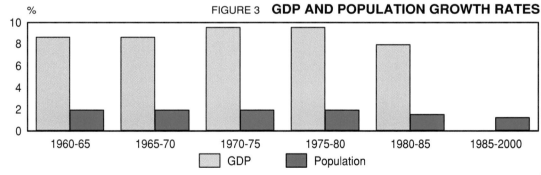

FIGURE 3 **GDP AND POPULATION GROWTH RATES** — GDP / Population

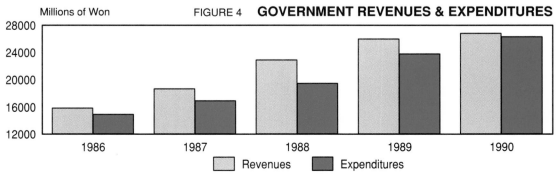

FIGURE 4 **GOVERNMENT REVENUES & EXPENDITURES** — Revenues / Expenditures

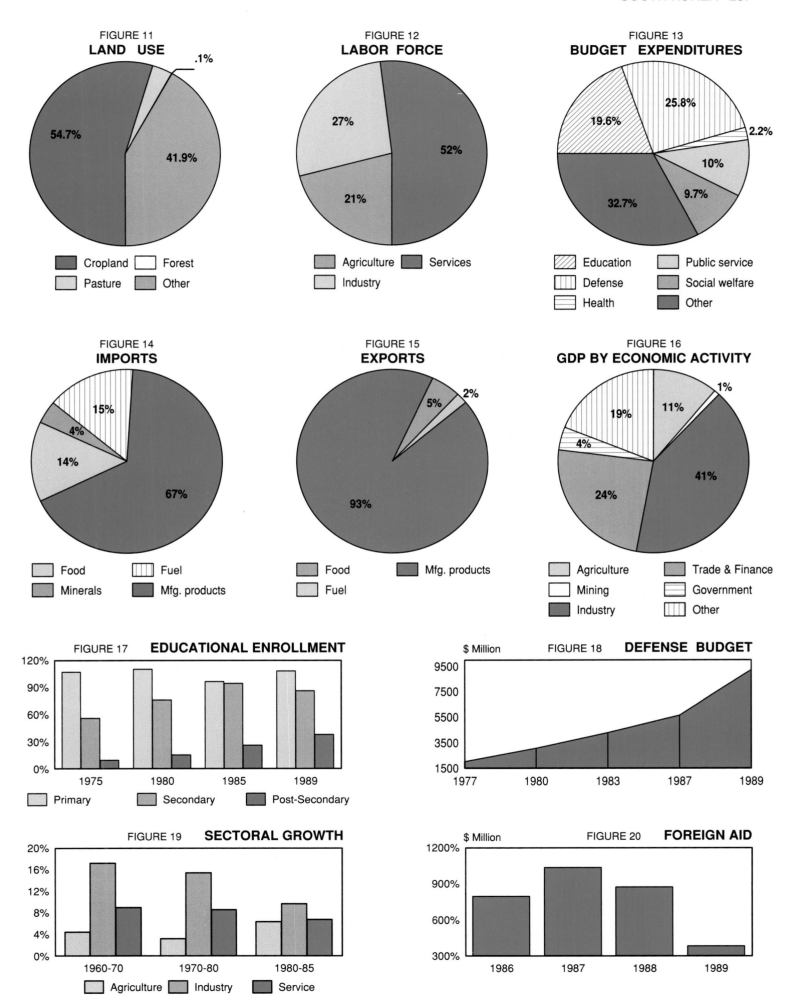

FIGURE 11
LAND USE

.1%
54.7%
41.9%

Cropland Forest
Pasture Other

FIGURE 12
LABOR FORCE

27%
52%
21%

Agriculture Services
Industry

FIGURE 13
BUDGET EXPENDITURES

25.8%
19.6%
2.2%
10%
9.7%
32.7%

Education Public service
Defense Social welfare
Health Other

FIGURE 14
IMPORTS

15%
4%
14%
67%

Food Fuel
Minerals Mfg. products

FIGURE 15
EXPORTS

2%
5%
93%

Food Mfg. products
Fuel

FIGURE 16
GDP BY ECONOMIC ACTIVITY

1%
19%
11%
4%
41%
24%

Agriculture Trade & Finance
Mining Government
Industry Other

FIGURE 17 EDUCATIONAL ENROLLMENT

120%
90%
60%
30%
0%
1975 1980 1985 1989

Primary Secondary Post-Secondary

$ Million FIGURE 18 DEFENSE BUDGET

9500
7500
5500
3500
1500
1977 1980 1983 1987 1989

FIGURE 19 SECTORAL GROWTH

20%
16%
12%
8%
4%
0%
1960-70 1970-80 1980-85

Agriculture Industry Service

$ Million FIGURE 20 FOREIGN AID

1200%
900%
600%
300%
1986 1987 1988 1989

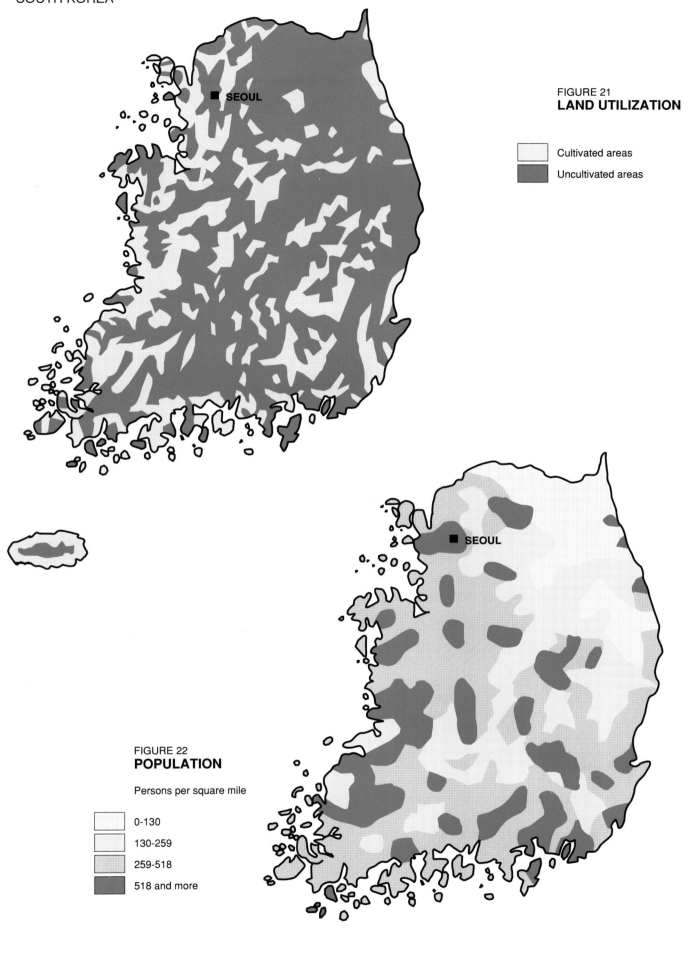

FIGURE 21
LAND UTILIZATION

Cultivated areas

Uncultivated areas

SEOUL

FIGURE 22
POPULATION

Persons per square mile

0-130

130-259

259-518

518 and more

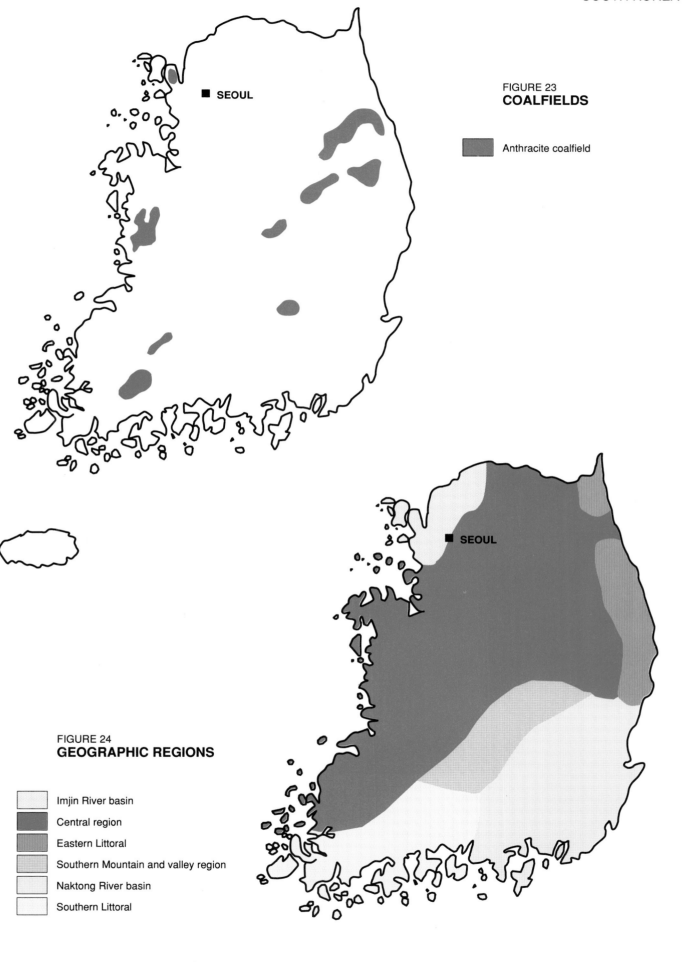

FIGURE 23
COALFIELDS

▮ Anthracite coalfield

FIGURE 24
GEOGRAPHIC REGIONS

Imjin River basin
Central region
Eastern Littoral
Southern Mountain and valley region
Naktong River basin
Southern Littoral

SEOUL

SEOUL

LAOS

One of the five landlocked countries in Asia, Laos ranks 80th in land and 102nd in population. Long after the end of the civil war that lasted nearly 20 years, Laos remains among the least developed nations of the world. The Marxist government's policies, such as collectivized farming and stringent barriers affecting internal trade, met with more resistance in the countryside than Vientiane had anticipated. The Laotian monetary unit, the kip, once the weakest currency in the world, was replaced with the liberation kip, in an effort to reduce the money supply. The food prices paid to farmers were raised in order to inhibit smuggling and induce higher production. Extra pay was offered to civil servants to reduce the exodus of trained employees. The tax system was reformed and private traders were permitted to import without limit from Thailand. These reforms helped to restore some vital signs to what once appeared to be a dying economy. A new constitution was drafted in 1990 which dropped all reference to socialism and stated its commitment to a market economy. The economy grew by about 4% in 1989 and was growing even faster in 1990.

I.M.F.
INFORMATION
NOT
AVAILABLE

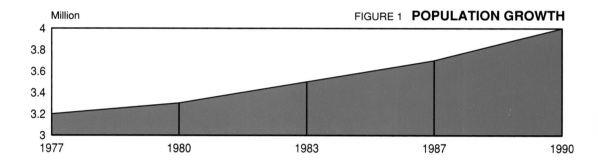

FIGURE 1 **POPULATION GROWTH**

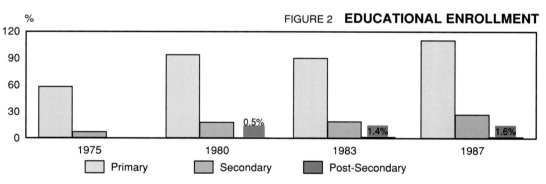

FIGURE 2 **EDUCATIONAL ENROLLMENT**

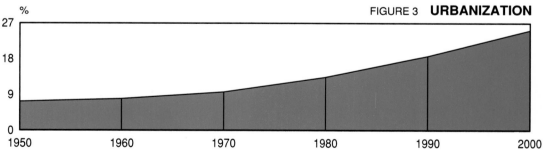

FIGURE 3 **URBANIZATION**

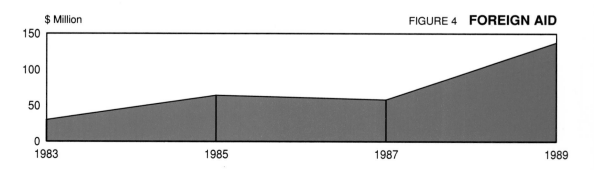

FIGURE 4 **FOREIGN AID**

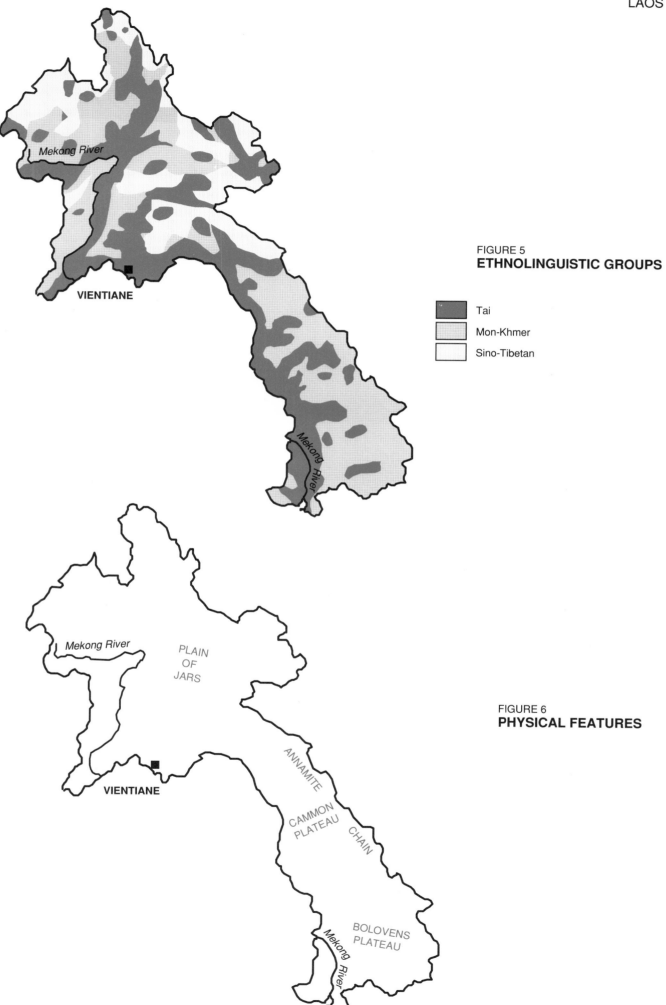

FIGURE 5
ETHNOLINGUISTIC GROUPS

Tai

Mon-Khmer

Sino-Tibetan

FIGURE 6
PHYSICAL FEATURES

LEBANON

Once known as the "Switzerland of Asia," strife-torn Lebanon ranks 146th in land area and 106th in population. Until the civil war, Beirut was the focal point of trading activity in the Middle East, especially in such service areas as banking, insurance, tourism and shipping. Lebanese universities attracted students from all over the Arab world. The civil war changed all this within the closing years of the seventies, and the state of Lebanon became more a fiction than a fact. As most statistical activities have been suspended, little significant economic information has been collected or published for nearly a decade. Nearly half of the nation's GNP is believed to have been lost between 1975 and 1977 and 700,000 skilled workers emigrated to other countries during this period. Nevertheless, the economy has proved remarkably resilient—owing much to the entrepreneurial ability of the populace—and could make a strong recovery once peace is restored.

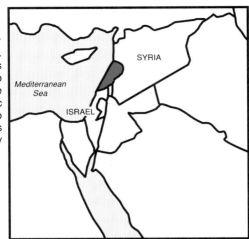

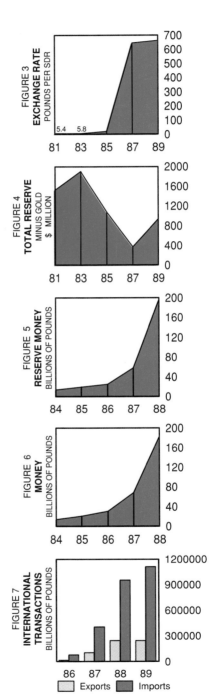

FIGURE 3 **EXCHANGE RATE** POUNDS PER SDR

FIGURE 4 **TOTAL RESERVE** MINUS GOLD $ MILLION

FIGURE 5 **RESERVE MONEY** BILLIONS OF POUNDS

FIGURE 6 **MONEY** BILLIONS OF POUNDS

FIGURE 7 **INTERNATIONAL TRANSACTIONS** BILLIONS OF POUNDS

☐ Exports ■ Imports

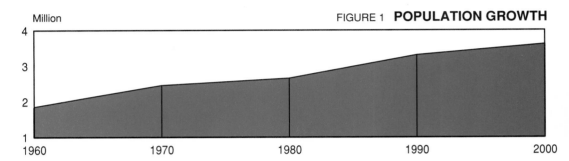

FIGURE 1 **POPULATION GROWTH**

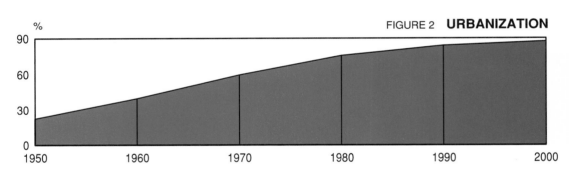

FIGURE 2 **URBANIZATION**

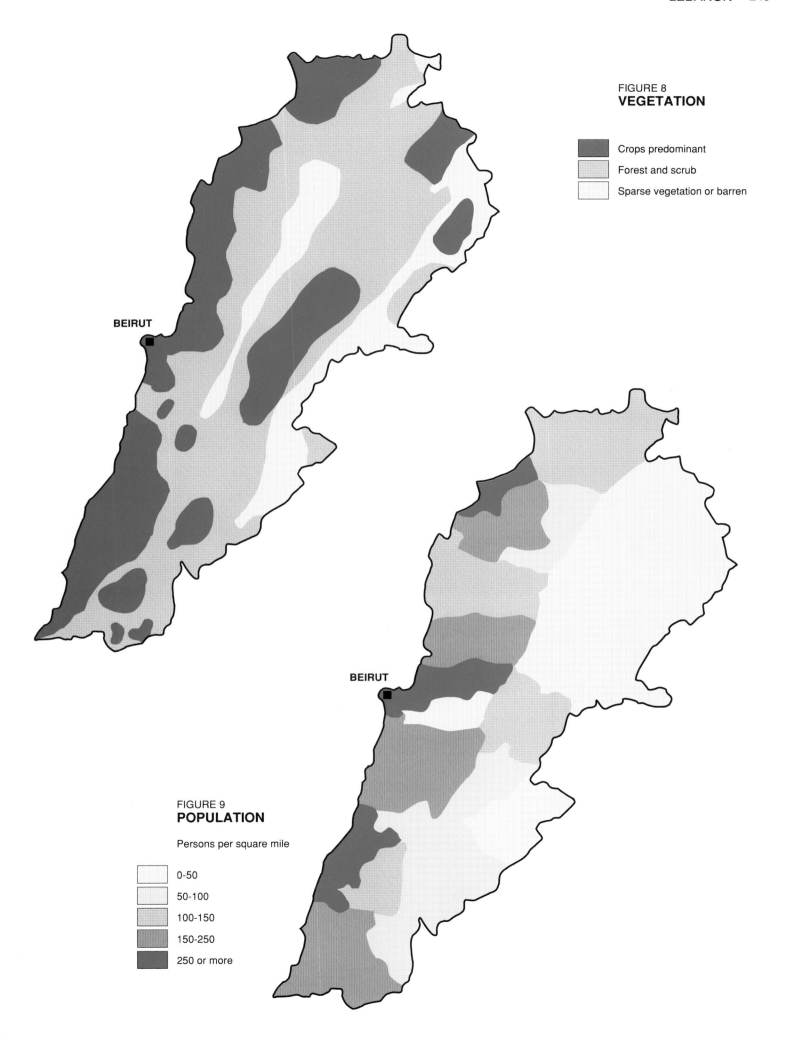

FIGURE 8
VEGETATION

Crops predominant

Forest and scrub

Sparse vegetation or barren

BEIRUT

BEIRUT

FIGURE 9
POPULATION

Persons per square mile

0-50

50-100

100-150

150-250

250 or more

LIBERIA

The oldest black republic in Africa, Liberia ranks 104th in land area and 117th in population. Liberia is most closely identified with two things: ships and rubber. In terms of gross registered tonnage, the Liberian merchant marine is the world's largest because the Liberian flag is the most popular flag of convenience. Rubber plantations initiated by the U.S. rubber manufacturer Firestone have made Liberia the World's sixth ranking natural rubber producer. More recently, rubber has been superseded by iron ore, which accounts for approximately 75% of Liberian exports. Although Samuel Doe pledged a return to civilian rule after he corrected the country's economic ills, his reputation for brutality began soon after the 1980 coup that brought him to power. Doe was killed in 1990 by rebels fighting to overthrow him in a civil war. Leaders of the warring factions signed a cease-fire in 1991 and set up an interim government until free elections could be held. The Liberian civil war displaced about half of the nation's 2.5 million citizens, killed tens of thousands, and wrecked the country's economy.

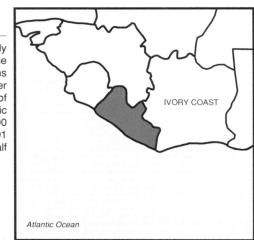

IVORY COAST

Atlantic Ocean

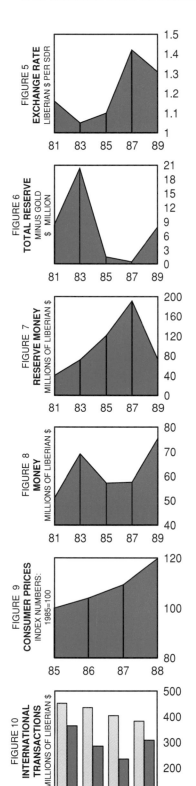

FIGURE 5 EXCHANGE RATE — LIBERIAN $ PER SDR

FIGURE 6 TOTAL RESERVE — MINUS GOLD $ MILLION

FIGURE 7 RESERVE MONEY — MILLIONS OF LIBERIAN $

FIGURE 8 MONEY — MILLIONS OF LIBERIAN $

FIGURE 9 CONSUMER PRICES — INDEX NUMBERS: 1985=100

FIGURE 10 INTERNATIONAL TRANSACTIONS — MILLIONS OF LIBERIAN $
Exports Imports

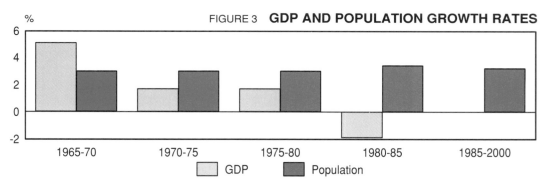

FIGURE 1 **POPULATION GROWTH**

Million

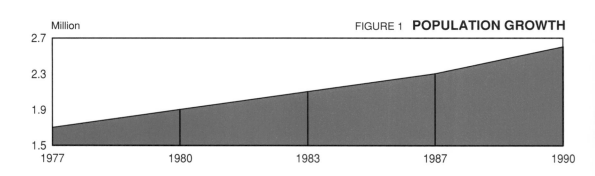

$ Million

FIGURE 2 **GROSS NATIONAL PRODUCT**

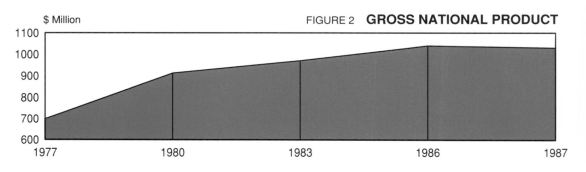

%

FIGURE 3 **GDP AND POPULATION GROWTH RATES**

GDP   Population

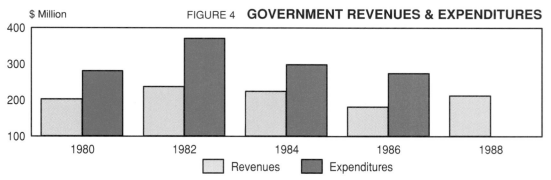

$ Million

FIGURE 4 **GOVERNMENT REVENUES & EXPENDITURES**

Revenues   Expenditures

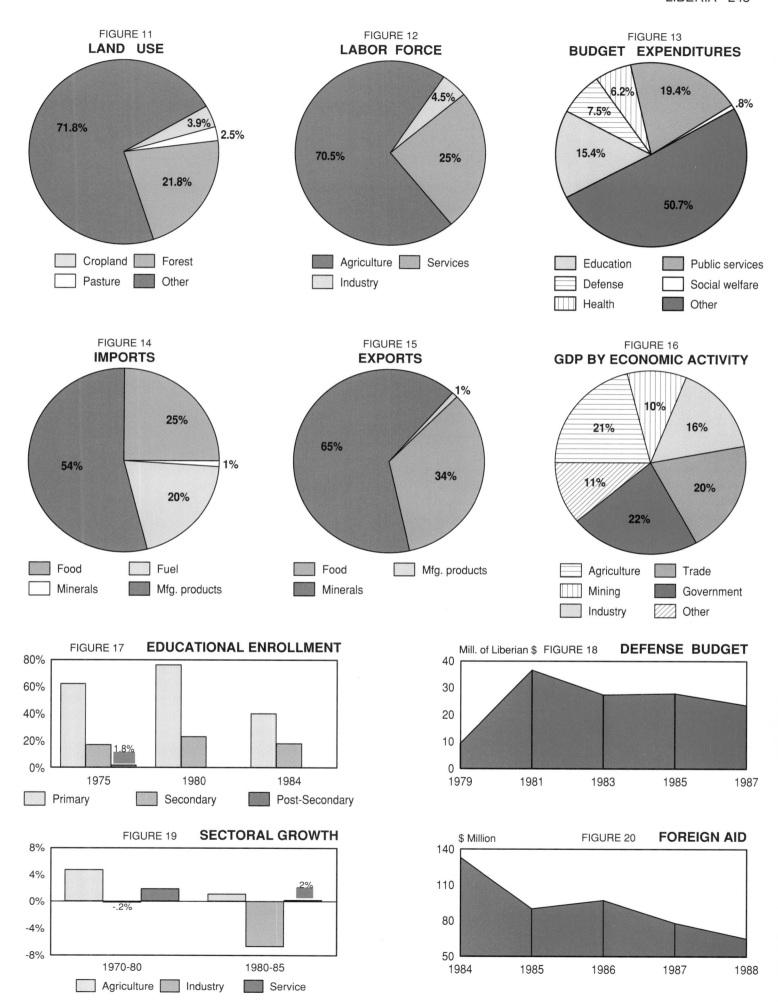

FIGURE 11
LAND USE

71.8%
3.9%
2.5%
21.8%

Cropland Forest
Pasture Other

FIGURE 12
LABOR FORCE

4.5%
70.5%
25%

Agriculture Services
Industry

FIGURE 13
BUDGET EXPENDITURES

6.2% 19.4%
7.5% .8%
15.4%
50.7%

Education Public services
Defense Social welfare
Health Other

FIGURE 14
IMPORTS

25%
54% 1%
20%

Food Fuel
Minerals Mfg. products

FIGURE 15
EXPORTS

1%
65%
34%

Food Mfg. products
Minerals

FIGURE 16
GDP BY ECONOMIC ACTIVITY

10% 16%
21%
11% 20%
22%

Agriculture Trade
Mining Government
Industry Other

FIGURE 17 **EDUCATIONAL ENROLLMENT**

80%
60%
40%
20% 1.8%
0%
1975 1980 1984

Primary Secondary Post-Secondary

Mill. of Liberian $ FIGURE 18 **DEFENSE BUDGET**

40
30
20
10
0
1979 1981 1983 1985 1987

FIGURE 19 **SECTORAL GROWTH**

8%
4%
-.2% 2%
0%
-4%
-8%
1970-80 1980-85

Agriculture Industry Service

$ Million FIGURE 20 **FOREIGN AID**

140
110
80
50
1984 1985 1986 1987 1988

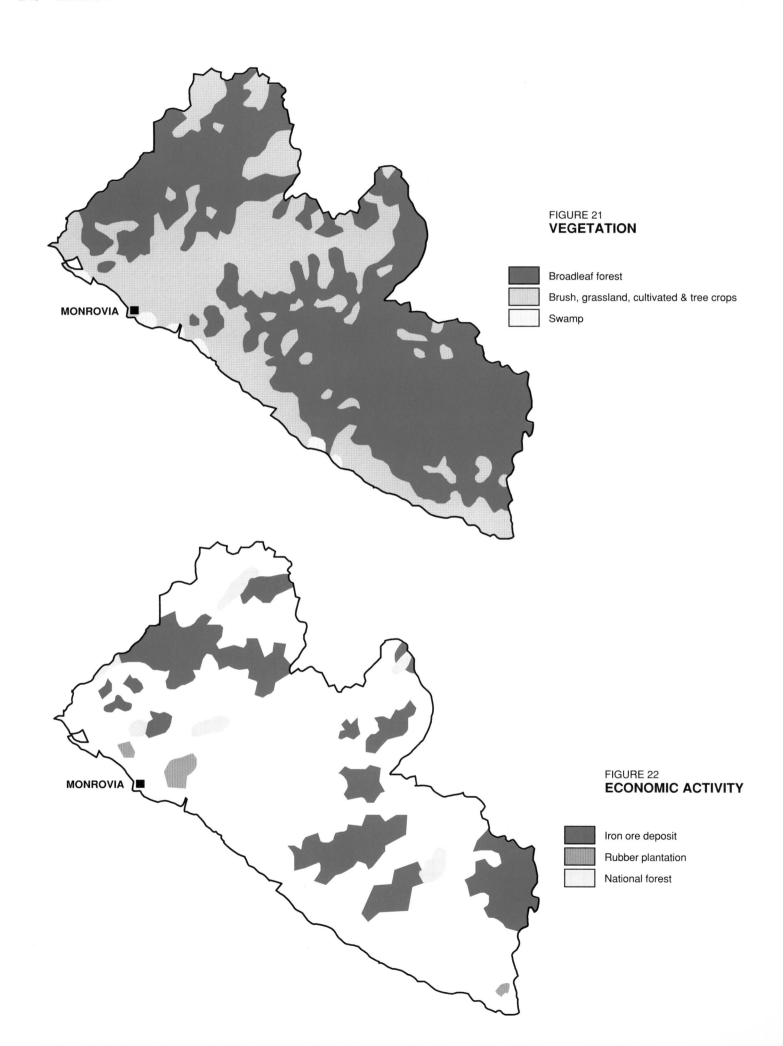

FIGURE 21
VEGETATION

Broadleaf forest

Brush, grassland, cultivated & tree crops

Swamp

MONROVIA

MONROVIA

FIGURE 22
ECONOMIC ACTIVITY

Iron ore deposit

Rubber plantation

National forest

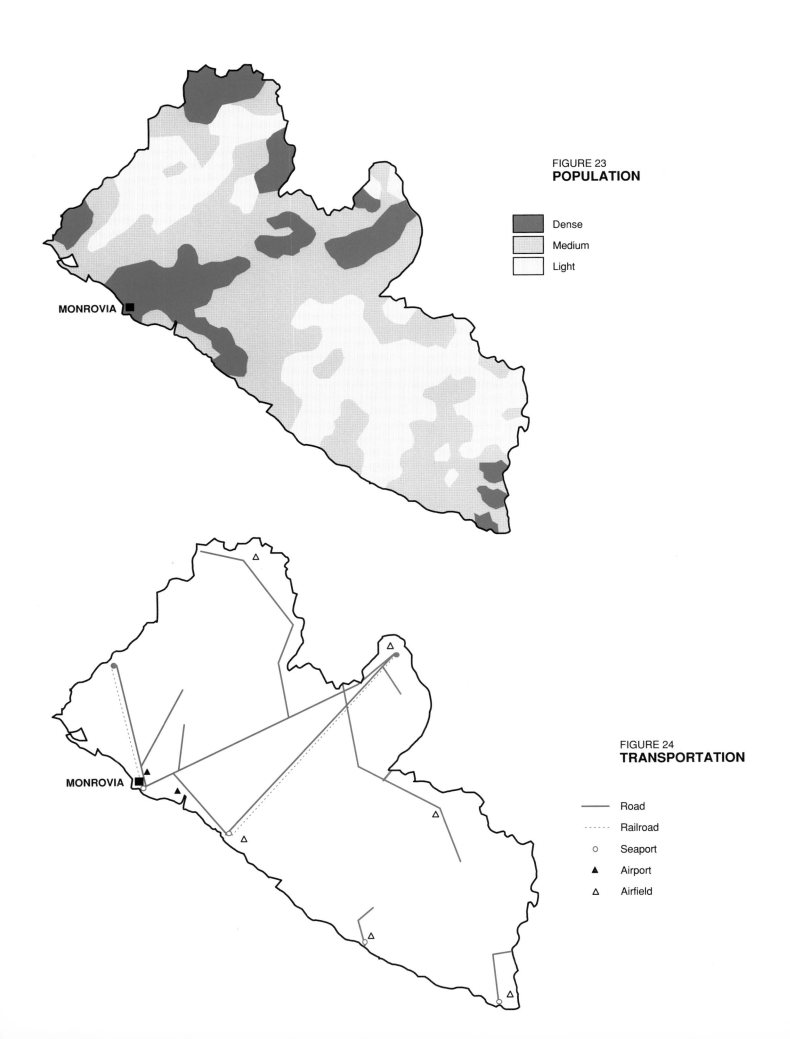

FIGURE 23
POPULATION

Dense
Medium
Light

FIGURE 24
TRANSPORTATION

MONROVIA

Road
Railroad
○ Seaport
▲ Airport
△ Airfield

LIBYA

The enfant terrible of the Arab world, Libya ranks 16th in land area but only 101st in population. Whereas the country had been classified in 1954 by the World Bank as one of the world's poorest countries, its per capita income in the early 1980s was the highest in Africa. During the same period the country witnessed a political transformation, moving from a conservative monarchy to an Islamic-Marxist jamahariya (roughly translated as state of the masses) whose ideology is nothing more than the sum total of the idiosyncrasies of its founder, Muammar Quadhafi. The petroleum industry, which employs only 10% of the labor force, contributes over one-half the country's GDP and more than 99% of its export earnings. Libya is also one of the most militant members of OPEC and was one of the first to nationalize foreign oil companies. Although Quadhafi disapproved of the 1990 Iraqi occupation of Kuwait, he did not support the U.S. leadership role in the UN force that drove the Iraqi's from Kuwait.

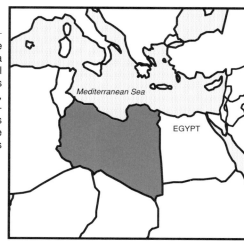

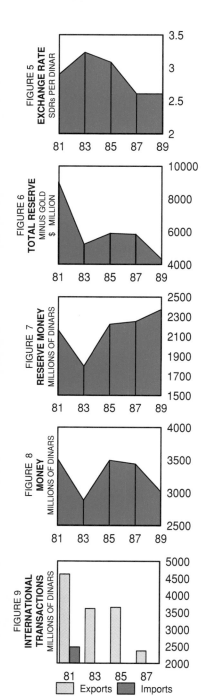

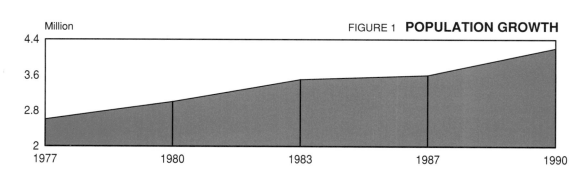

FIGURE 1 **POPULATION GROWTH**

FIGURE 2 **GROSS NATIONAL PRODUCT**

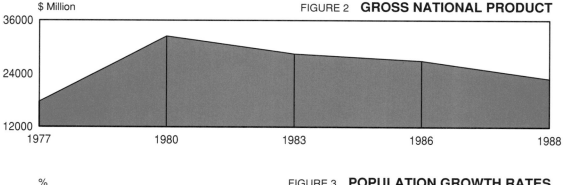

FIGURE 3 **POPULATION GROWTH RATES**

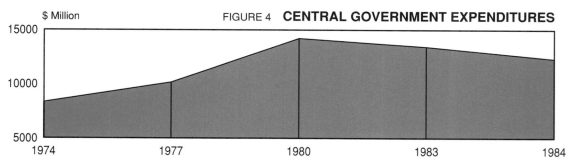

FIGURE 4 **CENTRAL GOVERNMENT EXPENDITURES**

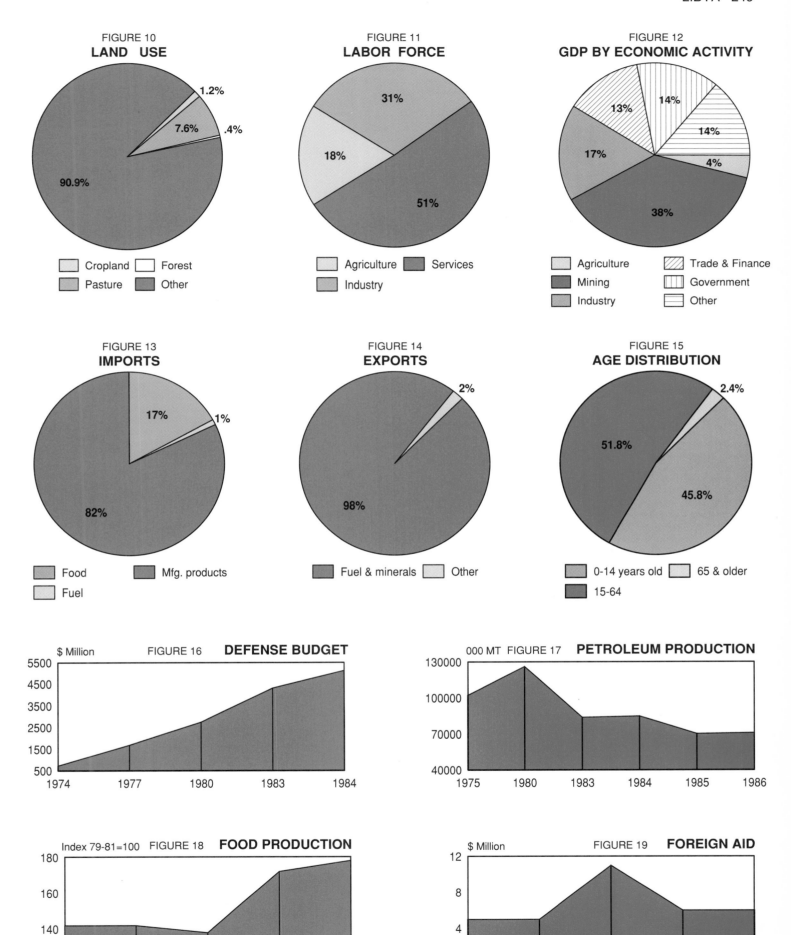

FIGURE 10
LAND USE

1.2%
7.6%
.4%
90.9%

Cropland　Forest
Pasture　Other

FIGURE 11
LABOR FORCE

31%
18%
51%

Agriculture　Services
Industry

FIGURE 12
GDP BY ECONOMIC ACTIVITY

13%　14%
14%
17%
4%
38%

Agriculture　Trade & Finance
Mining　Government
Industry　Other

FIGURE 13
IMPORTS

17%　1%
82%

Food　Mfg. products
Fuel

FIGURE 14
EXPORTS

2%
98%

Fuel & minerals　Other

FIGURE 15
AGE DISTRIBUTION

2.4%
51.8%
45.8%

0-14 years old　65 & older
15-64

$ Million　FIGURE 16　**DEFENSE BUDGET**

5500
4500
3500
2500
1500
500
1974　1977　1980　1983　1984

000 MT　FIGURE 17　**PETROLEUM PRODUCTION**

130000
100000
70000
40000
1975　1980　1983　1984　1985　1986

Index 79-81=100　FIGURE 18　**FOOD PRODUCTION**

180
160
140
120
1982　1983　1984　1985　1986

$ Million　FIGURE 19　**FOREIGN AID**

12
8
4
0
1984　1985　1986　1987　1988

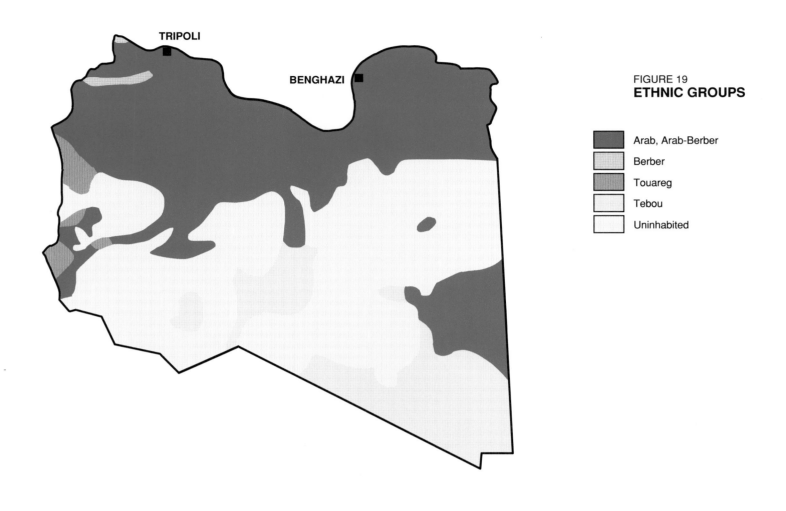

FIGURE 19
ETHNIC GROUPS

- Arab, Arab-Berber
- Berber
- Touareg
- Tebou
- Uninhabited

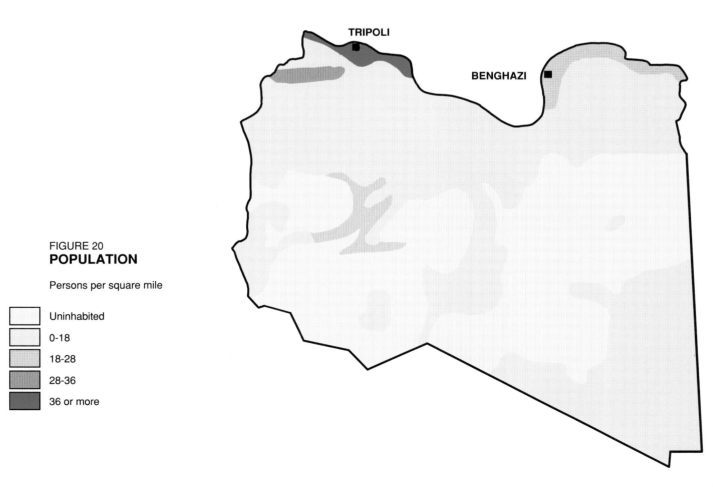

FIGURE 20
POPULATION

Persons per square mile

- Uninhabited
- 0-18
- 18-28
- 28-36
- 36 or more

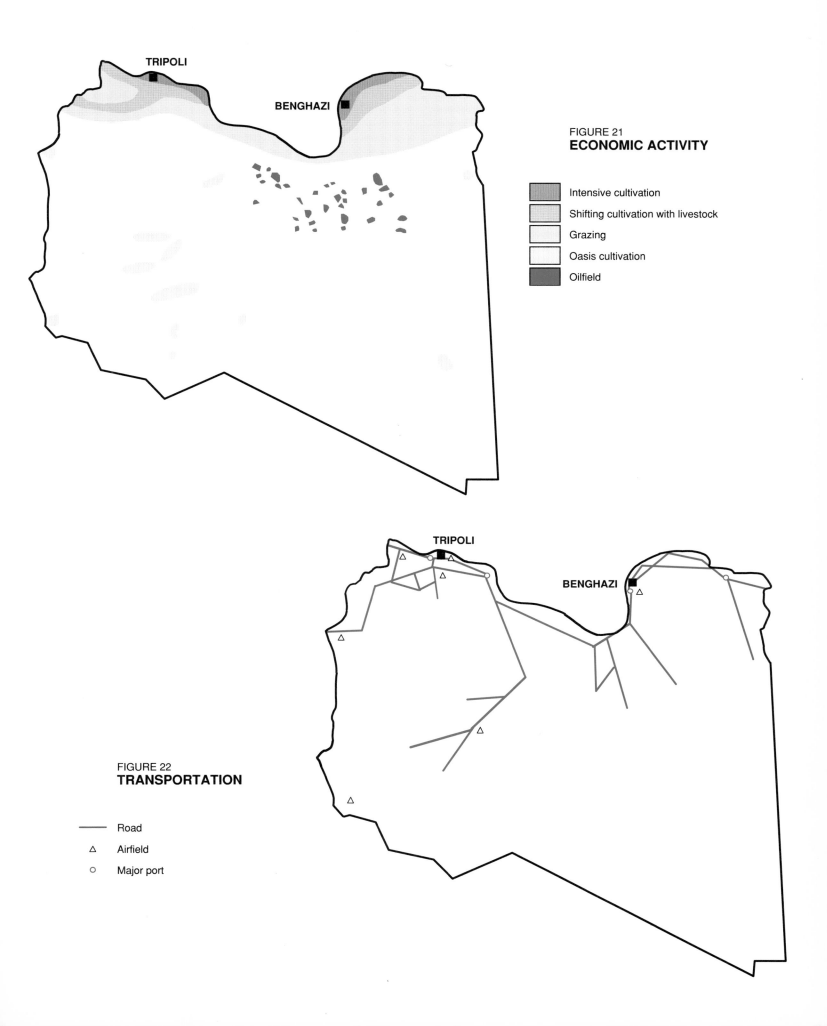

FIGURE 21
ECONOMIC ACTIVITY

Intensive cultivation

Shifting cultivation with livestock

Grazing

Oasis cultivation

Oilfield

FIGURE 22
TRANSPORTATION

—— Road

△ Airfield

○ Major port

MADAGASCAR

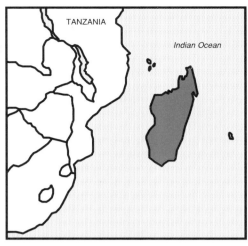

The world's fourth largest island, Madagascar ranks 43rd in land area and 59th in population. The turning point in Malagasy economic history was the socialist orientation introduced by President Didier Ratsiraka in the mid-1970s. Under his rule the government successfully nationalized all major industrial sectors, including plantations established under the French rule. Whereas the government owned or controlled only 13% of the economy's productive base in 1975, the proportion had risen to 75% by 1986. Agriculture remains the mainstay of the economy, contributing 45% of the GDP and employing nearly 80% of the economically active population. The principal crops are coffee (which accounts for nearly half the total export earnings), vanilla, and cloves; Madagascar is the world's leading producer of these last two. Until the 1970s foreign investors controlled approximately 85% of the industrial sector; currently direct foreign investment is limited to minority participation.

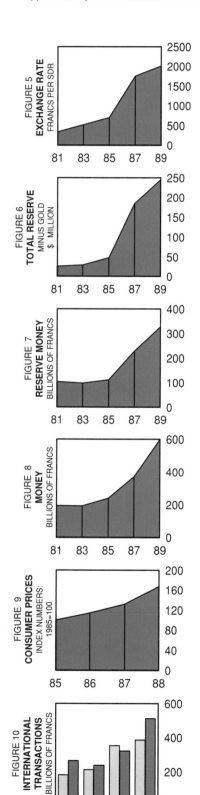

FIGURE 5 EXCHANGE RATE FRANCS PER SDR

FIGURE 6 TOTAL RESERVE MINUS GOLD $ MILLION

FIGURE 7 RESERVE MONEY BILLIONS OF FRANCS

FIGURE 8 MONEY BILLIONS OF FRANCS

FIGURE 9 CONSUMER PRICES INDEX NUMBERS: 1985=100

FIGURE 10 INTERNATIONAL TRANSACTIONS BILLIONS OF FRANCS
Exports   Imports

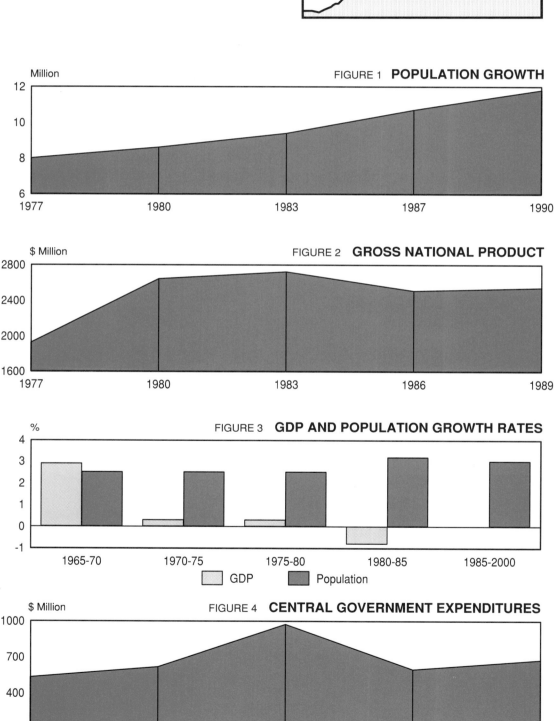

FIGURE 1 **POPULATION GROWTH**

FIGURE 2 **GROSS NATIONAL PRODUCT**

FIGURE 3 **GDP AND POPULATION GROWTH RATES**
GDP   Population

FIGURE 4 **CENTRAL GOVERNMENT EXPENDITURES**

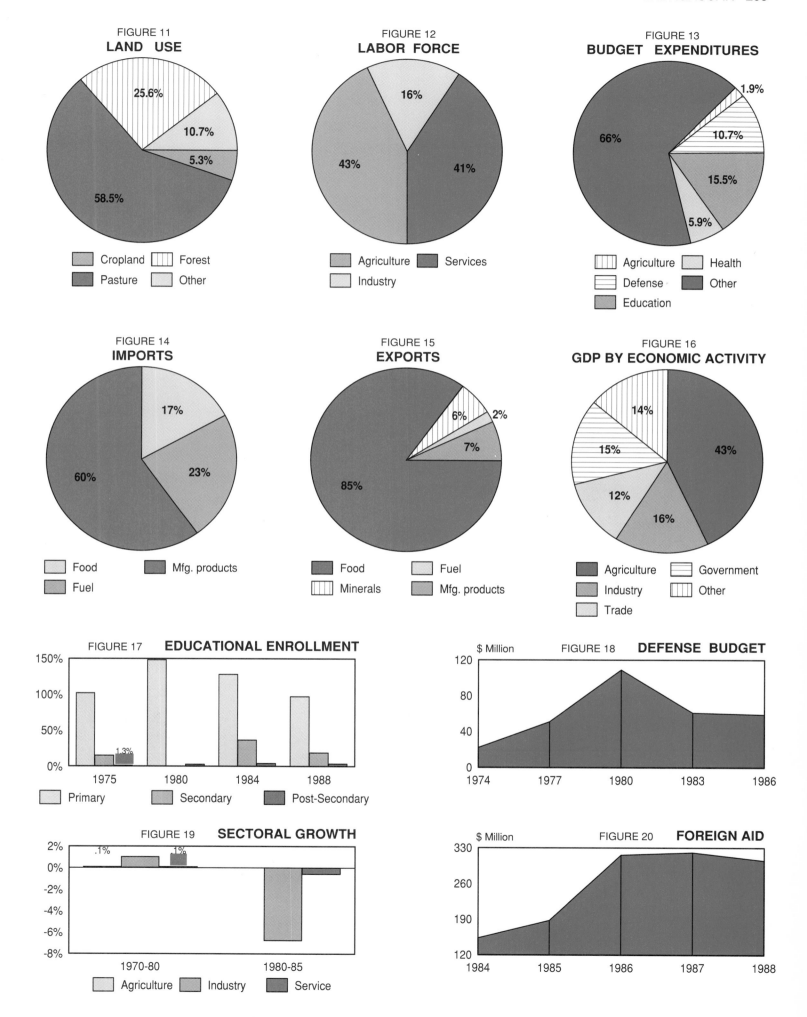

FIGURE 11
LAND USE

25.6%
10.7%
5.3%
58.5%

Cropland Forest
Pasture Other

FIGURE 12
LABOR FORCE

16%
43%
41%

Agriculture Services
Industry

FIGURE 13
BUDGET EXPENDITURES

1.9%
10.7%
66%
15.5%
5.9%

Agriculture Health
Defense Other
Education

FIGURE 14
IMPORTS

17%
60%
23%

Food Mfg. products
Fuel

FIGURE 15
EXPORTS

6% 2%
7%
85%

Food Fuel
Minerals Mfg. products

FIGURE 16
GDP BY ECONOMIC ACTIVITY

14%
15%
43%
12%
16%

Agriculture Government
Industry Other
Trade

FIGURE 17 **EDUCATIONAL ENROLLMENT**

150%
100%
50%
1.3%
0%
1975 1980 1984 1988

Primary Secondary Post-Secondary

$ Million FIGURE 18 **DEFENSE BUDGET**

120
80
40
0
1974 1977 1980 1983 1986

FIGURE 19 **SECTORAL GROWTH**

2%
.1% 1%
0%
-2%
-4%
-6%
-8%
1970-80 1980-85

Agriculture Industry Service

$ Million FIGURE 20 **FOREIGN AID**

330
260
190
120
1984 1985 1986 1987 1988

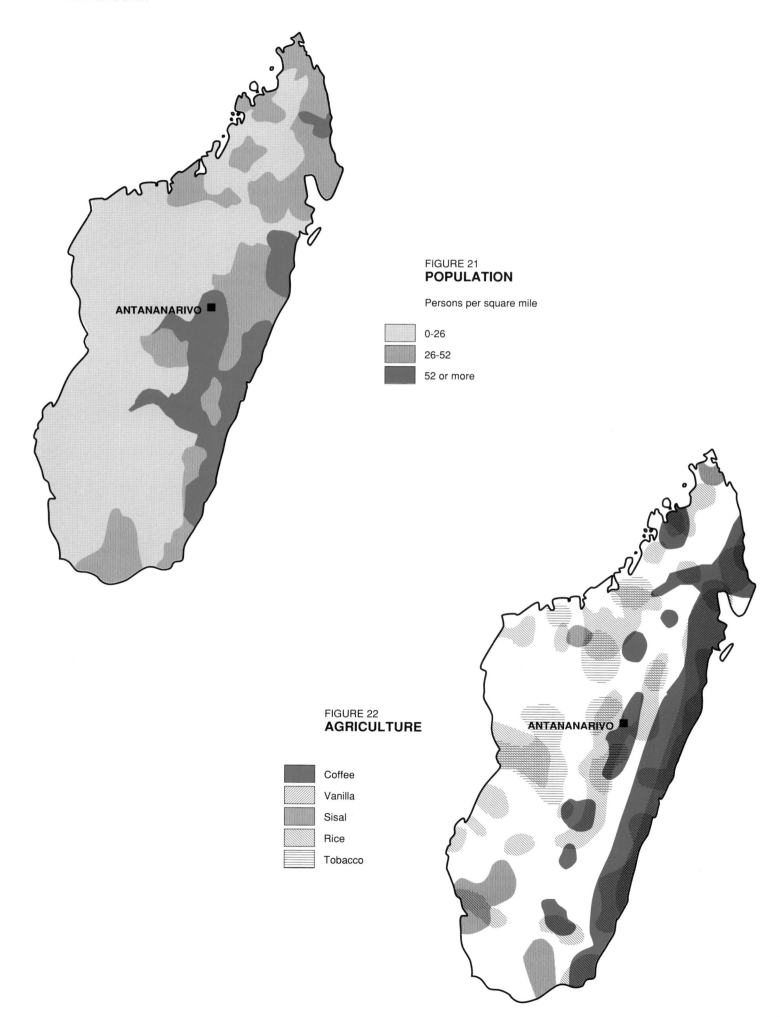

FIGURE 21
POPULATION

Persons per square mile

- 0-26
- 26-52
- 52 or more

FIGURE 22
AGRICULTURE

- Coffee
- Vanilla
- Sisal
- Rice
- Tobacco

ANTANANARIVO

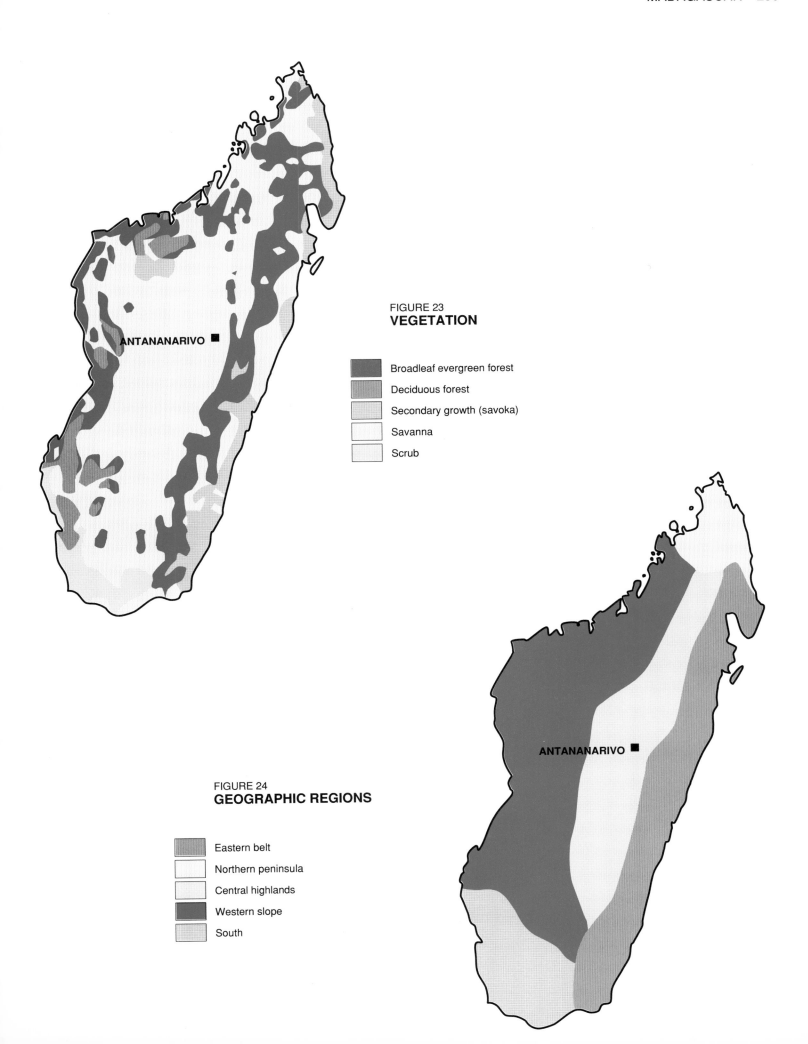

FIGURE 23
VEGETATION

Broadleaf evergreen forest
Deciduous forest
Secondary growth (savoka)
Savanna
Scrub

FIGURE 24
GEOGRAPHIC REGIONS

Eastern belt
Northern peninsula
Central highlands
Western slope
South

ANTANANARIVO

ANTANANARIVO

MALAWI

A landlocked nation on the western side of the lake that bears the same name, Malawi ranks 95th in land area and 77th in population. While the population growth rate is not much higher than the African average, the country experienced a steady growth in per capita GNP throughout most of the 1970s. Much of the growth was accounted for by the agricultural sector, particularly the small holdings. Malawi is among the few African countries totally self-sufficient in basic foodstuffs. Another reason for Malawi's remarkable growth record is its ability to attract the right type of foreign donors and investors. Several of the nations's largest agricultural estates and manufacturers are foreign owned, including the Imperial Group, Lonrho, and Portland Cement. A pragmatist, President H. Kamuzu Banda has maintained close ties with Pretoria, even at the expense of alienating his black neighbors, but the same pragmatism may dictate a closer relationship with the latter in the future, particularly in the areas of transportation, communication, and energy.

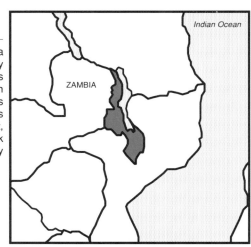

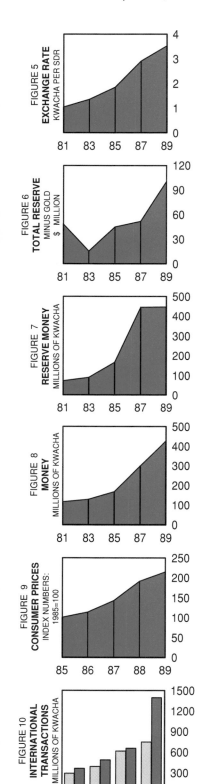

FIGURE 5 **EXCHANGE RATE** KWACHA PER SDR

FIGURE 6 **TOTAL RESERVE** MINUS GOLD $ MILLION

FIGURE 7 **RESERVE MONEY** MILLIONS OF KWACHA

FIGURE 8 **MONEY** MILLIONS OF KWACHA

FIGURE 9 **CONSUMER PRICES** INDEX NUMBERS: 1985=100

FIGURE 10 **INTERNATIONAL TRANSACTIONS** MILLIONS OF KWACHA

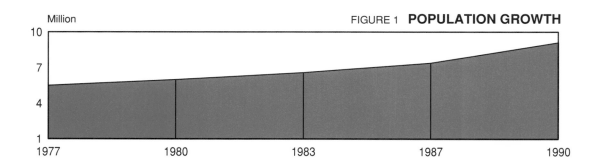

FIGURE 1 **POPULATION GROWTH**

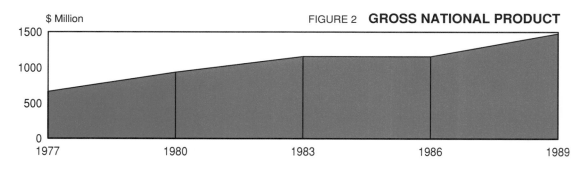

FIGURE 2 **GROSS NATIONAL PRODUCT**

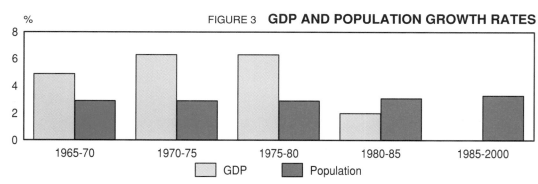

FIGURE 3 **GDP AND POPULATION GROWTH RATES**

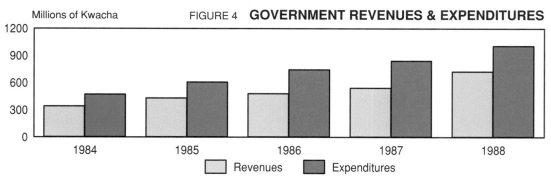

FIGURE 4 **GOVERNMENT REVENUES & EXPENDITURES**

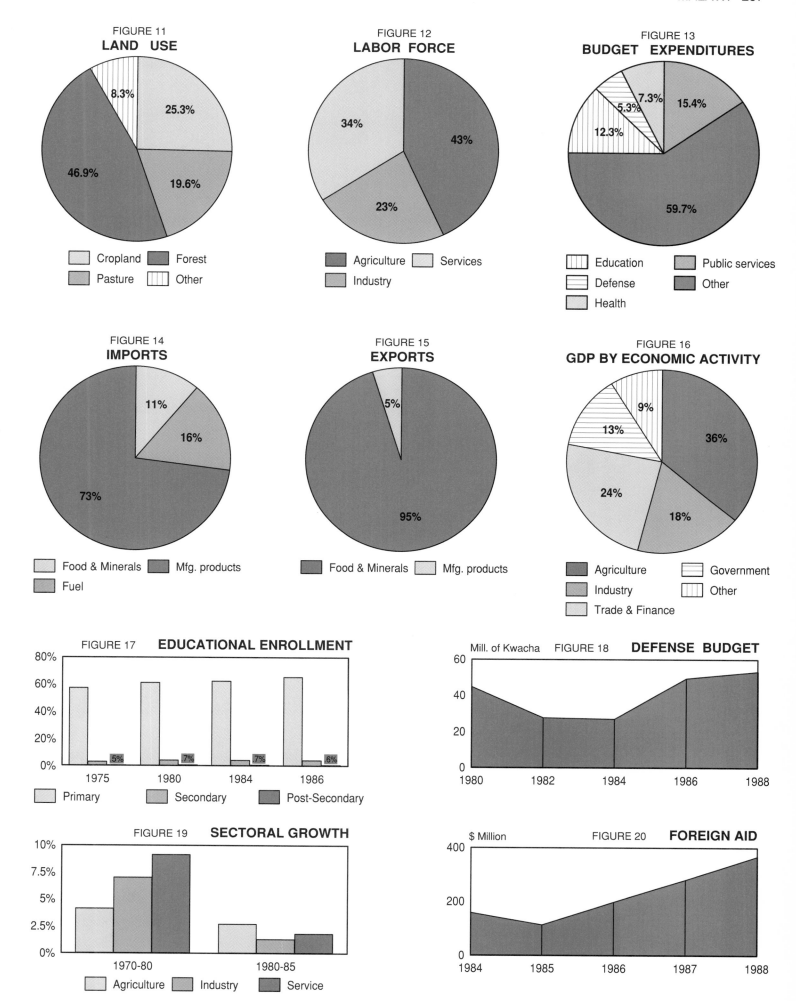

FIGURE 11
LAND USE

8.3%
25.3%
46.9%
19.6%

Cropland — Forest
Pasture — Other

FIGURE 12
LABOR FORCE

34%
43%
23%

Agriculture — Services
Industry

FIGURE 13
BUDGET EXPENDITURES

7.3% 15.4%
5.3%
12.3%
59.7%

Education — Public services
Defense — Other
Health

FIGURE 14
IMPORTS

11%
16%
73%

Food & Minerals — Mfg. products
Fuel

FIGURE 15
EXPORTS

5%
95%

Food & Minerals — Mfg. products

FIGURE 16
GDP BY ECONOMIC ACTIVITY

9% 36%
13%
24%
18%

Agriculture — Government
Industry — Other
Trade & Finance

FIGURE 17 **EDUCATIONAL ENROLLMENT**

80%
60%
40%
20%
0%
1975   1980   1984   1986
5%   7%   7%   6%

Primary   Secondary   Post-Secondary

Mill. of Kwacha   FIGURE 18   **DEFENSE BUDGET**

60
40
20
0
1980   1982   1984   1986   1988

FIGURE 19   **SECTORAL GROWTH**

10%
7.5%
5%
2.5%
0%
1970-80   1980-85

Agriculture   Industry   Service

$ Million   FIGURE 20   **FOREIGN AID**

400
200
0
1984   1985   1986   1987   1988

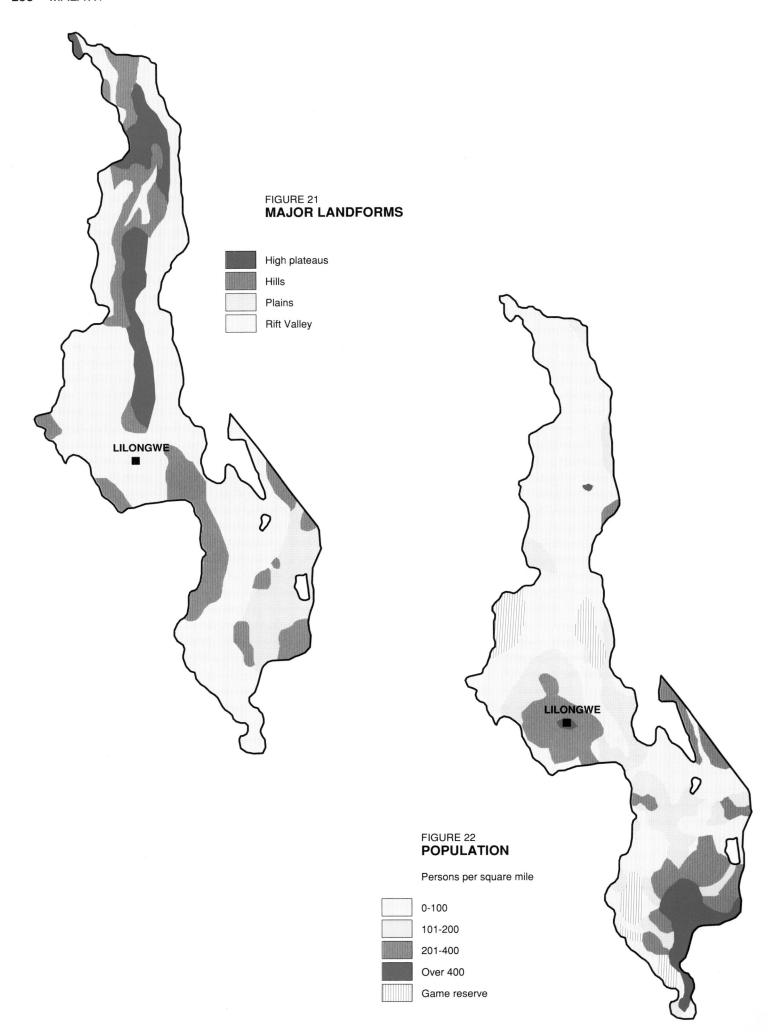

FIGURE 21
MAJOR LANDFORMS

High plateaus
Hills
Plains
Rift Valley

LILONGWE

FIGURE 22
POPULATION

Persons per square mile

0-100
101-200
201-400
Over 400
Game reserve

LILONGWE

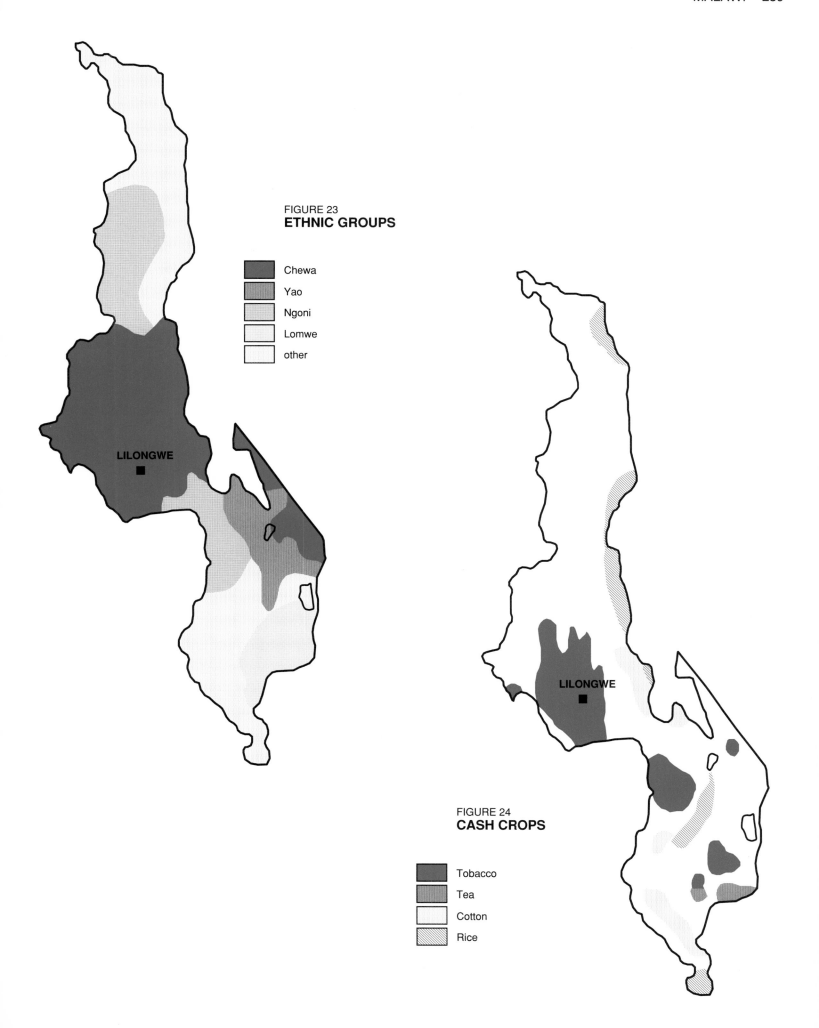

FIGURE 23
ETHNIC GROUPS

Chewa
Yao
Ngoni
Lomwe
other

LILONGWE

FIGURE 24
CASH CROPS

Tobacco
Tea
Cotton
Rice

LILONGWE

MALAYSIA

Located partly on the southern half of the Malay Peninsula and partly on the northern quarter of Borneo, Malaysia ranks 61st in land area and 48th in population. Malaysia's economy is dominated by three commodities: tin, rubber, and oil; the country is among the top producers of the first two. Malaysia's rich natural resources have been by and large well managed in terms of monetary and development policy. It has had consistent trade surpluses for over a decade because the prices of its traditional exports have remained firm while at the same time these surpluses have enabled it to diversify into other commodities, such as timber. Petroleum and manufactured products have overtaken rubber as the principal foreign exchange earners since 1980. In 1990, Malaysia's economy grew at a rate of 8.5% Ethnic and religious rivalries ripple through the economy periodically and the government has the task of monitoring and moderating these rivalries so that they do not tear apart the carefully balanced political and economic system.

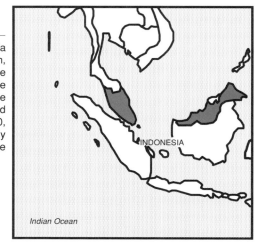

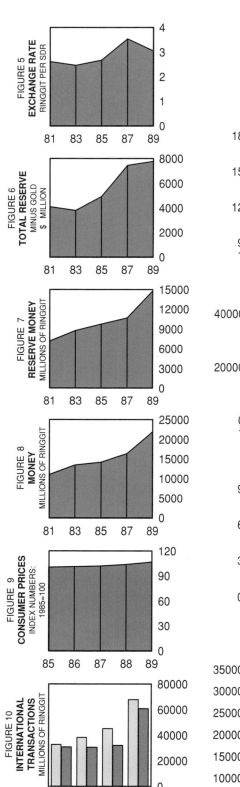

FIGURE 5 **EXCHANGE RATE** RINGGIT PER SDR

FIGURE 6 **TOTAL RESERVE** MINUS GOLD $ MILLION

FIGURE 7 **RESERVE MONEY** MILLIONS OF RINGGIT

FIGURE 8 **MONEY** MILLIONS OF RINGGIT

FIGURE 9 **CONSUMER PRICES** INDEX NUMBERS: 1985=100

FIGURE 10 **INTERNATIONAL TRANSACTIONS** MILLIONS OF RINGGIT — Exports ▢ Imports

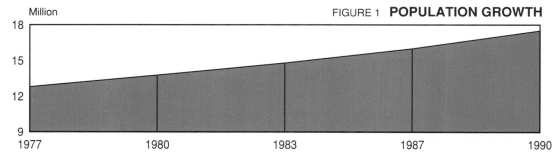

FIGURE 1 **POPULATION GROWTH** — Million

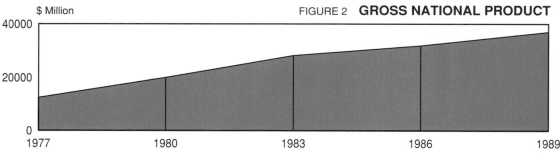

FIGURE 2 **GROSS NATIONAL PRODUCT** — $ Million

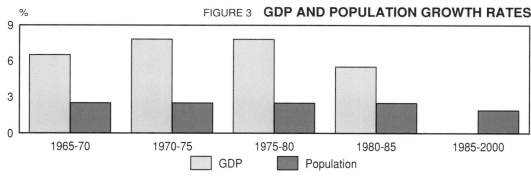

FIGURE 3 **GDP AND POPULATION GROWTH RATES** — % — GDP ▢ Population

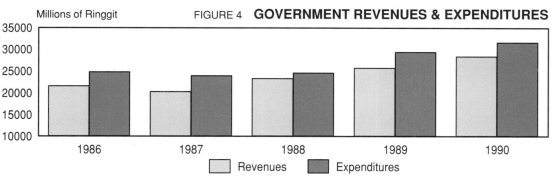

FIGURE 4 **GOVERNMENT REVENUES & EXPENDITURES** — Millions of Ringgit — Revenues ▢ Expenditures

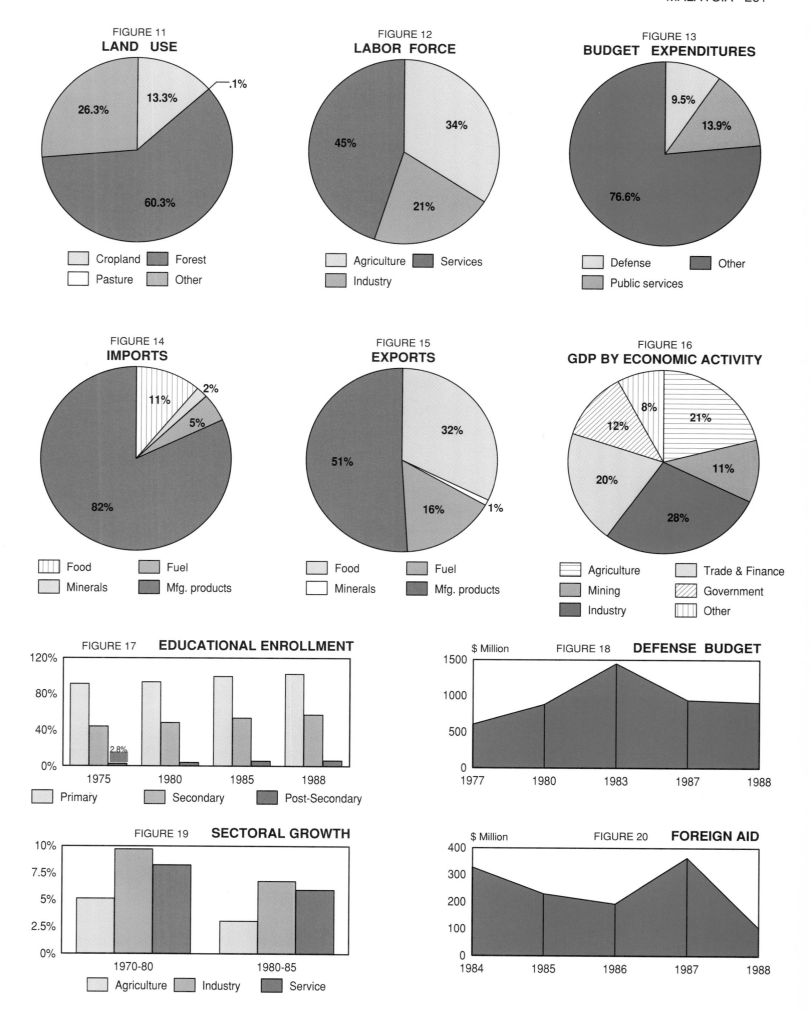

FIGURE 11
LAND USE

.1%
13.3%
26.3%
60.3%

Cropland Forest
Pasture Other

FIGURE 12
LABOR FORCE

34%
45%
21%

Agriculture Services
Industry

FIGURE 13
BUDGET EXPENDITURES

9.5%
13.9%
76.6%

Defense Other
Public services

FIGURE 14
IMPORTS

11%
2%
5%
82%

Food Fuel
Minerals Mfg. products

FIGURE 15
EXPORTS

32%
51%
16%
1%

Food Fuel
Minerals Mfg. products

FIGURE 16
GDP BY ECONOMIC ACTIVITY

8%
12%
21%
20%
11%
28%

Agriculture Trade & Finance
Mining Government
Industry Other

FIGURE 17 EDUCATIONAL ENROLLMENT

120%
80%
40%
2.8%
0%
1975 1980 1985 1988

Primary Secondary Post-Secondary

$ Million FIGURE 18 DEFENSE BUDGET

1500
1000
500
0
1977 1980 1983 1987 1988

FIGURE 19 SECTORAL GROWTH

10%
7.5%
5%
2.5%
0%
1970-80 1980-85

Agriculture Industry Service

$ Million FIGURE 20 FOREIGN AID

400
300
200
100
0
1984 1985 1986 1987 1988

FIGURE 21
AGRICULTURE AND LAND USE

▨	Rubber, oil palm
☐	Rice
▨	Rubber, rice, coconuts
▨	Tropical rain forest and swamp

KUALA LUMPUR ■

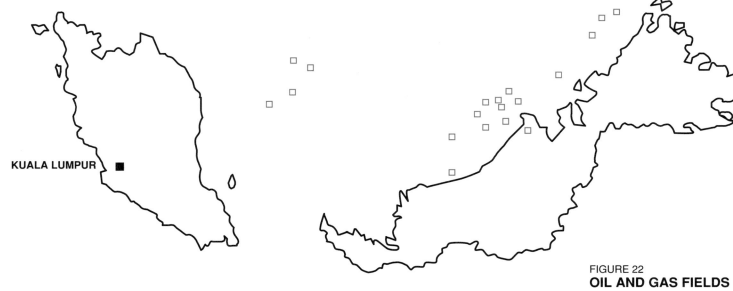

KUALA LUMPUR ■

FIGURE 22
OIL AND GAS FIELDS

☐   Oil/gasfield

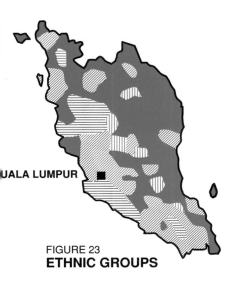
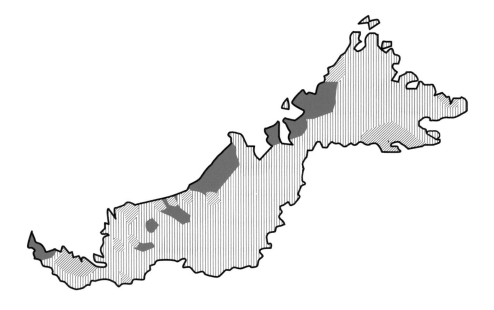

FIGURE 23
ETHNIC GROUPS

Chinese	
Malay	
Indian	
other	

KUALA LUMPUR ■

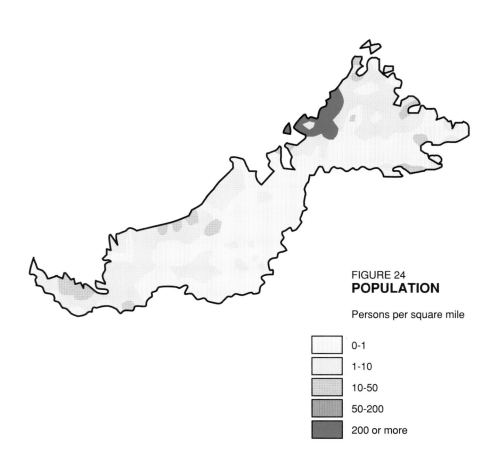

FIGURE 24
POPULATION

Persons per square mile

0-1	
1-10	
10-50	
50-200	
200 or more	

MAURITANIA

A large expanse of the Sahara Desert, Mauritania ranks 28th in land area and 123rd in population, a disparity characteristic of all desert countries. About 90% of all Mauritanians live in rural areas as nomadic herdsmen, constituting the traditional subsistence sector of the Mauritanian economy. The modern sector accounts for about 20% of the GDP, with mining contributing two-thirds of that share. The most important natural resource is the large deposit of high-grade iron ore in the F'Derick region, exports of which account for 70% of the country's foreign exchange earnings. The cessation of hostilities with the Polisario Front enabled the government to turn its attention once again to pressing economic problems, such as the need to control desertification and thus prevent a possible recurrence of the Sahelian drought. However, the 1989 border war with Senegal placed an extra burden on the economy as 200,000 refuges from Senegal flooded the country and caused food shortages. Little progress towards a permanent settlement of the dispute was made in 1990.

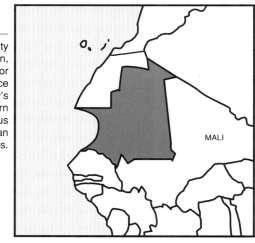

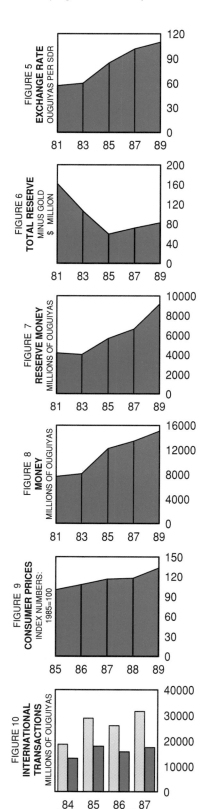

FIGURE 5 **EXCHANGE RATE** OUGUIYAS PER SDR

FIGURE 6 **TOTAL RESERVE** MINUS GOLD $ MILLION

FIGURE 7 **RESERVE MONEY** MILLIONS OF OUGUIYAS

FIGURE 8 **MONEY** MILLIONS OF OUGUIYAS

FIGURE 9 **CONSUMER PRICES** INDEX NUMBERS: 1985=100

FIGURE 10 **INTERNATIONAL TRANSACTIONS** MILLIONS OF OUGUIYAS
Exports Imports

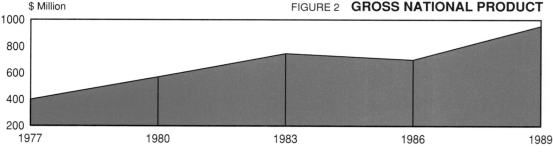

FIGURE 1 **POPULATION GROWTH**

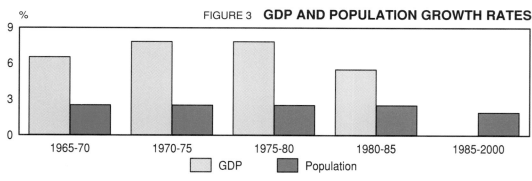

FIGURE 2 **GROSS NATIONAL PRODUCT**

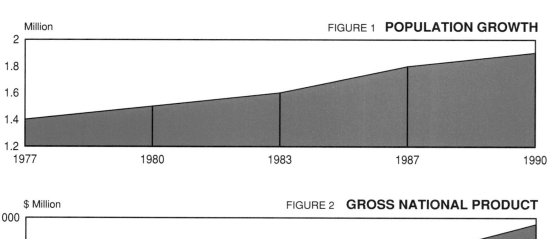

FIGURE 3 **GDP AND POPULATION GROWTH RATES**
GDP Population

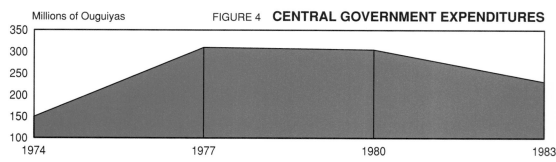

FIGURE 4 **CENTRAL GOVERNMENT EXPENDITURES**

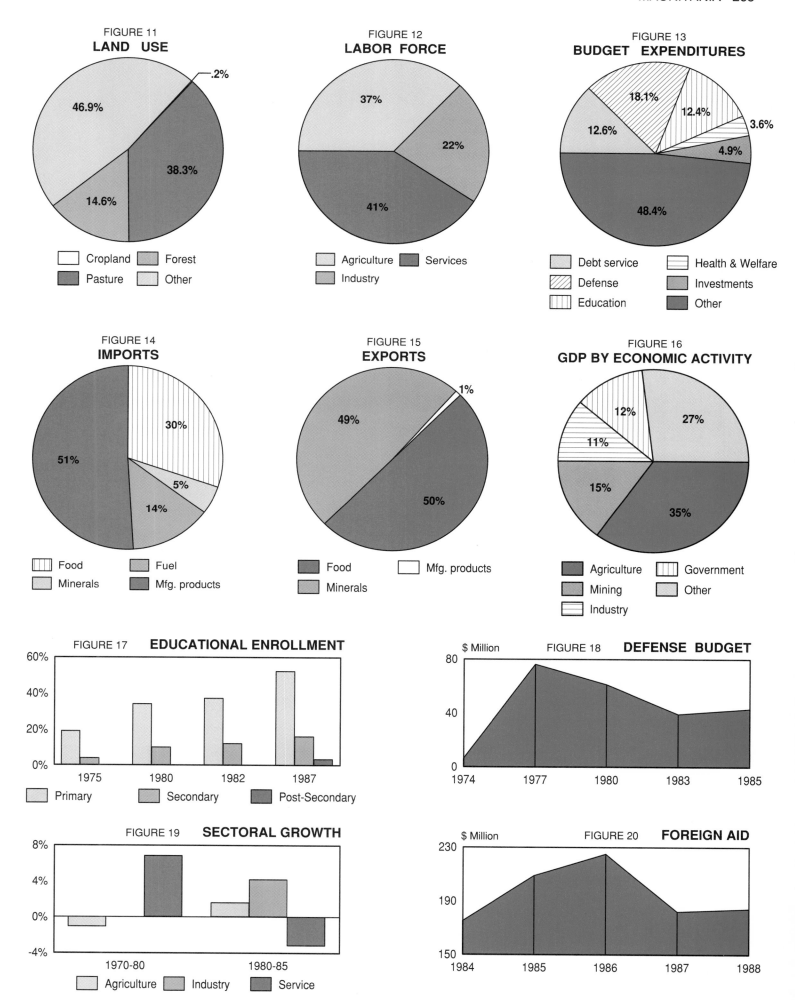

FIGURE 11
LAND USE

.2%
46.9%
38.3%
14.6%

Cropland — Forest
Pasture — Other

FIGURE 12
LABOR FORCE

37%
22%
41%

Agriculture — Services
Industry

FIGURE 13
BUDGET EXPENDITURES

18.1%
12.4%
3.6%
12.6%
4.9%
48.4%

Debt service — Health & Welfare
Defense — Investments
Education — Other

FIGURE 14
IMPORTS

30%
51%
5%
14%

Food — Fuel
Minerals — Mfg. products

FIGURE 15
EXPORTS

1%
49%
50%

Food — Mfg. products
Minerals

FIGURE 16
GDP BY ECONOMIC ACTIVITY

12%
27%
11%
15%
35%

Agriculture — Government
Mining — Other
Industry

FIGURE 17 **EDUCATIONAL ENROLLMENT**

60%
40%
20%
0%
1975   1980   1982   1987

Primary — Secondary — Post-Secondary

FIGURE 18 **DEFENSE BUDGET**

$ Million
80
40
0
1974   1977   1980   1983   1985

FIGURE 19 **SECTORAL GROWTH**

8%
4%
0%
-4%
1970-80   1980-85

Agriculture — Industry — Service

FIGURE 20 **FOREIGN AID**

$ Million
230
190
150
1984   1985   1986   1987   1988

MAURITIUS

An island in the southwest Indian ocean, Mauritius ranks 157th in land surface and 131st in population. The island is one of the most overpopulated countries in the world and ranks ninth in density. The population explosion that followed the eradication of malaria during World War II has been more or less brought under control and the growth rate is now a modest 1.4% while the GNP growth rate has jumped to an encouraging 7.1%. The economy remains predominantly dependent on sugar and, like all one-product countries, suffers from boom and bust cycles induced by erratic international markets. It also shares many of the problems of mini-economies: climbing energy prices, rising government expenditures, falling foreign exchange reserves, and high inflation. Mauritius represents a confluence of four cultures: English, French, Indian, and African. Given such diverse and disparate elements, it has fused together a viable identity with few ethnic conflicts.

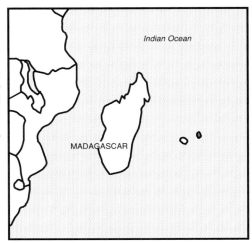

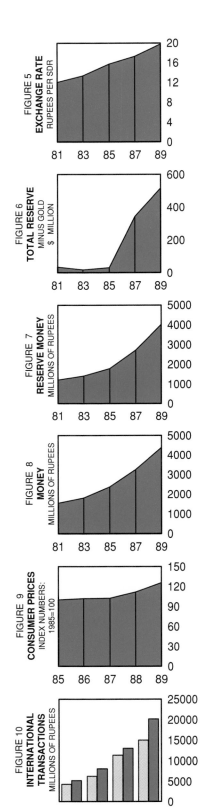

FIGURE 5 EXCHANGE RATE RUPEES PER SDR

FIGURE 6 TOTAL RESERVE MINUS GOLD $ MILLION

FIGURE 7 RESERVE MONEY MILLIONS OF RUPEES

FIGURE 8 MONEY MILLIONS OF RUPEES

FIGURE 9 CONSUMER PRICES INDEX NUMBERS: 1985=100

FIGURE 10 INTERNATIONAL TRANSACTIONS MILLIONS OF RUPEES
Exports Imports

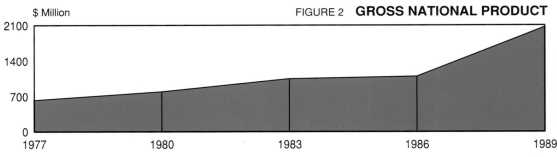

FIGURE 1 **POPULATION GROWTH**

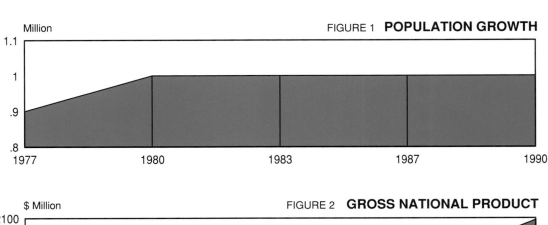

FIGURE 2 **GROSS NATIONAL PRODUCT**

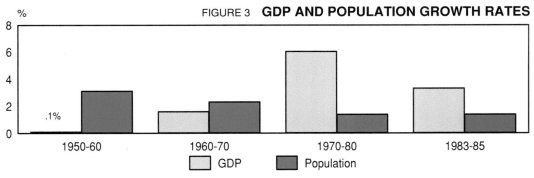

FIGURE 3 **GDP AND POPULATION GROWTH RATES**

GDP Population

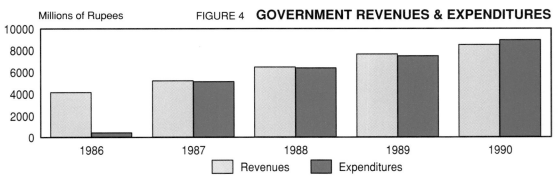

FIGURE 4 **GOVERNMENT REVENUES & EXPENDITURES**

Revenues Expenditures

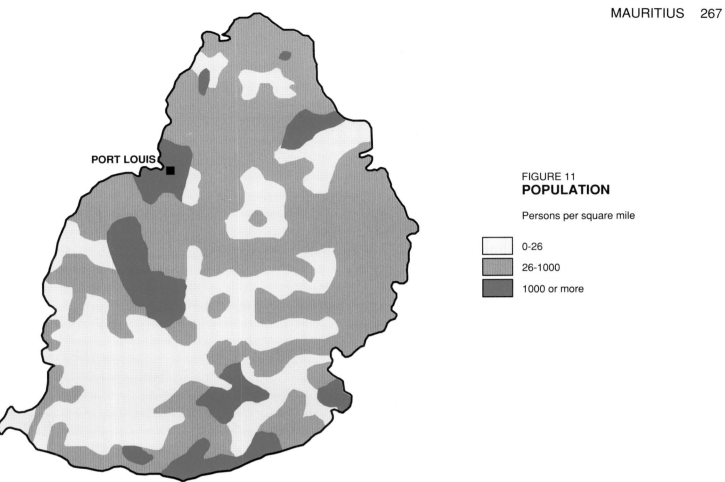

FIGURE 11
POPULATION

Persons per square mile

0-26

26-1000

1000 or more

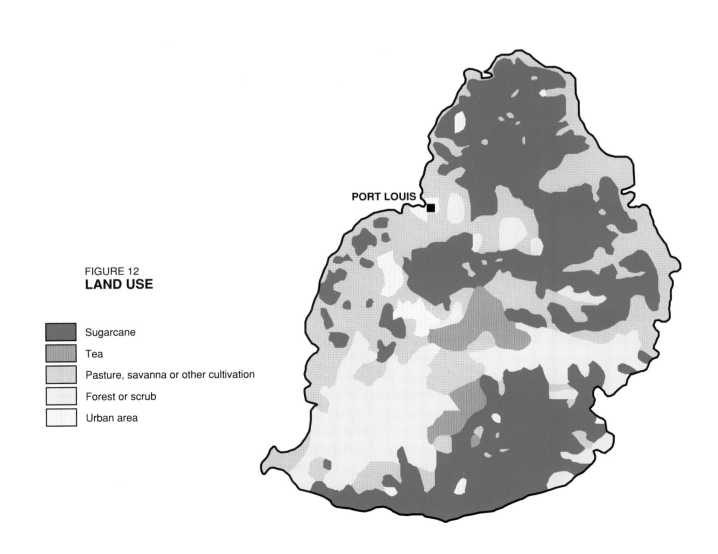

FIGURE 12
LAND USE

Sugarcane

Tea

Pasture, savanna or other cultivation

Forest or scrub

Urban area

MEXICO

The third largest country in Latin America, the 14th largest in the world, the 11th most populous, and the largest Spanish-speaking country in the world, Mexico has all the attributes of a great nation but somehow misses that title because of institutional shortcomings that neither historians nor economists have been able to pinpoint. With its immense natural resources, it should appear among the top 10 in a broad array of indicators but surprisingly it does not. It has no solid strength in any particular area. Recently, the surge in oil production had led observers to call it the Saudi Arabia of the Western Hemisphere. The economic momentum these expectations generated has not been sustained; further, substantial increases in oil exports have not prevented an overall deterioration in the trade balance, largely because of imports required for escalating ill-concieved development plans. It is saddled with one of the largest debt burdens of any country. In an effort to stimulate its economy, Mexico agreed in 1990 to begin formal negotiations with the U.S. for a comprehensive free-trade agreement.

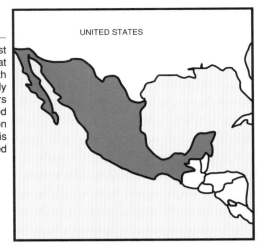

UNITED STATES

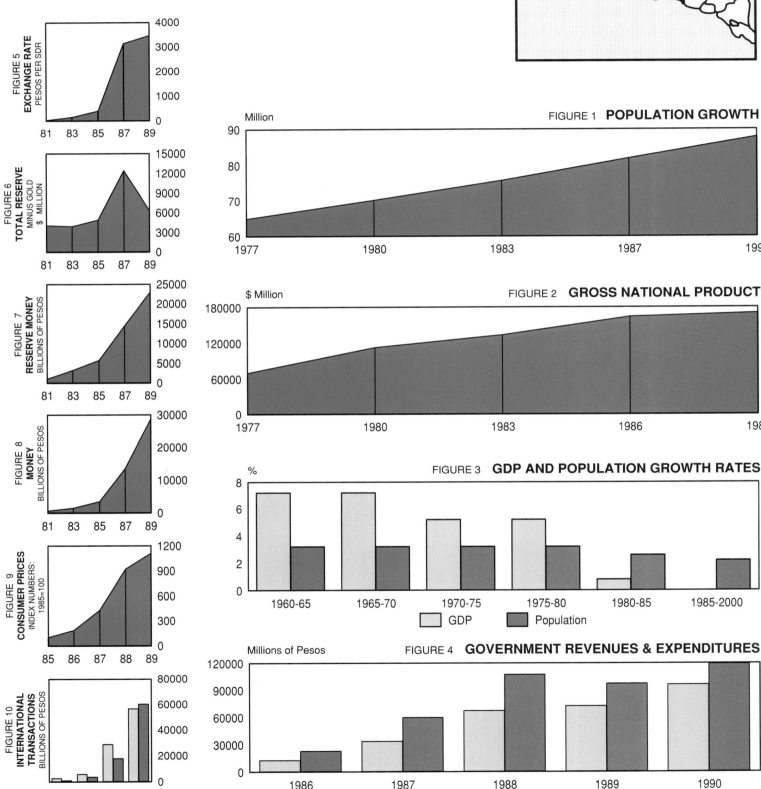

FIGURE 5 EXCHANGE RATE PESOS PER SDR

FIGURE 6 TOTAL RESERVE MINUS GOLD $ MILLION

FIGURE 7 RESERVE MONEY BILLIONS OF PESOS

FIGURE 8 MONEY BILLIONS OF PESOS

FIGURE 9 CONSUMER PRICES INDEX NUMBERS: 1985=100

FIGURE 10 INTERNATIONAL TRANSACTIONS BILLIONS OF PESOS
Exports Imports

Million FIGURE 1 **POPULATION GROWTH**

$ Million FIGURE 2 **GROSS NATIONAL PRODUCT**

% FIGURE 3 **GDP AND POPULATION GROWTH RATES**
GDP Population

Millions of Pesos FIGURE 4 **GOVERNMENT REVENUES & EXPENDITURES**
Revenues Expenditures

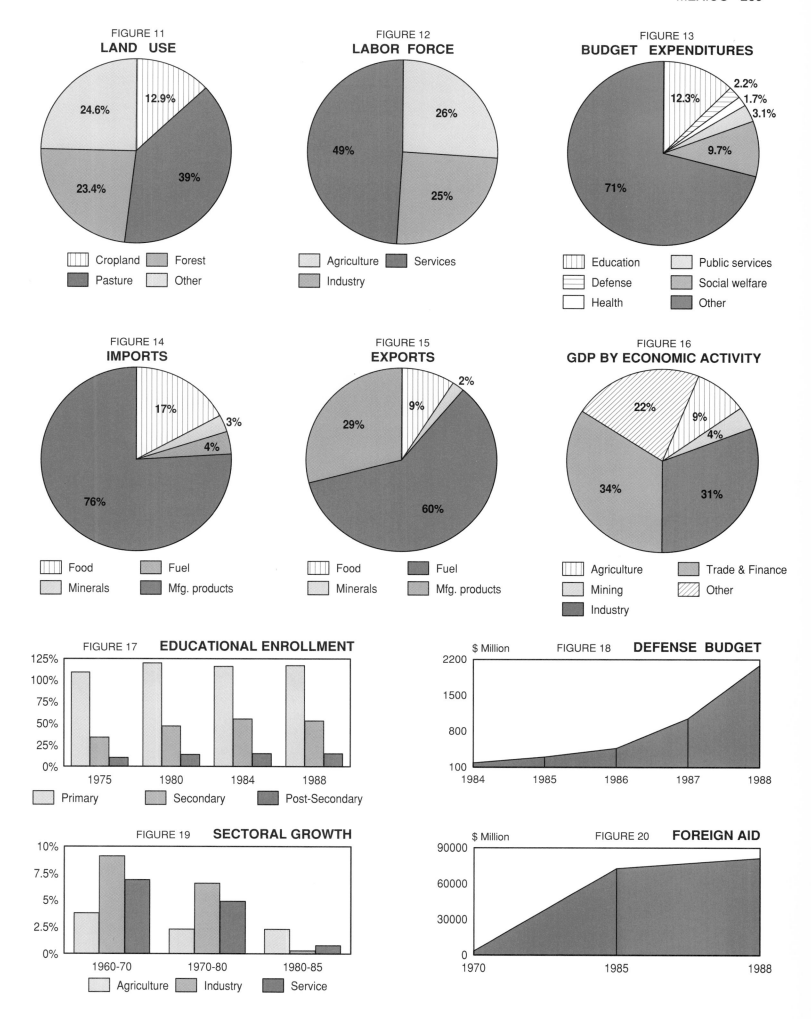

FIGURE 11
LAND USE

12.9%
24.6%
39%
23.4%

Cropland   Forest
Pasture   Other

FIGURE 12
LABOR FORCE

26%
49%
25%

Agriculture   Services
Industry

FIGURE 13
BUDGET EXPENDITURES

12.3%
2.2%
1.7%
3.1%
9.7%
71%

Education   Public services
Defense   Social welfare
Health   Other

FIGURE 14
IMPORTS

17%
3%
4%
76%

Food   Fuel
Minerals Mfg. products

FIGURE 15
EXPORTS

9%
2%
29%
60%

Food   Fuel
Minerals Mfg. products

FIGURE 16
GDP BY ECONOMIC ACTIVITY

22%
9%
4%
34%
31%

Agriculture   Trade & Finance
Mining   Other
Industry

FIGURE 17 **EDUCATIONAL ENROLLMENT**

125%
100%
75%
50%
25%
0%
1975   1980   1984   1988

Primary   Secondary   Post-Secondary

FIGURE 18 **DEFENSE BUDGET**

$ Million
2200
1500
800
100
1984   1985   1986   1987   1988

FIGURE 19 **SECTORAL GROWTH**

10%
7.5%
5%
2.5%
0%
1960-70   1970-80   1980-85

Agriculture   Industry   Service

FIGURE 20 **FOREIGN AID**

$ Million
90000
60000
30000
0
1970   1985   1988

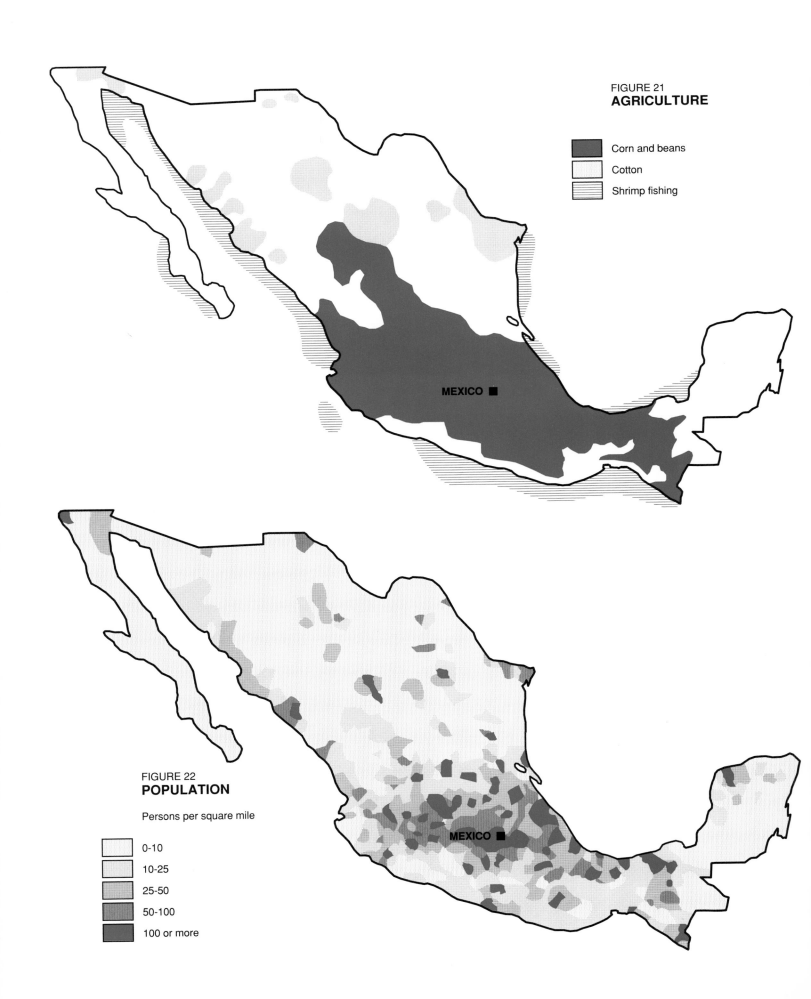

FIGURE 21
AGRICULTURE

Corn and beans
Cotton
Shrimp fishing

MEXICO ■

FIGURE 22
POPULATION

Persons per square mile

0-10
10-25
25-50
50-100
100 or more

MEXICO ■

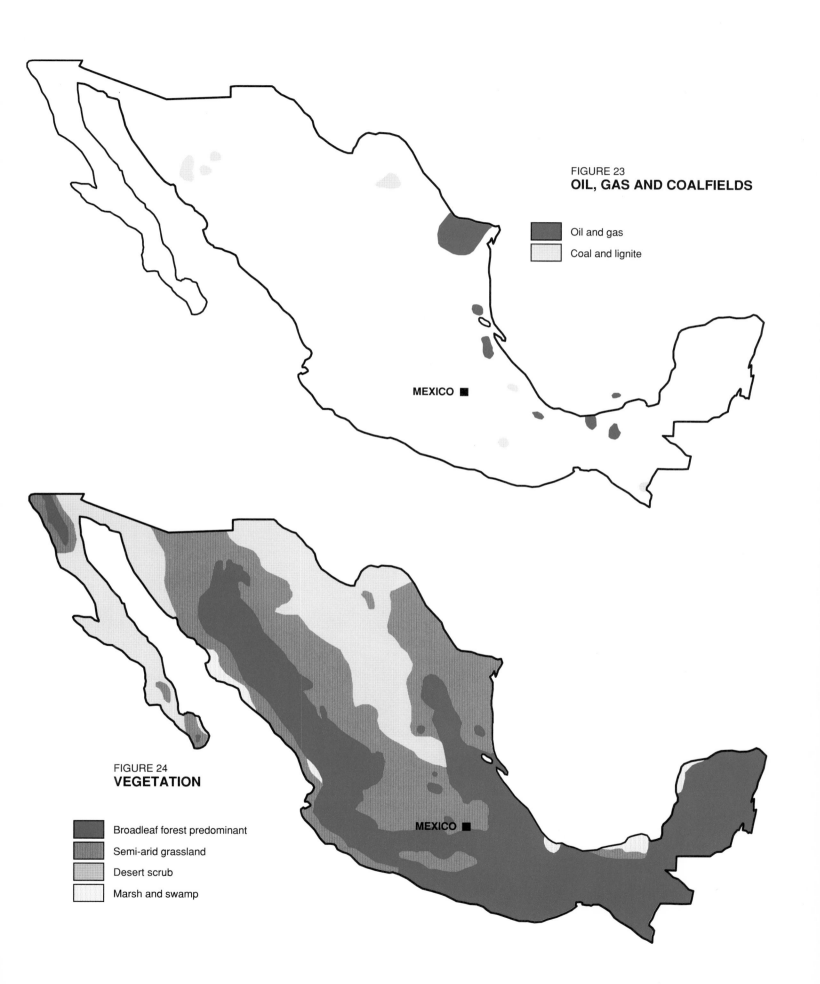

FIGURE 23
OIL, GAS AND COALFIELDS

Oil and gas

Coal and lignite

MEXICO ■

FIGURE 24
VEGETATION

Broadleaf forest predominant

Semi-arid grassland

Desert scrub

Marsh and swamp

MEXICO ■

MOROCCO

Morocco ranks 51st in land area and 32nd in population. Politically stable, Morocco has not experienced the kind of violent upheavals that sister Arab nations have had to confront. The economic implications of this stability are evident: Morocco is the favorite North African destination of western tourists as well as of French and U.S. capital. The continued fighting in Western Sahara has been a political and economic liability and has alienated Morocco from its neighbors. Despite frequent setbacks, the UN initiative for peace in the Western Sahara made progress during 1990. Outweighing these disadvantages is the fact that the issue has served to unify the nation and divert its attention from internal problems. While mining contributes only a small percentage of the GDP, it accounts for 30 to 50% of export earnings. Over 90% of mining output consists of phosphate, of which Morocco is the world's leading exporter. With the decline in phosphate prices beginning in the mid-1970s, Morocco recorded massive trade deficits which the remittances of Moroccan workers abroad only partially offset.

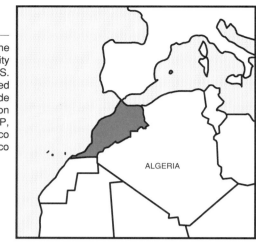

ALGERIA

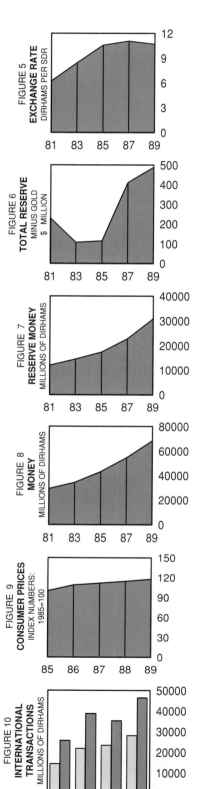

FIGURE 5 **EXCHANGE RATE** DIRHAMS PER SDR

FIGURE 6 **TOTAL RESERVE** MINUS GOLD $ MILLION

FIGURE 7 **RESERVE MONEY** MILLIONS OF DIRHAMS

FIGURE 8 **MONEY** MILLIONS OF DIRHAMS

FIGURE 9 **CONSUMER PRICES** INDEX NUMBERS: 1985=100

FIGURE 10 **INTERNATIONAL TRANSACTIONS** MILLIONS OF DIRHAMS

Exports Imports

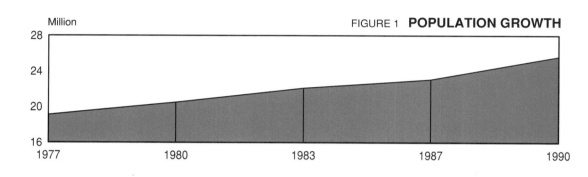

Million

FIGURE 1 **POPULATION GROWTH**

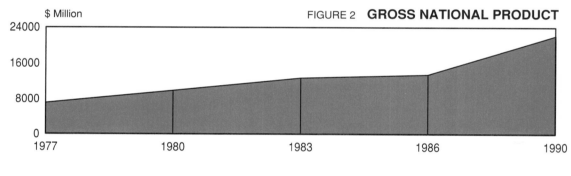

$ Million

FIGURE 2 **GROSS NATIONAL PRODUCT**

FIGURE 3 **GDP AND POPULATION GROWTH RATES**

%

GDP Population

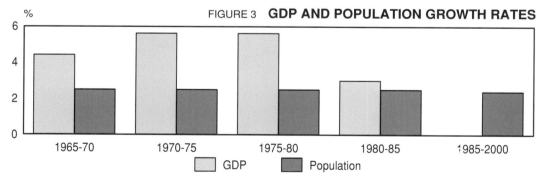

Millions of Dirhams

FIGURE 4 **GOVERNMENT REVENUES & EXPENDITURES**

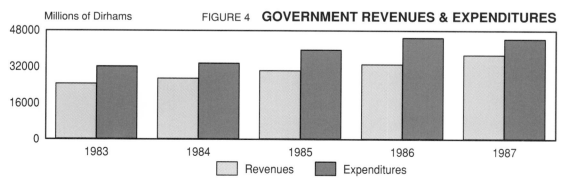

Revenues Expenditures

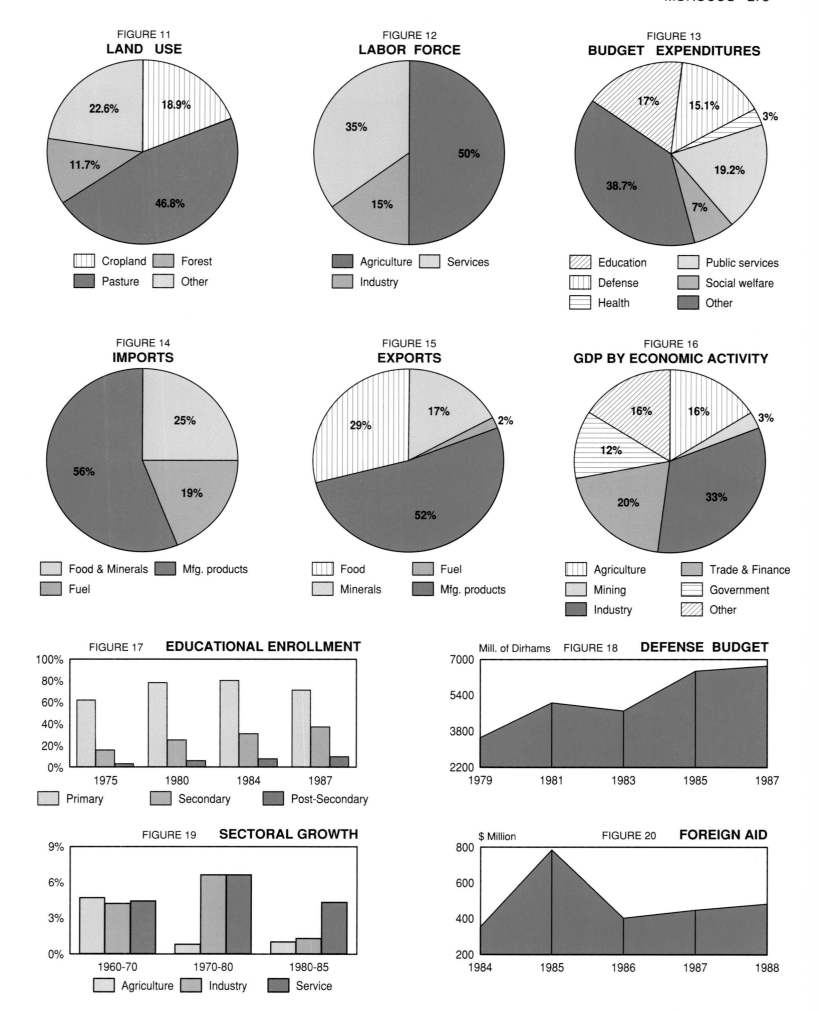

FIGURE 11
LAND USE

Cropland 18.9%
Forest 22.6%
Pasture 46.8%
Other 11.7%

Cropland | Forest
Pasture | Other

FIGURE 12
LABOR FORCE

Agriculture 50%
Services 35%
Industry 15%

Agriculture | Services
Industry

FIGURE 13
BUDGET EXPENDITURES

Education 17%
Defense 15.1%
Health 3%
Public services 19.2%
Social welfare 7%
Other 38.7%

Education | Public services
Defense | Social welfare
Health | Other

FIGURE 14
IMPORTS

Food & Minerals 25%
Mfg. products 56%
Fuel 19%

Food & Minerals | Mfg. products
Fuel

FIGURE 15
EXPORTS

Food 17%
Fuel 2%
Minerals 29%
Mfg. products 52%

Food | Fuel
Minerals | Mfg. products

FIGURE 16
GDP BY ECONOMIC ACTIVITY

Agriculture 16%
Mining 16%
Government 3%
Other 12%
Trade & Finance 33%
Industry 20%

Agriculture | Trade & Finance
Mining | Government
Industry | Other

FIGURE 17 **EDUCATIONAL ENROLLMENT**

Primary | Secondary | Post-Secondary

FIGURE 18 **DEFENSE BUDGET**

Mill. of Dirhams

FIGURE 19 **SECTORAL GROWTH**

Agriculture | Industry | Service

FIGURE 20 **FOREIGN AID**

$ Million

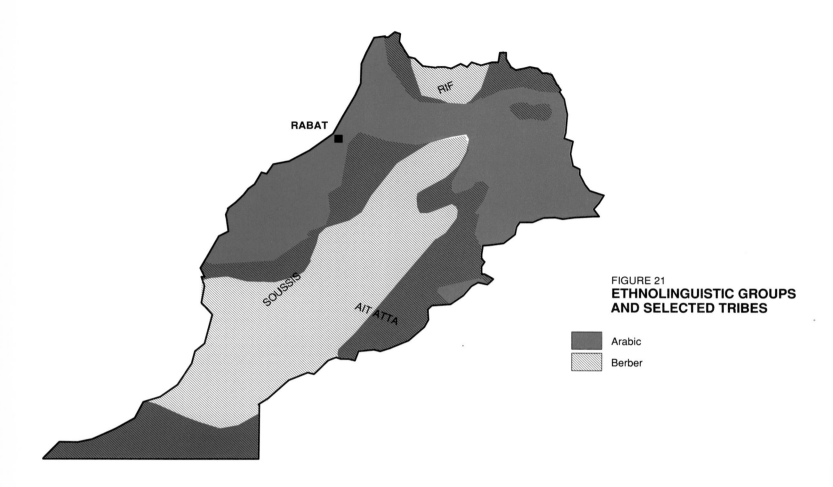

FIGURE 21
ETHNOLINGUISTIC GROUPS AND SELECTED TRIBES

Arabic

Berber

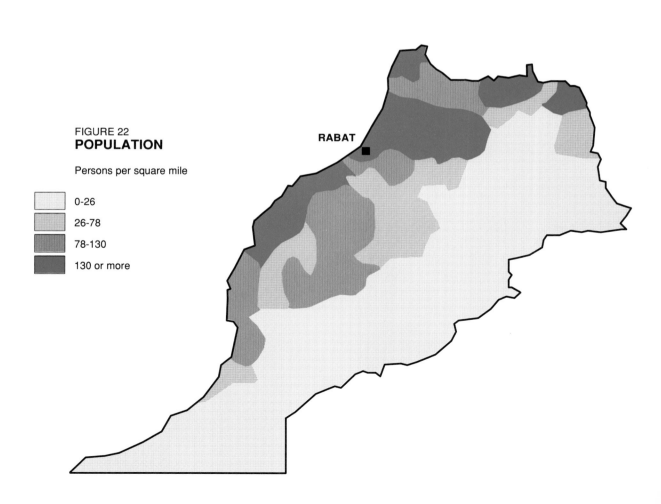

FIGURE 22
POPULATION

Persons per square mile

0-26

26-78

78-130

130 or more

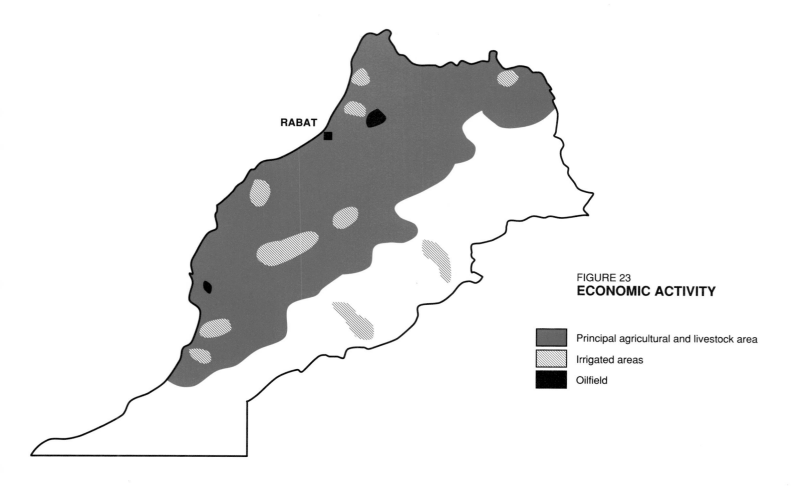

FIGURE 23
ECONOMIC ACTIVITY

RABAT

Principal agricultural and livestock area

Irrigated areas

Oilfield

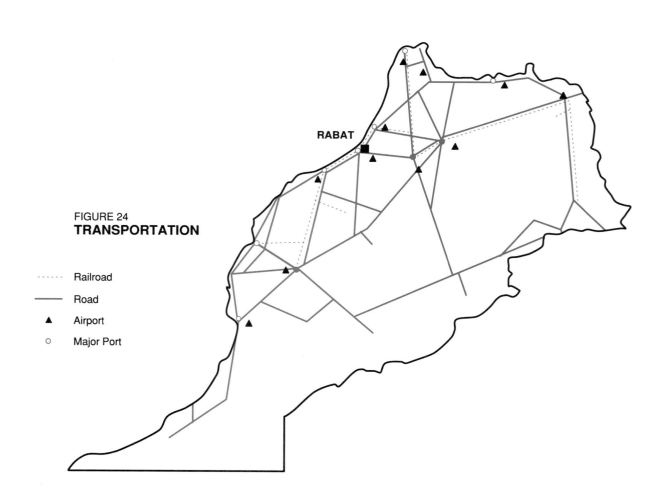

FIGURE 24
TRANSPORTATION

RABAT

Railroad

Road

▲ Airport

○ Major Port

MOZAMBIQUE

One of the youngest independent nations in Africa and one of the poorest countries in the world, Mozambique ranks 35th in land area and 53rd in population. The country is heavily urbanized, a legacy of Portuguese rule, and ranks first in Africa in this respect. The establishment of black rule in Zimbabwe lifted one of the principal burdens on the country's economy. Agriculture remains the mainstay of the economy, but with the exodus of white and Asian farmers, output has fallen below pre-independence levels and Mozambique has had to import as much as 40% of its food requirements in recent years. The government abandoned Marxism-Leninism in 1989, promising a free-market economy and allowing the people to choose between a one-party and a multiparty system. These proposals appeased the rebels and were expected to lead to an end of the civil war.

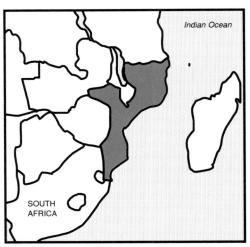

FIGURE 1 **POPULATION GROWTH**

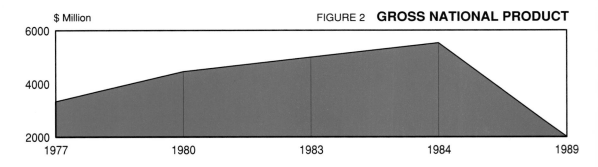

FIGURE 2 **GROSS NATIONAL PRODUCT**

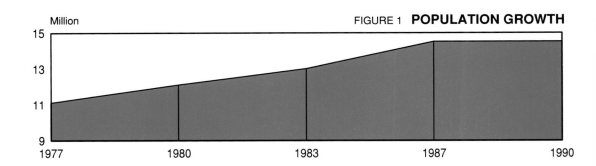

I.M.F.
INFORMATION
NOT
AVAILABLE

FIGURE 3 **GDP AND POPULATION GROWTH RATES**

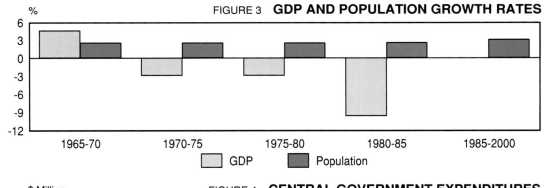

FIGURE 4 **CENTRAL GOVERNMENT EXPENDITURES**

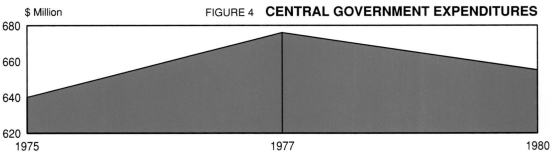

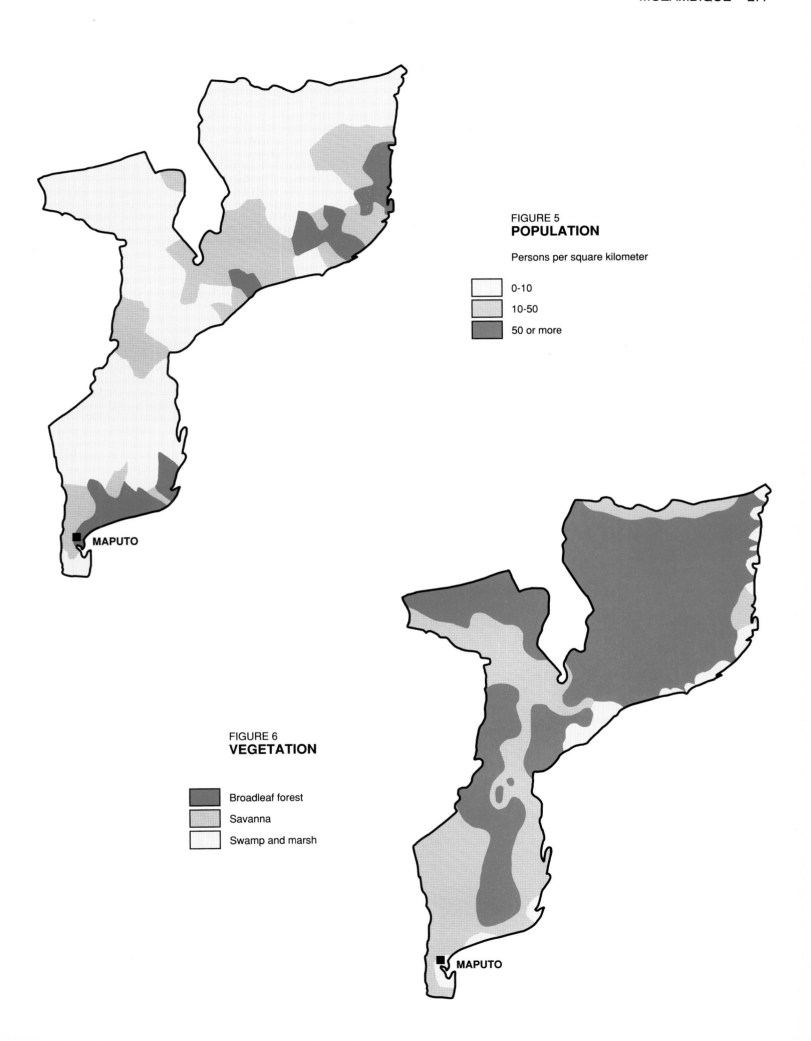

FIGURE 5
POPULATION

Persons per square kilometer

	0-10
	10-50
	50 or more

MAPUTO

FIGURE 6
VEGETATION

	Broadleaf forest
	Savanna
	Swamp and marsh

MAPUTO

MYANMAR

Myanmar, the largest country in mainland Southeast Asia, is the 39th largest country in the world and the 25th most populous. During 1978-86 the population growth rate was curbed while the GNP per capita growth rate rose. Much of this progress was achieved through three successive four-year plans which gave priority to agriculture, forestry, and mining, rather than to industry. The economy is still primarily agricultural, and is dependent on rice cultivation, which accounts for 60% of the nation's export earnings. Another important component of the economy is the mineral and petroleum sector. Myanmar has also a substantial underground economy and a flourishing black market that supplies all foreign-made consumer goods at prices well above the official levels. Because of its ideological commitment to socialism, there was no direct foreign investment in Myanmar after 1963 and even foreign borrowing was limited until the 1970s. The National League for Democracy, born of a nationwide pro-democracy uprising in 1988, won a massive general election victory in 1990, but the country's military rulers refuse to relinquish power.

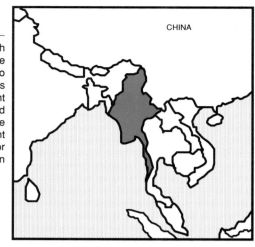

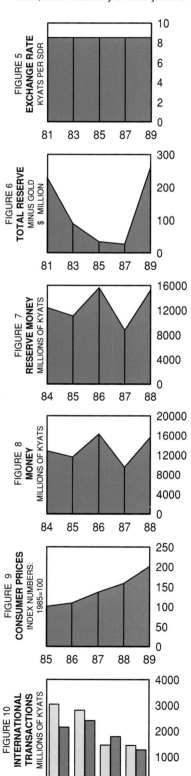

FIGURE 5 **EXCHANGE RATE** KYATS PER SDR

FIGURE 6 **TOTAL RESERVE** MINUS GOLD $ MILLION

FIGURE 7 **RESERVE MONEY** MILLIONS OF KYATS

FIGURE 8 **MONEY** MILLIONS OF KYATS

FIGURE 9 **CONSUMER PRICES** INDEX NUMBERS: 1985=100

FIGURE 10 **INTERNATIONAL TRANSACTIONS** MILLIONS OF KYATS

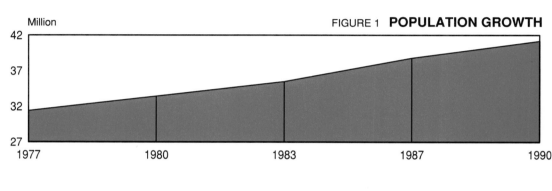

FIGURE 1 **POPULATION GROWTH**

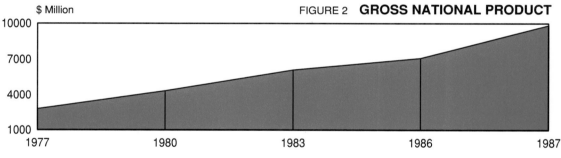

FIGURE 2 **GROSS NATIONAL PRODUCT**

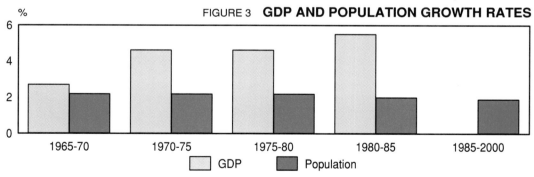

FIGURE 3 **GDP AND POPULATION GROWTH RATES**

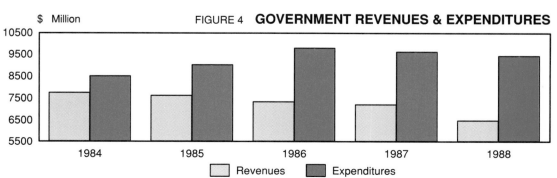

FIGURE 4 **GOVERNMENT REVENUES & EXPENDITURES**

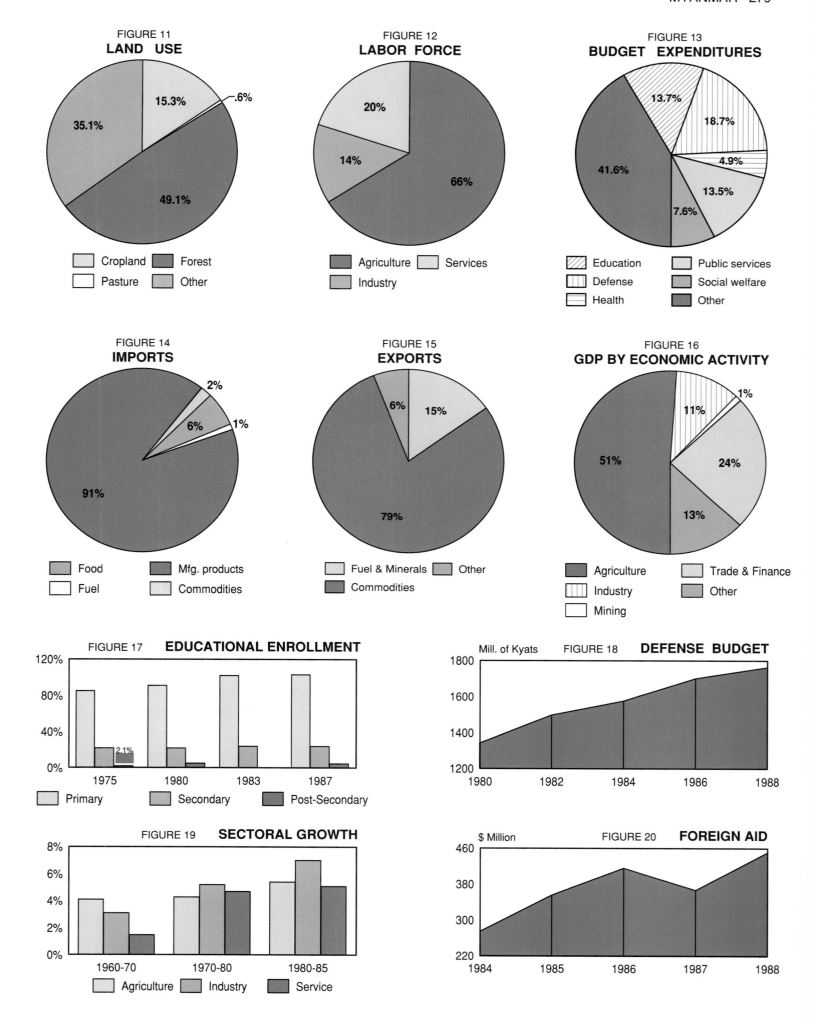

FIGURE 11
LAND USE

15.3%
.6%
35.1%
49.1%

Cropland
Forest
Pasture
Other

FIGURE 12
LABOR FORCE

20%
14%
66%

Agriculture
Services
Industry

FIGURE 13
BUDGET EXPENDITURES

13.7%
18.7%
4.9%
41.6%
7.6%
13.5%

Education
Public services
Defense
Social welfare
Health
Other

FIGURE 14
IMPORTS

2%
6%
1%
91%

Food
Mfg. products
Fuel
Commodities

FIGURE 15
EXPORTS

6%
15%
79%

Fuel & Minerals
Other
Commodities

FIGURE 16
GDP BY ECONOMIC ACTIVITY

1%
11%
51%
24%
13%

Agriculture
Trade & Finance
Industry
Other
Mining

FIGURE 17 **EDUCATIONAL ENROLLMENT**

120%
80%
40%
2.1%
0%
1975 1980 1983 1987

Primary
Secondary
Post-Secondary

Mill. of Kyats FIGURE 18 **DEFENSE BUDGET**

1800
1600
1400
1200
1980 1982 1984 1986 1988

FIGURE 19 **SECTORAL GROWTH**

8%
6%
4%
2%
0%
1960-70 1970-80 1980-85

Agriculture
Industry
Service

$ Million FIGURE 20 **FOREIGN AID**

460
380
300
220
1984 1985 1986 1987 1988

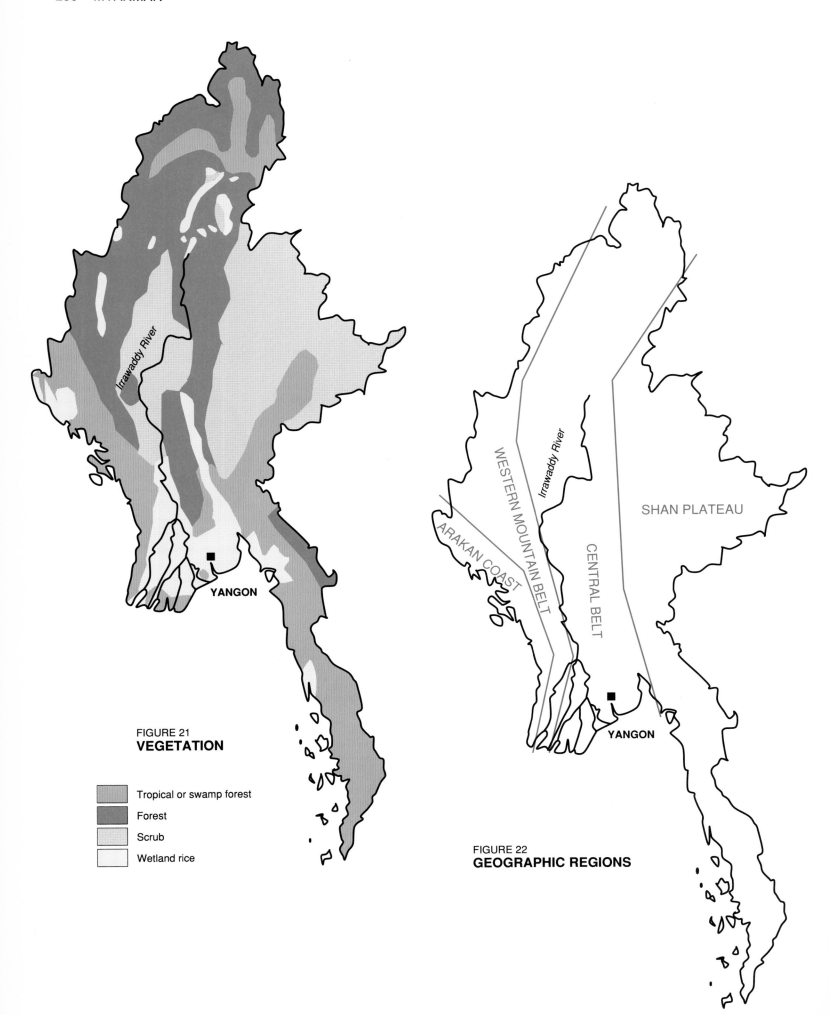

FIGURE 21
VEGETATION

Tropical or swamp forest
Forest
Scrub
Wetland rice

Irrawaddy River

YANGON

FIGURE 22
GEOGRAPHIC REGIONS

ARAKAN COAST

WESTERN MOUNTAIN BELT

Irrawaddy River

CENTRAL BELT

SHAN PLATEAU

YANGON

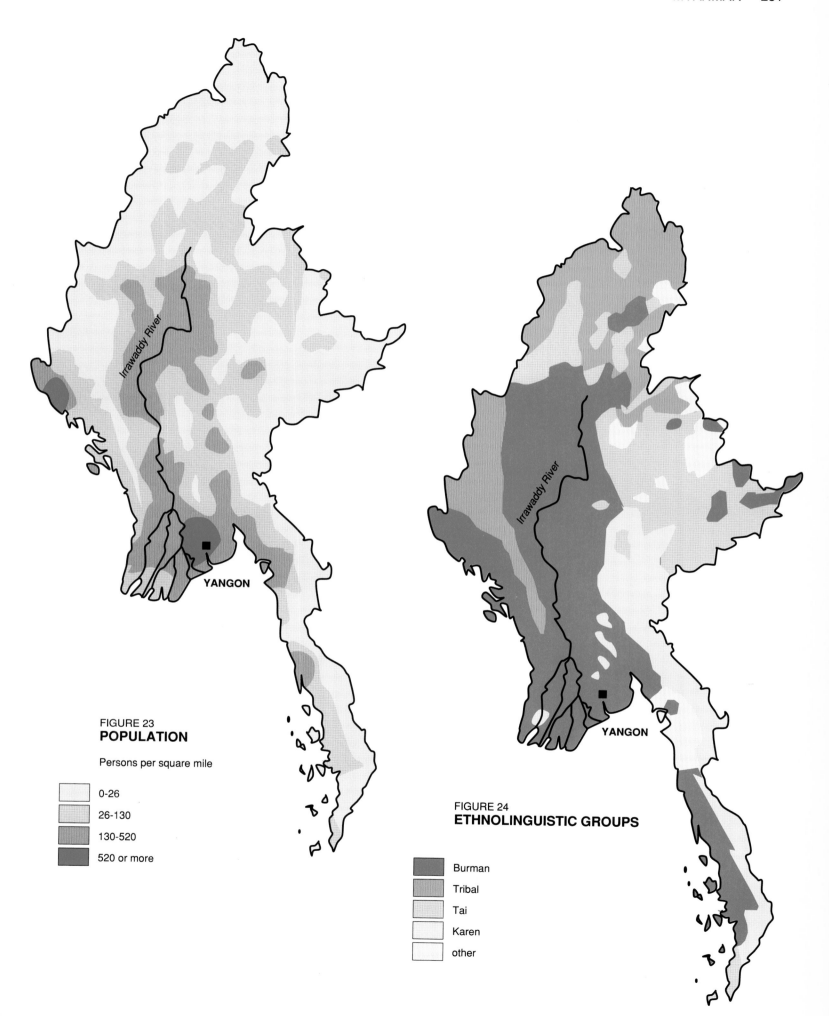

FIGURE 23
POPULATION

Persons per square mile

0-26

26-130

130-520

520 or more

FIGURE 24
ETHNOLINGUISTIC GROUPS

Burman

Tribal

Tai

Karen

other

YANGON

Irrawaddy River

NEPAL

The world's only Hindu kingdom, located on the southern slopes of the Himalayas, Nepal ranks 89th in land area and 43rd in population. Sandwiched between two of the largest nations in the world, without any access to the sea, Nepal has no strategic or political leverage; further, its economic resources are meager to begin with, affording little opportunity for development. Nearly 93% of the work force is engaged in agriculture, at or below subsistence level. Only about 30% of the land is farmed, while a third or more is forested. Two institutions—cooperatives (organized in units called sajahas) and a cluster of government agricultural agencies—sustain agricultural activities. While foreign trade has shown large and growing deficits, these deficits have been offset by positive balances in the services and transfers accounts, especially remittances by tourists and the famed Gurkha troops serving abroad. Over a million Indians are believed to live in Nepal and they control much of the import and export businesses. Nepal took a giant leap toward democracy in 1990 when the king approved a new constitution guaranteeing multiparty democracy and human rights.

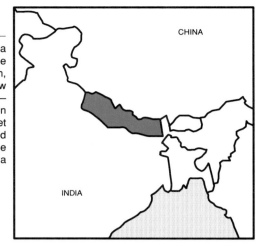

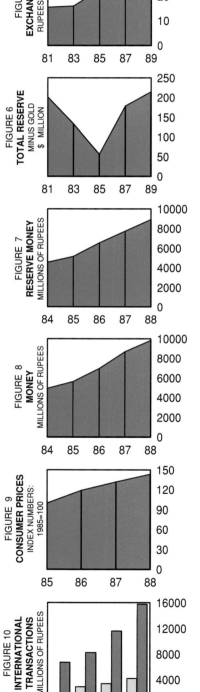

FIGURE 5 **EXCHANGE RATE** RUPEES PER SDR

FIGURE 6 **TOTAL RESERVE** MINUS GOLD $ MILLION

FIGURE 7 **RESERVE MONEY** MILLIONS OF RUPEES

FIGURE 8 **MONEY** MILLIONS OF RUPEES

FIGURE 9 **CONSUMER PRICES** INDEX NUMBERS: 1985=100

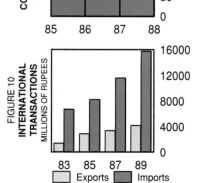

FIGURE 10 **INTERNATIONAL TRANSACTIONS** MILLIONS OF RUPEES

□ Exports ■ Imports

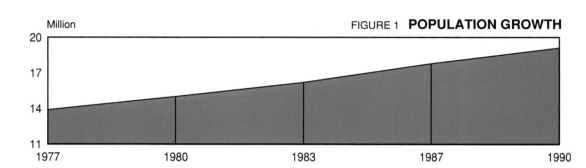

Million   FIGURE 1 **POPULATION GROWTH**

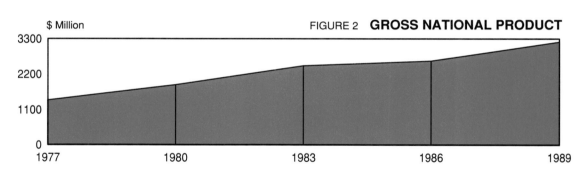

$ Million   FIGURE 2 **GROSS NATIONAL PRODUCT**

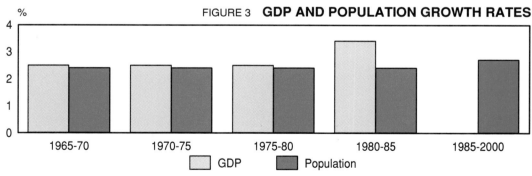

%   FIGURE 3 **GDP AND POPULATION GROWTH RATES**

□ GDP ■ Population

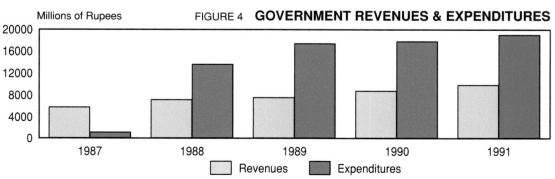

Millions of Rupees   FIGURE 4 **GOVERNMENT REVENUES & EXPENDITURES**

□ Revenues ■ Expenditures

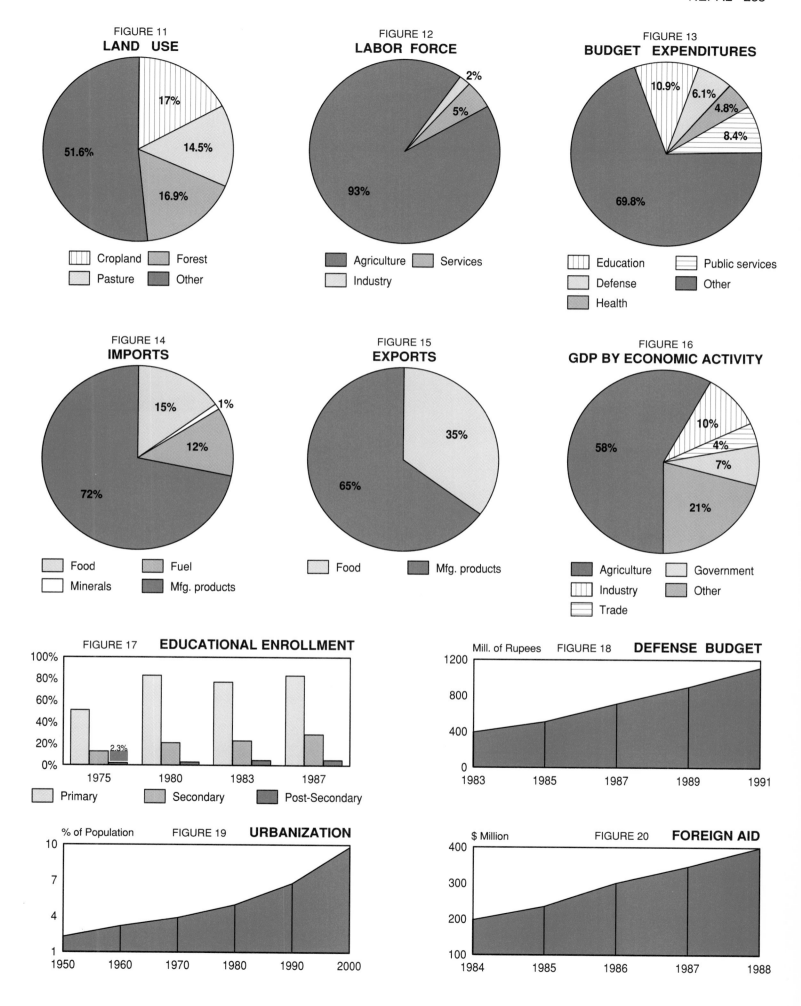

FIGURE 11
LAND USE

17%
14.5%
51.6%
16.9%

Cropland   Forest
Pasture   Other

FIGURE 12
LABOR FORCE

2%
5%
93%

Agriculture   Services
Industry

FIGURE 13
BUDGET EXPENDITURES

10.9%   6.1%
4.8%
8.4%
69.8%

Education   Public services
Defense   Other
Health

FIGURE 14
IMPORTS

15%   1%
12%
72%

Food   Fuel
Minerals   Mfg. products

FIGURE 15
EXPORTS

35%
65%

Food   Mfg. products

FIGURE 16
GDP BY ECONOMIC ACTIVITY

10%
4%
58%
7%
21%

Agriculture   Government
Industry   Other
Trade

FIGURE 17 **EDUCATIONAL ENROLLMENT**

100%
80%
60%
40%
20%
2.3%
0%
1975   1980   1983   1987

Primary   Secondary   Post-Secondary

Mill. of Rupees   FIGURE 18   **DEFENSE BUDGET**

1200
800
400
0
1983   1985   1987   1989   1991

% of Population   FIGURE 19   **URBANIZATION**

10
7
4
1
1950   1960   1970   1980   1990   2000

$ Million   FIGURE 20   **FOREIGN AID**

400
300
200
100
1984   1985   1986   1987   1988

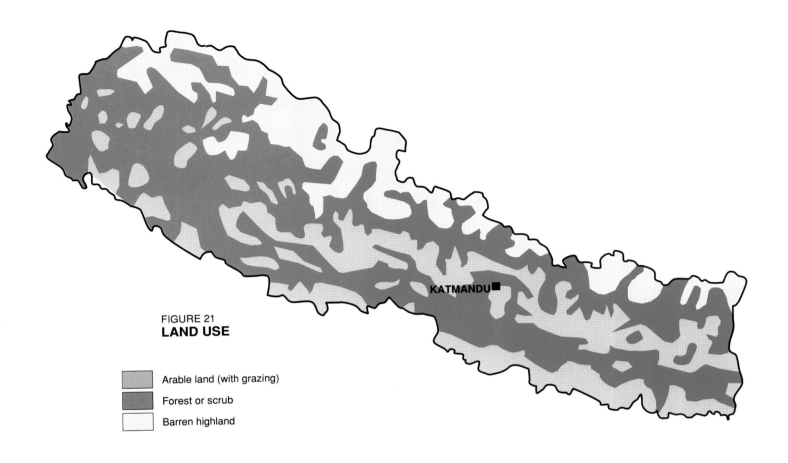

FIGURE 21
LAND USE

Arable land (with grazing)

Forest or scrub

Barren highland

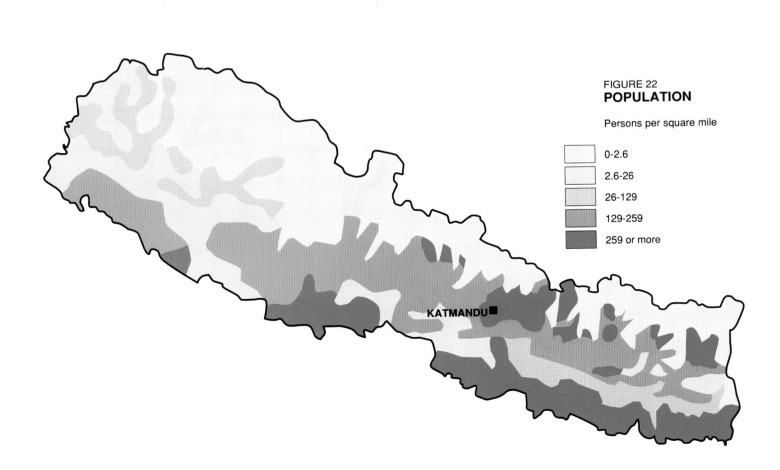

FIGURE 22
POPULATION

Persons per square mile

0-2.6

2.6-26

26-129

129-259

259 or more

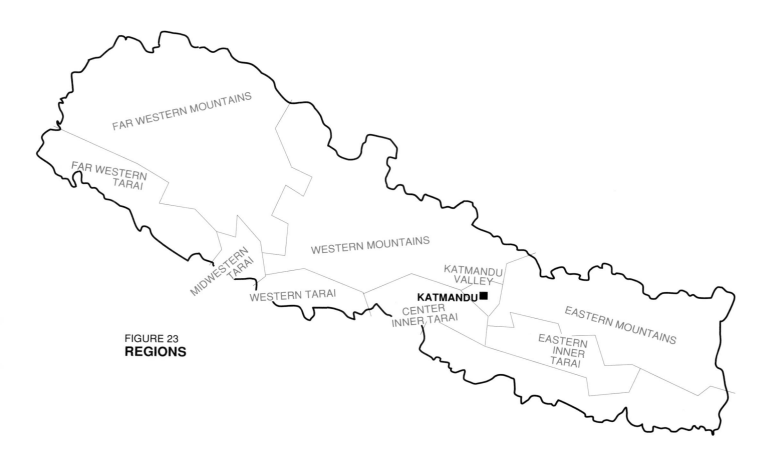

FIGURE 23
REGIONS

FAR WESTERN MOUNTAINS

FAR WESTERN TARAI

MIDWESTERN TARAI

WESTERN MOUNTAINS

WESTERN TARAI

CENTER INNER TARAI

KATMANDU VALLEY

KATMANDU

EASTERN MOUNTAINS

EASTERN INNER TARAI

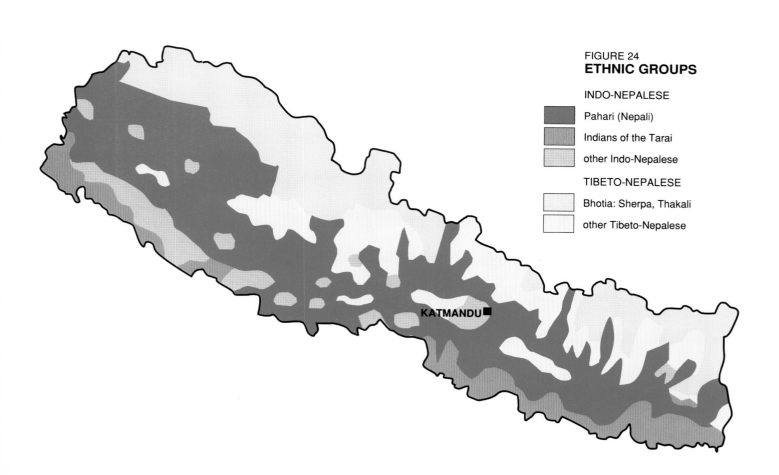

FIGURE 24
ETHNIC GROUPS

INDO-NEPALESE

Pahari (Nepali)

Indians of the Tarai

other Indo-Nepalese

TIBETO-NEPALESE

Bhotia: Sherpa, Thakali

other Tibeto-Nepalese

KATMANDU

NICARAGUA

The largest of the Central American republics, Nicaragua ranks 93rd in land area and 107th in population. Relatively prosperous until the 1970s, the Nicaraguan economy has suffered two major reverses since then: the earthquake that struck Managua in 1972 and the civil war that began in 1979. One of the first acts of the Sandinistas after they overthrew Somoza and came to power in 1979 was to nationalize the vast interest controlled by the Somoza family and the Somocistas, the ex-president's associates, that formerly comprised one-tenth of the Nicaraguan economy. While this step proved relatively easy, further progress was lost to conflicting pressures; within the junta communist counsel prevailed and the split between moderates and extremists became sharper. In a 1990 national election, the Sandinistas were soundly defeated by a U.S.-backed opposition coalition led by Violeta Chamorro. Upon taking office, she faced severe economic problems, rifts within her coalition, and a threat by the outgoing Sandinistas to "rule form below."

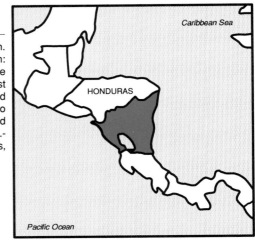

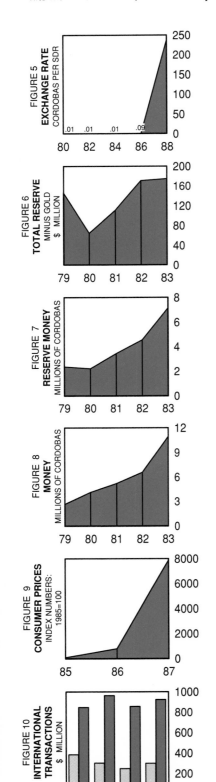

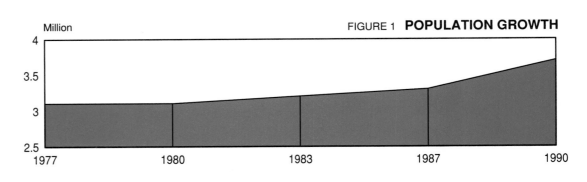

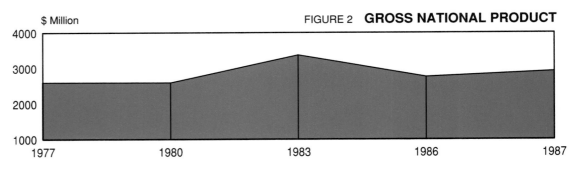

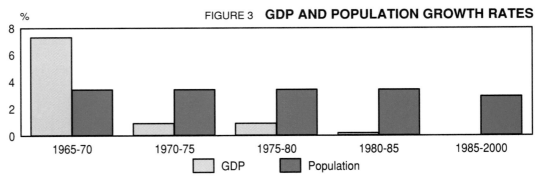

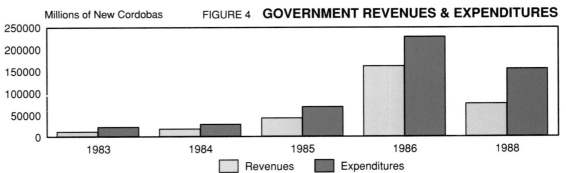

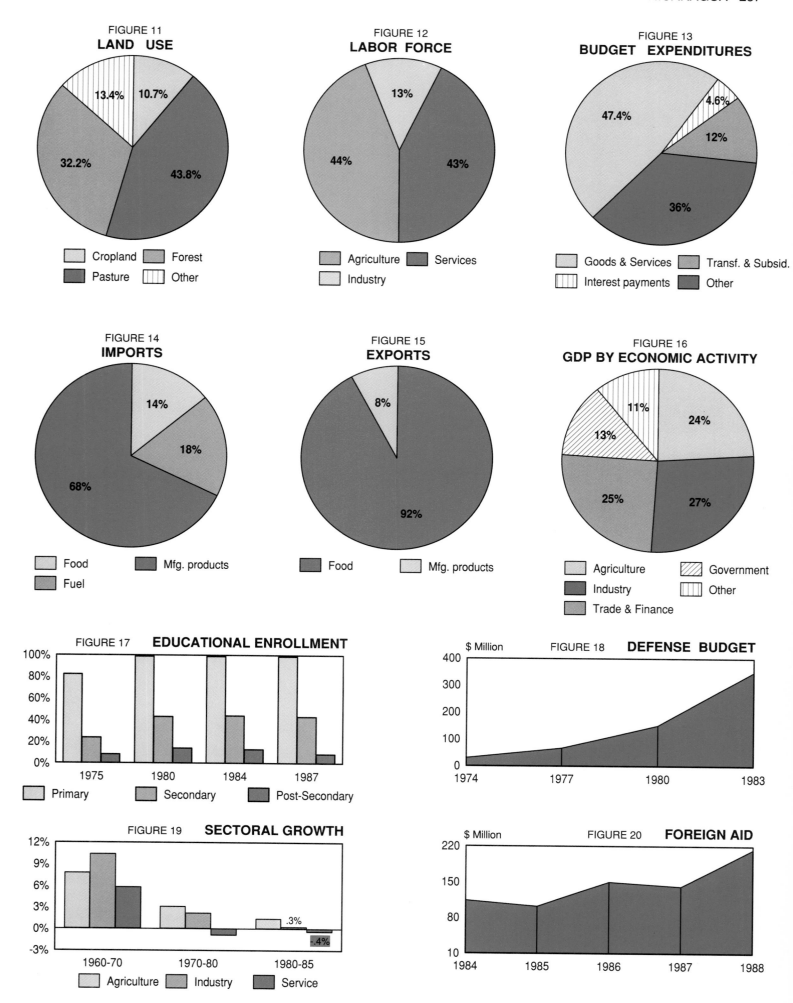

FIGURE 11
LAND USE

13.4% 10.7%
32.2% 43.8%

Cropland / Forest
Pasture / Other

FIGURE 12
LABOR FORCE

13%
44% 43%

Agriculture / Services
Industry

FIGURE 13
BUDGET EXPENDITURES

47.4% 4.6%
12%
36%

Goods & Services / Transf. & Subsid.
Interest payments / Other

FIGURE 14
IMPORTS

14%
18%
68%

Food / Mfg. products
Fuel

FIGURE 15
EXPORTS

8%
92%

Food / Mfg. products

FIGURE 16
GDP BY ECONOMIC ACTIVITY

11% 24%
13%
25% 27%

Agriculture / Government
Industry / Other
Trade & Finance

FIGURE 17 **EDUCATIONAL ENROLLMENT**

100%
80%
60%
40%
20%
0%
1975   1980   1984   1987

Primary / Secondary / Post-Secondary

FIGURE 18 **DEFENSE BUDGET**

$ Million
400
300
200
100
0
1974   1977   1980   1983

FIGURE 19 **SECTORAL GROWTH**

12%
9%
6%
3%
0%
-3%
1960-70   1970-80   1980-85
.3%
-.4%

Agriculture / Industry / Service

FIGURE 20 **FOREIGN AID**

$ Million
220
150
80
10
1984   1985   1986   1987   1988

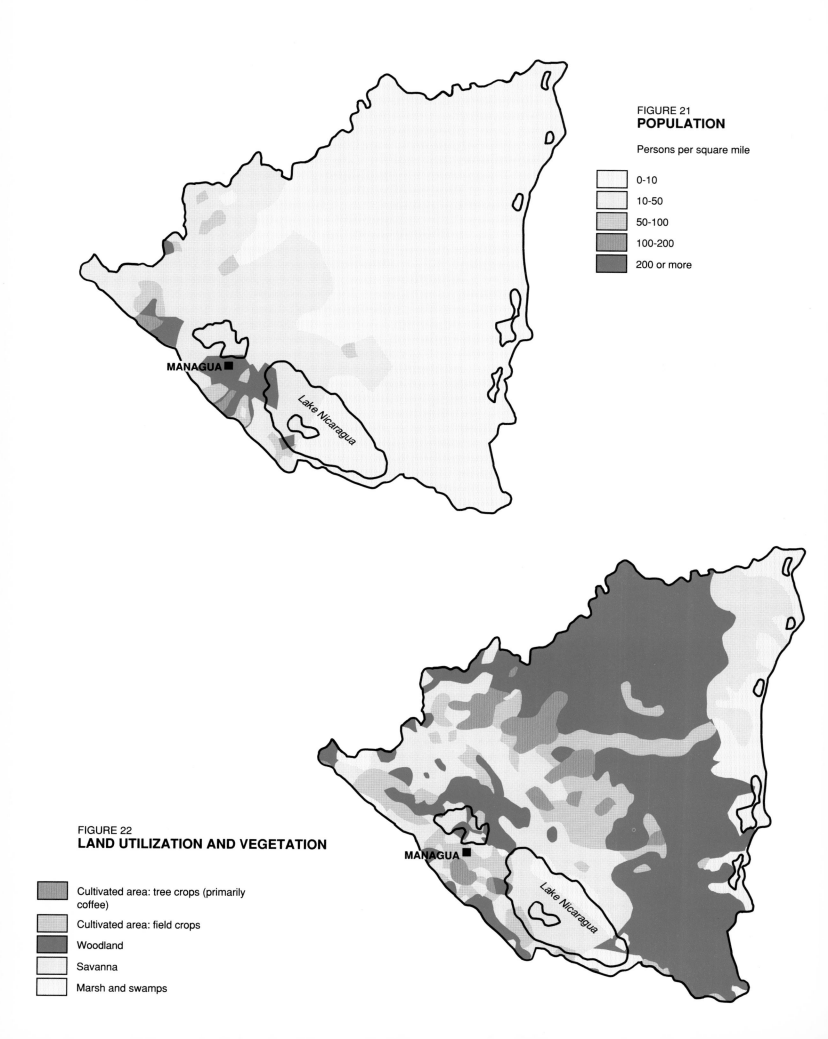

FIGURE 21
POPULATION

Persons per square mile

0-10
10-50
50-100
100-200
200 or more

MANAGUA ■

Lake Nicaragua

FIGURE 22
LAND UTILIZATION AND VEGETATION

Cultivated area: tree crops (primarily coffee)

Cultivated area: field crops

Woodland

Savanna

Marsh and swamps

MANAGUA ■

Lake Nicaragua

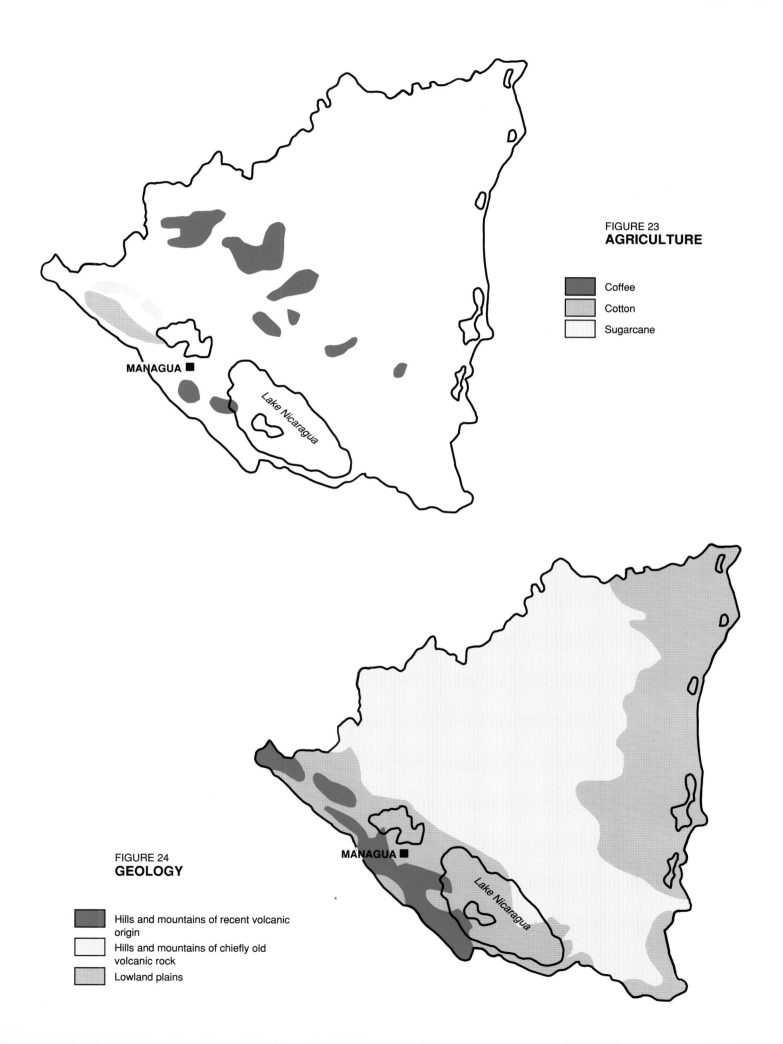

FIGURE 23
AGRICULTURE

Coffee
Cotton
Sugarcane

MANAGUA ■

Lake Nicaragua

FIGURE 24
GEOLOGY

Hills and mountains of recent volcanic origin

Hills and mountains of chiefly old volcanic rock

Lowland plains

MANAGUA ■

Lake Nicaragua

NIGER

Landlocked Niger, located on the southern fringe of the Sahara Desert, ranks 25th in land area and 80th in population. Land size is misleading because only 3% of the land is cultivable. Livestock raising, the traditional activity of the nomads, is only slowly recovering from the great Sahelian drought that resulted in the loss of two-thirds of the country's cattle stock. Niger's destitution is reflected in the fact that it has one of the highest death rates in the world. The most promising economic sector is mining; the country is rich in uranium and coal. Uranium production accounts for approximately tow-thirds of the country's trade receipts, projected at over $1 billion annually. Known reserves total more than 100,000 tons. France, the country's major trade partner, absorbs the bulk of its uranium exports.

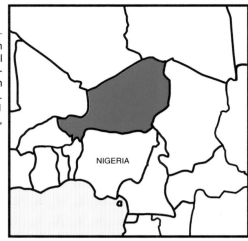

NIGERIA

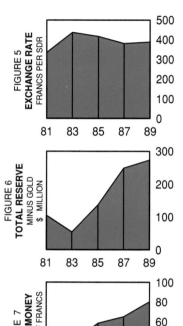

FIGURE 5 **EXCHANGE RATE** FRANCS PER SDR

FIGURE 6 **TOTAL RESERVE** MINUS GOLD $ MILLION

FIGURE 7 **RESERVE MONEY** BILLIONS OF FRANCS

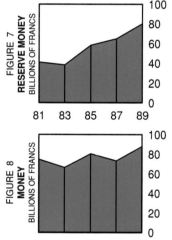

FIGURE 8 **MONEY** BILLIONS OF FRANCS

FIGURE 9 **CONSUMER PRICES** INDEX NUMBERS: 1985=100

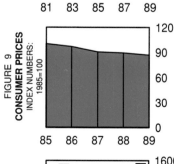

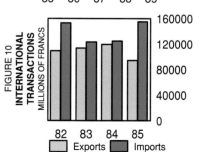

FIGURE 10 **INTERNATIONAL TRANSACTIONS** MILLIONS OF FRANCS

Exports   Imports

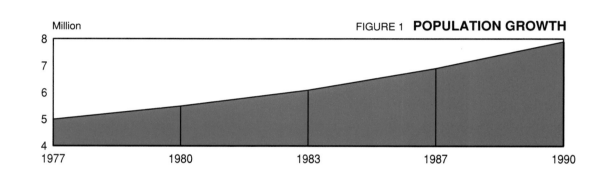

Million   FIGURE 1 **POPULATION GROWTH**

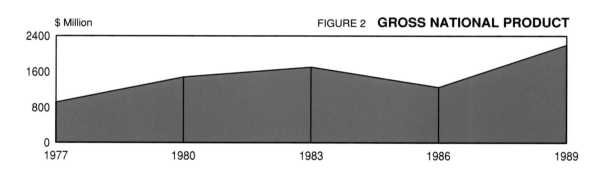

$ Million   FIGURE 2 **GROSS NATIONAL PRODUCT**

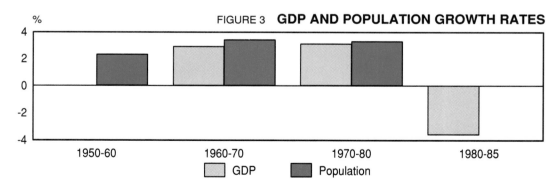

%   FIGURE 3 **GDP AND POPULATION GROWTH RATES**

GDP   Population

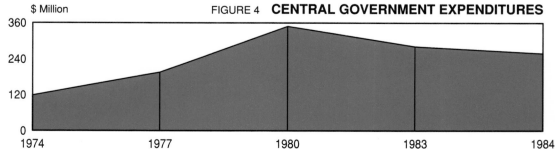

$ Million   FIGURE 4 **CENTRAL GOVERNMENT EXPENDITURES**

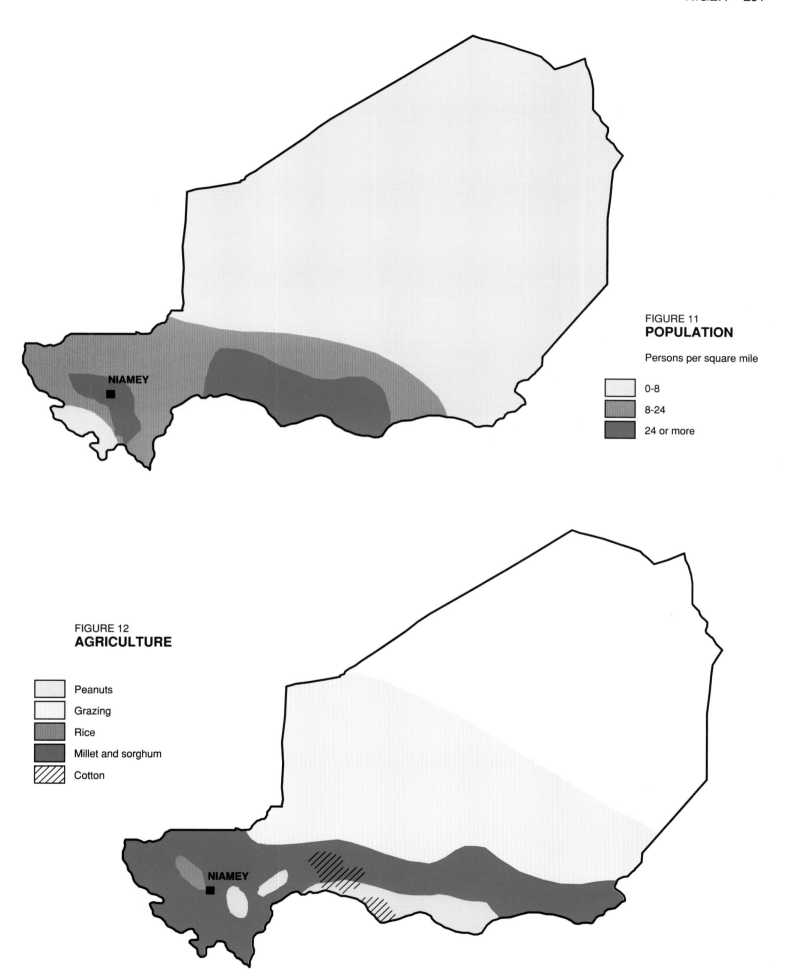

FIGURE 11
POPULATION

Persons per square mile

0-8

8-24

24 or more

NIAMEY

FIGURE 12
AGRICULTURE

Peanuts

Grazing

Rice

Millet and sorghum

Cotton

NIAMEY

NIGERIA

The most populous country in Africa, accounting for 25% of black Africa's population, Nigeria ranks 31st in land area and 8th in population. Its population density is twice as high as the African average. According to Ray Cline, it is also the most powerful nation in Africa, with the highest GNP, the largest standing army, and the largest crude oil production. Despite such attributes of power, Nigeria is in effect a low-income country and its economy is not much different from those of its African neighbors. Ethnic conflicts, political unrest, pervasive bureaucratic inefficiency, corruption, and sectoral imbalances all tend to distort economic growth patterns and slow development initiatives. Nevertheless, oil wealth, estimated at over $2 billion per year, has brought new opportunities and an expanded national vision. The impact of oil is felt in every area, but especially in construction, industry, and transportation. A number of large-scale industrial projects have been planned in collaboration with overseas firms. Despite recent diversification programs, the oil industry dominates the economy and in 1990 oil production rose to about 2.4 million bbl per day.

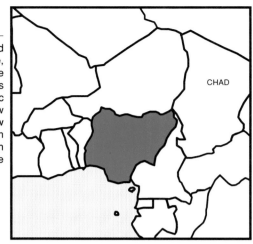

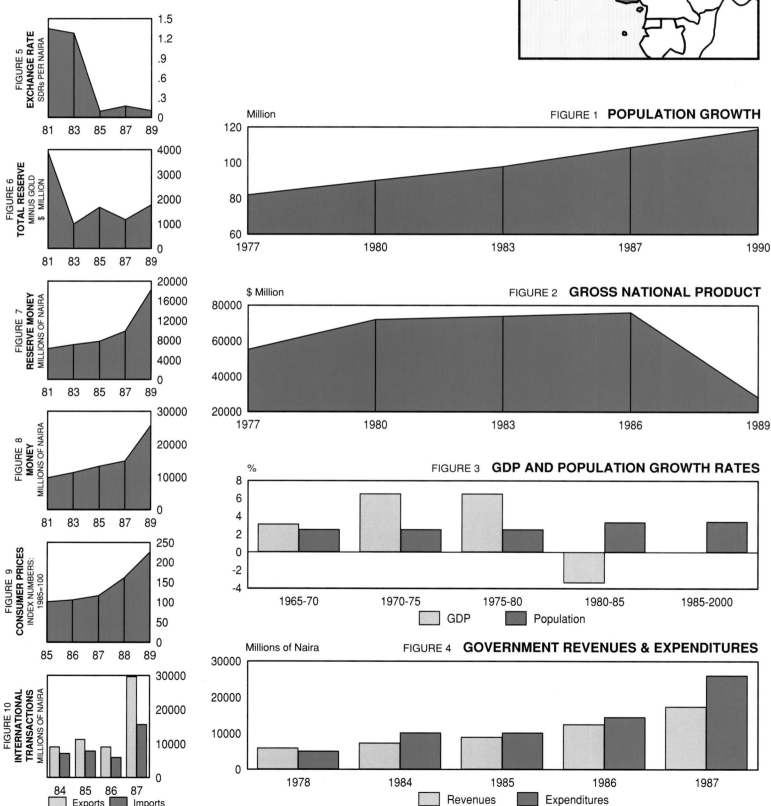

FIGURE 5 EXCHANGE RATE SDRs PER NAIRA

FIGURE 6 TOTAL RESERVE MINUS GOLD $ MILLION

FIGURE 7 RESERVE MONEY MILLIONS OF NAIRA

FIGURE 8 MONEY MILLIONS OF NAIRA

FIGURE 9 CONSUMER PRICES INDEX NUMBERS: 1985=100

FIGURE 10 INTERNATIONAL TRANSACTIONS MILLIONS OF NAIRA
Exports Imports

FIGURE 1 **POPULATION GROWTH**
Million

FIGURE 2 **GROSS NATIONAL PRODUCT**
$ Million

FIGURE 3 **GDP AND POPULATION GROWTH RATES**
%
GDP Population

FIGURE 4 **GOVERNMENT REVENUES & EXPENDITURES**
Millions of Naira
Revenues Expenditures

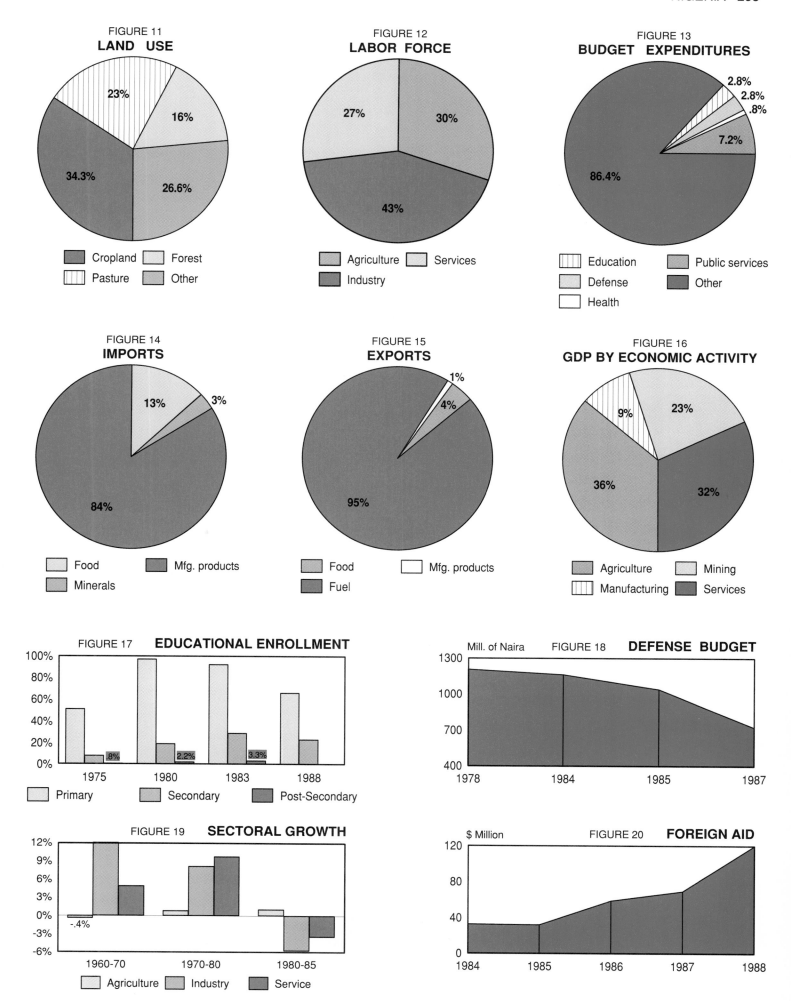

FIGURE 11
LAND USE

23%
16%
34.3%
26.6%

Cropland   Forest
Pasture   Other

FIGURE 12
LABOR FORCE

27%   30%
43%

Agriculture   Services
Industry

FIGURE 13
BUDGET EXPENDITURES

2.8%
2.8%
.8%
7.2%
86.4%

Education   Public services
Defense   Other
Health

FIGURE 14
IMPORTS

13%   3%
84%

Food   Mfg. products
Minerals

FIGURE 15
EXPORTS

1%
4%
95%

Food   Mfg. products
Fuel

FIGURE 16
GDP BY ECONOMIC ACTIVITY

9%   23%
36%   32%

Agriculture   Mining
Manufacturing Services

FIGURE 17 EDUCATIONAL ENROLLMENT

100%
80%
60%
40%
20%
0%
      1975   1980   1983   1988
8%   2.2%   3.3%

Primary   Secondary   Post-Secondary

FIGURE 18 DEFENSE BUDGET
Mill. of Naira

1300
1000
700
400
    1978   1984   1985   1987

FIGURE 19 SECTORAL GROWTH

12%
9%
6%
3%
0%
-3%
-6%
    1960-70   1970-80   1980-85
-.4%

Agriculture   Industry   Service

FIGURE 20 FOREIGN AID
$ Million

120
80
40
0
    1984   1985   1986   1987   1988

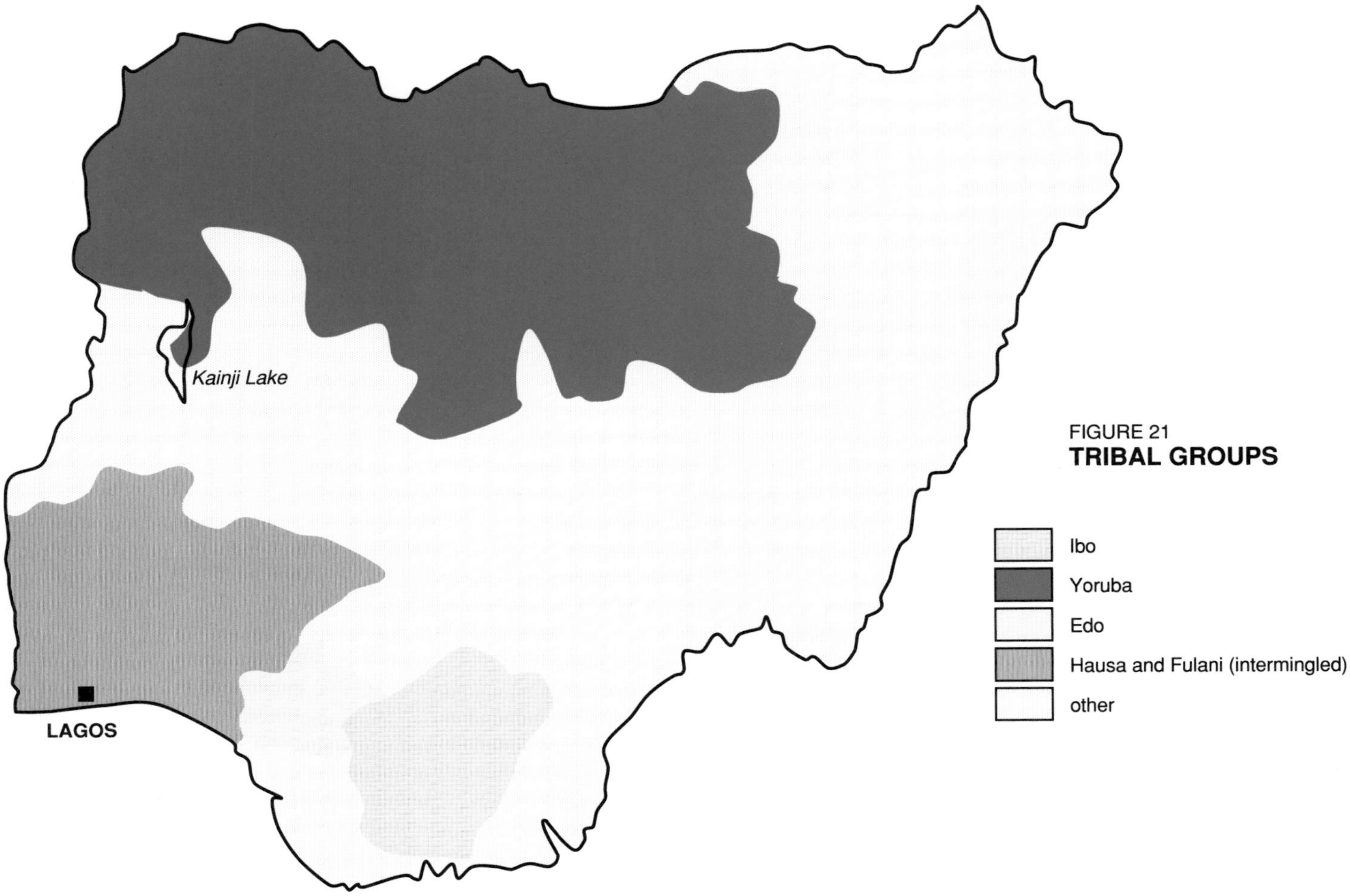

FIGURE 21
TRIBAL GROUPS

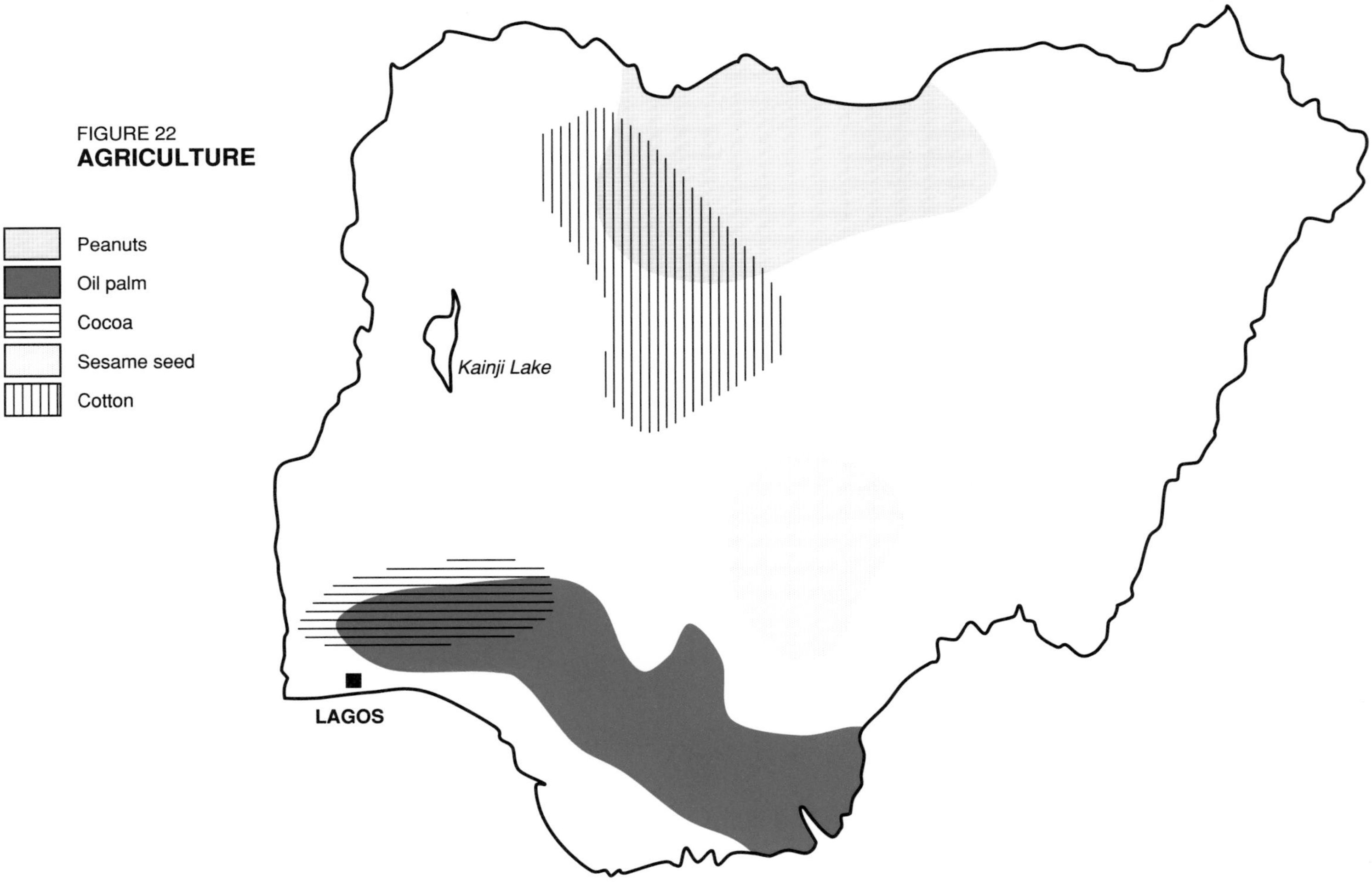

Ibo

Yoruba

Edo

Hausa and Fulani (intermingled)

other

Kainji Lake

LAGOS

FIGURE 22
AGRICULTURE

Peanuts

Oil palm

Cocoa

Sesame seed

Cotton

Kainji Lake

LAGOS

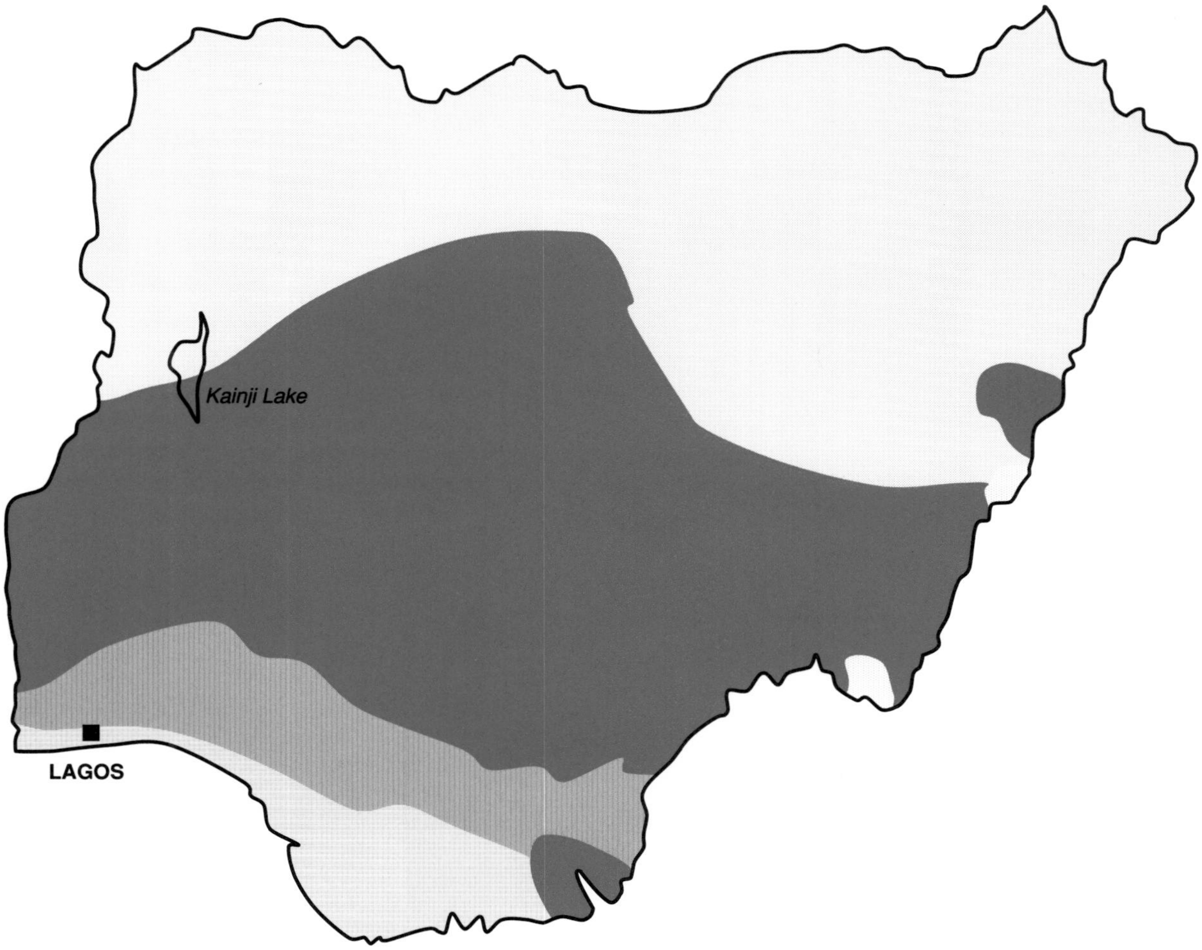

FIGURE 23
VEGETATION

Montane vegetation

Short-grass or
Sudan savanna

Tall-grass savanna

High rain forest

Swamp

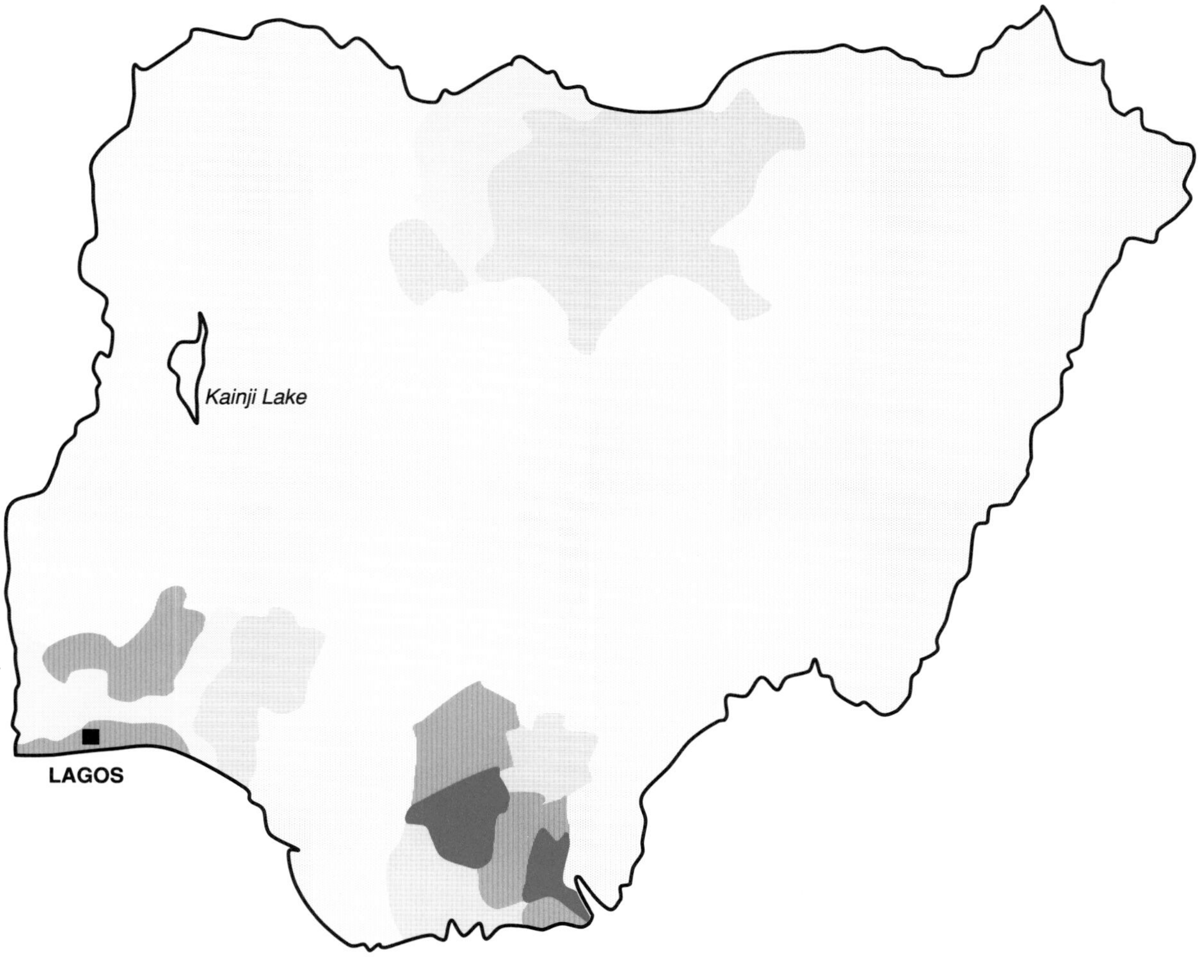

Kainji Lake

LAGOS

FIGURE 24
POPULATION

Persons per square mile

0-200

200-300

300-450

450-1000

1000 or more

Kainji Lake

LAGOS

PAKISTAN

Carved out of the old Indian empire, Pakistan ranks 35th in land area and 10th in size of population. Unlike India, Pakistan's political history since independence has been troubled: three wars with India, border skirmishes with Afghanistan, the secession of Bangladesh, separatist movements of Pathans and Baluchis, and a succession of authoritarian regimes have scarred the national ego. The so-called Islamization, launched by President Zia, only served to legitimize an increasingly authoritarian regime. The Pakistani economy displays all the negative characteristics of underdevelopment. The Zia government, on the one hand, loosened central government's direct involvement in the economy; on the other hand, martial law was used to interfere in routine business activities and to harass both business and labor. Zia died in a mysterious helicopter explosion in 1988. Benazin Bhutto, the Muslim world's only elected woman leader, served as prime minister from 1988 until 1990. National elections took place later that year with Bhutto's party suffering a decisive defeat.

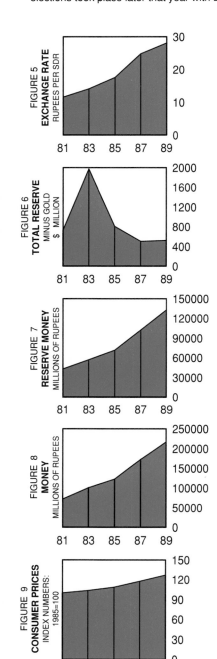

FIGURE 5 EXCHANGE RATE RUPEES PER SDR

FIGURE 6 TOTAL RESERVE MINUS GOLD $ MILLION

FIGURE 7 RESERVE MONEY MILLIONS OF RUPEES

FIGURE 8 MONEY MILLIONS OF RUPEES

FIGURE 9 CONSUMER PRICES INDEX NUMBERS: 1985=100

FIGURE 10 INTERNATIONAL TRANSACTIONS MILLIONS OF RUPEES
Exports Imports

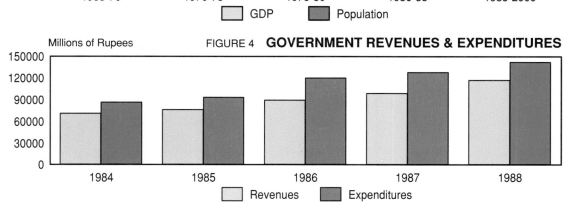
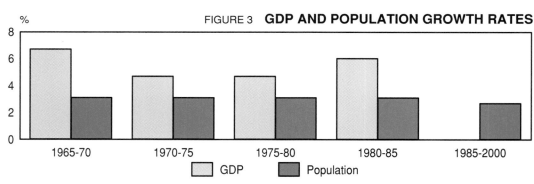
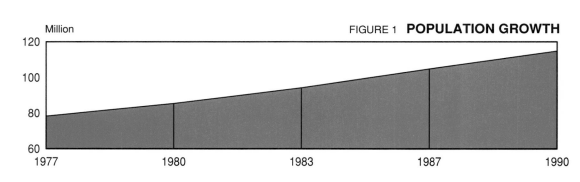
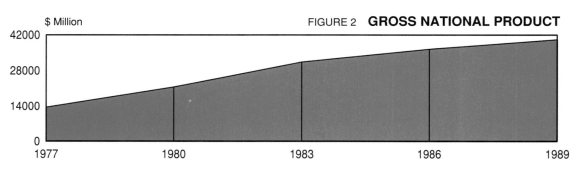

FIGURE 1 **POPULATION GROWTH**
Million

FIGURE 2 **GROSS NATIONAL PRODUCT**
$ Million

FIGURE 3 **GDP AND POPULATION GROWTH RATES**
%
GDP   Population

FIGURE 4 **GOVERNMENT REVENUES & EXPENDITURES**
Millions of Rupees
Revenues   Expenditures

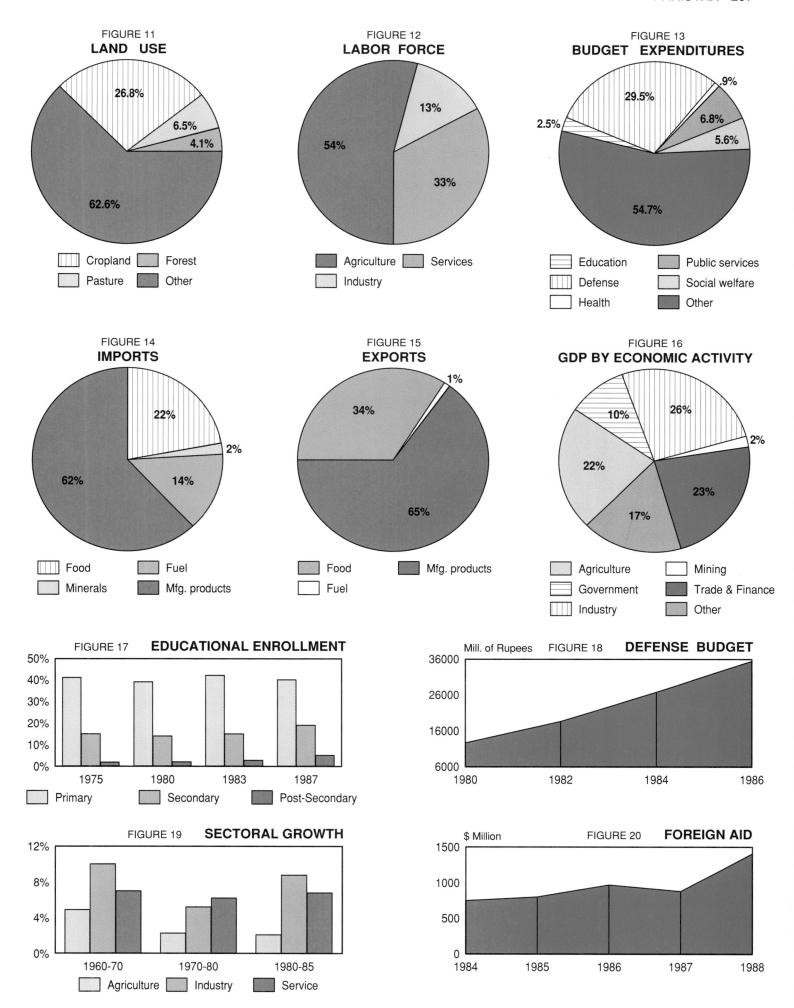

FIGURE 11
LAND USE

26.8%
6.5%
4.1%
62.6%

Cropland   Forest
Pasture   Other

FIGURE 12
LABOR FORCE

13%
54%
33%

Agriculture   Services
Industry

FIGURE 13
BUDGET EXPENDITURES

29.5%
.9%
2.5%
6.8%
5.6%
54.7%

Education   Public services
Defense   Social welfare
Health   Other

FIGURE 14
IMPORTS

22%
2%
62%
14%

Food   Fuel
Minerals   Mfg. products

FIGURE 15
EXPORTS

1%
34%
65%

Food   Mfg. products
Fuel

FIGURE 16
GDP BY ECONOMIC ACTIVITY

10%
26%
2%
22%
23%
17%

Agriculture   Mining
Government   Trade & Finance
Industry   Other

FIGURE 17   **EDUCATIONAL ENROLLMENT**

50%
40%
30%
20%
10%
0%

1975   1980   1983   1987

Primary   Secondary   Post-Secondary

Mill. of Rupees   FIGURE 18   **DEFENSE BUDGET**

36000
26000
16000
6000

1980   1982   1984   1986

FIGURE 19   **SECTORAL GROWTH**

12%
8%
4%
0%

1960-70   1970-80   1980-85

Agriculture   Industry   Service

$ Million   FIGURE 20   **FOREIGN AID**

1500
1000
500
0

1984   1985   1986   1987   1988

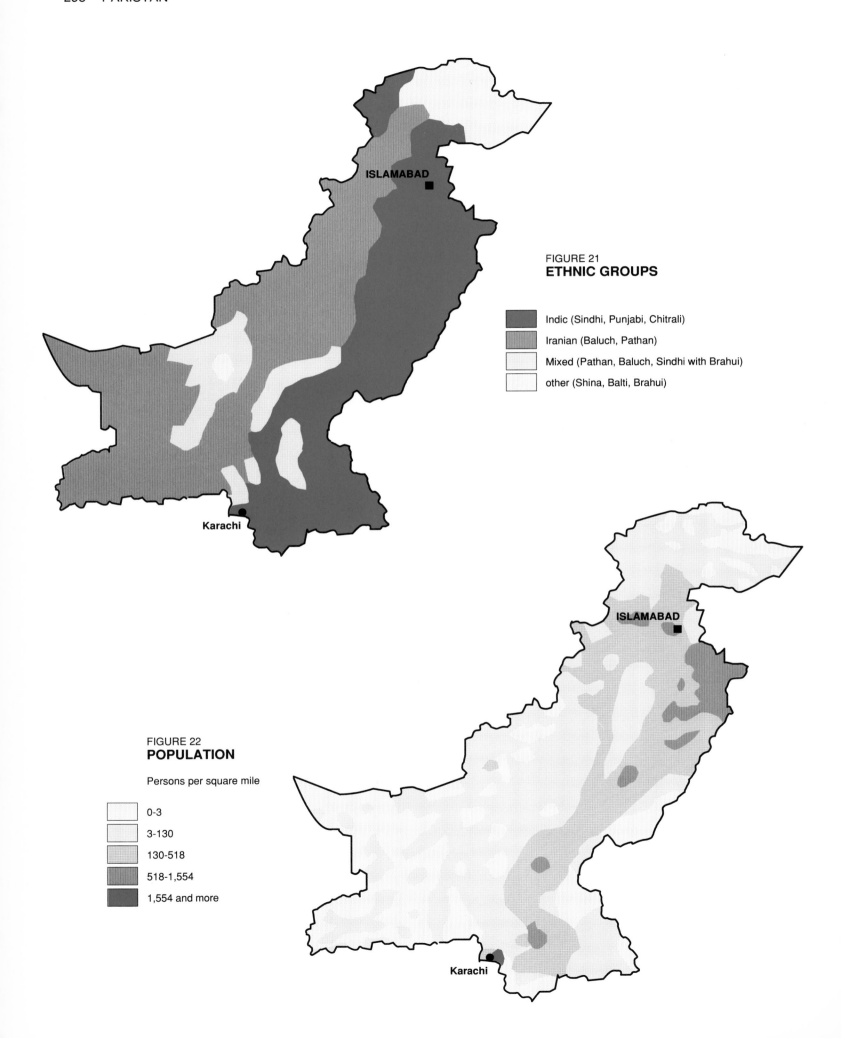

FIGURE 21
ETHNIC GROUPS

Indic (Sindhi, Punjabi, Chitrali)

Iranian (Baluch, Pathan)

Mixed (Pathan, Baluch, Sindhi with Brahui)

other (Shina, Balti, Brahui)

ISLAMABAD

Karachi

FIGURE 22
POPULATION

Persons per square mile

0-3

3-130

130-518

518-1,554

1,554 and more

ISLAMABAD

Karachi

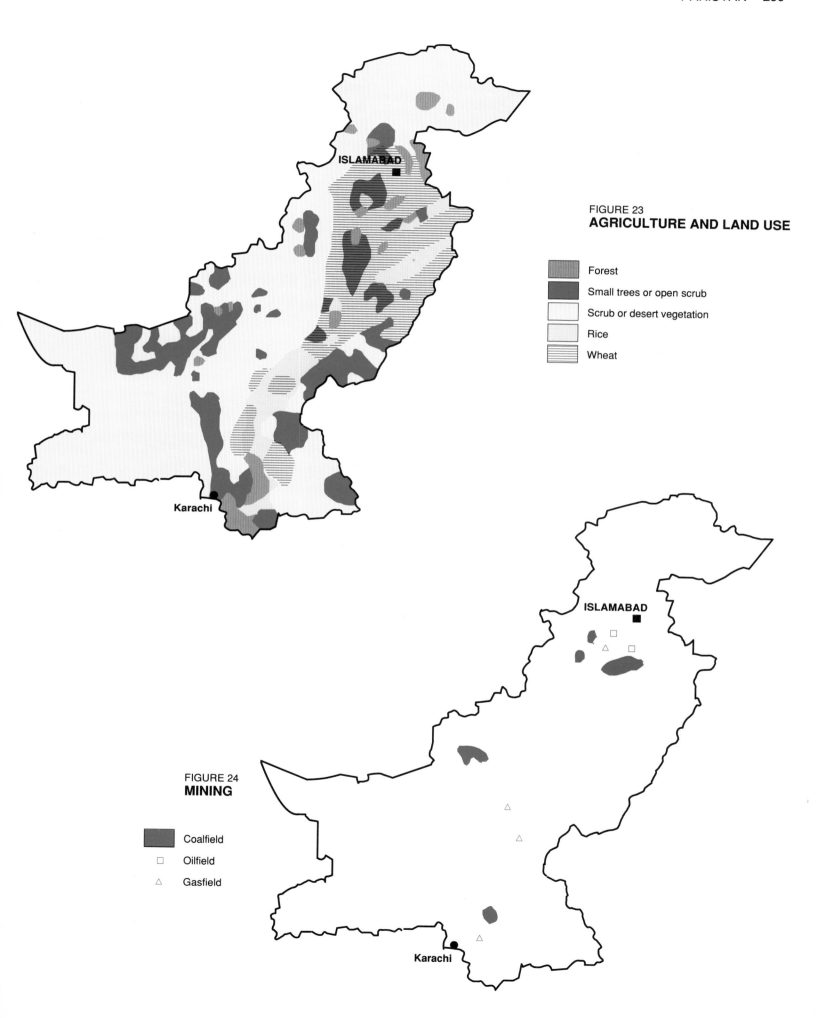

FIGURE 23
AGRICULTURE AND LAND USE

Forest

Small trees or open scrub

Scrub or desert vegetation

Rice

Wheat

ISLAMABAD

Karachi

FIGURE 24
MINING

Coalfield

Oilfield

Gasfield

ISLAMABAD

Karachi

PANAMA

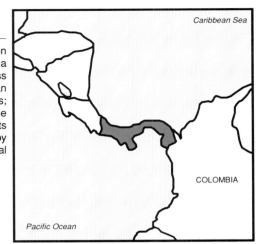

Panama ranks 119th in population and 111th in land area in the world. The Panamanian economy is based on banking, transit operations through the Canal, and use of its flag as a flag of convenience. Since 1968 Panama has developed into a major international banking and financial center. Although second to Liberia in the gross registered tonnage flying its flag, Panama has been gaining ground, with the number of ships on the Panamanian registry growing at 14% annually. Revenues from traffic through the canal have reached record levels; nevertheless, the Canal itself is less significant for the economy than the free zone at Colon which has become in recent years the hub of a vast commercial and industrial complex as well as a distribution point for exports to all Latin America. In the 1980s Panama gained the notoriety of being the only country in the world ruled by a person accused of drug trafficking. In 1989, the United States invaded Panama to topple strongman General Manuel Antonio Noriega and restore constitutionally elected president Guillermo Endara.

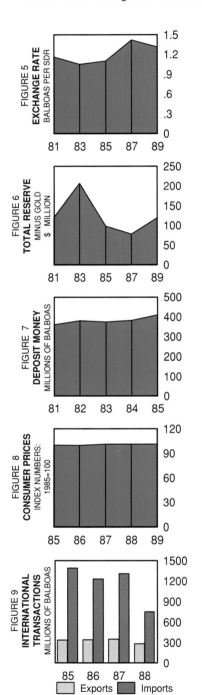

FIGURE 5 — EXCHANGE RATE — BALBOAS PER SDR

FIGURE 6 — TOTAL RESERVE — MINUS GOLD — $ MILLION

FIGURE 7 — DEPOSIT MONEY — MILLIONS OF BALBOAS

FIGURE 8 — CONSUMER PRICES — INDEX NUMBERS: 1985=100

FIGURE 9 — INTERNATIONAL TRANSACTIONS — MILLIONS OF BALBOAS — Exports — Imports

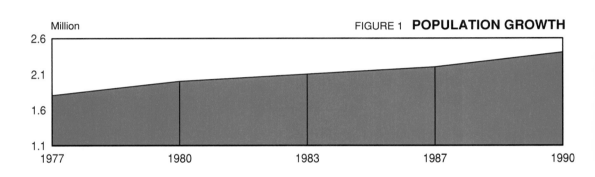

FIGURE 1 **POPULATION GROWTH**

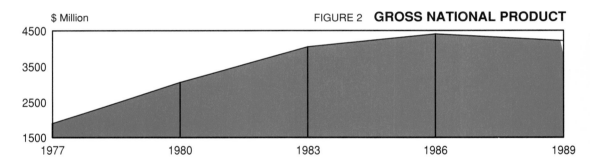

FIGURE 2 **GROSS NATIONAL PRODUCT**

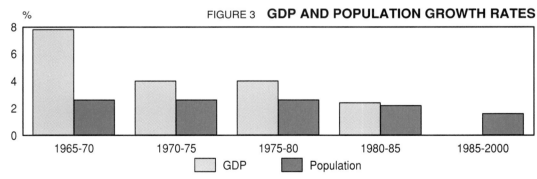

FIGURE 3 **GDP AND POPULATION GROWTH RATES**

GDP   Population

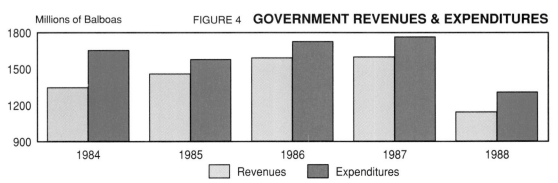

FIGURE 4 **GOVERNMENT REVENUES & EXPENDITURES**

Revenues   Expenditures

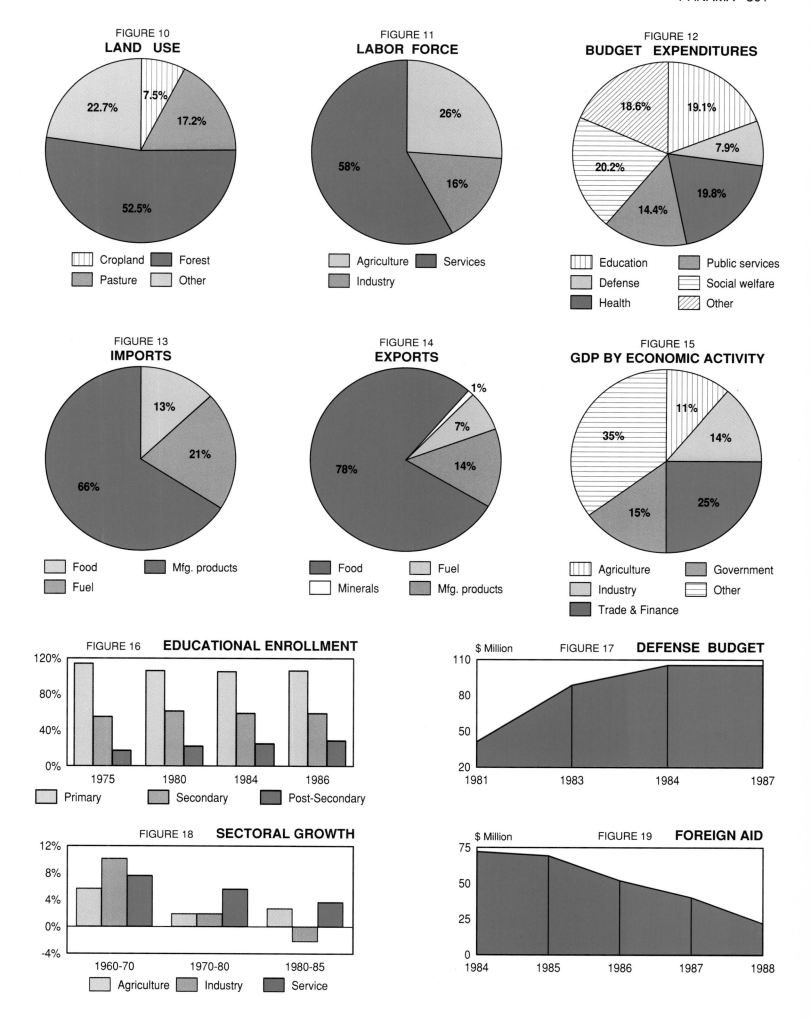

FIGURE 10
LAND USE

Cropland 7.5%
Forest 17.2%
22.7%
52.5%

Cropland | Forest
Pasture | Other

FIGURE 11
LABOR FORCE

26%
58%
16%

Agriculture | Services
Industry

FIGURE 12
BUDGET EXPENDITURES

18.6% | 19.1%
7.9%
20.2%
19.8%
14.4%

Education | Public services
Defense | Social welfare
Health | Other

FIGURE 13
IMPORTS

13%
21%
66%

Food | Mfg. products
Fuel

FIGURE 14
EXPORTS

1%
7%
78% | 14%

Food | Fuel
Minerals | Mfg. products

FIGURE 15
GDP BY ECONOMIC ACTIVITY

11%
35% | 14%
25%
15%

Agriculture | Government
Industry | Other
Trade & Finance

FIGURE 16 **EDUCATIONAL ENROLLMENT**

120%
80%
40%
0%
1975 1980 1984 1986

Primary | Secondary | Post-Secondary

FIGURE 17 **DEFENSE BUDGET**

$ Million
110
80
50
20
1981 1983 1984 1987

FIGURE 18 **SECTORAL GROWTH**

12%
8%
4%
0%
-4%
1960-70 1970-80 1980-85

Agriculture | Industry | Service

FIGURE 19 **FOREIGN AID**

$ Million
75
50
25
0
1984 1985 1986 1987 1988

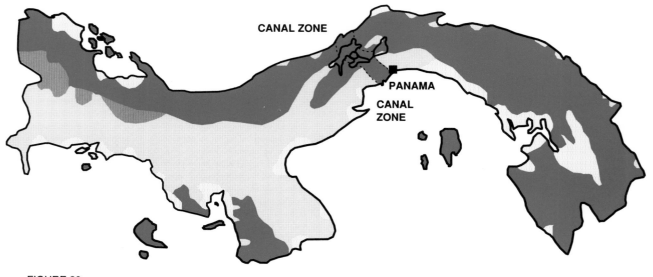

FIGURE 20
VEGETATION

Forest

Dwarfed mountain forest and alpine meadow

Grassland, scrub, secondary forest, and crops

Swamp and marsh

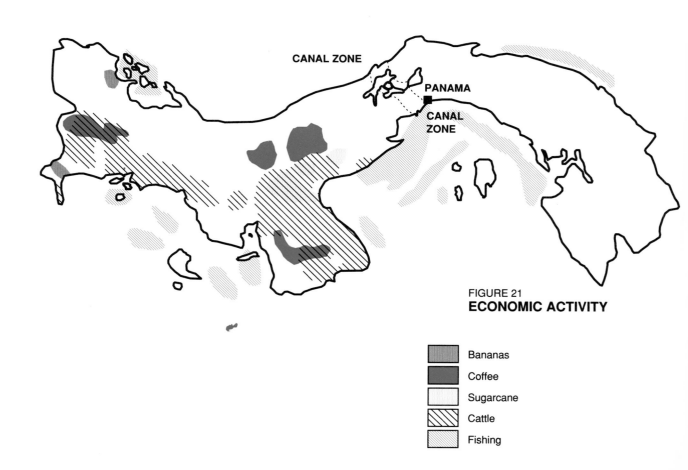

FIGURE 21
ECONOMIC ACTIVITY

Bananas

Coffee

Sugarcane

Cattle

Fishing

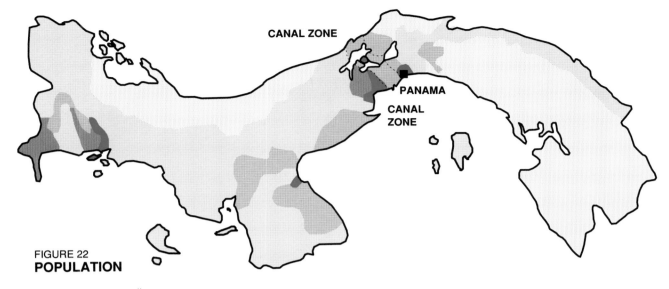

FIGURE 22
POPULATION

Persons per square mile

	0-13
	13-65
	65-130
	130-260
	260 and more

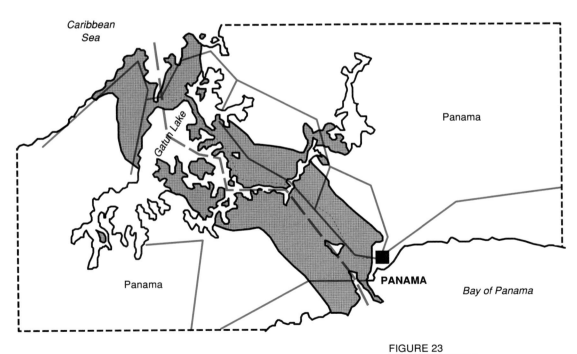

FIGURE 23
CANAL ZONE
(United States Administration)

	Canal Zone
- - -	PANAMA CANAL
....	Railroad
——	Highway

PERU

The third largest country in Latin America, Peru is the 19th largest in the world and the 40th most populous. Its fabled wealth in minerals and precious metals still contributes to the economy, accounting for over half the country's exports. Peru is the world's fourth ranking exporter of silver and eight ranking exporter of copper. It is among the top six producers of molybdenum in the world and leads South America in the extraction of seven other minerals, including zinc and lead. Since 1950, Peru has built up a large fishing industry and until the depletion of anchovy stocks in the mid-1970s, provided nearly half the world's supply of fishmeal. Agriculture and industry are dominated by the country's wealthy elite, contributing to manifest inequality with the poorest 20% receiving only 2% of the national income while the top 10% receive over 45%. In the first eight months of 1990, inflation reached 12,000%. Facing an extremely troubled economy, newly-elected President Alberto Fujimori began negotiations in 1990 with the IMF for $2 billion in loans.

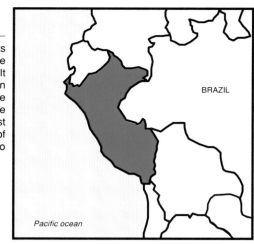

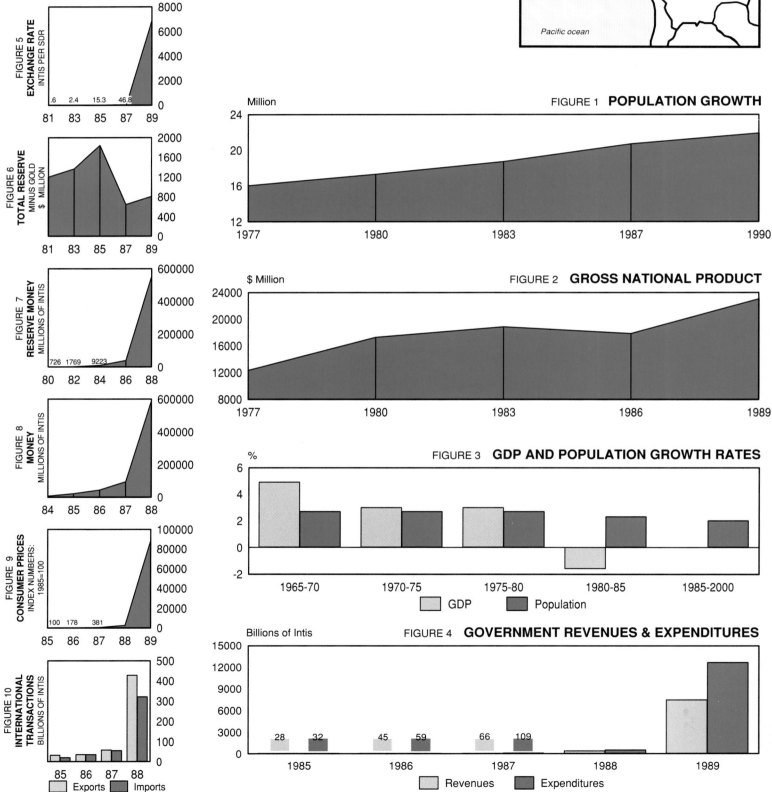

FIGURE 5 **EXCHANGE RATE** INTIS PER SDR

FIGURE 6 **TOTAL RESERVE** MINUS GOLD $ MILLION

FIGURE 7 **RESERVE MONEY** MILLIONS OF INTIS

FIGURE 8 **MONEY** MILLIONS OF INTIS

FIGURE 9 **CONSUMER PRICES** INDEX NUMBERS: 1985=100

FIGURE 10 **INTERNATIONAL TRANSACTIONS** BILLIONS OF INTIS
Exports Imports

FIGURE 1 **POPULATION GROWTH**

FIGURE 2 **GROSS NATIONAL PRODUCT**

FIGURE 3 **GDP AND POPULATION GROWTH RATES**
GDP Population

FIGURE 4 **GOVERNMENT REVENUES & EXPENDITURES**
Revenues Expenditures

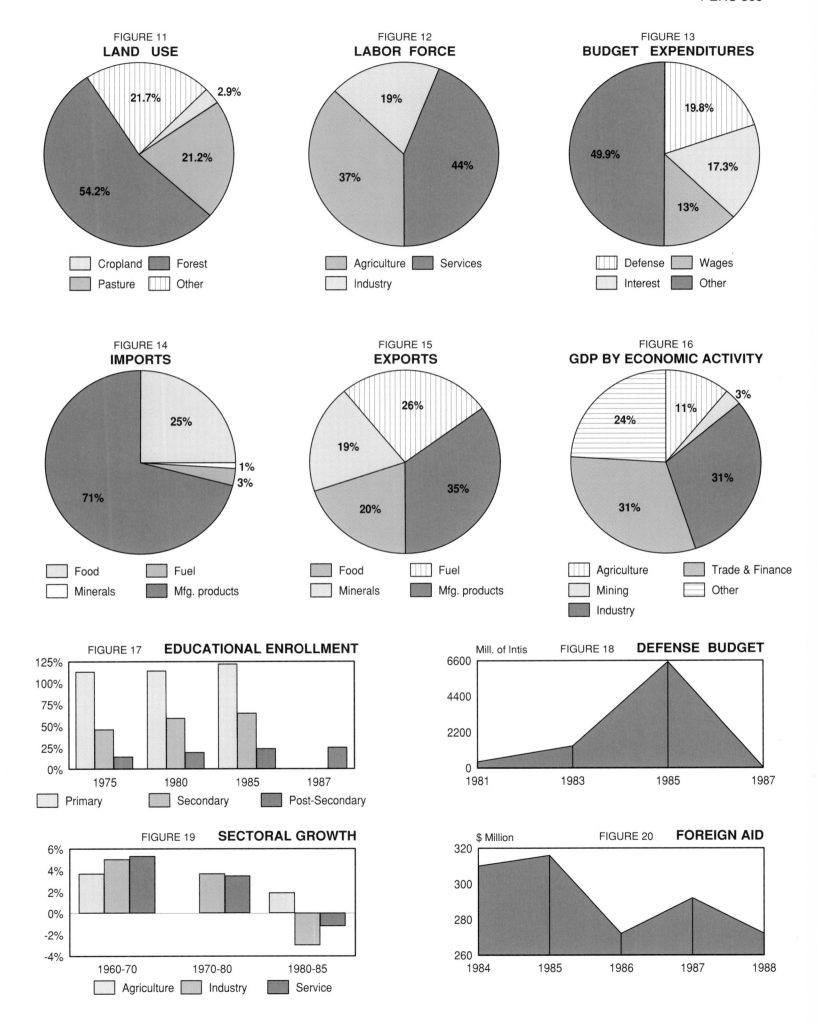

FIGURE 11
LAND USE

Cropland — Forest
Pasture — Other

FIGURE 12
LABOR FORCE

Agriculture — Services
Industry

FIGURE 13
BUDGET EXPENDITURES

Defense — Wages
Interest — Other

FIGURE 14
IMPORTS

Food — Fuel
Minerals — Mfg. products

FIGURE 15
EXPORTS

Food — Fuel
Minerals — Mfg. products

FIGURE 16
GDP BY ECONOMIC ACTIVITY

Agriculture — Trade & Finance
Mining — Other
Industry

FIGURE 17 **EDUCATIONAL ENROLLMENT**

Primary — Secondary — Post-Secondary

FIGURE 18 **DEFENSE BUDGET**
Mill. of Intis

FIGURE 19 **SECTORAL GROWTH**

Agriculture — Industry — Service

FIGURE 20 **FOREIGN AID**
$ Million

PHILIPPINES

An archipelago of some 7,000 islands and islets, the Philippines ranks 67th in land area and 13th in population. Despite adequate natural resources, the Philippines has remained a backward country by and large, and even the authoritarian rule of President Ferdinand Marcos did not help its economy to match the spectacular growth of neighbors such as South Korea, Taiwan, and Singapore. Ironically, the exodus of some half a million workers has turned into a blessing, as their remittances are helping to ease the country's balance of payments shortage. As a result of IMF intervention, the government has agreed to adopt a series of measures designed to bring down the inflation rate, set limits on government and commercial borrowing, introduce new taxes, and promote exports. The fall of Marcos in 1986 and the rise to power of president Corazon Aquino, while a major event in political history, has had little impact on the economy. Aquino struggled during 1990 to cope with military dissidents, economic shocks, a major earthquake, and other problems, giving rise to widespread apprehension about the country's future.

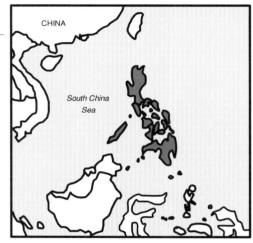

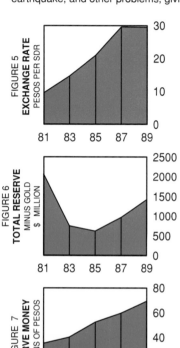

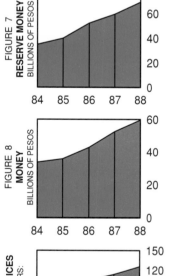

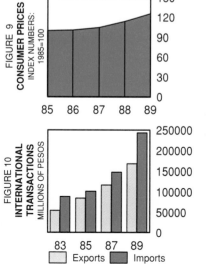

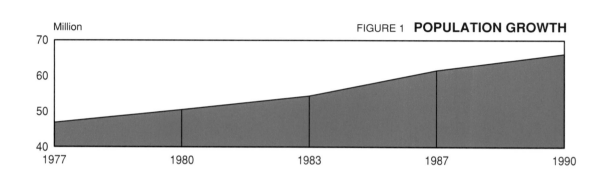

FIGURE 1 **POPULATION GROWTH**

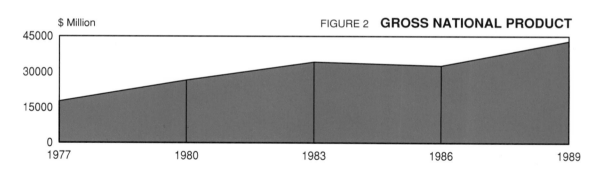

FIGURE 2 **GROSS NATIONAL PRODUCT**

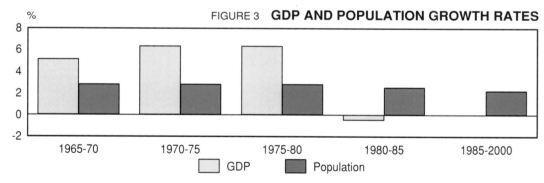

FIGURE 3 **GDP AND POPULATION GROWTH RATES**

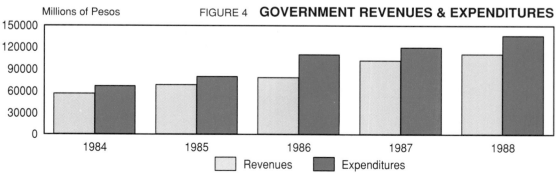

FIGURE 4 **GOVERNMENT REVENUES & EXPENDITURES**

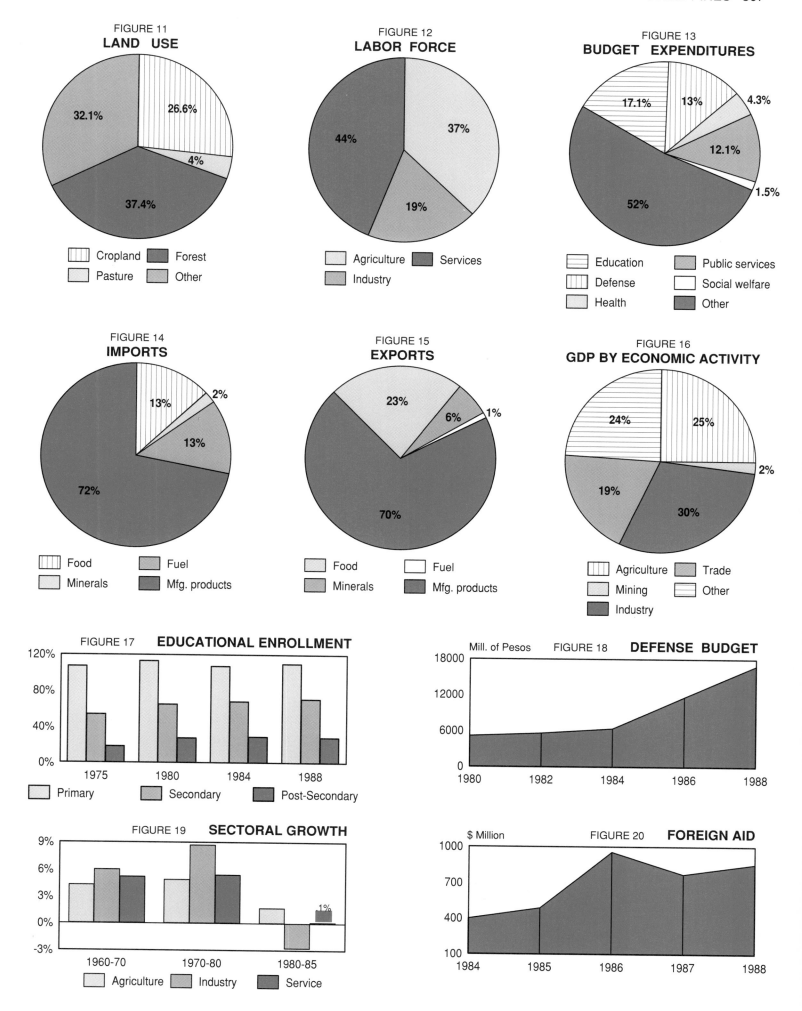

FIGURE 11
LAND USE

32.1%
26.6%
4%
37.4%

Cropland   Forest
Pasture   Other

FIGURE 12
LABOR FORCE

44%
37%
19%

Agriculture   Services
Industry

FIGURE 13
BUDGET EXPENDITURES

17.1%   13%   4.3%
12.1%
52%
1.5%

Education   Public services
Defense   Social welfare
Health   Other

FIGURE 14
IMPORTS

13%   2%
13%
72%

Food   Fuel
Minerals   Mfg. products

FIGURE 15
EXPORTS

23%
6%   1%
70%

Food   Fuel
Minerals   Mfg. products

FIGURE 16
GDP BY ECONOMIC ACTIVITY

24%   25%
2%
19%
30%

Agriculture   Trade
Mining   Other
Industry

FIGURE 17 EDUCATIONAL ENROLLMENT

120%
80%
40%
0%
1975   1980   1984   1988

Primary   Secondary   Post-Secondary

Mill. of Pesos   FIGURE 18   DEFENSE BUDGET

18000
12000
6000
0
1980   1982   1984   1986   1988

FIGURE 19   SECTORAL GROWTH

9%
6%
3%
0%
1%
-3%
1960-70   1970-80   1980-85

Agriculture   Industry   Service

$ Million   FIGURE 20   FOREIGN AID

1000
700
400
100
1984   1985   1986   1987   1988

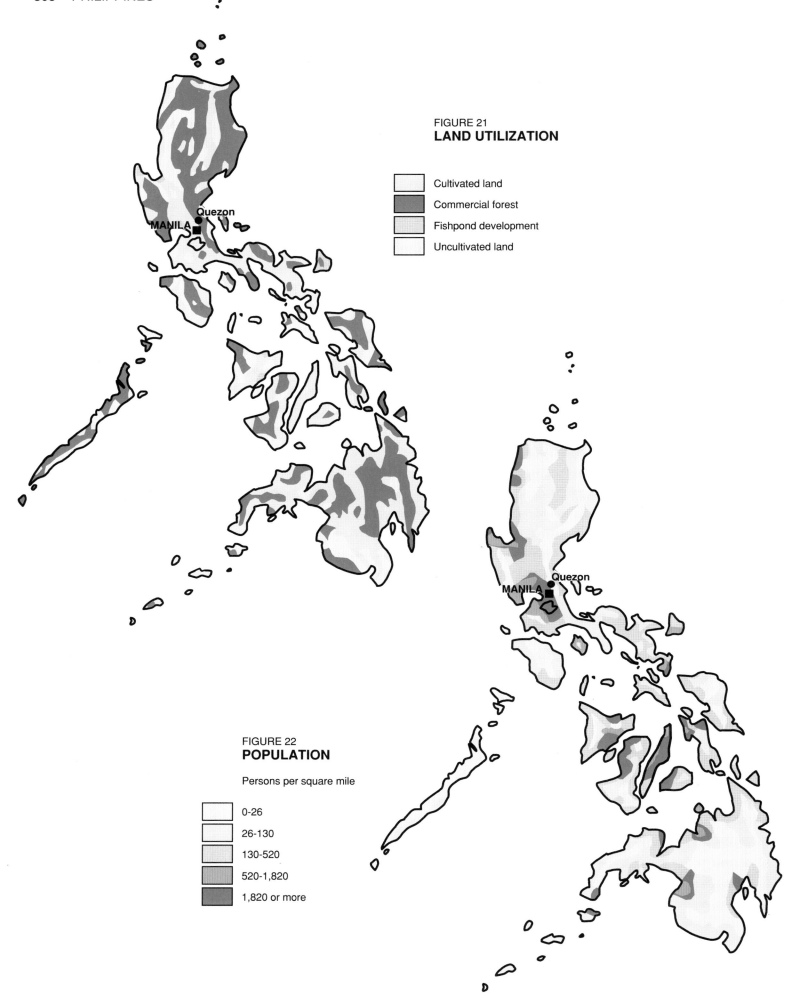

FIGURE 21
LAND UTILIZATION

Cultivated land

Commercial forest

Fishpond development

Uncultivated land

Quezon
MANILA

FIGURE 22
POPULATION

Persons per square mile

0-26

26-130

130-520

520-1,820

1,820 or more

Quezon
MANILA

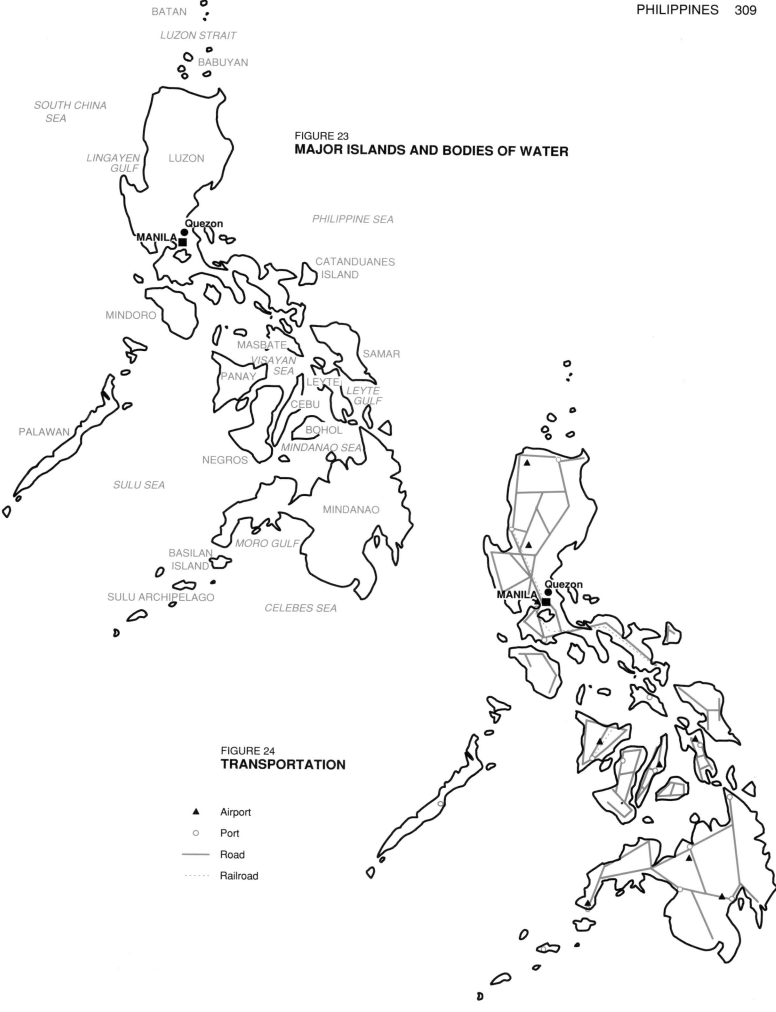

FIGURE 23
MAJOR ISLANDS AND BODIES OF WATER

BATAN

LUZON STRAIT

BABUYAN

*SOUTH CHINA
SEA*

*LINGAYEN
GULF*

LUZON

Quezon

MANILA

PHILIPPINE SEA

CATANDUANES
ISLAND

MINDORO

MASBATE

*VISAYAN
SEA*

SAMAR

PANAY

LEYTE

*LEYTE
GULF*

CEBU

PALAWAN

BOHOL

MINDANAO SEA

NEGROS

SULU SEA

MINDANAO

BASILAN
ISLAND

MORO GULF

SULU ARCHIPELAGO

CELEBES SEA

FIGURE 24
TRANSPORTATION

▲ Airport

○ Port

—— Road

----- Railroad

Quezon

MANILA

SAUDI ARABIA

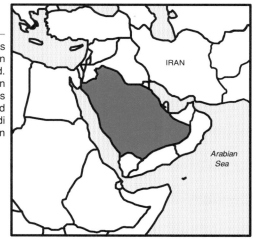

A preeminent producer of petroleum, Saudi Arabia occupies about four-fifths of the Arabian Peninsula and ranks 12th in land area and 51st in population. However, it must be borne in mind that a true census has never been held in the country and in any official enumeration, nomads are left out and women are generally underreported. Saudi Arabia appears in the top 10 in virtually all energy-related rankings including energy production, production of crude petroleum, natural gas reserves, petroleum reserves and balance of trade. The ripple effect of oil is felt in all other sectors, especially in industrial growth rate, construction, defense expenditures, education, and consumption. The 1990 Iraqi occupation of Kuwait threatened Saudi Arabia as Iraqi forces built up on the Saudi border. In an unprecedented move, King Fahd asked Western and Arab forces to deploy in the kingdom in support of Saudi defense forces. The nation played a leading role in the 1991 Persian Gulf War.

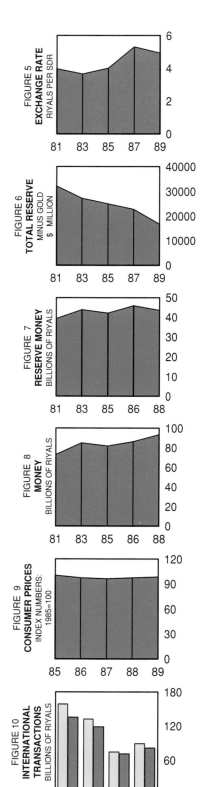

FIGURE 5 EXCHANGE RATE — RIYALS PER SDR

FIGURE 6 TOTAL RESERVE — MINUS GOLD — $ MILLION

FIGURE 7 RESERVE MONEY — BILLIONS OF RIYALS

FIGURE 8 MONEY — BILLIONS OF RIYALS

FIGURE 9 CONSUMER PRICES — INDEX NUMBERS: 1985=100

FIGURE 10 INTERNATIONAL TRANSACTIONS — BILLIONS OF RIYALS — Exports, Imports

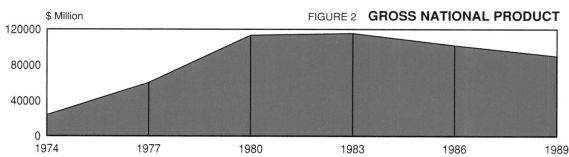

FIGURE 1 **POPULATION GROWTH**

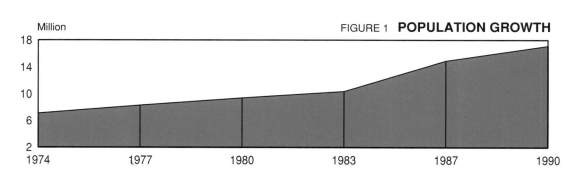

FIGURE 2 **GROSS NATIONAL PRODUCT**

FIGURE 3 **GDP AND POPULATION GROWTH RATES**

GDP   Population

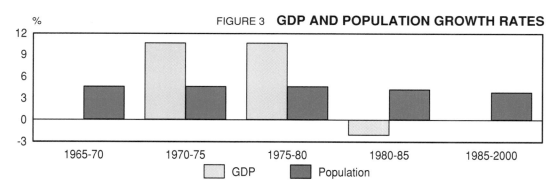

FIGURE 4 **CENTRAL GOVERNMENT EXPENDITURES**

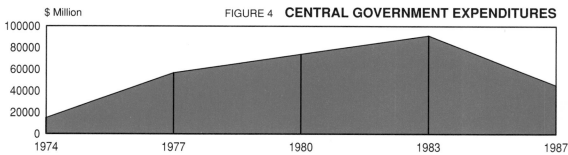

FIGURE 11
LAND USE

11%

89%

■ Total cropland □ Other

FIGURE 12
LABOR FORCE

16%

56%

28%

□ Agriculture ■ Services
■ Industry

FIGURE 13
BUDGET EXPENDITURES

7%

14.6%

28.7%

14%

35.7%

■ Defense ▦ Transportation & communication
▨ Human resource administration □ Other
▨ Public administration

FIGURE 14
IMPORTS

17%

1%

82%

▨ Food ■ Mft. products
□ Minerals

FIGURE 15
EXPORTS

13%

2%

85%

▨ Food □ Mft. products
■ Fuels

FIGURE 16
OFFICIAL DEVELOPMENT ASSISTANCE TO OTHER COUNTRIES ($ Million)

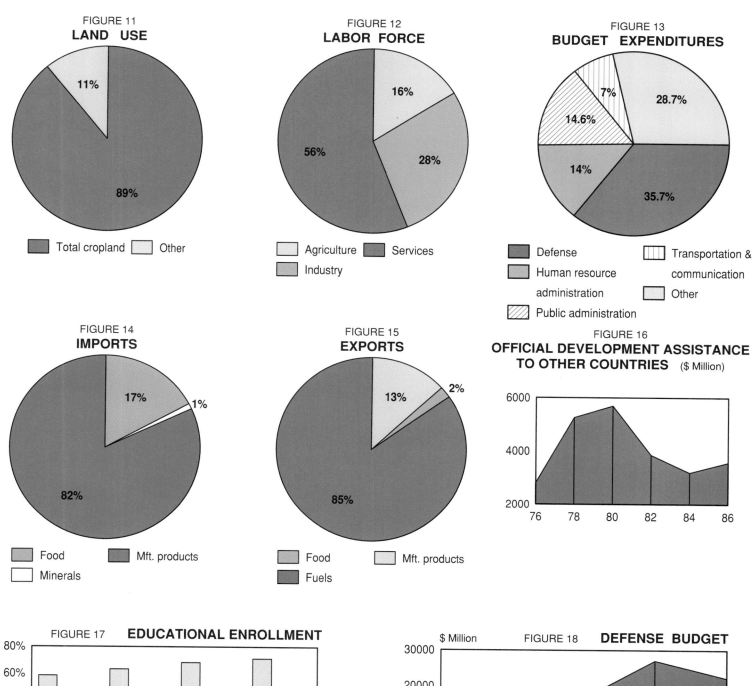

6000

4000

2000

76   78   80   82   84   86

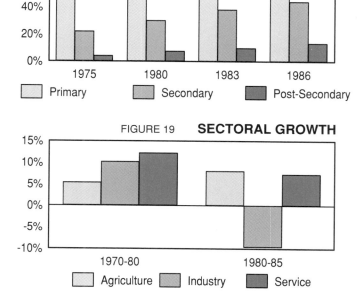

FIGURE 17 **EDUCATIONAL ENROLLMENT**

80%

60%

40%

20%

0%

1975   1980   1983   1986

□ Primary ▨ Secondary ■ Post-Secondary

FIGURE 19 **SECTORAL GROWTH**

15%

10%

5%

0%

-5%

-10%

1970-80   1980-85

□ Agriculture ▨ Industry ■ Service

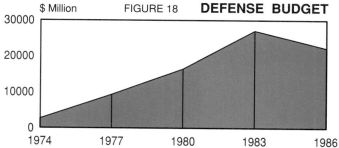

$ Million   FIGURE 18 **DEFENSE BUDGET**

30000

20000

10000

0

1974   1977   1980   1983   1986

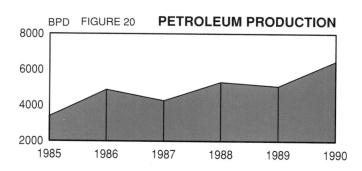

BPD   FIGURE 20   **PETROLEUM PRODUCTION**

8000

6000

4000

2000

1985   1986   1987   1988   1989   1990

FIGURE 21
**MAJOR MILITARY AND
NATIONAL GUARD INSTALLATIONS**

▲   Air force

□   National Guard

△   Army

○   Navy

RIYADH ■

● Mecca

FIGURE 22
PRINCIPAL TRIBES

ANAYZAH

HARB

MUTAYR

RIYADH ■

UTAYBAH

● Mecca

QAHTAN

AL MURRAH

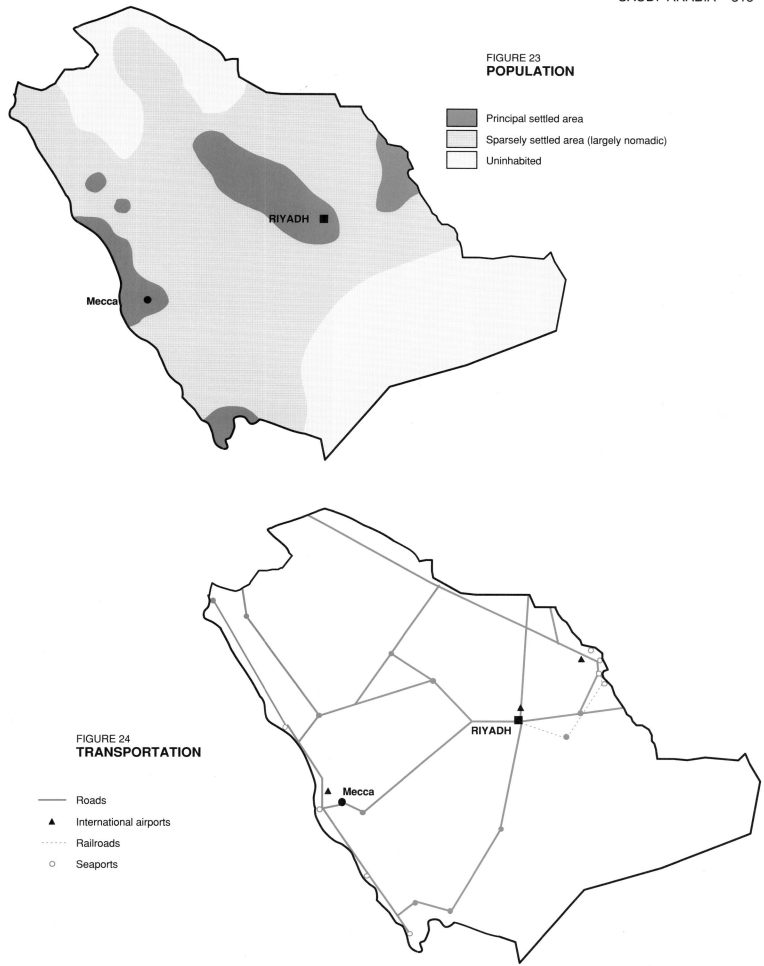

FIGURE 23
POPULATION

Principal settled area
Sparsely settled area (largely nomadic)
Uninhabited

RIYADH ■

Mecca ●

FIGURE 24
TRANSPORTATION

RIYADH ■▲

Mecca ●▲

—— Roads
▲ International airports
····· Railroads
○ Seaports

SENEGAL

Located close to the middle of the western bulge of Africa, Senegal ranks 82nd in land area and 79th in population. Senegal has been one of the showcases of francophone Africa, although it has not been spared the difficulties that most other Sahelian nations have experienced. Since the export of peanuts (the principal crop, in the production of which Senegal ranks fourth in the world) provides about 80% of export earnings, a single bad harvest can throw the economy into a downward spiral. Former President Leopold Senghor's policy of gradualist socialism led the state to play an increasingly active role in the economy. Although Senegal's growth potentials are limited, it can always count on generous aid from France, its principal financial patron, and from other EC countries and international agencies. Senegal's border war with Mauritania and ongoing dispute over territorial waters with Guinea-Bissau moved no closer to solution in 1990.

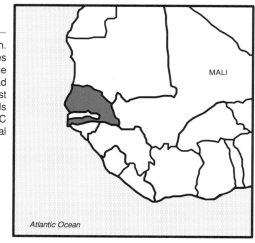

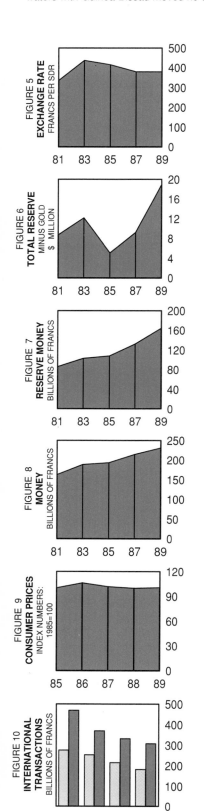

FIGURE 5 — EXCHANGE RATE — FRANCS PER SDR

FIGURE 6 — TOTAL RESERVE — MINUS GOLD — $ MILLION

FIGURE 7 — RESERVE MONEY — BILLIONS OF FRANCS

FIGURE 8 — MONEY — BILLIONS OF FRANCS

FIGURE 9 — CONSUMER PRICES — INDEX NUMBERS: 1985=100

FIGURE 10 — INTERNATIONAL TRANSACTIONS — BILLIONS OF FRANCS — Exports — Imports

FIGURE 1 **POPULATION GROWTH**

Million

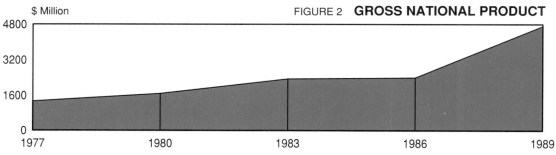

FIGURE 2 **GROSS NATIONAL PRODUCT**

$ Million

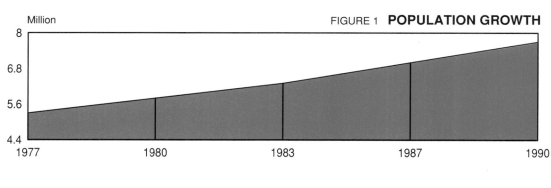

FIGURE 3 **GDP AND POPULATION GROWTH RATES**

% — GDP — Population

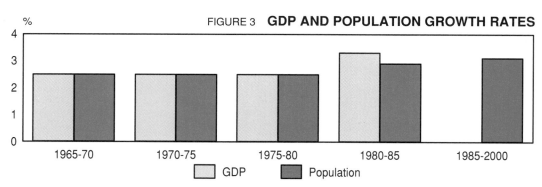

FIGURE 4 **GOVERNMENT REVENUES & EXPENDITURES**

Billions of Francs — Revenues — Expenditures

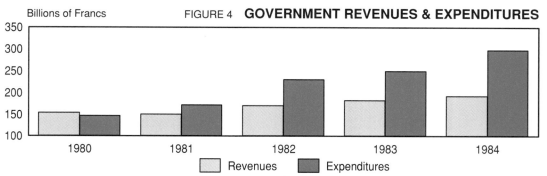

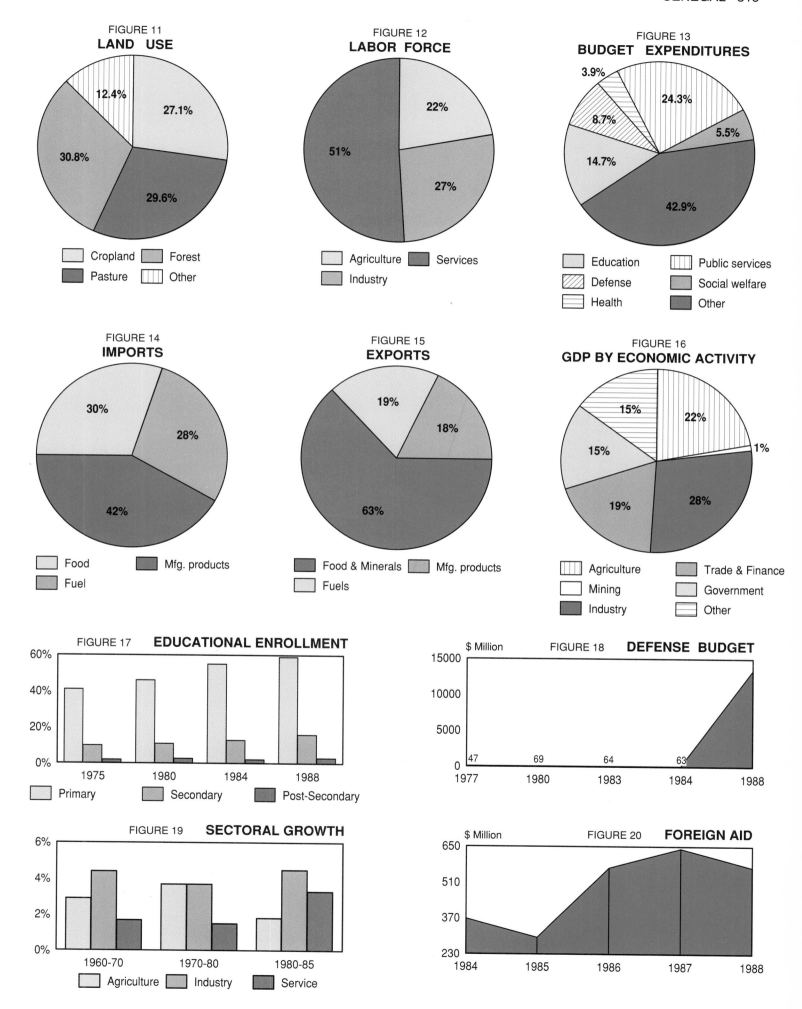

FIGURE 11
LAND   USE

27.1%
12.4%
30.8%
29.6%

Cropland   Forest
Pasture   Other

FIGURE 12
LABOR   FORCE

22%
51%
27%

Agriculture   Services
Industry

FIGURE 13
BUDGET   EXPENDITURES

3.9%
24.3%
8.7%
14.7%
5.5%
42.9%

Education   Public services
Defense   Social welfare
Health   Other

FIGURE 14
IMPORTS

30%
28%
42%

Food   Mfg. products
Fuel

FIGURE 15
EXPORTS

19%
18%
63%

Food & Minerals   Mfg. products
Fuels

FIGURE 16
GDP BY ECONOMIC ACTIVITY

15%
22%
15%
1%
19%
28%

Agriculture   Trade & Finance
Mining   Government
Industry   Other

FIGURE 17   **EDUCATIONAL ENROLLMENT**

60%
40%
20%
0%
1975   1980   1984   1988

Primary   Secondary   Post-Secondary

$ Million   FIGURE 18   **DEFENSE   BUDGET**

15000
10000
5000
0
47   69   64   63
1977   1980   1983   1984   1988

FIGURE 19   **SECTORAL GROWTH**

6%
4%
2%
0%
1960-70   1970-80   1980-85

Agriculture   Industry   Service

$ Million   FIGURE 20   **FOREIGN AID**

650
510
370
230
1984   1985   1986   1987   1988

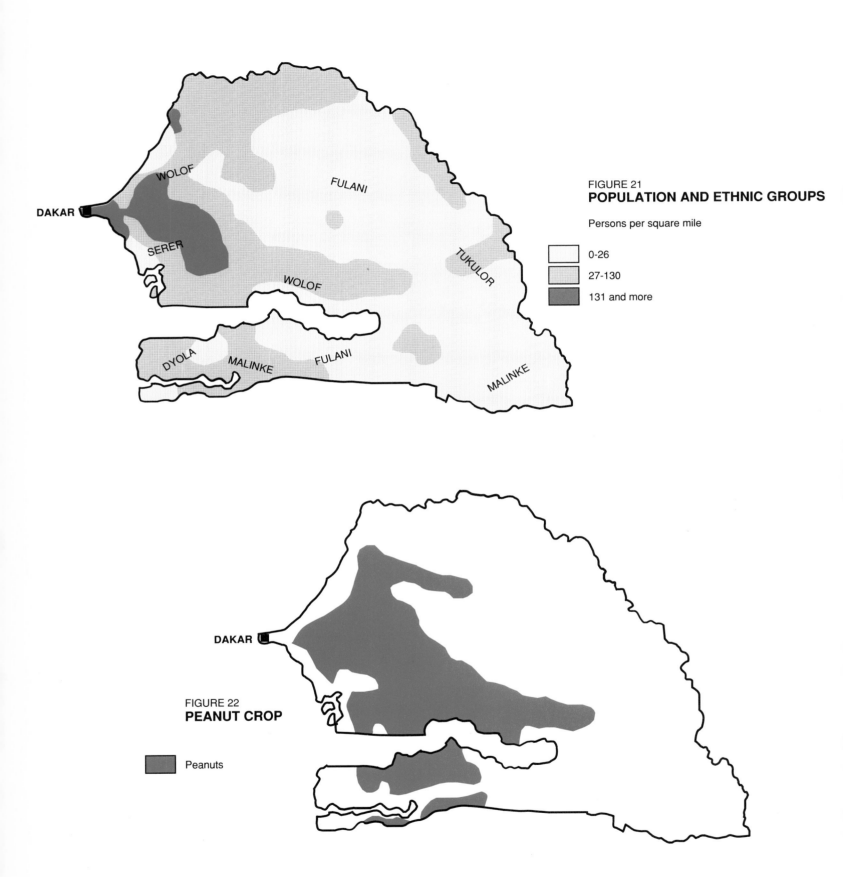

FIGURE 21
POPULATION AND ETHNIC GROUPS

Persons per square mile

0-26

27-130

131 and more

WOLOF

DAKAR

FULANI

SERER

TUKULOR

WOLOF

DYOLA   MALINKE   FULANI

MALINKE

FIGURE 22
PEANUT CROP

Peanuts

DAKAR

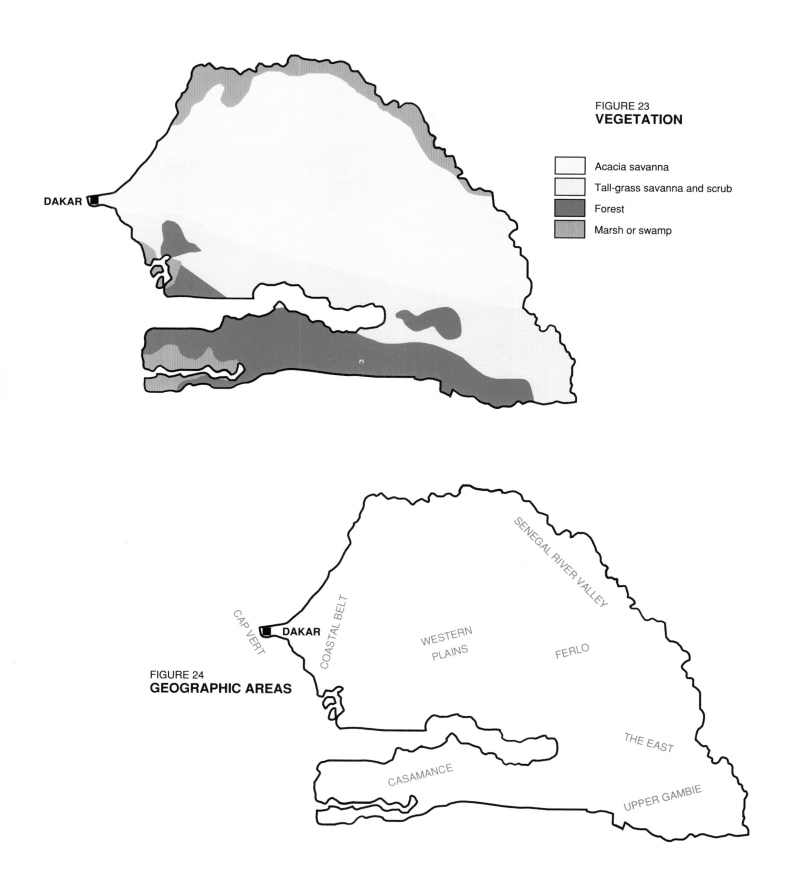

FIGURE 23
VEGETATION

Acacia savanna

Tall-grass savanna and scrub

Forest

Marsh or swamp

DAKAR

FIGURE 24
GEOGRAPHIC AREAS

CAP VERT

COASTAL BELT

DAKAR

WESTERN PLAINS

SENEGAL RIVER VALLEY

FERLO

THE EAST

CASAMANCE

UPPER GAMBIE

SIERRA LEONE

Located in West Africa, wedged in between Liberia and Guinea, Sierra Leone ranks 112th in land area and 100th in population. Even though agriculture employs two-thirds of the economically active population, mining is the major economic activity. The principal minerals produced are diamonds, iron ore, bauxite, and titanium, which together account for 80% of the country's exports by value. The country also claims the third largest deposit of rutile, a form of titanium oxide. Although economically troubled, the country's difficulties have not turned foreign creditors away primarily because the country has a substantial resource base in terms of mineral deposits and considerable potential for expansion of agriculture. Two international aid agreements with the EC and China in 1990 promised to boost the economy.

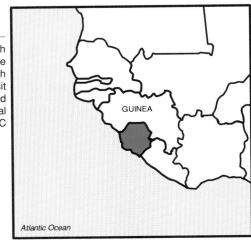

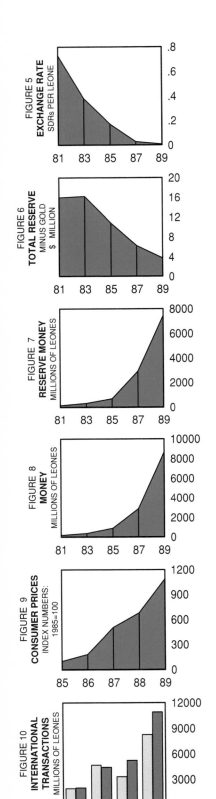

FIGURE 5 **EXCHANGE RATE** SDRs PER LEONE

FIGURE 6 **TOTAL RESERVE** MINUS GOLD $ MILLION

FIGURE 7 **RESERVE MONEY** MILLIONS OF LEONES

FIGURE 8 **MONEY** MILLIONS OF LEONES

FIGURE 9 **CONSUMER PRICES** INDEX NUMBERS: 1985=100

FIGURE 10 **INTERNATIONAL TRANSACTIONS** MILLIONS OF LEONES

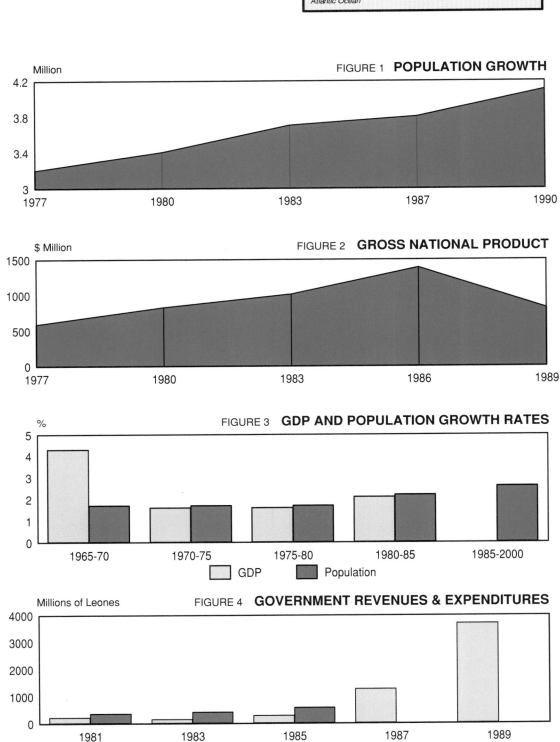

FIGURE 1 **POPULATION GROWTH**

FIGURE 2 **GROSS NATIONAL PRODUCT**

FIGURE 3 **GDP AND POPULATION GROWTH RATES**

FIGURE 4 **GOVERNMENT REVENUES & EXPENDITURES**

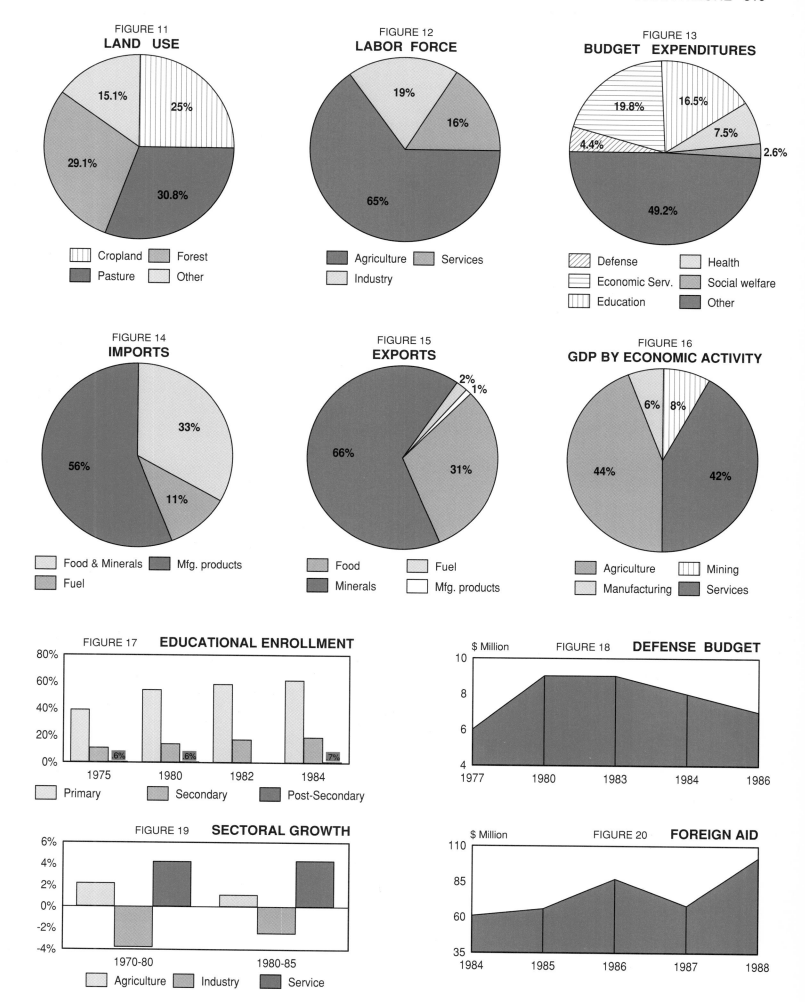

FIGURE 11
LAND USE
- Cropland
- Forest
- Pasture
- Other

FIGURE 12
LABOR FORCE
- Agriculture
- Services
- Industry

FIGURE 13
BUDGET EXPENDITURES
- Defense
- Health
- Economic Serv.
- Social welfare
- Education
- Other

FIGURE 14
IMPORTS
- Food & Minerals
- Mfg. products
- Fuel

FIGURE 15
EXPORTS
- Food
- Fuel
- Minerals
- Mfg. products

FIGURE 16
GDP BY ECONOMIC ACTIVITY
- Agriculture
- Mining
- Manufacturing
- Services

FIGURE 17 **EDUCATIONAL ENROLLMENT**
- Primary
- Secondary
- Post-Secondary

FIGURE 18 **DEFENSE BUDGET**
$ Million

FIGURE 19 **SECTORAL GROWTH**
- Agriculture
- Industry
- Service

FIGURE 20 **FOREIGN AID**
$ Million

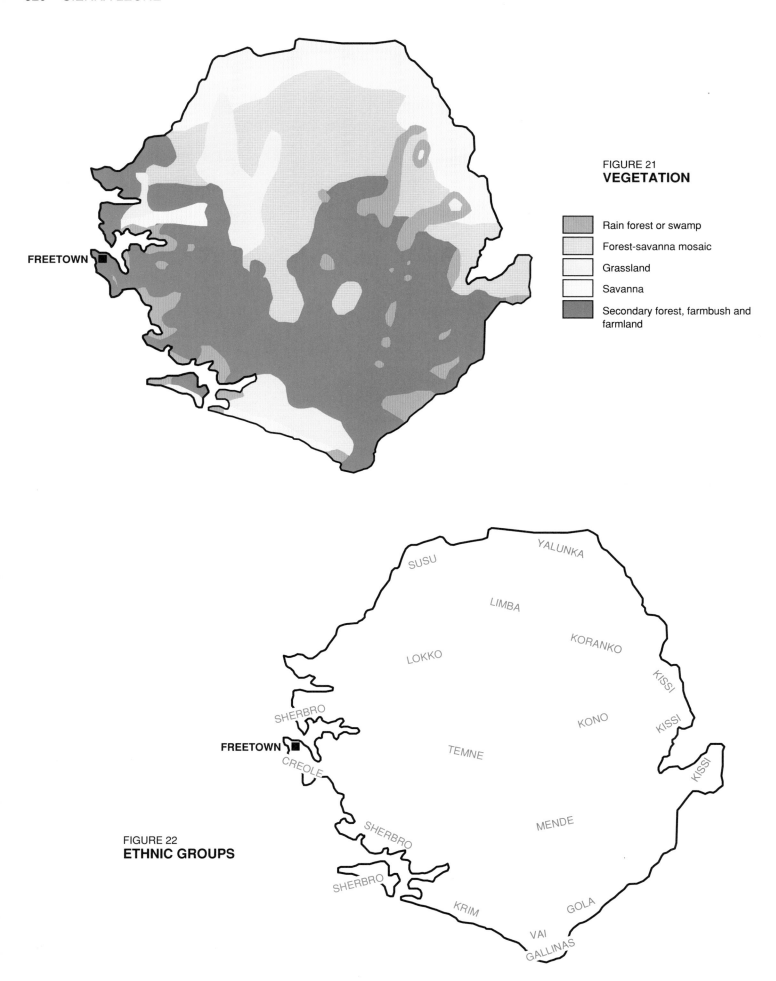

FIGURE 21
VEGETATION

Rain forest or swamp

Forest-savanna mosaic

Grassland

Savanna

Secondary forest, farmbush and farmland

FREETOWN ■

FIGURE 22
ETHNIC GROUPS

FREETOWN ■

SUSU

YALUNKA

LIMBA

KORANKO

LOKKO

KISSI

SHERBRO

KONO

KISSI

TEMNE

KISSI

CREOLE

SHERBRO

MENDE

SHERBRO

KRIM

GOLA

VAI

GALLINAS

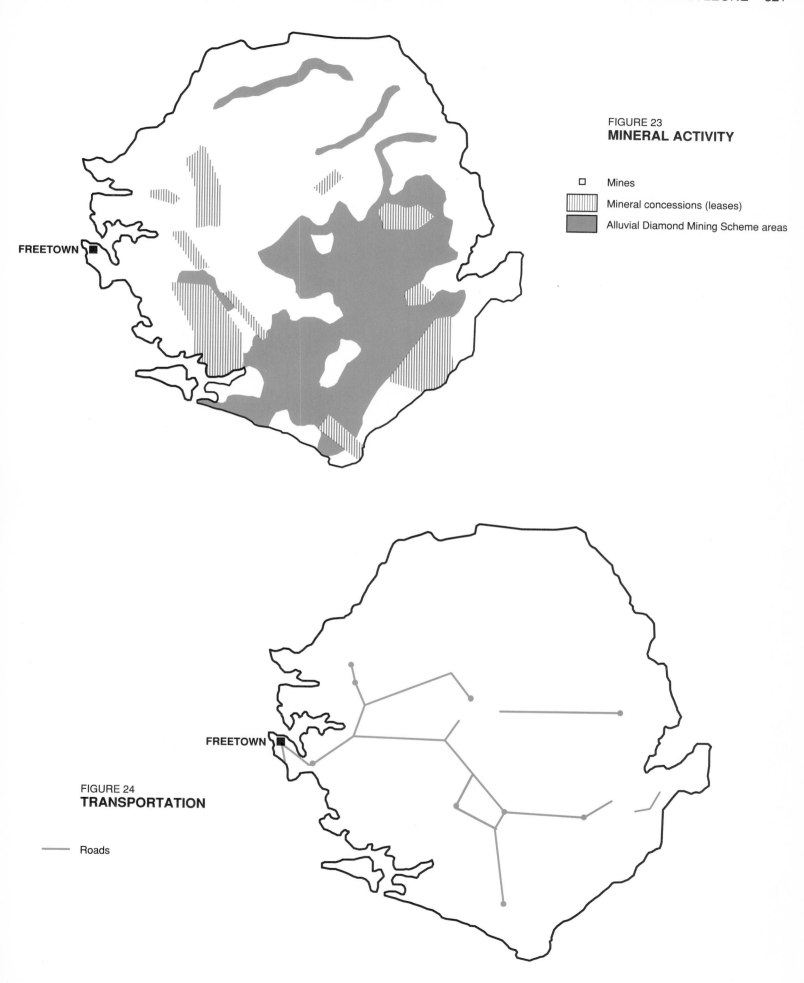

FIGURE 23
MINERAL ACTIVITY

☐ Mines

Mineral concessions (leases)

Alluvial Diamond Mining Scheme areas

FREETOWN

FIGURE 24
TRANSPORTATION

— Roads

FREETOWN

SINGAPORE

One of the world's great commercial centers and entrepots, Singapore ranks 170th in land area but is the fourth most densely populated and urbanized country. It is also an interesting amalgam of three important Asian races: Chinese, Malay, and Indian. Because of its high per capita income the UN ranks it a developed country. Traditionally geared to the entrepot trade, it ranks fourth in the world in exports and imports per capita and the port of Singapore is the fourth largest in the world in cargo handled. However, in recent years the government has shifted its economic strategy to place greater emphasis on industrialization, making Singapore a regional leader in shipbuilding, electronics, and oil refining. Singapore has also developed a reputation as an international financial center, competing with the Bahamas in attracting offshore U.S. dollars. Singapore's move into capital-intensive, technologically sophisticated industries paid off in the eighties, reinforcing its status as the linchpin of the southeast Asian economy. Oil refining was given a boost in 1990-91 before and during the Persian Gulf War, as foreign whole-salers turned to alternative sources.

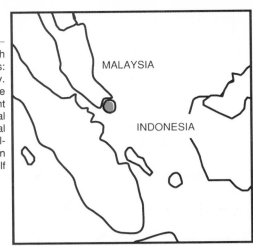

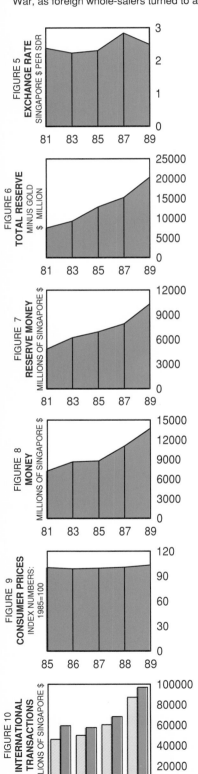

FIGURE 5 EXCHANGE RATE SINGAPORE $ PER SDR

FIGURE 6 TOTAL RESERVE MINUS GOLD $ MILLION

FIGURE 7 RESERVE MONEY MILLIONS OF SINGAPORE $

FIGURE 8 MONEY MILLIONS OF SINGAPORE $

FIGURE 9 CONSUMER PRICES INDEX NUMBERS: 1985=100

FIGURE 10 INTERNATIONAL TRANSACTIONS MILLIONS OF SINGAPORE $

Exports Imports

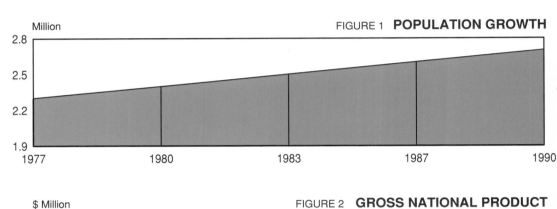

FIGURE 1 **POPULATION GROWTH**

Million

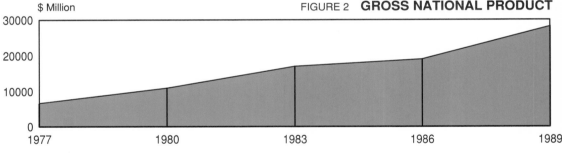

FIGURE 2 **GROSS NATIONAL PRODUCT**

$ Million

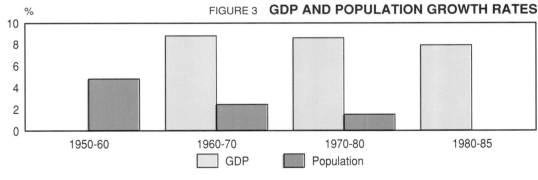

FIGURE 3 **GDP AND POPULATION GROWTH RATES**

%

GDP Population

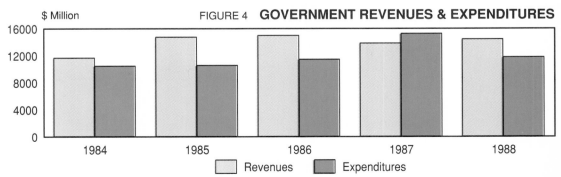

FIGURE 4 **GOVERNMENT REVENUES & EXPENDITURES**

$ Million

Revenues Expenditures

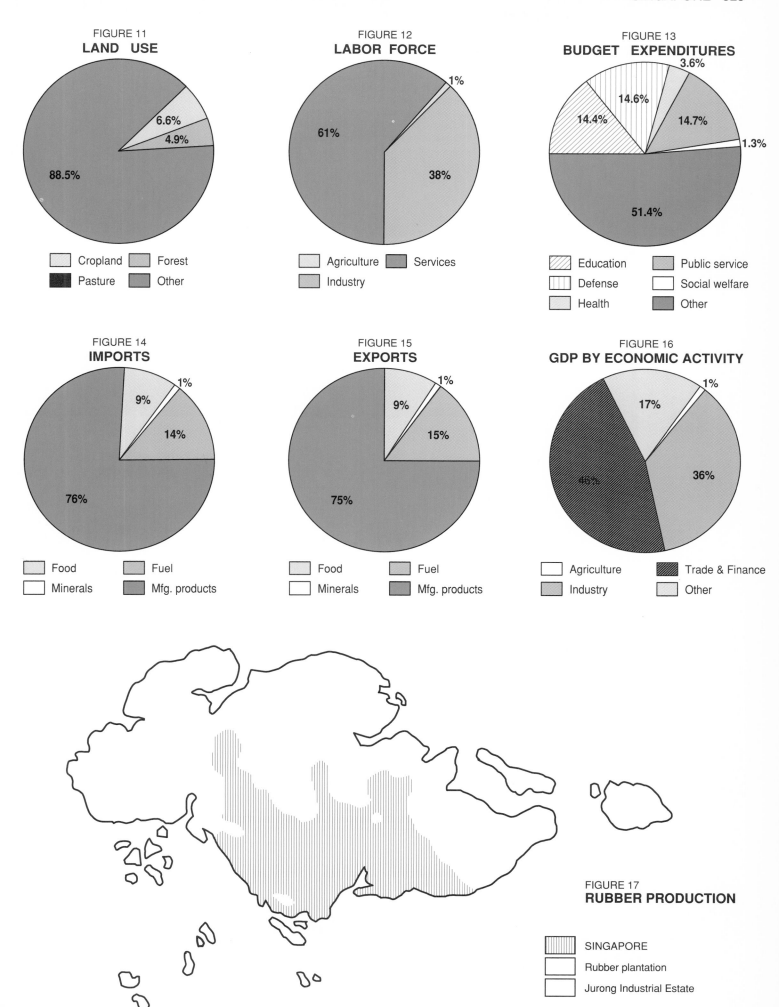

FIGURE 11
LAND USE

6.6%
4.9%
88.5%

Cropland Forest
Pasture Other

FIGURE 12
LABOR FORCE

1%
61%
38%

Agriculture Services
Industry

FIGURE 13
BUDGET EXPENDITURES

3.6%
14.6%
14.4%
14.7%
1.3%
51.4%

Education Public service
Defense Social welfare
Health Other

FIGURE 14
IMPORTS

1%
9%
14%
76%

Food Fuel
Minerals Mfg. products

FIGURE 15
EXPORTS

1%
9%
15%
75%

Food Fuel
Minerals Mfg. products

FIGURE 16
GDP BY ECONOMIC ACTIVITY

1%
17%
36%
46%

Agriculture Trade & Finance
Industry Other

FIGURE 17
RUBBER PRODUCTION

SINGAPORE
Rubber plantation
Jurong Industrial Estate

SOMALIA

The tip of the horn of Africa, Somalia ranks 41st in land area and 74th in population. Already among the poorest nations of the world, Somalia suffered crushing losses in the 1977-78 war with Ethiopia; it also had to feed nearly a million refugees from the Ogaden region at a time when the nation had lost a fourth of its livestock and suffered severe setbacks in agricultural production as a result of drought. Despite problems of such awesome magnitude, the economy is limping along and has actually made progress in some areas. Under the 1979-81 three-year development plan a dam was built across the Juba at Bardera providing irrigation for half a million acres of cropland and yielding 115 million kwh of hydroelectric power annually. Most Western investment in the economy was eliminated through large-scale nationalization measures in 1975. After three years of civil war, in 1991 much of Somalia was in the hands of rebel groups.

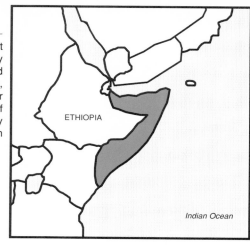

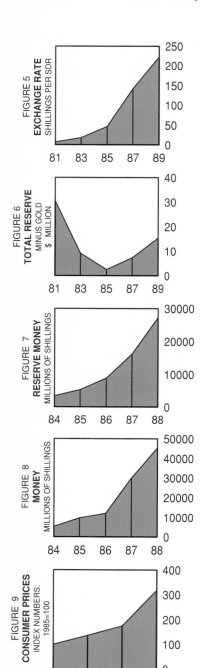

FIGURE 5 EXCHANGE RATE SHILLINGS PER SDR

FIGURE 6 TOTAL RESERVE MINUS GOLD $ MILLION

FIGURE 7 RESERVE MONEY MILLIONS OF SHILLINGS

FIGURE 8 MONEY MILLIONS OF SHILLINGS

FIGURE 9 CONSUMER PRICES INDEX NUMBERS: 1985=100

FIGURE 10 INTERNATIONAL TRANSACTIONS MILLIONS OF SHILLINGS

Exports   Imports

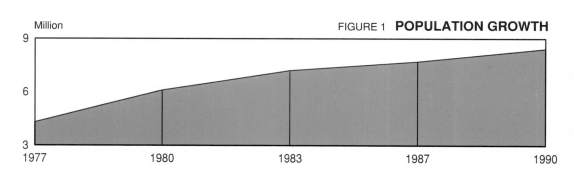

FIGURE 1 **POPULATION GROWTH**

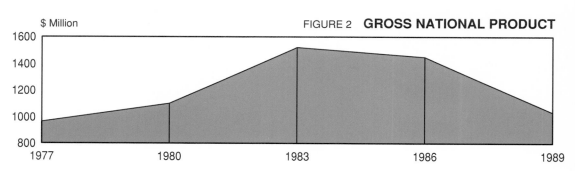

FIGURE 2 **GROSS NATIONAL PRODUCT**

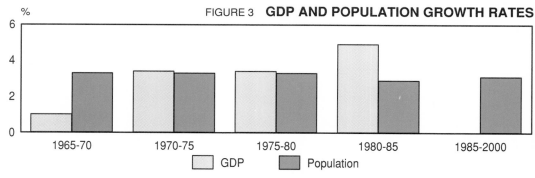

FIGURE 3 **GDP AND POPULATION GROWTH RATES**

GDP   Population

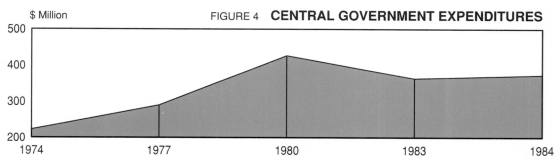

FIGURE 4 **CENTRAL GOVERNMENT EXPENDITURES**

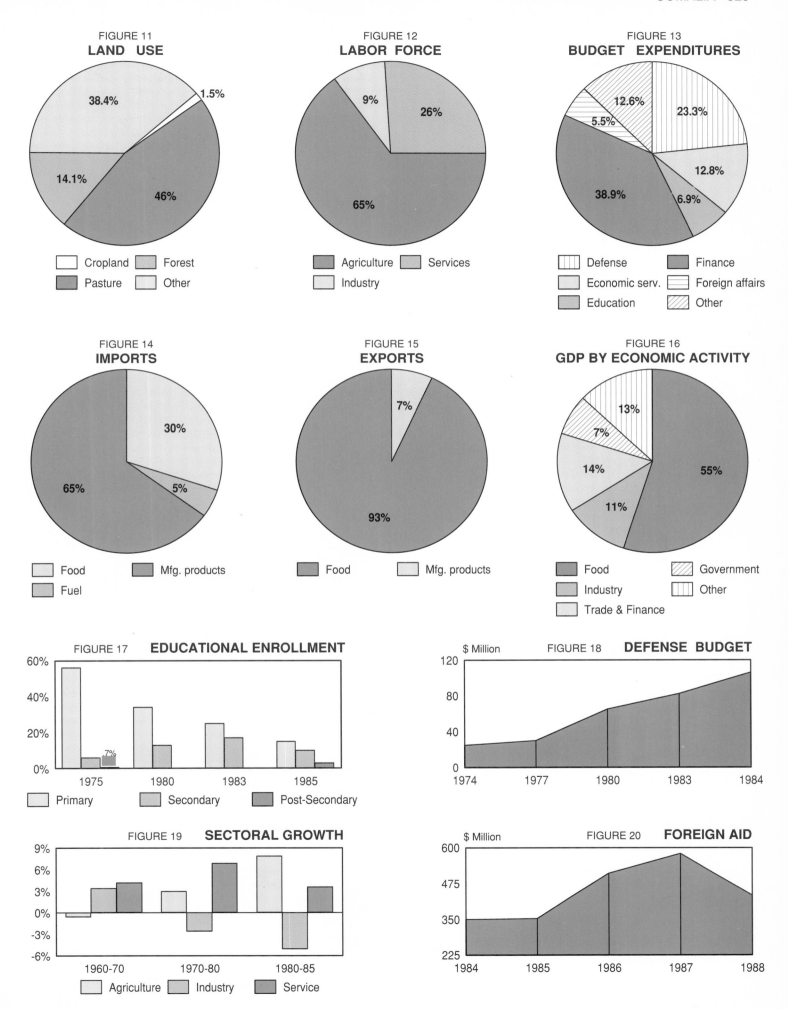

FIGURE 11
LAND USE

38.4%
1.5%
14.1%
46%

Cropland | Forest
Pasture | Other

FIGURE 12
LABOR FORCE

9%
26%
65%

Agriculture | Services
Industry

FIGURE 13
BUDGET EXPENDITURES

12.6%
23.3%
5.5%
38.9%
6.9%
12.8%

Defense | Finance
Economic serv. | Foreign affairs
Education | Other

FIGURE 14
IMPORTS

30%
65%
5%

Food | Mfg. products
Fuel

FIGURE 15
EXPORTS

7%
93%

Food | Mfg. products

FIGURE 16
GDP BY ECONOMIC ACTIVITY

13%
7%
14%
55%
11%

Food | Government
Industry | Other
Trade & Finance

FIGURE 17 **EDUCATIONAL ENROLLMENT**

60%
40%
20%
0%
7%
1975 | 1980 | 1983 | 1985

Primary | Secondary | Post-Secondary

$ Million   FIGURE 18   **DEFENSE BUDGET**

120
80
40
0
1974 | 1977 | 1980 | 1983 | 1984

FIGURE 19 **SECTORAL GROWTH**

9%
6%
3%
0%
-3%
-6%
1960-70 | 1970-80 | 1980-85

Agriculture | Industry | Service

$ Million   FIGURE 20   **FOREIGN AID**

600
475
350
225
1984 | 1985 | 1986 | 1987 | 1988

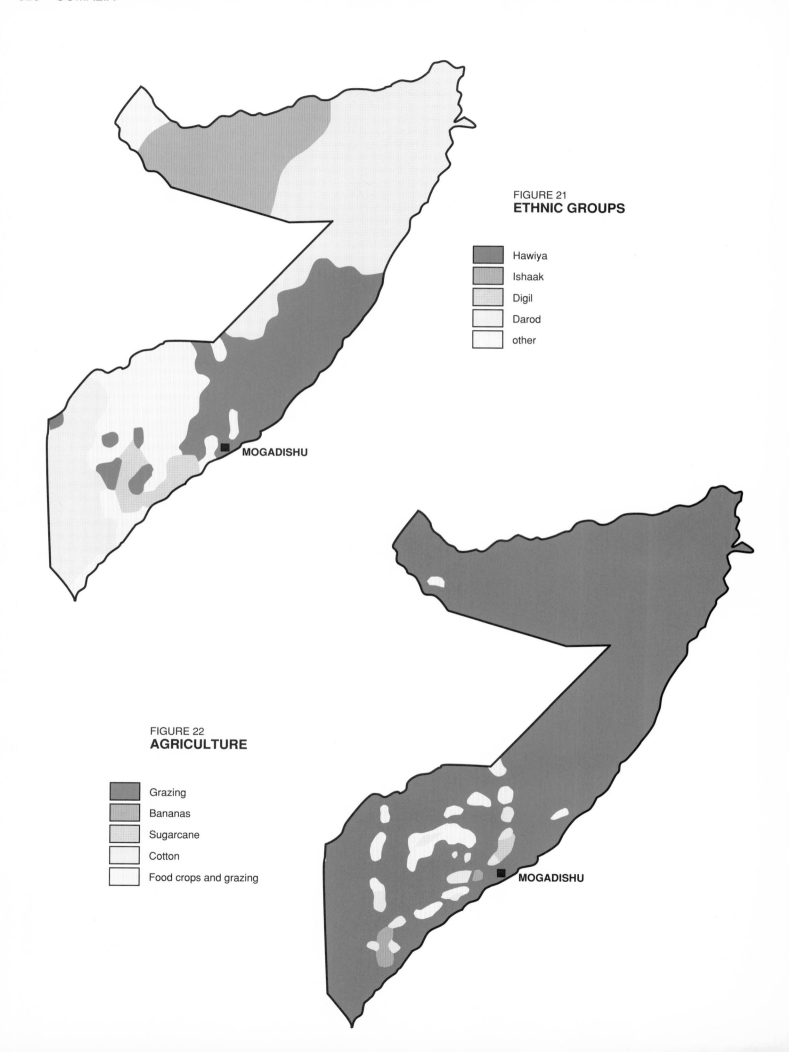

FIGURE 21
ETHNIC GROUPS

Hawiya
Ishaak
Digil
Darod
other

MOGADISHU

FIGURE 22
AGRICULTURE

Grazing
Bananas
Sugarcane
Cotton
Food crops and grazing

MOGADISHU

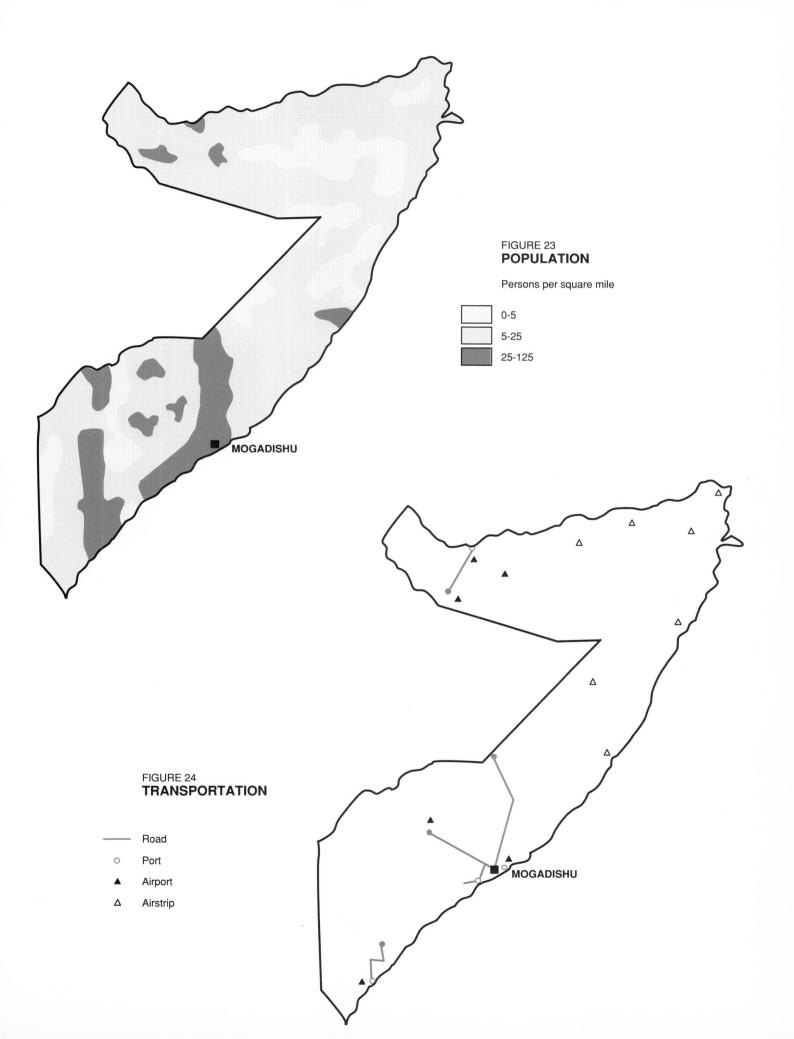

FIGURE 23
POPULATION

Persons per square mile

0-5

5-25

25-125

■ MOGADISHU

FIGURE 24
TRANSPORTATION

—— Road

○ Port

▲ Airport

△ Airstrip

■ MOGADISHU

SRI LANKA

A pear-shaped island in the Indian Ocean southeast of India, Sri Lanka ranks 114th in land area and 46th in population. Along with all other countries in the Indian subcontinent, it is officially classified as a low-income country. However, it fares better than other countries in the region on the physical quality of life index. Three major plantation crops account for by far the bulk of Sri Lankan exports: tea, rubber, and coconuts. Despite declining production, it remains the world's second largest exporter of tea. Official economic policies have swung from extreme leftist under the two Bandaranikes to free-enterprise under the Senanaikes and Presidents Jayawardene and Premadasa. The economy is expected to benefit as a result of the relaxation of controls both on domestic business as well as foreign investors. Nevertheless, some 60% of the economy is still in government hands and many of the socialist programs of the Bandaranaike governments remain. The Tamil revolt in the northern provinces has created conditions of near-anarchy and led to much bloodshed, although the Tamils have indicated a willingness to hold formal peace talks with the government in 1991.

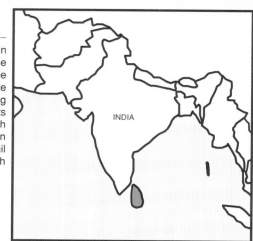

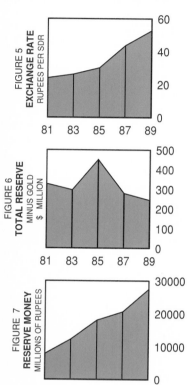

FIGURE 5 EXCHANGE RATE RUPEES PER SDR

FIGURE 6 TOTAL RESERVE MINUS GOLD $ MILLION

FIGURE 7 RESERVE MONEY MILLIONS OF RUPEES

FIGURE 8 MONEY MILLIONS OF RUPEES

FIGURE 9 CONSUMER PRICES INDEX NUMBERS: 1985=100

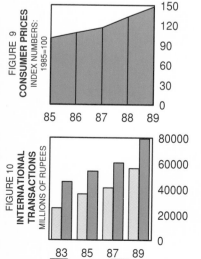

FIGURE 10 INTERNATIONAL TRANSACTIONS MILLIONS OF RUPEES

Exports   Imports

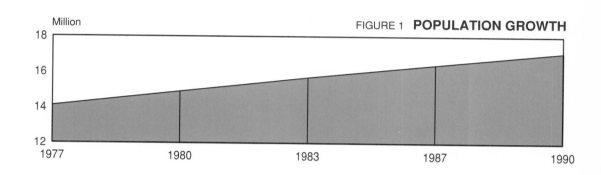

FIGURE 1 **POPULATION GROWTH**

Million

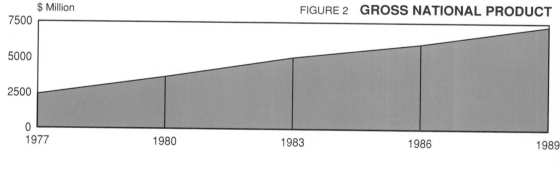

FIGURE 2 **GROSS NATIONAL PRODUCT**

$ Million

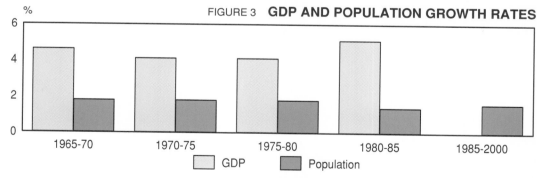

FIGURE 3 **GDP AND POPULATION GROWTH RATES**

%

GDP   Population

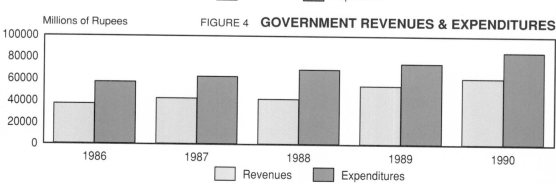

Millions of Rupees

FIGURE 4 **GOVERNMENT REVENUES & EXPENDITURES**

Revenues   Expenditures

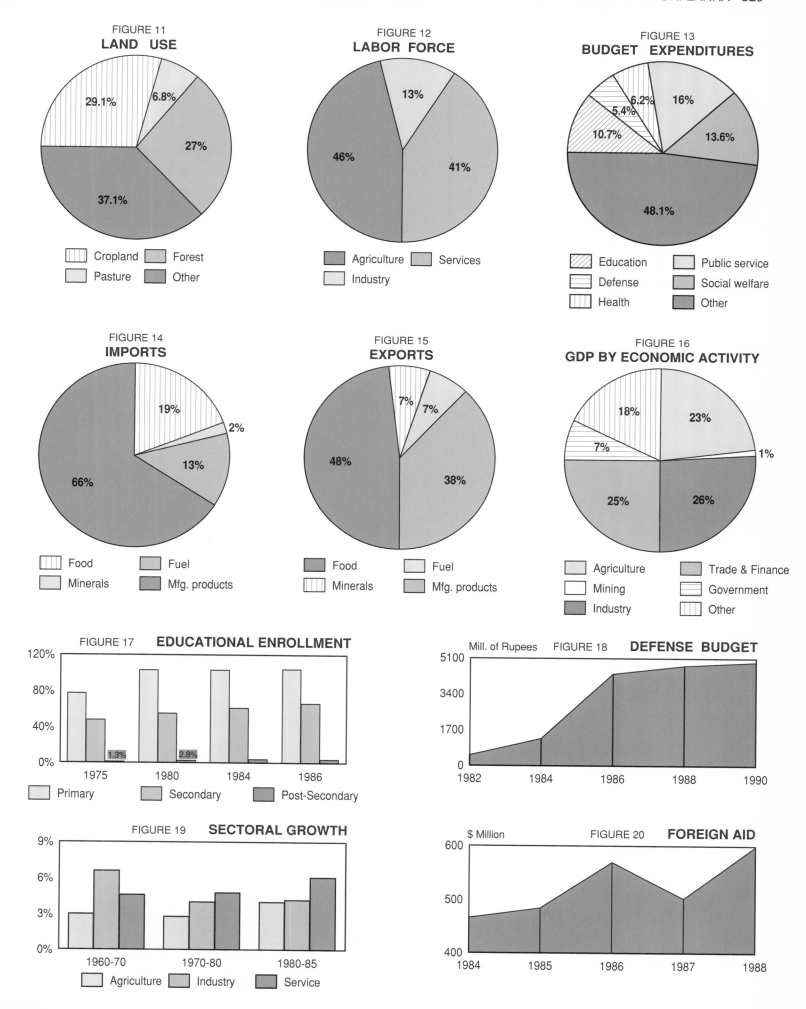

FIGURE 11
LAND USE

29.1%
6.8%
27%
37.1%

Cropland
Pasture
Forest
Other

FIGURE 12
LABOR FORCE

13%
46%
41%

Agriculture
Industry
Services

FIGURE 13
BUDGET EXPENDITURES

6.2%
5.4%
10.7%
16%
13.6%
48.1%

Education
Defense
Health
Public service
Social welfare
Other

FIGURE 14
IMPORTS

19%
2%
13%
66%

Food
Minerals
Fuel
Mfg. products

FIGURE 15
EXPORTS

7%
7%
48%
38%

Food
Minerals
Fuel
Mfg. products

FIGURE 16
GDP BY ECONOMIC ACTIVITY

18%
23%
7%
1%
25%
26%

Agriculture
Mining
Industry
Trade & Finance
Government
Other

FIGURE 17 EDUCATIONAL ENROLLMENT

120%
80%
40%
0%

1.3%
2.8%

1975   1980   1984   1986

Primary   Secondary   Post-Secondary

Mill. of Rupees   FIGURE 18   DEFENSE BUDGET

5100
3400
1700
0

1982   1984   1986   1988   1990

FIGURE 19   SECTORAL GROWTH

9%
6%
3%
0%

1960-70   1970-80   1980-85

Agriculture   Industry   Service

$ Million   FIGURE 20   FOREIGN AID

600
500
400

1984   1985   1986   1987   1988

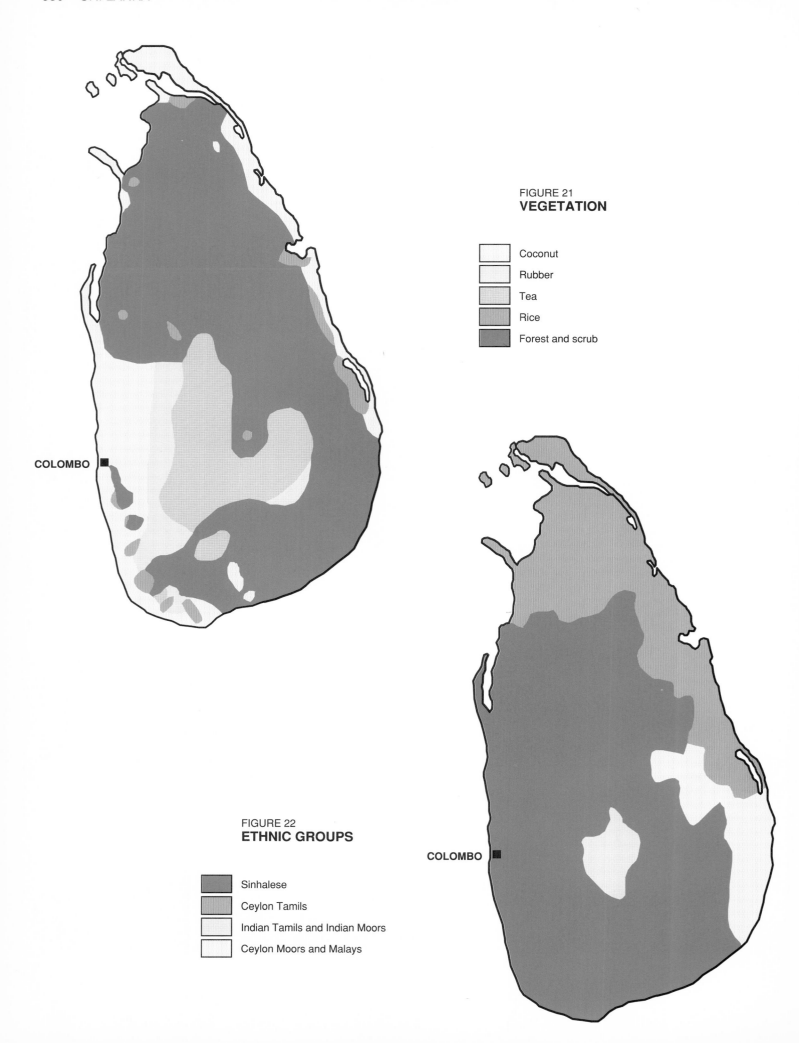

FIGURE 21
VEGETATION

Coconut

Rubber

Tea

Rice

Forest and scrub

COLOMBO

FIGURE 22
ETHNIC GROUPS

Sinhalese

Ceylon Tamils

Indian Tamils and Indian Moors

Ceylon Moors and Malays

COLOMBO

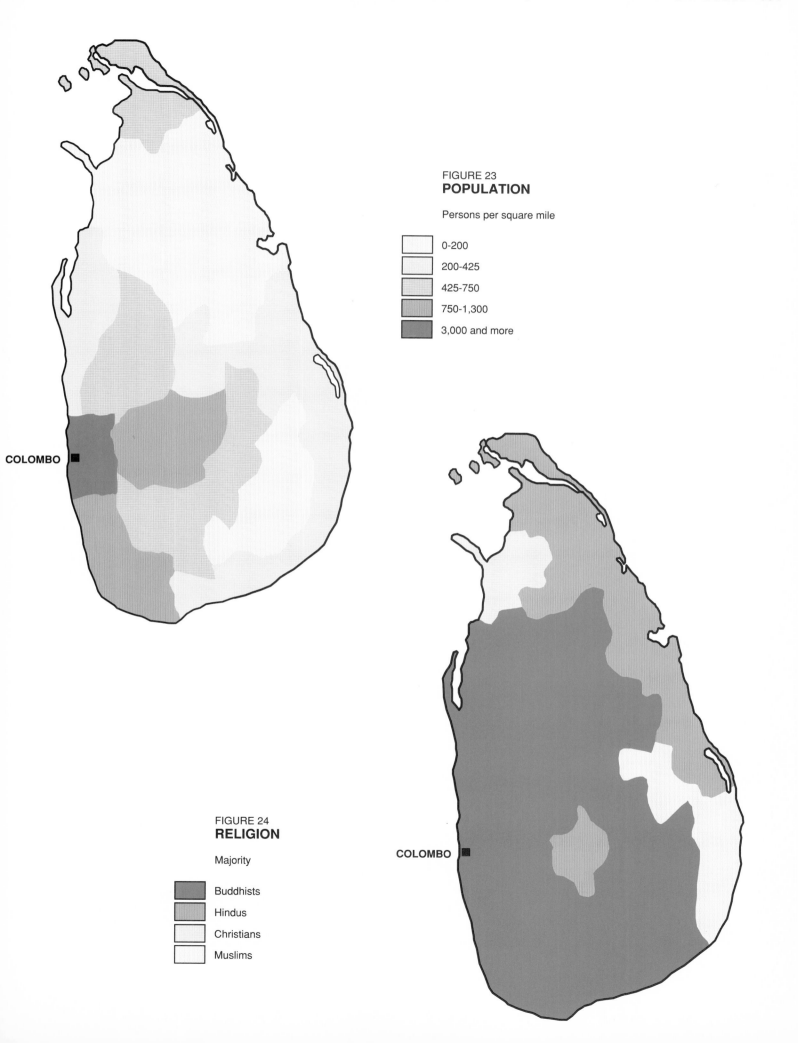

FIGURE 23
POPULATION

Persons per square mile

- 0-200
- 200-425
- 425-750
- 750-1,300
- 3,000 and more

COLOMBO

FIGURE 24
RELIGION

Majority

- Buddhists
- Hindus
- Christians
- Muslims

COLOMBO

SUDAN

The largest country in Africa, Sudan ranks ninth in land area but only 33rd in population. The potentials for growth that flow from sheer physical size have only been partially realized. A number of reasons have been advanced for such underdevelopment: inadequate transportation facilities, presence of nearly half a million refugees from Eritrea, Uganda, Chad, and other countries, misallocation of resources in the agricultural sector, political instability, ethnic rivalries between the predominantly Muslim north and the non-Muslim south, and chronic trade deficits. Of the 200 million acres of cultivable land (which, if properly utilized, could turn the country into the breadbasket of Africa), only 10% is being cultivated. In 1991 the UN estimated that 7.1 million people across Sudan were threatened with famine, the result of severe drought and damage caused by the country's seven-year-old civil war. Historically, cotton has been the principal commodity but most people tend to associate the country with gum arabic, of which Sudan produces four-fifths of the world's supply. One sign of the future direction of the economy is Saudi Arabia's and the United Arab Emirates' substantial investments in Sudanese development projects, in gratitude for which Sudan is turning into a Muslim fundamentalist country.

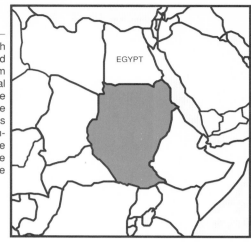

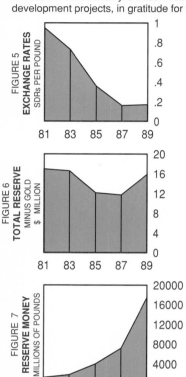

FIGURE 5 **EXCHANGE RATES** SDRs PER POUND

FIGURE 6 **TOTAL RESERVE** MINUS GOLD $ MILLION

FIGURE 7 **RESERVE MONEY** MILLIONS OF POUNDS

FIGURE 8 **MONEY** MILLIONS OF POUNDS

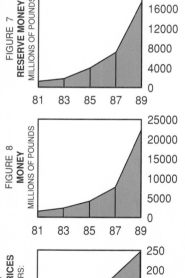

FIGURE 9 **CONSUMER PRICES** INDEX NUMBERS: 1985=100

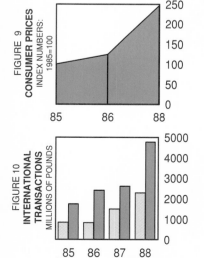

FIGURE 10 **INTERNATIONAL TRANSACTIONS** MILLIONS OF POUNDS

☐ Exports ☐ Imports

FIGURE 1 **POPULATION GROWTH**

Million

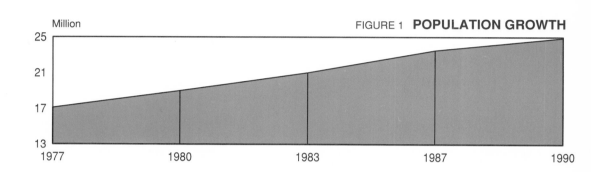

FIGURE 2 **GROSS NATIONAL PRODUCT**

$ Million

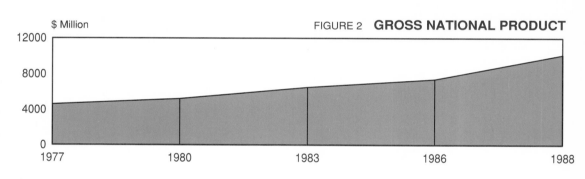

FIGURE 3 **GDP AND POPULATION GROWTH RATES**

%

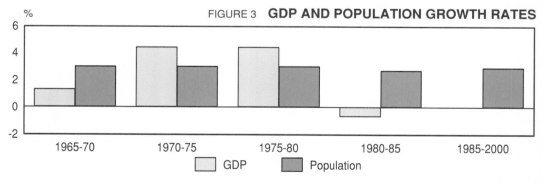

☐ GDP ☐ Population

FIGURE 4 **CENTRAL GOVERNMENT EXPENDITURES**

$ Million

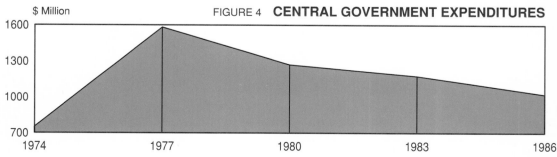

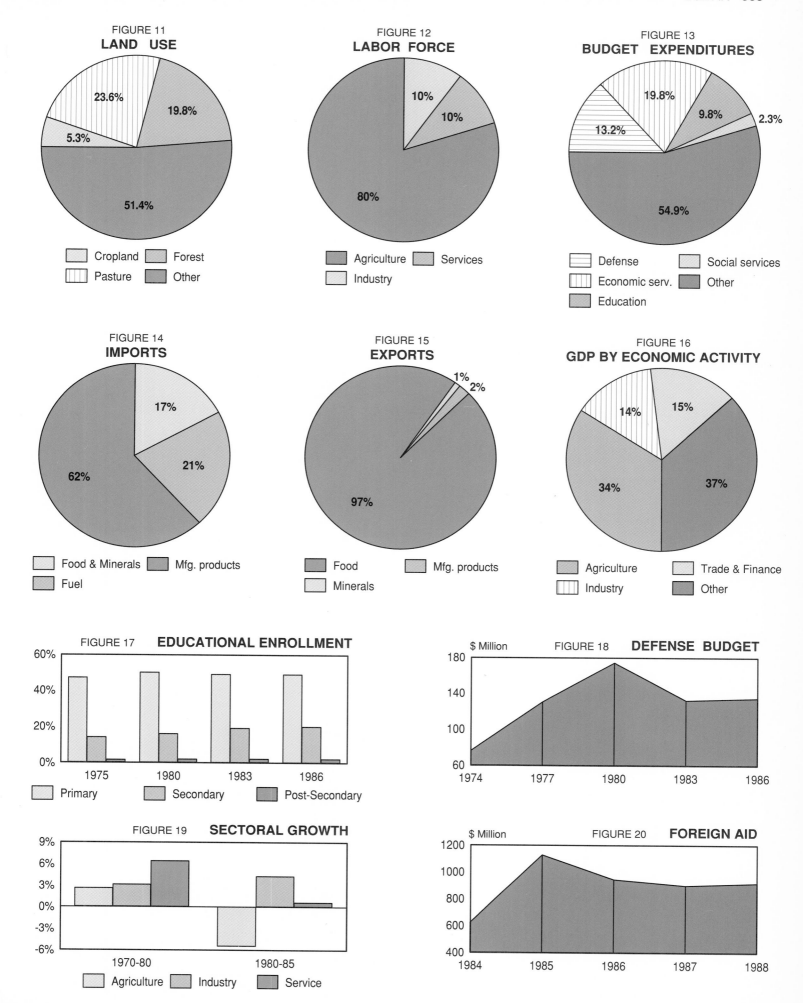

FIGURE 11
LAND USE

23.6%
19.8%
5.3%
51.4%

Cropland Forest
Pasture Other

FIGURE 12
LABOR FORCE

10%
10%
80%

Agriculture Services
Industry

FIGURE 13
BUDGET EXPENDITURES

19.8%
9.8%
13.2%
2.3%
54.9%

Defense Social services
Economic serv. Other
Education

FIGURE 14
IMPORTS

17%
62%
21%

Food & Minerals Mfg. products
Fuel

FIGURE 15
EXPORTS

1%
2%
97%

Food Mfg. products
Minerals

FIGURE 16
GDP BY ECONOMIC ACTIVITY

14%
15%
34%
37%

Agriculture Trade & Finance
Industry Other

FIGURE 17 **EDUCATIONAL ENROLLMENT**

60%
40%
20%
0%
1975 1980 1983 1986

Primary Secondary Post-Secondary

FIGURE 18 **DEFENSE BUDGET**

$ Million
180
140
100
60
1974 1977 1980 1983 1986

FIGURE 19 **SECTORAL GROWTH**

9%
6%
3%
0%
-3%
-6%
1970-80 1980-85

Agriculture Industry Service

FIGURE 20 **FOREIGN AID**

$ Million
1200
1000
800
600
400
1984 1985 1986 1987 1988

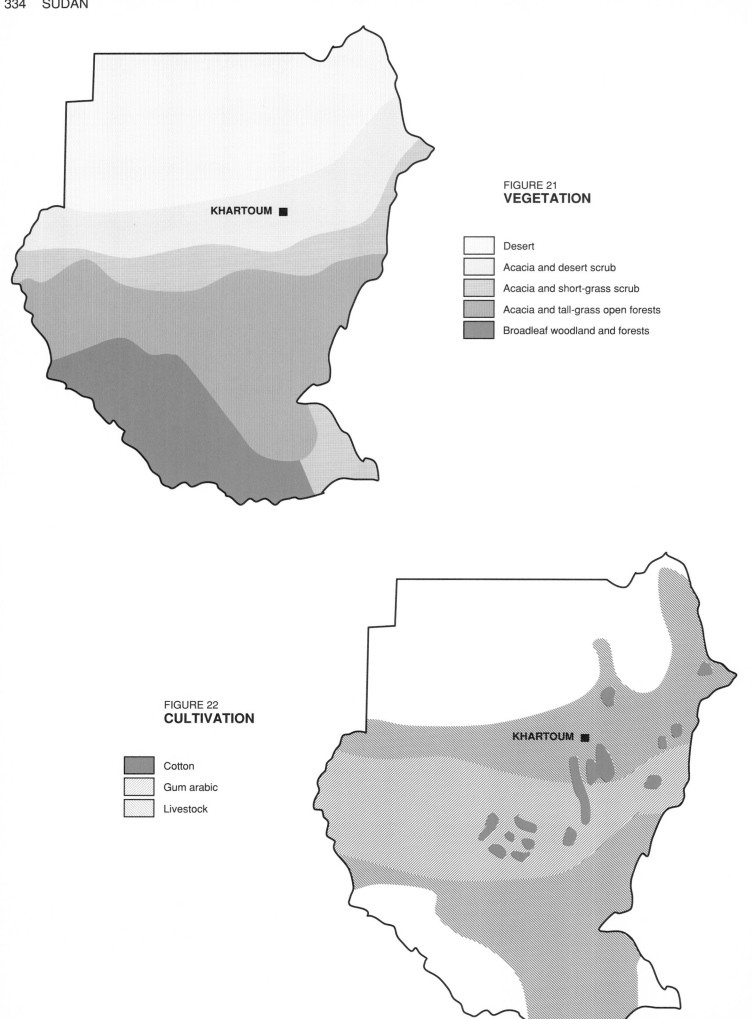

KHARTOUM ■

FIGURE 21
VEGETATION

Desert

Acacia and desert scrub

Acacia and short-grass scrub

Acacia and tall-grass open forests

Broadleaf woodland and forests

FIGURE 22
CULTIVATION

Cotton

Gum arabic

Livestock

KHARTOUM ■

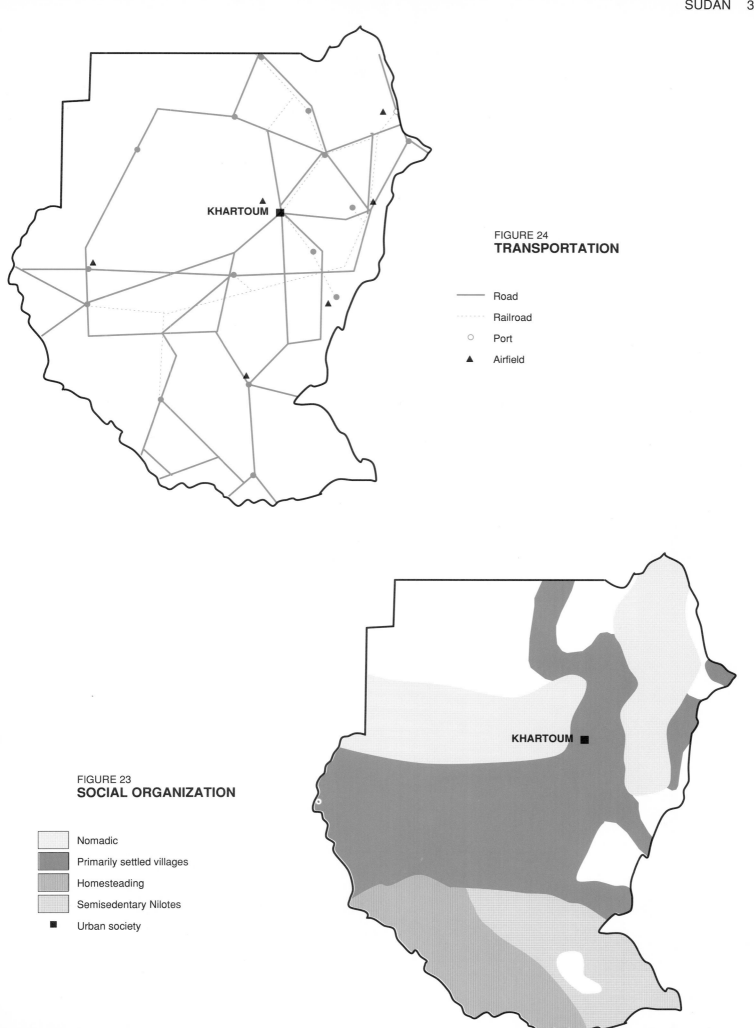

FIGURE 24
TRANSPORTATION

——— Road

· · · · · Railroad

○ Port

▲ Airfield

KHARTOUM ■

FIGURE 23
SOCIAL ORGANIZATION

Nomadic

Primarily settled villages

Homesteading

Semisedentary Nilotes

■ Urban society

KHARTOUM ■

SYRIA

Ranking 84th in land area and 57th in population, Syria, once a byword for political instability, has become, since the rise of President Assad to power in 1971, one of the most stable nations in the region, although internal dissensions continue to erupt off and on. During 1974-75 the economy reached an annual growth rate of 14% and, despite inflationary pressures, maintained a growth rate of 5.5 for the first half of the 1980s. Major factors contributing to such a performance were massive aid from richer Arab nations, realistic economic planning and higher prices for oil exports. Although highly centralized and state-controlled, the economy retains some private sector flavor. After 1987, declining oil production and the burden of maintaining troops in Lebanon placed a severe financial strain on the nation's economy, although in 1989 the economy grew stronger and Syria recorded its first trade surplus in 35 years.

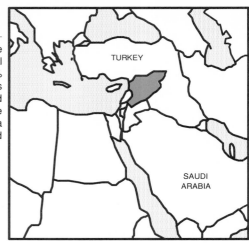

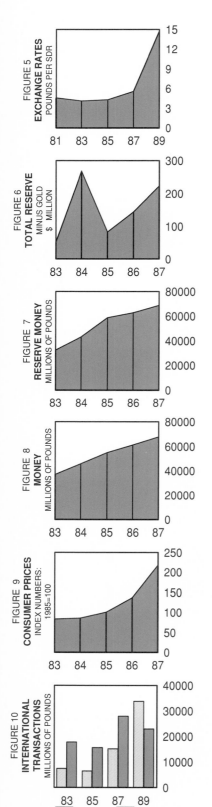

FIGURE 5 EXCHANGE RATES POUNDS PER SDR

FIGURE 6 TOTAL RESERVE MINUS GOLD $ MILLION

FIGURE 7 RESERVE MONEY MILLIONS OF POUNDS

FIGURE 8 MONEY MILLIONS OF POUNDS

FIGURE 9 CONSUMER PRICES INDEX NUMBERS: 1985=100

FIGURE 10 INTERNATIONAL TRANSACTIONS MILLIONS OF POUNDS
Exports Imports

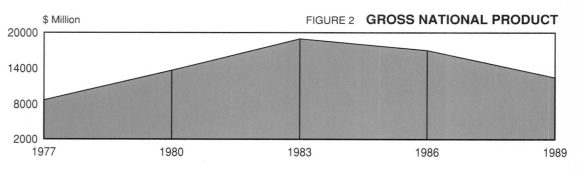

FIGURE 1 **POPULATION GROWTH**

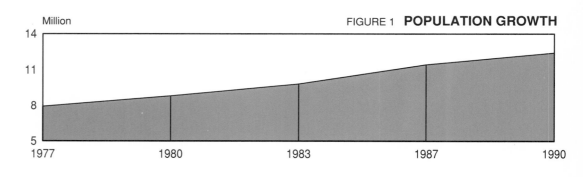

FIGURE 2 **GROSS NATIONAL PRODUCT**

FIGURE 3 **GDP AND POPULATION GROWTH RATES**

GDP Population

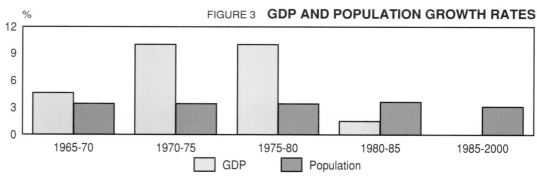

FIGURE 4 **GOVERNMENT REVENUES & EXPENDITURES**

Revenues Expenditures

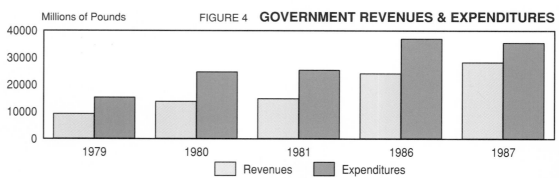

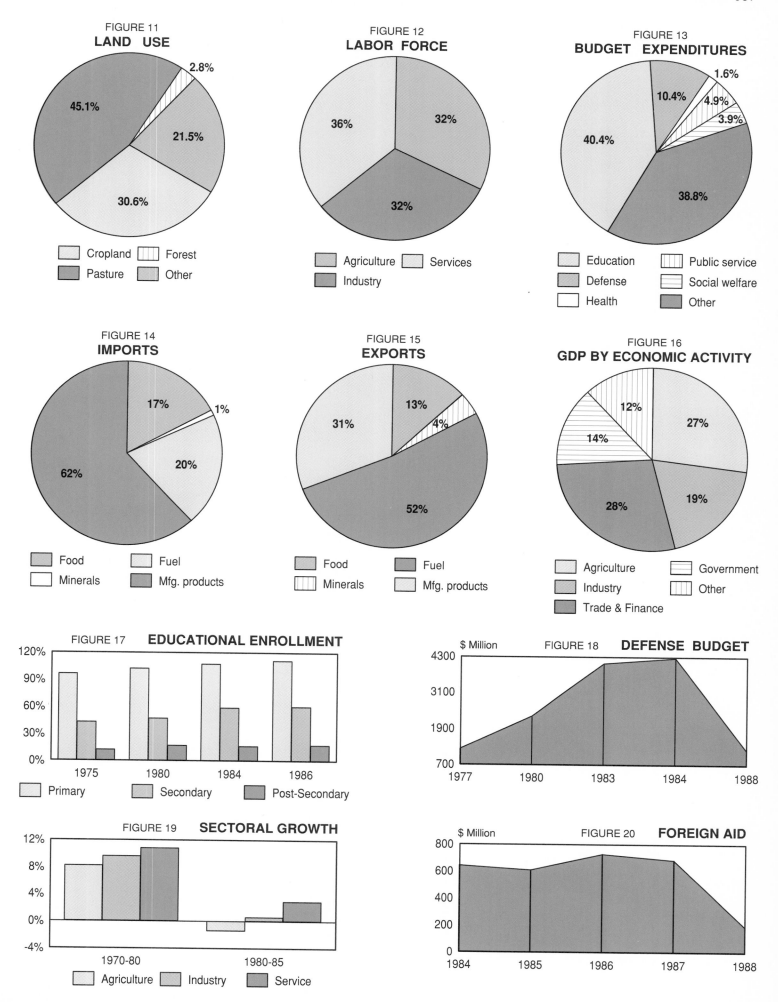

FIGURE 11
LAND USE

2.8%
45.1%
21.5%
30.6%

Cropland Forest
Pasture Other

FIGURE 12
LABOR FORCE

36% 32%
32%

Agriculture Services
Industry

FIGURE 13
BUDGET EXPENDITURES

1.6%
10.4% 4.9%
3.9%
40.4%
38.8%

Education Public service
Defense Social welfare
Health Other

FIGURE 14
IMPORTS

17% 1%
62% 20%

Food Fuel
Minerals Mfg. products

FIGURE 15
EXPORTS

13%
31% 4%
52%

Food Fuel
Minerals Mfg. products

FIGURE 16
GDP BY ECONOMIC ACTIVITY

12% 27%
14%
28% 19%

Agriculture Government
Industry Other
Trade & Finance

FIGURE 17 **EDUCATIONAL ENROLLMENT**

120%
90%
60%
30%
0%
1975 1980 1984 1986

Primary Secondary Post-Secondary

FIGURE 18 **DEFENSE BUDGET**

$ Million
4300
3100
1900
700
1977 1980 1983 1984 1988

FIGURE 19 **SECTORAL GROWTH**

12%
8%
4%
0%
-4%
1970-80 1980-85

Agriculture Industry Service

FIGURE 20 **FOREIGN AID**

$ Million
800
600
400
200
0
1984 1985 1986 1987 1988

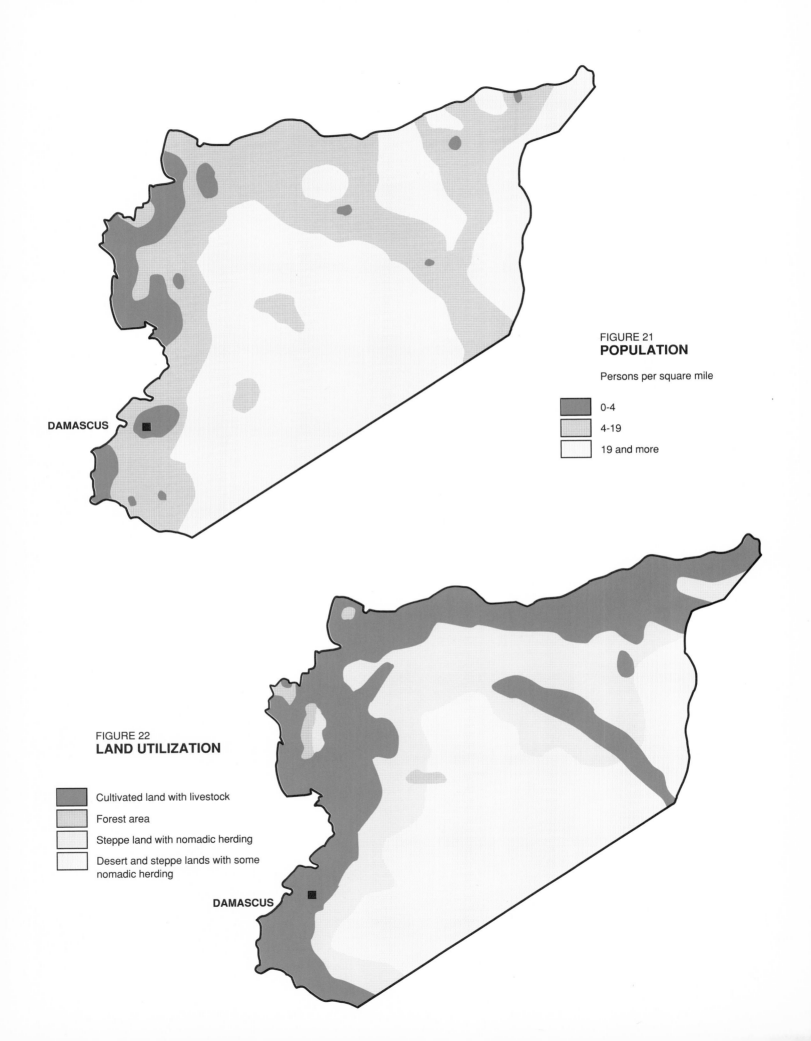

FIGURE 21
POPULATION

Persons per square mile

0-4
4-19
19 and more

DAMASCUS

FIGURE 22
LAND UTILIZATION

Cultivated land with livestock
Forest area
Steppe land with nomadic herding
Desert and steppe lands with some
nomadic herding

DAMASCUS

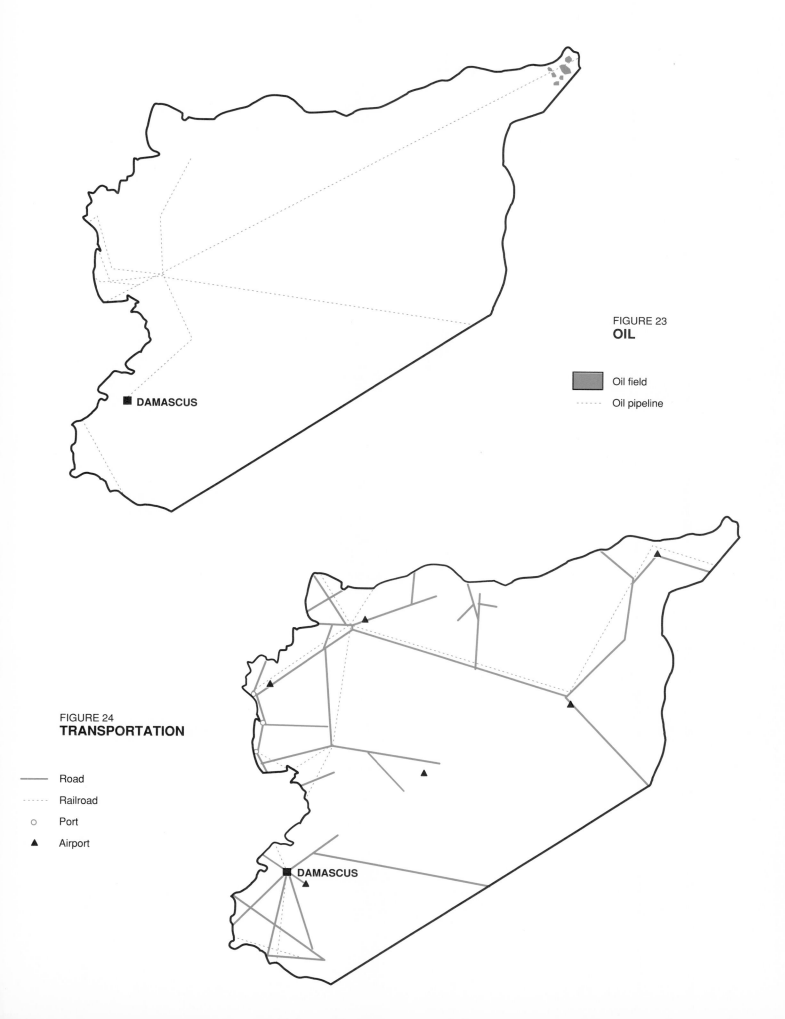

FIGURE 23
OIL

Oil field

Oil pipeline

DAMASCUS

FIGURE 24
TRANSPORTATION

Road

Railroad

○ Port

▲ Airport

DAMASCUS

TANZANIA

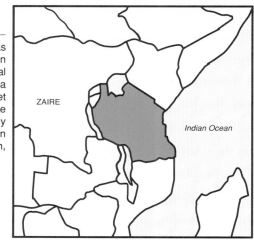

Located in East Africa, Tanzania ranks 30th in land area and 34th in population. The basic philosophy that has guided its economic and political development since independence was set forth in the 1967 Arusha Declaration and is embodied in the concept known as ujamaa (Swahili for familyhood). Ujamaa is a practical form of rural organization in which the communal village is the basic unit of development planning. The post-Arusha development strategy of egalitarianism, self-reliance, and social transformation has borne some fruits; yet Tanzania remains one of the world's poorest countries, with nearly 30% of the GDP derived from subsistence activities. During the latter half of the 1970s, the country experienced severe economic distress—principally caused by its war against Idi Amin, estimated to have cost it $500 million—and survived only through foreign aid. President Nyerere stepped down in 1985. The new government was less enthusiastic about socialism, and in 1990 leaders of the country were contemplating multiparty politics.

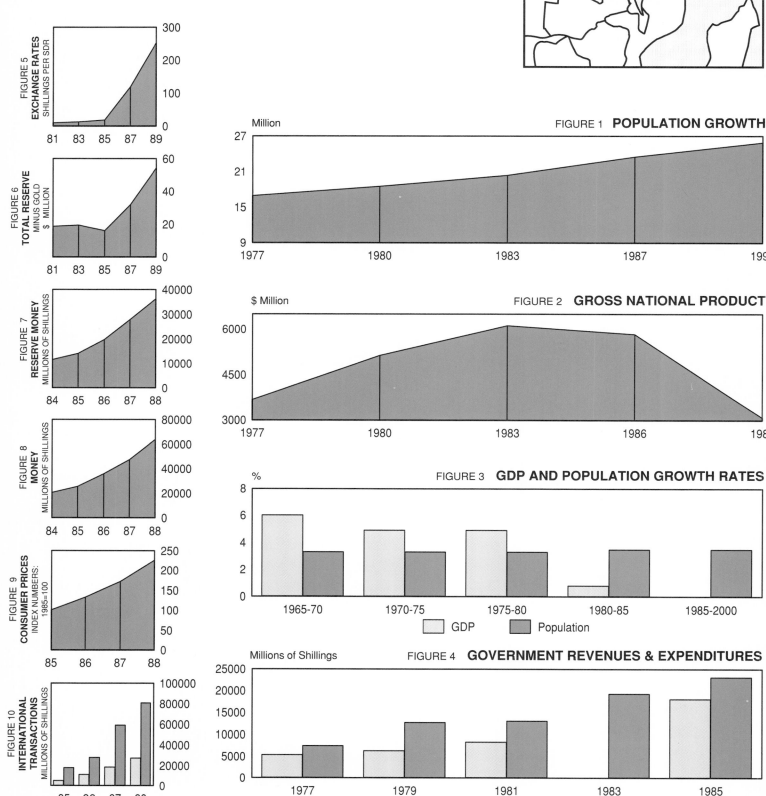

FIGURE 5 EXCHANGE RATES SHILLINGS PER SDR

FIGURE 6 TOTAL RESERVE MINUS GOLD $ MILLION

FIGURE 7 RESERVE MONEY MILLIONS OF SHILLINGS

FIGURE 8 MONEY MILLIONS OF SHILLINGS

FIGURE 9 CONSUMER PRICES INDEX NUMBERS: 1985=100

FIGURE 10 INTERNATIONAL TRANSACTIONS MILLIONS OF SHILLINGS
Exports   Imports

FIGURE 1 **POPULATION GROWTH**
Million

FIGURE 2 **GROSS NATIONAL PRODUCT**
$ Million

FIGURE 3 **GDP AND POPULATION GROWTH RATES**
%
GDP   Population

FIGURE 4 **GOVERNMENT REVENUES & EXPENDITURES**
Millions of Shillings
Revenues   Expenditures

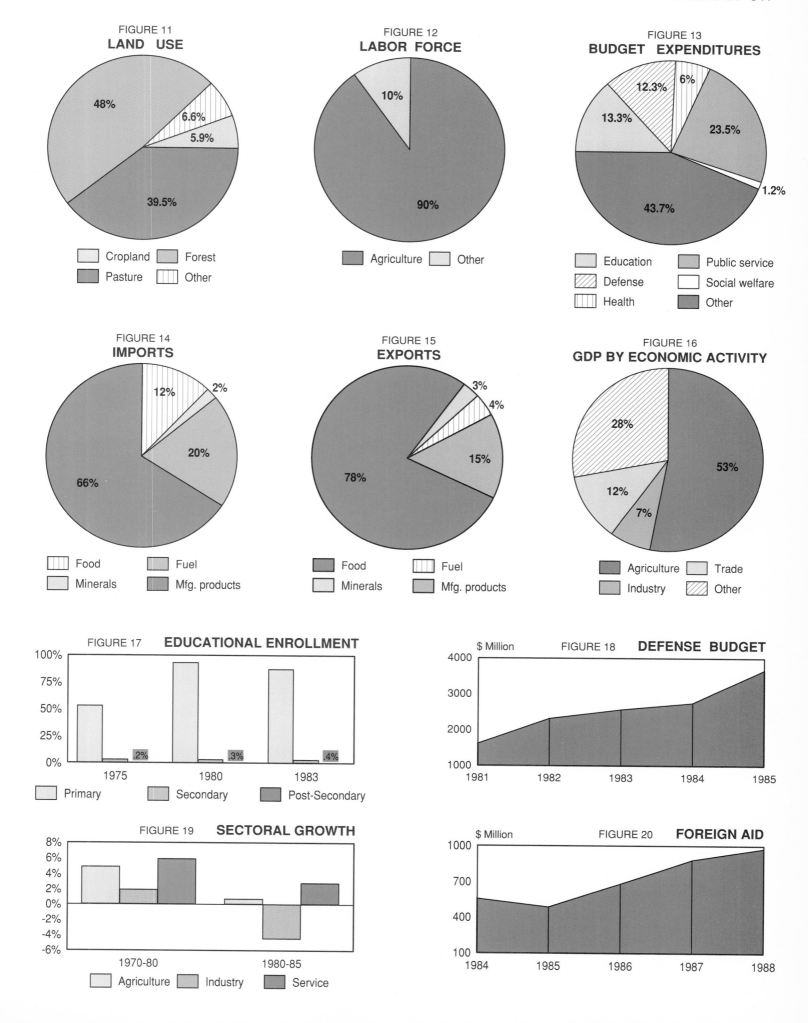

FIGURE 11
LAND USE

48%
6.6%
5.9%
39.5%

Cropland | Forest
Pasture | Other

FIGURE 12
LABOR FORCE

10%
90%

Agriculture | Other

FIGURE 13
BUDGET EXPENDITURES

12.3% | 6%
13.3%
23.5%
43.7%
1.2%

Education | Public service
Defense | Social welfare
Health | Other

FIGURE 14
IMPORTS

12% | 2%
20%
66%

Food | Fuel
Minerals | Mfg. products

FIGURE 15
EXPORTS

3%
4%
15%
78%

Food | Fuel
Minerals | Mfg. products

FIGURE 16
GDP BY ECONOMIC ACTIVITY

28%
12%
7%
53%

Agriculture | Trade
Industry | Other

FIGURE 17 EDUCATIONAL ENROLLMENT

| | 1975 | 1980 | 1983 |
| .2% | .3% | .4% |

Primary | Secondary | Post-Secondary

FIGURE 18 DEFENSE BUDGET

$ Million

4000
3000
2000
1000

1981 1982 1983 1984 1985

FIGURE 19 SECTORAL GROWTH

8%
6%
4%
2%
0%
-2%
-4%
-6%

1970-80   1980-85

Agriculture | Industry | Service

FIGURE 20 FOREIGN AID

$ Million

1000
700
400
100

1984 1985 1986 1987 1988

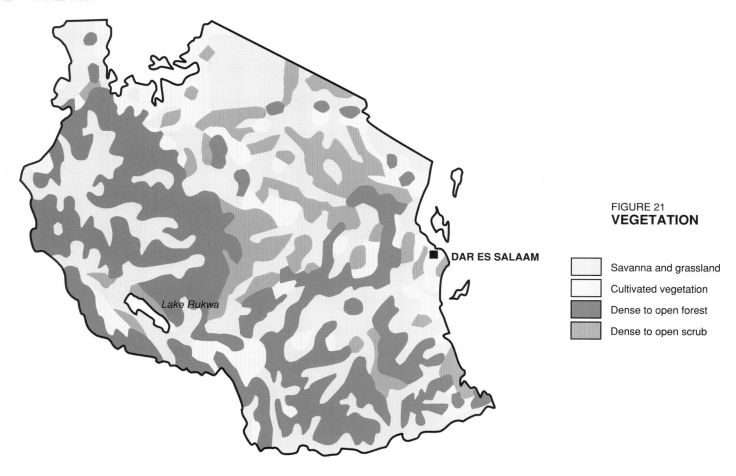

FIGURE 21
VEGETATION

Savanna and grassland
Cultivated vegetation
Dense to open forest
Dense to open scrub

Lake Rukwa

■ DAR ES SALAAM

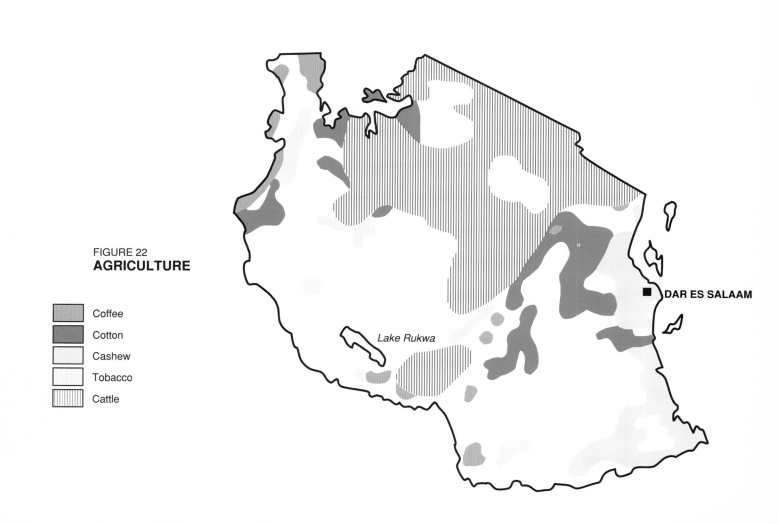

FIGURE 22
AGRICULTURE

Coffee
Cotton
Cashew
Tobacco
Cattle

Lake Rukwa

■ DAR ES SALAAM

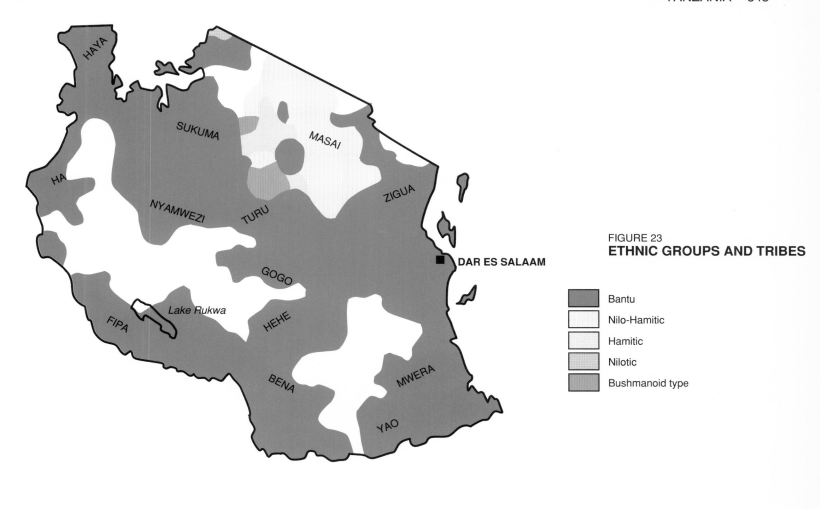

FIGURE 23
ETHNIC GROUPS AND TRIBES

Bantu

Nilo-Hamitic

Hamitic

Nilotic

Bushmanoid type

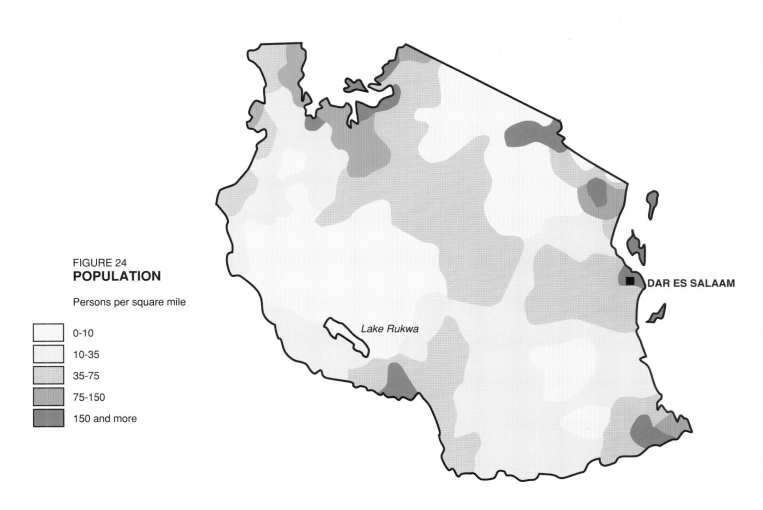

FIGURE 24
POPULATION

Persons per square mile

0-10

10-35

35-75

75-150

150 and more

THAILAND

The world's largest Buddhist nation, Thailand ranks 47th in land area and 18th in population. An island of stability in a region ravaged by war and insurgency, Thailand emerged from the seventies with fewer economic scars than her neighbors. The challenges and threats were many and serious, including one of history's largest influxes of refugees and the withdrawal of U.S. military bases. Yet the character of the economy remained unchanged and economic crises never reached flash point. Agriculture employs 71% of the labor force and contributed 17% of the GDP. The country's conservative fiscal policies have helped it to earn a solid international credit rating. External debt remains a small percent of GDP and debt servicing constitutes less than 16% of the value of exported goods and services. Although the country is hospitable to foreign capital, there is considerable nationalist sentiment (expressed in periodic demonstrations) against Japanese domination of the market; over 500 Japanese firms are believed to have substantial investment in Thailand.

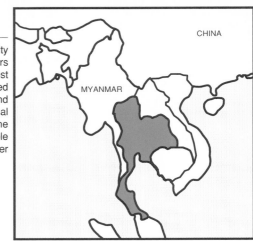

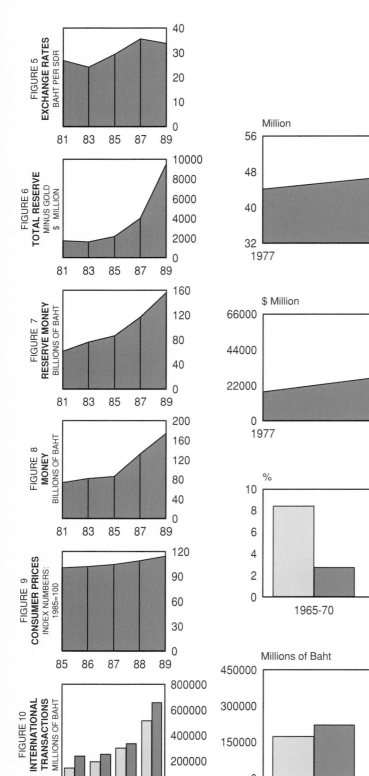

FIGURE 5 **EXCHANGE RATES** BAHT PER SDR

FIGURE 6 **TOTAL RESERVE** MINUS GOLD $ MILLION

FIGURE 7 **RESERVE MONEY** BILLIONS OF BAHT

FIGURE 8 **MONEY** BILLIONS OF BAHT

FIGURE 9 **CONSUMER PRICES** INDEX NUMBERS: 1985=100

FIGURE 10 **INTERNATIONAL TRANSACTIONS** MILLIONS OF BAHT
Exports Imports

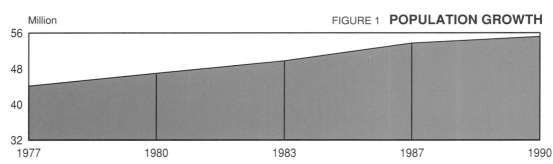

FIGURE 1 **POPULATION GROWTH**

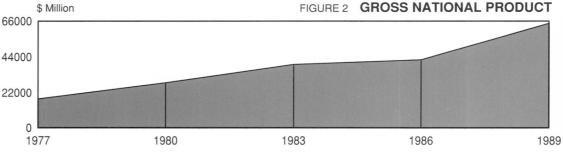

FIGURE 2 **GROSS NATIONAL PRODUCT**

FIGURE 3 **GDP AND POPULATION GROWTH RATES**

GDP Population

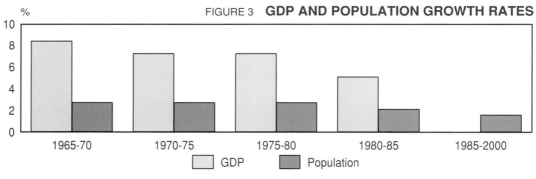

FIGURE 4 **GOVERNMENT REVENUES & EXPENDITURES**

Revenues Expenditures

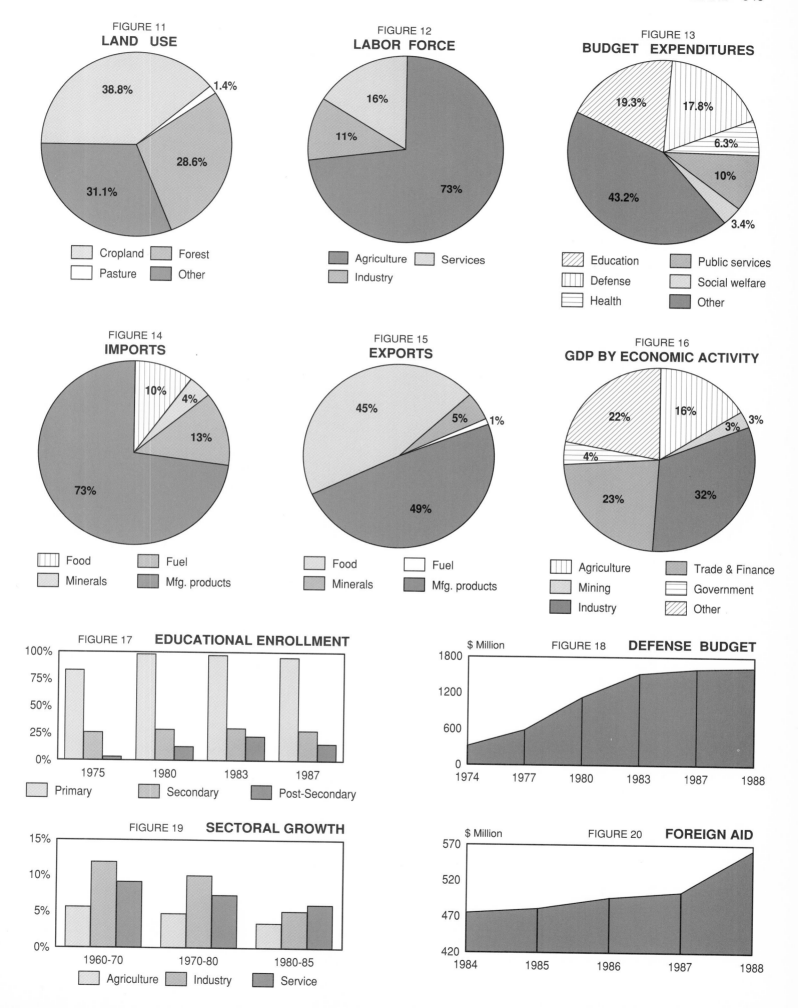

FIGURE 11
LAND USE

38.8%   1.4%
28.6%
31.1%

☐ Cropland   ☐ Forest
☐ Pasture   ☐ Other

FIGURE 12
LABOR FORCE

16%
11%
73%

☐ Agriculture   ☐ Services
☐ Industry

FIGURE 13
BUDGET EXPENDITURES

19.3%   17.8%
6.3%
10%
43.2%
3.4%

☐ Education   ☐ Public services
☐ Defense   ☐ Social welfare
☐ Health   ☐ Other

FIGURE 14
IMPORTS

10%   4%
13%
73%

☐ Food   ☐ Fuel
☐ Minerals ☐ Mfg. products

FIGURE 15
EXPORTS

45%   5%   1%
49%

☐ Food   ☐ Fuel
☐ Minerals ☐ Mfg. products

FIGURE 16
GDP BY ECONOMIC ACTIVITY

22%   16%   3% 3%
4%
23%   32%

☐ Agriculture   ☐ Trade & Finance
☐ Mining   ☐ Government
☐ Industry   ☐ Other

FIGURE 17 EDUCATIONAL ENROLLMENT

☐ Primary   ☐ Secondary   ☐ Post-Secondary

FIGURE 18 DEFENSE BUDGET
$ Million
1974 1977 1980 1983 1987 1988

FIGURE 19 SECTORAL GROWTH

1960-70   1970-80   1980-85
☐ Agriculture   ☐ Industry   ☐ Service

FIGURE 20 FOREIGN AID
$ Million
1984 1985 1986 1987 1988

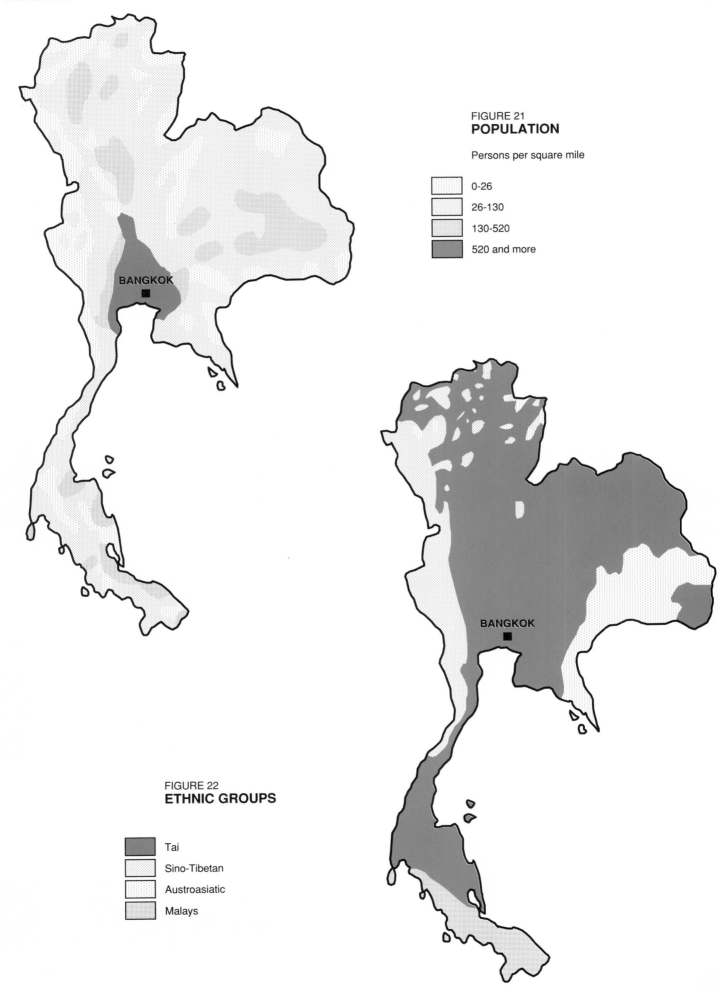

FIGURE 21
POPULATION

Persons per square mile

0-26

26-130

130-520

520 and more

BANGKOK

FIGURE 22
ETHNIC GROUPS

Tai

Sino-Tibetan

Austroasiatic

Malays

BANGKOK

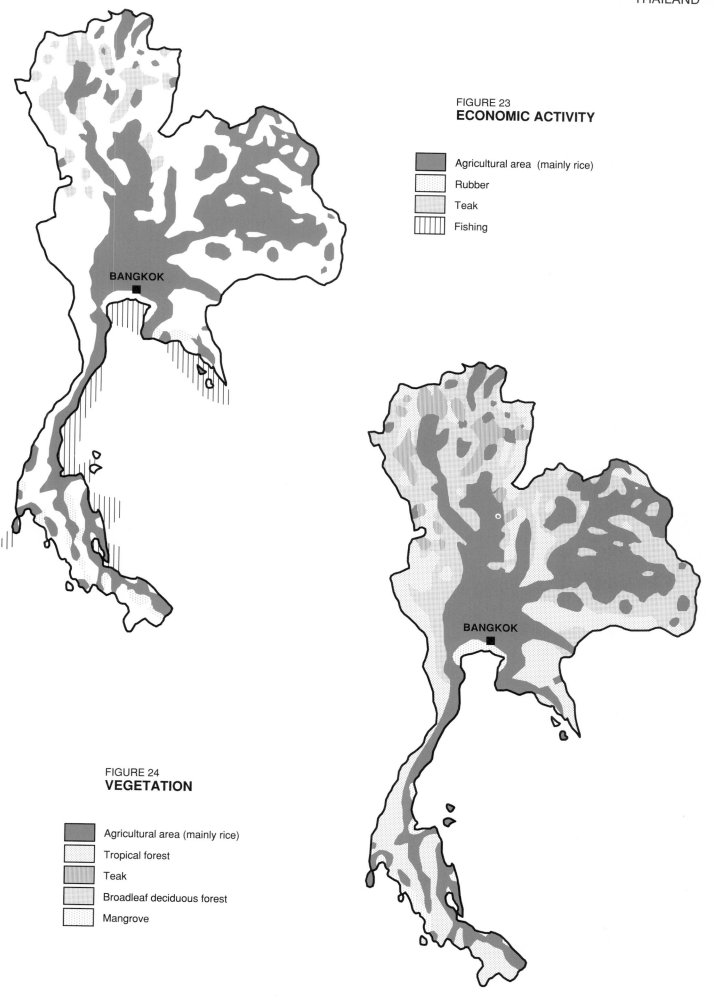

FIGURE 23
ECONOMIC ACTIVITY

- Agricultural area (mainly rice)
- Rubber
- Teak
- Fishing

BANGKOK

FIGURE 24
VEGETATION

- Agricultural area (mainly rice)
- Tropical forest
- Teak
- Broadleaf deciduous forest
- Mangrove

BANGKOK

TUNISIA

Located on the eastern end of the Maghrebian littoral, Tunisia ranks 88th in land area and 76th in population. Until 1987 Tunisia had known only one president, Habib Bourguiba. After a long spell of indifferent economic performance, the country began to rally in the mid-1970s and the annual growth rate of per capita GNP rose to 5.7% through the seventies. The key factor in this turnaround was the abandonment of the socialist programs of earlier years and the move toward a mixed economy with adequate incentives for private investment. The relative share of agriculture in the GDP fell from 24% in 1961 to 16% in 1986 while that of industry rose to 33% from 18%. The discovery of petroleum in 1964 also helped to spur the economy and cushion it against erratic performance in other sectors. Economic problems in 1990 were caused by a weak agricultural sector and serious flooding. Production is dominated by foreign companies, with the state being only a limited participant.

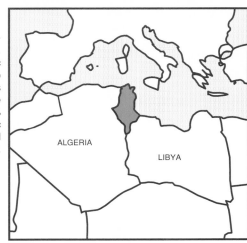

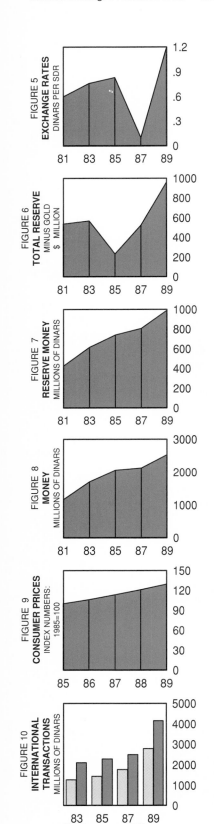

FIGURE 5 EXCHANGE RATES DINARS PER SDR

FIGURE 6 TOTAL RESERVE MINUS GOLD $ MILLION

FIGURE 7 RESERVE MONEY MILLIONS OF DINARS

FIGURE 8 MONEY MILLIONS OF DINARS

FIGURE 9 CONSUMER PRICES INDEX NUMBERS: 1985=100

FIGURE 10 INTERNATIONAL TRANSACTIONS MILLIONS OF DINARS
Exports Imports

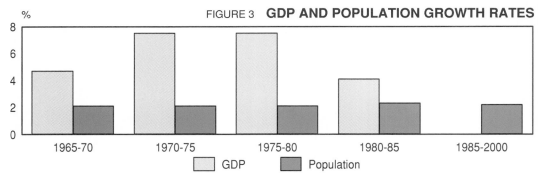

FIGURE 1 **POPULATION GROWTH**

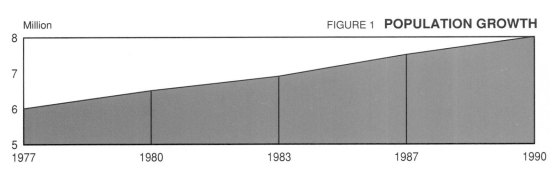

FIGURE 2 **GROSS NATIONAL PRODUCT**

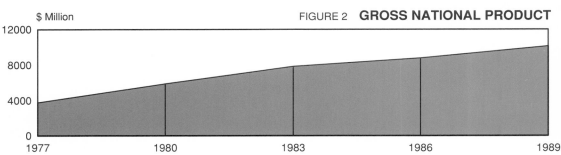

FIGURE 3 **GDP AND POPULATION GROWTH RATES**

GDP Population

FIGURE 4 **GOVERNMENT REVENUES & EXPENDITURES**

Millions of Dinars

Revenues Expenditures

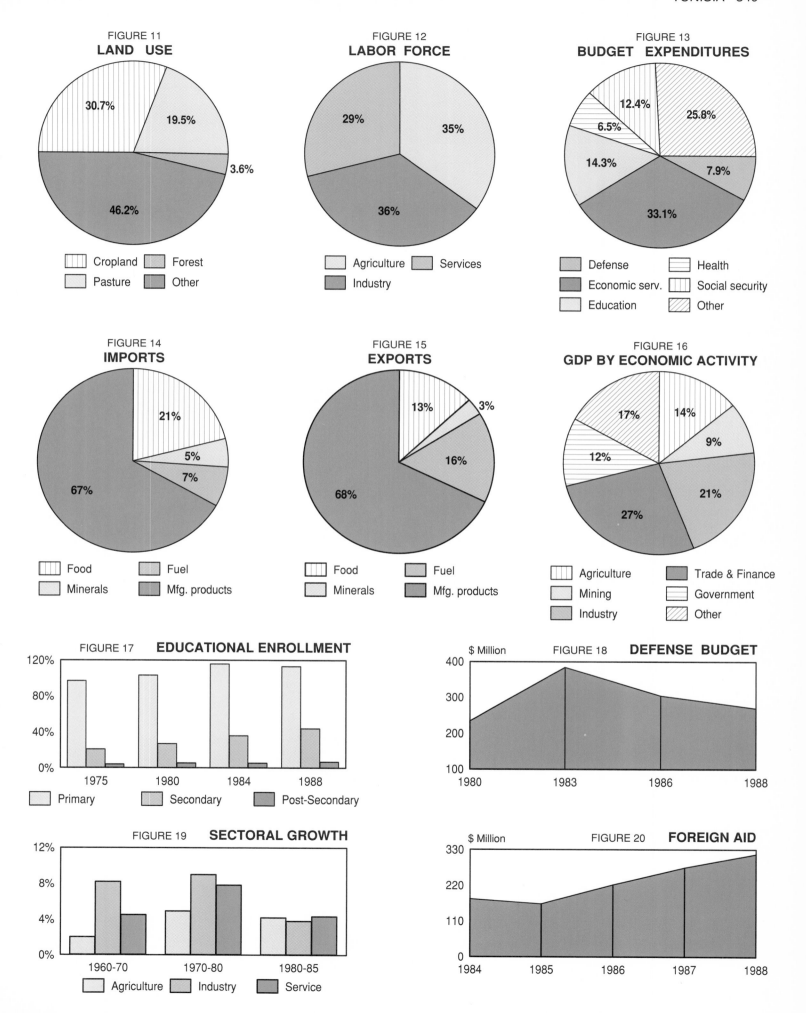

FIGURE 11
LAND USE

30.7%
19.5%
3.6%
46.2%

Cropland | Forest
Pasture | Other

FIGURE 12
LABOR FORCE

29%
35%
36%

Agriculture | Services
Industry

FIGURE 13
BUDGET EXPENDITURES

12.4%
6.5%
14.3%
25.8%
7.9%
33.1%

Defense | Health
Economic serv. | Social security
Education | Other

FIGURE 14
IMPORTS

21%
5%
7%
67%

Food | Fuel
Minerals | Mfg. products

FIGURE 15
EXPORTS

13%
3%
16%
68%

Food | Fuel
Minerals | Mfg. products

FIGURE 16
GDP BY ECONOMIC ACTIVITY

17%
14%
9%
12%
21%
27%

Agriculture | Trade & Finance
Mining | Government
Industry | Other

FIGURE 17 **EDUCATIONAL ENROLLMENT**

120%
80%
40%
0%
1975 1980 1984 1988

Primary | Secondary | Post-Secondary

FIGURE 18 **DEFENSE BUDGET**

$ Million
400
300
200
100
1980 1983 1986 1988

FIGURE 19 **SECTORAL GROWTH**

12%
8%
4%
0%
1960-70 1970-80 1980-85

Agriculture | Industry | Service

FIGURE 20 **FOREIGN AID**

$ Million
330
220
110
0
1984 1985 1986 1987 1988

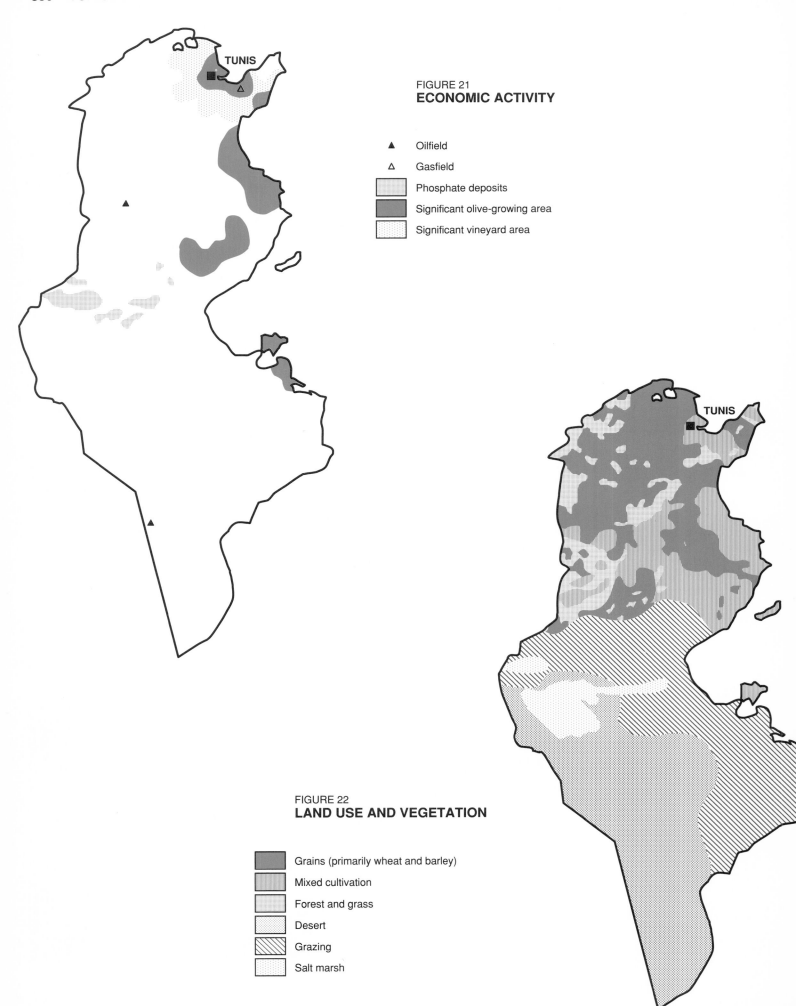

FIGURE 21
ECONOMIC ACTIVITY

▲ Oilfield

△ Gasfield

Phosphate deposits

Significant olive-growing area

Significant vineyard area

FIGURE 22
LAND USE AND VEGETATION

Grains (primarily wheat and barley)

Mixed cultivation

Forest and grass

Desert

Grazing

Salt marsh

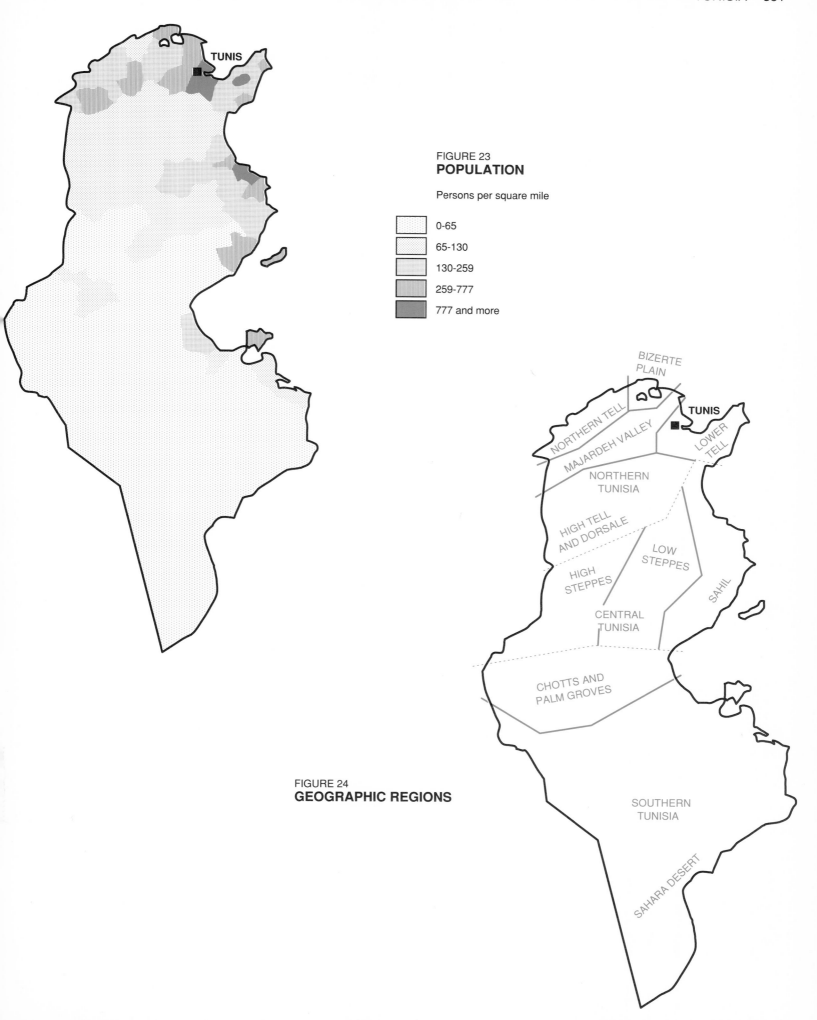

FIGURE 23
POPULATION

Persons per square mile

0-65

65-130

130-259

259-777

777 and more

TUNIS

FIGURE 24
GEOGRAPHIC REGIONS

BIZERTE
PLAIN

NORTHERN TELL

MAJARDEH VALLEY

TUNIS

LOWER
TELL

NORTHERN
TUNISIA

HIGH TELL
AND DORSALE

LOW
STEPPES

HIGH
STEPPES

SAHIL

CENTRAL
TUNISIA

CHOTTS AND
PALM GROVES

SOUTHERN
TUNISIA

SAHARA DESERT

TURKEY

Straddling Europe and Asia, Turkey ranks 36th in land area and 19th in population. Still the "sick man of Europe," Turkey does not fall into neat political, social, or cultural categories; it is neither European nor Asian, neither democratic nor authoritarian, neither modernized and secular nor medieval and sectarian. This anomaly extends to the economy: its population growth rate is typically Asian, 2.3% during the late 1980s, its per capita income is lower than that of any European country, and in indicators of modernization, it ranks in the middle of developing countries. Yet the government is committed to bring Turkey into the European Community and to pursue full membership, which it is unlikely to obtain because of Greece's potential veto. Political instability has made it difficult to formulate and sustain a coherent economic strategy over a sufficiently long period of time. The country continues to depend on worker remittances from Europe (generally over $1 billion every year) to meet the balance of payments deficits.

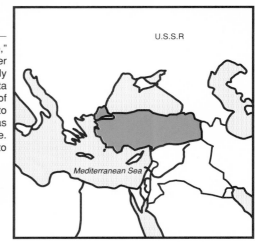

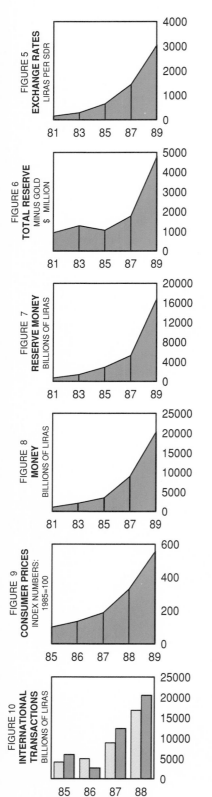

FIGURE 5 EXCHANGE RATES — LIRAS PER SDR

FIGURE 6 TOTAL RESERVE — MINUS GOLD $ MILLION

FIGURE 7 RESERVE MONEY — BILLIONS OF LIRAS

FIGURE 8 MONEY — BILLIONS OF LIRAS

FIGURE 9 CONSUMER PRICES — INDEX NUMBERS: 1985=100

FIGURE 10 INTERNATIONAL TRANSACTIONS — BILLIONS OF LIRAS
Exports ▢ Imports ▢

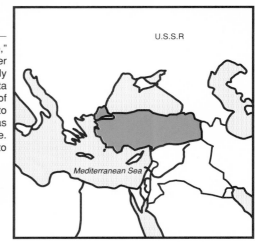

Million

FIGURE 1 POPULATION GROWTH

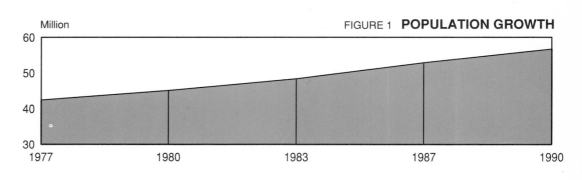

$ Million

FIGURE 2 GROSS NATIONAL PRODUCT

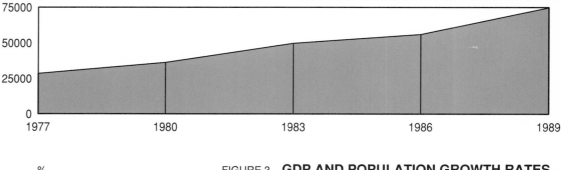

%

FIGURE 3 GDP AND POPULATION GROWTH RATES

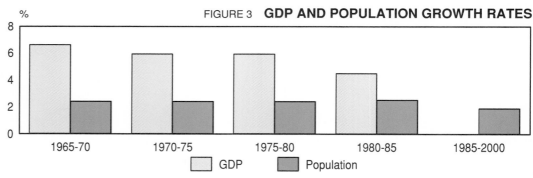

GDP ▢   Population ▢

Billions of Liras

FIGURE 4 GOVERNMENT REVENUES & EXPENDITURES

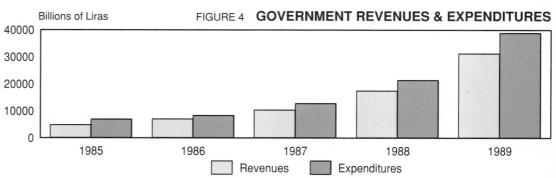

Revenues ▢   Expenditures ▢

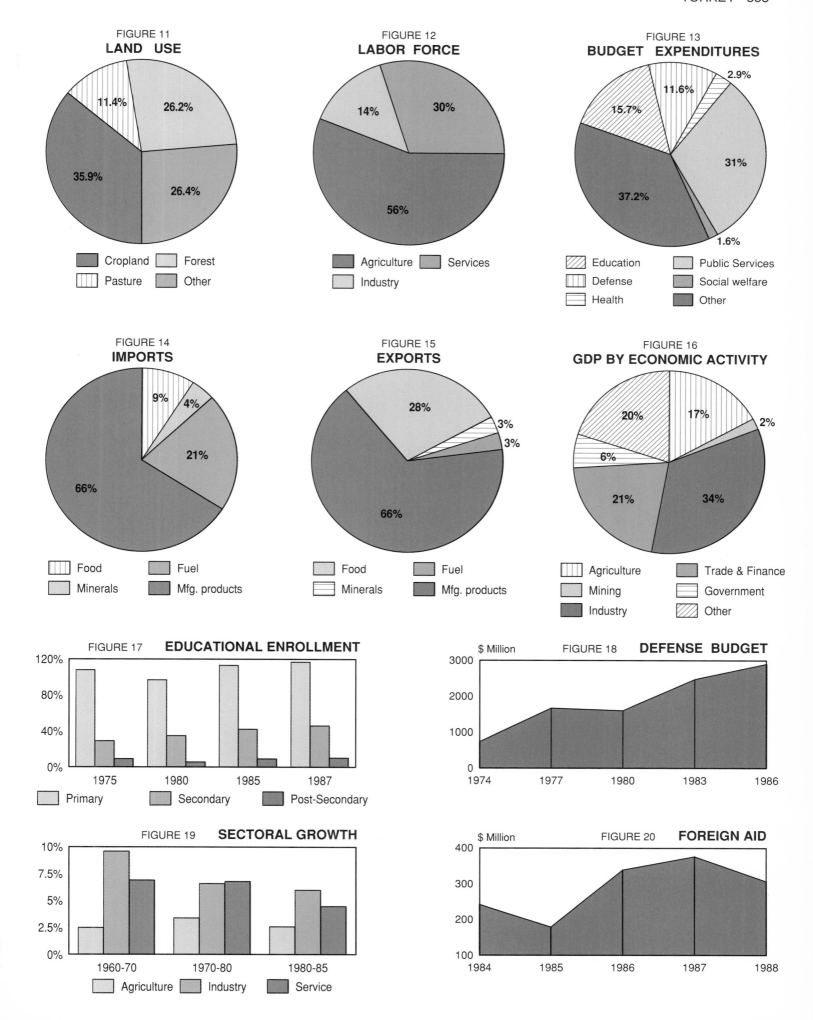

FIGURE 11
LAND USE

11.4%
26.2%
35.9%
26.4%

Cropland
Forest
Pasture
Other

FIGURE 12
LABOR FORCE

14%
30%
56%

Agriculture
Services
Industry

FIGURE 13
BUDGET EXPENDITURES

2.9%
11.6%
15.7%
31%
37.2%
1.6%

Education
Public Services
Defense
Social welfare
Health
Other

FIGURE 14
IMPORTS

9%
4%
21%
66%

Food
Fuel
Minerals
Mfg. products

FIGURE 15
EXPORTS

28%
3%
3%
66%

Food
Fuel
Minerals
Mfg. products

FIGURE 16
GDP BY ECONOMIC ACTIVITY

20%
17%
2%
6%
21%
34%

Agriculture
Trade & Finance
Mining
Government
Industry
Other

FIGURE 17 **EDUCATIONAL ENROLLMENT**

120%
80%
40%
0%
1975   1980   1985   1987

Primary
Secondary
Post-Secondary

$ Million   FIGURE 18   **DEFENSE BUDGET**

3000
2000
1000
0
1974   1977   1980   1983   1986

FIGURE 19   **SECTORAL GROWTH**

10%
7.5%
5%
2.5%
0%
1960-70   1970-80   1980-85

Agriculture
Industry
Service

$ Million   FIGURE 20   **FOREIGN AID**

400
300
200
100
1984   1985   1986   1987   1988

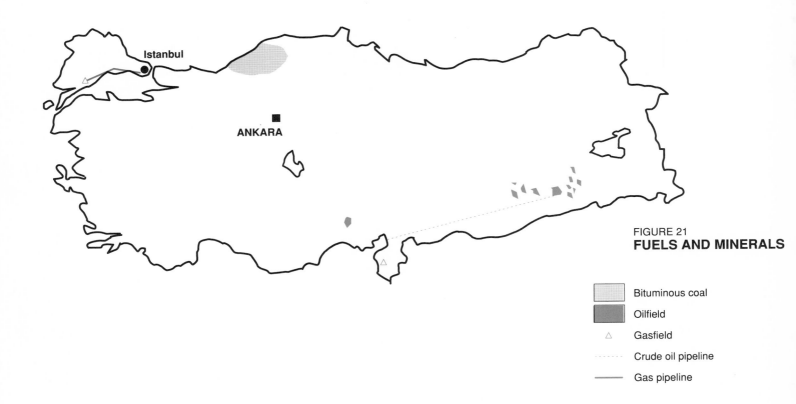

FIGURE 21
FUELS AND MINERALS

Bituminous coal

Oilfield

△ Gasfield

Crude oil pipeline

Gas pipeline

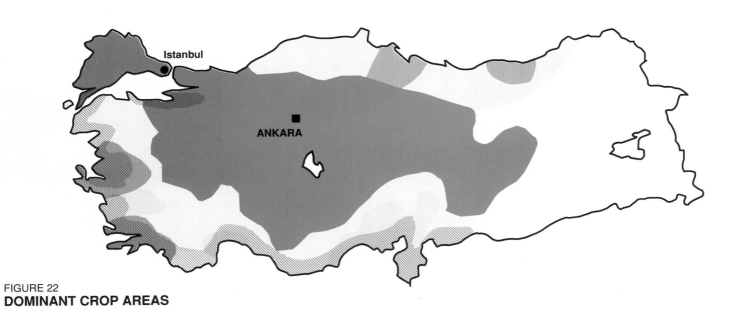

FIGURE 22
DOMINANT CROP AREAS

Wheat

Tobacco

Cotton

Mixed farming

Olives

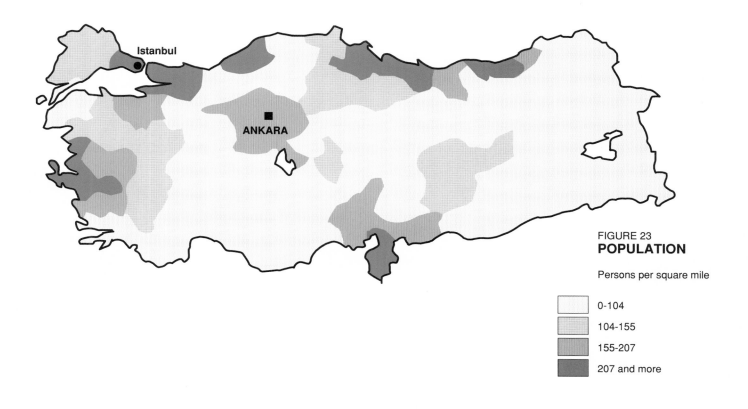

FIGURE 23
POPULATION

Persons per square mile

0-104

104-155

155-207

207 and more

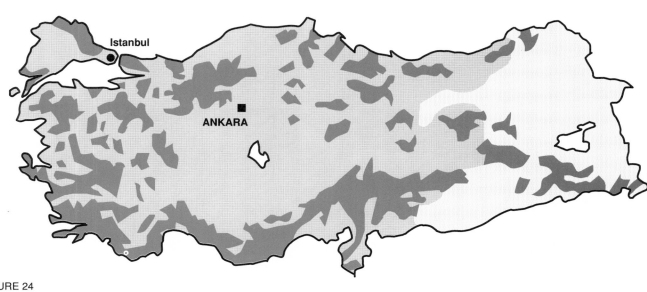

FIGURE 24
LAND USE

Forest

Cultivated areas with livestock grazing

Grazing areas with scattered cultivation

UGANDA

A landlocked nation in central Africa, Uganda ranks 77th in land area and 49th in population. Still recovering from the locust years of Idi Amin's rule, Uganda has found the process of rebuilding to be slow and frustrating, often one step forward and two steps back. Not merely is the cost of rebuilding, estimated at over $3 billion, beyond its reach, but political unrest and outbreaks of criminal violence continue to disrupt even existing economic activities. Although many of the foreign and Asian enterprises confiscated by Idi Amin have been restored to their former owners, there is little prospect of substantial private investment in the country. During 1979-80, Uganda regained its position as the third largest coffee grower and fifth largest cottonseed producer, although problems of transit through Kenyan territory made export of these commodities difficult. In 1990, the economy was badly hit by the low price of coffee on the world market.

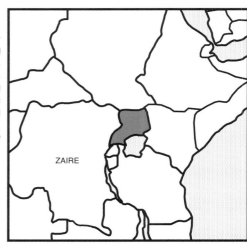

ZAIRE

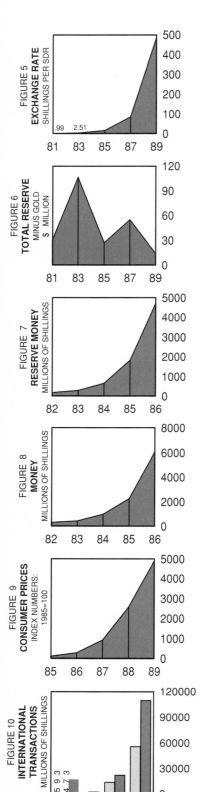

FIGURE 5 EXCHANGE RATE — SHILLINGS PER SDR

FIGURE 6 TOTAL RESERVE — MINUS GOLD $ MILLION

FIGURE 7 RESERVE MONEY — MILLIONS OF SHILLINGS

FIGURE 8 MONEY — MILLIONS OF SHILLINGS

FIGURE 9 CONSUMER PRICES — INDEX NUMBERS: 1985=100

FIGURE 10 INTERNATIONAL TRANSACTIONS — MILLIONS OF SHILLINGS — Exports / Imports

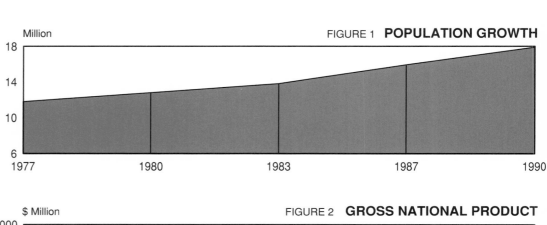

FIGURE 1 **POPULATION GROWTH**

Million

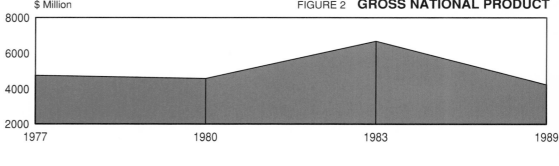

FIGURE 2 **GROSS NATIONAL PRODUCT**

$ Million

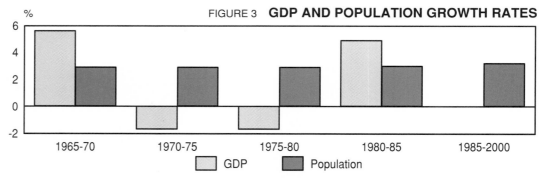

FIGURE 3 **GDP AND POPULATION GROWTH RATES**

% — GDP / Population — 1965-70 · 1970-75 · 1975-80 · 1980-85 · 1985-2000

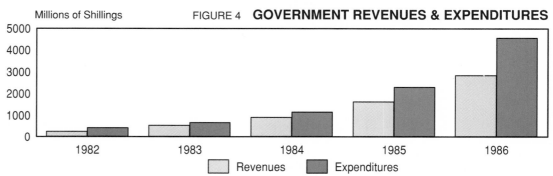

FIGURE 4 **GOVERNMENT REVENUES & EXPENDITURES**

Millions of Shillings — Revenues / Expenditures — 1982 · 1983 · 1984 · 1985 · 1986

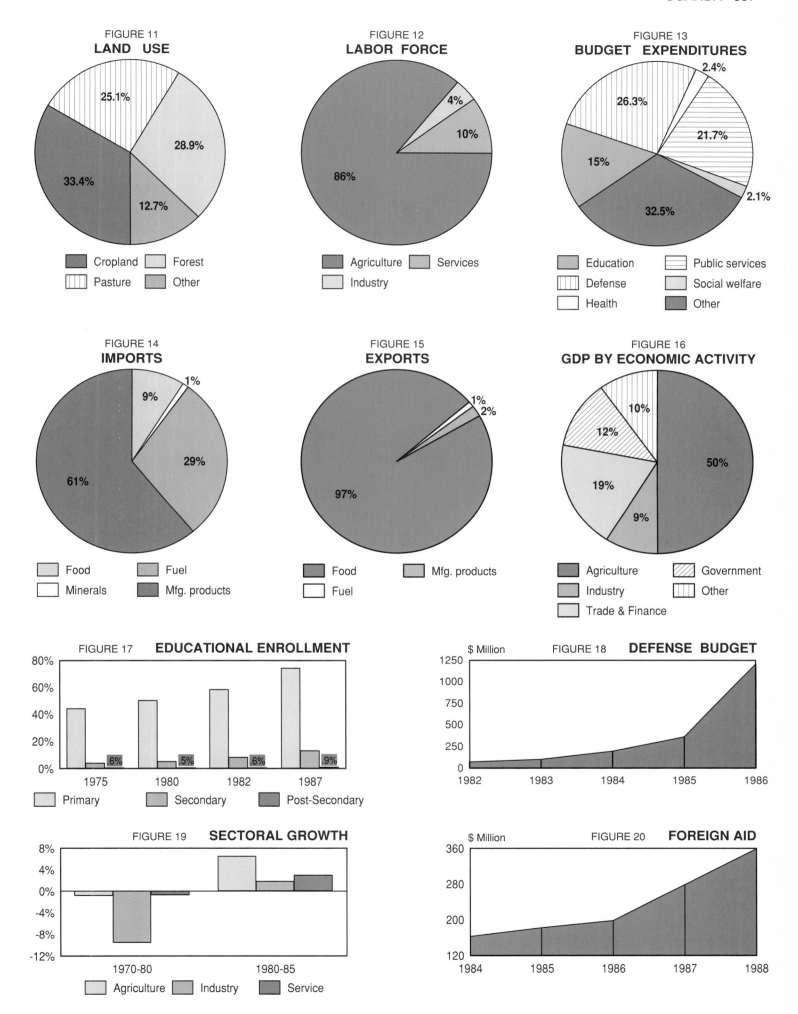

FIGURE 11
LAND USE

25.1%
28.9%
33.4%
12.7%

■ Cropland ▨ Forest
▥ Pasture ▨ Other

FIGURE 12
LABOR FORCE

4%
10%
86%

■ Agriculture ▨ Services
▨ Industry

FIGURE 13
BUDGET EXPENDITURES

2.4%
26.3%
21.7%
15%
32.5%
2.1%

▨ Education ▥ Public services
▥ Defense ▨ Social welfare
□ Health ■ Other

FIGURE 14
IMPORTS

1%
9%
29%
61%

▨ Food ▨ Fuel
□ Minerals ■ Mfg. products

FIGURE 15
EXPORTS

1%
2%
97%

■ Food ▨ Mfg. products
□ Fuel

FIGURE 16
GDP BY ECONOMIC ACTIVITY

10%
12%
19%
9%
50%

■ Agriculture ▨ Government
▨ Industry ▥ Other
▨ Trade & Finance

FIGURE 17 **EDUCATIONAL ENROLLMENT**

80%
60%
40%
20%
0%

.6% .5% .6% .9%

1975 1980 1982 1987

▨ Primary ▨ Secondary ■ Post-Secondary

$ Million FIGURE 18 **DEFENSE BUDGET**

1250
1000
750
500
250
0

1982 1983 1984 1985 1986

FIGURE 19 **SECTORAL GROWTH**

8%
4%
0%
-4%
-8%
-12%

1970-80 1980-85

▨ Agriculture ▨ Industry ■ Service

$ Million FIGURE 20 **FOREIGN AID**

360
280
200
120

1984 1985 1986 1987 1988

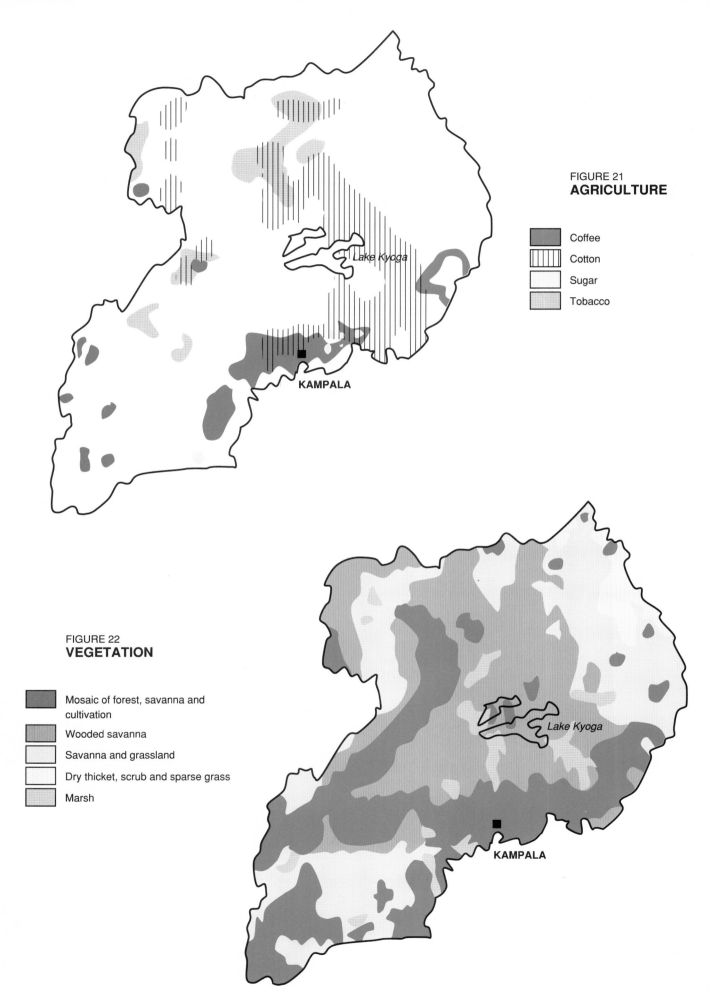

FIGURE 21
AGRICULTURE

Coffee
Cotton
Sugar
Tobacco

Lake Kyoga

KAMPALA

FIGURE 22
VEGETATION

Mosaic of forest, savanna and cultivation

Wooded savanna

Savanna and grassland

Dry thicket, scrub and sparse grass

Marsh

Lake Kyoga

KAMPALA

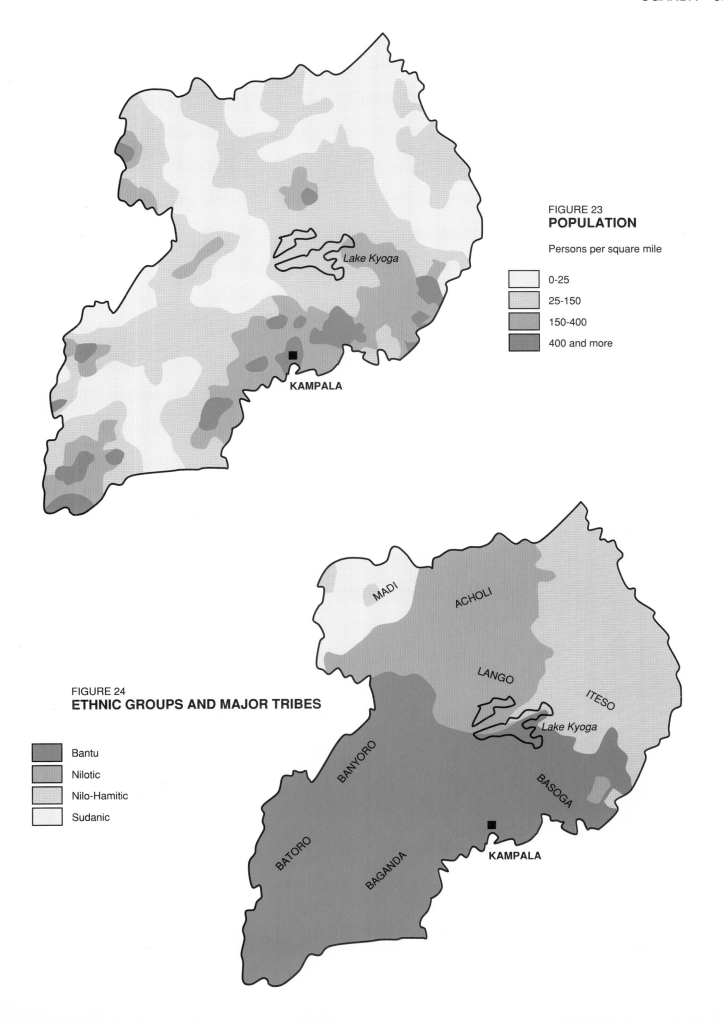

FIGURE 23
POPULATION

Persons per square mile

0-25

25-150

150-400

400 and more

Lake Kyoga

KAMPALA

FIGURE 24
ETHNIC GROUPS AND MAJOR TRIBES

Bantu

Nilotic

Nilo-Hamitic

Sudanic

MADI

ACHOLI

LANGO

ITESO

Lake Kyoga

BANYORO

BASOGA

BATORO

BAGANDA

KAMPALA

URUGUAY

The second smallest independent country in South America, Uruguay ranks 86th in land area and 111th in population. Hard hit by the fourth highest rate of inflation, its per capita GNP has been declining by 0.3% annually, and it ranks third in all three gauges of inflation: the wholesale price index, the consumer price index, and the rent index. Uruguay's richest resource is its livestock, raised on 70% of its agricultural land, and it ranks high in all indicators related to livestock. The rising costs of the country's extensive domestic social programs and the declining market for agricultural exports have placed its economy in a double bind and might produce the kind of social unrest that led to military intervention over a decade ago.

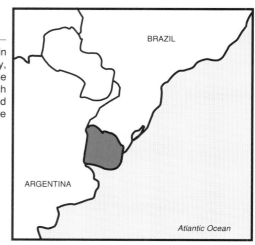

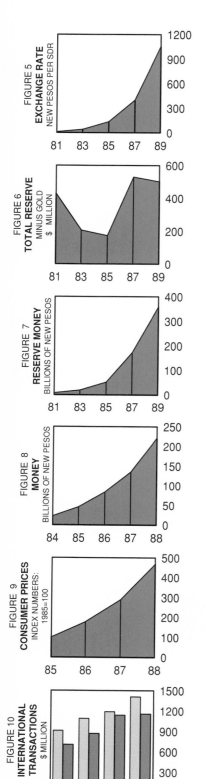

FIGURE 5 EXCHANGE RATE — NEW PESOS PER SDR

FIGURE 6 TOTAL RESERVE — MINUS GOLD $ MILLION

FIGURE 7 RESERVE MONEY — BILLIONS OF NEW PESOS

FIGURE 8 MONEY — BILLIONS OF NEW PESOS

FIGURE 9 CONSUMER PRICES — INDEX NUMBERS: 1985=100

FIGURE 10 INTERNATIONAL TRANSACTIONS — $ MILLION — Exports Imports

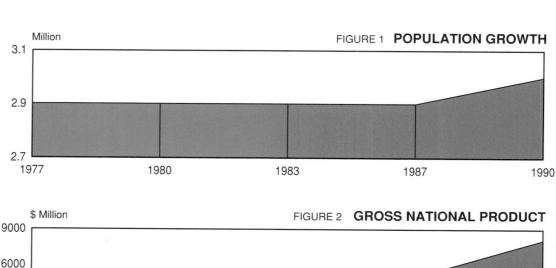

Million — FIGURE 1 **POPULATION GROWTH**

$ Million — FIGURE 2 **GROSS NATIONAL PRODUCT**

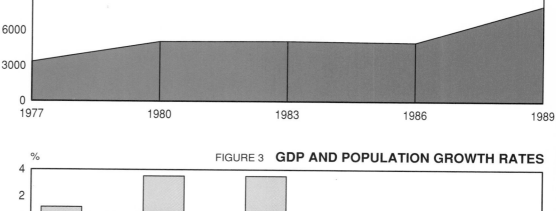

% — FIGURE 3 **GDP AND POPULATION GROWTH RATES** — GDP Population

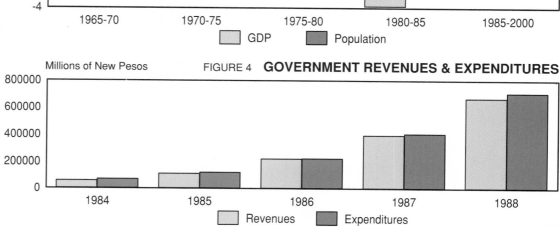

Millions of New Pesos — FIGURE 4 **GOVERNMENT REVENUES & EXPENDITURES** — Revenues Expenditures

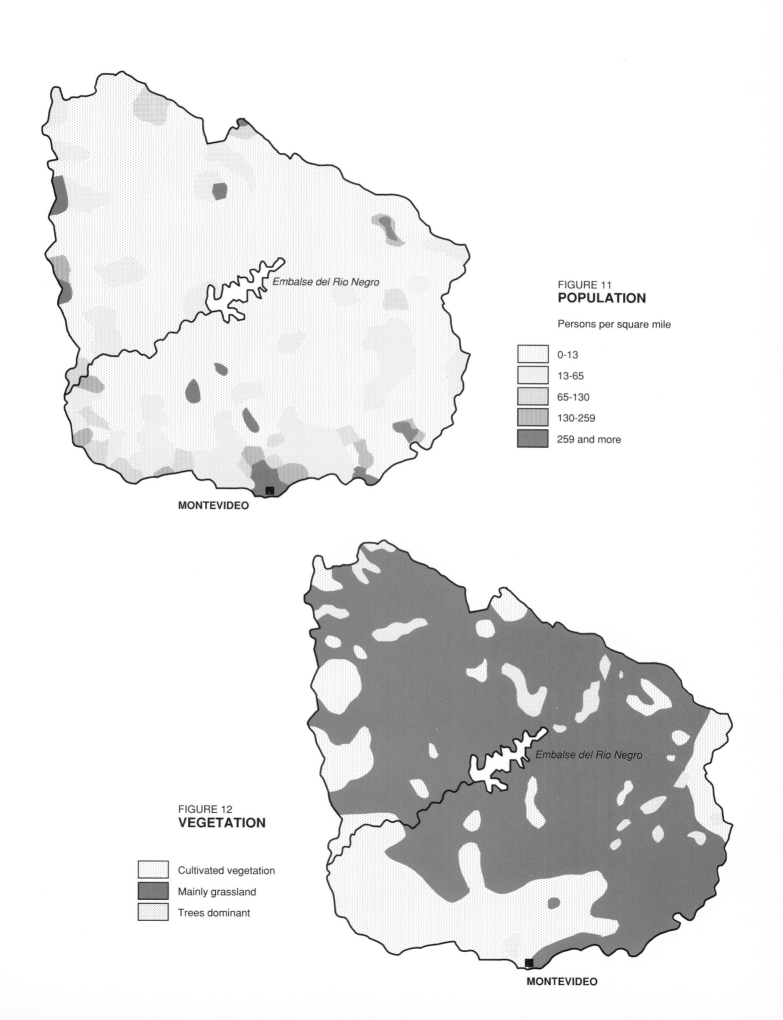

FIGURE 11
POPULATION

Persons per square mile

- 0-13
- 13-65
- 65-130
- 130-259
- 259 and more

Embalse del Rio Negro

MONTEVIDEO

FIGURE 12
VEGETATION

- Cultivated vegetation
- Mainly grassland
- Trees dominant

Embalse del Rio Negro

MONTEVIDEO

VENEZUELA

The country with the highest per capita GNP in Latin America, Venezuela ranks 32nd in land area and 42nd in population. It is one of the world's major oil-producing and oil-exporting nations, ranking sixth in production and third in exports. Petroleum accounts for nearly one-third of GDP, two-thirds of government revenues, and over 90% of export earnings. The rise in oil prices following the 1990 Iraqi invasion of Kuwait greatly benefited Venezuela, which increased output 25% by the year's end. Venezuela is also a major producer of iron ore and bauxite. Over 60% of the economy remains in private hands and this proportion is not likely to change dramatically in the future. Despite substantial oil revenues, Venezuela has above average foreign indebtedness, estimated at over $24.5 billion. Debt service is unusually high. The government is gambling on exploiting the heavy oil belt complex at Orinoco, a project estimated to cost $8 billion. The future of Venezuela's economy will hinge on the success of this project.

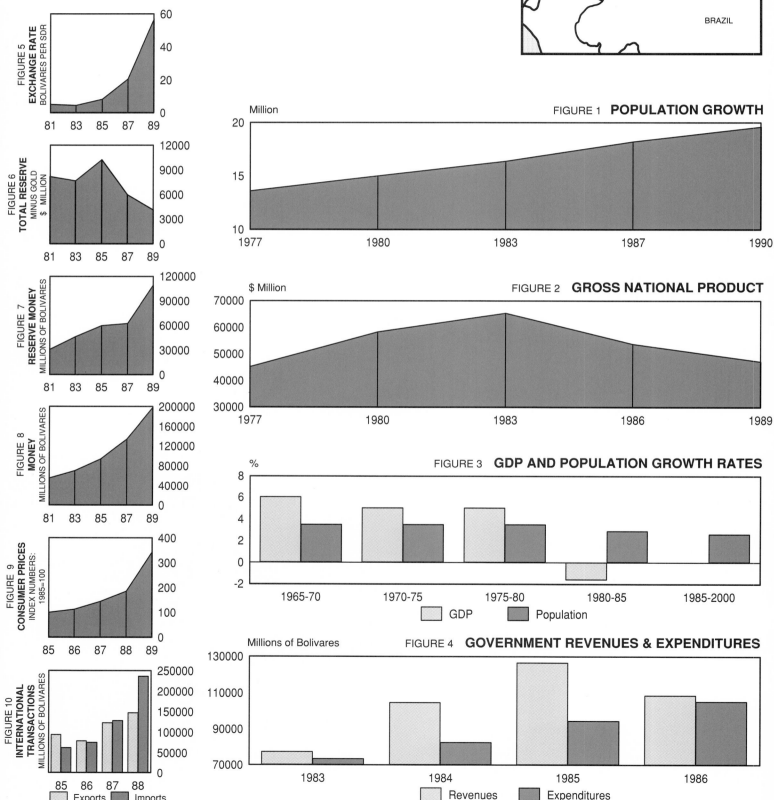

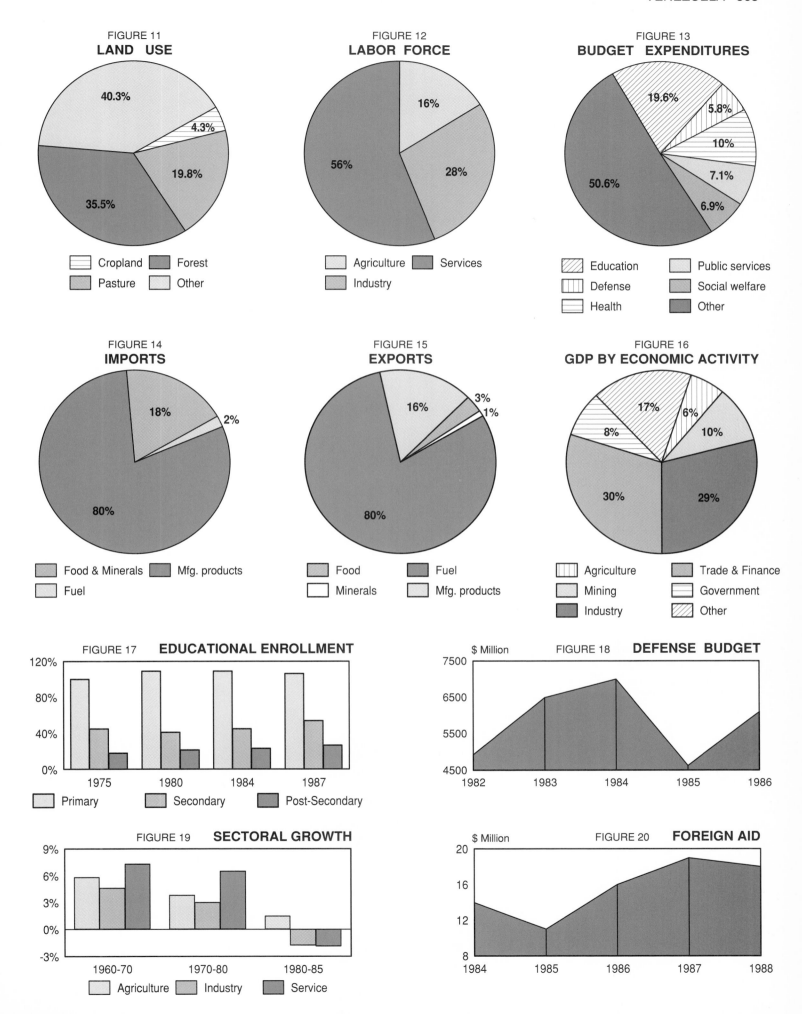

FIGURE 11
LAND USE

40.3%
4.3%
19.8%
35.5%

Cropland — Forest
Pasture — Other

FIGURE 12
LABOR FORCE

16%
28%
56%

Agriculture — Services
Industry

FIGURE 13
BUDGET EXPENDITURES

19.6%
5.8%
10%
7.1%
6.9%
50.6%

Education — Public services
Defense — Social welfare
Health — Other

FIGURE 14
IMPORTS

18%
2%
80%

Food & Minerals — Mfg. products
Fuel

FIGURE 15
EXPORTS

16%
3%
1%
80%

Food — Fuel
Minerals — Mfg. products

FIGURE 16
GDP BY ECONOMIC ACTIVITY

17%
6%
8%
10%
30%
29%

Agriculture — Trade & Finance
Mining — Government
Industry — Other

FIGURE 17 **EDUCATIONAL ENROLLMENT**

120%
80%
40%
0%
1975   1980   1984   1987

Primary — Secondary — Post-Secondary

$ Million   FIGURE 18   **DEFENSE BUDGET**

7500
6500
5500
4500
1982   1983   1984   1985   1986

FIGURE 19   **SECTORAL GROWTH**

9%
6%
3%
0%
-3%
1960-70   1970-80   1980-85

Agriculture — Industry — Service

$ Million   FIGURE 20   **FOREIGN AID**

20
16
12
8
1984   1985   1986   1987   1988

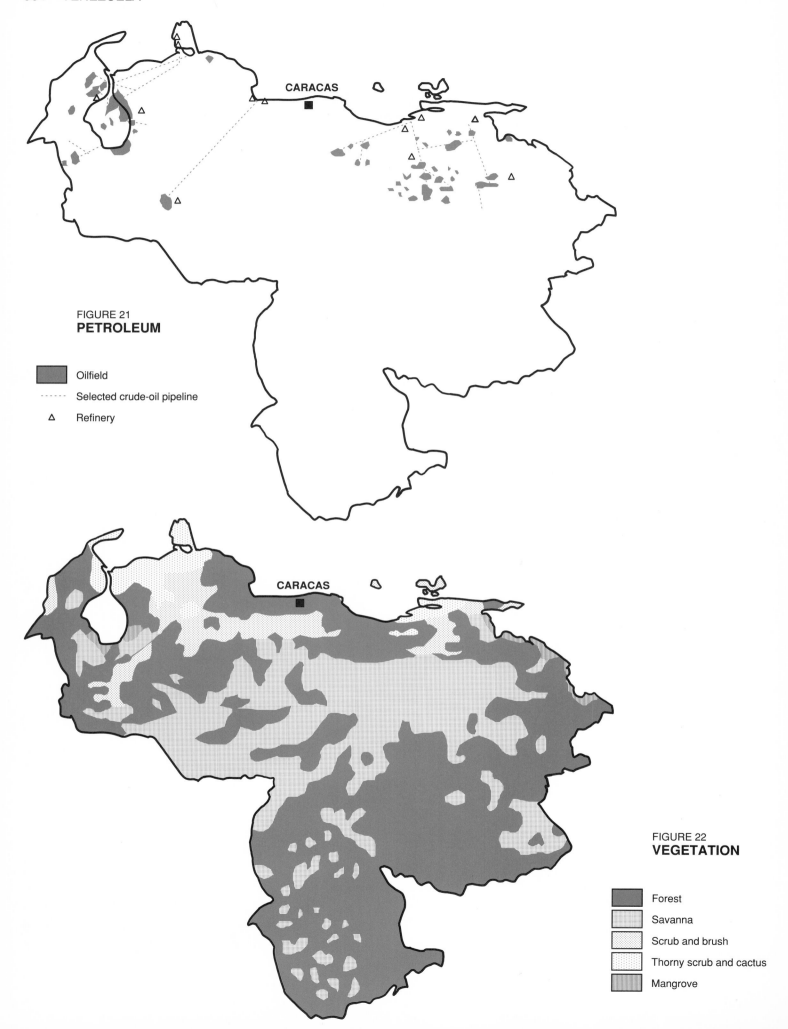

FIGURE 21
PETROLEUM

Oilfield

Selected crude-oil pipeline

△ Refinery

CARACAS

FIGURE 22
VEGETATION

Forest

Savanna

Scrub and brush

Thorny scrub and cactus

Mangrove

CARACAS

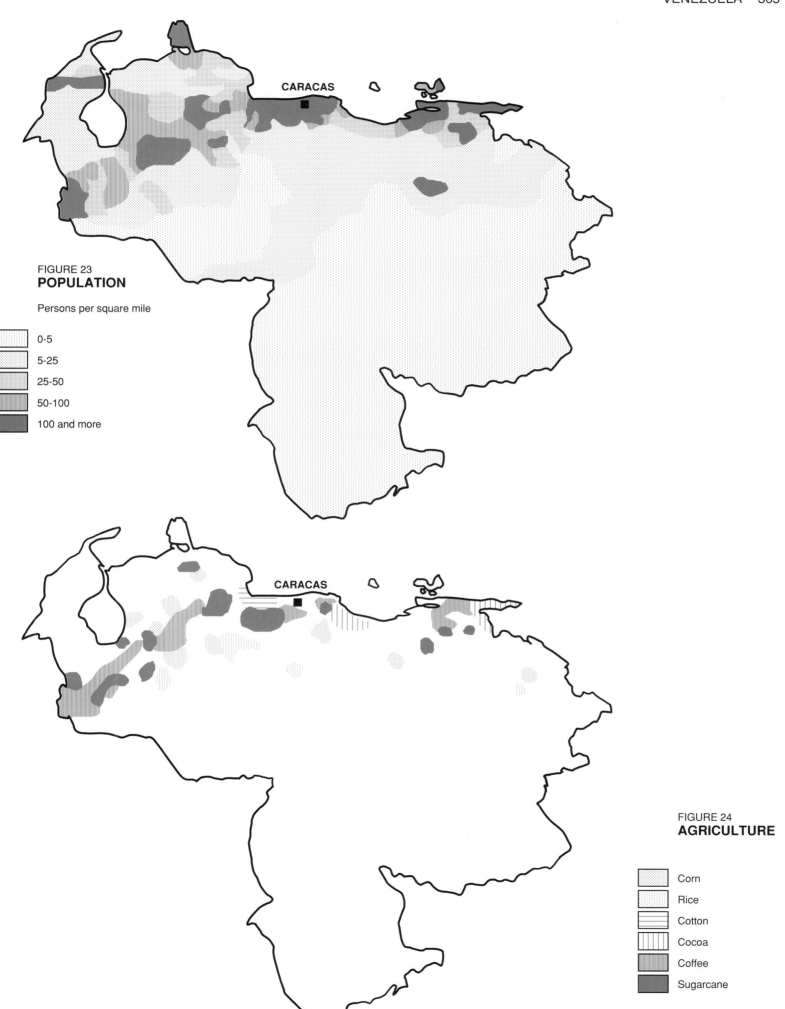

FIGURE 23
POPULATION

Persons per square mile

0-5
5-25
25-50
50-100
100 and more

CARACAS

FIGURE 24
AGRICULTURE

Corn
Rice
Cotton
Cocoa
Coffee
Sugarcane

VIETNAM

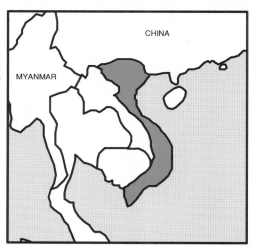

The easternmost country in mainland southeast Asia, Vietnam ranks 60th in land area and 12th in population. One of the great giantkillers in military history, it established its formidable reputation by defeating and humiliating two major Western powers, France and the United States. It has not lost a war since 1945. It followed up its victory over the United States by conquering Cambodia in the early 1980s in a matter of weeks. Unfortunately, it was a Pyrrhic victory which isolated and impoverished the country. Doing worse in peace than in war, its economic performance in the mid-1980s was disastrous. After the Communist Party congress in 1987, Hanoi announced the most extensive leadership changes in four decades and launched a renovation campaign to rescue the country's economy, including measures to encourage private enterprise and strengthen the dong. The reining in of the economy in 1989 stabilized the exchange rate and the gold price and kept inflation down in 1990.

I.M.F.
INFORMATION
NOT
AVAILABLE

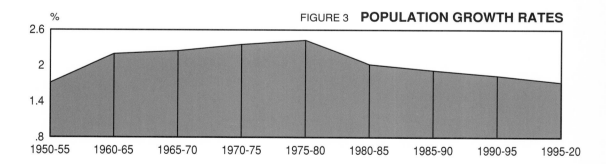

FIGURE 1 **POPULATION GROWTH**

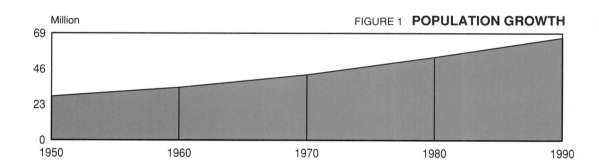

FIGURE 2 **GROSS NATIONAL PRODUCT PER CAPITA**

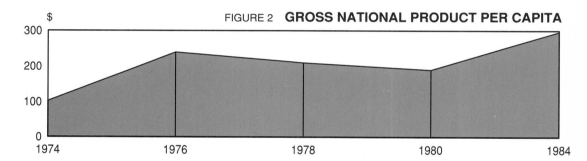

FIGURE 3 **POPULATION GROWTH RATES**

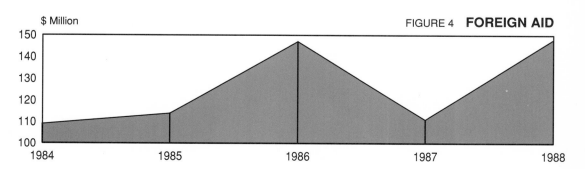

FIGURE 4 **FOREIGN AID**

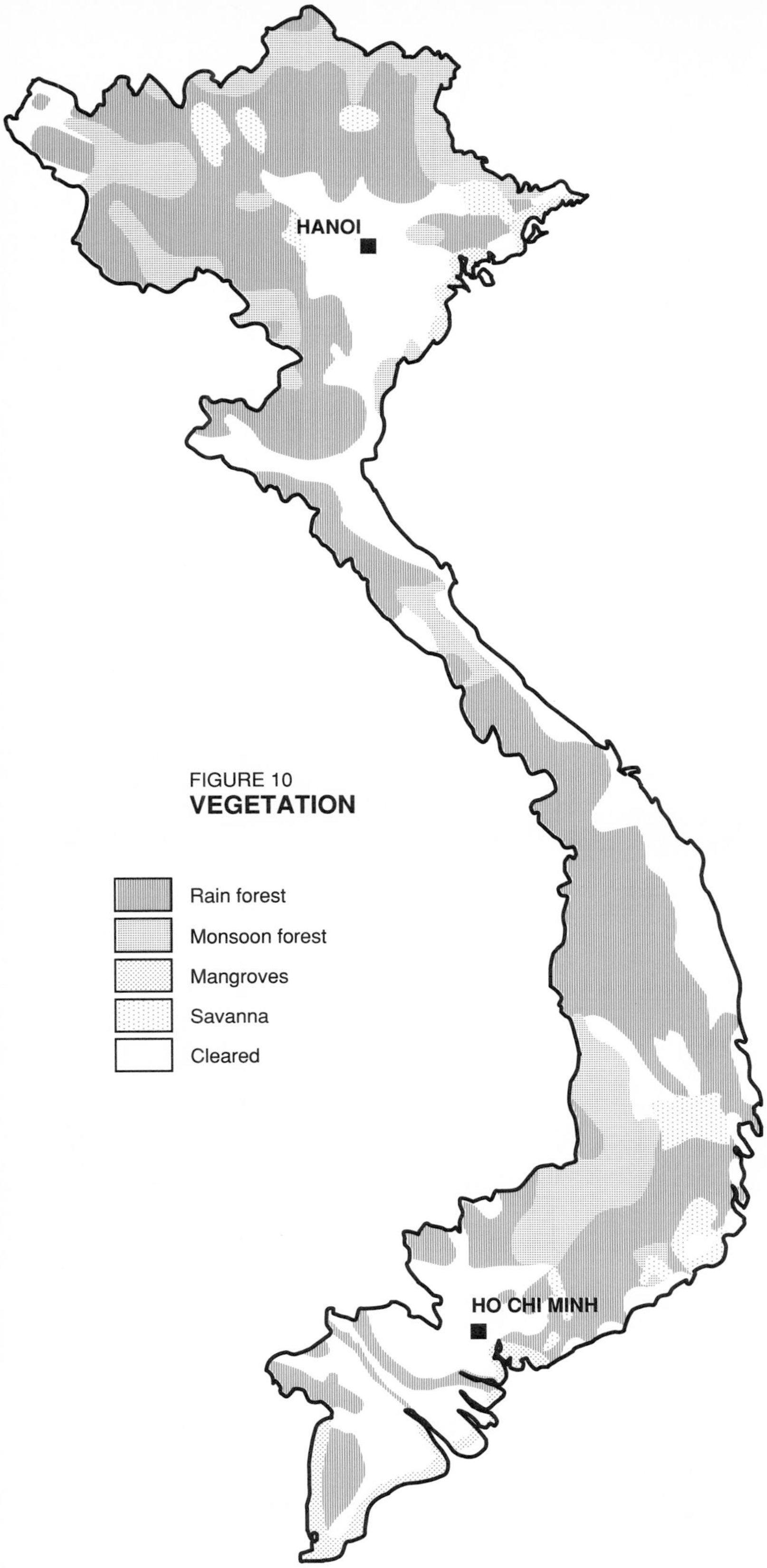

FIGURE 10
VEGETATION

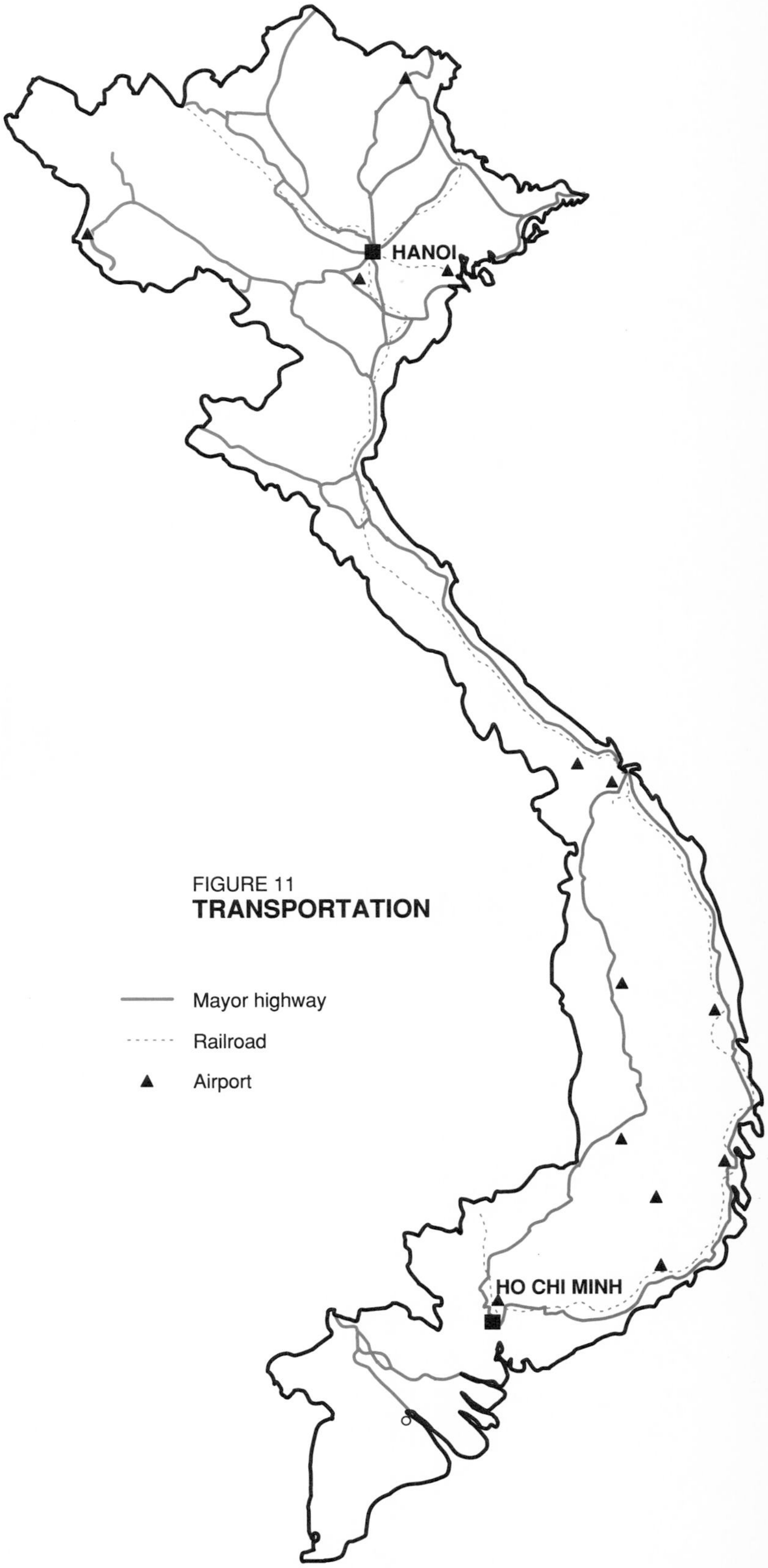

- Rain forest
- Monsoon forest
- Mangroves
- Savanna
- Cleared

HANOI

HO CHI MINH

FIGURE 11
TRANSPORTATION

Mayor highway

Railroad

▲ Airport

HANOI

HO CHI MINH

YEMEN ARAB REPUBLIC*

A country out of the Middle Ages, the Yemen Arab Republic ranked 83rd in land area and 118th in population before unification with the People's Democratic Republic of Yemen in 1990. What is significant about its economy was neither its agriculture nor its manufacturing, but the fact that nearly half the GDP was generated by 1 million Yemenis—half the country's adult male work force—who are working abroad. Remittance from these workers were estimated at over $1.5 billion. In addition to these remittances, the economy was supported by Saudi Arabian subsidies, motivated partly by the political necessity of having a buffer against the Marxist-dominated Southern Yemen. Nearly 90% of the population had no piped water or electricity and the vast majority was illiterate. But for a country that, until the civil war of 1962, was a stranger to modern civilization, it made a remarkable transformation, riding on the coattails of richer Arab neighbors, right into the 20th century.
*Statistics are not yet available for a unified Yemen.

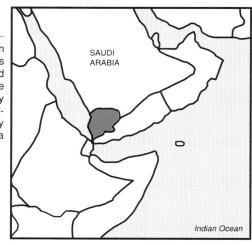

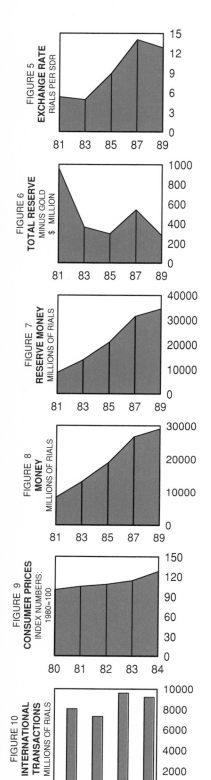

FIGURE 5 EXCHANGE RATE RIALS PER SDR

FIGURE 6 TOTAL RESERVE MINUS GOLD $ MILLION

FIGURE 7 RESERVE MONEY MILLIONS OF RIALS

FIGURE 8 MONEY MILLIONS OF RIALS

FIGURE 9 CONSUMER PRICES INDEX NUMBERS: 1980=100

FIGURE 10 INTERNATIONAL TRANSACTIONS MILLIONS OF RIALS — Exports, Imports

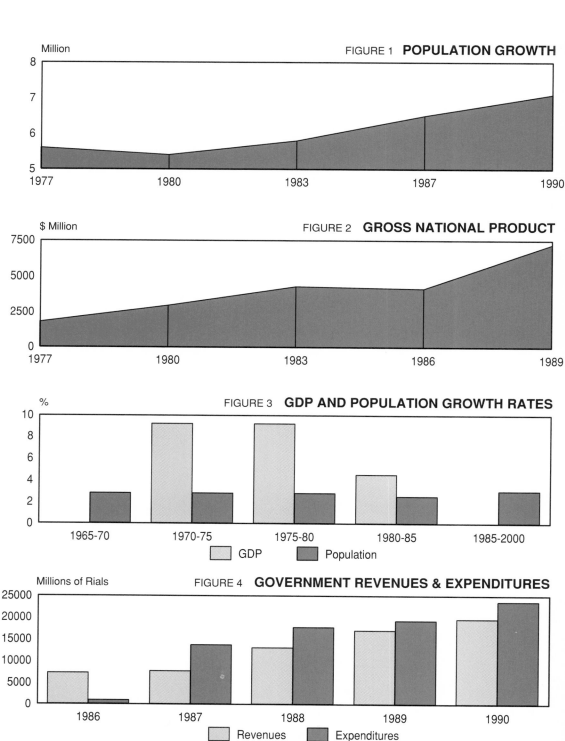

FIGURE 1 **POPULATION GROWTH** (Million)

FIGURE 2 **GROSS NATIONAL PRODUCT** ($ Million)

FIGURE 3 **GDP AND POPULATION GROWTH RATES** (%) — GDP, Population

FIGURE 4 **GOVERNMENT REVENUES & EXPENDITURES** (Millions of Rials) — Revenues, Expenditures

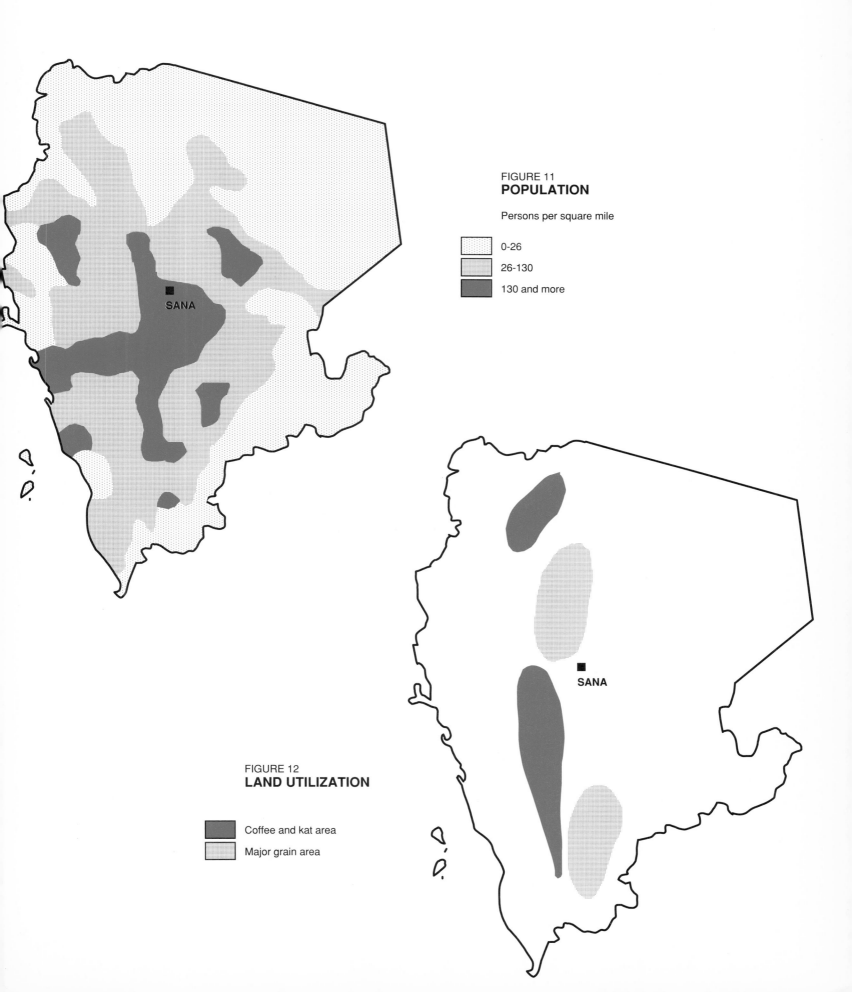

FIGURE 11
POPULATION

Persons per square mile

0-26

26-130

130 and more

SANA

FIGURE 12
LAND UTILIZATION

Coffee and kat area

Major grain area

SANA

PEOPLE'S DEMOCRATIC REPUBLIC OF YEMEN*

Located on the southeastern coast of the Arabian Peninsula, Southern Yemen ranked 59th in land area and 86th in population before unification with the Yemen Arab Republic in 1990. It shared with the other Yemen its status as one of the least developed low-income countries. Once a tranquil British colony noted for its port of Aden with its oil refinery, after independence it became the Cuba of the Middle East. A clear Soviet military presence was established with Socotra Island as a Soviet naval station. Ironically, the country received foreign aid not only from the Soviet bloc but also from Kuwait, UAE, and Iraq, and these subsidies, along with remittances from Yemeni workers abroad (estimated at over $300 million annually), enabled PDRY to maintain a respectable balance of payments and even provide capital for investment.

*Statistics are not yet available for a unified Yemen.

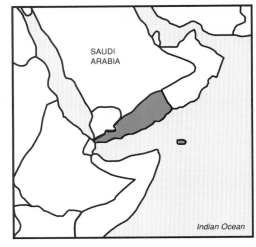

SAUDI ARABIA

Indian Ocean

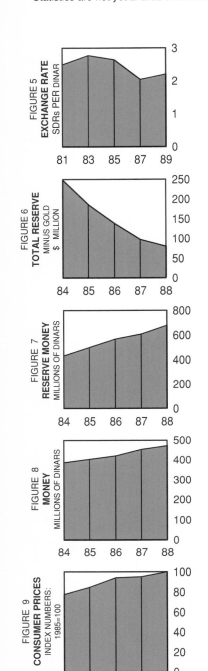

FIGURE 5 **EXCHANGE RATE** SDRs PER DINAR

FIGURE 6 **TOTAL RESERVE** MINUS GOLD $ MILLION

FIGURE 7 **RESERVE MONEY** MILLIONS OF DINARS

FIGURE 8 **MONEY** MILLIONS OF DINARS

FIGURE 9 **CONSUMER PRICES** INDEX NUMBERS: 1985=100

FIGURE 10 **INTERNATIONAL TRANSACTIONS** MILLIONS OF DINARS

☐ Exports ■ Imports

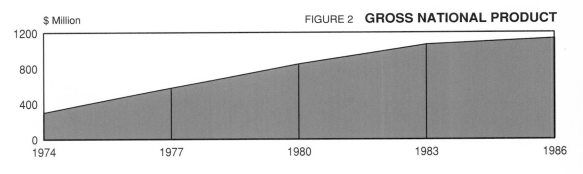

FIGURE 1 **POPULATION GROWTH**

Million

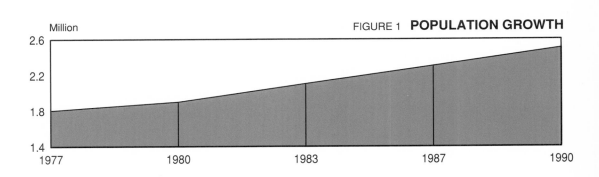

FIGURE 2 **GROSS NATIONAL PRODUCT**

$ Million

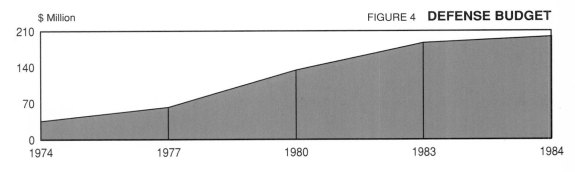

FIGURE 4 **DEFENSE BUDGET**

$ Million

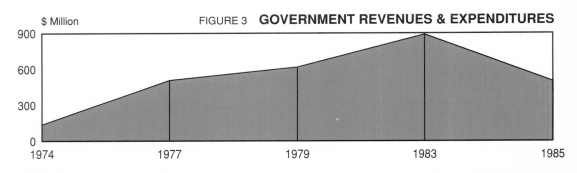

FIGURE 3 **GOVERNMENT REVENUES & EXPENDITURES**

$ Million

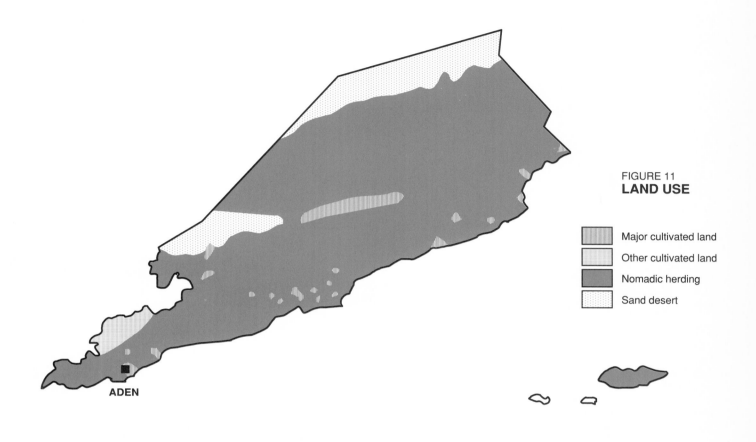

FIGURE 11
LAND USE

Major cultivated land

Other cultivated land

Nomadic herding

Sand desert

ADEN

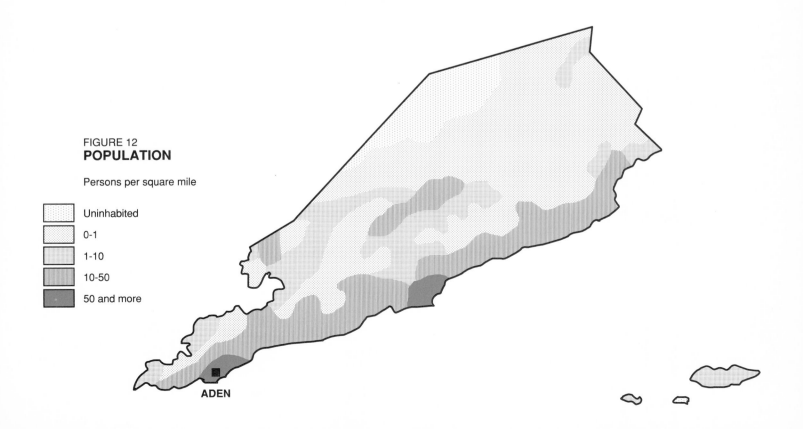

FIGURE 12
POPULATION

Persons per square mile

Uninhabited

0-1

1-10

10-50

50 and more

ADEN

ZAIRE

Located in south central Africa, Zaire is the third largest country in Africa and ranks 11th in land area and 28th in population in the world. Drained by one of the longest rivers in Africa, Zaire ranks sixth in inland navigation and its hydroelectric potential is estimated at 13% of the world total. It is a treasurehouse of minerals, from cobalt and industrial diamonds (in both of which it leads all countries) to copper, tin, and manganese. Yet it has been plagued throughout the first three decades of independence by political and administrative failures that have resulted in a staggering foreign debt, an inflation rate of over 50% and a scandalous inequality of wealth. The crisis reached flash point in the late 1970s and the economy was rescued from imminent collapse by a team of international aid agencies. Zaire entered the 1990s with mixed economic prospects; while mining appeared to be holding its own, the other sectors were collapsing under the weight of rampant corruption and mismanagement.

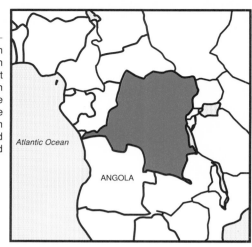

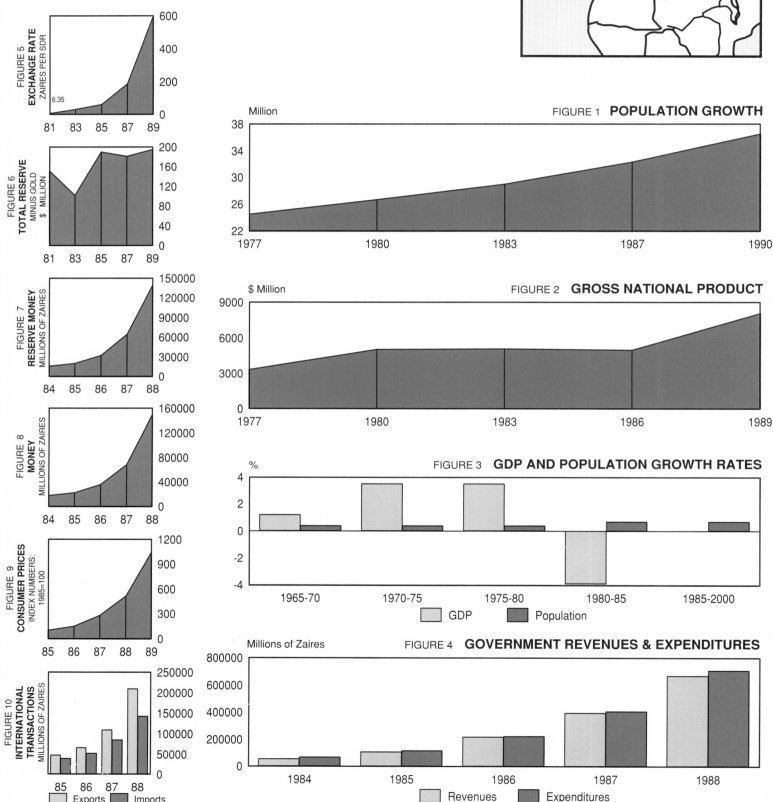

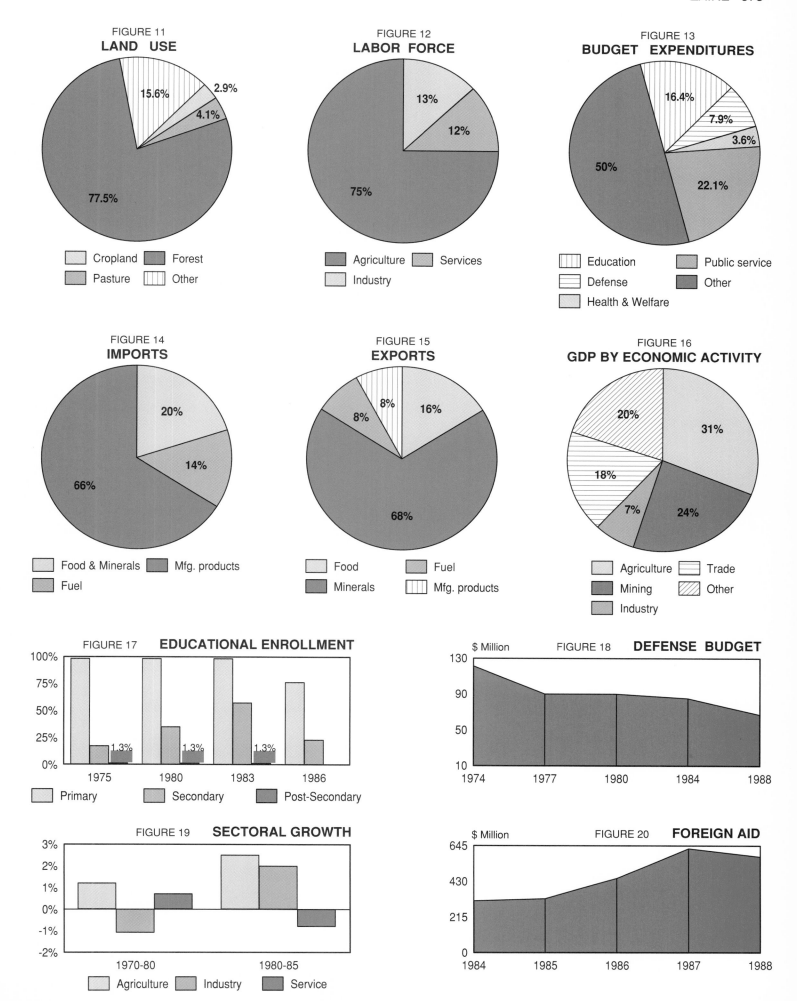

FIGURE 11
LAND USE

- 15.6%
- 2.9%
- 4.1%
- 77.5%

Cropland   Forest
Pasture   Other

FIGURE 12
LABOR FORCE

- 13%
- 12%
- 75%

Agriculture   Services
Industry

FIGURE 13
BUDGET EXPENDITURES

- 16.4%
- 7.9%
- 3.6%
- 50%
- 22.1%

Education   Public service
Defense   Other
Health & Welfare

FIGURE 14
IMPORTS

- 20%
- 14%
- 66%

Food & Minerals   Mfg. products
Fuel

FIGURE 15
EXPORTS

- 8%
- 8%
- 16%
- 68%

Food   Fuel
Minerals   Mfg. products

FIGURE 16
GDP BY ECONOMIC ACTIVITY

- 20%
- 31%
- 18%
- 7%
- 24%

Agriculture   Trade
Mining   Other
Industry

FIGURE 17   **EDUCATIONAL ENROLLMENT**

100%
75%
50%
25%
0%

1.3%   1.3%   1.3%

1975   1980   1983   1986

Primary   Secondary   Post-Secondary

$ Million   FIGURE 18   **DEFENSE BUDGET**

130
90
50
10

1974   1977   1980   1984   1988

FIGURE 19   **SECTORAL GROWTH**

3%
2%
1%
0%
-1%
-2%

1970-80   1980-85

Agriculture   Industry   Service

$ Million   FIGURE 20   **FOREIGN AID**

645
430
215
0

1984   1985   1986   1987   1988

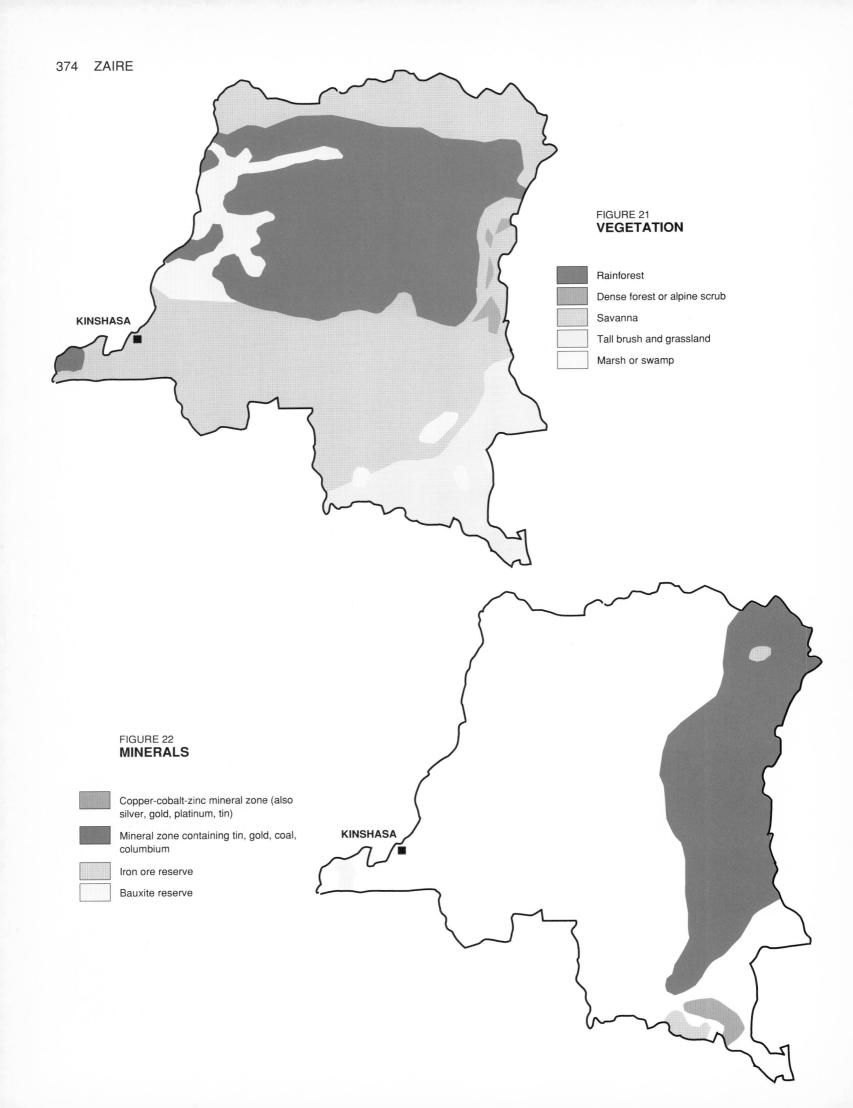

FIGURE 21
VEGETATION

Rainforest
Dense forest or alpine scrub
Savanna
Tall brush and grassland
Marsh or swamp

KINSHASA

FIGURE 22
MINERALS

Copper-cobalt-zinc mineral zone (also silver, gold, platinum, tin)

Mineral zone containing tin, gold, coal, columbium

Iron ore reserve

Bauxite reserve

KINSHASA

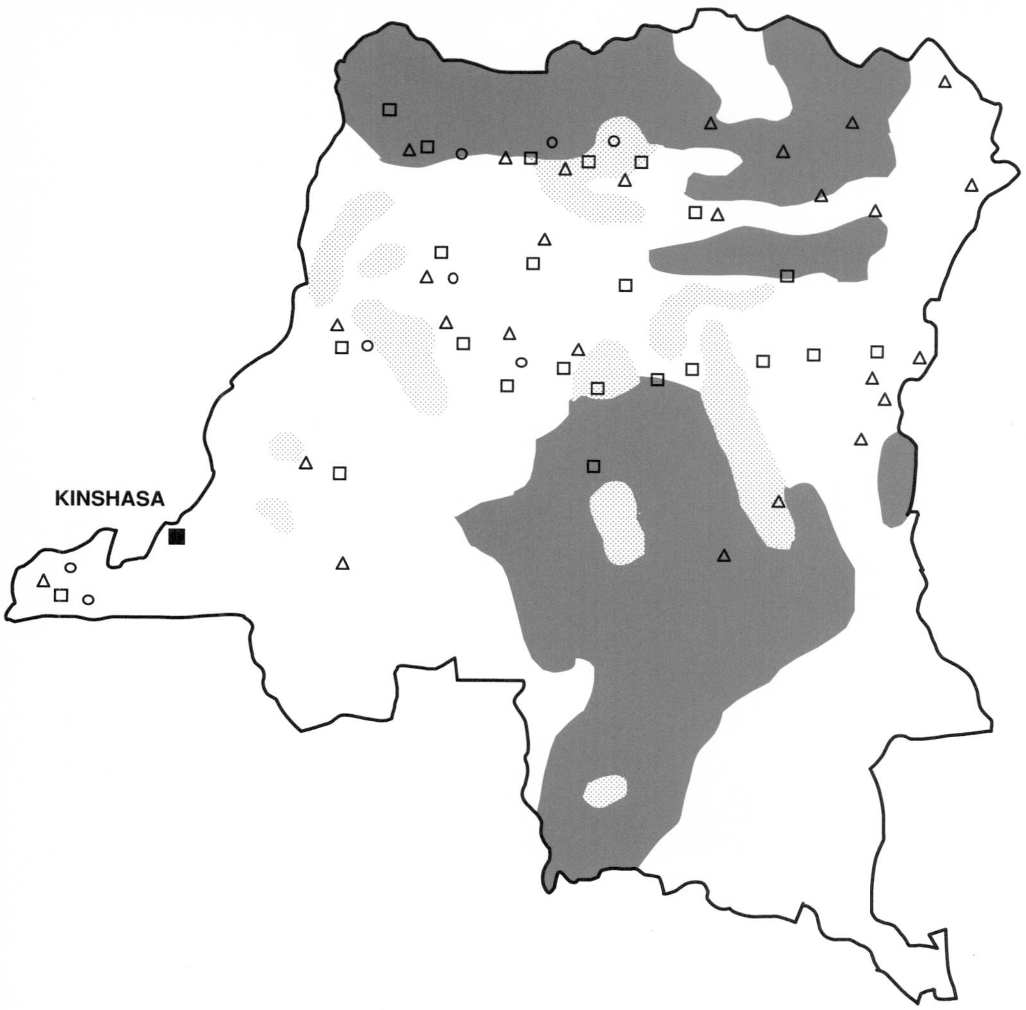

FIGURE 23
AGRICULTURE

Cotton

Rice

△ Coffee

○ Cocoa

□ Rubber

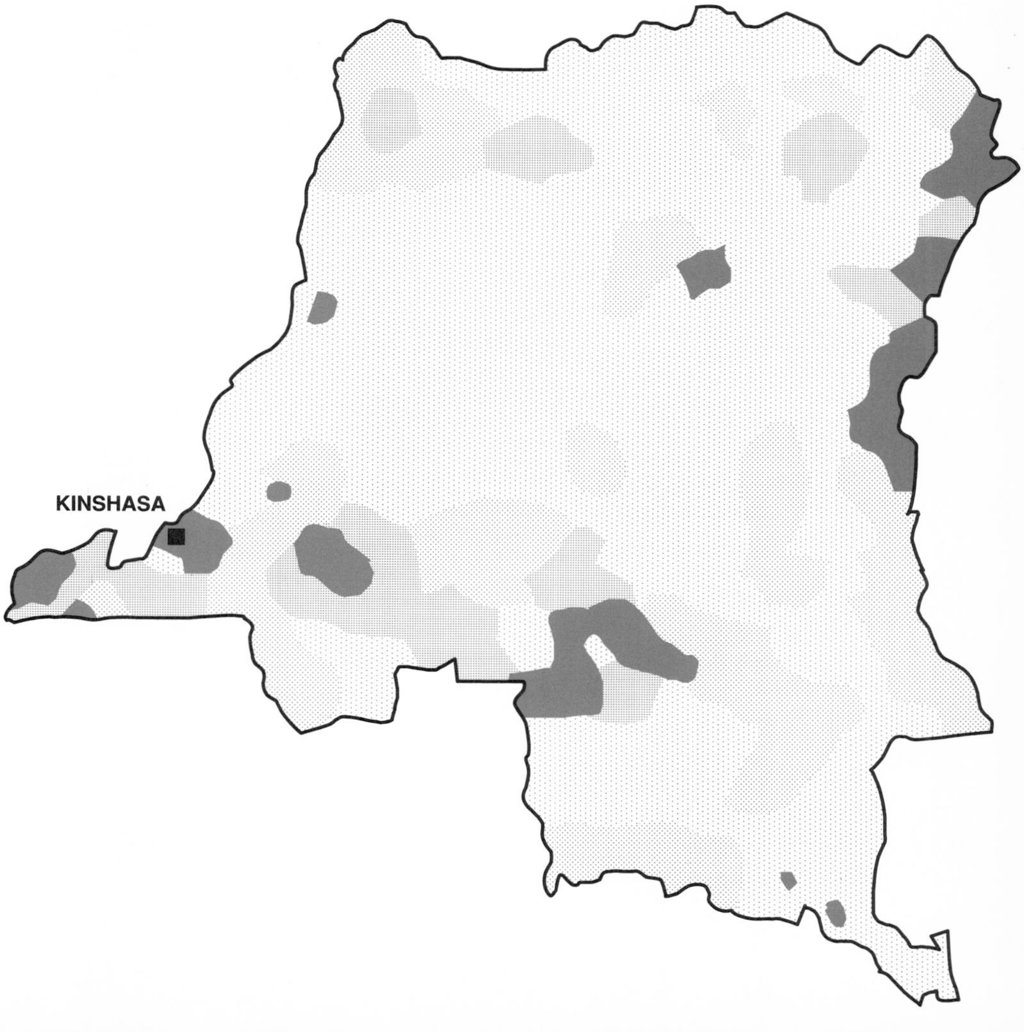

KINSHASA

FIGURE 24
POPULATION

Persons per square mile

0-15

15-35

35-75

75 and more

KINSHASA

ZAMBIA

A landlocked country in central Africa, Zambia ranks 38th in land area and 78th in population. It is considered a lower middle-income country, a relatively high status for African countries, but it owes that label solely to the fact that it is the world's fourth largest copper producer. The country's official ideology is an African variety of socialism based on traditional egalitarianism and communality. The collapse of the world copper market in the mid-1970s reduced the share of copper mining in the Zambian GDP from 45% to 13%. As a result, all sectors declined, unemployment rose by 7.5% and the GDP fell by 4%. The establishment of Zimbabwe and recent surges in world market prices for copper and cobalt have restored some stability to the economy, although by the end of 1989 inflation had reached 122.5%. The government reached an agreement with the IMF and the World Bank in 1990, and President Kaunda forecast a reduction in inflation to 15% by 1993.

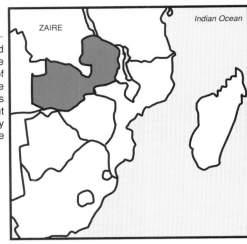

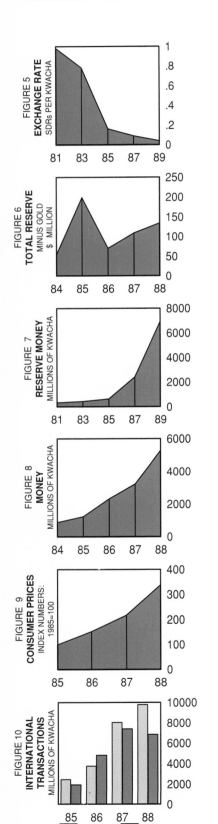

FIGURE 5 EXCHANGE RATE — SDRs PER KWACHA

FIGURE 6 TOTAL RESERVE — MINUS GOLD — $ MILLION

FIGURE 7 RESERVE MONEY — MILLIONS OF KWACHA

FIGURE 8 MONEY — MILLIONS OF KWACHA

FIGURE 9 CONSUMER PRICES — INDEX NUMBERS: 1985=100

FIGURE 10 INTERNATIONAL TRANSACTIONS — MILLIONS OF KWACHA — Exports — Imports

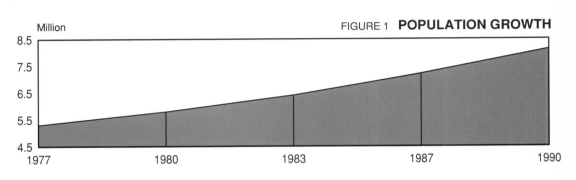

FIGURE 1 **POPULATION GROWTH**

Million

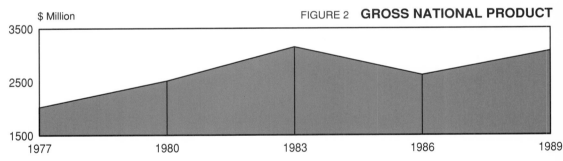

FIGURE 2 **GROSS NATIONAL PRODUCT**

$ Million

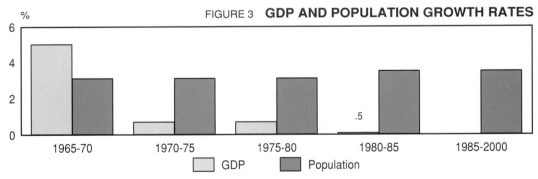

FIGURE 3 **GDP AND POPULATION GROWTH RATES**

%

GDP — Population

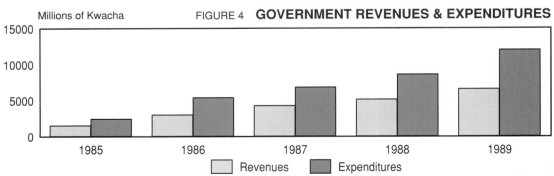

Millions of Kwacha — FIGURE 4 **GOVERNMENT REVENUES & EXPENDITURES**

Revenues — Expenditures

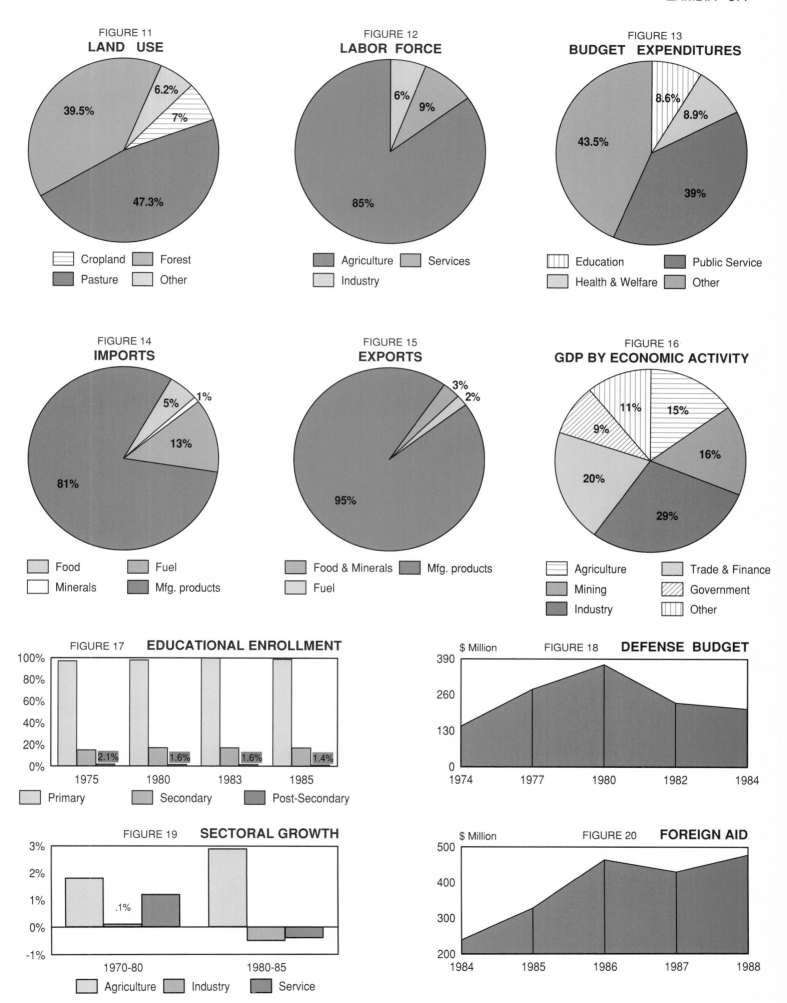

FIGURE 11
LAND USE

6.2%
39.5%
7%
47.3%

Cropland
Forest
Pasture
Other

FIGURE 12
LABOR FORCE

6%
9%
85%

Agriculture
Services
Industry

FIGURE 13
BUDGET EXPENDITURES

8.6%
8.9%
43.5%
39%

Education
Public Service
Health & Welfare
Other

FIGURE 14
IMPORTS

5% 1%
13%
81%

Food
Fuel
Minerals
Mfg. products

FIGURE 15
EXPORTS

3%
2%
95%

Food & Minerals
Mfg. products
Fuel

FIGURE 16
GDP BY ECONOMIC ACTIVITY

11% 15%
9%
20% 16%
29%

Agriculture
Trade & Finance
Mining
Government
Industry
Other

FIGURE 17 **EDUCATIONAL ENROLLMENT**

100%
80%
60%
40%
20%
2.1%   1.6%   1.6%   1.4%
0%
1975   1980   1983   1985

Primary
Secondary
Post-Secondary

FIGURE 18 **DEFENSE BUDGET**

$ Million
390
260
130
0
1974   1977   1980   1982   1984

FIGURE 19 **SECTORAL GROWTH**

3%
2%
1%
.1%
0%
-1%
1970-80   1980-85

Agriculture
Industry
Service

FIGURE 20 **FOREIGN AID**

$ Million
500
400
300
200
1984   1985   1986   1987   1988

ZIMBABWE

Zimbabwe ranks 55th in land area and 67th in population. Its economy, while already well established through the years of white rule, had only a few years to adjust to the responsibilities and opportunities of freedom after independence in 1980. The Robert Mugabe government began on a moderate note—surprising those who had expected his performance to match his Marxist rhetoric—but was soon prodded by extremists as well as opposition from the Joshua Nkomo group into more hardline positions. The funds needed for reconstruction and social reform, including land redistribution, estimated at $2 billion, can only be forthcoming from Western nations if the government forswears its professions of socialism and nationalization. Given political moderation and stability, Zimbabwe's economic prognosis is unusually bright. By African standards, it already has a well-developed infrastructure and a strong agricultural and industrial base, painfully built up during the white rule.

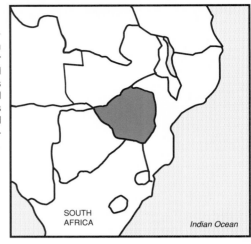

SOUTH AFRICA

Indian Ocean

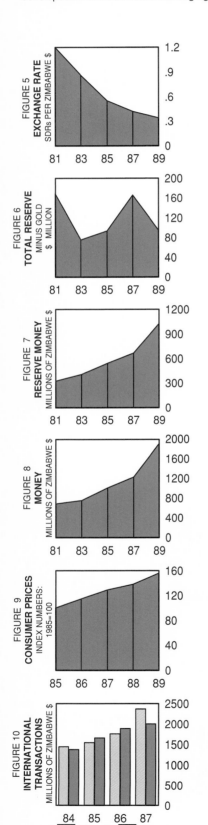

FIGURE 5 **EXCHANGE RATE** SDRs PER ZIMBABWE $

FIGURE 6 **TOTAL RESERVE** MINUS GOLD $ MILLION

FIGURE 7 **RESERVE MONEY** MILLIONS OF ZIMBABWE $

FIGURE 8 **MONEY** MILLIONS OF ZIMBABWE $

FIGURE 9 **CONSUMER PRICES** INDEX NUMBERS: 1985=100

FIGURE 10 **INTERNATIONAL TRANSACTIONS** MILLIONS OF ZIMBABWE $

Exports   Imports

FIGURE 1 **POPULATION GROWTH**

Million

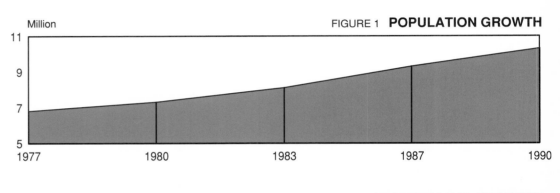

FIGURE 2 **GROSS NATIONAL PRODUCT**

$ Million

FIGURE 3 **GDP AND POPULATION GROWTH RATES**

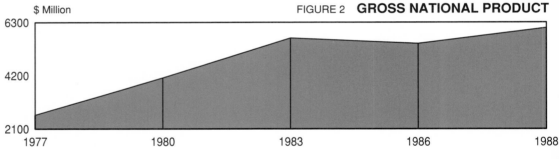

%

GDP   Population

FIGURE 4 **GOVERNMENT REVENUES & EXPENDITURES**

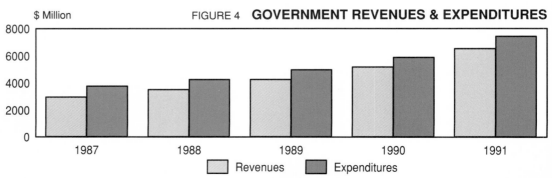

$ Million

Revenues   Expenditures

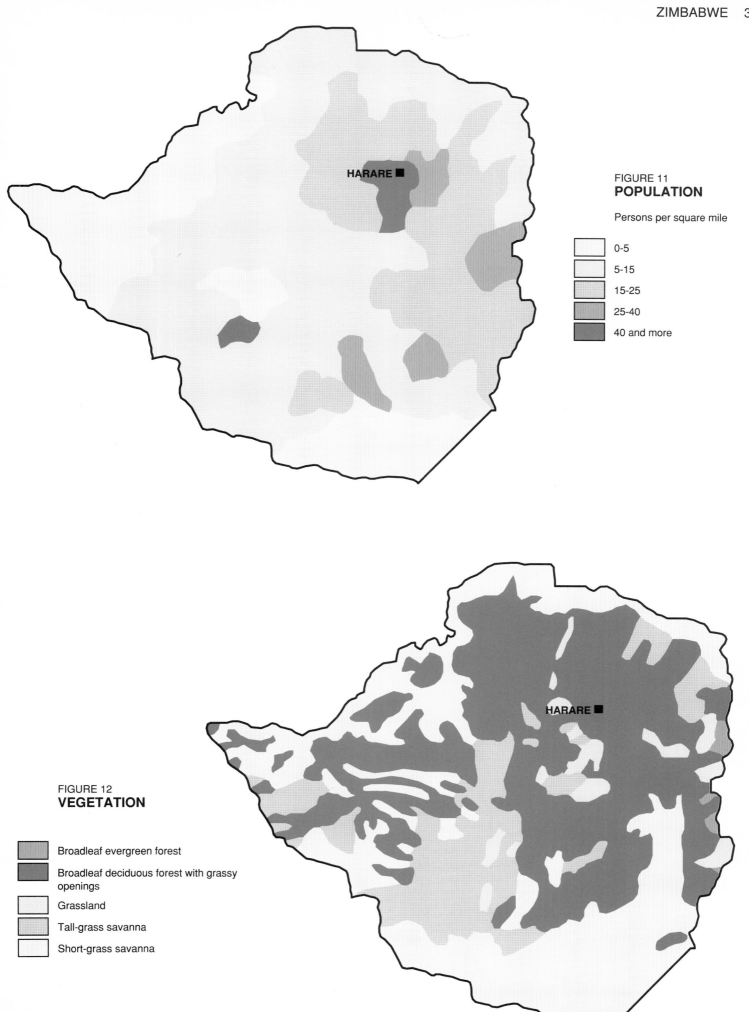

FIGURE 11
POPULATION

Persons per square mile

HARARE ■

- 0-5
- 5-15
- 15-25
- 25-40
- 40 and more

FIGURE 12
VEGETATION

- Broadleaf evergreen forest
- Broadleaf deciduous forest with grassy openings
- Grassland
- Tall-grass savanna
- Short-grass savanna

HARARE ■

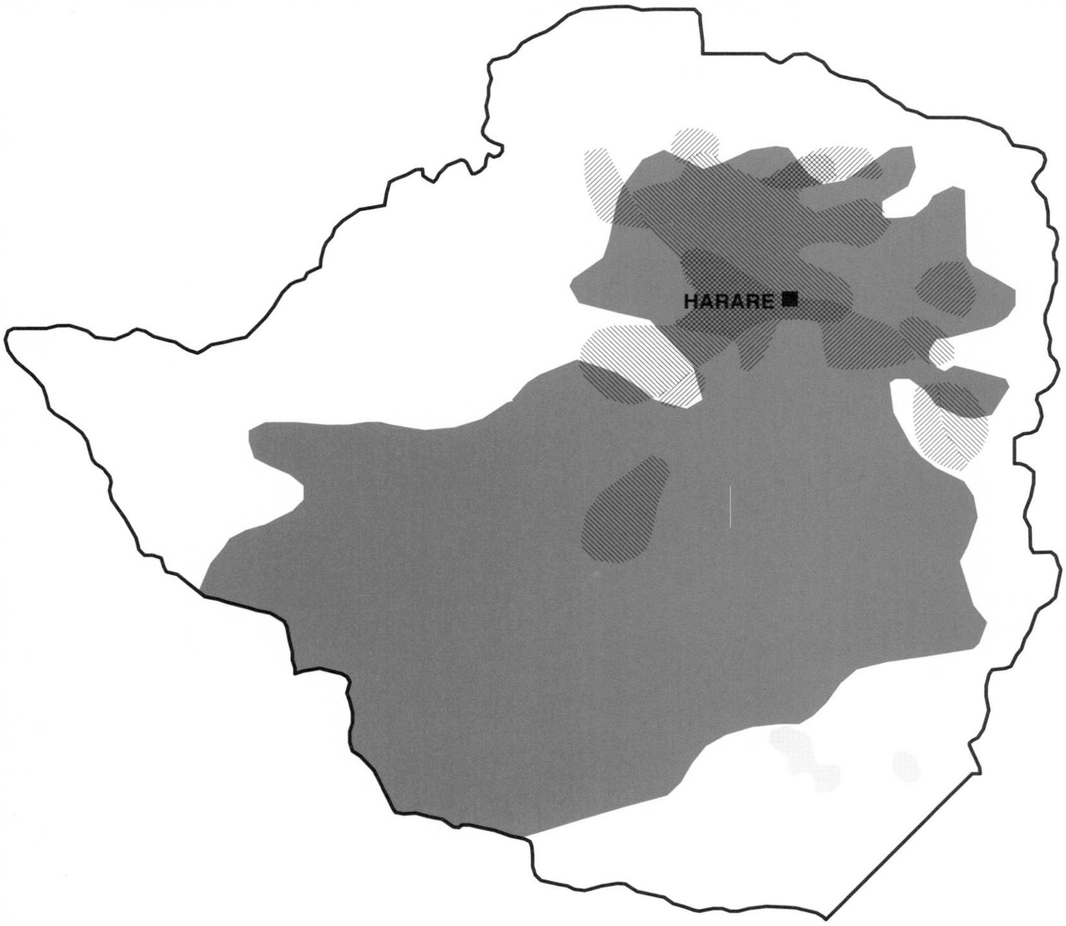

FIGURE 13
AGRICULTURE

Corn
Tobacco
Cattle
Sugarcane

FIGURE 14
MINING

Goldfield
Coalfield
Great Dyke

INDEX

Boldface numbers indicate chapter or national profiles.

Aberdare National Park 232
Abidjan 220–221
Accra 184–185
Addis Ababa 176–177
Aden 370–371
Afghanistan, Republic of **104–107**, 296
Africa—*See also specific country*
  agriculture 40, 47–49
  debt 32, 33–35
  defense 77–78
  economy 23–24
  energy 57, 61
  industry 56
  media and communication 98–99
  population of 11
Age 16, 20—*See also specific country*
Agriculture **39–53**—*See also specific country and crop*
Aid—*See Foreign aid*
Air Force, U.S. 229
Airports and Airfields—*See specific country*
Akan 184, 221
Alexandria 168–169
Algeria, Democratic and Popular Republic of 33, **108–111**
Algiers 110–111
Allende Gossens, Salvador 144
Altitude 201
Aluminum and Alumina 76, 136
Amerindian 195
Amin Dada, Maj. Gen. Idi 340, 356
Amman 228–229
Anchovies 304
Andean Common Market 162
Andean Foreign Investment Code 162
Angola, People's Republic of **112–113**
Animals 51
Animist-Christian 143
Ankara 354–355
Antananarivo 254–255
Antimony 126
Aquino, Corazon 306
Arab and Arabic 250, 274
Arabian Peninsula 310, 370
Argentina (Argentine Republic) 33, **114–117**
Armaments 77–78, 81
Armed Forces 78
Arms—*See Armaments*
Army, U.S. 229
Artibonite Plain 197
Arusha Declaration 340
Asia—*See also specific country*
  agriculture 40, 47–49
  debt 32, 33–35
  defense 77–78
  economy 23
  energy 57, 61
  industry 56
  media and communication 98–99
  population 11
Assad, Hafez al- 336
Austroasiatic 346

Baghdad 216–217
Bahamas, Commonwealth of the 322
Bakota 180
Balance of Trade—*See specific country*
Bali 208
Balinese-Sasak 208

Baluchis 296
Bananas
  Ecuador 164
  Guatemala 186
  Honduras 198
  Jamaica 224
  Panama 302
  Somalia 326
Banda, Dr. Hastings Kamuzu 256
Bangkok 346–347
Bangladesh, People's Republic of 11, 48, **118–121**, 296
Banks and Banking 34, 242
Bantu 233, 343, 359
Bardera 324
Barley 212, 350
Bases, Military 229, 312
Bauxite 70, 76
  Burkina Faso 132
  Guinea 190
  Guyana 192
  Jamaica 222, 225
  Sierra Leone 318
  Venezuela 362
  Zaire 374
Beans 270
Beirut 242–243
Belgium, Kingdom of 6
Benghazi 250–251
Benin, People's Republic of **122–125**
Berber 250, 274
Bhutto, Benazir 296
Birth Rates 12
Bismuth 126
Bizerte Plain 351
Black Mountains 197
Blacks 151, 195
Bogota 150–151
Bolivia, Republic of **126–127**
Bolovens Plateau 241
Bombay 204–205
Books 98
Brahmaputra River 118
Brasilia 130–131
Brazil, Federative Republic of 11, 33, **128–131**
Brazzaville 152
Brush—*See specific country*
Buddhists and Buddhism 331, 344
Budget Expenditures—*See specific country*
Buenos Aires 116–117
Buman 281
Burkina Faso (formerly Upper Volta) **132–133**
Burma—*See Myanmar*
Business—*See Industry*

Cairo 168–169
Calcutta 204–205
Calories 47
Cambodia, State of **134–135**, 366
Cameroon, Republic of **136–139**
Cammon Plateau 241
Canals 169
Canal Zone—*See Panama Canal Zone*
Caracas 364–365
Cashews 342
Casmance 317
Cassava 50
Castes 205
Cattle—*See Livestock*
Cayemites 197
Celebes 208
Central America 47, 49, 57—*See also Latin America*
Cereal 47–48, 111, 228—*See also specific grain*
Chad **140–143**, 332

Chahar Aimak 106
Chewa 259
Children 16, 96
Chile, Republic of 33, **144–147**
China, People's Republic of 11, 48, 77, 234
China, Republic of (Taiwan) 236
Chinese 263
Christians and Christianity 331
Cities 21–22
Citrus Fruit 111, 224
Climate 142
Cline, Ray 292
Cloves 76, 252
Coal 60–61
  Colombia 148
  Iran 212
  Mexico 271
  Niger 290
  Pakistan 299
  South Korea 239
  Turkey 354
  Zaire 374
  Zimbabwe 380
Cobalt 372, 374, 376
Cocoa 76
  Brazil 131
  Cameroon 136, 139
  Colombia 148
  Ecuador 164
  Ghana 182, 185
  Ivory Coast 218, 220
  Jamaica 224
  Nigeria 294
  Venezuela 365
  Zaire 375
Coconut Palm 139
Coconuts 224, 262, 328, 330
Coffee 76
  Brazil 131
  Cameroon 136, 139
  Colombia 148, 151
  Cuba 158
  Ecuador 164
  El Salvador 173
  Ethiopia 176
  Guatemala 186, 188
  Honduras 198
  Indonesia 209
  Ivory Coast 218, 220
  Jamaica 224
  Madagascar 252, 254
  Nicaragua 289
  North Yemen 369
  Panama 302
  Tanzania 342
  Uganda 356, 358
  Venezuela 365
  Zaire 375
Colombia, Republic of **148–151**
Colombo 330–331
Colon 299
Columbium 374
Commodities 76—*See also specific commodity*
Communications **98–102**—*See also specific country*
Communism 147, 156, 366—*See also Marxism*
Conakry 191
Congo, People's Republic of the **152–153**
Construction—*See specific country*
Consumer Prices 24—*See also specific country*
Consumption 57
Contraceptives 17
Copper 70, 76
  Angola 112
  Chile 147

Peru 304
Zaire 372, 374
Zambia 376
Copra 76, 209
Corn 50–51
  Argentina 117
  Ecuador 164
  Indonesia 209
  Mexico 270
  Venezuela 365
  Zimbabwe 380
Costa Rica, Republic of **154–155**
Cotton
  Argentina 117
  Benin 124
  Brazil 131
  Cameroon 136, 139
  Colombia 151
  Ecuador 164
  Egypt 166
  El Salvador 173
  Guatemala 188
  Malawi 259
  Nicaragua 289
  Niger 291
  Nigeria 294
  Somalia 326
  Sudan 332, 334
  Tanzania 342
  Turkey 354
  Uganda 356, 358
  Venezuela 365
  Zaire 375
Council For Mutual Economic Assistance (Comecon) 156
Cropland—*See Agriculture*
Crops 40–41, 46–47, 49—*See also specific country and crop*
Cuba, Republic of 38, 112, **156–159**, 370
Current Account Balance 71

DAC—*See Development Assistance Committee*
Dakar 316–317
Damascus 338–339
Dams and Reservoirs 169
Dar es Salaam 342–343
Darod 326
Dates 212
Death Rates—*See Mortality Rates*
Debt **31–38**—*See also specific country*
Defense **77–82**—*See also specific country*
Deforestation 68
Deserts and Desertification 69—*See also specific country*
Developing Countries—*See Third World*
Development Assistance Committee (DAC) 33
Dhaka 120–121
Diamonds 76
  Angola 112
  Ghana 185
  Sierra Leone 318, 321
  Zaire 372
Diet 51
Digil 326
Doe, Gen. Samuel K. 244
Dominican Republic **160–161**
Dos Santos, Jose Eduardo 112
Drought 264, 290, 324
Drugs, Illegal 148, 299
Duvalier, Jean-Claude 196
Dyola 316
Earthquakes 286
Eastern Europe—*See also specific country*
  agriculture 47
  debt 33
  population 11

East Indians 195
EC—*See European Community*
Economy and Econometrics
22–30—*See also specific country*
Ecuador, Republic of **162–165**
Edo 294
Education **83–86**—*See also specific country*
Egypt, Arab Republic of 11, **166–169**
Electricity 59
Electronics 322
El Salvador, Republic of **170–173**
Emeralds 148
Energy **57–61**—*See also specific country*
English Language 8, 136
Environment **66–70**—*See also specific country*
Eritrea 174, 332
Eshira 180
Ethiopia, People's Democratic Republic of **174–177**, 324
Ethiopian Orthodox Church 177
Ethnic Groups—*See specific country*
Ethnolinguistic Groups 106, 208, 241, 274, 281
Euphrates River 214, 216–217
Europe—*See also specific country*
  agriculture 47, 49
  defense 77–78
  media and communication 98–99
European Community (EC) 33
Ewe 184
Exchange Rates—*See specific country*
Exports 23, 39, 45, 72–75, 78—*See also specific country*

Family Planning 15, 17
Fang 180
Far East—*See Asia*
Farming—*See Agriculture*
Ferlo 317
Fertility Rates 19
Fertilizer 49
Films 99
Finance—*See specific country*
Firetone Tire & Rubber Co. 244
Fish and Fishing Industry 40–41, 49
  Benin 124
  Mexico 270
  Panama 302
  Peru 304
  Thailand 347
Food **39–53**—*See also specific country*
Foreign Aid 35, 37–38, 44—*See also specific country*
Foreign Deposit 36
Foreign Exchange Reserves—*See specific country*
Forests—*See specific country*
Fossil Fuel 60—*See also specific kind*
France (French Republic)
  and Algeria 108
  and Benin 122
  and Burkina 132
  and Chad 140
  as colonial power 6
  as foreign deposit source 36
  and Mauritius 266
  and Morocco 272
  and Niger 290
  population of 11
  and Senegal 314
  and Vietnam 366
Freetown 320–321
French Language 136, 196
Fruits 147, 228—*See also specific fruit*
Fuels—*See specific kind*

Fulani 316

Ga-Adangbe 184
Gabon (Gabonese Republic) **178–181**
Game Reserves—*See Wildlife Reserves*
Ganges River 204–205
Gas, Natural 60–61
  Afghanistan 104
  Algeria 108
  Egypt 168
  Iran 212
  Malaysia 262
  Mexico 271
  Pakistan 299
  Saudi Arabia 310
  Tunisia 350
  Turkey 354
Gatun Lake 303
Georgetown 194–195
Germany, Federal Republic of (West) 6, 11, 36, 73
Ghana, Republic of **182–185**
GNP—*See Gross National Product*
Gold 132, 374, 380
Gonave Island 197
Goods and Services—*See Service Industries*
Government Expenditures—*See specific country*
Grain 176, 350, 369—*See also specific kind*
Grapes 228
Grassland—*See Savanna*
Grazing—*See Livestock*
Great Britain & Northern Ireland, United Kingdom of (UK)—*See also specific country*
  as colonial power 6
  as economic comparison 23–25
  as foreign deposit source 36
  and Ghana 182
  and Guyana 192
  as investment source 36
  and Kenya 230
  and Mauritius 266
  population of 11, 23–25, 36
Gross Domestic Product (GDP) 23–24, 39, 43, 54, 85—*See also specific country*
Gross National Product (GNP) 23, 26–28, 32—*See also specific country*
Ground Nuts 76, 139
Growth Rates 18, 22–23, 28—*See also specific country*
Guatemala, Republic of **186–189**
Guatemala City 188–189
Guinea, Republic of **190–191**
Gum Arabic 332, 334
Gurkha Troops 282
Guyana, Cooperative Republic of **192–195**

Haiti, Republic of **196–197**
Hamitic 233, 343
Hanoi 366–367
Harare 379–380
Harbors and Ports—*See specific country*
Hausa and Fulani 294
Havana 158–159
Hawiya 326
Hazara 106
Health **87–97**—*See also specific country*
Henequen 158
Herding—*See Livestock*
Hindus and Hinduism 282, 331
Ho Chi Minh City 367
Homesteading 335
Honduras, Republic of **198–201**

Hong Kong (British colony) 36, 236
Hospital Beds 92
Hotte Mountains 197
Houphouet-Boigny, Felix 218
Hydroelectric Power 324, 372

Ibo 294
IMF—*See International Monetary Fund*
Imjin River Basin 239
Immigration 14
Immunization 91
Imperial Group 256
Imports 23, 45, 57, 72, 74, 77–78—*See also specific country*
Income 25—*See also specific country*
India, Republic of 11, 48, **202–205**, 266, 282, 296
Indian 263, 282
Indian Ocean 328
Indic 298
Indo-Nepalese 285
Indonesia, Republic of 11, 33, 36, 48, **206–209**
Industry **54–56**—*See also specific country*
Infant Mortality 95
Inflation 30
Insurance 242
International Bank for Reconstruction and Development—*See World Bank*
International Monetary Fund (IMF) 34
Investment 35—*See also specific country*
Iran, Islamic Republic of 11, **210–213**, 214
Iranian 298
Iraq, Republic of 210, **214–217**, 336, 370
Iron 70, 76
  Afghanistan 104
  Angola 112
  Chile 147
  Gabon 178, 181
  Ivory Coast 220
  Liberia 244, 246
  Mauritania 264
  Sierra Leone 318
  Venezuela 362
Irrawaddy River 280–281
Irrigation 49, 107, 275
Ishaak 326
Islam—*See Muslims*
Islamabad 298–299
Israel, State of 166, 226
Istanbul 354–355
Italy 6, 11
Ivory Coast, Republic of the **218–221**
Izabal, Lake 188–189

Jakarta 208–209
Jamaica **222–225**
Japan 11, 36, 73, 344
Java 206
Javanese 208
Jordan, Hashemite Kingdom of **226–229**
Juba River 324
Jurong Industrial Estate 323

Kabul 106–107
Kainji Lake 295
Kalimantan 208
Kampala 358–359
Kampuchea—*See Cambodia*
Karachi 298–299
Karen 281
Kat 369
Katmandu 284–285

Kaunda, Kenneth 376
Kenya, Republic of **230–233**
Kerekou, Mathieu 122
Khartoum 334–335
Khmer 135
Khmer Loeu 135
Kim Il Sung 234
Kingston 224–225
Kinshasa 374–375
Kip (Laotian monetary unit) 240
Korea, Democratic People's Republic of (North Korea) **234–235**
Korea, Republic of (South Korea) 33, **236–239**
Krou 221
Kuala Lumpur 262–263
Kuwait, State of 370
Kyoga, Lake 359

Labor **62–65**—*See also specific country*
Lagoon 221
Lagos 294–295
Lakes—*See key word*
Land Use 40, 46—*See also specific country*
Languages 8, 136, 196
Lao 135
Laos (Lao People's Democratic Republic) **240–241**
Latin America—*See also specific country*
  agriculture 40, 47–49
  debt 32, 35
  defense 77–78
  economy 23
  energy 57, 61
  industry 56
  media and communication 98–99
  population of 11
Lead 132, 304
Lebanon, Republic of, **242–243**, 336
Liberia, Second Republic of **244–247**
Libreville 180–181
Libya (Socialist People's Libyan Arab Jamahiriya) 140, **248–251**
Life Expectancy 94
Lifestyle 110
Lilongwe 258–259
Linguistic Groups—*See specific country*
Literacy 83–84
Livestock 40, 48, 76
  Argentina 114
  Chile 147
  Ecuador 164
  Jamaica 224
  Libya 251
  Morocco 275
  Niger 290–291
  Panama 302
  Somalia 326
  Sudan 334
  Syria 338
  Tanzania 342
  Tunisia 350
  Turkey 355
  Uruguay 360
  Zimbabwe 380
Lomwe 259
Lonrho PLC 256
Luanda 113
Lumber 131, 136, 181, 218, 260

Machinery—*See specific country*
Madagascar, Democratic Republic of **252–255**
Maghrebian Littoral 108, 348
Maize—*See Corn*
Majardeh Valley 351

Malaria 266
Malawi, Republic of **256–259**
Malayo-Polynesian 135
Malays 208, 263, 330, 346
Malaysia 36, **260–263**
Malinke 316
Managua 286, 288–289
Mande (Lobi) 221
Manganese 132, 147, 372
Mangrove—*See specific country*
Manila 308–309
Manufacturing—*See Industry*
Maputo 277
Marasbit National Park 232
Marcos, Ferdinand Edralin 306
Marshes—*See Swamps*
Marxism 122, 152, 240, 276
Mateaux Mountains 197
Mauritania, Islamic Republic of **264–265**
Mauritius **266–267**
Meadows and Pastures—*See specific country*
Meat 41
Mecca 312–313
Media **98–102**—*See also specific country*
Meghna River 118
Mekong River 241
Mekong Valley 134
Meru National Park 232
Mexico (United Mexican States) 11, 33, 36, **268–271**
Mexico City 270–271
Middle East—*See also specific country*
 agriculture 40, 47–49
 debt 32–35
 defense 77–78
 economy 23
 energy 61
 industry 56
 media and communication 98–99
Migrant Labor 64
Military Expenditures 77, 79
Millet 50–51, 143, 291
Minangkabau 208
Minerals and Mineral Deposits 70—*See also specific country*
Mines and Mining—*See specific country*
Mogadishu 326–327
Moi, Daniel arap 230
Molybdenum 304
Money Supply—*See specific country*
Mon-Khmer 241
Monrovia 246–247
Montevideo 361
Moors 330
Morocco, Kingdom of **272–275**
Mortality Rates 12, 95–97, 290
Mt. Elgon National Park 232
Mt. Kenya National Park 232
Mozambique, People's Republic of **276–277**
Mugabe, Robert 378
Muslims 143, 177, 331
Myanmar, Union of (formerly Burma) **278–281**

Nairobi 232–233
Naktong River Basin 239
Narcotics—*See Drugs, Illegal*
National Guard 312
National Parks 66, 232—*See also specific park*
NATO—*See North Atlantic Treaty Organization*
Natural Gas—*See Gas, Natural*
Navy, U.S. 229
N'djamena 142–143

Near East—*See Middle East*
Nepal, Kingdom of **282–285**
Netherlands, Kingdom of the 6, 36
Neto, Agostino 112
New Delhi 204–205
Ne Win 278
Newspapers 98
Newsprint 99
Ngoni 259
Niamey 291
Nicaragua, Lake 288–289
Nicaragua, Republic of **286–289**
Nickel 132, 156–157
Niger, Republic of **290–291**
Nigeria, Federal Republic of 11, 33, **292–295**
Nile River 166, 168–169
Nilo-Hamitic 233, 343, 359
Nilotic 233, 343, 359
Nitrates 49, 147
Nkomo, Joshua 378
Nkrumah, Kwame 182
Nomads and Nomadic Life 110–111, 176, 335, 338, 371
Noriega, Gen. Manuel Antonio 300
North America—*See also specific country*
 agriculture 47, 49
 defense 78
 energy 57
 media and communication 98–99
North Atlantic Treaty Organization (NATO) 77, 80–81
North Yemen—*See Yemen Arab Republic*
Nyerere, Julius 340

OCA—*See Official Commitments to Agriculture*
Oceania—*See also specific country*
 agriculture 47, 49
 debt 35
 defense 77–78
 energy 57, 61
 media and communication 98–99
Oceans and Seas 309
ODA—*See Overseas Development Assistance*
OECD—*See Organization of Economic Cooperation and Development*
Official Commitments to Agriculture (OCA) 40
Ogaden Region 324
Oil and Fats—*See Palm Oil*
Oil and Oilfields—*See Petroleum*
Oilseed Crops 176
Olives 111, 228, 350, 354
Omiene 180
OPEC—*See Organization of Petroleum Exporting Countries*
Organization of Economic Cooperation and Development (OECD) 23, 33, 73
Organization of Petroleum Exporting Countries (OPEC) 33–34
Ottoman Empire 6
Ouagadougou 133
Output—*See Production*
Overseas Development Assistance (ODA) 33

Pakistan, Islamic Republic of 11, 104, **296–299**
Palm Oil
 Benin 124
 Cameroon 139
 Indonesia 209
 Malaysia 262
 Nigeria 294

Panama, Republic of **299–303**
Panama Canal 299, 303
Panama Canal Zone 302–303
Panama City 302–303
Pan-American Highway 165
Papuan 208
Parks—*See National Parks*
Pastures—*See Meadows*
Pathans 296
Peanuts
 Cameroon 136
 Chad 143
 Niger 291
 Nigeria 294
 Senegal 314, 316
Peru, Republic of **304–305**
Peten Itza, Lake 188–189
Petroleum 25, 60–61, 71, 76
 Algeria 108
 Angola 112
 Chile 147
 Ecuador 162
 Egypt 168
 Gabon 178
 Indonesia 206
 Iran 210, 212
 Iraq 214–215, 217
 Libya 248–249, 251
 Malaysia 260, 262
 Mexico 268, 271
 Morocco 275
 Myanmar 278
 Nigeria 292
 Pakistan 299
 Saudi Arabia 310–311
 Singapore 322
 Syria 336, 339
 Tunisia 348, 350
 Turkey 354
 Venezuela 362, 364
Philippines, Republic of the 11, **306–309**
Phnom Penh 135
Phosphate 49, 226, 272, 350
Physical Quality of Life Index (PQLI) 87, 328
Physicians 93
Pinochet Ugarto, Gen. Augusto 144
Plain of Jars 241
Plantain 50
Platinum 374
Point-Noire 152
Police 119
Polisario Front 264
Political Divisions **5–9**—*See also specific country*
Population **11–22**, 47, 52–53, 93—*See also specific country*
Port-au-Prince 196–197
Portland Cement Co. 256
Port Louis 267
Porto-Novo 124–125
Portugal (Portuguese Republic) 6, 112, 276
Potash 49
Potatoes 50, 164
Poverty 29, 174, 190, 196
PQLI—*See Physical Quality of Life Index*
Precipitation—*See Rain*
Pretoria 256
Production 56–57—*See also specific product*
Public Administration—*See specific country*
Public Education—*See Education*
Public Health—*See Health*
Public Utilities—*See Utilities*
Public Works 149
Pushtun 106

Pyongyang 235

Qaddafi, Col. Muammer el- 248
Quebracho 117
Quezon 308–309
Quito 164–165

Rabat 274–275
Radios 99, 101
Railroads—*See specific country*
Rain 131, 204
Rain Forests
 Gabon 181
 Guyana 194
 Ivory Coast 220
 Jamaica 224
 Nigeria 295
 Sierra Leone 320
 Vietnam 367
 Zaire 374
Ratsiraka, Didier 252
Rawlings, Lt. Jerry 182
Religions 177, 216, 331—*See also specific country*
Rice 48, 50–51
 Chad 143
 Cuba 158
 Guyana 192, 195
 Indonesia 206, 209
 Iran 212
 Malawi 259
 Malaysia 262
 Myanmar 278
 Niger 291
 Pakistan 299
 Sri Lanka 330
 Thailand 347
 Venezuela 365
 Zaire 375
Rio de Janeiro 130–131
Riyadh 312–313
Roads—*See specific country*
Root Crops 47–48, 51
Roundwood 49
Rubber
 Cameroon 136
 Indonesia 209
 Liberia 244, 246
 Malaysia 260, 262
 Singapore 323
 Sri Lanka 328, 330
 Thailand 347
 Zaire 375
Rudolf, Lake 232–233

Sahal 351
Sahara Desert 108, 140, 264, 290, 351
Sajahas (Nepalese cooperatives) 282
Sana 369
Sandinistas 286
Sanitation 90
San Salvador 172–173
Santiago 144, 146–147
Sao Paulo 130–131
Saudi Arabia, Kingdom of 226, **310–313**, 332, 368
Savanna and Grassland—*See specific country*
School Enrollment 86—*See also specific country*
Seaports—*See Harbors and Ports*
Sectoral Growth—*See specific country*
Selle Mountains 197
Senegal, Republic of **314–317**
Senegal River Valley 317
Senghor, Leopold 314
Senoufo 221

Seoul 238–239
Seren 316
Service Industries 56—*See also specific country*
Sesame Seed 294
Shan Plateau 280
Ships and Shipping 165, 242, 244, 299, 322
Shrimp 270
Sierra Leone, Republic of **318–321**
Silver 304, 374
Singapore, Republic of 36, 236, **322–323**
Sinhalese 330
Sino-Tibetan 241, 346
Sisal 254
Socialism 108, 192, 234, 252, 278, 314, 328, 340, 348, 376, 378
Social Security—*See specific country*
Social Services 119, 175
Somalia (Somali Democratic Republic) **324–327**
Somoza Debayle, Gen. Anastasio 286
Sorghum 51, 143, 291
South America—*See Latin America*
South East Asia 77–78
South Korea—*See Korea, Republic of*
South Yemen—*See Yemen, People's Democratic Republic of*
Soviet Union—*See Union of Soviet Socialist Republics*
Spain, Kingdom of 6
Sri Lanka, Democratic Socialist Republic of **328–331**
Staple Crops 50—*See also specific country and crop*
Steppe 177, 338
Sub-Sahara 78, 98–99
Subsidies and Grants-in-Aid 119
Sudan, Republic of the **332–335**
Sudanic 359
Sugar and Sugarcane 76
    Argentina 117
    Brazil 131
    Colombia 151
    Cuba 156, 158
    Ecuador 164
    Guatemala 186
    Guyana 192, 195
    Jamaica 224
    Mauritius 266–267
    Nicaragua 289
    Panama 302
    Somalia 326
    Uganda 358

Venezuela 365
    Zimbabwe 380
Sumatra 208
Sunnis 216
Swamps and Marshes—*See specific country*
Syria (Syrian Arab Republic) **336–339**

Tai 241, 281, 346
Taiwan—*See China, Republic of*
Tajik 106
Tamils 328, 330
Tanzania, United Republic of **340–343**
Tea
    Cameroon 136
    Indonesia 209
    Iran 212
    Malawi 259
    Mauritius 267
    Sri Lanka 328, 330
Teak 347
Tebou 250
Tegucigalpa 200–201
Tehran 210, 212–213
Telephones 100
Televisions 99, 102
Thailand, Kingdom of 11, 48, 240, **344–347**
Third World—*See also specific country and topic*
Tibeto-Nepalese 285
Tigris River 214, 216–217
Timber—*See Lumber*
Timor 208
Tin 126, 260, 372, 374
Titanium 318
Tobacco
    Cameroon 136
    Cuba 158
    Indonesia 209
    Madagascar 254
    Malawi 259
    Tanzania 342
    Turkey 354
    Uganda 358
    Zimbabwe 380
Tojoa, Lake 201
Topography 197
Torture Island 197
Touareg 250
Toure, Ahmed Sekou 190
Tourism 222, 242, 272, 282
Trade 71–76, 78, 81—*See also specific country*

Transportation—*See specific country*
Travel—*See Tourism*
Tribes 124, 143, 221, 233, 281, 312, 343, 359
Tripoli 250–251
Trujillo Molina, Rafael Leonidas 160
Tsavo National Park 232
Tukulor 316
Tunis 350–351
Tunisia, Republic of **348–351**
Turkey, Republic of 11, **352–355**
TV—*See Television*

Ubangi River 152
Uganda, Republic of 332, **356–359**
Ujamaa (familyhood) 340
UN—*See United Nations*
Unionization 63, 236
Union of Soviet Socialist Republics (USSR)
    and Afghanistan 104
    and Cuba 156
    media and communication in 98, 100
    military presence of 80
    and North Korea 234
    population of 11
    and South Yemen 370
    trade by 11
United Arab Emirates (UAE) 332, 370
United Fruit Co. 186
United Kingdom (UK)—*See Great Britain*
United Nations (UN) 33, 42
United States
    as colonial power 6
    defense and armed forces 77
    as foreign deposit source 36
    and Honduras 198
    and Jordan 226
    and Morocco 272
    and Nicaragua 286
    ODA aid from 33
    and Panama 300
    population of 11
    and Vietnam 366
Upper Gambia 317
Upper Volta—*See Burkina Faso*
Uranium 76, 178, 290
Urbanization—*See specific country*
Uruguay, Oriental Republic of **360–361**
Utilities, Public—*See specific country*

Valparaiso 144

Vanadium 132
Vanilla 252, 254
Vegetation—*See specific country*
Venezuela, Republic of 33, 36, **362–365**
Vientiane 240–241
Vietnam, Socialist Republic of 11, 48, **366–367**
Vietnamese 135
Vineyards 111, 350
Volta, Lake 184–185

Wages and Salaries 199
War Casualties 82
Warsaw Pact 38, 77, 80
Wasteland 175, 193, 199, 213, 215
Water and Water Supply 40, 67, 89, 193
Welfare—*See Social Services*
Wheat 50–51
    Argentina 117
    Iran 212
    Pakistan 299
    Tunisia 350
    Turkey 354
Wilderness Areas 66
Wildlife Reserves 66, 232
Wolof 316
Women
    in labor force 65
    literacy of 84
Wood—*See Lumber*
Woodland—*See specific country*
World Bank (International Bank for Reconstruction and Development) 33

Yams 50
Yangon 280–281
Yao 259
Yaounde 138–139
Yemen, People's Democratic Republic of (South Yemen) **370–371**
Yemen Arab Republic (North Yemen) **368–369**
Yoruba 294
Youth 62

Zaire, Republic of **372–375**
Zaire River 152
Zambia, Republic of **376–377**
Zia ul-Haq, Gen. Muhammad 296
Zimbabwe, Republic of 276, **378–380**
Zinc 132, 304, 374